THE QUEST FOR FREEDOM

A LIFE OF ALEXANDER KERENSKY
THE RUSSIAN UNICORN

Peter Alexander Thompson

By the same author

- ***The Battle for Singapore***: *Britain's Greatest Military Disaster*
- ***Pacific Fury***: *How Australia and her Allies defeated the Japanese*
- ***Anzac Fury***: *The Battle of Crete 1941*
- ***Shanghai Fury***: *Australian Heroes of Revolutionary China*
- ***Wesfarmers 100***: *The People's Story (1914-2014)*

With Robert Macklin
- ***The Battle of Brisbane***: *Australians and Americans at War*
- ***Operation Rimau***: *The Commando Raid on Singapore*
- ***The Adventures of Morrison of China***
- ***Keep off the Skyline***: *The Diggers in Korea*
- ***The Big Fella***: *The Rise and Rise of BHP Billiton**

With Anthony Delano
- ***Maxwell***: *A Portrait of Power*

With Marcella Evaristi
- ***The Private Lives of Mayfair***

* Winner of the Blake Dawson Prize for Business Literature

Copyright © Peter Thompson All rights reserved, 2020.

ISBN: 978-1-09831-968-7

Peter Thompson has asserted his right under the Copyright, Designs and Patents Act 1988 to be identified as the author of this work. No part of this publication may be reproduced, stored in a retrieval system, or transmitted, in any form or by any means, electronic, mechanical, photocopying, recording or otherwise, without the prior permission of the author.

For Stephen Kerensky

'Unfortunately Russians today have completely lost their ability to kill tyrants.'
Vladimir Nabokov during the Stalin years

Contents

Author's Note 1
Prologue: The Russian Unicorn 5

PART I: RESISTANCE (1854-1914) 15
1. The Doomed Dynasty 16
2. The Sons of Simbirsk 28
3. The Distorting Mirror 44
4. The Young Madmen 65
5. The Calamitous Kaiser 81
6. The Accidental Terrorist 100
7. The Dress Rehearsal 112
8. The Romantic Assassin 131
9. The Kerensky Ascent 150

PART II: REVOLUTION (1914-1917) 177
10. The Damn Fool Thing 178
11. The Iron Hurricane 199
12. The Great Retreat 217
13. The Flashes of Lightning 239
14. The February Revolution 259
15. The End of Tsarism 281
16. The Return of the Exiles 304
17. The Poison Chalice 327
18. The Bolshevik Rising 348

PART III: RETRIBUTION (1917-1924) 381
19. The Kornilov Revolt 382
20. The October Coup 400
21. The Death of Freedom 428

22. The Lubianka Prisoners 448
23. The Entente Outsider 462
24. The Dragon's Teeth..479
25. The Suspicious Alien 500
26. The Hungry Years 514

PART IV: REDEMPTION (1924-1970) 537
27. The French Connection..538
28. The Incurable Romantic 555
29. The Fury of Comrade Stalin 570
30. The Flight from Paris...592
31. The Last Ship Out..611
32. The Death of Nell Tritton 625

Epilogue: The Tiger of History 643
Bibliography 649
Endnotes...669
Index 724

Author's Note

Cambridge, January 2020

The Quest for Freedom is a testament to the extraordinary life of Alexander Kerensky, 'the Russian Unicorn', before, during and after the Russian Revolution of February 1917, which saw the collapse of the Romanov Autocracy and the abdication of Tsar Nicholas II after a century of agitation and martyrdom. Every step of the road to freedom was paved with danger and heartbreak. Kerensky recorded many of the milestones in seven books but he never managed to capture the sheer improbability of his own story - the Tolstoyan epic of a young lawyer from the Middle Volga who devoted his life to fighting for the freedom of his fellow Russians.

My sources were two of his grandchildren, Stephen Kerensky and his sister Libby Hudson, the children of Alexander and Olga Kerensky's younger son Gleb; his three volumes of memoirs (*The Catastrophe*, 1927, *The Crucifixion of Liberty*, 1934, *Russia and History's Turning Point,* 1965), his monograph on the Kornilov Affair, *The Prelude to Bolshevism*, and three volumes of documents on *The Russian Provisional Government 1917* (with Robert P. Browder); as well as documents in the Kerensky Family Papers at the Cadbury Research Library at the University of Birmingham, and the Kerensky Collection of his grandson Stephen Kerensky.[1]

This last collection contains Olga Kerenskaya's 1935 memoirs; Gleb Kerensky's 1950 manuscript *Only One Freedom*; and the 'Grandfather' chapter from the 1991 manuscript of Oleg Kerensky Jr., son of Alexander and Olga's elder son, Oleg. I also read the unclassified security dossier on Alexander Kerensky at the British National Archives, Kew; the unclassified security dossier at the Australian National Archives, Canberra; and some of his letters at the Harry Ransom Centre of the University of Texas, Austin.

I am also extremely grateful to my friend Jean Baptiste Hugo, who provided intimate details and photographs of Kerensky's friendship with his father, the French artist and war hero Jean Hugo, and his great grandmother, Aline Ménard-Dorian, the model for the salonniere Madame Verdurin in Proust's *À la recherche du temps perdu*.

Alexander Kerensky was married to two remarkable women, firstly to Olga Baranovskaya who suffered greatly at the hands of the Bolsheviks and whose courage, resilience and love saved the lives of their sons, and secondly to Lydia Ellen Tritton, whose courage and determination rescued him from the Nazis, though at great personal cost. The story of Olga's ordeal is a damning indictment of Bolshevism under Lenin and Trotsky following the October Coup when millions of their 'class enemies' were displaced, imprisoned, starved or murdered. Her survival was due to the selfless heroism of one man, Dr Boris Sokolov, a humanitarian who risked his own life to save her and her children. Olga and her sons arrived in Britain as refugees in 1920. Despite her separation and divorce from Alexander Kerensky, she remained one of his most loyal supporters for the rest of her life.

Both of their sons became brilliant engineers who were involved in bridge-building and hydroelectric projects, including the Sydney Harbour Bridge and the Snowy Mountains Hydroelectric Scheme in Australia. They also contributed to the British war effort, Oleg as one of the engineers who built the portable Mulberry harbours for the Normandy landings and Gleb as an officer in the Corps of Royal Electrical and Mechanical Engineers (REME) who served in France and Holland after D-Day.

Kerensky's second wife, Lydia Ellen Tritton, was known at various times as Nellé Tritton, Thérèse Nadejine (from her first marriage to a Russian opera singer) and Thérèse Kerensky after her marriage to Alexander Fyodorovich. Her Australian family called her Nell and for the sake of simplicity I have followed their example. Nell Tritton was an Australian journalist and poet who arrived in Europe in 1925. She worked with Alexander Kerensky on anti-Communist newspapers in France in the 1930s and they were married in the United States on 20 August 1939.

Following the sweetheart deal between Stalin and Hitler and the outbreak of World War II in September that year, Nell accompanied Alexander back to France to campaign against the Soviet threat to the Western war effort. As German forces surrounded Paris in June 1940, they were instrumental in helping Russian émigrés escape to Britain and the United States.

Slipping through the net themselves, they reached South-Western France thanks to Nell's driving skills and escaped in the very last British ship to cross the Channel from a French port. The ordeal irreparably damaged her health and contributed to her early death.

I am enormously grateful to the late Andy Anderssen, a friend since schooldays, who provided me with introductions to Nell Tritton's relatives, Lavinia Tritton in Brisbane and Pat Tritton in Kent. They supplied information, newsletters and photographs relating to the Tritton family history, as did Elizabeth-Anne Peters, whose parents Lilian and Bill Tomlinson, knew Nell Tritton and met Kerensky at 'Elderslie', the Tritton family home, in 1945.

My interest in Australian history also brought me into contact with the stories of Jean Turner, a young Brisbane woman who joined her husband, Robert Bruce Lockhart, in Moscow in 1913, and Fyodor 'Artem' Sergeyev, 'the Brisbane Bolshevik', whose son, Tomik 'Artyom' Sergeyev, was adopted by Stalin following his death in 1921.

Much of my research on the Russian Revolutions (January 1905, February 1917 and October 1917) was conducted with the help of the staffs at the Cambridge University Library, the British Library, London, the Australian National Library, Canberra, the Queensland State Library, Brisbane, the Saint John's College Library, Cambridge, the British National Archives, Kew, the Australian National Archives, Canberra, and Simon Blundell, the Librarian of the Reform Club, London. My thanks also go to the staff of Saint John's College, Cambridge, and West Court at Jesus College, Cambridge, for their assistance during my stays in those colleges.

My friends Robert Macklin, Clive Lyon and Anthony Delano contributed enormously to my knowledge of the subject. At his home in Norfolk Clive Lyon guided me through his extensive collection of books on World War I and the Revolutions. Robert Macklin and Stephen Kerensky read the work-in-progress and made many valuable suggestions about the content and structure of the book. Stephen and his wife Sandie were generous hosts on my trips to Lancashire.

The books I read ranged from some of the earliest texts on the Russian Revolutions to the very latest, and included Richard Abraham's absorbing biography, *Alexander Kerensky: The First Love of the Revolution* (1987), and the family memoir *It was Farewell to Russia, Goodbye to Everything: The Emigration of the Baranovsky Family after the Russian Revolution of 1917*, by Jan Doets and André Birukoff. None was more valuable than Alexander Solzhenitsyn's autobiography, *Between Two Millstones, Book I, Sketches of Exile 1974-1978*, and his *Red Wheel* novels *August 1914*, *November 1916* and *March 1917*, which contain an immense amount of intensely researched, historically accurate material.

At the time of the Russian Revolution Russia used the Julian (or Old Style) calendar. In the Nineteenth Century this was twelve days behind the Gregorian (or New Style) calendar of Western Europe. From 1900 the gap became thirteen days until midnight on 31 January 1918 when the country switched to the Gregorian calendar and the date jumped to 14 February. I've given dates relating to events in Russia in both styles (e.g. 1/13 March 1817 or 1/14 March 1917) until the country converted to New Style.

For the sake of readability I have used Anglicised versions of many Russian names (Alexander Kerensky instead of Alexandr Kerenskii) but I have mostly retained the masculine and feminine endings of Russian surnames (Alexander Kerensky, Olga Kerenskaya). In some cases I have taken the preferred spelling in keeping with the best Anglicised practice, for example Tsar Nicholas II instead of Tsar Nikolai II but Kaiser Wilhelm II instead of Kaiser William II.

While the term 'White Russians' applies specifically to people from present-day Belarus, I have also used it in a generic sense to refer to anti-Communist forces during the Russian Civil War 1917-1921. For the sake of clarity, I have simplified some of Kerensky's more complicated prose. I have also taken the liberty of using the present tense in attributing some quotes – for example, 'he says' – when a specific recollection may in fact have taken place years earlier.

Prologue

The Russian Unicorn

In the summer of 1963, a few months before the assassination of President John F. Kennedy at the hands of a pro-Soviet former United States Marine armed with a $19.95 rifle, an elderly man dressed for an earlier time in a three-piece tweed suit, his white hair cut in the style known in France as en brosse but which was popular in America as the crewcut, turned up at a party for newspaper and publishing people in the Manhattan apartment of Anthony Delano of the London *Daily Mirror*. 'I forget who brought him and I didn't know who he was,' Tony Delano says. 'He was introduced to me as Alexander Kerensky and he spent the evening sitting quietly in an armchair until it was time to go home.'[1]

Ah, yes – Alexander Fyodorovich Kerensky, the Socialist Revolutionary who personified the February Revolution, the great reformer who led the Provisional Government for one hundred days and who is best remembered today, if at all, as 'the man who lost Russia'.

In 1963 Kerensky was in his eighty-third year, half-deaf, blind in one eye, his bearing slightly stooped, his complexion sallow from a kidney condition and needing his bone-handled walking stick to get around. All of these failings indicated decrepitude and yet, as the publication of his final book of memoirs showed, he was still capable of great passion.

At first hand he had witnessed the slaughter of liberty - the liberty that Marx cherished – under Lenin and Trotsky, and then, in exile, he had seen Stalin take the Soviet system to grotesque new depths. Reviewing *Russia and History's Turning Point* (Duell, Sloan & Pearce 1965), Malcolm Muggeridge concluded, 'Despite his years of exile, Kerensky remains indomitably and admirably a Russian democrat and patriot, embittered and infuriated, as well he might be, by the feebleness and asininity of many of those outside Russia who were nominally on his side.'[2]

Kerensky was living on the top floor of a redbrick townhouse at 109 East 91st Street, the home of Helen Simpson, widow of his great friend and political ally Kenneth F. Simpson, a United States Congressman and Republican leader of New York County. Survival had been a Pyrrhic victory. While Lenin, Trotsky and Stalin enjoy a global multimedia afterlife as historical celebrities, Kerensky has been reviled and is all but forgotten.

He was frequently reminded that it would have been easy for him to have retained power in 1917 had he betrayed Russia's Allies in World War I and signed a separate peace with Germany, as Lenin did a few months later; had he turned a blind eye to the illegal seizure and partition of farmland instead of pleading with the peasants for patience until the necessary legislation could be passed; and, above all, had he executed Lenin and Trotsky for treason when he had the chance.[3]

Kerensky refused to take extreme measures to defeat the Bolsheviks and the consequences of that refusal proved irreversible until 1991 when the Soviet Union collapsed under the weight of its own deficiencies. But, as the *New York Times* noted, there was a glimpse of forces at work during the Provisional Government's brief existence 'seeking to turn the vast land into a democracy, and to create a new society whose citizens would enjoy both freedom and prosperity'.[4]

Lenin's genius was to transform Marxism into a fighting creed that had but one aim: total power. Instead of 'peace, bread, land' in a Communist Utopia, as he had promised, the Russians got civil war, starvation and seven decades of the most crushing autocracy of modern times.

In 2016 so many books were in production to mark the Centenary of the Russian Revolution in 2017 that it proved impossible to find a publisher for this one. Typical of numerous rejection notices, one leading British publisher wrote, 'As publicity is so crucial these days, the fact that the Provisional Government failed makes it hard for us to make real claims for Kerensky's place in history.' This sort of evaluation isn't unusual. Kerensky has no historic value today because the Bolsheviks destroyed the Provisional Government and smashed the Russian Republic he had established on 1 September 1917.

When the books were published, they invariably supported this view. Yet the fact that Kerensky failed in his mission could be viewed in an entirely different light: that it ranks as one of the greatest and most tragic misses of all time. The fact that his failure owed much to the hostility of Lloyd George, Balfour, Churchill and Clémenceau, and the indifference of Woodrow Wilson makes it even more imperative that he should be given a hearing today.

In his massive work on the Revolution, Leon Trotsky consigned Kerensky to his proverbial 'dustbin of history'. 'Kerensky was not a revolutionist,' he said, 'he merely hung around the revolution.' Lenin was equally dismissive. 'Kerensky,' he sneered, 'is a balalaika on which they play to deceive the workers and peasants.'[5]

The Marxist-Leninist view of Soviet hagiographers was that the Bolshevik Party had been at the vanguard of all three Russian revolutions: the 'dress rehearsal' of 1905, the overthrow of the Tsar in February 1917 and 'the Great October Socialist Revolution' later that year. Any historian who deviated from that line was denounced as a 'bourgeois falsifier'.[6] The Bolshevik influence in the 1905 Revolution was, in fact, minimal and neither Lenin nor Trotsky, much less Stalin, Zinoviev, Kamenev or any of the other 'professional revolutionaries', were anywhere to be seen when the Romanov Autocracy collapsed virtually overnight in February 1917 (Old Style).

Alexander Kerensky, a thirty-five-year-old member of the State Duma, the lower house of the Russian Parliament, seized the moment. As an excited crowd of revolutionary citizens and mutinous soldiers approached the Tauride Palace, the Duma's home beside the River Neva, he shouted to his colleagues, 'May I tell them that the State Duma is with them, that it assumes all responsibility, that it will stand at the head of the movement?'

Getting no coherent answer, he dashed outside and addressed the troops. 'Citizen Soldiers,' he cried, 'on you falls the great honour of guarding the State Duma…. I declare you to be the First Revolutionary Guard!'

He had committed the Duma to the Revolution.[7]

By any standard, Kerensky's hubris-inducing career in 1917 was phenomenal. As the Petrograd Soviet's only member in the Provisional Government's first cabinet, he was Minister of Justice (March-May) and in the second cabinet War and Naval Minister (May-September), then Prime Minister (July-August), Supreme Commander of the

Armed Forces (August-October), and Minister-President (September-October).

'There is no other statesman living whose accession to the Premiership would fill us with the same enthusiasm and hope,' the Irish nationalist Robert Lynd wrote of Kerensky in the London *Daily News* in July 1917. 'He is the representative of the world's hope. With his defeat, the light of the world would go out.'

That light was indeed extinguished.

By definition the Provisional Government was a stop-gap measure to tackle Russia's most pressing problems and, inevitably, those problems overwhelmed it. His grandson Stephen Kerensky says, 'It is remarkable that the anti-Kerensky case made by politicians and historians, both in London and Saint Petersburg, is still founded on the idea that the Provisional Government should have solved all the social, political, economic and military disasters resulting from Nicholas II's rule within six months of taking office.'

The biggest problem was the war. Attempting to revive morale in the Russian Army (and to aid Russia's Allies on the Western Front) Kerensky planned an offensive for spring 1917. However, a power struggle between the government and the Petrograd Soviet delayed the start of the operation until 18 June, with fatal results for the Russian Army and the nascent Russian democracy.[8]

Then, as Prime Minister in August, Kerensky was confronted with a rightwing revolt from the Army's new Supreme Commander, General Lavr Kornilov. It was Kerensky's defeat of Kornilov's forces with Soviet (and Bolshevik) help that fatally weakened his support among the military. When Red Guards and Baltic Fleet sailors attacked the Winter Palace on the night of 25-26 October, officers and soldiers alike sat back and did nothing as he was driven from office. Forced into hiding, he was lucky to escape with his life. Louise Bryant, an American journalist and a socialist, lamented his fall in her book *Six Months in Red Russia*:

> I had a tremendous respect for Kerensky when he was head of the Provisional Government. He tried so passionately to hold Russia together, and what man at this hour could have accomplished that? He was never wholeheartedly supported by any group. He attempted to carry the whole weight of the nation on his frail shoulders, keep up a front against the Germans, keep down the warring political factions at home.[9]

So what had he achieved in those months? As Minister of Justice, Kerensky signed decrees that granted women full civil and political rights, including the right to vote, and established equality for all religions and ethnicities. This edict officially terminated 'the Pale' - the iniquitous Pale of Permanent Jewish Settlement, the territory in Western Russia to which 95 per cent of the Empire's Jewish population were confined by imperial order after 1791 - thus giving Jews the right to live wherever they pleased, including Moscow and Petrograd (as wartime Saint Petersburg had been renamed). Henceforth, Jewish children were allowed to attend public schools and universities without being subjected to repressive Tsarist-imposed quotas. He also abolished the death penalty and he banned the whipping of prisoners and the use of straitjackets to restrain them.

For the rest of his life, Kerensky argued that the Bolsheviks' celebrated victory was not what it seemed. There was no popular uprising in Russia in October 1917 but rather a coup by an armed, anti-democratic minority. The real revolution – the one that had been the dream of the Russian masses for centuries, the one that had deposed the Tsar and ended the autocracy – had started six months earlier on 23 February/8 March 1917, with Nicholas's abdication following eight days later.

Alexander Solzhenitsyn, the author who did more than any other human being to bring the Soviet Union to its knees, acknowledged this fact in an interview in 2007. 'The "October Revolution" is a myth generated by the winners, the Bolsheviks, and swallowed whole by progressive circles in the West,' he said. 'On 25 October 1917 a violent twenty-four-hour coup d'état took place in Petrograd. It was brilliantly and thoroughly planned by Leon Trotsky - Lenin was still in hiding then to avoid being brought to justice for treason. What we call "the Russian Revolution of 1917" was actually the February Revolution.'[10]

Nevertheless, the Bolsheviks took control of the capital and other key cities in October-November that year and used brutal methods, including summary executions, to enforce their will on the population. They then rewrote history to legitimise the takeover. 'There was only one Russian Revolution, which brought Kerensky to power,' says the author Vladimir Nabokov. 'Communism, what has it given us? Well-organised police.' Indeed, Russia became an even more brutal police state than it had been under the Romanovs.[11]

In early 1918 Lenin destroyed all meaningful opposition when he turned the dictatorship of the proletariat (a phrase borrowed from the French economist Jérôme-Adolphe Blanqui) into the dictatorship of a single political party: the All-Russian Communist Party. Lenin did not invent the Gulag but he used it mercilessly. Within six months of the coup, he demanded that 'unreliable elements' be locked up in concentration camps.

Lenin's victims included many of the people who had fought valiantly to bring down the autocracy. He then attacked the clergy with medieval ferocity. Bishops, priests, monks and nuns were tortured and murdered. Women were raped, men castrated. Many were disembowelled, buried alive, crucified upside down, or, in midwinter, simply drenched with water and frozen solid like grotesque statues.

The Communist state became a rigid theocracy with its own dogma, saints and heretics. The 'bogus' Mensheviks and Socialist Revolutionaries were suppressed with the venom of religious zealots. Dissidents were denounced as 'counter-revolutionaries', a crime that led to imprisonment or a bullet in the back of the head. To be *'burzhui'* – a derivation of 'bourgeois' - was enough to damn any man or woman, irrespective of their political beliefs.

Literature was heavily censored. Lenin hated Tolstoy, the former artillery officer-turned-pacifist, because he preached a peaceful revolution through universal brotherhood, while his wife, Nadezhda Krupskaya, campaigned to have Pushkin's books banned from public libraries. Under the Communists truth was mutilated, language perverted and power abused. *Pravda*, whose name means *Truth*, published absurd distortions similar to George Orwell's doublethink slogans in *1984*: 'War is Peace/ Freedom is Slavery/ Ignorance is Strength'.[12]

Through the whole of 1917 Alexander Kerensky, the main obstacle to Bolshevik supremacy, was a sick man. In April 1916 he had had a tubercular kidney removed and throughout the revolutionary period relied on injections of intravenous morphine to keep himself going. Even in robust good health, he could never have matched the unbounded ferocity and single-minded fanaticism of Lenin or the dynamism and ruthlessness of Trotsky - few people could – but he was not the 'weak' man of numerous academic studies.

On the contrary his downfall owed much to the weakness and folly of his colleagues in the Provisional Government, to the hostility of Bolshevik enablers in the Petrograd Soviet, to the wiles of his Allies in the Triple Entente and to the superiority of German generals who inflicted horrific losses on the Russian Army without ever annihilating it.[i] [13]

Despite numerous setbacks in the decades that followed, Kerensky's belief in the inherent decency and goodness of the Russian people never wavered. No matter how often he was attacked – sometimes physically – he maintained his dignity and never played the victim or the spurned hero. His criticisms were reserved for Lenin, Trotsky, Stalin and his other political enemies. Always, he insisted, his argument was with the Soviet rulers and not with the Russian people.

At the heart of his message was the conviction that the enforcement of Bolshevik power was nothing less than a continuation of Tsarist autocracy in a different, more brutal form. 'The history of Europe,' he wrote in 1934, 'knows no dictatorship more reactionary, more absolute, more disastrous for the people and the country, than the dictatorship of the Bolsheviks.'[14]

Dr Jonathan Smele, Senior Lecturer in Modern European History at Queen Mary University of London, afforded Kerensky a backhanded compliment when he described him as 'one of the most famous forgotten men in history'.[15] As if to prove the point, one author claimed in his 2017 opus that 'Kerensky remained in hiding inside Russia or in Finland throughout the Civil War that followed, hoping for a triumphal return to Petrograd. Eventually he accepted it would be unlikely to happen and left for Berlin in 1922, and subsequently Paris…'

The reader was thus denied any knowledge of Kerensky's hair-raising escape to Scotland in a British Secret Service trawler in June 1918; his meeting with Lloyd George at 10 Downing Street; his trip to Paris to see Clémenceau; and his efforts to be recognised at the 1919 Paris Peace Talks as the last legitimate head of the Russian state before the Bolshevik apocalypse. All the while the bloodhounds of European and Russian security agencies, Red and White, followed him around Europe, scoured his mail and interviewed his enemies for evidence of

---

i It was the Soviet's Order Number 1, published on 2 March 1917, that effectively destroyed the Russian Army's discipline and attacking capability.

conspiracy, or espionage, or some other crime – any crime - for which he might be prosecuted or declared persona non grata.

All of this happened to Alexander Kerensky, though you would never know it from many of the books on the Revolution. The main charges against him were that he was 'all impulse and emotion', that he had 'Bonapartist ambitions', that he was undone by 'weakness of will'. Kerensky actually detested Bonaparte for his brutality and it is difficult to imagine Napoleon sans grapeshot. Stephen Kerensky told this author:

> My grandfather is still being written off as an idiot, lost in folie de grandeur and Napoleonic delusions, who had no idea at all what he ought to be doing. Worse still is the impression that he floundered about like a bad actor in a melodrama, spouting torrents of overemotional and empty rhetoric.
>
> His great strength was his mandate from the people, which developed during his legal work from 1905 to 1917. In particular, he became a national hero for his attacks on Nicholas following his Duma-appointed investigation into the massacre of 200 miners on the Lena Goldfields in Northern Siberia in April 1912.
>
> He knew how to appeal to revolutionary peasants and even mutinous troops, but, even so, the Russian people at large had either read Dostoyevsky's description of nihilistic anarchists like Lenin, or had heard them being read out in the regular village-hall meetings that were such a feature of rural life.
>
> Lenin's espousal of mass-murder ran contrary to the Russian Orthodox version of Christianity, which did not celebrate Christmas with an orgy of food and drink but centred on Easter and its emphasis on poverty, compassion, forgiveness and the sacrifice of one's own life for the good of others - watchwords of the vast majority of the revolutionary movement.
>
> It is the most unbelievable arrogance of Western Europeans to say that the Russian people's hero was a weak-kneed fool who, like Ophelia, was 'incapable of [his] own distress'.

Robert Bruce Lockhart, the British diplomat and secret agent, judged Kerensky 'a kind and, above all, a humane man with a deep sense of decency'. 'I had been one of the first, if not the very first, British official to meet Kerensky,' he says. 'I had known him in the days of his greatness. I had seen him in the years of adversity and of dwindling hope. I had never once noticed the smallest change in his demeanour or heard from his lips one word of criticism of those who had sought his favour in success and had cursed him in his failure.'[16]

To the Russian symbolist poet Zinaida Hippius, Kerensky was 'the first love of the Revolution'. To his first wife, Olga Kerenskaya, he was 'a dedicated and brilliant man […] there was never anything tawdry or Bonapartist about him'. To his second wife, the Australian poet and journalist Nell Tritton, he was 'my beloved unicorn' for his uniqueness of character and his vulnerability to extinction. And in the estimation of his biographer, Richard Abraham, he could be 'an irresistibly lovable person'.[17]

Nevertheless, as his family learned to their cost, he could also be headstrong, self-centred and unfaithful. Olga Kerenskaya, the abandoned mother of his two sons, Oleg and Gleb, could not forget the hardship and terror she suffered following the Bolshevik coup of 1917. After fifteen years in Britain, she wrote in her 1935 autobiography that these memories 'still torture me and I spend sleepless nights crying'.

Her son Gleb said in an introduction to the memoirs, 'Being back in Russia was the subject of her nightmares. Russia was a desecrated cemetery of friends, hopes and ideals. It was Russian culture and Russian ambiance that she loved but in England there were few Russians and most were hostile because the Revolution had turned into a disaster.' Olga suffered from post-traumatic stress disorder (PTSD) and without any kind of therapy it remained untreated for the rest of her life.

Kerensky's married lover, Elena 'Lilya' Baranovsky-Birukova, also experienced hunger and persecution following the Bolshevik coup. She broke off all contact with him in the 1920s and brought up their child, Irena, under her deceased husband's name.

Bernard Butcher, who met Kerensky when he taught at Stanford University in the 1960s, posed the key questions: 'Looking back, should we consider him - and the Provisional Government in which he played such a prominent part - merely a footnote to history? Or was there a chance that this frail old man could, in his prime, have led Russia toward a constitutional democracy? Was perhaps the most pivotal development of the Twentieth Century, Russia's long experiment with totalitarian communism, really inevitable?'[18]

Those questions are examined here and the answers are neither straight-forward nor exculpatory. In 1945, in Melbourne, an Australian reporter asked Alexander Kerensky whether he had any regrets.

> Well, he replied, someone had once said that he should have done away with his enemies while he ruled Russia. But that was not his way. He believed that a great pity and kindness were what bound humanity together and how, believing this, could he approve bloodshed and the ruthless liquidation of his enemies?[19]

Alexander Kerensky died of heart disease in a New York hospital on 11 June 1970 in his ninetieth year, making him one of the longest-living Russian politicians of his generation. To the very end, he considered himself the legal head of the Russian state. He was the humane face of Russian socialism, the romantic who loved too many women and the humanitarian who refused to murder his opponents. Ridiculed and then forgotten, he deserves more than the passing references granted him during the Revolution's hundredth anniversary year.

PART I
RESISTANCE
(1854-1914)

1
The Doomed Dynasty

The Russia that Alexander Kerensky grew up in was a nation of dangerous uncertainty, suspicious of the future, uncomfortable in the present and with one foot planted firmly in the past. The exploits of Peter the Great in extending the rule of Muscovy to the Baltic and Alexander I's glorious victory over Napoleon's Grande Armée in 1812 were seared into the national conscience.[i] It took the defeat of Alexander's successor, the incorrigibly tyrannical Nicholas I, in the Crimean War to persuade his son, Alexander II, of the simple truth that free men fight harder than slaves.

According to Alexander Kerensky, the fall of Sevastopol disclosed to the world the bankruptcy of the Romanov Dynasty. After a siege lasting 336 days, the collapse of the great naval base on the Black Sea threatened to bring down the three pillars of Romanov rule - Autocracy, Orthodoxy and Nationality.[ii] 'Sevastopol was the price of thirty years of tyranny,' he says. 'Like some terrible thunderbolt from the gods, it brought Russia out of her stupor.'[1]

'Nicholas the Flogger' had turned Russia into a police state. 'I cannot permit that any individual should dare defy my wishes,' he warned. Any perceived challenge to the autocracy was met with an atavistic fury involving whips, chains, dungeons and the scaffold. Siberia, which comprised roughly seventy-five per cent of his kingdom, presented him with a dumping ground for dissidents and criminals, while *katorga*, or forced labour, in its forests, mines and

---

i Peter the Great founded Saint Petersburg on the Neva marshes in 1703 as a bastion against Swedish, Polish, Lithuanian, Finnish and German invaders. Local people have always referred to their city as 'Peter'.

ii 'The Triad of Official Nationality' was the creation of the Minister of National Enlightenment, Sergei Uvarov (1786-1855), in an 1833 circular letter to subordinate educators. Nicholas loved the idea and embraced it.

fisheries enriched his treasury.[iii] [2]

After the suppression of the Polish uprising of 1830-31, no fewer than 180,000 Polish patriots joined the miserable caravansaries heading east. The people condemned to this hellish existence included the Decembrist conspirators, Catholics, moderate politicians and suspect writers.[iv] Fyodor Dostoevsky, author of *Crime and Punishment*, served four years shackled hand and foot in a cramped communal barracks at Omsk in south-western Siberia for his involvement in the Petrashevsky Circle, a reading group that met secretly in Saint Petersburg to study the work of the French socialist Charles Fourier. He described the Tsarist heart of darkness thus: 'Here was a world all its own, unlike anything else; here were laws unto themselves, manners and customs unto themselves, a house of the living dead, a life unlike anywhere else, with distinct people unlike anyone else.'[3]

Punishment for breaking the camp rules included flogging, extended sentences, solitary confinement and banishment to an even more inhospitable place. Women were bartered and prostituted. The cruelty of Nicholas's regime alienated more liberal European countries to the point of Russophobia. Since time immemorial the most common adjectives applied to Russia were 'barbarous', 'Asiatic' and 'despotic'. It was not on the grand-tour itinerary and very few visitors from 'civilised' Europe ever travelled there. The vast distances, unreliable transport and poor accommodation were powerful deterrents.

However, the Marquis de Custine, the celebrated French traveller, ignored all of these difficulties and embarked on a fact-finding visit to Russia in 1839. He was appalled at the inhumanity he encountered. After meeting the Tsar in Saint Petersburg, he decided he was two-faced like Janus and that the face hidden from view would be engraved 'Violence, Exile, Oppression, or their equivalent, Siberia'.

Receiving Nicholas at Windsor Castle in the summer of 1844,

---

iii In 1845 Nicholas abolished the *knout*, a vicious whip of multiple metal-tipped rawhide thongs inherited from the Tatars. He replaced it with the *pleti*, a whip with three thongs tipped with pleated leather in place of metal talons. The number of lashes was limited to one hundred.

iv The Decembrists were a small clique of noble officers who failed to overthrow Nicholas I on his accession to the throne in December 1825. The leaders were thrown into the Alekseyevsky Ravelin in the western part of the Peter and Paul Fortress. Five were executed and thirty-one were sentenced to hard labour in Siberia.

Queen Victoria thought his profile '*beautiful*', though she found that 'the expression of the eyes is *formidable*, and unlike anything I ever saw before'.[4]

> He is stern and severe – with fixed principles of *duty* which *nothing* on earth will make him change: very *clever* I do *not* think him, and his mind is an uncivilised one; his education has been neglected; politics and military concerns are the only things he takes great interest in; the arts and all softer occupations he is insensible to, but he is *sincere*, I am certain, sincere even in his most despotic acts, from a sense that it is the only way to govern.[5]

Nicholas had been raised to believe that Holy Russia had a God-given right to reclaim the legacy of the Byzantine Empire and seize Constantinople (Tsargrad to the Russians) the spiritual capital of the Orthodox Church. It was also his ambition to open up the Turkish Straits – the Bosphorus, the Sea of Marmara and the Dardanelles - and thus enable his Black Sea Fleet to enter the Mediterranean and join Britain, France, Germany, Italy, Spain and Portugal in exploiting the treasure-houses of the Middle East.

He conceived a clumsy plan to divide the territorial assets of the ailing Ottoman Empire among the Great Powers. In February 1853 he asked the British Ambassador in Saint Petersburg, Sir Hamilton Seymour, whether Britain would be satisfied with Cyprus and Egypt. 'We have a sick man on our hands, a very sick man,' he said. 'It would be a pity if he slipped away before we had made arrangements for his funeral.'[6]

While the real casus belli was Nicholas's determination to carve up the Ottoman Empire, hostilities broke out over Russia's demand that the Sultan find in favour of the Orthodox Church in a squabble with French Catholics over protection of the Holy Places in Palestine, and a second demand that the Sultan recognise Russia's right to protect all Orthodox subjects living under Turkish rule. As this second demand affected Turkey's sovereignty and opened the way to Russian intervention in Turkish affairs, possibly leading to the occupation of Constantinople, it brought a strong reaction from Britain and France who were determined to keep Russia out of the Mediterranean.[7]

Through self-interest, an Anglo-French coalition rallied to the aid of the Sublime Porte. The coalition had to make do without Prussia when King Friedrich Wilhelm IV refused to attack his friend, Tsar Nicholas, a refusal that intensified anti-German feeling towards the House of Hanover that ruled the United Kingdom of Great Britain and Ireland. The Queen, three-quarters German, and her husband Prince Albert, wholly German, were hissed as their carriage conveyed them down Whitehall to the Palace of Westminster for the State Opening of Parliament in January 1854.[v] [8]

Two months later Britain was at war with Russia, though it was early September before the British Expeditionary Army landed at Calamita Bay on the west coast of the Crimean Peninsula in the Black Sea. On paper, the Russian Army of 1.75 million men enjoyed a huge numerical advantage over an Allied force one-fifth that size; in reality, the battle-worthiness of the Tsar's troops was greatly exaggerated. The vast majority were serfs - peasant conscripts who were poorly trained and badly armed. Their officers were incompetent and often corrupt, while the Russian musket was inferior to French and British rifles in terms of range and rate of fire.[9]

Once Lord Raglan, the sixty-five-year-old British Commander, had been reminded he was fighting Russia and not France, the armies clashed at the Alma and then at Balaclava (which saw the notorious Charge of the Light Brigade) and finally at Inkerman. These battles ended in stalemate and the front settled into the long-running Siege of Sevastopol, leading to horrendous privation on both sides.[10]

In December 1854 Count Leo Tolstoy, a twenty-six-year-old artillery officer, took charge of a battery in the Fourth Bastion, the most exposed point of the Sevastopol defences. He watched 'doctors with their arms blood-stained above the elbow, and with pale, stern faces' going about their work in a makeshift hospital:

> You see the sharp, curved knife enter the healthy, white body, you see the wounded man suddenly regain consciousness with a piercing cry and curses, you see the army surgeon fling the amputated arm into a corner... you behold war, not from its conventional, beautiful, and brilliant side, with music and drumbeat, with fluttering flags and galloping generals, but you behold war in its real phase - in blood, in suffering, in death.[11]

---

v Albert had no official position in the Kingdom but possessed a talent for interference. His unpopularity did not stop him from complaining to the beleaguered Prime Minister, Lord Aberdeen, about the rude behaviour of certain cabinet ministers towards his wife.

It was scenes like this amputation that inspired Tolstoy to write about the miserable lot of the Russian peasant. To Nicholas's *'sincere, uncivilised mind'*, however, the Russian Army was the supreme expression of the Russian State – it was the autocracy made flesh – and he found its failure to expel the invaders unbearable. After declaring, 'My successor must do as he pleases; for myself I cannot change,' he expired in the Imperial Family's official residence, the reddish-brown Winter Palace on the south bank of the River Neva, on 2 March 1855. Officially, he died of pneumonia but it was rumoured he had committed suicide.

Such was Russia's technical backwardness that his successor, Alexander II, had to rely on news reports telegraphed to Saint Petersburg from Paris and London to find out what was happening at the front. Sevastopol fell six months after his father's death.[12]

The Treaty of Paris, which ended the Crimean War in March 1856, closed the Black Sea to all warships and demilitarised the Crimean coastline. If Russia were to survive as a Great Power, she would have to undertake the painful process of modernising along Western lines until she was strong enough to overturn the treaty and rebuild her Black Sea Fleet.

On 19 February 1861 Alexander celebrated the sixth anniversary of his succession by signing the Liberation Statute emancipating Russia's serfs, the slaves who constituted about one-third of the population and almost half the peasantry. At the stroke of a pen more than twenty-three million people ceased to be the chattels of their masters, to be bought and sold, given as gifts, offered in payment for debts or simply worked to death. 'It is better to abolish serfdom from above,' the Tsar declared, 'than to wait for the time when it will begin to abolish itself from below.'[13]

The Liberation Statute, coupled with other legal and temporal reforms over the next few years, earned Alexander the title of 'The Liberator', though at heart he was no less autocratic than his father. His primary purpose in making concessions was to save his Empire from disintegration.[14]

The Tsar introduced an independent judiciary, trial by jury for serious criminal offences (though not in Poland, the Caucasus, Central Asia or Siberia) and an autonomous Bar. Flogging was abolished for soldiers, while the period of service was reduced from twenty-five years to fifteen years' active service and ten years' 'leave'. Elected local councils (the *zemstvos* in rural districts, the *dumas* in the towns and cities) were set up to provide roads, schools and medical services funded by local taxes. Most importantly for Russia's educated class, the lifting of restrictions on the press meant that new magazines and newspapers could flourish.

Despite these reforms, the monarchy itself remained innately medieval and stubbornly autocratic. Alexander had enraged the aristocracy and the landed gentry to whom most serfs had been bonded. This tiny but powerful minority demanded so many exemptions from the new laws that many of the newly liberated serfs, who believed they had a God-given right to the land ('We are yours but the land is ours'), found themselves worse off than under serfdom.

Keeping the best farmland for themselves, the landlords of the great estates sold off inferior plots to the peasants through the commune or *mir*, the village assembly of all male heads of households. Not only did the serfs get the worst farmland but by far the greater part of the land that changed hands between 1861 and 1905 went not to peasants but to townspeople. There were many anomalies. State serfs received more land than privately-owned serfs, while serfs employed inside manor houses received none at all. Overall, the agrarian peasant's average holding was thirteen per cent smaller than the one he had previously cultivated.[15]

While struggling to feed themselves, the peasants had to keep up with crippling mortgage repayments spread over forty-nine years, which meant that an entire generation and their children were lumbered with a massive burden of debt. Alexander Kerensky conceded that the villages had been freed from the power of the landlord but the peasant still had no defence against the grain merchant and the land jobber, an iniquity that led to 'poverty, sorrow and tears'.[16]

Indeed, the peasant, or *muzhik*, innately conservative, deeply religious and highly superstitious, was still a slave of his *mir* and he could be birched at the discretion of the rural district courts. Nor did the *zemstvos* provide much relief for the poor and underprivileged for the simple reason that suffrage was restricted to the wealthy, whose overriding concern was to maintain the status quo. The final bitter blow was that the nobility and the clergy were exempt from taxation and it was the peasant who provided about five-sixths of the state's revenue in taxes collected through his *mir*.[17]

Such was the anger over these blatant injustices that outbreaks of peasant disorder, mostly disturbances aimed at the landlords, increased alarmingly in the provinces. Local police easily suppressed these uprisings but the peasants remained angry and unhappy, and their plight attracted the makers of revolution. Some of the most alienated peasants were given permission to leave their *mir* and join the new urban class of industrial workers who were herded into unhygienic barracks and treated abominably. The barracks and the factories in which they laboured, many of them owned by British, French and German investors, provided an even richer breeding ground for socialist agitators than the villages, where troublesome strangers were often handed over to the police.[18]

'Alexander the Liberator' was no more humane than his father in curbing dissent. Political suspects could be incarcerated indefinitely before being charged with an offence, after which a secret commission would decide their fate. Many were held in underground dungeons beneath the Fortress of Peter and Paul, Saint Petersburg's Bastille, on tiny Zayachy Island off the north bank of the Neva. Thick stone walls kept the Tsar's enemies quiet and the golden spire of its cathedral marked the resting place of his ancestors. The Marquis de Custine noted the twin identities of the fortress as both prison and tomb, and added that 'the dead appeared to me to be freer than the living'.[19]

Half of the 'politicals' – prisoners of conscience - were arrested on the word of a spy, or for simply knowing a revolutionary. Some would be released after one or two years when the authorities could find no evidence to charge them with any crime; others were not so fortunate. One of the unluckiest was Nikolai Chernyshevsky, a priest's son and a disciple of Charles Fourier, who wrote and published his revolutionary novel *What Is To Be Done?* in 1863 while imprisoned in the fortress. Born in Saratov on the Volga in 1828, Chernyshevsky was a gentle, thoughtful, mild-mannered man and yet his book ignited revolutionary fires. After two years in the fortress, he was exiled to Siberia, first as a prisoner and then in almost life-long banishment.

In *What Is To Be Done?*, the author presented the *mir* as the birth-place of a socialist society in which men and women had equal rights and all nationalist and religious prejudices were abandoned. One of the characters, Rakhmetov, was a dedicated revolutionary. Ascetic in his habits and ruthlessly disciplined, he became a role model for many young men and women. Indeed, the novel was regarded as the bible of the *narodniks*, or Populists, in the pre-Marxist era. Its influence was so great that many historians credit Nikolai Chernyshevsky with being the true founding father of Bolshevism.[20]

After the underground dungeons were closed in the 1860s, the casemates of the Trubetskoi Bastion, the triangular fortifications at the front of the fortress, were rebuilt into a two-storey political prison consisting of sixty-nine cells. Prince Kropotkin, the anarchist son of an ancient land-owning family, was imprisoned there for revolutionary activism in 1874.[vi] He described his treatment in the Trubetskoi Ravelin:

> This room of mine was a casemate destined for a big gun and the window, cut in a wall five feet thick and protected by an iron grating and a double iron window frame, was an embrasure. The prisoner hears no human voice and sees no human being, except two or three jailers, deaf and mute when addressed by the prisoners. …You never hear a sound, excepting that of a sentry continually creeping like a hunter from one door to another to look through the 'Judas' into the cells. You are never alone, an eye is continually kept upon you; and yet you are always alone. The absolute silence is interrupted only by the bells of the clock which ring a change every quarter of an hour, each hour a canticle and each twelve hours 'God Save The Tsar'. The cacophony of the discordant bells is horrible and I do not wonder that nervous persons consider these bells one of the plagues of the fortress.[21]

The most glaring omission among the Great Reforms was Alexander II's failure to create an elected parliament. This was largely due to the anti-democratic rigidity of his legal adviser Konstantin Petrovich Pobedonostsev, Professor of Civil Law at Moscow University, who considered the reforms a 'criminal error'. Pobedonostsev's father, an Orthodox priest, had drilled into him the belief that man was by nature 'weak, vicious, worthless and rebellious'. Starting from that negative premise, his son denounced any sort of progressive thinking and preached 'Land, Family and Church' as the three legs of stable

---

vi Kropotkin renounced his princely title aged twelve and was known thereafter as Peter Kropotkin. As a geographer, he discovered that the Ice Age ended far more recently than previously supposed.

government. To him, Fourier was an 'inspired madman' whose socialist teaching 'incites the people to infamous misdeeds'.[22]

He also defended Russia's rule over her conquered minorities and advocated their cultural and political Russification, a self-defeating policy that weakened rather than strengthened the bonds of empire. Strict censorship prevented dangerous ideas being imported from those sinks of iniquity, republican Paris and democratic London. In 1872, however, three thousand copies of the Russian edition of Karl Marx's classic work, *Das Kapital*, were permitted to enter Russia after the censors decided it was a 'strictly scientific work that very few people in Russia will read and even fewer will understand'.[23]

The book sold out within a matter of months. It was indeed 'scientific' but the censors had failed to realise that what it preached was 'scientific socialism'. Marx's theory that capitalism must inevitably collapse interested one unlikely reader in Princess Victoria, the eldest daughter of Victoria and Albert, who was married to the Crown Prince of Germany. After reading *Das Kapital* in 1878, she sent an emissary to meet the London-based author, who had moved out of proletarian Soho and was living among the bourgeoisie of Belsize Park.

Sir Mountstuart Elphinstone Grant Duff, a Liberal Member of Parliament, invited him to the Devonshire Club, an old Whig establishment in Saint James's, on 31 January 1879. The next day Grant Duff reported on his mission in a letter to the Princess in which he described Marx, a Jewish atheist, as 'a short, rather small man with grey hair and beard which contrast strangely with a still dark moustache'.

> The face is somewhat round, the forehead well shaped and filled up - the eye rather hard but the whole expression rather pleasant than not, by no means that of a gentleman who is in the habit of eating babies in their cradles - which is, I daresay, the view which the Police takes of him.
>
> He looks, not unreasonably, for a great and not distant crash in Russia; thinks it will begin by reforms from above which the old bad edifice will not be able to bear and which will lead to its tumbling down altogether. As to what would take its place he had evidently no clear idea, except that for a long time Russia would be unable to exercise any influence in Europe.

To reassure the Princess that the monarchies were in no imminent danger, he concluded optimistically, '[His] ideas about the near future of Europe are too dreamy to be dangerous; there was no trace of bitterness or savagery - plenty of acrid and dissolvent criticism but nothing of the Marat tone. I would gladly meet him again. It will not be he who, whether he wishes it or not, will turn the world upside down.'[vii]

Eight months after that meeting, in October 1879, the People's Will (*Narodnaya Volia*), the most extreme political group Russia had seen so far, was formed in Saint Petersburg. Its aims were to destroy the Tsarist state through acts of violence and give birth to a people's republic. Its members were young revolutionary socialist intellectuals who had broken away from an earlier terrorist group, Land and Liberty (*Zemlya I Volya*), which had decided to pursue a more moderate, evolutionary course under Georgi Plekhanov, one of the first Russian Marxists.

On the afternoon of Sunday 1 March 1881 Sofia Perovskaya, the terrorist daughter of a former Governor-General of Saint Petersburg, waved a white handkerchief by the side of the Catherine Canal. This was the signal for a fellow terrorist, Nikolai Rysakov, to throw a bomb under the horses' hooves of Alexander II's bulletproof carriage as it passed him on its way from the Winter Palace to the capital's main street, Nevsky Prospekt.[viii]

The explosion killed the horses and mortally wounded one of the Tsar's Cossack escorts. It also killed a butcher's boy who happened to be passing on his way to deliver an order to a customer. It was then 2.15 pm. The Tsar was unharmed but insisted on leaving his carriage to check on the wounded.

'Are you all right, Sire?' one of his aides inquired.

'Yes, thank God!' Alexander replied.

'It's too early to thank God!' yelled Rysakov's Polish comrade, Ignacy Hryniewiecki, throwing a second bomb, which exploded with great force, killing the bomb thrower instantly. Colonel Adrian

---

vii Indeed, Marx's years in London had persuaded him that Britain could perhaps evolve towards socialism without a violent revolution.

viii Nevsky Prospekt was named after Prince Alexander Nevsky, the warrior-saint who defeated the Swedish invaders at the Neva River in 1240 and, two years later, beat the Teutonic Knights in 'the Battle on the Ice' at Lake Peipus.

Dvorzhitsky, who was travelling in a sleigh in front of the royal carriage, recalls that moment:

> I was deafened by the new explosion, burned, wounded and thrown to the ground. Suddenly, amid the smoke and snowy fog, I heard His Majesty's weak voice cry, 'Help!' Gathering what strength I had, I jumped up and rushed to the Emperor. His Majesty was half-lying, half-sitting, leaning on his right arm. Thinking he was merely wounded, I tried to lift him but the Tsar's legs were shattered and blood poured out of them.
>
> Twenty people, with wounds of varying degree, lay on the sidewalk and on the street. Some managed to stand, others to crawl, still others tried to get out from beneath bodies that had fallen on them. Through the snow, debris and blood you could see fragments of clothing, epaulets, sabres and bloody chunks of human flesh.[24]

'Take me to the Winter Palace,' Alexander gasped before drifting into unconsciousness. He was bleeding to death but instead of rushing him to hospital the faithful colonel complied with his master's command. Alexander was carried to the palace and placed on the divan in his study. Priests gave him communion and administered the last rites, while his physician, Dr Sergei Botkin, tried to stop the bleeding.

The Tsar's twelve-year-old grandson, Nicholas Alexandrovich, whom he called 'my sunray', dashed to the palace:

> My parents were already in the study. My uncle and aunt were standing near the window [Nicholas says]. Nobody said a word. My grandfather was lying on the narrow camp bed on which he always slept. He was covered with the military greatcoat that served as his dressing gown. His face was mortally pale; it was covered with small wounds. My father led me up to the bed. 'Papa,' he said, raising his voice, 'your sunray is here.'
>
> I saw a fluttering of his eyelids. The light blue eyes of my grandfather opened. He tried to smile. He moved his finger, but could not raise his hand and say what he wanted, but he undoubtedly recognised me.

His Imperial Majesty was able to swallow a little of the holy wine before he breathed his last. At 3.30 that Sunday afternoon his personal standard was lowered from the mast of the Winter Palace and the hopes and dreams of the reformers sank with it. The surviving members of the plot were rounded up and Sofia Perovskaya and four other terrorists, including Nikolai Rysakov, went to the gallows on 3 April 1881 without knowing that the assassination would achieve the exact opposite of what they had intended.

Ironically, on the day he was murdered, Alexander II had signed a modest first step towards a constitution, which would have permitted elected representatives of the people to collaborate with the government in reviewing the Great Reforms. This initiative died with him. His murder proved to his son, Alexander III, that greater freedom had failed to stabilise the Empire. The new Tsar disclosed his feelings in a letter to his wife, the Empress Maria Fyodorovna: 'All the scum burst out and swallowed all that was holy. The guardian angel flew away and everything turned to ashes, culminating in the dreadful incomprehensible of the first of March.' His grief would manifest itself in an all-consuming rage against liberalisation. Like a malevolent phoenix, the autocracy would rise again over the Winter Palace and spread disunity, hardship and terror among his subjects.[25]

2
The Sons of Simbirsk

Three weeks after Alexander II's assassination Fyodor Mikhailovich Kerensky, a staunch supporter of the monarchy and a devout communicant of the Orthodox Church, celebrated the birth of his first son, Alexander. Through a trick of fate, Alexander Fyodorovich Kerensky and his nemesis, Vladimir Ilyich Ulyanov, a.k.a. Vladimir Ilyich Lenin, were born within a few hundred yards of one another in Simbirsk, an ancient hillside town overlooking the Middle Volga. According to the Julian calendar, their birthdays both fell in April - Lenin on 10 April 1870 and Kerensky eleven years later on 22 April 1881.

Fyodor Mikhailovich, a tall, broad-shouldered man, with an enormous head, close-cropped hair and intelligent eyes set in a massive forehead, belonged to a Russian clan with monks and priests in its bloodline. The family name was derived from Kerensk, a settlement on the River Kerenka, 300 miles southeast of Moscow, with the stress on the first syllable: Kérensky. 'My parents met in Kazan, where my father held his first teaching post after leaving university,' Kerensky says. 'My mother was one of his pupils and they were married shortly after she left school.'[1]

Apart from their common birthplace Lenin and Kerensky shared another connection: their fathers were friends who worked closely together to advance the prospects of Simbirsk's younger generation. 'My father was principal of the two local gymnasiums, one for boys and the other for girls,' Kerensky says. 'Lenin's father, Ilya Ulyanov, was inspector of elementary schools. All his children were educated in the local high schools under my father's supervision.'[2]

Alexander, 'Sasha' to his family, was the Kerenskys' fourth child. His older sisters were Elena (Lyolya), Anna (Nyeta) and Nadezhda (Nadya), and his younger brother was Fyodor (Fedya). They had no Jewish ancestry but that didn't stop Alexander's enemies from claiming he was Jewish to discredit him in the eyes of the antisemitic Court and the antisemitic Russian masses. Henry Ford's newspaper, the *Dearborn Independent*, would claim in 1920 that Jewish propaganda had falsified Kerensky's paternity:

> His name is Adler. His father was a Jew and his mother a Jewess. Adler, the father, died, and the mother married a Russian named Kerensky, whose name the young child took. Among the radicals who employed him as a lawyer, among the forces that put him forward to drive the first nail into Russia's cross, among the soldiers who fought with him, his Jewish descent and character have never been doubted.[i] [3]

This mishmash of malice and make-believe emanated from the fact that Kerensky's mother, Nadezhda Alexandrova Adler, was the daughter of General Alexander Adler, a Tsarist officer who had fought with distinction in the armies of Nicholas I. She was also the niece of the Professor of Divinity at the University of Kazan. The Alder name was correct but the Jewish connection was untrue, as Kerensky's grandson Stephen Kerensky confirmed to *The Times of Israel*.[ii]

Lenin's father, Ilya Nikolaevich Ulyanov, was born at Astrakhan, the illustrious port-city on the Caspian Sea, into a family of former serfs of Russian and Kalmyk descent. Throwing off the shackles of the past, he graduated in physics and mathematics at the University of Kazan and then trained as a teacher. His wife, Maria Alexandrovna Blank, born in Saint Petersburg, was the daughter of a wealthy German-Swedish Lutheran mother and a Russian Jewish father whose family had converted to Christianity.

In 1869, six years after their wedding, Ilya Ulyanov was appointed Inspector of Popular Schools in Simbirsk and five years later he was promoted to inspector for the whole province, with the immense task of founding some 450 primary schools as part of the government's plans for modernisation. His dedication earned him the Order of Saint Vladimir, giving him the status of an hereditary nobleman.

---

[i] Henry Ford helped to fund the Nazi Party's rise to power in Germany. A grateful Hitler displayed Ford's portrait in his office from 1922 to 1924

[ii] Sir George Buchanan, the British Ambassador to Saint Petersburg, wrongly described Kerensky as the son a Jewish mother in his memoirs.

Ilya Ulyanov was a God-fearing member of the Orthodox Church and his younger son Vladimir, known as 'Volodya', was baptised in that faith six days after his birth. There were six surviving children: Anna, Alexander, Vladimir, Olga, Dmitri and Maria. Vladimir's head was so large and his legs so weak that he often toppled over. He used to bang his head on the floor, making his mother, Maria Alexandrovna, worry that he might be retarded. Maria had been raised a Lutheran but, in adulthood, she had become largely indifferent to Christianity, an attitude that turned some of her children – certainly Vladimir - against organised religion.

Alexander Kerensky has only one memory of his enemy in their Simbirsk days and it is more a fleeting impression than a clear picture:

> The school chapel on a festive occasion: the Holy Gates are opened, the priest comes out to administer communion to the children; the headmaster's two little sons are led up to him: they are in white, with pink bows under their Eton collars; and behind them, from among the orderly rows of schoolboys, dressed in tight-fitting blue uniform with silver buttons, looking at them, is the exemplary pupil (religiously educated and first in his class): Vladimir Ulyanov.'[4]

One week after Alexander Kerensky's birth Alexander III, guided by Konstantin Pobedonostsev, published the 'Manifesto on Unshakeable Autocracy' in which he proclaimed his faith in 'the justice and power of the autocracy'.[iii] Through a series of draconian laws, he dragged the monarchy back into the Dark Ages without actually restoring serfdom. The effect of these laws was to place an icy medieval grip on freedom of expression and freedom of worship.

Schools were forced to raise their fees to prevent the poorer classes from receiving an education. The press was heavily censored. Thousands of revolutionaries were sentenced to hard labour in Siberia. Any judge or government official suspected of liberal ideas was instantly dismissed. To limit the growth of Catholicism, the Tsar

---

iii In 1861, the year serfdom was abolished, Alexander II had invited Pobedonostsev to instruct his son and heir, Nicholas, in the theory of law and administration. When young Nicholas died four years later, the Professor was asked to teach his brother Alexander the same subjects. Master and pupil remained close for the next thirty years. Alexander also inherited Nicholas's fiancée, Princess Dagmar of Denmark, who became the Empress Maria Fyodorovna.

made it an offence for any of his subjects to convert from the Orthodox Church to another faith. Harsh penalties were reserved for anyone challenging Romanov power. Richard Pipes, who made a study of the autocratic Tsarist regime, wrote:

> Politics was declared the exclusive preserve of the government and its high functionaries. Any meddling in them on the part of unauthorised personnel, which included all private citizens, was a crime punishable by law. The enforcement of this principle was entrusted to a Department of Police and a Corps of Gendarmes whose exclusive concern was with crimes against the state. They had the power to search, arrest, interrogate, imprison and exile persons either guilty of political activity or suspected of it.[5]

Germans, Poles, Lithuanians, Latvians, Armenians and every other minority living under Romanov rule in Western Europe, Ukraine and the Caucasus (and later Finland) were required to speak Russian. The Poles, following the brutal suppression of their 1863 insurrection, had to read Polish literature in Russian. Absurdly, it was a crime for two schoolboys to have a conversation in their own language. Moreover, hundreds of thousands of Polish children were declared illegitimate because their parents had been married according to the rites of the Catholic Church.[6]

The Tsar reserved his greatest spite for Russia's five million Jews, the people he blamed for 'the murder of Jesus Christ'.[7] It was the German-born Catherine the Great who had established the Pale of Permanent Jewish Settlement, which stretched from Lithuania in the north to the Black Sea in the south, from Poland in the west to 'White Russia' and Ukraine in the east.[iv]

Ever since the Revolutions of 1848 had swept across Europe and terrified reactionary Christian monarchs, Jewish people had been portrayed as the agents of revolutionary subversion. It was a matter of great concern to the Romanovs that Jews did not see themselves as Russian nationals but as Russian citizens of Jewish nationality, even though no Jewish state existed. 'Alexander III and his son Nicholas II sowed the seeds of bitter national hatred in every corner of the Empire,' Alexander Kerensky says. 'But of all the sins of the last two

---

iv The archaic English term pale is derived from the Latin palus, a stake, extended to mean the area enclosed by a fence or boundary

Tsars, their greatest, unequalled, crime was their fanatical, one may even say maniacal, antisemitism.'[8]

Conspiratorial antisemites spread rumours that the Tsar's assassins were Jewish and hinted that the government had given the go-ahead for revenge attacks on Jewish communities. The first part was a lie; the second part was fundamentally true. Viacheslav von Pleve, a lawyer-turned-policeman who had arrested many members of the People's Will in the aftermath of the assassination, was the instigator of pogroms in Ukraine in which hundreds of Jews were killed and wounded, and thousands made homeless.[v] The most violent attacks took place in Kiev over three days in May 1881 and were described by the authorities as 'spontaneous demonstrations of an outraged people', so spontaneous that the local police had been informed in advance that they would take place and trainloads of extreme nationalists were brought in to ensure the maximum carnage.[9]

Pleve, the Chief of the Gendarmerie, and Count Nikolai Ignatiev, the new Minister of the Interior, had no scruples about protecting the autocracy from dangerous alien ideas. More than 600 statutes were drafted to deal with 'the Jewish Question' and even Jews who had been permitted to move into Russian towns and cities because they had special abilities or possessed a certain amount of wealth were persecuted.

Ignatiev's Temporary Regulations banned Jews from owning or managing land, buildings or farms outside the towns of the Pale; forbidding them from trading on Christian holy days including Sundays; and severely restricting Jewish numbers at university. Having been stripped of their businesses and forced to sell their homes at knockdown prices, more than 400,000 Jewish people emigrated from the Russian Empire in the 1890s, many sailing to a new life in the Americas.[10]

Alexander III's antisemitism became an international scandal in 1891 when his brother, Grand Duke Sergei Alexandrovich, refused to accept his appointment as Governor-General of Moscow 'unless the city is cleared of Jews'. On 28 April that year the Tsar signed the first of a series of laws allowing Sergei to expel the Jews from Moscow. Jewish artisans, distillers, brewers, general craftsmen, workmen and even discharged Jewish soldiers – 20,000 people in all, including

---

v Pogrom is Russian for devastation.

wives and children - were deported. Jewish women were allowed to remain in the city only if they registered as prostitutes.[11]

Leon Trotsky wrote in his biography *Young Lenin*, 'Whoever is born on the Volga carries her image through life.' This was certainly true of Alexander Kerensky. Life would take him to Britain, France, Germany, Czechoslovakia, the United States and Australia but his thoughts would always return to his home town and, in his mind's eye, he would see the hillside covered in apple and cherry blossom and hear the nocturnal song of the nightingale.

The Kerenskys' home was a large state-owned apartment on top of the hill in the fashionable part of town known as 'the Crown'. The apartment had so many rooms that, according to Alexander, the lives of the children 'were only remotely stirred by the excitement of big receptions'. He went to dancing lessons with elegant little girls and played with ragged, barefoot village boys. His first ambition was to be the church bell-ringer, 'to stand on a high steeple, above everybody, near the clouds, and thence to call men to the service of God with the heavy blows of a huge bell'.[12]

But it was the mighty river that most captivated him. Aged about seven, he watched the spring thaw:

> The Volga freed herself from her icy yoke and in a joyous outburst flooded the meadows on the left bank. The distant roar of the spring waters filled the air and I ran off to gaze at the river. Spellbound by the beauty of the scene, I experienced a sense of elation that grew almost to the point of spiritual transfiguration. Then, suddenly overcome by an unaccountable feeling of terror, I ran away. For me that moment was decisive in choosing the spiritual path that I was to follow throughout my life.[13]

Elation and terror - the river would become a metaphor for Russia's quest for liberty. 'From the very beginning of my conscious existence,' he says, 'the history of the Russian political struggle became a living thing for me, the long unbroken development of a single action – the fight for freedom.'

Simbirsk was a good starting point. Despite an abundance of natural beauty, it was one of the most backward, most repressed places in the Empire. 'All around the town, on the steep shores of the river and hidden among wooded glades and thickets, were the country manors of the squires,' Kerensky says. 'The manors were surrounded by villages inhabited by peasants who had but recently been serfs. The great reforms of Alexander II evoked no enthusiasm there; the government had never been forgiven for the liberation of the peasants, particularly liberation accompanied by land-endowment which "had ruined the landed gentry".'[14]

One of Tsar Alexander's meanest acts was to give the Church control over all primary schools. This enabled Pobedonostsev, who had been elevated to Procurator-General of the Most Holy Synod in 1880, making him not only the most powerful layman in the Orthodox Church but also Minister of Religion, to emasculate the syllabuses that reformers such as Ilya Ulyanov had painstakingly compiled in creating the network of elementary schools. His aim was to keep each person in that station in life into which he had been born and to restrict higher education to the upper classes.[15]

In 1883, the year of Karl Marx's death, Ilya Ulyanov's elder son Alexander won the gold medal as the most outstanding student at the Simbirsk Classical Gymnasium. A glowing testimonial from Fyodor Kerensky helped him to gain a place at the University of Saint Petersburg to study natural sciences. He was two years into a course on Zoology when his father was struck down by a fatal stroke on 12 January 1886. Ilya Ulyanov's last years had been unhappy. He had been forced into retirement four years earlier than was customary and, as well as being professionally humiliated, he had struggled to raise his family. After his death, Fyodor Kerensky stepped in and became the children's guardian. He also mentored young Vladimir in his studies.[16]

The Ulyanov brothers were completely dissimilar in character. Kerensky says Alexander was known for being 'infinitely kind, generous and self-denying... he bewitched and conquered people at first sight and forever'. Vladimir, on the other hand, had a cruel streak. It was said that as a boy he 'liked to shoot at stray cats, or to break a crow's wing with his airgun'. According to his biographer Robert Service, 'There was a malicious aspect to his behaviour and the rest of the family did not like it.'[17]

While at university, Alexander Ulyanov joined the *narodniki*, a group of revolutionary Populists who plotted to kill Alexander III on the sixth anniversary of his father's death, 1 March 1887. The Okhrana, the Tsarist secret police force, got wind of the plot and all the conspirators were arrested. Alexander, the bomb-maker, accepted full responsibility and refused to recant. 'There is no finer death than death for one's country,' he told the judges at his trial. 'Such a death holds no terror for sincere and honest men. I had but one aim: to help the unfortunate Russian people.' He was hanged in the Shlisselburg Fortress, an island prison in Lake Ladoga at the head of the River Neva, on 8 May 1887 and his family was ostracised from Simbirsk society.

Vladimir, who was sixteen at the time, was sitting his final exams. Even then a pragmatist, he summed up his brother's actions in one sentence: 'It must mean that he had to act like this; he couldn't act in any other way.'[18] Despite the family catastrophe, Vladimir achieved a five – the highest mark – in all ten of his subjects and came top of his year. Fyodor Kerensky acknowledged his achievement in a testimonial which gained him a place at the University of Kazan to study law:

> Very gifted, always neat and assiduous, Ulyanov was first in all subjects and upon completing his studies received a gold medal as the most deserving pupil with regard to his ability, progress and behaviour. Neither in the school nor outside, has a single instance been observed when he has given cause for dissatisfaction by word or deed to the school authorities and teachers. His mental and moral instruction has always been thoroughly looked after, first by his parents and upon the death of his father in 1886 by his mother alone... Religion and discipline were the basis of this upbringing, the fruits of which are apparent in Ulyanov's behaviour. Looking more closely at Ulyanov's character and private life, I have had occasion to note a somewhat excessive tendency to avoid contact with acquaintances, even with the very best of his schoolfellows outside school hours. Ulyanov's mother intends to be with him throughout his university career.[19]

Vladimir's isolation probably stemmed from a monk-like dedication to his studies, though after Alexander's arrest he became noticeably antisocial and melancholic. He also lost any connection with the Almighty; from then on, he described himself as an atheist. Alexander Kerensky had no doubt that it was the fate of his 'noble-minded and brilliant brother' that would turn Vladimir into 'a sadistically vengeful cynic'.[20]

Alexander Ulyanov entered Kerensky's life only fleetingly but he left an indelible mark. 'The mere mention of his name evoked the picture of a mysterious carriage with drawn green blinds driving through the town at night to take people away,' he says. 'The frightened talk of the grown-ups about these dreadful events penetrated into our nursery and, owing to the close connection between our parents and the Ulyanovs, we soon learned of the execution of their talented son. Such was my initial contact with the revolutionary movement.'[21]

Shortly after Alexander Ulyanov's execution Sasha Kerensky was stricken with tuberculosis of the hip and had to be segregated from his siblings. An iron brace was fitted to his right knee to prevent him bending his leg. When he complained, his mother told him, 'You don't want to be lame for the rest of your life.' For six months he lay in bed. Books and magazines, historical novels, travel and scientific texts, stories about Native American tribes and the lives of the saints were his salvation. 'I fell under the spell of Pushkin, Lermontov (the poet of the Caucasus) and Tolstoy,' he says. 'I could not put down *Dombey and Son* and I shed bitter tears over *Uncle Tom's Cabin*.'[vi]

Sasha made a good recovery and was able to remove the brace from his leg and go for morning walks with his brother Fyodor and their nursemaid, Ekaterina. Their route took them from the Kerensky home at the top of the hill, past the Governor's Mansion, the Simbirsk Classical Gymnasium and the Simbirsk Library and down a tree-lined boulevard towards the waterfront. One morning they came upon a group of prisoners being led to the quayside. The men had been condemned to exile in Siberia and were to be loaded on to a steamer for the journey to the nearest railhead. 'The grim procession, guarded by a convoy of soldiers, was followed by a wagon crowded with women and children,' Kerensky says. 'To us children, the convicts were frightening with their half-shaven heads and their clanking chains, and my brother and I started to run away.'

Ekaterina stopped them. 'Do you really think they're going to hurt you?' she said. 'Who are we to judge them? You should take pity on these poor wretches.' She bought some *kalach* bread from one of the

---

vi Harriet Beecher Stowe's classic about an African slave's attempts to escape from an American plantation was also the favourite book of young Vladimir Ulyanov.

vendors walking beside the prisoners. 'You must ask the soldiers to let you give it to these poor men,' she said. 'Not only will they enjoy it, but it will make you feel good, too.' Sasha distributed the bread and the image of those gaunt, shaven-headed figures came back to haunt him whenever 'Siberian exile' was mentioned. Just as the Volga had inspired elation and terror in the young Kerensky, this incident generated the first stirrings of a social conscience.[22]

Meanwhile, Vladimir Ulyanov's legal studies at the University of Kazan had ended abruptly after only three months with his expulsion in December 1887 for taking part in a harmless student protest. According to a police report based on information provided by informers at the university, his behaviour prior to the incident 'gave grounds for suspicion that he was fomenting trouble and that he was meditating some improper behaviour: he spent much time in the common room, talking to the less desirable students, he went home and came back again with some object the others had asked for, and in general behaved very strangely'.[23]

Then, on 4 December, the day of the protest, he had burst into the assembly hall, rushed shouting down a corridor and waved his arms 'as though to encourage the others'. Given his family background, this was enough for the police 'to believe him fully capable of unlawful and criminal demonstrations of all kinds'.

Despite a letter from Fyodor Kerensky to the university authorities making the point that Alexander Ulyanov had been hanged only eight months earlier and speculating that Vladimir 'might have lost the balance of his mind as the result of the catastrophe that has shattered the unhappy family', he was obliged to spend most of 1888 in exile on the Blank family's estate at Kokushino with his mother, Maria Alexandrovna, and elder sister, Anna Ilinichna, who had also been exiled.

Maria was shocked to see that while at university her son had taken up smoking. When he lit a cigarette after dinner, the normally contained matriarch exploded, 'Volodya, you have no income apart from the money I provide. You have no right to squander our family funds on tobacco.' Vladimir never lit another cigarette. He came to loathe smoking in his presence, so much so that smokers at his meetings were obliged to face the fireplace and exhale up the chimney.

Exile provided him with the opportunity to devote himself to books. 'Never later in my life, not in prison in Petersburg or in Siberia, did I read so much as in the year after my exile to the countryside from Kazan,' he said later. 'This was serious reading, from early morning to late at night.'[24] His reading list included the works of Chernyshevsky, Nechayev, Marx, Georgi Plekhanov and Pyotr Nikitich Tkachev, the last a revolutionary theorist sometimes described as 'the first Bolshevik'. The first volume of *Das Kapital* had an electrifying effect on him. Gesticulating wildly, he told his sister Anna about 'the principles of Marxist theory and the new horizons it was opening to him'.[25]

In one of his early pamphlets Marx, a former Hegelian, argued that 'philosophers have only interpreted the world in various ways, the point is to change it'. He and his collaborator Friedrich Engels provided the antidote to philosophy in 'The Communist Manifesto', published in German as *Manifest der Kommunistischen Partei* just three days before the 1848 Revolution forced the abdication of Louis-Philippe in France.

The manifesto opened with the words, 'A spectre is haunting Europe - the spectre of communism. All the powers of old Europe have entered into a holy alliance to exorcise this spectre'. The text ended with a call-to-arms: 'The proletarians have nothing to lose but their chains. They have a world to win. Working men of all countries, unite!' None of this was original: Marat, the French revolutionary, was the first to say 'The proletarians have nothing to lose but their chains,' while the German socialist Karl Schapper coined the slogan 'Working men of all countries, unite'. Nevertheless, Marx and Engels had provided Communists with a manual setting out 'their views, their aims and their tendencies'.[26]

The manifesto was not translated into Russian until 1869 when the anarchist Mikhail Bakunin produced an unauthorised, and partly inaccurate, version. Marx and Engels wrote a new preface for the 1882 Russian edition, which was translated by Georgi Plekhanov from his sanctuary in Geneva. The authors pondered the question of whether Russia could turn communist directly or whether she would first have to become a capitalist society in the pre-ordained socialist manner.

Lenin preferred Plekhanov's interpretation in his pamphlet *So-*

cialism and Political Struggle (1883) and his book *Our Differences* (1885), which explained Marxism from a Russian standpoint and delineated its differences from the Populist movement. Plekhanov argued that capitalism already existed in Russia, primarily in the textile industry but also in agriculture, and that a working class was beginning to emerge among the peasants. It was this expanding working class, he believed, that would ultimately and inevitably bring about socialist change in Russia.[27]

Lenin incorporated elements from all these works, plus the conspiratorial politics of the People's Will, in his own revolutionary doctrine in which he reached the same conclusion as Marx: that the end justified the means. For Lenin, Marxism became a convenient vehicle that could be turned left or right, or even put into reverse, to suit changing circumstances. Planted firmly in the driving seat, he would make history as he went along.[28]

At the end of Lenin's exile the Ulyanovs moved to a 200-acre farm purchased by Maria at Alakaevka, thirty miles from Samara on the Volga between Simbirsk and Astrakhan. For the first time in his life Lenin made contact with peasants in their natural habitat. As he was their landlord, they treated him with suspicion and his efforts to speak to them about their lives were largely unproductive. His main interest was in meeting local activists and reading as much political literature as he could digest.

He also studied law as an external student of the University of Saint Petersburg and in November 1891 passed his final examinations with a first in all subjects. For the next eighteen months he practised law in Samara, working primarily with peasants and artisans, an experience that confirmed his loathing of the class bias in the Tsarist legal system. Moving to Saint Petersburg on 31 August 1893, his law work served as a cover for his growing involvement with revolutionary Marxism. The most important development was his participation with Julius Martov (real name Yuly Tsederbaum) and others to form the Union of Struggle for the Liberation of the Working Class, a political organisation that united twenty Marxist study groups with the aim of educating the workers in the principles of Marxism.

The union was partly responsible for organising a strike of textile workers in Saint Petersburg in 1896, the first mass action by Russia's industrial workers. Lenin and Martov, however, played little or no part in the strike - they had been arrested before it began, Lenin in December 1895 and Martov a month later. After spending a year in prison, Lenin was sentenced on 29 January 1897 to three years' 'free exile' in Eastern Siberia for belonging to a radical organisation.[29]

'Free exile' meant he could travel to his place of confinement unescorted and, once there, do pretty much as he pleased. He settled down in Shushenskoe, a village beside a lake in the Minusinsk district of Yenisei Province. His lover, Nadezhda 'Nadya' Krupskaya, an activist who had been sentenced for her own political activities to exile in Ufa, 300 miles east of Samara, was allowed to join him on condition that they married. Although both despised the concept of holy matrimony, they were joined together as husband and wife on 22 July 1898.

Lenin had been nervous and ill when he arrived in Siberia but married life, fresh air, fishing, hunting and swimming gave him a healthy glow. Most of his hair had fallen out by then and he had assumed the familiar goatee'd look of a crusty academic. Nadezhda, who had been born into an impoverished noble family, was twenty-eight to his twenty-seven. Her school friend, Ariadne Tyrkova, described her as 'a tall, quiet girl who did not flirt with the boys... one of those who are forever committed'.[30]

Alexander Kerensky had lost touch with the Ulyanov family in early 1889 when his father was appointed Chief Inspector of Schools for Turkestan, literally 'Land of the Turks', an immense territory at the Central Asian frontier of the Russian Empire, with Siberia to the north and Iran, Afghanistan and Tibet to the south. Alexander had never heard of the place and the journey opened his eyes to the immensity of his country. 'The morning of our departure, our closest friends came to bid us farewell and sit down with us in silent prayer,' he says. 'Then we made the sign of the cross, embraced each other and set out for the boat landing.'[31]

The Kerenskys sailed down the Volga to Astrakhan, the scene of Ivan the Terrible's 1556 victory over the Kazan and Astrakhan Tatars of the Golden Horde which had opened up the south to Russian expansion.[vii] From Astrakhan, the family crossed the Caspian to Uzun-Ada and took the single-track Transcaspian Railway to Samarkand,

---

vii Gold was the colour of Batu Khan's royal tent.

Tamerlane's one-time capital whose capture in 1868 had completed Russia's conquest of Turkestan. Their destination was Tashkent, the current capital, located in a fertile river valley with the snow-capped Pamir Mountains just visible in the distance.

As the railway line ended at Samarkand, the Kerenskys made the final 200-mile leg of their journey in the springless, hooded carriage known as a *tarantas*. The total distance covered was 1595 miles after which Alexander found himself in an exotic Eastern world of brightly coloured people, jostling bazaars, sweet-smelling *chai-khanas* (teahouses) and tinkling caravans of two-humped dromedaries.

The Central Asians were Turkic peoples, mostly Sunni Muslims. They ranged from Uzbeks, who had built Tashkent, Samarkand and the holy city of Bokhara, to the nomadic Kazakhs, who lived in *yurts* (circular tents) and drove their horses and cattle from the grasslands of the treeless steppes to the cool of the mountains. Tashkent itself was an ancient Islamic city of shady alleys that connected houses, mosques and minarets to the central bazaar, one of the most important trading hubs on the Silk Road. The city had a population of 150,000 but only a quarter were Russians, who lived primarily in a well-planned new town of broad streets and large, cool houses. Almost every street was lined with a double avenue of trees – poplar, elm, chinar, oak, mulberry and acacia – and running water from the irrigation system gushed down the gutters, acting as an al fresco air-conditioning system for the teahouses.[32]

Since annexation in 1865 Tashkent had served as the nerve centre of Russian military operations in Central Asia, the 'vast chessboard' on which the Great Game of espionage and subversion was played between Britain and its Russian occupiers. The previous year George Curzon, the future British Foreign Secretary, had made an epic journey from Saint Petersburg to Tashkent to spy on Russia's military preparations for invading India. He called the city a 'refuge of [men with] damaged reputations and shattered fortunes, whose only hope of recovery lay in the chances afforded on the battlefield'.[33]

The policy of the local Tsarist officials was to rule the region peacefully without any attempt at Russification, so the population's Muslim faith and traditions were left untouched. The Russian judicial system, minus trial by jury, operated side by side with sharia law. Slavery had been abolished but inside the broad white walls of

Bokhara murderers and thieves were still hurled to their deaths from the top of a minaret.[34] Kerensky thought that, on the whole, the effects of Russian rule in Turkestan 'reflect nothing but credit on Russia':

> Turkestan had no gentry longing for the days of serfdom, nor had its development been influenced by an impoverished peasantry. It had not experienced the absurd government campaign against literacy in rural areas, the pernicious policies of barring the children of the 'lower classes' from school and of suppressing any expression of independent thought in colleges, the press and civic organisations. Turkestan was too remote to be the target of reactionary officials who were trying to turn the empire, with its many different peoples, into a Muscovite kingdom.[35]

The planned extension of the railway from Samarkand to Tashkent, plus new agricultural and irrigation projects, drew the Turkic peoples into the Russian economy. Towns and cities were surrounded by flowering fields of cotton and other lucrative cash crops. Even the Russophobic Curzon, in his 1889 book *Russia in Central Asia and the Anglo-Russian Question*, had to admit that Russian rule had brought considerable benefits to the region. But he warned his compatriots that once the railway joined Moscow to Tashkent the Russians would be able to concentrate as many as 100,000 troops on the Afghan frontier to threaten India.

While the British worried about the Raj, the Russian Army pulled off a coup of its own through Captain Lavr Kornilov, a Cossack graduate of the General Staff Academy. 'Kornilov spent little time in fashionable drawing-rooms and had no liking for the ladies of the social set,' says Kerensky. 'He was regarded as rather shy and a bit of a savage.' Disguising himself as a merchant, Kornilov made his way into Afghanistan, the buffer state between Russian Turkestan and British India, on a secret mission to spy on Afghan defences. This was forbidden territory to all foreigners but Kornilov, slim and wiry with slanting Kalmyk eyes, had mastered one of the local dialects and he was able to mix easily with Afghans in their marketplaces. He returned to Tashkent with a great deal of useful military intelligence.

News of his mission created a sensation. Aged just twenty-two, he was marked down as an enterprising officer with a great future. It was typical of his doughty character, however, that he turned his back on celebrity. 'He astonished high society by marrying the daughter of a minor official in my father's department,' says Kerensky. 'This was too much: the doors of society were closed to him.'

One of the most important events during Kerensky's time in Tashkent was the arrival in 1894 of Colonel Vsevolod Stephanovich Baranovsky to serve as examining magistrate in the halls of justice. Vsevolod and his wife Lydia, née Vasilieva, had three daughters, Vera, Olga and Elena, and two sons, Vladimir and Svetoslav. Over the next eight years the Baranovsky and Kerensky children would become firm friends, with Alexander very much the leader of the pack. Thirteen when they met, he described himself as 'gregarious, fond of social life and girls, and an enthusiastic partner in games and dances'. His heart was set on an acting career and such was his ardour that a year or so later he signed a letter to his parents, 'The future Artist of the Imperial Theatre, A. Kerensky'.

His greatest success on the local gymnasium's stage was his portrayal of Khlestakov, the main character in Gogol's comedy of errors *The Inspector General*, which satirises human greed, stupidity and the rampant political corruption of Imperial Russia. Although Kerensky stuck to his acting ambitions throughout his secondary schooling, it was his friend Vera Baranovskaya who would become a leading actor at the Moscow Art Theatre and one of the Soviet Union's best-loved film stars. Olga, the second Baranovsky sister, would also become an actress, but it was the youngest girl, Elena, known as Lilya, who would make the greatest impact on Kerensky's life. She would become his lover and would bear him a daughter out of wedlock.

3

The Distorting Mirror

While Alexander Kerensky was an ethnic Russian with a bloodline that stretched back for generations in the Penza Province southeast of Moscow, Nicholas II, Emperor of All the Russias, had almost no Russian blood at all. Even the humblest *muzhik* toiling in the fields for a few kopeks was more Russian than his fabulously wealthy master could ever claim to be. Indeed, Maurice Paléologue, the French Ambassador to Saint Petersburg, estimated that Nicholas was only 1/256th Russian.[1]

The Tsar was a distant, almost mythical figure to the vast majority of his subjects but, unlike millions of others, Kerensky had actually caught a glimpse of him in the flesh. As he was walking past the Winter Palace late one evening during the Easter of 1900 or 1901, he saw the monarch standing on an overhanging balcony. 'I stopped involuntarily,' he says. 'He was quite alone, deep in thought. I had a keen presentiment and it pursued me for a long time.'[2]

By then the young Kerensky had become a staunch anti-Tsarist. He was convinced that one day their paths would cross and that he would appear on that same balcony in a position of power. If Nicholas was 'God's Anointed One' with a divine right to rule Russia as a supreme autocrat, then he would be one of the revolutionaries who would bring him down.

Nicholas Alexandrovich Romanov, the eldest son of Alexander III, was born on the night of 6 May 1868 at the Alexander Palace at Tsarskoe Selo, the 'Tsar Village' fifteen miles south of the capital. His mother, Maria Fyodorovna, was the former Princess Dagmar of Denmark, sister of Princess Alexandra, wife of the future King Edward VII of Great Britain. It was an astonishing feature of European Royalty that just as Edward and Alexandra's offspring would be overwhelmingly German and Danish rather than British, so the children of

Alexander and Maria would be overwhelmingly German and Danish rather than Russian.

Following their wedding in 1866, Alexander and 'Minnie', as the Tsarina was known to her family, started married life in the Anichkov Palace on Nevsky Prospect. They raised their five surviving children, Nicholas, George, Michael, Olga and Xenia, in the rarefied atmosphere of imperial palaces, or in the palaces and castles of their Danish, British and German relatives.[i] They travelled between one exotic location and another on royal yachts or in royal trains, with the curtains drawn to prevent the hoi polloi from getting even a glimpse of their private world.[3]

After his father's death, Alexander was obliged to move into the Winter Palace but he found it uncomfortable and there were too many memories of the assassination in its cold, draughty corridors. When another plot was uncovered, the Imperial Family moved twenty-five miles southwest of Saint Petersburg to the Great Gatchina Palace, which was reassuringly close to the barracks of several regiments. Contact with ordinary Russians was even more minimal than before. There were picnics, bicycle rides and bear hunts on private estates. On an almost daily basis Michael went shooting and reported to his French tutor, Ferdinand Thormeyer, how many bears he had shot on that particular outing.[4]

Minnie made the mistake of treating 'Nicky' as a child for far too long. She dressed him in little sailor suits and called him 'my dear little soul'. He was still playing hide-and-seek well into his twenties. While he adored his mother, he was terrified of his autocratic father, a black-bearded giant who ruled Russia with an iron fist. The Tsar's favourite sport was slaughtering game and having the kill laid out for the admiration of his family. He was so strong he could twist iron pokers into knots with his bare hands.[5]

Despite an age advantage over his siblings, Nicholas – his grandfather's 'sunray' – had not lived up to expectations. George, the most intelligent brother, was his mother's favourite, while his father favoured Michael (Misha), the bear killer, for his reckless spirit and love of hunting. He considered the son who would follow him on to the

---

i The second-born child, named Alexander, died of meningitis in 1870, one month before his first birthday. George died in 1899 aged twenty-eight, making Michael the Tsarevich until the birth of Nicholas's son Alexei in 1904.

throne a weakling and called him 'girlie'. As a result, Nicholas grew up with a crippling sense of inferiority. When ministers suggested the time had come to give the Tsarevich some responsibility, Alexander was astonished. 'What? Have you ever had a serious conversation with him? He is still absolutely a child; he has only infantile judgments.'[6]

Nicholas was painfully shy and acutely aware of his shortcomings, starting with his height - five feet seven inches compared with his father's strapping six feet three inches - but he was far from retarded. Specialists had been brought to the palace to teach him French, English and German, mathematics, history, geography and chemistry. His first tutor on law and history was Michael Katkov, the Slavophile editor of *Moscow Gazette*, with the back-up of his father's mentor, Professor Pobedonostsev.[7]

Nicholas's principal tutor, however, was Charles Heath, a tophatted, frockcoated Cambridge graduate. While Pobedonostsev and Katkov drummed the sanctity of the autocratic state into his head, Heath taught him to speak English with an upper-class accent and to curb his quick temper. 'Aristocrats are born but gentlemen are made,' his tutor told him firmly. As a result, Nicholas mastered his temper and achieved a high degree of self-control.

Nicky grew to manhood without realising he was looking at life through a distorting mirror that altered the true state of Russia and her people. He was taught that everybody was in their rightful place according to God's will and that the peasant was happy with his lot, so long as he was spared the attentions of socialist agitators. As the historian Dominic Lieven put it, 'An innocent childhood and an education devoted to inculcating purity of heart and selfless patriotism were a poor preparation for a working life at the heart of Russian politics.'[8]

On 23 June 1887 Nicholas joined the Preobrazhensky Lifeguard Regiment, one of the oldest and most elite Guards regiments of the Imperial Russian Army, with the rank of second-lieutenant, rising to staff captain seven days later. He remained on active service with the regiment for two years before joining units of the Guards' Cavalry and Horse Artillery.

There was also his sex education to consider. Once Nicky had turned twenty-one, Alexander took him to a graduation ceremony at the Imperial School of Theatrical Dance. After the ceremony, Nicky was introduced to one of the graduating class, a bewitching seventeen-year-old Polish ballerina named Matilda-Marie Feliksovna Kshesinskaya. Unbeknown to him, his father had chosen her as his first mistress. At the graduation supper Alexander placed the sloe-eyed dancer next to himself and put Nicky on her other side.

'Careful!' he chuckled. 'Not too much flirting.'[9]

Alexander had chosen unwisely. The Bolshoi historian Simon Morrison described Matilda as 'a black swan capable of extreme malice before the idea of the black swan had even been devised'. Nicholas was putty in her hands. She noted triumphantly in her diary, 'He will be mine.'[10] Matters of state intervened to interrupt his seduction. The biggest project of the age was the Trans-Siberian Railway to link Moscow in the west with Vladivostok in the east.[ii] Alexander saw the 5564-mile rail link principally as a way of uniting his empire through faster, more efficient communications. Its construction, however, was always going to bring Russia into conflict with the Japanese, who had ambitions in the Chinese vassal state of Korea and in Manchuria, the Qing's Manchu homeland.

To the outside world, Japan was the Sphinx of Asia, a feudal riddle wrapped in a modern enigma; a country where business magnates in top hats and frockcoats mingled with peasants in costumes as old as antiquity. The Emperor Mutsuhito (1825-1912), known posthumously as Meiji ('the Great'), had ascended the Chrysanthemum Throne as a fifteen-year-old in 1867. Dating from the Emperor Jimmu, who ruled from 660 BC to 585 BC, the Imperial Line of Japan was by far the oldest reigning dynasty in the world. Compared with the Japanese royals, the Romanovs were upstarts.[11]

In early 1891 Alexander III sent the Tsarevich halfway round the world to take part in the ceremonies marking the start of construction of the Trans-Siberian Railway at its eastern terminus. After visiting Greece, Egypt, India and Indochina (Vietnam), Nicholas and his travelling companion, his cousin Prince George of Greece, stopped off in Japan to visit the Japanese Emperor. A few days later Nicholas

---

ii The 1860 Treaty of Peking - the foundation of Russia's Pacific power - set the eastern boundary between the Russian and Chinese Empires along the Amur and Usuri Rivers. The Usuri boundary gave Russia possession of what became the Maritime Province, with Vladivostok as capital.

arrived in Golden Horn Bay, Vladivostok, with a dragon tattoo on his right arm and a livid scar on the right side of his forehead.

He received the scar while returning to Kyoto after a day trip to Otsu in Shiga Prefecture when a deranged member of his police escort swung at his head with a sabre. The sword caught him a glancing blow on the forehead and it was only the quick thinking of Prince George, who parried a second blow with his bamboo cane, that saved his life. After having the wound treated in hospital, Nicholas headed back to the Russian Fleet at Kobe and sailed for Vladivostok. The Meiji Emperor's public expression of sorrow at Japan's lack of respect towards her guest did little to diminish the physical pain which would recur for the rest of Nicholas's life. From then on, he nursed a burning hatred of the Japanese, an obsession that would shake the very foundations of the Romanov Dynasty.

Returning to Saint Petersburg through Siberia, the wounded hero resumed his pursuit of Matilda Kshesinskaya. 'This evening flew to my MK and spent the very best evening with her up to now,' he told his diary. 'I am still under her spell – the pen is shaking in my hand.' He had finally lost his virginity.[12]

Given her nature, it was no surprise to Matilda's sister ballerinas that she developed an instantaneous sense of entitlement. She moved into in a mansion at Nicky's expense, dined on caviar and champagne, took her holidays in European resorts and started collecting diamonds and emeralds. Grand dukes fell at her feet – one even fathered a child with her. Matilda made it clear to the ballet master of the Imperial Ballet, Marius Petipa, that she enjoyed the protection of the Court and should be treated as a diva. Petipa, a volatile Franco-Russian martinet, referred to her in his diaries as 'that nasty little swine'.[13]

It was symptomatic of Russia's contradictory character that while the Tsar had been applying the thumbscrew to his subjects' civil liberties, the country was undergoing a remarkable industrial revolution, largely due to the efforts of Sergei Yulevich Witte, a huge, bearded, bear-like man whose heart burned with a fiery passion for Russia. Born on 17 June 1849 to a gentrified Georgian civil servant and the daughter of a Russian princess, he had qualified as an engineer in Odessa, the Ukrainian port-city on the Black Sea, and had then devoted his technical skills to becoming an expert on the country's rail network.

In early 1892 Alexander appointed him Minister of Transport and later that year promoted him to Minister of Finance with a brief to accelerate the progress of the Trans-Siberian Railway. He responded with a bold empire-building scheme. 'I conceived the idea of building the railway straight across Chinese territory, principally Mongolia and northern Manchuria, toward Vladivostok,' he says.[14]

Witte's personal life, however, presented a problem in his dealings with the Court. His first wife had died in 1890 and while working in Odessa he had fallen in love with Matilda Ivanovna Lisanevich, a married woman, after meeting her at the theatre one evening. Matilda was a Jewess who had converted to Orthodoxy. After divorcing her 'profligate and worthless' husband, she and Witte were wed in Saint Petersburg according to the rites of the Orthodox Church.

Hearing Witte had acquired a Jewish wife, Alexander III asked him, 'Is it true you are in sympathy with the Jews?'

> The only way I can answer this question [Witte replied] is by asking Your Majesty whether you think it is possible to drown all the Russian Jews in the Black Sea. To do so, of course, would be a radical solution to the problem. But if Your Majesty will recognise the right of the Jews to live, then conditions must be created which will enable them to carry on a human existence. In that case, gradual abolition of the disabilities is the only solution of the Jewish problem.[15]

Alexander said nothing and Witte took his silence to mean he accepted his answer. 'As Minister of Finance,' he says, 'I vigorously opposed all measures intended to restrict the rights of the Jews, but it was not in my power to repeal the existing laws against them. Many of these laws were unjust and did much harm to Russia and Russians.'

Witte's enemies, who vastly outnumbered his friends, found him boastful, coarse, opinionated and devious. Some called him a dyed-in-the-wool conservative; others thought him a dangerous radical. His marriage to Matilda, which made him a happy man for the rest of his life, cost him many of his connections with the nobility. The Tsar, however, refused to dismiss him. 'When Alexander discovered Witte,' says Alexander Kerensky, 'he put the right man in the right place. Russia moved forward in bounds, taking whole centuries of progress in its stride and catching up with the best that Western Europe could show.'[16]

The results of his financial policies astonished Western economists and investors. From an admittedly low base, Russia in the 1890s achieved an annual growth rate of just over eight per cent, the highest on the planet. Witte placed the rouble on the Gold Standard and encouraged British, German and French financiers to fund the budding industrial Colossus. Russia's coal, iron, steel and oil production tripled between 1890 and 1900. His most controversial move was to make the production and sale of vodka a state monopoly. At a stroke, it earned billions for the treasury.[17]

Ever since his ascension, Alexander III had encouraged rapprochement with France, even though it had become a republic again following the collapse of the Second Empire during the Franco-Prussian War of 1870-71. His chances of reaching a deal with the Quai d'Orsay improved immeasurably when Count Otto von Bismarck, the first Chancellor of the German Empire, resurrected the Triple Alliance of Germany, Austria-Hungary and Italy. The pact represented a threat to both France and Russia, and led to the Russian and French fleets exchanging courtesy visits. These acts of friendship culminated in 1893 with the signing of a secret alliance between the foreign ministers of the two countries.

When the news leaked out, Tolstoy denounced the Franco-Russian Alliance as a flagrant violation of the principles of right and freedom. In an open letter to the press he condemned the fact that the French Republic had given its moral authority to the autocracy, the enemy of Russian liberty. Censorship forbade publication of the letter in Russia, so it was circulated privately in lithographic form. Fyodor Kerensky brought one of the copies home and young Alexander deduced from the conversation at the dinner table that his parents intended to read it that evening.

'I sneaked quietly back to the dining room,' he says, 'and there, from behind a curtain, listened with bated breath to Tolstoy's biting, angry, accusing words, words as fatal as sword thrusts. By the emotion in my father's voice as he was reading, I knew that Tolstoy had written something great and true, and that to some extent my father agreed with him.'[18]

Back among the lakes and gardens of Gatchina, Nicholas was plucking up the courage to take the most important step of his rite of passage into adulthood. His nerves were so bad that he started smoking – 'Couldn't help myself [and am] assuring myself this is all right,' he confided to his diary. Whenever a decision had to be made, he would light a *papierosy* and remain inscrutable; that is, until it came to the question of choosing his life's partner. In that respect, his mind was made up. Even while he was bedding 'Little K', his thoughts were on a pale, blonde German princess.[iii]

He had met Princess Alix of Hesse-Darmstadt in 1884 at the wedding of his Uncle Sergei to Alix's sister Elizabeth, in Saint Petersburg. Alix, known as Alicky, was twelve; Nicholas was sixteen. They danced together and he tried to give her a present – a diamond brooch – but she was too shy to accept it.[19] When Alix returned to Russia to visit her sister five years later, they fell in love. Nicholas wrote in his diary, 'It is my dream to one day marry Alix H. I have loved her for a long time, but more deeply and strongly since 1889 when she spent six weeks in Petersburg. For a long time, I have resisted my feeling that my dearest dream will come true.'

Alix's mother, Princess Alice, was the third child of Queen Victoria and Prince Albert. During the Crimean War, Her Majesty had taken the emotionally sensitive eleven-year-old to visit the wounded in hospital. She never forgot those horrific scenes. During Bismarck's wars that tore Europe apart in the 1860s she worked tirelessly to help the wounded in Hesse-Darmstadt and, advised by Florence Nightingale, revolutionised nursing in the German States. From her mother, however, Alice had inherited the Haemophilia B gene that prevented the blood from clotting. She would transmit this disorder to her son Friedrich (and through her daughters to three grandsons). Friedrich, known as 'Frittie', died of bleeding in May 1873 aged three. Barely four years later Alix lost her mother and sister May, her 'inseparable companion', to diphtheria.[20]

Alix's parents had called her 'Sunny' because of her sunny disposition but grief turned her into an unsmiling melancholic. Queen Victoria, the mother of nine children herself, announced that 'poor dear Alicky has no one but me' and took a close interest in her upbringing. She saw to it that her granddaughter spent much of her

---

iii A papierosy was a cylindrical cardboard cartridge filled with tobacco.

time learning to be a young lady in the placid suburban surrounds of Kensington Palace in which she had been raised herself.

On 1 January 1893 Nicholas returned to the Preobrazhensky Guards to take command of the 1st Battalion as Colonel. He was now a fully-fledged soldier and it showed in his determination to marry Alix. He proposed to her during a visit Darmstadt for the wedding of her brother Ernie. At first she turned him down. She was deeply religious and would not contemplate converting from her Lutheran faith to Russian Orthodox. But Nicholas persisted and the day after the wedding Alix relented. They became officially engaged on 20 April 1894. 'You are locked in my heart,' she wrote to him. 'The little key is lost and now you must stay there forever.'[21]

His mother Minnie opposed the union. She was Alix's godmother but thought Nicholas could do much better than this sad, unsmiling, German-born member of a minor royal family who had been raised an Englishwoman. Nicholas, however, ignored all criticisms; she was his Alix and he was locked in her heart. Queen Victoria, who made no secret of her hatred for 'those horrible, deceitful, cruel Russians', wrote to Alix's sister, Victoria, Princess Louis of Battenberg, on 21 October 1894:

> All my fears about her future marriage now show themselves so strongly and my blood runs cold when I think of her so young most likely placed on that very unsafe throne, her dear life and above all her husband's constantly threatened and unable to see her but rarely. It is a great additional anxiety in my declining years! Oh, how I wish it was not to be that I should lose my sweet Alicky.

The Romanovs might have survived had Alexander III stuck to shooting game or his other favourite pastime, playing the trumpet. To Minnie's distress, however, her husband was addicted to strong liquor. According to his security chief (and drinking buddy), Adjutant-General Peter Cherevin, he would get so drunk that he 'lay on his back and waved his arms and legs about, behaving like a child, trying to get to his feet and then falling down, grabbing the legs of anyone who walked past'.[22]

By mid-October 1894 the Tsar was dying of acute nephritis – a kidney disease, probably alcohol-related - in the Imperial Family's neo-Renaissance palace at Livadia near Yalta in the Crimea. Nicholas pleaded with Alix to come as quickly as possible. By the time she arrived, Alexander was almost blind and very weak but he insisted on getting out of bed and greeting the next Tsarina in full dress uniform. He died on 20 October at the relatively young age of forty-nine, having made few preparations for his succession. At Witte's urging the Tsarevich had presided over the Siberian Railway Committee but apart from that role he had been given almost no responsibility. 'Uncle Bertie' – Edward, Prince of Wales – thought his Romanov nephew 'deplorably unsophisticated, immature and reactionary'.[23]

At twenty-six, Nicholas Alexandrovich was a man of medium height, with a fit, lean figure, bright blue eyes and a pointed ginger beard. Physically, he could have passed for the identical twin of his cousin, Bertie's son George, the future King George V. He was a good dancer (the quadrille, mazurka, waltz and polonaise), a fine horseman and an excellent marksman. He was also a chain-smoking, tongue-tied, untrustworthy neurotic.[iv]

Cutting short the period of official mourning, the marriage of Nicky and Alicky took place in the Winter Palace on 14 November, a date that coincided with the birthday of his disapproving mother, now the Dowager Empress Maria Fyodorovna. Forsaking her Protestant faith, the bride was canonised in the Orthodox Church as Alexandra the Passion-Bearer.

Her bejewelled wedding dress was so heavy that she could not stand up unaided. There was no reception. The newlyweds began married life with a quiet dinner in one of Nicholas's childhood homes, the Anichkov Palace. Alix had a headache, so they went to bed early. Within days, Nicky and Alicky moved into their apartments in the Winter Palace, which Alicky furnished in the English style from the catalogue of Maples of Tottenham Court Road.

'A completely new life has started for me,' Nicholas wrote to his brother Georgy, the new Tsarevich. 'I can't thank God enough for the treasure He's sent me in my wife.' His only complaint was that the munching of English biscuits sometimes kept him awake.[24]

Alicky adapted to the physical side of married life with enthusiasm. 'Never did I believe there could be such utter happiness in this world.

---

iv When Nicholas visited Balmoral Castle in 1896, Queen Victoria, an irritable, bad-tempered matriarch, banished him to a smoking room that was kept even colder than the rest of the castle.

I love you!' she wrote in her husband's diary. And again: 'I burn with impatience to see you as soon as possible, to feel myself in your arms. I long for you terribly.' They referred to their sexual organs as 'boysy' and 'lady', as in 'Tell boysy that lady sends him her tenderest love and kisses'. He had only to whistle and she would dash to his side.

In Tashkent, Alexander Kerensky wept when he heard about Alexander III's death. He attended mass and a requiem service for the Tsar and collected small contributions from his classmates to buy a wreath in his memory. 'The grown-ups did not weep,' he says. 'They were expecting from the youthful Emperor that for which they had waited in vain under his father: a bold move ahead, the sacred word – Constitution.'[25]

These hopes were dashed after the Zemstvo of Tver, in its loyal address to the new Tsar, expressed the hope that 'the voice of the people would be listened to' during his reign and that the law would stand 'above the changing views of the individual instruments of supreme power'. The imperial watchdog Pobedonostsev detected revolutionary nuances in these apparently mild aspirations. Indeed, the authors of the address, Fyodor Rodichev and Ivan Petrunkevich, were opponents of the autocracy. To make sure there was no room for misunderstanding, Pobedonostsev drafted a reply which Nicholas delivered to a delegation of the nobility and the *zemstvos* at the Winter Palace on 17 January 1895, 'Some people in *zemstvo* assemblies have let themselves be carried away by senseless daydreams of participation by *zemstvo* representatives in matters of internal administration. I shall defend the principles of autocracy as firmly and unswervingly as did my late and unforgettable parent.'

His reference to 'senseless daydreams' was music to the ears of his reactionary Romanov relatives who feared he might have possessed a more liberal streak than his father. From Berlin his cousin Kaiser Wilhelm II sent his congratulations: 'I am delighted by your magnificent address. The principle of the monarchy must be maintained in all its strength.'[v]

This was easier said than done. The Russian Empire covered almost one-sixth of the Earth's landmass and contained more than a hundred ethnic, linguistic and nationalist groups. There were so many different

---

v The titles Kaiser and Tsar were both derived from the Roman word Caesar.

nationalities that Russia was sometimes described as 'a state without a people'. The 1897 national census numbered Nicholas's subjects at 129.4 million (including the three million citizens of the Grand Duchy of Finland, which had been annexed in 1809).

Fewer than half of that total were Russians. Russia, as such, constituted just one-quarter of the Empire, while the remainder were territories of conquest or colonisation. Poland (which had been partitioned among Russia, Prussia and Austria in the Eighteenth Century), the Baltic Provinces, White Russia (the eastern part of present-day Belarus), Little Russia (Ukraine and Belarus) and the Caucasus paid reluctant tribute to the Romanov's double-headed eagle, as did the Turkic peoples of Central Asia and the Yakuts and Buriats of Siberia. Given the multiplicity of political aspirations and religious beliefs, it would have been nonsensical to speak of 'national unity' or the 'national psyche'.[vi]

The vast realm of tundra, forest and steppe was virtually ungovernable. Not a day passed without the assassination of a Romanov official or an insurrection breaking out in some corner of the Empire. Defending her borders and suppressing rebellions required more soldiers and more military equipment than the Ministry of War could afford, even on a budget twice that of France or Germany.[26]

Russia's geographic shape also put her at a disadvantage with regard to trade. Having sold Alaska to the United States in 1867 for US$7.2 million (US$125 million today), Russia enjoyed the favour of no overseas territories. Moreover, her Baltic and Pacific ports were iced up for many months of the year and, as we have seen, traffic from the Black Sea to the Mediterranean depended on the goodwill of the Turkish Sultan. Not only was her navy split into Baltic, Black Sea and Pacific fleets but her rivals controlled key choke points that limited the movement of her ships. Britain, for example, had Gibraltar and the Suez Canal between Europe and the Middle East.[27]

Nicholas's relations with Sergei Witte were fractious, all the more

---

vi By 1897 the Russian Empire had twenty-two million Ukrainians, eight million Poles, six million White Russians (from present-day Belarus), five million Jews, four million Balts, three and a half million Georgians, Armenians and other Caucasian peoples, more than seven million Kazakhs, Uzbeks, Turkmens and other Central Asians, four million Tatars, nearly two million Germans and half a million Mongols.

so because Alexandra, who was taking an increasing interest in the workings of the state, hated him. Shortly after their marriage he had used his influence to oppose the idea that, in the advent of her husband's premature death, she would rule the Empire as regent. For his part, Witte judged his new master harshly. 'His good breeding conceals all his shortcomings,' he said. 'His outstanding failing is his lamentable lack of will power. Though benevolent and not unintelligent, this shortcoming disqualifies him totally as the unlimited autocratic ruler of the Russian people. Poor, unhappy Emperor! He was not born for the momentous historical role which fate has thrust upon him.'[28]

The distorting mirror also affected the Tsar's servants and advisers. Everybody from the most decorated minister down to the lowest courtier was too frightened or too overawed to tell him the truth. Romanov survival depended on maintaining his image as the nation's patriarch, a wise and gentle father-figure capable of performing miracles; an able statesman adept at handling troublesome foreigners; and, in times of war, a fearless warrior. The Tsarina, however, recognised him for what he was: a weak, vacillating political novice.[29]

Knowing that his ministers compared him unfavourably with his father, Nicholas was secretive and devious, shunting the blame for his mistakes on to hapless courtiers or concealing the truth beneath a tissue of lies. 'He is incapable of playing fair,' Witte says, 'and he always seeks underhand means and underground ways. He has a veritable passion for secret notes and methods.'[30]

By far the most populous group in the Empire were its eighty-five million peasants. Nicholas took their loyalty for granted. 'I conceive of Russia as a landed estate,' he declared, 'of which the proprietor is the Tsar, the administrator is the nobility and the workers are the peasantry.' He neglected to mention that, of the three, the only indispensable element was the humble peasant who produced the grain that not only fed the population but also provided Russia with about half her export revenue to pay off the overseas loans that enabled the state to function.

To increase these profits, Sergei Witte's predecessor as Minister of Finance had forced farmers to sell their grain at reduced prices. In time, this measure depleted food reserves in the countryside to such an extent that the failure of crops along the Volga in 1891 and 1892 resulted in a catastrophic famine. People in the cereal-producing provinces of Samara and Saratov suffered the greatest hardship – it was reported that more than half the population of Samara was destitute, while the total death toll was estimated at 400,000.[31]

Alexander Kerensky, who had been born and raised in the stricken region, blamed the disaster on 'the criminal neglect on the part of the government':

> Leo Tolstoy wrote his famous articles on famine and went himself to organise help in the villages. Russia seemed to awake from a heavy slumber. There was a new will for action, for a struggle to obtain the right to a share in constructive social and political work. The eyes of the intelligentsia were opened, not only to the famine but also to the terrible poverty of the peasantry, [which had been] left at the mercy of economic forces.[32]

From then on, the intelligentsia - cultured aristocrats, moderate academics and prominent literary figures – supported terror as a means of forcing reform on the Tsar. They demanded amnesties for exiles and reprieves for convicted terrorists. 'Terror' in all its forms from bomb-throwing to extortion and 'expropriation' (i.e., armed robbery) became the physical manifestation of their political dreams.

As a means of diminishing Russia's influence in Europe, Bismarck had urged Nicholas's father to exploit Asia. 'Russia has nothing to do in the West,' he said. 'There she can only catch Nihilism and other diseases. Her mission is in Asia; there she represents civilisation.'[vii] Since 1890 Germany's foreign policy had been in the hands of Cousin Willy, who had sacked Bismarck over his refusal to create a world-class battle fleet on the sensible grounds that such a move would drive Britain and France closer together. Willy worked hard to shift Nicky's eyes away from Russia's spheres of influence in the Balkans and turn them eastwards.[33]

'It is the great task of the future for Russia to cultivate the Asian continent and to defend Europe from the great inroads of the Great Yellow Race,' he wrote to his cousin on 16 April 1895. 'In this you will always find me on your side ready to help you as best I can. You have well understood that call of Providence and have quickly

---

vii The Nihilists were young radicals who defied convention, eschewed religion and accepted no guide but reason.

grasped the moment; it is of immense political and historical value and much good will come of it.'[34]

The young Tsar liked the idea. Based on his travels to Vladivostok in 1891, he saw himself as an expert on the Asia-Pacific region. The Franco-Russian Alliance had deposed Britain as the most dominant power in China and Nicholas was all too willing to believe that the time had come to convert that power into territory. According to General Aleksei Kuropatkin, his Minister of War, the Tsar intended to extend his Empire across the whole of Asia to include Manchuria and Korea and then take Tibet, Afghanistan and Persia. Quite apart from any local objections, he seemed unperturbed that this would bring him into conflict with Britain in India and Japan in the Pacific.[35]

Nicholas hated the English for their arrogance and military superiority. In conversations with Sergei Witte, he called them 'Jews', using the abusive term *zhidy*.[36] The Japanese were referred to, even in official documents, as *macaques* (a small species of monkey indigenous to East Asia). Witte says, 'He became involved in the Far Eastern adventure because of his youth, his natural animosity against Japan, where an attempt had been made on his life (he never speaks of that occurrence), and, finally, because of a hidden craving for a victorious war.'[37]

Impressive though it was, Russia's industrial progress did not compare with the Japanese achievement, which had created a new state under the Meiji Emperor capable of competing with Western countries on equal economic and military terms. The task of transforming Japan from a reclusive feudal state into a modern industrialised nation had fallen to a new industrial class, the *zaibatsu*, headed by family holding companies such as Mitsui, Mitsubishi, Sumitomo, Yasuda and later Nissan. That the Japanese, a brave, industrious and resourceful people, achieved this goal in the first generation of the Meiji era rates as the most remarkable feat of any country in modern times. To end the samurai's traditional role, Meiji's advisers, the *genro*, reintroduced emperor worship, or *Kami no michi*: 'the Way of the Gods', which promoted the Emperor to the status of deity. Nicholas might have been anointed by God but Meiji was actually a god in his own right.

Armed with the latest Western weapons, Japan exploded on to the Asian scene in the early 1890s after the founder of the modern Japanese Army, Count Aritomo Yamagata, warned the Meiji Emperor that the Trans-Siberian Railway, which was creeping across the steppes towards the Pacific, posed the threat of Russian domination in the East.[38]

The friction between Russia and Japan increased in August 1894 when Japan picked a fight with the Qing Dynasty over conflicting interests in Korea and sent an expeditionary force to the Asian mainland. The ensuing Sino-Japanese War was nominally about wresting control of Korea from China but Tokyo's real purpose was to prevent further Russian encroachment into Manchuria. Once China had been defeated, Japan would join the 'eagles' – Mahan's epithet for the Western powers – in slicing up the Chinese 'carcass'.[viii]

China's army and navy were easily defeated and hostilities ended in the Treaty of Shimonoseki of April 1895 under which China ceded to Japan the island of Formosa (today's Taiwan), the key port of Jiaozhou (Kiaochow, the birthplace of Confucius) on the Shandong Peninsula and the strategic ice-free anchorage at Port Arthur on the Yellow Sea. In addition, she lost control of Korea and agreed to pay an indemnity of 230 million ounces of silver, six times the annual income of the Japanese Government at that time.

The terms of the treaty were regarded with horror in Saint Petersburg. 'It appeared obvious to me,' says Witte, 'that it was imperative not to allow Japan to penetrate into the very heart of China.' As a result, Russia prevailed upon France and Germany to join her in denying Japan the fruits of her victory. Posing as the protectors of Chinese independence, they forced the Japanese to relinquish most of their gains, including the Shandong Peninsula (which was colonised by Germany to give the Kaiser his 'place in the sun') and Port Arthur (which the Russian fleet forcibly occupied shortly afterwards).

The Japanese were rightly incensed but the Meiji Emperor, counselled by Britain and the United States to adopt a conciliatory attitude, exhorted his subjects to 'endure the unendurable' and accept this humiliating reverse.[39]

China's defeat confirmed what the Confucian literati and a growing number of merchants and students already knew: that their Manchu

---

[viii] Alfred Thayer Mahan (1840–1914) was the American author of *The Influence of Sea Power Upon History* in which he argued that sea power went hand in hand with economic advancement. It was inevitable, Mahan said, that the expansion of the United States merchant fleet across the Pacific would bring her into conflict with other nations, probably Japan and possibly Britain.

rulers, once a proud warrior race, were now decadent, foolhardy and fallible. This realisation became one of the driving forces behind the Chinese Revolution, which would depose the Qing in 1911 and turn China into the first Asian republic.[40]

On 3 November 1895 there were celebrations throughout the Russian Empire when Alicky made Nicky a father with the birth of Olga, the first of their four daughters. 'I'm glad the child is a girl,' he told her thoughtfully. 'Had it been a boy, he would have belonged to the people. Being a girl she belongs to us.'

Nicholas's coronation was held in the Cathedral of the Assumption inside the Kremlin Palace on 14 May 1896. Dressed in his Preobrazhensky colonel's uniform, he was crowned with the Silk Imperial Crown of Russia. 'In the sight of my Maker,' he told his mother, 'I have to carry the burden of a terrible responsibility, ready to render an account to Him of my actions.'

During the ceremonies Muscovites got their first sight of the new Tsarina. Alexandra was conscious of the fact that she was taller than her husband, so she crouched forward and bobbed her head like a clockwork toy. She was also badly dressed and, in the absence of fluent Russian, spoke poorly accented French. 'No one liked the Tsarina,' Zinaida Hippius wrote. 'Her sharp face, beautiful but ill-tempered and depressed, with thin, tightly pressed lips, did not please; her German, angular height did not please.'

An augury of Nicholas's ill-starred reign took place four days later when more than a thousand spectators were crushed to death in a stampede at a public feast in his honour. The tragedy happened after false rumours swept the immense crowd on Khodynka Field, a military training ground outside Moscow, that free commemorative enamel mugs contained a gold coin. As the crowd charged towards the booths, people fell into the trenches that pitted the field and were crushed to death.[41]

While the bodies were being removed that night, the Tsar was persuaded against his better judgment to attend the French Ambassador's ball. Almost immediately, he regretted the decision and spent the next morning visiting the wounded in their hospital beds. Nor was the Imperial Couple's ordeal over. The following evening Matilda Kshesinskaya danced at a Bolshoi gala performance of *The Pearl* in front of her former lover and his wife.

Nicholas spent the first years of his reign sitting behind a large mahogany desk in the Winter Palace being bellowed at by ferocious grand dukes and manipulated by oleaginous ministers, while his wife took an increasing interest in the workings of the state. In the summer of 1898 Sergei Witte suggested that he hold a conference to find a way of giving the peasants more protection under the law. Witte had prolonged the period of grain seizure, thus exacerbating resentment in the villages and providing fertile ground for agitators.[42] He expressed his concerns in a letter to the Tsar, who was holidaying with his family in Crimea:

> The peasant was freed from his landowner but he is still a slave of his community as represented by the *mir* meetings and also of the entire hierarchy of petty officials who make up the rural administration. The peasants' rights and obligations are not clearly defined by law. His welfare and his very person are at the mercy of the arbitrary rulings of the local administration. In a word, Sire, it is my profound conviction that the peasant problem is at present the most vital problem of our existence. It must be dealt with immediately.[43]

Nicholas did not reply to Witte's letter. He spent much of his holiday playing games of hide and seek with his children, tennis (in military jacket, breeches and cap) and dominoes (his favourite board game). He also went hunting, proudly recording the kill in his diary: 'Total game killed: 100 deer, 56 goats, 50 boar, 110 foxes, 27 hares – 253 in 11 days.' When he returned to the capital, he pointedly never referred to Witte's scheme and so the peasant remained a slave to arbitrariness, lawlessness and prejudice.

Meanwhile, racial prejudice under the Romanovs produced a new political movement that would become the leitmotif of opposition to the autocracy. For generations, Jewish workers had suffered even greater economic and political oppression than their Russian brethren. At the end of September 1897 thirteen Jews - eleven men and two women - met in the attic of a farmhouse near Vilna (today's Vilnius in Lithuania), the cultural centre of Russian Jewry, to form the General Jewish Labour Bund. The aim of this unique body was to unite all Jewish workers in fighting for a democratic and socialist Russia.

According to historian Mark Mazower, the grandson of a leading Bundist, the Bund 'played an absolutely critical role in the birth of leftwing party politics in the Tsarist Empire'.[44] Indeed, Arkadi Kremer, the 'Father of the Bund', was partly instrumental in bringing together the forty Marxist intellectuals who formed the Russian Social Democratic Labour Party (RSDLP), the harbinger of the All-Russian Communist Party. The rebels met in the Belarus capital of Minsk on 1 March 1898, the seventeenth anniversary of the assassination of Alexander II. It was an article of faith among the Bundists that the task of fighting antisemitism belonged to Jewish workers rather than the working class as a whole, so the congress unanimously accepted their request for autonomy in all Jewish matters.[ix][45]

It was also agreed that Peter Struve, a fiery, doctrinaire redhead who spoke at the 'Legal Marxist' debates of the Free Economic Society, should write the new party's manifesto.[x] Published in April 1898, it demanded the political freedom of the Russian proletariat and declared that 'the proletariat *alone* can win for itself that political freedom'.[46]

The Bundists and the Social Democrats now had an identity and a creed but they had barely come into existence when the Okhrana pounced. Betrayed by informers, the leaders of both movements were arrested and thrown into prison.

The biggest issue of the age was the arms race among the Great Powers. Helmuth von Moltke the Younger, the rising star of the German Army, speculated that weapons of mass destruction could become so powerful as to make war an impossibility. 'It is up to us,' he said, 'to determine whether we have reached the stage at which war has become not only destructive but politically futile.' Indeed, Friedrich Engels had warned as long ago as 1887 that Prussia-Germany 'can no longer fight any war but a world war; and a world war of hitherto unknown dimensions and ferocity. Eight to ten million soldiers will strangle each other and in the process decimate Europe as no swarm of locusts ever did'.[47]

Russia was in the process of rearming her infantrymen with new

---

ix The Bund's demands for Jewish national autonomy within a Russian federation were later rejected by RSDLP, including Trotsky, who put class interest above nationalism.

x 'Legal Marxists' were so-named because they published their work in legally recognised publications.

rifles when Aleksei Kuropatkin learned that Austria was about to equip her artillery with the latest heavy guns at vast expense. He discussed the situation with Witte, who knew that the cost of matching Austria's expenditure on siege and field pieces would place an impossible burden on the treasury. Never short of good ideas, he suggested that Russia initiate a plan for the global limitation of arms. The Foreign Minister, Count Muraviov, put the plan to Nicholas, who reacted positively. The idea of stepping into the international arena in the name of disarmament had immense appeal: if his grandfather had been 'Alexander the Liberator', he would become 'Nicholas the Peacemaker'.

In May 1899 the First International Peace Conference of all the Great Powers, including the newly emergent United States and Japan, was convened in his name at The Hague to discuss arms limitation and the founding of an international court to settle disputes between nations. It was a bold idea. In his keynote speech Nicholas warned the assembled heads of state that 'the accelerating arms race is transforming the armed peace into a crushing burden that weighs on all nations and, if prolonged, will lead to the very cataclysm it seeks to avert.'[48]

The conference had barely settled down to its work when another of Karl Marx's predictions to Grant Duff twenty years earlier - that efforts to reduce arms would fail - was proved scarily true. 'All sorts of fears and jealousies will make that impossible,' Marx had said. 'It is a vicious circle - there is no escape from it.' Indeed, the British Government, fearing Nicholas's motives towards India and the Far East, ordered their delegates to thwart his aims.

Nevertheless, the conference had some success. It set up the International Court at The Hague and, with a commendable eye to the future, voted to limit the aerial bombardment of civilians with a five-year ban on balloon warfare. Unfortunately, membership of the International Court was voluntary and most nations carried on as before. Germany's attitude was wholly obstructive. The Kaiser, who saw an arms moratorium as the thin end of the wedge to weaken Germany, sneered at 'Little Nicky's' peacekeeping efforts. 'I shit on all their resolutions,' he said.[49]

Brusque, impatient and restless, Wilhelm was indispensable to Germany's militarists because he alone could make the decision to declare war. He was the *Kaiserreich*'s Supreme Warlord and to convey that image he had his portrait painted as Mars, the God of War.[50]

'The Hague Peace Conference revealed the unwillingness of all imperialist governments to cut down their armed forces,' Alexander Kerensky says. 'This was particularly true of the expanding sea powers, which were frantically vying with one another and with England. But in that age of vehement expansionism, no stigma was attached to the concept of imperialism. The great powers regarded it as a mission to be fulfilled for the benefit of mankind.'[51]

4

The Young Madmen

Kerensky graduated with honours from the Tashkent Classical Gymnasium in the summer of 1899 and, in autumn that year, arrived at the University of Saint Petersburg on Vasilevsky Island to read History and Philology in the Faculty of Arts on a monthly stipend of sixty roubles from his father. As the privileged son of a liberal-minded though thoroughly conventional bureaucrat, his upbringing had given him an interest in all aspects of Russian history, culture and literature. He had also been taught to draw his own conclusions from events and, in the months ahead, the events in Saint Petersburg would seriously test his beliefs in a Christian God and the Tsarist regime.

At eighteen, he was five feet ten inches tall with a lean body, oval face and bright blue eyes. He was vain about his appearance. Photographs from this time show that his hair was close-cropped like his father's but, unlike his father, he was clean-shaven like an actor of the period. He had also developed the habit of placing his right hand inside his jacket, a teenage affectation that no one took seriously. Diagnosed with myopia, he refused to wear spectacles. His short-sightedness led to the practice of speaking with his eyes half-closed (a habit he shared with Lenin, who had undiagnosed myopia in his left eye).[1]

Hand on heart, he would have said he practised the five virtues of justice, temperance, courage, piety and wisdom to the best of his ability. Honour was important. Many years hence his political mistakes could be traced to the moral and ethical beliefs learned in his youth. However, it was his rich baritone voice, strong enough to hit the back of the hall, that set him apart from other teenaged youths. Abandoning his ambition to become an actor, he decided 'to serve my people as my father had done all his life'. His voice, his dramatic flair and a tendency towards emotionalism would make him an outstanding political orator.

By the end of the century, Russian women were studying at universities, entering the medical profession and organising cooperative movements. Kerensky's elder sister Anna, who had been enrolled at the Conservatoire, made the long journey from Tashkent to Saint Petersburg with him. His eldest sister, Elena, was also in the capital, studying medicine at the Medical Institute for Women. Traditionally, Russia's institutions of higher learning were the only outlets for the political pressures of national life, so three of Fyodor Kerensky's children were exposed to this stimulus at a time of mounting civil disobedience and growing opposition to the autocracy.

Kerensky moved into one of the halls of residence surrounding the university's courtyard, a pleasing location on the Neva Embankment with views of the Admiralty and the Senate building on the square in which the Decembrists had made their stand against Nicholas I. 'We newcomers experienced an exhilarating sense of freedom,' he says. 'Most of us had been living at home and were now for the first time at liberty to do as we liked.'[2]

The students came from all parts of the Empire and represented all classes and nationalities. Here mingled intellectuals, apprentice revolutionaries, young nobles, embryonic lawyers, future literary and artistic luminaries and those whom Kerensky described as 'young madmen'. Students of noble birth tended to keep to themselves but the vast majority were from poor families and relied on state subsidies to pay for their studies. Politically astute members of the fraternity informed the freshmen that the main source of discontent was the Tsarist decree of 1884 which had stripped all Russian universities of autonomy and placed their affairs under police control. Student clubs had been banned and, most threatening of all, troublesome students could be conscripted into the army.

Undergraduates lived in a friendly, closely united community in which elected leaders handled matters of communal concern. 'But,' Kerensky says, 'if something exceptional happened in the country that hurt the moral feelings of youth or touched our pride, then the students rose as one man.' Such an issue was the death of Maria Vetrova, a student who had killed herself in the Peter and Paul Fortress on 12 February 1897. Her suicide had thrown the undergraduates into a state of turmoil.³

Born to a peasant woman in the Chernigov Province of Ukraine in 1870, Maria had been brought up in an orphanage. In 1894, after completing her secondary schooling and working as a teacher for several years, she had enrolled in one of the Courses of Higher Learning for Women in Saint Petersburg. 'Short rather than tall, and shabbily, carelessly dressed', she was described as ferociously independent. Invited to dine at someone's house, she supposedly replied, 'I only eat what I have earned but I will gladly come to talk with you.'⁴

Secretly, Maria had joined one of the People's Will groups that had survived Pleve's crackdown following the murder of Alexander II. In December 1896 she was arrested when the group's printing press was discovered during a police raid. Taken to the Peter and Paul Fortress, she was entombed in the Trubetskoi Ravelin. To deaden all sound, the stone floor was carpeted in felt and the walls were covered in felt pasted on to sheets of canvas. The prison warders wore felt boots and even the 'Judas' spy shutter was opened and closed noiselessly. Absolute silence was compulsory; even singing was forbidden.

As the rays of the sun never penetrated Maria's cell, she was permitted a lamp to light the way from her iron bed to the washstand or to the stool beside a small oak table. Two months after her incarceration that cold, dark place reverberated to the agonised screams of its young occupant. As a protest against these harsh conditions, Maria had poured oil from the lamp over herself and struck a match. The students' reaction was instantaneous. On 4 March 1897 a crowd of 5000 attended her funeral at Kazan Cathedral. After the service, demonstrators attempted to march down Nevsky Prospekt but were surrounded by mounted police and whipped until they dispersed. Within days, Maria's martyrdom had become a cause célèbre among students from Moscow to Kiev.

Two years of intermittent unrest followed. On 8 February 1899, the anniversary of the University of Saint Petersburg's founding, protesters interrupted the official ceremony of remembrance. Storming out of the hall with the intention of marching across Palace Bridge into the city centre, they were set upon by mounted police and Cossacks and flogged once again.

Emotions were running high in autumn that year when Alexander Kerensky joined the collegiate fray. 'It was under these conditions,' he says, 'that I gradually changed my views about the supposedly benevolent rule of the Tsar.' The students wanted an official apology for the brutality on the Neva Embankment, the restoration of the pre-1884 freedoms and the removal of the 'Temporary Regulations' under which they could be called up into the army.[5]

'We became enemies of the autocracy almost as soon as we entered the university,' Kerensky says. 'There were no arguments among the students whether the autocracy was to be fought or not. This was understood. The only argument was as to where the real truth was to be found: with the Marxists or with the *narodniki*.'[6]

As memories of his childhood in Simbirsk drew him towards the peasantry, Kerensky's sympathies lay with the *narodniki*. 'The whole history of the *narodniki* movement, its entire substance, was inseparably connected with the idea of absolute political freedom, with the idea of democracy, the will of the people,' he says. The orderly logic of Marxism, on the other hand, 'tallied very badly with the social structure of Russia and with our general outlook on life'.[7]

Fyodor Kerensky had provided his son with introductions to senior bureaucrats among the Saint Petersburg hierarchy and Alexander found himself dancing with their daughters at upper-class parties. This went down badly with his contemporaries in radical student circles. He quickly dropped all social pretentions and, at the end of his first year, identified himself as 'one of the young madmen'.

From the tone of his letters home, his father became concerned that his son was heading for trouble. 'Last year's insult has not been forgotten, and cannot be,' he wrote to his parents in February 1900. 'The repressions were uncivilised, that is what disturbs us, and those who ordered them (i.e., the ministers) do not deserve respect!' Fyodor Kerensky would have been distraught had he known that his son, preferring the spirit of collegiality to social acceptance, had become a staunch republican who considered His Imperial Highness 'an irreconcilable enemy of freedom'.[8]

In addition to History and Philology, Kerensky studied Jurisprudence in the Faculty of Law, a practical subject that might lead to a career as a lawyer. When his second year began in autumn 1900, however, the authorities introduced a new ordinance prohibiting students from studying in more than one faculty at a time. This restriction was intended to thwart agitators who enrolled as students in several courses in order to spread disorder as widely as possible.

Kerensky decided to abandon the Faculty of Arts and, like Marx and Lenin before him, study law, a decision that would delay his graduation for a year. After graduating he intended to take up postgraduate work in criminal law, leading eventually to a professorship at one of the universities. 'I sought out and found professors who confirmed my own instinctive feelings about the world,' he says. His most influential teachers were Leo Petrazhitsky, a liberal jurist who had developed a psychological theory of law, and twenty-eight-year-old Nicholas Lossky, a neo-Kantian philosopher who lecturer on intuitivism, or mystical empiricism.[9]

Kerensky was just settling into his course work when one of his new friends, an engineering student named Sergei Vasiliev, introduced him to his cousin, Olga Baranovskaya, a seventeen-year-old student at an unofficial women's university, the Bestuzhev-Ryumin Course of Higher Learning for Girls. Olga, a clear-headed woman whose wistful, brown-eyed beauty masked a ferocious willpower, was one of the leading young rebels. 'I never met on my life's path,' Kerensky told her many years later, 'a more intense and beautiful woman than you.'

Alexander and Olga – 'Olya' to her family - belonged to a student group who met to discuss Russian and foreign literature and to quote poetry (Pushkin, Baudelaire) to one another. 'We were ardent theatregoers,' Kerensky says, 'and the brilliant performances of the Moscow Art Theatre under Stanislavsky and Nemirovich-Danchenko during the spring season left us spellbound for weeks.'[10]

They first noticed each other in April that year when Sergie Vasiliev invited his friend to join the guard of honour at the funeral of their grandfather, Professor Vasily Pavlovich Vasiliev, one of Russia's leading sinologists. Professor Vasiliev had been head of the Department of Oriental Studies at the University of Saint Petersburg and was a member of the Russian Academy of Science. Alexander took his duties seriously. He turned up at the funeral in his suit and, according to his family, Olga thought his formal, upper-class manner pretentious and ribbed him about it. He pretended to ignore her but secretly he was intrigued. Back at their literary group, Alexander and Olga discussed politics and it was clear that she was more revolutionary than him (and would remain so for the rest of their lives). Their younger son Gleb remarked many years later, 'The motto "*Do right and fear no man*" might have been devised for my mother.'

As Kerensky came to know the Baranovsky family history, he realised that Olga's passion for radical politics emanated from her unhappy experiences as a child. Olga Lvovna Baranovskaya was born in Kazan on 26 November 1883 to Colonel Lev Stephanovich Baranovsky and his wife Maria Vasilieva. Maria's mother, Sophia Ivanovna Simonova, had died in childbirth aged just thirty-two. 'My grandfather, Vasily Vasiliev, adored her and never remarried,' Olga says, 'although he was left a widower with six children, the eldest of whom was twelve and the youngest a baby.'

Leaving his children in the care of a housekeeper, Professor Vasiliev threw himself into academic pursuits, including authorship of Russia's first Chinese and Manchu dictionaries. He became an emotionally remote figure in the lives of his three beautiful daughters, Olga, Lydia and Maria.

In 1877, shortly after Olga, the eldest daughter (after whom Olga Baranovskaya was named), finished her studies at the Smolny Institute for Girls of the Nobility, she and Lydia attracted the interest of two brothers, Lev and Vsevolod Baranovsky, both officers in the Cuirassier Life Guard Regiment. After the social protocols had been observed, the engagements were announced of Olga, nineteen, to Lev, twenty-six, and Lydia, seventeen, to Vsevolod, twenty-five.

Their futures seemed assured. After a happy day out, the two young couples arrived at the girls' house at six o'clock in the evening to find Professor Vasiliev in a rage. He accused his daughters of ingratitude and loose morals. The protests of the Baranovsky brothers that their fiancées' honour was still intact had no effect in assuaging his anger. Before anyone could intercede, Olga ran to an upstairs window and jumped to her death.[11]

Despite the suicide of her sister, Lydia went ahead and married Vsevolod Baranovsky in April 1879. The following year Lev Baranovsky proposed to Lydia's younger sister, Maria Vasilieva, then seventeen, even though she was now his sister-in-law. This relationship was within the Orthodox Church's prohibited degrees of consanguinity. Professor Vasiliev, making amends for his treatment of Olga, sought the necessary dispensation from Alexander II. The Tsar sanctioned the union and Maria and Lev were married in August 1881. Three children, Vladimir, Olga and Elena, quickly followed.[i]

Ten years later, after the family had moved to Omsk, Lev Baranovsky fell in love with the seventeen-year-old daughter of a state councillor. Maria refused to divorce him and took her daughters Olga and Elena back to Saint Petersburg to live with her father in his official apartment near the university on Vasilevsky Island. Her son Vladimir stayed with his father and his new love, Yevgenia Mikhailova.[12]

In the spring of 1896 Maria learned to her consternation that, in order to marry Yevgenia, Lev had had her own marriage declared null and void; she was now considered to be the mother of three illegitimate children. Maria appealed to the Imperial Court to have the children's birthright restored, citing Alexander II's authorisation of her marriage.

When the Holy Synod's archives were searched, it was discovered that the Court had failed to inform the Church of the Tsar's decision. The papers were located in the Royal Chancellery and the legitimacy of the three children was restored. This public humiliation at the hands of their father caused his children immense pain. As the paternity issue had only recently been resolved, Olga's rebellious attitude was understandable. Gleb Kerensky says:

> My mother was very proud of her ancestors and relatives but she did not care for her father, to put it mildly, because he divorced her mother (or rather, had the marriage annulled) on a technicality. Olga lived with the belief that once his wife's dowry had been spent and he had found a new object of affection, he sent his wife packing. That her father was now a general didn't interest her in the slightest. What mattered to her was that the family was star-studded with distinguished men of learning and practical achievement. This attitude was partly due to the fact that the academics were mainly on her mother's side of the family.[13]

After her parents' marital break-up, Olga Baranovskaya had the further misfortune to be raised in the home of Professor Vasiliev, who

---

i To complicate matters, Lev's brother Vsevolod Baranovsky also named three of his children Vladimir, Olga and Elena. Elena, or Lilya, would become Kerensky's lover.

subjected her and her sister Elena to a life of puritan severity. Olga says the only dress the girls were permitted to wear was their Smolny school uniform. Make-up was forbidden and they were not allowed to mix with boys. The fact that Professor Vasiliev had driven her namesake aunt to suicide made Olga even more hostile towards him.[14] 'I am proud of my family not because they were rich or influential but because everything they achieved was due to their brains, their devotion to science and their inherent integrity, which is the only inheritance my children received from them,' Olga says.

> Vasily Vasiliev rowed 500 kilometres down the Volga from Nizhny-Novgorod[ii] to enrol at the University of Kazan to study Chinese and Sanskrit. He spent ten years in China in the days when even foreigners had to wear a queue as a sign of submission to the Manchu Dynasty. His wife, Sophia Ivanova, was the daughter of Ivan Simonov, who received his education in Germany. When he came back to Russia, he was appointed Professor of Astronomy at the University of Kazan. As navigator, astronomer and biologist, he took part in the Russian expedition to the Antarctic in 1819-1821. The Bolsheviks, who liked to boast even of the achievements of the class of people they had massacred, published some of my grandfather's diaries in America trying to prove that the Russians went further towards the South Pole than any other nation.

The Tsar's greatest advantage in his war against reform was the rivalry, antipathy and disunity among his revolutionary enemies. Divisive personalities and doctrinal differences split the movement into warring factions whose arguments did as much to destroy them as the secret police. Few personalities were more divisive than Vladimir Lenin. He revelled in dispute, nursed resentments and thrived on factionalism, while denouncing it as a vice in his rivals. His intolerance of other views and his espousal of Nihilistic violence were anathema to most socialists. His first split was with the Marxist Economist Group, who argued that the RSDLP should concentrate on assisting the workers to obtain better conditions, as well as supporting the liberals' campaign for constitutional reform through which socialism, with its promise of popular sovereignty and social and economic equality, might be

---

ii From 1932 to 1990 Nizhny-Novgorod was known as Gorky after the author Maxim Gorky, who was born there in 1868.

achieved.[iii]

'The tactics of the Social Democrats,' says Vladimir Akimov, the Economists' spokesman, 'were simply to educate a number of workers who, grouped in circles, would become conscious Marxists and enjoy influence among their fellows.'[15] Lenin regarded 'Economism' as a deviation from Marxism and was determined to purge its influence from the party. When his Siberian exile ended on 10 February 1900 he accompanied Nadezhda to Ufa, where she would serve the final year of her own confinement. He then returned to Saint Petersburg but did not stay long. At the time of his second wedding anniversary in July that year, he left Russia for Western Europe.

By December, Lenin had joined Georgi Plekhanov, Paul Axelrod, Vera Zasulich, Alexander Potresov and Julius Martov in Leipzig to publish the first Marxist newspaper, *Iskra* (Spark). The objective was to produce a vehicle which would forge independent Marxist groups into a single unified organisation. The title was taken from a line by the Decembrist poet Alexander Odoevsky: 'Out of this spark will come a conflagration'.

The chances of this sextet working harmoniously together were slim. Plekhanov was notoriously disputatious and his ally Paul Axelrod was a renegade *narodnik*, while Lenin was determined to get his own way in all political matters. Nevertheless, *Iskra* was published in Munich, then London and Geneva, and was smuggled into Russia through a distribution system established by Martov and some of his family members.

As published, it was not so much a newspaper as a political weapon in Lenin's battle with the Economists. In numerous articles he preached that Marxists should form a tightly centralised, highly disciplined vanguard of professional revolutionaries to politicise the working class. It was this narrow focus that set his faction apart from other socialist parties across Europe, including the Social Democratic Party of Germany, one of the very first Marxist-influenced parties in the world.[iv] [16]

[iii] The Economists were disciples of Eduard Bernstein, a member of the German Social Democratic Party who saw flaws in orthodox Marxism. He believed that developed capitalist states would inevitably evolve into socialist democracies irrespective of class conflict.

[iv] Lenin quit *Iskra* after his proposal to reduce the editorial board to three - himself, Martov and Plekhanov - was vehemently opposed.

Meanwhile, a new political party that condoned terrorism had been activated in the capital and one of its first acts was to assassinate the students' arch enemy, the Minister of Education, Nikolai Bogolepov, a martinet who saw it as his mission to discourage liberal tendencies among the young. He had been serving as Professor of Roman Law at the University of Moscow when his ultra-conservative views attracted the Tsar's attention. Since becoming minister, his most notorious act was to punish 500 students who had been arrested for holding an illegal protest meeting at the University of Kiev. He ordered that 183 of the rebels should be conscripted into the army and the remainder expelled.[17]

In early 1901 Bogolepov decided to pay a visit to Alexander Kerensky's dormitory to see how the students were living. Entering the library, he was completely ignored. 'It was a silent but eloquent protest,' Kerensky says. 'Some students just sat there sullenly, some pretended to be absorbed in their books and others looked at newspapers. Bogolepov was left in no doubt as to the students' frame of mind.'

On 14 February Peter Karpovich, a student who had been expelled from the University of Moscow for taking part in student riots in 1896, sought permission to petition Bogolepov about his case. The minister remembered Karpovich and made the mistake of agreeing to see him. The student walked up to him in the Ministry of Education, produced a pistol from his coat pocket and calmly shot him in the neck.[18]

Two days after Bogolepov's death, 3000 students gathered in front of Kazan Cathedral in memory of Maria Vetrova and to protest against student conscription. Waving red flags, they burst into a lusty rendition of the 'Marseillaise', which had become the anthem of the international revolutionary movement. The author Maxim Gorky was delivering a speech condemning the government's action when a squadron of Cossacks appeared from behind the Cathedral and charged into the crowd on their sturdy little ponies, striking the students with whips and batons.[19]

Thirteen people were killed and hundreds wounded in the ensuing stampede. The injured included Peter Struve, who roared in disbelief, 'How dare they whip me! Me!' Some 1500 students were rounded up and imprisoned, many of them in the Peter and Paul Fortress. Struve's friend, the feminist writer Ariadne Tyrkova, was jailed for ten days.[20]

Alexander Kerensky missed the drama - at the time of the demonstration he was at a friend's funeral – but Olga Baranovskaya had taken part despite her mother's objections and although she hadn't been arrested she was withdrawn from the Higher Women's Courses and sent to the family's country estate until things settled down.

At his trial for Bogolepov's murder Peter Karpovich addressed the court for an hour about student troubles under the minister's rule. He described his victim as the 'baleful spirit of reaction' and said he was indifferent as to whether he had been killed or wounded. Karpovich's life was spared – instead of being hanged he was sentenced to twenty years' *katorga* in Siberia.[21]

Kerensky wrote in his 1965 memoirs that the assassin belonged to no political movement but it was later established that he had joined the newly formed Party of Socialist Revolutionaries (PSR), whose founding members Andrei Argunov, Mikhail Gotz, Catherine Breshko-Breshkovskaya, Grigory Gershuni and Viktor Chernov were heirs to the *narodnik* tradition. There was one important distinction: whereas the Populists drew their support from the peasantry and advocated common ownership of the land, the PSR was oriented towards the 'toilers' – the peasants *and* the workers, thus giving party members a voice in both rural and urban communities.

The Socialist Revolutionaries wanted to remove the Tsar, distribute agricultural land among the peasantry according to need, establish a democratically elected Constituent Assembly and introduce an eight-hour day for factory workers. Grigory Gershuni, whose parents had been killed in a Tsarist-inspired pogrom, formed a Battle Group similar to the People's Will which would unleash terror on ministers and other state officials to achieve these political aims.[22]

While Alexander Kerensky supported the students' cause, he belonged to no political group and, in the eyes of Olga Baranovskaya and Sergei Vasiliev, was still a political novice. He had never travelled abroad and his social life had been spent among the bourgeoisie. He committed his first political act just before the end of the Easter semester in 1901 when a group of students gathered noisily on the staircase of the main university building to air their grievances. Pushing his way to the top of the stairs, Kerensky launched into a fiery speech demanding that the student body maintain its support for the liberation struggle. He received a round of applause.

The next day he was summoned to the Rector's office for a dressing-down. 'Young man, I would expel you from the university were it not for your honourable father and his service to the country,' the Rector told him. 'I suggest you take a vacation and stay with your family for a while.'

Such a suggestion was tantamount to exile from the capital and when Kerensky reached Tashkent the local youths treated him as a hero. Any enjoyment he might have felt over his sudden notoriety was negated by his father's disapproval. His son had brought shame on the family and he feared he could go the same way as the Ulyanov brothers. Fyodor made his son promise that he would refrain from political activity until he had completed his law course. It made little difference: for the rest of his time at university Alexander was recognised as a rebel.

An official report on student disturbances for the year 1901 warned the government that student protests had assumed 'an openly anti-government nature', with the leaders of the student movement 'enticing scholastic youth at illegal meetings on to the path of political agitation'. Moreover, the student body had made contact with revolutionary groups and had indulged in 'criminal propaganda' with the objective of organising street demonstrations to achieve its goals.[23]

'We could see Russia marshalling its political troops for a new assault against the autocracy,' Kerensky says. 'These were not the small revolutionary societies of the 1870s [but] party committees drawing on the intelligentsia for their strength and firmly in touch with the new social force – the urban workman. The new movement had a clear and definite aim: to change the existing system of government. Henceforth, no police barriers would hold back the fight for political liberty.' Despite his promise to his father, Kerensky described himself as 'a rank-and-file participant' in these illegal activities. 'It would be quite wrong to imagine that I was a politician then: even when I was completing my studies, I did not think of political work. I was preparing for an academic career.'[24]

Meanwhile, in March 1902, Lenin declared in a pamphlet called *What Is to Be Done?*, a title that reprised Chernyshevsky's novel: 'Class political consciousness can be brought to the workers *only from without*; that is, only from outside the economic struggle, from outside the sphere of relations between workers and employers.' The subtitle, *Burning Questions of Our Movement*, issued a challenge: Lenin rejected the orthodox Marxist view that the liberal bourgeoisie must be the natural leaders of the revolution. He preached centralisation, discipline and ideological unity.

Many Marxists interpreted this to mean that the party's rank-and-file members would have to agree to obey military-style commands from the leadership (i.e., from Lenin himself). '"Freedom" is a grand word,' he said, 'but under the banner of freedom for industry the most predatory wars were waged, under the banner of freedom for labour, the working people were robbed.' In their interests, therefore, there would be no personal freedom in the Bolshevik state.[25]

Internecine arguments regarding Lenin's strategy were so bitter that in August 1903 the Social Democrats split into two parties over the precise wording of the first article of the statute defining party membership. Lenin wanted it limited to party activists who would be controlled by a nucleus of professional revolutionaries, while Julius Martov wanted to accept anyone who, as in other European socialist parties, recognised the party manifesto. After winning a vote at the Second Congress of the RSDLP in London, Lenin named his faction the 'majoritarians' (*bol'sheviki* or Bolsheviks), and Martov foolishly followed his lead and called his faction the 'minoritorians' (*men'sheviki* or Mensheviks), thus giving Lenin a psychological advantage in recruiting new believers.

The Menshevik supporters included Pavel Axelrod, Fyodor Dan, Georgi Plekhanov, Leon Trotsky, Irakli Tsereteli, Moisei Uritsky and Vera Zasulich. Those who flocked to the Bolshevik banner included Alexander Bogdanov, Felix Dzerzhinsky, Lev Kamenev, Maxim Litvinov, Anatoli Lunacharsky, Grigory Ordzhonikidze, Alexei Rykov, Josef Stalin, Yakov Sverdlov and Grigory Zinoviev. The battlelines had been drawn for the political struggle that would ultimately decide Russia's future.

One of Lenin's new recruits was Fyodor Sergeyev, a stocky nineteen-year-old who had fled to France in 1902 after serving six months' imprisonment for revolutionary activities. He went by the nom de guerre 'Artem' (pronounced Artyom in Russian). Fyodor Andreievich Sergeyev was born on 18 March 1883 at Glebovo, a village in the Fatezh district of Kursk in Central Russia. His father,

Andrei Arefievich Sergeyev, was a contractor in the building industry. When Fyodor was five, the family moved to Yekaterinoslav (now Dnipro) in South-Central Ukraine in search of a better life.

After graduating from high school, Fyodor attended Moscow Higher Technical School but was expelled in 1901 for organising a campus protest. The following year he joined the Russian Social Democratic Labour Party and started mixing with older revolutionaries. During the Bolshevik-Menshevik split he became attached to the Leninist wing of the RSDLP and never deviated from it.[26]

Meanwhile, the Socialist Revolutionaries' Battle Group claimed its second high-profile victim on 2 April 1902 when the Minister of the Interior, Dmitri Sipyagin, was assassinated by another dissident student. Disguising himself as a government officer delivering a letter, Stephan Balmashev walked up to his victim in the Marinsky Palace, the seat of the Imperial Government on the south side of Saint Isaac's Square, and shot him several times. Security was unbelievably lax: the only guard was an unarmed liveried doorman. Sentenced to death, Balmashev refused to ask for a reprieve and was hanged in the Shlisselburg Fortress.

Faced with violence on an unprecedented scale, the Tsar appointed Pleve as Minister of the Interior with instructions to use every method of detection to track down the new breed of revolutionary assassin. From its base at 16 Fontanka Embankment, the Okhrana invaded the privacy of the Russian people as never before. Telephones were tapped, mail intercepted, political groups infiltrated and assemblies of any kind were banned. One of his main targets was the student body: students risked arrest if they walked down the street together, while provocateurs were employed to stir up trouble in their ranks. Anyone holding a party for more than a few people had to obtain written permission from the police.

As Russia's leading antisemite, Nicholas blamed the Jews for many of the regime's troubles. Pleve had no particular hatred of the Jews himself but he pandered to the Tsar's lust for blood. In a new wave of officially sanctioned pogroms thousands of Jews were killed or wounded and their property destroyed. The carnage began after publication in the Saint Petersburg newspaper *The Banner (Znamya)* of extracts from an antisemitic tract, *The Protocols of the Elders of Zion*. Claiming to describe a Jewish plot for world domination, *The*

Protocols were written by Paul Krushevan, an antisemitic ideologue and newspaper editor. His handiwork was not so much a work of original fiction as a plagiarised copy of an existing French satirical tract, whose author, Maurice Joly, was not writing about the Jews at all but about the strutting French dictator, Louis Napoleon.

At the time, however, *The Protocols* whipped up anti-Jewish agitation in many parts of the Empire, most horrifically at Kishinev, a Bessarabian city near the Austro-Hungarian border.[v] On 6 February 1903 Krushevan, writing in his local newspaper held the Jews responsible for the murder of a Christian boy. He claimed the victim had been ritualistically murdered and that the killers used his blood to make matzo biscuits for Passover.

The Kishinev Pogrom started in April with children throwing stones at Jewish shops and developed into a full-scale riot when about 2000 adults, goaded by Orthodox seminarians, broke into Jewish homes and looted Jewish businesses. Forty-seven Jews were killed and 600 raped or wounded.[27] Pleve encouraged local police to turn a blind eye to the violence. As a result, they refused to intervene until the end of the second day when the damage had been done. Facing an outcry from the intelligentsia, the government was forced to punish some of the rioters.

Witte warned Pleve that his policies had made his own assassination inevitable. Pleve, however, was not concerned about his safety - his most effective double-agent was Evno Azev, the head of the PSR Battle Group. A brutish-looking fellow in a bowler hat, Azev betrayed dozens of his SR comrades to the Okhrana while playing the part of a terrorist. He was also the son of a Jewish tailor and when the party hierarchy insisted that Pleve must pay with his life for his crimes against the Jews, he remained silent about the Battle Group's plans.[28]

The task of killing Pleve was handed to Boris Savinkov, Azev's morphine-addicted number two, who had been expelled from the Faculty of Law of University of Saint Petersburg for being involved in the 1899 student riots. Born in Kharkov, Ukraine, on 19 January 1879, Savinkov had grown up in Warsaw and strongly supported the Polish national cause. A short wiry man with a debonair moustache

---

[v] Nicholas was said to have thought The Protocols were fabricated and yet he kept a copy with him throughout his imprisonment at the hands of the Bolsheviks. The book was found among his belongings following his murder in July 1918.

and head of reddish-brown hair, he was quite happy to murder Pleve. The minister survived one attack in 1903 and two in 1904 but his luck was running out. According to Peter Struve, 'the life of the Minister of the Interior is ensured only insofar as there are technical difficulties in putting him to death'.[29]

5

The Calamitous Kaiser

After defeating the French at Trafalgar in 1805, Britain emerged from the Napoleonic Wars unchallenged at sea. The story goes that when the question 'What do we do now?' was raised at the Admiralty, one admiral replied, 'We can do whatever we like.' The biggest prizes were to be found in the East, where no fewer than eight European monarchies took part in the armed occupation euphemistically labelled 'the scramble for China'.[i]

The British saw themselves as an enlightened people extending the benefits of Christian civilisation to pagans. Whenever opposition stood in the way of imperial progress, the gunboats were sent in. Imposing British rule (and Indian-grown opium) on the Chinese in the Opium War of 1842 was a dastardly crime, and so was the Anglo-French destruction of the Summer Palace in 1860 at the conclusion of the Second Opium War.[ii] In Paris, Victor Hugo wrote, 'One day two bandits entered the Summer Palace. One plundered, the other burned… We Europeans are the civilised ones, and for us the Chinese are the barbarians. This is what civilisation has done to barbarism.'[1]

Nevertheless, George Curzon dedicated his 1894 book, *Problems of the Far East*, 'to those who believe that the British Empire is, under Providence, the greatest instrument for good that the world has seen,

---

i The countries were Britain (Saxe-Coburg-Gotha), Germany (Hohenzollern), Russia (Romanov), Austria-Hungary (Habsburg), Belgium (Saxe-Coburg-Gotha), Spain (Bourbon), Italy (Savoy) and the Netherlands (Orange-Nassau). It was Sir Claude MacDonald, the British Minister in Peking, who called the battle for concessions 'a general, and not very edifying, scramble'.

ii Lord Elgin ordered the destruction of the *Yuan ming yuan* and the five surrounding palaces as 'a solemn act of retribution' for the torture and murder of Thomas Bowlby, The Times correspondent with the British forces. More than 200 pavilions, halls and temples were systematically pillaged and then burned down. 'You can scarcely imagine the beauty and the magnificence of the places we burnt,' Captain Charles Gordon (later of Khartoum fame), wrote to his mother.

and who hold, with the writer, that its work in the Far East s not yet accomplished'. Britain's main rivals in this civilising mission were Tsar Nicholas and his cousin Kaiser Wilhelm, both of whom would prove disastrously inept as colonisers. Nicky's blundering in China would lead to the Russo-Japanese War, while ten years later Willy's meddling in Balkan affairs would ignite 'the Great War', the global catastrophe that would obliterate their thrones.

The Calamitous Kaiser, Friedrich Wilhelm Victor Albert Hohenzollern of the royal family of Brandenburg-Prussia, was the first-born of Victoria and Albert's forty-two grandchildren. He was also the most aggressive. A short man with an atrophied left arm that was six inches shorter than his right arm and the possessor of a moustache that was shaved and waxed to resemble the letter W, Wilhelm was known in his circle of aesthetic German aristocrats as *'das Liebchen'* ('Little Darling' or 'Sweety').

His father, whom he viewed with contempt, was Emperor Friedrich III, 'Fritz' to his friends, while his mother, the Empress Friedrich for whom he nursed a pathological hatred, was Victoria and Albert's eldest daughter, Victoria ('Vicky'). It had been her parents' dream that Europe should find ever-lasting peace through the creation of a stabilising Anglo-German Dynasty. Fritz and Vicky were at the heart of the dynastic plan, which backfired spectacularly when Fritz died of throat cancer in June 1888 after only ninety-nine days on the throne.

Suspicious that his parents had been plotting with the British, Willy ordered troops to surround his mother's palace and then had it searched for evidence of anti-German conspiracies. He would have been outraged had he read the passages relating to Germany in Grant Duff's interview with Karl Marx:

> He thinks that the [revolutionary] movement will spread to Germany, taking there the form of a revolt against the existing military system. To my question 'But how can you expect the army to rise against its commanders?' he replied, 'You forget that in Germany now the army and the Nation are nearly identical. These Socialists you hear about are trained soldiers like anybody else. You must not think of the standing army only. You must think of the *Landwehr* - and even in the standing army there is much discontent. Never was there an army in which the severity of the discipline led to so many suicides. The step from shooting oneself to shooting one's officer is not long, and an example of the kind, once set, is soon followed.'

Willy would have regarded the letter – and his mother's role in approaching Germany's number one enemy through a third party - as rank treason. Fortunately for Vicky, the incriminating document was not discovered; nevertheless, the mother-son relationship remained toxic. 'His conduct towards you is simply revolting,' her brother Bertie wrote to her, 'but alas he lacks the feelings and usages of a gentleman. The time may come quicker than he expects when he will be taught that neither Germany nor Russia will stand an autocrat at the end of the Nineteenth Century.' It did not help the mother-son relationship that Vicky told her friends, 'Willy is mad. I mean just what I say! It is literal: Willy is mad.'[2]

Willy's problems had started with his birth, a protracted breech delivery on 27 January 1859 at his parents' home, the *Kronprinzenpalais* (the Crown Prince Palace) in Berlin. For a time, the Anglo-German medical team feared for the lives of both mother and child. Willy's legs were folded up against his chest and his left arm was behind his head. One of the surgeons used considerable force with a pair of forceps to free this arm, pulling it from its socket and causing severe damage to the nerves and muscles.

Nor was the baby breathing. It took some time – perhaps a few minutes - before chest massage and the application of ice resulted in the first signs of life. Deprived of oxygen, it is probable that Wilhelm suffered brain damage in that time. It was three days before a midwife noticed that his arm had been dislocated, too late to rectify the damage. He would suffer from Erb's Palsy, a form of paralysis, for the rest of his life. Many years later the Kaiser confided to his homosexual friend, Count Eulenburg, 'Something is missing in me that others have. All poetic feeling in me is dead, has been killed.'[3]

To Vicky, his deformed arm was repugnant. She blamed a fall on a slippery parquet floor when she was five months' pregnant for the baby being in a 'false position' in her womb.[4] 'It cuts me to the heart when I see all other children with the use of all their limbs and that mine is denied that,' she wrote to her mother. 'The thought of him remaining a cripple haunts me. I long to have a child where everything is perfect about it just like everybody else.'

Willy grew up knowing his mother regarded him as inferior to his physically unimpaired younger brothers. He spent his entire life trying to prove that he was in no way inferior to anybody. No less an authority than Freud concluded that it was Vicky's abhorrence of his defect and the withdrawal of maternal love that accounted for Willy's inadequacies as an adult.[5]

Even so, the young man coped valiantly with his useless arm. In formal pictures, he posed with his gloved left hand resting on the pommel of his sword to disguise its shortened length. His clothes were tailored with high pockets and his left hand was invariably tucked into one of them. He chopped wood daily with his right arm to increase its strength and became adept at shooting and riding one-handed.

As a boy, he was devoted to his grandfather, Wilhelm I, standing beside the old man's desk while he worked on his papers. Young Willy acted as the office boy responsible for sealing and opening packages, and seeing that the Kaiser's inks and pens were in order. He took his duties seriously and performed them with commendable diligence.[6]

In 1881, at the age of twenty-two, Willy married Augusta Victoria of Schleswig-Holstein-Sonderburg-Glücksburg-Augustenburg. Known as Dona, his bride's Anglophobia and innate conservatism widened the gulf between Willy and his liberal parents. They raised six sons and a daughter, though Willy, who found his wife dull, was often away on army manoeuvres, hunting trips or carousing with Viennese prostitutes.[7]

The most repugnant thing about him was not his withered arm but his bloodlust. Like Alexander III, he liked nothing better than blazing away at defenceless animals. One of the 'cures' that Willy endured as a child was to have his withered arm placed inside the warm carcass of a freshly killed hare in the hope that the heat might revive the shrivelled tissue. Not surprisingly, this quack method failed to work and the experience seems to have given him a loathing of wildlife.[iii]

Gamekeepers on his country estates, such as his Prussian hunting castle at Rominten near the Russian border, would drive wild creatures – stags, deer, boars and game birds - into huge pens where the Kaiser slaughtered them by the thousand. His hunting registry for 1902 recorded, 'On this day the All Highest killed his 50,000th creature: a white cock pheasant.'[8]

At the start of his reign Nicky was critical of Cousin Willy, reflecting his father's dislike of the Kaiser's 'weakness for stage effects and

---

[iii] Willy's doctors also placed him in a metal cage in an effort to even up his shoulders.

spectacular splurges' and his Danish mother's hatred of Prussia over the loss of the Schleswig-Holstein Duchies to Prussia in 1864. As Nicky believed that, in the eyes of the world, Willy was grander and more regal than himself, there was an element of envy in his hostility.

After their first meeting as rulers, postcards were released in Russia with a photograph of the Kaiser resting his good arm on Nicky's shoulders in a pose that made it seem he was slightly taller than his cousin. Nicky ordered the postcards to be confiscated.[9]

German public opinion was strongly anti-British. Willy made no secret of the fact that he envied Britain her empire and her navy. Having taken all day to sail through the Grand Fleet during Queen Victoria's Diamond Jubilee in 1897, he returned to Berlin determined to catch up. 'One cannot have enough hatred for England,' he said. Admiral Count Alfred von Tirpitz was recalled from retirement and made head of the Admiralty with orders to build capital ships for the Home Fleet (*Heimatflotte*) that could match those of the Royal Navy in quality if not in quantity. The first naval law of 1898 required him to produce twelve battleships and thirty-three cruisers within six years.[10]

Willy saw Germany as a lusty young nation whose historic dismemberment had unfairly handicapped her in the race for colonies. He firmly believed that Britain should recognise his country as the greatest European power and make concessions to her claims for overseas territories. Britain, however, showed no sign of doing so. The Kaiser, therefore, promoted the racist line that the English were a 'Germanic' people who had been infected by the decadent French; like the 'Latin' nations, they 'merely possessed a civilisation; only the Germans possessed a higher, spiritual *Kultur*'.[11]

Meanwhile, Nicky was steaming ahead with his Eastern scheme. One of the most important foreign guests at his 1896 coronation was the Chinese Emperor's representative Li Hongzhang, who had been invited as part of Sergei Witte's plan to divert the Trans-Siberian Railway through Mongolia and Manchuria. Now very elderly after a lifetime of service to the Qing, Li Hongzhang looked up to no one: he was well over six feet tall, with long limbs, a drooping Manchu moustache, very small, bright eyes and a brilliant academic mind. Born in 1823 in the province of Anhwei adjacent to Shanghai, he was China's leading moderniser in everything except politics in which his aim was to uphold the Qing while getting fabulously wealthy himself.

With Li's agreement, the Chinese Government signed the 'Mutual Defence Treaty' with Russia to protect both countries against Japanese aggression. The pact allowed Russia to build the Chinese Eastern Railway, which shortened the Trans-Siberian line by 340 miles and placed Russia in pole position to take control of Manchuria. Two years later Witte bribed Li with half a million roubles to acquire a twenty-five-year lease of the Liaodong Peninsula, rent-free, with the right to build a branch line, the Southern Manchurian Railway, down through Harbin and Mukden to the ports of Dairen (Dalian) and Port Arthur (Lüshun), thus looping even more of Manchuria on to the Russian Empire.

The West's indecent conspiracies to seize China's treaty ports, build her railways and extract her mineral wealth revitalised many of the Celestial Kingdom's secret societies. The sect which most effectively captured the mood of suppressed rage was the *I-ho-ch'uan*, or the 'Society of Righteous and Harmonious Fists'. Western missionaries watched its emergence with concern. Noting its adherents' practice of shadow-boxing as part of an elaborate ritual to make themselves bullet-proof, they gave them a nickname: 'the Boxers'.[12]

The Boxer Rising of 1900 was initially directed against the Manchu regime but was cleverly diverted by the Qing's Dowager Empress Cixi into an insurgency against foreigners. The Boxers moved among the peasantry, propagating the belief that Catholics and Protestants 'have vilified our gods and sages, destroyed Buddhist images and seized our people's graveyards. This has angered Heaven'.[13]

To Sir Robert Hart, the Ulsterman in charge of the Chinese Maritime Customs Service, the Boxers were freedom fighters whose primary aim was 'to terrify foreigners, frighten them out of the country and thus free China from foreign trespass, contamination and humiliation'. He blamed 'missionary propagandism' for much of the trouble: the Chinese, he said, saw the teaching of the Gospel as 'the corroding influence of a foreign cult'.[14]

By June 1900 Peking was besieged and the Boxers were hacking Christian converts to pieces and attacking the barricades protecting foreign diplomats in their legations. Cixi's plan to exterminate the foreign devils was on the brink of success.[15] However, an international expeditionary force commanded by a British general, Sir Alfred Gaselee, fought its way from Tianjin to the walls of Peking and the Siege of the Legations was lifted after fifty-five days.

By early September the China Field Force - 75,000 troops from Britain, Germany, France, Russia, Japan and Australia – had occupied the capital and its surrounding districts. Thousands of Chinese – many of them innocent of any involvement with the Boxers - were rounded up and executed and their villages destroyed in punitive expeditions into the countryside. The Dowager Empress summoned Li Hongzhang from Shanghai to Peking to negotiate a peace settlement with the foreign devils.[16]

Fighting had also broken out between China and Russia in Manchuria after Chinese imperial troops attacked Russian settlements along the Chinese Eastern Railway. As a result, the Russian Governor of the Liaodong Peninsula, Admiral Evgeni Ivanovich Alekseyev, forced the local Chinese authorities at the Manchurian capital of Mukden (Shenyang today) to sign a secret agreement which sanctioned a virtual Russian takeover of Manchuria.

Having invested a large portion of the Romanov fortune in Manchuria, Nicholas had appointed Alekseyev as Viceroy of the Far East and Commander in Chief of Russia's fighting forces there, with instructions to exploit the region's railways and natural resources. 'The appointment was the height of absurdity,' says Sergei Witte. 'Alekseyev was not an army man. He could not even ride on horseback.'[17] Indeed, Alekseyev had risen to the top of the Russian hierarchy thanks to his friendship with Alexander III's brother, Grand Duke Alexei. As a young man, Alexei had gone on a drinking spree in a Marseilles bordello and been arrested for violent behaviour. Alekseyev, then a young naval officer, persuaded the French police that he was the guilty party and took the punishment himself. The Tsar appointed Alexei Minister of the Navy and elevated his protégé to General-Admiral.[18]

In September 1901 Li Hongzhang signed the Boxer Protocol in his last act for the Qing - he died two months later aged seventy-eight. For the deaths of their nationals and damage to property, China agreed to pay reparations of 450 million ounces of silver in varying amounts to Britain, Russia, Germany, France, the United States and Japan. Russia would receive the biggest chunk – almost a third of the total - and America, which was promoting an open-door policy to prevent the wholesale carve-up of Chinese territory, the smallest.[19]

Alekseyev pushed Russian forces along the wide, meandering

Yalu River bordering Korea, thus threatening Japanese interests in the Hermit Kingdom. Nicholas made the mistake of listening to Alexander Bezobrazov, a Russian speculator who had submitted a petition to the throne urging an aggressive policy towards Japan. The former cavalry officer wanted to establish a private company, the Yalu Timber Company, to work a timber concession along the river. As protection, Russian soldiers would be moved into Korea disguised as workers and railway guards to establish military strongholds.

Despite Witte's vigorous opposition, Nicholas not only approved the plan but appointed Bezobrazov as one of his ministers. 'Witte had done his best to oppose the pro-war policy of the Tsar's new favourite, State Secretary Bezobrazov,' Alexander Kerensky said. 'At the end of 1901 the famous Japanese statesman Marquis Ito visited Saint Petersburg in the hope of settling the impending conflict by peaceful means. Despite Witte's urgings, the Tsar gave him a very frigid welcome.' There was no official greeting – indeed, the visitor was completely ignored. When he tried opening negotiations through correspondence, his letters to the Tsar and the Foreign Ministry were met with silence or rudeness.

Marquis Ito left Russia in despair and travelled to London, where the Japanese Ambassador, Hayashi Tadasu, was negotiating a treaty with Britain. Hayashi used the Tsar's treatment of Marquis Ito as proof of Russia's belligerence and, as a result of these talks, the Anglo-Japanese Alliance - the first treaty between a European country and an Asiatic power against a Western rival - was signed in January 1902. It was also an admission that the Royal Navy could no longer police the globe. *Pax Britannica*, which had ruled the waves since Trafalgar, was in decline and Britain would shortly need all her naval resources to counter the challenge of the German High Seas Fleet (*Hochseeflotte*).

Cousin Willy missed no opportunity to urge the diversion of Russian forces to the East and thus give him a free hand in the West. As the two royal yachts parted at the end of the Russian Navy's manoeuvres at Reval (now Estonia's capital Tallinn) in the summer of 1902, Willy flashed a message to his cousin: 'The Admiral of the Atlantic Ocean salutes the Admiral of the Pacific'. Nicky lapped up the accolade. He had added 300,000 square miles of Manchuria to the Russian Empire and the Trans-Siberian Railway to Vladivostok was well on the way to completion. The great eastward trek of Russian immigrants, accompanied by thousands of political exiles in iron-barred carriages, had assumed gigantic proportions.

But Nicholas was a dangerous amateur in foreign affairs. 'Not that he had a definite programme of conquest,' says Witte. 'He was merely possessed by an unreasoned desire to seize Far Eastern lands.' After ten years in post, Witte received a note from Nicholas on 1 January 1903 thanking him for strengthening the country's defences and improving its prosperity, stabilising the currency and increasing state revenues. Eight months later he was summoned to Peterhof and sacked as Minister of Finance for opposing his East Asian adventure. He was kicked upstairs as chairman of the Committee of Ministers, a largely ceremonial post.[20]

One of the most vocal imperialists was Viacheslav Pleve, who declared that nothing would be more effective in averting a revolution in Russia than a small victorious war against the Japanese. 'Russia was made by bayonets, not diplomacy,' he said. When one of his assistants suggested the Japanese might be too strong for Russia, he snorted that it was a simple question of arithmetic. 'Which population is greater,' he asked the doubting Thomas, '50 million or 150 million?'

Russia's obstinacy continued to frustrate Japanese attempts at a diplomatic settlement into 1904. At a soiree in the Winter Palace, the Japanese Ambassador, Shin'ichiro Kurino, begged Witte to impress on the Foreign Minister, Count Lamsdorff, the necessity of replying to Japan's latest note without delay. Witte wrote in his memoirs, 'Japan was at the end of her patience, Kurino declared, and if within a few days no reply was given, hostilities would break out.' Lamsdorff could do nothing to break the deadlock – the Tsar had handed negotiations over to the man least likely to settle with the Japanese: Admiral Alekseyev.[21]

The Japanese emulated the great powers in dispensing with a formal declaration of war until after hostilities had commenced. At midnight on 25 January/7 February 1904, the Russian Pacific Fleet was at anchor in the roads outside the harbour walls of Port Arthur. Two destroyers were on routine patrol and searchlights played across the freezing waters. It was the lights which told Admiral Heihachiro Togo's striking force that it had found its target. Twenty minutes later, at 12.20 a.m. on the eighth, blacked-out Japanese destroyers attacked with torpedoes, inflicting serious damage on the fleet's newest battleships *Tsarevich* and *Retvizan* and incapacitating the cruiser *Pallada*.

On 26 January Nicholas wrote in his diary: 'Went to the theatre at 8 – they were doing *Rusalka*. Very good. Returning home, received a telegram from Alekseyev with the news that that night Japanese torpedo boats had carried out an attack against *Tsarevich*, *Pallada*, etc., which were at anchor, and put holes in them. Is this undeclared war? Then may God help us!'[22]

There were no outraged howls from Washington over the surprise attack; indeed, American newspapers heaped praise on Togo's ingenuity, with the *New York Times* leading the pack in saluting 'the prompt, enterprising and gallant feat of the Japanese'. The audacity of the attack caused great indignation in Saint Petersburg, where the Japanese were stigmatised as 'traitors and aggressors' for launching an attack without first declaring war.[23]

The Russo-Japanese War would be the first conflict in which weapons of mass destruction - new types of machineguns, field mortars and batteries of eleven-inch howitzers - were employed on the battlefield. David Garnett, who was visiting Saint Petersburg with his mother Constance, the translator of Turgenev, Tolstoy, Gogol, Dostoevsky and Chekov, painted a vivid picture of the military cavalcade: 'The streets were thick with officers in white blouses, peaked caps and epaulettes, high boots of Russian leather, jingling spurs, sabres worn in the Russian manner, back to front, and rolled grey overcoats worn slung around the body like bandoliers. There were Cossacks, Circassians, Generals of enormous size, military of all arms and all ranks, and the saluting was incessant.'[24]

The enemy were depicted in the press as monkeys succumbing to the heroic Russian bear but despite acres of propaganda the euphoria was far from universal. Tolstoy expressed his disgust with the autocracy in another of his open letters: 'Again war. Again sufferings, necessary to nobody, utterly uncalled for; again fraud, again the universal stupefaction and brutalisation of war.'[25]

Censorship forbade the publication of his letter in Russia but it appeared in *The Times* of London and translations of the text were circulated in Russian cities. Mobilisation went off smoothly, though there was a distinct lack of public enthusiasm as the trains rolled east. Knowing that Witte had opposed the war, many Russians saw difficult times ahead and feared a disastrous outcome.[26]

Kerensky's elder sisters supported the war effort. Elena suspended her medical studies to treat wounded soldiers, while Anna volunteered as a nurse. Olga Baranovkaya fell out with her brother Vladimir, who was about to graduate as an artillery officer in the Guards. 'The years of the Japanese war were a cruel spiritual torture,' Kerensky says. 'It brought strife into the friendliest relations and divided nearly every family into two hostile camps. The memory of those long, sleepless nights, spent in frenzied arguments about the war are still painful to me.'[27]

In the spring of 1904 he wrote to his parents to tell them he would not be coming home to Tashkent after his graduation. Instead, he and Olga had decided to get married. This news caused a sensation in his family. Fyodor Kerensky was convinced that Sasha, the light of his life, was being led astray by a revolutionary femme fatale. He saw the union not as gaining a daughter but as losing a son.

Elena and Anna wrote to Olga begging her to postpone the wedding until their brother was older and more able to support a family. Olga, who was working as a typist at the head office of the Nikolaevsky Railway Company, knew she was perfectly capable of making ends meet, while Alexander was confident he would soon find a job in the legal profession. Their minds were made up and they ignored the girls' plea.

Shortly after Alexander graduated in June that year, he and Olga took the train from Saint Petersburg to Kazan, sailed up the Volga to Sviazhsk and then travelled by open carriage to the Vasiliev estate in the village of Kainki, near Sviazhsk. The estate, which had been part of Sophia Ivanovna's dowry, included a house, an orchard and farmland. Since childhood, Olga had spent her holidays there and she knew the area well. 'When the peasants were still serfs, my grandfather and grandmother looked after them,' she recalls.

> Grandmother Sophie had great compassion for pregnant peasant women and she used to go to the fields during harvest time and when she saw a pregnant woman working she would call her to come and sit beside her for a long rest. The bailiff supervising the work did not dare to send her back to work.
>
> When my three uncles married and had families, Grandfather Vasily divided the estate among them, leaving himself only his house, garden and enough land to grow produce for him on his summer holiday. We

adored the place, so much so that when my mother took my two cousins and myself on a three-month trip through Germany, Italy, Switzerland and Austria, whenever we saw some beautiful scenery we'd exclaim, "It's just as beautiful as our Kainki!" My uncle Alexander, who inherited the house after Grandfather's death, was very good to me.[28]

Peasant welfare remained a priority for Olga's family. Her uncle Alexander Vasilievich Vasiliev, Sergei Vasiliev's father, was Professor of Mathematics at Saint Petersburg University. He was also a prominent *zemstvo* activist, a member of the First Duma and a member of the State Council. He believed that peasants should be educated, so every year he sponsored one or two peasant boys from the village school to go on to higher education, often sending them abroad.[29]

Kerensky had spent very little time in the countryside and he loved the experience of farm life. The farmland had been leased to the local peasants, many of whom had known Olga all her life and were overjoyed to be introduced to her young fiancé. The following month Olga and Alexander were married in the village church next to the Vasiliev house. The bride was twenty-two, the groom twenty-three. No one from either of their families was present. The newlyweds spent an idyllic honeymoon walking through orchards of cherry and hazelnut trees, crossing flowering meadows, swimming in the fish pond and sleeping 'with the windows wide open and waking up to the fresh air and the sun'.

Saint Petersburg rarely intruded. 'One day my wife and I went for a stroll by the edge of a wood, taking the newly arrived newspapers with us,' Kerensky says. 'The first thing that caught our eyes was a report that in Saint Petersburg on July 15, while on his way along the Zabalkansky Avenue to see the Tsar, Pleve had been killed by a bomb thrown by a former university student named Igor Sazonov. It is difficult to describe the mixture of feelings that the news aroused in me: a combination of joy, relief and the expectation of great change.'[30]

So many ministers and public officials were being assassinated to destabilise the autocracy that murder had become an occupational hazard for everyone in authority. The Tsar hardly mourned the victims any longer. After the murder of Dmitri Sipyagin, he had written in his diary, 'We must endure the trials the Lord sends us for our own good with humility and steadfastness.' Pleve's departure elicited this epitaph: 'I have lost a friend and an indispensable interior minister. The Lord has vented his wrath upon us. Thus is His sacred will.'

The advantage of accepting everything as God's will made misfortune easier to bear but his faith in the Almighty was about to face its most daunting test. Fifteen days after Pleve's murder, on 30 July 1904, Empress Alexandra's prayers were answered when she gave birth to a son. 'A great never-to-be-forgotten day when the mercy of God has visited us so clearly,' Nicholas wrote in his diary. 'Alix gave birth to a son at one o'clock.'[31]

The new Tsarevich, fair-haired with blue eyes and weighing eight pounds, was born at Peterhof, Peter the Great's summer palace, and christened Alexei after his father's favourite Tsar, the autocratic Alexei Mikhailovich (1645-1676). Six weeks after his birth Alexei bled from the navel for three days. Having lived with a haemophilic brother, Alexandra feared her son was carrying what she called 'our inherited curse', the Haemophilia B gene. The slightest bump could cause internal bleeding and lead to his death.

Had his frail condition become known to the world, it would have destroyed the Tsarina's reputation and raised questions about the succession, so her baby's affliction became a state secret. The effect on the Imperial Family was profound. All of a sudden, Nicholas had to apply his fatalism to his own family, while Alexandra regarded the tragedy as a punishment from God. If this were God's will, then what else lay in store for them?

Instead of the Winter Palace in Saint Petersburg, the Imperial Family spent months at a time at the Alexander Palace in Tsarskoe Selo, where Alexandra subjected her four daughters – Olga, Tatiana, Maria and Anastasia - to a Spartan upbringing within the bounds of strict Victorian morality – cold baths, bed-making, constant supervision, religion. The girls referred to themselves by the acronym OTMA, which was expanded to OTMAA to include Alexei. The girls' isolation grew more extreme in order to protect the secret of their brother's haemophilia.

Pierre Gilliard, who joined the Imperial Court in 1905 as tutor to Olga and Tatiana and stayed for with them for the rest of their lives, developed a certain sympathy for the Tsarina. 'I learned to realise by certain signs that the reserve which so many people had taken as an affront was a mask covering her sensitivity,' he said. But Alexandra was also sick. She had suffered from sciatica (pain in the lower back) since her teenaged years and a succession of other ailments – crippling migraine headaches, terrifying palpitations of the heart and a string of psychosomatic conditions resulting from the belief that she had an enlarged heart – had turned her into an invalid who was often confined to a sofa or wheelchair.

Having isolated her children from the outside world, Alexandra now shut herself away from her daughters inside the Alexander Palace. She devised a code to indicate the intensity of her pain: 'No. 1' meant the least severe pain; 'No. 2' intense pain and 'No. 3' the most severe pain. Unable to speak to her for days on end, the girls sent her plaintive notes: 'So sorry that your heart is No. 2. I'm so sorry not to see you today. 1000 kisses from your own loving Maria.'

Meanwhile, Nicholas visibly cheered up when two Japanese battleships, the 12,320-ton *Yashima* and the 15,300-ton *Hatsuse*, sank in a Russian minefield off Port Arthur. Their loss eliminated one-third of Japan's battleship force and made the Japanese Fleet vulnerable to attack. Instead of seizing this opportunity, the Russian admirals played safe and kept their ships in port. Shortly afterwards General Maresuke Nogi, the Japanese commander of the Third Army, attacked Port Arthur from the landward side. After breaching the two outer defensive lines in the eastern hills, he was confident of a quick victory.

Admiral Alekseyev had fled to Mukden in May and command of the Port Arthur garrison at had been left in the hands of an even bigger scoundrel, Baron Anatoli Mikhailovich Stoessel. Despite Stoessel's interference, two of his subordinates, Generals Smirnov and Kondratenko, built up a formidable array of defences, consisting of forts, miles of trenches and batteries containing guns salvaged from the crippled Pacific Squadron. Reaching the outskirts of the township, General Nogi threw wave after wave of Japanese troops into full-frontal assaults against these well-prepared positions. The Russian line buckled but it did not break.[32]

Nicholas ordered Vice Admiral Rozhdestvensky to take the Baltic Fleet to the East to relieve Port Arthur. The mission started badly when Rozhdestvensky mistook some British fishing boats on the Dogger Bank in the North Sea for Japanese torpedo boats and attacked them, killing two fishermen. 'All this is very awkward,' Nicky told his mother. 'The English are very angry [and are] getting their squadrons ready for action.' He sent his regrets to Uncle Bertie but refused to apologise, as though an apology was beneath his dignity.[iv]

Britain avenged the Dogger Bank Incident by honouring the terms of the 1902 Anglo-Japanese Alliance and closing the Suez Canal to the Baltic Fleet. Rozhdestvensky was obliged to sail around the Cape of Good Hope to reach the Indian Ocean.

When Alexander and Olga Kerensky returned to Saint Petersburg in the autumn of 1904, Olga was pregnant with their first child. The gloom of four months earlier, when Pleve's secret police were in full cry, had been replaced by a new mood of hope. The new Minister of the Interior, Prince 'Pepka' Svyatopolk-Mirsky, was a cultured man who preached 'mutual trust' and went out of his way to accommodate the regime's opponents. 'There began a political springtime,' Kerensky says. 'All educated Russia was at one in a common demand for a Constitution.'[33]

Alexander and Olga moved into a three-room flat on the fifth floor of an apartment block in Grodnensky Alley, near the Preobrazhensky Barracks. 'It was in a good part of Petersburg and it cost sixty-five roubles a month,' Olga says. 'Alexander was receiving from his father the same allowance as in his student days – sixty roubles per month. My mother had given up her flat and let me have all her furniture and kitchen equipment. She also gave me one thousand roubles.'

Self-belief had never been a problem for Kerensky but he lacked basic homemaking skills. Olga provided him with stability. She not only made a home for him but also earned a regular wage. His hopes of becoming a Professor of Law had dissolved in the same way as his dream of becoming an actor. 'Deep inside,' he says, 'I already felt that this was not to be and that my place was among the active opponents of the autocracy.' He applied to join the Saint Petersburg Bar to enable him to work as a political defender. For references, he listed a former governor, a former public prosecutor and a judge of the nation's highest court, the Senate. Appalled at the applicant's 'bureaucratic friends', the Council of Assistant Lawyers rejected his application.[34]

Once he had recovered from the shock, Kerensky saw the point of their objection. He found more suitable referees and was duly

---

iv The International Court at The Hague ordered Russia to pay £65,000 (£7.8 million today) in compensation to the fishermen's families.

admitted to the Bar as a junior barrister. 'I had no intention whatsoever of dealing with any but political cases,' he says. 'But I had no contacts in the main with leftwing parties and bore the label of a "bureaucratic background".' Nothing, however, could stop him from offering free advice to victims of the autocracy about their legal rights.

He worked in the Ligovsky People's House,[v] the purpose-built headquarters of a charitable organisation founded by Countess Sofia Panina to provide the working class with a legal aid centre, library, reading room, theatre and cafeteria. Ligovsky was on the impoverished southern edge of Saint Petersburg and Kerensky's legal work brought him into contact with what he called 'the lowest strata of the urban population'.

It also brought him into the realm of Countess Panina who, although apolitical herself, was surrounded by the everyday dramas of working-class life. 'I never belonged to any political party and my interests were concentrated on questions of education and general culture,' she wrote in her memoirs. 'I was deeply convinced these could provide a firm foundation for a free political order.'[35]

Sofia Vladimirovna Panina was born on 23 August 1871 into two of Russia's richest and most influential noble families, the Maltsevs and the Panins. Her father, Count Vladimir Viktorovich Panin, was the son of a long-serving Minister of Justice, and her stepfather, Ivan Illitch Petrunkevish, was one of the founders of the liberal movement opposed to the autocracy.

In January 1904 Petrunkevish had been elected chairman of the Union of Liberation, an illegal political alliance created by Peter Struve, who had abandoned Marxism and was editing the influential *Liberation* magazine in Stuttgart. The union's supporters included the radical historian Paul Miliukov, whose involvement with political issues had cost him his teaching post in 1895, and the *zemstvo* activist Fyodor Rodichev, once described as 'the very flower of Russian liberalism in its highest and broadest sense'.[36]

'The legal work engrossed me completely,' Kerensky says. 'The people – above all the women – would talk for hours, complaining about all sorts of things and pouring out their troubles. I worked with capable barristers, one of whom would become head of my private office when I was in government.' This was David Soskice, who had

---

v Ligovskii Narodnyi Dom (LND)

arrived in Saint Petersburg as correspondent for the London-based newspaper *The Tribune*. It was the beginning of a lasting friendship between the forty-year-old powerfully built revolutionary and the pale twenty-five-year-old civil rights lawyer.

Born on 27 March 1866 in Berdichev, the most Jewish of Ukrainian cities in the Pale, Soskice had been radicalised while studying at the University of Kiev after three young students were hanged for distributing socialist literature. 'I considered myself a socialist—or a revolutionist, which is the same thing,' he said. Over the next few years he hid revolutionaries from the police and took part in secret political meetings. It was only a matter of time before he attracted the attention of the Okhrana. His lodgings were repeatedly searched and police harassment forced him to abandon his studies in Kiev and then Saint Petersburg. Finally, he graduated in law at Odessa and moved to Kazan to set up a practice.[37]

Soskice's revolutionary activities led to his arrest in 1890 and he was taken to Saint Petersburg and locked up in the Trubetskoi Ravelin. As the law stood then, he should have been released within a month, or charged and put on trial. Instead, he spent the next twelve months in solitary confinement apart from a short daily walk in the courtyard and a monthly steam bath. The prison diet was so poor he developed scurvy. Several times the Okhrana dragged him out of his cell for questioning but he was never charged with any offence.[38]

Having spent three years in one prison or another without being charged with any offence, Soskice escaped to Paris and then settled in England, where he joined the Society for Friends of Russian Freedom, whose aims were to publicise the evils of Romanov regime and to encourage peaceful democratic change in Russia.[vi] His English friend David Garnett described him as 'a squarely built man, with a curly black beard, a square forehead and the simplest ideas of right and wrong which he put into practice with little regard for consequences'. In Paris, for instance, he had found himself in the midst of a vast crowd howling for the death of Captain Alfred Dreyfus, the Jewish officer who had been wrongly convicted of treason. Believing Dreyfus to be innocent, he had shouted, *'Vive Dreyfus!'* and was lucky to escape with his life.[39]

---

vi Some of Juliet's friends thought her husband humourless but they hadn't witnessed pogroms as he had done in Kiev, been harassed by the Tsar's secret police or been held for a year in the Trubetskoi Ravelin.

Soskice was not only a Doctor of Law but also a skilled journalist who collaborated with George Perris, *Tribune*'s Foreign Editor in London, to arrange such a devilish anti-Tsarist coverage of Russian affairs for British readers that the Russian Ambassador described the newspaper as his 'bête noire' and its Saint Petersburg correspondent as an 'execrable scoundrel'.[40]

By the turn of the century, the militant intelligentsia were eager to find a legal way to replace the autocracy with a constitutional monarchy. 'It was during the years of merciless Tsarist dictatorship that the mind of Russia was being prepared for the great era of liberal reforms,' Kerensky says. 'The seeds of revolution had been sown not through weighty political treatises but through the poems, novels and plays of Pushkin, Gogol, Tolstoy, Turgenev, Dostoevsky and Chekhov.'[41]

'Pepka' Mirsky's main concession was to permit the Union of Liberation and the General Zemstvo Congress to organise public banquets to commemorate the Great Reforms of the 1860s. These events proved extremely popular. Guests drank toasts to freedom and chanted 'Long live the Constituent Assembly', the first time anyone could mention such a thing in a public place without being arrested. The unspoken slogan was 'Down with the Autocracy'.

Guest speakers included Vladimir Dmitrievich (V. D.) Nabokov, the son of a former Minister of Justice (and father of the author Vladimir Nabokov), on the failures of the Tsarist judicial system, and Paul Miliukov on the advantages of the American Constitution. As one of the few women present at a Saint Petersburg banquet, Ariadne Tyrkova was called upon to give a female point of view. She received a round of applause 'for my courage, the fact that I was younger than most of them, and because I was a woman'.[42]

Kerensky was too young to expect an invitation to the banquets, so he undertook secretarial duties for the organisers, one of whom was Ivan Petrunkevich. Within a matter of months, he had made useful contacts in the wider world of politics. 'The banquets were in effect a parade of the political forces current among the intelligentsia and in the professions,' he says. 'There were always seats for workers, although few of them were ever filled. The keynote was the demand for a constitution.'[43]

At Port Arthur the Russians were hanging on grimly and casualties on both sides were running into the thousands. General Nogi called in batteries of eleven-inch howitzers to hurl huge explosive shells into the town and blast the blockaded Russian fleet at its moorings. Some of the ships were scuttled by their own officers who then retired ashore in the hope of avoiding further risk of annihilation.

On 23 December 1904/5 January 1905 General Stoessel surrendered Port Arthur after secretly accepting a Japanese bribe and arranging safe passage for himself back to Moscow. 'It is not hard to die for one's country,' he said in his last proclamation to his troops, 'but I must be brave enough to surrender.' Nicholas received the news while travelling to Minsk to inspect soldiers boarding the Trans-Siberian Railway on their way to the front. 'One had hoped that the army would prevail,' he wrote in his diary. 'Yet the defenders are heroes and did more than what might have been expected. It is God's will!'[44]

This was no consolation to the defenders. The Australian correspondent of *The Times*, George Morrison, accompanied General Nogi on his triumphal entry into the captured fortress. 'No foreign officer can explain the reason for the capitulation,' he wrote after the Japanese uncovered huge stores of food and ammunition. 'All accounts agree that no man who ever held a responsible command less deserved the title of hero than General Stoessel.'[45]

Nicholas would gladly have spent every waking moment with his family at Tsarskoe Selo but on Thursday 6 January 1905 - the Feast of the Epiphany marking the baptism of Jesus – custom required him to be in Saint Petersburg for the annual Blessing of the Waters. As he stood on the banks of the frozen Neva, a cannon employed in the ceremonial salute fired a live round from the Peter and Paul Fortress. Pieces of metal wounded a policeman and shattered some of the windows in the Winter Palace.

A hasty investigation established that caseshot had been loaded into the gun instead of a blank charge. Nicholas was unharmed but rumours spread around the Court that it was an assassination attempt. Some took it as a bad omen that the policeman's name was Romanov.[46]

6

The Accidental Terrorist

The sun rose in Saint Petersburg at 8.37 a.m. on Sunday 9 January 1905 in the old Julian calendar. 'A more perfect and lovely day never dawned,' recalls Robert Wilton, *The Times* correspondent who was staying at the Hotel Angleterre on Saint Isaac's Square. 'There were five degrees of frost. The air was crisp and invigorating and almost cloudless. The gilded domes of the cathedrals and the churches and the frost-encrusted roofs and facades of the houses, brilliantly illuminated by the sun, formed a superb panorama as I looked out of the hotel windows, wondering what the day would bring forth.'[1]

It would be a day like no other in Russia's modern history; a day that no one who lived through it would ever forget. As the sun set that afternoon, the snow would be stained with the blood of innocent people and Tsar Nicholas II's reputation as the 'Little Father of All the Russias' *(tsar-batyushka)* would have been trampled in the urban slush. It was the day that would put 'Bloody Sunday' into the Russian vocabulary.

Down at street level that morning, Alexander Kerensky was watching thousands of men, women and children assemble on the crackling snow. 'It was an amazing sight,' he says. 'Along the Nevsky Prospekt from the direction of the working-class districts came row upon row of orderly and solemn-faced workers, all dressed in their best clothes.' The idea of joining thousands of working men and women to present a petition - 'A Humble and Loyal Address' - to the Tsar at his own front door appealed enormously to Kerensky's democratic spirit.

The petition was the idea of a young Orthodox priest, Father Georgi Gapon, a popular figure among the Saint Petersburg working class. The previous year he had founded one of the only legal trade unions, a police-sponsored body called the Assembly of Russian Factory and

Mill Workers, which had branches in many of the biggest industrial plants. 'His influence on the masses was staggering,' Kerensky says, 'and in Saint Petersburg the Gaponist movement assumed huge proportions. The priest's speeches, in which he urged the workers to go directly to the Tsar, appealed to his listeners and the idea of voicing their grievances in a mass demonstration quickly gained support.'[2]

Industrial workers numbered 300,000 among the city's population of 1.5 million. They had many causes for complaint – food shortages were common and prices were going up. The Russian industrial employee worked an eleven-hour shift (ten hours on Saturday) and he was lucky if he earned a rouble a day. Conditions in the factories were harsh and little concern was shown for his health or safety. Many families were on the verge of starvation.

Nevertheless, the vast majority of the workforce remained staunchly conservative and devoutly Orthodox. Rather than embrace the mystifying polemics of the intelligentsia or the radical propaganda of the socialist parties, they stuck to their peasant roots and believed with a blind faith born of ignorance that the Tsar would never fail them in their hour of need.[3]

It was the Tsar's uncle, Grand Duke Sergei Alexandrovich, the Governor-General of Moscow, who had introduced police-sponsored labour organisations into Russian industry through the recently departed Viacheslav Pleve. He borrowed the idea from Bismarck, who had seen such bodies as a means of neutralising the influence of socialism among the workers.[4] The task of making 'police socialism' work in Russia was given to Sergei V. Zubatov, a revolutionary turncoat who had risen to chief of the Okhrana's Moscow office. Union meetings were permitted but were carefully controlled. Each meeting began with the Lord's Prayer and ended with the national anthem, a combination of God and flag that might have salved the members' consciences but failed to solve the problems bedevilling their lives.[5]

Zubatov fell from grace when a march to commemorate the 1861 Emancipation of the Serfs attracted a potentially troublesome crowd of 50,000. The government's concerns about the growth and influence of 'police socialism' were soon confirmed. 'In 1903, Zubatov was removed from his post,' Kerensky says. 'The new movement had become too "successful", inasmuch as some of his agents had taken part in, or even organised, general strikes.'[6]

All through the autumn and early winter of 1904 the strikes had grown larger and more threatening. The measures taken against the strikers – flailing Cossack whips and rifle butts – completely failed to curb the militancy. By the New Year, 90,000 workers were on strike throughout Saint Petersburg over the sacking of four union members at the arms-producing Putilov Iron Works in the southwest of the city.[i][7]

This was the issue that had inspired Father Gapon's petition to the Tsar calling for the recognition of free trades unions, an eight-hour day, higher pay, the release of political prisoners, freedom of speech and a Constituent Assembly elected by secret ballot. Such was the disunited state of the nation on Saturday 8 January, the eve of the great march. Father Gapon sent two messengers to the Winter Palace bearing a letter to the Tsar to explain his motives:

> Sire,
> I fear that your Ministers have not told you the whole truth about the state of affairs in the capital. Be assured that the workmen and the people of Saint Petersburg, trusting in you, have irrevocably decided to appear tomorrow at 2 p.m. before the Winter Palace, in order to present to you a statement of their needs and those of the whole Russian people. If, hesitating in your heart, you do not show yourself to your people, and if innocent blood be shed, the moral tie which has existed between you and your people will be broken, and the trust which the people have in you will disappear forever. Come, then, tomorrow with confidence before your people, and receive with an open mind our petition. I, the representative of the workmen, and my brave comrades guarantee the safety of your person at the price of our lives.[8]

The letter was signed 'G. Gapon, Priest'. Father Gapon never heard from his messengers again; they had probably been arrested as soon as they approached the palace and were, even then, languishing in the Vyborg One-Night Prison, the jail for 'politicals' commonly known as Kresty (The Cross) on the banks of the Neva.[ii] Prince Sviatopolk-

---

[i] The founder of the Putilov Company was one of Russia's greatest metallurgists, Nikolai Ivanovich Putilov (1820-1880). The Imperial Russian Government saved the company from bankruptcy in the 1880s and it became a gigantic industrial complex in the later part of the Nineteenth Century.

[ii] The prison was built in the form of a cross with a central tower overlooking all four wings.

Mirsky, however, had been given a copy of the letter, so the Tsar would probably have been informed about its contents.

Unbeknown to Father Gapon and his supporters, Nicholas had already rejoined his family at Tsarskoe Selo for a pleasant weekend of tennis, billiards, bezique and dominoes. On Saturday night he scribbled in his diary, 'Since yesterday all the factories and workshops in Saint Petersburg have been on strike. Troops have been brought in from the surroundings to strengthen the garrison. The workers have conducted themselves calmly hitherto. Their number is estimated at 120,000. At the head of the workers' union is some priest, a socialist named Gapon. Mirsky came in the evening with a report of the measures taken.'

Father Georgy Apollonovich Gapon was not a socialist but he was committed to social reform. He had been born in the village of Beliki in the Cossack heartlands of Ukraine on 5 February 1870. His father was a Cossack, his mother a peasant, and, according to him, they sometimes struggled financially. Soviet historians maintain that the family were prosperous peasants – *kulaks* – but, of course, both versions could be true.[9]

The militant political parties of Saint Petersburg were opposed to police-sponsored unions on principle and Father Gapon's protest march did not have their backing. But Father Gapon had something that neither Bolsheviks, Mensheviks nor Socialist Revolutionaries possessed: personal contact with the grass roots of the working class. That his action in confronting the forces of autocracy in a peaceful protest could trigger a revolution would never have occurred to him. He was a mesmeric preacher, a weaver of spells, and the people believed in his magic. Politically, however, he was an innocent novice, a charismatic naïf, an accidental terrorist.

As outlined by Mirsky, the measures taken to protect the Tsar from the crude embrace of the mob were extreme. Overnight, the centre of Saint Petersburg had been turned into an armed camp of cavalry, infantry and artillery regiments totalling 12,000 men accompanied by ambulances and mobile kitchens. Their commanding officers had been briefed to prevent the marchers from reaching the Winter Palace, an order that would inevitably lead to confrontation. Angry Petersburgers were bound to remind the soldiers that instead of blocking a legitimate protest march they should be fighting the Japanese on the other side of the world.

Every Russian soldier on duty that night was painfully aware that the army's reputation had hit a new low in Manchuria. Even as they were setting up roadblocks on bridges over the Neva, the Prussian-trained Japanese Army was celebrating the seizure of Port Arthur.

Meanwhile, the government had ordered Father Gapon to call off his march and notices were posted in the city centre warning that 'resolute measures' would be taken against any group who dared to gather on the streets. The turbulent priest refused to be cowed; the march must go ahead, he said, to bring these important social matters to the Tsar's notice. At eleven o'clock on Saturday morning – the starting hour of the march – the level of excitement rose in every working class district across the city. The crowd, estimated at 150,000, set off from six different points with the aim of converging on Palace Square, actually a great semi-circular arena in front of the Winter Palace. Father Gapon's column, numbering 20,000, would travel four miles from the industrialised Narva District to the square via the Narva Gates at the Triumphal Arch celebrating Russia's victory over Napoleon in 1812.

The priest told representatives of the Socialist Revolutionary and Social Democratic Parties, 'When I enter the Winter Palace, I will have with me two flags, one white and one red. If the Tsar receives the deputation I will signal with the white flag; if he refuses, with the red flag; and in that case you may raise your own red flag and do what you think necessary.'[10]

To keep tabs on Father Gapon, the SR leaders ordered one of their members, Pinhas 'Peter' Rutenberg, a Jewish engineer who had worked at the Putilov plant, to join the march. Just prior to setting off, Gapon invited him to address the marchers. Rutenberg warned that they might come under fire and if that happened he informed them of places where they could obtain weapons to fight back.

Gapon, however, insisted that the march must be peaceful and he asked his followers whether any of them were carrying weapons. When he was satisfied they had none, he said, 'We will go unarmed to our Tsar.' As the columns set off, the people linked arms and sang the national anthem, 'God Save the Tsar'. There was no outward sign of hostility or rebellion; no red flags and no guns. When one marcher started singing a revolutionary song, fellow marchers silenced him with the rebuke, 'You are violating order; it is necessary to conduct oneself as orderly as possible.'[11]

On Nevsky Prospekt Alexander Kerensky kept pace with the marchers as they set off, with the distant Admiralty spire acting like the needle point of a compass indicating their destination. Palpably excited, they reached the Anichkov Bridge with its bronzed sculptures of the four Horse Tamers glinting in the sunlight. Crossing the Fontanka River, they passed baroque palaces, gilded churches and fabulous shops in which they would never be permitted to set foot. Heads swung to the left and people crossed themselves as they passed the Kazan Cathedral with its ribbed cupola and priceless icon to Our Lady of Kazan behind whose image was God, and then swung to the right to marvel at the richly decorated Art Nouveau Singer Building behind whose image was American capitalism.[iii]

Emerging from their Sunday morning services, husbands in top-hats and frockcoats and wives swathed in expensive furs gazed in amazement at this rare vision of working-class solidarity. On their way to church that morning the gentry had seen the Imperial Standard fluttering over the Winter Palace and assumed that all was right with the world. Nothing could have been further from the truth. Saint Petersburg was about to undergo a gigantic convulsion.

As the marchers reached the Alexander Garden beside Palace Square, Kerensky heard the sound of a bugle. Everybody halted, uncertain as to its meaning. When a detachment of police standing to their right showed no signs of hostility, they moved off again towards the palace. Almost immediately, a squadron of Cossack Cavalry rode into them from the left flank, the blades of their sabres flashing in the sunshine. On the far side of Palace Square, opposite the Admiralty, a company of the Preobrazhensky Guards, the Tsar's own regiment, took this as their signal to open fire. The Guards' first volley went into the air but the second hit the crowd and a number of people fell to the ground. Panic-stricken, the marchers fled for their lives through the

---

iii The building was opened in 1904 as the Russian head office of the Singer Manufacturing Company, maker of the Singer sewing machine. It was briefly home to the US Embassy during the First World War and soon after the October Revolution it was given to the state publishing company Petrogosizdat (later Lenizdat). Today it is home to Saint Petersburg's largest and most famous bookshop, Dom Knigi (House of the Book).

gardens towards the Admiralty, towards the Neva Embankment, or back along Nevsky Prospekt.

'They were now being fired on from behind and we bystanders took to our heels along with the rest,' Kerensky says. 'I cannot describe the horror we felt at that moment. It was clear that the authorities had made a terrible mistake; they had totally misunderstood the intentions of the crowd.' As events in other parts of the city would show, this was no misunderstanding. The officers had been ordered to take all necessary measures to prevent the march reaching the palace.[12]

The marchers had planned to kneel down in Palace Square in the hope that the Tsar would make an appearance on the balcony of the Winter Palace and bless them. Alexandra Kollontai, the Marxist daughter of a Tsarist general, observed the 'trusting expectant faces, the fateful signal of the troops stationed around the palace, the pools of blood on the snow, the bellowing of the gendarmes, the dead, the wounded, the children shot.'[13]

At the Trinity Bridge next to the Peter and Paul Fortress, the Cossacks attacked a crowd of 10,000 people with their sabres. Most fled but not everyone got away.[14] Maxim Gorky lived nearby. His description of the killing of a single marcher illustrated the Cossacks' frenzy:

> The dragoon circled round him and, shrieking like a woman, waved his sabre in the air [and] slashed him across the face, cutting him open from the eyes to the chin. I remember the strangely enlarged eyes of the worker and the murderer's face, blushed from the cold and excitement, his teeth clenched in a grin and the hairs of his moustache standing up on his elevated lip. Brandishing his tarnished shaft of steel he let out another shriek and, with a wheeze, spat at the dead man through his teeth.[15]

No one was safe from attack. The ballet dancer Nijinsky received a savage blow to the head from a Cossack baton when the fleeing crowd swept him along Nevsky Prospekt.[16]

Alexander Kerensky, in common with many other witnesses, believed that Father Gapon was at the head of the Nevsky Prospekt march. Some claimed the priest was wearing a long white cassock and carrying a crucifix, which would have made him an easy target. Indeed, Robert Wilton reported in *The Times* that he had been shot and wounded.[17] In reality, the priest's column was making steady progress towards Palace Square along its south-western route. In the front row of marchers an old man carried a framed portrait of the Tsar, while others held aloft religious banners, crucifixes and icons. Father Gapon, wearing an overcoat over his cassock, was in the second row protected by his assistants and two bodyguards.

Two uniformed police officers walked ahead of the march to clear carriages and pedestrians out of the way. Despite the bitter cold, the marchers were bareheaded and sang hymns and the national anthem. Their sole aim was to see their Sovereign; as one of them put it, 'to cry out our griefs like children on the breast of the father'.

Approaching the Narva Gates, less than half a mile from the Winter Palace, a company of riflemen blocked the bridge over the Tarakanovka River and a squadron of Cossack Cavalry was drawn up in front of the infantry. Father Gapon's stewards asked him, 'Shall we march straight to the Gates or avoid the soldiers?' The priest remembers shouting, 'No, straight through them. Courage! Death or freedom.' The crowd shouted 'Hurrah!' and surged forward, singing the Tsar's hymn, 'God Save Thy People'. Father Gapon recalls:

> In front of me were my two bodyguards and a yellow fellow with dark eyes from whose face his hard labouring life had not wiped away the light of youthful gaiety. On the flanks of the crowd ran the children. Some of the women insisted on walking in the first rows, in order, as they said, to protect me with their bodies, and force had to be used to remove them.
>
> Suddenly the company of Cossacks galloped rapidly towards us with drawn swords. So, then, it was to be a massacre after all! There was no time for consideration, for making plans, or giving orders. A cry of alarm arose as the Cossacks came down upon us. Our front ranks broke before them, opening to right and left, and down the lane the soldiers drove their horses, striking on both sides.
>
> I saw the swords lifted and falling, the men, women and children dropping to the earth like logs of wood, while moans, curses and shouts filled the air. Again we started forward, with solemn resolution and rising rage in our hearts.[18]

Reaching the back of the procession, the Cossacks turned around and rode through the whole column again, slashing at helpless marchers all the way. Satisfied with their bloody work, they galloped back to the Narva Gates, where the infantrymen stepped aside to let them through. The squadron commander later claimed two shots had been fired from the crowd and that marchers had struck his men with their crosses. The infantry then took aim at the crowd which, though depleted, was still advancing slowly towards the gates.

> We were not more than thirty yards from the soldiers when, without any warning, I heard the crack of many rifle-shots [Father Gapon says]. Vasiliev, with whom I was walking hand in hand, suddenly sank upon the snow. Immediately, one of the two police officers shouted out, 'What are you doing? How dare you fire upon a portrait of the Tsar!' This had no effect – both he and the other officer were shot down. I heard afterwards one was killed and the other dangerously wounded.[19]

The old man carrying the Tsar's portrait fell to the ground. Another elderly marcher picked up the portrait but was felled by the next volley. Stumbling around, Father Gapon could be heard repeatedly shouting, 'There is no God. There is no Tsar.'

The massacre plunged Saint Petersburg into a state of open revolt. Workers and students on Vasilevsky Island pulled down telegraph poles and wrenched benches from their bases to make barricades. Looters broke into shops and houses, and raided an arsenal for weapons. Power supplies were cut off. 'The passions of the mob broke loose like a bursting dam,' Robert Wilton wrote. 'The people, seeing the dead and dying carried away in all directions, the snow on the streets and pavements soaked with blood, cried aloud for vengeance.'

Peter Rutenberg, who had remained close to Father Gapon, extricated him from a mass of writhing bodies and led him away from the carnage. Taking out a pair of scissors attached to a knife, he cut off some of the priest's flowing locks, trimmed his beard and covered his head with a workman's cap. He spent his first night as a fugitive at Gorky's home in Kronversky Prospekt on Petersburg Side. The author wrote to his former wife, Ekaterina Peshkova, who was in Nizhny Novgorod, 'So, my dear, the Russian revolution has started. We are not daunted by the dead. History will be repainted in the colour of blood. Tomorrow will see even more drama and heroism....'

Safely tucked up in Alexander Palace, Nicholas wrote in his diary: 'A grievous day! Serious disorders occurred in Saint Petersburg because workers sought to reach the Winter Palace. Troops were compelled to fire in several parts of the city: many were killed and wounded. God, how painful and heart-breaking! Mama came from the city straight to church. Had lunch with everyone. Went for a walk with [brother] Misha. Mama stayed overnight.'[20]

The petition, which had been signed by Father Gapon and 135,000 members of the Assembly of Russian Factory and Mill Workers, was abandoned in the snow. It had been a strangely prophetic document. 'The awful moment has come,' Father Gapon had written in his address to the Tsar, 'when death is better than the prolongation of our unendurable tortures.'[21]

Bloody Sunday made an immense impression on Alexander Kerensky. 'The ninth of January,' he says, 'saw the creation of the proletariat as a new anti-dynastic political force.' In the coming days he joined volunteers from the Bar Council in visiting the families of the dead to offer legal advice about claiming compensation from the state. Some of the bereaved lived in well-furnished tenements, others in the meanest hovels but the reaction of the wives seemed to be identical: they lacked any sense of class-consciousness. 'These women had no feelings of resentment or hatred,' he says. 'They simply felt that something had happened that would change the whole course of their lives.'

Kerensky could not reconcile the fact that Russian soldiers who had proved so inept against the Japanese could turn their fury on innocent, unarmed Russian men, women and children. 'I wrote a letter to the officers of the Guards,' he said, 'reminding them that at a time when the Army was fighting for Russia, they at home, with all Europe looking on, had shot down defenceless workers and had thereby greatly harmed the country's prestige abroad.'

He signed the letter with his own name and sent copies to a number of officers, one of whom was his brother-in-law, Vladimir Baranovsky. There were no unpleasant consequences. 'Not one of them betrayed me or passed on my letter to the police,' he said. 'But from that time on, I broke off relations with all my friends and acquaintances in bureaucratic circles.'[22]

One of the greatest obstacles to reform was the Tsarina Alexandra. When Queen Victoria had suggested that the Imperial Couple's first duty was to win the love and respect of their subjects, Alicky replied,

'You are mistaken, my dear grandmamma; Russia is not England. Here we do not need to earn the love of the people. The Russian people revere their Tsars as divine beings.'[23]

All that changed on Bloody Sunday. From Odessa, Thomas E. Heenan, the American Consul, wired Robert McCormick, the American Ambassador in Saint Petersburg: 'All classes condemn the authorities and, more particularly, the Tsar. He has lost absolutely the affection of the Russian people and whatever the future of the dynasty, the Tsar will never be safe in the midst of his people.'

The final death toll was horrific: more than a thousand had been killed and 2000 seriously wounded. Mirsky was adamant he had not authorised the shooting of the marchers but before he was allowed to resign and join the ranks of disgraced Tsarist ministers, he was required to perform one final duty and take the blame for the massacre.

Alexander Pasternak, younger brother of the *Doctor Zhivago* author Boris Pasternak, decried 'the official tactic of metaphorically dousing down fire with paraffin'. The peaceful march, he said, had ended in 'a highway sown with dead and wounded. Soldiers and police shot them down indiscriminately and the official strength, that had failed so lamentably to put the Japanese to flight, now glowed in its dispersal of a defenceless crowd'.[24]

Though only a schoolboy in his twelfth year, Alexander says Bloody Sunday turned him into 'a whole-hearted revolutionary'. His first subversive act was to copy the texts of treasonable documents for the Social Democrats to distribute to the workers. Like all his school friends, he carried in his pocket a Browning automatic pistol carved from wood and painted black. 'Something hung over us,' he said, 'and everybody was preparing himself.'[25]

The Tsarina had always been as reactionary as her husband but had become even more so since the birth of her son because of the necessity to protect his inheritance. Five days after Bloody Sunday, she poured out her heart in a letter to her elder sister, Princess Victoria, wife of Prince Louis of Battenberg:

> My poor Nicky's cross is a heavy one to bear, all the more as he has nobody on whom he can thoroughly rely. He has had so many bitter disappointments, but through it all he remains brave and full of faith in God's mercy. He tries so hard, works with such perseverance, but the lack of what I call 'real' men is great. Had his father seen more

men, drawn them around him, we should have lots to fill the necessary posts; now [there are] only old men and quite young ones, [there is] no one to turn to.[26]

Father Gapon had been smuggled out of Saint Petersburg and across the border into Finland. From his hiding place, he sent a letter to Nicholas in which he damned him and his family to eternity. 'The innocent blood of workers, their wives and children lies forever between thee, oh soul destroyer, and the Russian people,' he wrote. 'Let all the blood that has to be shed, hangman, fall upon thee and thy kindred.'

7

The Dress Rehearsal

Bloody Sunday was the first day of the 1905 Revolution, a spontaneous uprising which was, in the words of Vladimir Lenin, a 'dress rehearsal' for the abolition of the Romanov Dynasty twelve years later. Harold Williams, the New Zealand-born correspondent of the *Daily Chronicle*, witnessed the rage that turned peaceful marchers into rioters, looters and arsonists. 'I saw these looks of hatred on every face, young and old, men and women,' he says. 'The Revolution was born. The popular ideal – myth or not – of a Good Tsar, which had sustained the regime for centuries, was suddenly destroyed.'

In late January Alexander Kerensky wrote to his father in Tashkent, 'I am sorry not to have written to you earlier, but we have been living here in such a state of shock that it was impossible to write. Oh, "these awful days" in Peter will remain forever in the memory of everybody who lived through them. Now there is silence, but it is the silence before the storm. Both sides are preparing and reviewing their own forces. Only one side can prevail. Either the demands of society will be satisfied (i.e., a freely elected legislature of people's representatives) or there will be a bloody and terrible conflict, no doubt ending in the victory of the reaction.'

Almost immediately serious strikes broke out in the capital and their violent repression during spring and summer triggered yet more strikes, not only in Saint Petersburg and Moscow but also in Warsaw, Kharkov, Vilna, Kovno, Kiev, Bialystok, Riga and Tiflis (today's Tbilisi, capital of Georgia). Kerensky concluded that Nicholas's birthright was to blame for his intransigence. 'From his youth he had been brought up to believe that his welfare and the welfare of the country were one and the same thing,' he says, '"Disloyal" workmen, peasants and students who were shot down, executed or exiled seemed to him mere monsters and outcasts of humanity who must be destroyed for the sake of the country and his "faithful subjects".'[1]

To avenge the Bloody Sunday atrocity, Boris Savinkov decided to assassinate Nicholas's uncle, Grand Duke Sergei Alexandrovich, the fifth son of Alexander II. In a macabre touch he decreed that the victim should be killed by a bomb thrown at his moving carriage, the same method that the People's Will had used to murder his father in 1881.

After breakfast on 5 February 1905, four weeks after the Bloody Sunday massacre, Alexander Pasternak was deep in conversation with his father in the family's Moscow flat overlooking the Polish Cathedral when an explosion rent the air. 'Within a few hours we heard that a bomb had been thrown into the carriage of the Grand Duke Sergei,' Alexander says. 'He was killed instantly as he drove into the Kremlin through the Nikolsky Gate.'[2]

Lenin called Savinkov 'a bourgeois with a bomb in his pocket' but it was Ivan Kaliaev, a disaffected aristocrat, and not Savinkov himself, who had thrown it. Badly wounded by the blast, the bomber was captured alive. Sergei's wife, the Tsarina's deeply religious sister Elizabeth, known as Ella, visited Kaliaev in prison and asked him to repent for killing her husband. The assassin told her that he had acted according to his conscience and regretted nothing. Turning her back on the Imperial Court, Ella took holy orders and founded a convent to help the poor.

Kaliaev was hanged three months after the assassination. He told the judge at his trial, 'I am not a defendant. I am your captive. We are two warring parties. You represent the imperial government, the hired servants of capital and violence. I am one of the people's avengers, a socialist and a revolutionary.'[3]

The Revolution reached into hitherto sheltered places. At the Saint Petersburg Conservatoire, Rimsky-Korsakov refused to teach in a building surrounded by the armed police. After thirty-five years as Professor of Music, the great composer was dismissed from his post and his much-loved musical compositions were temporarily banned from public performance.[4] At the Bear Restaurant the opera singer Fyodor Chaliapin was overcome with a rash of radical fervour. Rising from the supper table, it was said he gave his audience a beautifully rendered selection of revolutionary and prison songs. The impromptu performance endeared him to the masses but infuriated Nicholas, who refused to receive him at Court and declined invitations to his operas.[5]

While the Imperial Family kept out of sight to prevent another assassination, the Tsar's problems multiplied exponentially when a nationalist uprising broke out in Russian-occupied Poland. The country was in a state of anarchy, with assassinations and other terrorist acts occurring daily in the name of independence. The idea of revolution was understood more clearly in Poland than in Russia. Whereas the Russian peasant wanted land and liberty, and the Russian worker sought higher wages and improved conditions, the entire Polish nation was united in demanding freedom from its oppressors.[6]

Like an airborne epidemic, the revolutionary spirit raced across the Baltic provinces (Kurland, Livland and Estland – later, Lithuania, Latvia and Estonia) and leaped down to the Caucasus (Georgia, Armenia and Azerbaijan); even parts of Siberia were in a state of turmoil. Peasants attacked landowners and burned down their manor houses; students rioted; government officials were murdered.

Inevitably, Father Gapon was blamed for these violent spasms. The conservative Saint Petersburg press branded him a terrorist and Robert McCormick called him a paedophile (on the say-so of the Austro-Hungarian Ambassador) and 'a thorough-paced revolutionist' (on the say-so of the correspondent of the *Standard*). The most frequent allegation against him was that he was a police agent provocateur whose motive was not to lead the workers to salvation but to destroy them.

Gapon had fled abroad and, in the next few dizzy months, thoroughly enjoyed his notoriety in European cities. In Geneva he met most of the Russian political exiles there and succeeded in arguing with Georgi Plekhanov; briefly joined the Socialist Revolutionaries Viktor Chernov, 'Babushka' Brezhkovskaya and Evno Azev; and hobnobbed with Vladimir Lenin and the Social Democrats. Lenin found him fascinating. He inscribed his most recent pamphlet, 'Two Tactics of Social Democracy in the Democratic Revolution', 'To Georgi Gapon with respect, from the author.' He was also drawn to Gapon's slogan 'All the Land to the People', which was crisper, more far-reaching and more radical than his own feeble demand for cut-off strips of land to be handed to the peasants. Nadezhda Krupskaya, however, had her doubts about the visitor. She called him 'a sly priest'.[7]

Taking the train to Paris, Gapon met the socialist leader Jean Jaurès and the future Prime Minister George Clémenceau. In London, he was invited to stay with David Soskice, who had returned from his reporting assignment in Saint Petersburg. Soskice and his wife, Juliet Hueffer, a member of the pre-Raphaelite milieu through her grandfather, the artist Ford Madox Brown,[i] lived in Hammersmith and Gapon was their guest while he wrote his memoirs with the help of George Perris. *The Story of My Life* was published by E. P. Dutton in New York and was serialised in the *New York Times* under the headline 'Gapon, Hero of Bloody Sunday'.

The Tsar badly needed some good news from the Far East but none was forthcoming. The strategy of General Kuropatkin, the former Minister of War who had been appointed Commander of the Russian Army (although Admiral Alekseyev remained Commander in Chief, thus confusing the lines of command), had been to trade space for time. Reinforcements were arriving along the single-track Trans-Siberian Railway, with ferries carrying the trains across the gap in the line at Lake Baikal, at the rate of 35,000 men a month. Unfortunately for Kuropatkin, the Ministry of War was obliged to retain the most reliable troops in the west to put down peasant revolts, so he received mostly poorly trained reservists.[8]

At Mukden in March 1905 more than 600,000 troops clashed in the greatest land battle ever fought. Almost half the Russian force of 380,000 were killed, wounded or captured and the rest were saved from annihilation only because Kuropatkin ordered yet another retreat.[9] Even schoolboys like Alexander Pasternak knew about the incompetence and corruption that had undermined the Russian armed forces. 'Our maps were so bad they led the commanding officer into catastrophic miscalculations,' he says. 'Our old-fashioned army was ill-equipped for the unexpected mountainous terrain; instead of essential packhorses, our transport consisted of wagons whose wheels broke constantly, making it impossible for our troops to manoeuvre quickly. Could it really be true that a second-year schoolboy knew more than the high command?'[10]

Kerensky became a father when his first son Oleg was born on 3

---

[i] Juliet's aunt and uncle were Christina and Dante Gabriel Rossetti, and her brother was the author Ford Madox Ford. For a time David Soskice had funded Ford's literary magazine, The English Review. When Ford slipped off to France for a holiday with his lover Violet Hunt without informing him, he appointed John Galsworthy as temporary editor. Ford was enraged on his return to find the great novelist ensconced in his office.

April 1905. The family's joy over his birth was diminished by the news from Tashkent that Nadezhda Kerenskaya had died suddenly. Fyodor Kerensky was stricken with grief: his devoted companion on his journey to educate Russian children, his soulmate for life and the mother of his children was barely fifty.

Meanwhile, the Baltic Fleet had seemingly disappeared somewhere in the Indian Ocean after rounding the Cape of Good Hope and passing Madagascar. The Royal Navy, however, had kept the Russian ships under surveillance and knew exactly where they were. Contrary to the laws of neutrality, Russia's ally France had permitted Admiral Rozhdestvensky to shelter in Camranh Bay in French Indochina. Japan was notified that the fleet had been at anchor there since 15 April and was filling its bunkers with coal and loading fresh provisions.[11]

As Britain was bound under the terms of the Anglo-Japanese Alliance to prevent a third party from interfering in the war on Russia's side, the Foreign Office remonstrated with the French who, in the spirit of the new Entente Cordiale, replied that nothing of the sort had occurred. 'The growing indignation felt by the Japanese respecting the use made by the Baltic Fleet of a neutral port is fully warranted,' the *Brisbane Courier* editorialised. 'It is only an historical accident that the Russian Armada is directed against Japan instead of Australia.'[12]

Rozhdestvensky had taken so long to reach the China Seas that his mission – the relief of Port Arthur – was now pointless. Instead of instructing him to return home as best he could, Nicholas ordered him 'to seize control of the Sea of Japan'. Before undertaking this arduous task Rozhdestvensky decided to break through Japanese lines to replenish his fleet at Vladivostok.

In mid-May news reached Saint Petersburg that the Japanese Navy had inflicted a devastating defeat on the Baltic Fleet in the Tsushima Straits between Korea and Japan in what became known as the 'Trafalgar of the East'. Grand Duke Alexander Mikhailovich ('Sandro', a naval officer who was married to Nicholas's sister Xenia) recalls, 'Our picnic party at Gatchina was interrupted by a messenger: our fleet had been annihilated.' Twenty-one ships out of thirty-eight had been sunk at a cost of just three Japanese torpedo boats. The humiliation was overwhelming. Nicholas could not comprehend how such a thing could have happened. According to Sandro, he turned pale, lit a cigarette and said nothing.

The Australian journalist William Henry Donald, who had visited the Baltic Fleet while it was at anchor in Camranh Bay on its way to Tsushima, provided part of the answer: 'The officers were drunkards and the crews were untrained, undisciplined and unpatriotic men who had no shred of interest in their work and no concern as to the outcome of the battle.' Crew morale was at rock bottom because Sergei Witte had cut the navy's training budget to the bone in order to balance the books after the Tsar insisted on spending millions of roubles on new battleships.[13]

Closer to home, Witte's cost-cutting economies were also responsible for a mutiny aboard the battleship *Potemkin* of the Black Sea Squadron. The mutiny broke out at Odessa on 14 June after an officer shot a deckhand who had the gall to complain about cheap, maggot-ridden meat. The sailors killed the captain, threw their officers overboard and took control of the warship.[14] Crossing Odessa Harbour, the renegade vessel shelled the town with the intention of wiping out some generals who were holding a meeting in a theatre there but their aim was poor and they wrecked the soldiers' barracks instead. For several days the *Potemkin* bombarded settlements on the shores of the Black Sea before being grounded at Constanta on the coast of Romania. Some of the mutineers escaped, others were interned.[15]

The usual scapegoats – the Jews - were blamed for the Motherland's tribulations. Indeed, one of the common salutations of the time was, 'God save the Tsar and beat the Jews.' Antisemites spread rumours that the Jews had also been responsible for the murder of Uncle Sergei, bringing terror to many towns both inside and outside the Pale of Settlement. The Black Hundred, a militant gang of antisemites and extreme Russian nationalists, attacked Feodosiya in February 1905 and Melitopol in April, while in May a pogrom in the provincial capital of Zhitomir surpassed either of these in its ferocity.[16]

In Odessa the Municipal Governor issued a proclamation in which recent unrest in the port-city was attributed to Jewish troublemakers. Thomas Heenan, the American Consul, estimated that casualties in the ensuing pogrom ran into the thousands, with the Jewish death toll touching 500. Artillery, he said, was employed to suppress the rioting, while armed Jews had fought back, firing from upstairs windows at troops in the street.[17]

The Bund, which had withdrawn from the ranks of the RSDLP,

called on Jewish workers in Lodz, 'the Polish Manchester', to take industrial action. Felix Dzerzhinsky, leader of the Social Democratic Party of the Kingdom of Poland and Lithuania (and future head of Lenin's secret police, the Cheka), had many friends among the Bundists who joined his members in staging rolling factory sit-ins involving half the city's workforce.[18]

More than 1200 people, both Christian and Jewish, were killed in battles against police and troops during June. As a sign of things to come, officers of one regiment in Lodz refused to fire on defenceless people. These troops were quickly replaced with others who were prepared to obey orders. 'These are gloomy days for the Government of Russia,' the *New York Times* reported. 'Every new dispatch accentuates the situation in Poland and the Caucasus, where a state of almost open war exists. Reports of strikes, demonstrations and agrarian disorders are pouring in as if the volleys fired at Lodz had been the signal for an outbreak of general disorders like those following the events of Bloody Sunday.'[19]

Privately, Nicky breathed a sigh of relief when the American President, Theodore 'Teddy' Roosevelt, offered to act as mediator to end the Russo-Japanese War. Peace talks began in Portsmouth, New Hampshire, between a recalled Sergei Witte and Japan's Baron Jutaro Komura. Witte quickly won the public relations battle by giving interviews to the world's press and posing for photographs, while Komura, quiet, dignified and silent, went unnoticed in the background. The result was stalemate until Roosevelt exerted pressure on Komura to drop Japan's demand for reparations and the Treaty of Portsmouth was signed on 5 September.

Russia agreed to recognise Japanese control of Korea (as a preliminary step towards annexation of that country as a Japanese colony five years later) and transferred to Japan the Kwantung Leased Territory on the Liaodong Peninsula, including Port Arthur and the Southern Manchurian Railway. Japan also retained the sparsely populated southern half of Sakhalin Island (later discovered to be rich in oil and natural gas). Both countries agreed to restore Manchuria to Chinese sovereignty and to evacuate their forces, although Japan was permitted to retain enough troops to guard her new rail network.[20]

'Witte came to see us,' the Tsar wrote to his mother. 'He was very charming and interesting. After a long talk, I told him of his new honour. I am creating him a Count. He went quite stiff with emotion and then tried three times to kiss my hand!'

No amount of smoking, however, could lessen Nicholas's distress over the ruination of his East Asian dream. His humiliation at the hands of the Meiji Emperor was the turning point in East-West relations. The *Brisbane Courier* described Japan's triumph as 'a victory of outraged humanity against wanton aggression, despotism and that cruel bigotry which regards every land as the peculiar possession of white men'. The victory heralded the rise of Japanese militarism which would eventually challenge Western domination throughout the East.[21]

By early October 1905, a general strike had paralysed everyday life across the Russian Empire. All trains had stopped running and the shipyards and steelmills were deserted. There was no electric light, no newspapers, no post, no telegrams or telephones, no food deliveries. A student strike closed down the universities and the law courts had ceased to function. Anna Pavlova was among the stars of the Imperial Ballet who walked out at the Marinsky Theatre.[22]

'I remember the last few days: all the cabs had disappeared, the street lamps were dark and everywhere there was an uncanny silence,' Alexander Kerensky recalls. 'This silence was felt in the palace at Peterhof, too, where the Tsar and his family were living at the time.' Nicholas told his mother, the Dowager Empress, 'Petersburg and Moscow are entirely cut off from the interior. The only way to get to town is by sea. Nothing but new strikes in schools and factories, murdered policemen, Cossacks and soldiers, riots, disorder, mutinies. But the ministers, instead of acting with quick decision, gather like frightened hens and cackle.'[23]

Peterhof was within sight of the Kronstadt Naval Base on a long, low island in the Gulf of Finland. Two destroyers were on permanent standby in the harbour to whisk the Imperial Family to safety if things became too dangerous. Ministers communicated with their besieged monarch by military telegraph or made the trip to Peterhof by naval launch. The extraordinary thing was that the October strike happened in a country that had no means of organising it. As it was unorganised, there was no centralised force to engage in negotiations with the government. It seemed that the bourgeoisie, the proletariat and the peasantry had independently arrived at the same conclusion: that Russia needed an elected parliament.

Russia had reached a fork in the road to freedom. Defeated at home and abroad, Nicholas was desperate to find a solution that would preserve the autocracy while reestablishing the monarchy's mystique in the hearts and minds of the peasantry. At his mother's urging, he summoned the newly ennobled Count Witte to Peterhof on 9 October 1905. When Nicholas asked what could be done to end the crisis, the statesman replied, 'Man always strives for freedom. Civilised man strives for freedom and law. The slogan "freedom" must become the slogan of the government. There is no other way to save the country.'[24]

Witte offered Nicholas a stark choice: either impose a merciless military dictatorship to stamp out all dissent, or introduce 'a constitutional system of government on the basis of political liberty'. All Nicholas's instincts pointed to dictatorship; it was also the Tsarina's favoured option. As to the prospective dictator, Witte nominated the Tsar's first cousin once removed, Grand Duke Nicholas Nikolaevich.

At six feet five inches tall, he was a giant of a man who was known on account of his cruelty as 'Nikolasha the Terrible'- he had once cut one of his borzoi dogs in half to demonstrate the sharpness of a sword. Instead of embracing the opportunity to crush Russian dissidence, he was horrified at the prospect. Pulling out his revolver in the presence of the Minister of the Court, Count Vladimir Fredericks, he threatened to shoot himself unless Nicholas accepted Witte's proposals.[25]

Reluctantly, the Tsar accepted a revised version of Count Witte's reforms, including an end to the arbitrary rule of the law enforcement agencies; civil liberties for all Russian people; and the creation of a lower house of parliament, the State Duma. Witte was appointed President of the Council of Ministers, making him Russia's first-ever Prime Minister. He lost no time preparing the necessary decrees, as well as issuing an amnesty for political prisoners in Russian prisons and exiles in Siberia and abroad.

Even before the amnesty was announced Leon Trotsky, at twenty-five one of the most experienced young revolutionaries, had slipped into Saint Petersburg to join the Revolution. On Bloody Sunday he had been on a train heading for Geneva to meet his ideological heroes Georgi Plekhanov, Paul Axelrod and Vladimir Lenin. Finding them locked in debate about Marxist doctrine, he left them to it as soon as he heard about Bloody Sunday and returned to Russia through Ukraine on a fake passport.

Trotsky was born Lev Davidovich Bronstein on 26 October 1879, the son of a Jewish peasant farmer on the steppes. As a teenager, he had been arrested in Odessa for revolutionary activities and had spent two and a half years in Russian prisons before being exiled to Eastern Siberia. Escaping to Western Europe, he adopted the name of one of his jailers: Trotsky. Raymond Robbins, head of the American Red Cross Mission to Russia, described him as 'a poor kind of a son of a bitch but the greatest Jew since Christ'.[26]

On 10 October, the day after Witte's epoch-making meeting with Nicholas, Trotsky joined the workers of Saint Petersburg in forming the Petersburg Soviet of Workers' Deputies. The Soviet set up its base in the building of the Free Economic Society, with the leftwing lawyer Georgi Nosar (a.k.a. Petro Khrustalev) as its nominal leader. The real power rested in its two vice chairmen: Trotsky, a non-factional Social Democrat using the alias 'Comrade Yanovski' (the name of his birthplace), and Nikolai Avksentiev, a militant Socialist Revolutionary.[27]

The Soviet published its own newspaper, *Izvestia*, which not only promoted revolution but also tackled social issues including the regulation of food prices and the lowering of rents. The Soviet organised trade unions based on the Western model and established a strike fund to relieve hardship. Most alarming, as far as the new Minister of the Interior, Peter Nikolayevich Durnovo, was concerned, was the creation of its own militia to protect striking members from the state's police forces.

The Petersburg Soviet was not the first such body to be launched in Russia but it was the biggest and the most effective. Soon, fifty Soviets had been established among workers in industrial cities and the pressure on the regime for reform became irresistible. On 16 October 1905 the doorbell of the Kerenskys' apartment rang urgently. 'I thought it was the police who were searching houses and making political arrests,' he says, 'but it turned out to be my friend Ovsyannikov in a state of great excitement.'[28]

Alexander Ovsyannikov belonged to a Socialist Revolutionary group involved in printing militant leaflets. One of his contacts in the printing trade had given him a copy of a special edition of the *Government Messenger*. Hot off the presses, the official newspaper contained details of the Tsar's concessions.

Kerensky devoured the words hungrily. 'The Manifesto on the Improvement of State Order' granted basic civil liberties, such as the principles of inviolability of the person, freedom of conscience, speech, assembly and association, a parliament with a lower house (the Duma) elected with limited suffrage, and an upper house (the State Council). Half of the State Councillors would be appointed by the Tsar and half would be elected from various categories of society.

The newspaper also printed a message from the Tsar appealing to 'all true sons of Russia' to stop the unprecedented troubles that were tearing their native land apart 'and together with Us' reestablish peace and quiet. Kerensky took this plea on face value and spent the rest of the night in a state of elation. The struggle for the people's right to participate in the state affairs seemed to be over. '"Constitution" was no longer an empty slogan of the revolutionary movement,' he says. 'A wave of warmth and gratitude went through my whole being, and my childhood adoration of the Tsar revived.'

After Alexander Ovsyannikov's departure, the night seemed endless. Kerensky was impatient to join the jubilant crowds of intellectuals, factory workers, students and the bourgeoisie who would surely pour on to the streets to celebrate this great victory. At first light, he walked down Nevsky Prospekt. It was strangely deserted. Bewildered, he reached Palace Square, so recently the scene of the Bloody Sunday massacre. Instead of a celebration he found a handful of people holding black banners with 'Long Live Anarchy' inscribed in red letters.[29]

Kerensky returned home deflated. From telephone calls to friends he learned that the October Manifesto was being regarded in political circles as a sham. Indeed, it made no mention of a constitution at all, a deliberate omission which infuriated liberals and radicals alike but which enabled Nicholas to remain faithful to his coronation oath to uphold the principles of autocracy. Unsurprisingly, the 'true sons of Russia' had no difficulty interpreting the Tsar's call to reestablish peace and quiet in the most literal sense: through violence. According to one commentator, his purpose 'was to divert the excitement of the nation into channels of antisemitic and anti-revolutionary excess'.[30]

Nicholas surrounded himself with antisemitic ministers and the leaders of the Black Hundred and its political arm, the Union of the Russian People, which drummed up public support with the usual conspiracy theories about Jewish wealth and power. Pogroms authorised by his most reactionary ministers and carried out by Black Hundred thugs killed or maimed thousands of Jews in Kiev and elsewhere in the Ukraine. When Witte protested to the Tsar about the massacres, he remarked, 'But it is the Jews themselves who are to blame.' He used the abusive term *zhidy* instead of *yevrei*.[31]

Meanwhile, Nicholas's failure to embrace the educated elites continued to polarise Russian society. Paul Nikolaevich Miliukov, one of Russia's most prominent constitutionalists, chose this moment to return to Saint Petersburg from a lecture tour of the United States. An impressive figure with neatly trimmed greying locks, a wiry white moustache and an ego to match his erudition, Miliukov envisaged westernising Russia into a rule-of-law society. He judged the October Manifesto inadequate and declared, 'Nothing has changed; the war goes on.'[32]

Miliukov was alarmed to discover that the assassination of Grand Duke Sergei had turned the Party of Socialist Revolutionaries into the country's leading militant organisation. He decided the time was long overdue to unite various moderate groups into a political party whose main demand would be for a democratically elected Constituent Assembly to propose solutions to Russia's political impasse.

Earlier that year Miliukov had become chairman of the Union of Unions, a militant coalition of professional associations for lawyers, writer, actors, academics and teachers. Now, in October 1905, he was instrumental in founding the Constitutional Democratic Party (the Kadets from the abbreviation K-D of the party name) with the ultimate aim of uniting the entire opposition against the autocracy. The Kadet Party's rule-of-law emphasis was confirmed at its founding congress when nine lawyers and nine professors, including three professors of law, were elected to the twenty-six-man Central Committee.[33]

Party members included V. D. Nabokov, the *zemstvo* activists Rodichev and Petrunkevish, A. I. Shingarev, V. A. Maklakov and N. V. Nekrasov. One of the highlights of the congress was the clash between Miliukov and his suffragette wife, Anna Miliukova, over whether the party should support the equality of women in its manifesto. The delegates passed a resolution in favour of female suffrage but in deference to Miliukov it was made nonbinding.[ii] Instead, the manifesto

---

ii This policy would become mandatory after Ariadna Tyrkova made an impassioned speech to delegates at the Kadet Party's Second Congress.

focused on political reforms: a legislative parliament and civil rights, the democratisation of local government and more autonomy for Poland and Finland.[34]

The imperial amnesty for political exiles created a stampede to test the new political boundaries. Vladimir Lenin, Viktor Chernov, Julius Martov and Peter Struve were among the hundreds who returned to Saint Petersburg to join the Revolution. After an absence of five years, Lenin arrived at Finland Station on 8 November 1905 with papers that identified him as a Englishman called William Frey. No longer a gnomic figure hunched over his library books, he became the driving force behind a Bolshevik uprising. 'The point is not about victory but about giving the regime a shake and attracting the masses to the movement,' he said. 'That is the whole point. And to say that because we cannot win we should not stage an insurrection - that is simply the talk of cowards.'[35]

As though following Lenin's script, Peter Durnovo ordered police to round up the members of the Petrograd Soviet. 'Everyone is delighted that 260 important leaders of workmen's committees have been arrested,' Nicholas told his mother, 'all of which gives Witte courage to keep the right line of action.' The arrests, however, acted as a detonator. Four days later members of the Moscow Soviet took to the barricades in the working-class Presnia district and fighting broke out with the local police.

Nicholas authorised severe measures to crush the revolt. The Semenovsky Guards were despatched from Saint Petersburg with orders to inflict maximum punishment on the rioters. The regiment's commander, Colonel Georgi Min, detached the Third Battalion under Colonel Nikolai Riman to attack the barricades. Much of Presnia, the centre of the city's textile industry, was destroyed by heavy artillery barrages and the troops then opened fire with machineguns. Three thousand workers perished in the fighting or were executed without a trial. 'The armed rebellion in Moscow has been crushed,' Nicholas wrote. 'The abscess was growing ... now it has burst.' He praised Colonel Min for his ruthlessness and promoted him to his personal entourage with the rank of major-general.

The Social Democrats had chosen this moment to hold a conference in the Finnish town of Tammerfors (now Tampere). The delegate from

Georgia, one of the least loyal and most revolutionary provinces of the Empire, was known as Koba after an outlaw in a popular nineteenth-century novel. Anxious to make Lenin's acquaintance, he scanned the delegates assembled inside the hall and was astonished to be told that the short, balding, red-bearded non-entity talking animatedly to other delegates was the Bolsheviki's legendary leader.[36]

Koba, later known to the world as Stalin (from the Russian word *stal*, meaning 'steel'), was born Josif Vissarionovich Dzhugashvili on 6 December 1878 in the small town of Gori on the Kura River, forty-eight miles northwest of Tiflis, capital of Georgia. He was the son of a hard-drinking shoemaker whose wife was ambitious for her only surviving child. In adulthood he was five feet six inches tall, with a stocky, powerful build, pockmarked face, low forehead, thick moustache and prematurely greying hair. His dark, watchful eyes and impenetrable mien unsettled even his closest comrades. As a Georgian, he was neither a Slav like the Russians nor a Turk like the Tatars. Lenin believed that for this reason he would be useful in helping to secure the support of the Empire's minority ethnicities.

The conference adopted resolutions to boycott the elections for the First Duma and to restore party unity with other factions. Peacemakers among the delegates called for the merging of Bolshevik and Menshevik central organs on a basis of equality. Lenin, however, saw such a move as a retrograde step and had no intention of allowing it to occur. The December uprising had clarified the path to power in his mind. He recognised that the Soviets were the ideal messengers to spread the Bolshevik gospel among the proletariat.

After their deliberations, the delegates trooped into the woods where they indulged in some target practice with a variety of handguns and rifles. If Lenin ever took an active role in any sort of armed insurrection, he kept quiet about it. 'He displayed a virtual lust for violence,' says his biographer Robert Service. 'While he personally had no ambition to kill or main or even to witness any butchery, he took a cruel delight in recommending such mayhem.'[37]

Indeed, Lenin had urged his comrade-in-arms Artem Sergeyev to return to Russia in 1903 for exactly that purpose. His protégé was happy to do so and two years later he was head of the Bolshevik organisation in a large part of eastern Ukraine. In December that year he led an armed rebellion of factory workers that created havoc in the city of Kharkov, a daunting but exhilarating experience that ended in his arrest in 1906 and a period of incarceration in the dreadful Kharkov Prison.

Nicholas's pacification hammer had fallen on every rebellious part of the Empire. More than 15,000 peasants and workers were hanged or shot, 20,000 wounded, at least 70,000 arrested and 45,000 exiled to Siberia in the seven months between the issuing of the manifesto in October 1905 and the opening of the First Duma in April 1906.[38]

The Tsar's true feelings were revealed when Witte received a telegram from the Governor-General of the Reval district in Estonia requesting him to moderate the behaviour of one Captain Richter, 'who was executing people indiscriminately without the least semblance of legality'. When the Prime Minister referred this complaint to Nicholas, he scribbled 'Fine! A capital fellow!' beside Richter's name.[39]

One of the lucky ones was Leon Trotsky. After spending fifteen months in Kresty Prison (during which he published his doctrine of permanent revolution in his book *Results and Prospects*), he was found guilty of supporting an armed rebellion and sentenced to twenty-five years' exile in a penal colony north of the Arctic Circle. During the trek north he slipped away from his captors and hitched a lift in a reindeer-powered sleigh. Travelling across the tundra, he alighted at a remote railway station and caught a train to Finland.

In May 1907 Trotsky was in London for the RSDLP's Fifth Congress, the decisive event at which Bolshevism would achieve its ascendancy over the party's Menshevik wing for control of the working-class movement of Russia. The delegates included Artem Sergeyev, who, after escaping from Kharkov Prison, had spent the last two years as one of the leading figures in the Bolshevik organisation in the Urals.

The congress was held at the Brotherhood Church in proletarian Hackney. It was there that Trotsky met Lenin and Stalin, and that Lenin met Maxim Gorky. 'I can still see the bare walls of the ridiculously shabby wooden church in the suburbs of London, the lancet windows of a small narrow hall much like the classroom of a poor school,' Gorky wrote. 'When we were introduced he gripped my hand firmly, probed me with his penetrating eyes, and said in the humorous tone of an old friend, "I'm glad you came. You like a fight, don't you? Well, there's going to be a big scrap here".'

The Bolsheviks argued in favour of an armed uprising against the Russian autocracy, which Julius Martov on behalf of the Mensheviks denounced as 'putschist'. The rivals also disagreed over how the party should relate to the trade union movement. The Mensheviks wanted to set up a 'Workers' Congress' as a first step towards transforming the RSDLP into a European-style, legally acceptable Social Democratic Party. On both of these issues the Bolsheviks achieved winning majorities with the help of the Polish and Latvian contingents.

Returning to Russia, Artem Sergeyev's luck ran out when he was recognised and arrested again. After spending three years in another Tsarist prison in Perm, he was sentenced to lifelong exile in the Irkutsk region of Eastern Siberia, 3600 miles from Saint Petersburg. Far from destroying his faith in Bolshevism, his travails would turn him into an even more effective revolutionary.[40]

Meanwhile, a new star had arisen in the Petersburg firmament. Carrying the barnyard smell of a goat and using the metaphorical cunning of a fox, Grigory Rasputin probed the perimeter of the royal hencoop for its weakest point. Entry proved remarkably easy through two Montenegrin princesses known as 'the Black Crows', who had married into the Imperial Family (Stana to Grand Duke Nicholas Nikolaevich and Milica to his younger brother Peter Nikolaevich).[iii]

At the time of Alexander III's death, Konstantin Pobedonostsev expressed his fears that Nicholas might fall prey to evil influences owing to his youth and inexperience. He was thinking of the liberal menace; he could never have conceived a situation in which a degenerate like Rasputin would have power over the Imperial Family.

Nicholas and Alexandra met the man whose name would become synonymous with the fall of the Romanov Dynasty at Peterhof on 1 November 1905. During the three-hour meeting Rasputin, in a *muzhik*'s sleeveless coat, girdled shirt, greased boots and straggly beard, presented himself as a wise and perceptive *starets,* a holy man or spiritual adviser who put believers in touch with the Almighty. The Tsar recorded the encounter in his diary that night with the words,

---

[iii] For years it was claimed that Rasputin had been named after *rasputnyi,* the Russian word for 'debauched'. Sir George Buchanan, wrong again, claimed in his memoirs, 'The native of a Siberian village and the son of an uneducated *muzhik,* he had been nicknamed "Rasputin", or the Debauchee, on account of his dissolute life.' Rasputin was actually a family name going back generations.

'We made the acquaintance of a man of God – Grigory, from Tobolsk province.'[41] Rasputin shrewdly followed up this initial contact with a letter to the Tsar:

> Great Emperor, Tsar, and Autocrat of all Russia! Greetings to you! May God give you sage advice. When advice comes from God, the soul rejoices, our joy is genuine, but if it is stiff and formal, then the soul becomes despondent and our head is confused... Don't disdain our simple words. You, as our Master, and we, as your subjects, must do our best, we tremble and pray to God to keep you safe from all evil, to protect you from all wounds, now and in the future, so that your life will forever flow like a life-giving spring.

Having turned down Father Gapon's advice to listen to the people, Nicholas was inclined to indulge this dishevelled, wild-eyed holy man. While Gapon had sided with his enemies and damned him to eternity, Rasputin was offering to guide the autocracy through its darkest hour. Shortly after their first meeting, however, Rasputin returned to his family in the village of Pokrovskoe, 250 miles east of the Urals, and would not meet Nicholas and Alexandra again for nearly a year.

Meanwhile, Father Gapon had taken the opportunity to return to Saint Petersburg on false papers to avoid arrest for his crimes. His dwindling band of supporters shrank even further when he announced that he had performed a complete volte-face. His revolutionary outburst in January 1905, he said, had been a reaction to the Bloody Sunday massacre and he now realised he had more in common with the supporters of the regime than with the revolutionary parties. The accidental terrorist had become a defender of the Tsarist regime.[42]

When Gapon held a public meeting to relaunch the Assembly of Russian Factory and Mill Workers, the Okhrana gave him 30,000 roubles to open branches of the assembly, with the promise of higher sums if he could recruit Peter Rutenberg as an Okhrana informer. Naively, Gapon saw this as an opportunity to extract extra cash from the police by supplying them with bogus information through Rutenberg. He and Rutenberg arranged to discuss the matter in a cottage at Ozerki, a little town north of Saint Petersburg. Rutenberg, however, had informed the PSR's Central Committee about Gapon's treachery. The last thing Evno Azev wanted was for Rutenberg to start talking to his police handlers. He ordered him to murder the priest.

THE QUEST FOR FREEDOM 129

On 26 March 1906 Rutenberg arrived at the cottage first and placed three Battle Group assassins in an adjoining room to overhear the conversation. As soon as the priest repeated his proposal for Rutenberg to collaborate with the Okhrana, Rutenberg called them in. Gapon was overpowered and his hands were tied behind his back. He was then hanged from a coat-hook on the cottage wall. As the hook was too low to act as a proper gallows, the executioners sat on his shoulders, dragging his body down until he was strangled to death.

'I was not present at the execution,' Rutenberg claimed in his unreliable memoirs published in the *New York Times* in 1909. 'I entered the room only after I had been told that Gapon was dead. I saw him hanging on a hook. He was left hanging on the hook.'[43]

The cottage door was then locked and it was a month before the body was discovered (and photographed). Rutenberg asserted that he was merely carrying out the orders of Evno Azev and Boris Savinkov, who saw Gapon as 'a mortal danger to the terror and the Revolution'. 'I'm not sure to this day,' he admitted to Alexander Kerensky's lover Flora Solomon, 'whether his execution was justified, whether he was in fact an agent provocateur.'[44]

Alexander Kerensky also had his doubts. 'I cannot believe that he was from the very outset merely a police agent,' he said. 'I think he was genuinely carried away by the idea of working for the workers. It may well be that later on he was ensnared in political traps but I submit that he did not join the workers from the outset as a deliberate agent provocateur.'[45]

Meanwhile, 'Grishka' Rasputin[iv] had returned to Saint Petersburg. He sent Nicholas a telegram seeking permission to present him with an icon of Saint Simon Verkhotursky, the patron saint of the Ural region. He met with Nicholas and Alexandra at the Alexander Palace in October 1906 and was introduced to their children.

Shortly afterwards, when Alexei was three, he fell and bumped his leg, causing internal bleeding. 'The Tsarina's mind was now obsessed with one idea: Alexei must live and reign but foremost he must live,' Kerensky says. 'Rasputin was called in. He prayed with the boy and told him he would be all right. The following morning the swelling disappeared. Alexandra came to believe that Rasputin had been sent by God to relieve her son's suffering. He was to preserve the life of

---

iv 'Grishka' was a contemptuous abbreviation of his Christian name, Grigory.

Alexei while the Empress was to preserve intact his heritage – the autocratic powers of Tsardom. She seemed to regard the Emperor as no more than a guardian of that heritage. She was entirely in the power of her one obsession: Alexei must live to be an Autocrat.'

Ever since her marriage, Alexandra had attended séances and consorted with mystics, prophets and clairvoyants. Rasputin was merely the latest in a long line of charlatans, all of whom owed their presence to the Tsarina's religious mania for influencing events and foretelling the future. The *starets* seized on her superstitious beliefs like a dog with a bone. For the next nine years, he fed her such a litany of mumbo-jumbo that she even believed the dried crusts from his table - 'Rasputin rusks' - were imbued with miraculous powers.[46]

He never revealed the secret of his ability to relieve the Tsarevich's agony. People suspected he used hypnosis and/or drugs; some thought he showed up after the crisis had passed when recovery was assured. Whatever the method, the sudden appearance at his bedside of this wild-eyed creature smelling like a goat and breathing brandy fumes must have terrified the infant patient.

8

The Romantic Assassin

Alexander Kerensky viewed many of his friends as 'revolutionary romantics' who had little chance of challenging the autocracy. After struggling with his conscience, he decided to join the extremists in their mission to assassinate the Tsar. 'I had come to the conclusion that individual terrorism was inevitable,' he says. 'I was quite willing, if need be, to take upon myself the mortal sin of killing the incumbent of supreme power who was ruining the country.'[1]

There was nothing in Kerensky's upbringing, his schooling or his character that would mark him down as a regicide. His most revolutionary act so far had been to permit Olga's cousin Sergei Vasiliev, who had joined a student committee of the Party of Socialist Revolutionaries, to store some leaflets in their apartment. 'Sergei's proclamations were signed in the name of a formidable-sounding "Organisation of Armed Rebellion",' Kerensky says. 'I knew only too well that none of its members possessed firearms.'

Kerensky set his sights on joining the SRs' Battle Group, an entirely different proposition from the Organisation of Armed Rebellion. He knew that Boris Moiseenko, number three to Evno Azev and Boris Savinkov in the SR's assassination squad, was the brother of one of Olga's friends, Eugenia Moiseenko. Without informing Olga of his intentions, he told Eugenia he wanted to collaborate in the plot against the Tsar and asked her to arrange a meeting with her brother on his next visit to Saint Petersburg.

Eugenia was reluctant to do so – Olga was her friend and Alexander was the father of a nine-month-old son. When he persisted, she agreed somewhat tearfully to set up the meeting. Two weeks later, in the best cloak-and-dagger tradition, Eugenia told him to walk along Nevsky Prospekt to the corner of Liteiny in the direction of the Anichkov Bridge and then turn right into Fontanka. 'You will be approached by a clean-shaven man in an overcoat and Astrakhan hat who will ask for a light. Tell him briefly what you want. He will give you his answer and walk away.'

Kerensky followed the instructions and everything happened exactly as Eugenia had said it would. While Boris Moiseenko lit his cigarette, Kerensky explained his motives for wanting to join the Battle Group. Moiseenko grunted that he would be in touch in a few days' time and walked away. 'A few days later we met at the same hour and at the same corner,' Kerensky says. 'As he passed me, Boris said without turning his head, "Nothing doing".' Kerensky had been turned down. Eugenia explained that his offer had been rejected because of his inexperience. He later discovered that his request had gone as high as Azev, who had personally vetoed him. 'I had to laugh at the thought that I, too, had turned out to be just another revolutionary dreamer.' It was just as well. His friends could have told him that he lacked the killer instinct to be an assassin.

On the night of 21 December 1905 the Kerenskys were decorating a Christmas tree in their apartment when there was a loud knock on the front door. As Kerensky opened the door, the police burst in. They were looking for a fugitive who was wrongly reported to have visited the apartment. There was no sign of the fugitive but they discovered Sergei Vasiliev's incendiary leaflets, which provided clear evidence that Kerensky was in league with revolutionaries. He was hustled out of the building. 'There was no carriage with drawn green blinds such as I remembered from my childhood,' he says. 'There was only an ordinary droshky drawn by a miserable nag.'

The silvery light of dawn was breaking over the Neva when he was marched through the gates of Kresty Prison. The prison regulations were read out to him and he was locked up. 'My cell was six paces long and three paces wide, and the only daylight came from a small window set high in the outer wall,' he says. 'It was furnished with a bed, a table and chair, and a chamber-pot. There was a dim light in the middle of the ceiling which was never turned off. I slumped down on the narrow cot and mercifully was asleep in seconds.'[2]

Later that morning Kerensky was taken to the communal washroom, where he learned from another man that most of the prisoners were 'politicals'. Someone slipped a note into his pocket instructing him on how to communicate with other prisoners by tapping on the walls of his cell in a predetermined code. By this method, he learned that

Sergei Vasiliev had also been arrested and was in a cell on the floor above him.

Kerensky knew from his legal training that prisoners could not be held for more than two weeks without being informed of the reason for their arrest. 'As soon as the legal period of detention had expired,' he says, 'I wrote to the Assistant Public Prosecutor of the District Court that I would go on a hunger strike unless I was informed of the charges against me within five days.' Receiving no reply, he began to starve himself. Each day a plate of food was placed beside his bed and although he found the smell almost irresistible he remained abstinent. 'By the fourth day I felt quite numb and I fell into a state of semi-consciousness,' he says. 'I experienced hallucinations. I felt almost blissful.'

Three days later the deputy governor of the prison entered his cell with a couple of warders who dressed him and took him to the governor's office. While the warders held him up, the assistant public prosecutor charged him with complicity in the preparation of armed rebellion and membership of an organisation that aimed to overthrow the state system. He did not hear the end of the indictment – he had passed out.[3]

Kerensky's hunger strike was intended to draw attention to the fact that the law was still being violated despite the October Manifesto. Through a sympathetic warder, he managed to get word of his protest to friends on the outside in the hope that they would have it reported in the press. His friends, however, were concerned about the effect on Olga and kept the news to themselves.

Hearing from the warder about their concern for his wife's feelings, Kerensky decided there was no point in carrying on with the strike. 'Little did they know her,' he says. 'She would have had it published immediately.' According to her son Gleb, Olga 'was of the type who would go to the stake if necessary and she would cheerfully have let her husband do the same'.

Kerensky had been in prison for almost four months when the first sprigs of democratic government in the history of the Russian Empire took root in the uncertain Saint Petersburg soil. The franchise in the Duma election in the early spring of 1906 was far from universal but nevertheless a large proportion of the population had been able to vote. The results were announced in mid-April.

As the Socialist Revolutionaries, the Bolsheviks and the Mensheviks had boycotted the elections, the Kadets emerged with 179 seats after winning strong majorities in the main urban areas of European Russia. Finding themselves on the left of Duma spectrum, the Kadets opted for a revolutionary course and declared war on the government. It was said that Miliukov, who had been technically ineligible to stand for election, 'ruled the Duma from the buffet-room', an arrangement that would bring decidedly mixed benefits to the other members of the Kadet Party.[4]

Two other significant developments were that one hundred of the two hundred peasant deputies formed the Trudovik Group (the Toilists or Labour Party, including peasant deputies, radical intelligentsia and Socialist Revolutionaries), which was pledged to follow a simplified *narodnik* (Socialist Revolutionary) policy, while the national groups, comprising thirty-five Poles and twenty-five representatives of other minorities, merged to form the Union of Federalists in a bold step towards independence for their countries.

Nicholas regarded the existence of the Duma as 'a personal affront and a violation of the sacred trust reposed in him'. Four days before the Duma was due to open he enacted a new version of the 'Fundamental Laws of Empire' which overruled the concessions in the October Manifesto. The new statutes emphasised the 'supreme autocratic power' of the Tsar and gave him the power to veto any legislation he found unacceptable. He could also appoint and dismiss ministers whenever he felt like it and he could dissolve the Duma at a moment's notice if it incurred his displeasure.[5]

As the Tsar refused to set foot in the Duma's home, the Tauride Palace, a beautiful Palladian building on Shpalernaya Street in the large U-bend of the Neva northeast of the city centre, the ceremony to proclaim the new lower house would take place beneath the chandeliers of the Saint George Hall, the Great Throne Room in the Winter Palace. At 10 a.m. on 27 April the royal yacht *Standardt*, named after Peter the Great's flagship and escorted by gunboats, brought the Emperor and two Empresses from Peterhof and moored at the English Church on the English Embankment. A launch then took the imperial party to the Peter and Paul Fortress for a religious service in the Romanov mausoleum on the quayside.

To prevent demonstrations or a physical assault on the monarch, the area was sealed off: police raised the bridges and blocked all routes to the Winter Palace while the launch brought the imperial party across the river to a landing stage opposite the palace's main entrance. Troops appeared everywhere, each man carrying 180 rounds of ball cartridge. Squadrons of Cavalry occupied Palace Square. Detectives disguised as peasants and workers mingled with the courtiers. All businesses were closed. There was very little evidence of ordinary citizens celebrating the birth of Russia's first elected parliament.[6]

To reach the Winter Palace from the Tauride Palace, the Duma members - peasants in cotton shirts and baggy trousers tucked into their boots, lawyers in frockcoats, monks and priests in clerical black, Ukrainians, Poles and Tatars in national costume – walked along the Embankment, passing the Kresty Prison on the opposite side of the river.

'The windows of the prison wing that housed my cell gave on to the Neva,' Kerensky says. 'Violating prison regulations, we jumped on our tables and craned our necks to catch sight of the procession through the windows. As hundreds of deputies passed by in the direction of the Winter Palace, we waved whatever came to hand – handkerchiefs, towels, pillow cases – and yelled, "Long live the amnesty!"'[7]

The deputies, many of them veteran campaigners in the struggle for liberty, cheered and waved their hats. This expression of solidarity made the militants among them more determined than ever to free the 'politicals' – the men and women Nicholas described as 'monsters and outcasts' - from their torment. It was a defiant start to the Duma and a pointed challenge to the autocracy.

Inside Saint George Hall the full panoply of Romanov power was on show. The canopied throne, draped in ermine, stood in front of an immense coat of arms, with the imperial regalia – crown, sceptre, seal and orb - placed at its feet on four stools. Tsarist men wore bemedalled uniforms or morning dress, while every bejewelled Tsarist women flaunted the contents of the ancestral vault. Everything possible had been done to celebrate the alliance between the Crown, the State and the Church at the expense of the elected parliamentarians.[8]

The Tsar, a slight figure in his Preobrazhensky colonel's uniform, bowed to the icon of Peter the Great and stepped up to the throne. 'The voice of the Archdeacon thundered an invocation of God's blessing on the mightiest, most autocratic Sovereign and Lord, Nicholas,' Robert Wilton reported in *The Times*. 'Scarcely a score of villagers crossed themselves. The Duma remained stonily, icily passive. They would not pray for the Autocrat.'[9] Standing in front of the throne, the Tsar read out his speech:

> Divine Providence has laid on me the care of the welfare of the Fatherland and has moved me to summon representatives elected by the people to cooperate in the work of framing laws. With an ardent belief in a prosperous future for Russia, I welcome in you, the best men, to whose election I commanded my beloved to proceed. Difficult and complicated labours await you but I believe that the ardent wishes of the dear native land will inspire you and will unite you. I, for my part, will unswervingly uphold the institutions which I have granted in the firm conviction that you will devote all your powers to the self-sacrificing service of the Fatherland, to a clear presentation of the needs of the peasants, which lie so close to my heart, to the enlightenment of the people and to the development of its well-being. You must realise that for the great welfare of the state, not only is liberty necessary but also order as the basis of laws. May my ardent wishes be fulfilled, may I see my people happy and be able to bequeath to my son as his inheritance a firmly-established, well-ordered and enlightened State. May God bless me in conjunction with the Council of Empire and the Duma in the work before us and may this day prove the rejuvenation of Russia's moral outlook and the reincarnation of her best powers. Go to the work to which I have summoned you and justify worthily the trust of your Tsar and your country! May God help me and you!

It was a speech full of twisted meanings and vague promises of great things but with a heavy emphasis on the Autocrat's infallibility under God. His references to the needs of the peasants being close to his heart must have rankled with Sergei Witte, who had been dismissed as Prime Minister just before the Duma's convocation but was still a member of the State Council. He stood solemnly to attention in ceremonial dress throughout the Tsar's speech.

Not once did Nicholas glance towards the deputies, who received his words in silence on their side of the central aisle. On the other side, the massed ranks of ministers, courtiers, bureaucrats and priests filled the void with prolonged applause. Alexandra, crowned with a tiara and draped from head to foot in gold-encrusted white brocade, one hand encased in a long white leather glove and the other holding a fan, stood grimacing to the right of the throne. She was suffering from an attack of sciatica but looked as though an unpleasant smell was wafting towards her from the *muzhik* section of the Duma.

The Dowager Empress Maria Fyodorovna, dressed in mourning black, found the experience altogether horrifying. 'They looked at us as upon their enemies,' she said, 'and I could not stop myself from looking at certain faces, so much did they seem to reflect a strange hatred for us all.'

By 2.30 p.m. it was all over. Eight steamers returned the hundreds of deputies to the Tauride Palace for the Duma's opening session. Cheering crowds greeted them at the gates on Shpalernaya Street and escorted them into the courtyard. Peasants from Siberia were shaken by the hand; farmers from Ukraine were clapped on the back. As they entered their shiny new workplace, someone in the crowd cried, 'Get an amnesty for your comrades!'

Dating from 1789, the palace was a gift from Catherine the Great to her lover, Prince Grigory Potemkin, who had taken the title of Prince of Tauride. The two-storey building, crowned by a low cupola, was adorned with a six-columned Doric portico. Galleries connected the main building with a one-storey wing on either side. Behind the main entrance, a domed hall opened on to the grand columns gallery.[i]

The deputies held their deliberations in the magnificent Catherine Hall, where they sat in leather-bound seats behind wooden desks arranged in terraced, semi-circular rows. The desks had sliding tops to prevent the banging of lids and there were no inkpots which could be used as missiles. Pencil and paper were provided for note-taking. The hall was painted white and adorned with frescoes from Potemkin's time. Facing the deputies from behind the President's dais, three large bay windows provided a view of the landscaped English gardens. The tribune, or rostrum, from which members addressed the House occupied a central position in front of the President, with seats on either side for the Duma's two secretaries.

Beside the tribune were benches for the ministers, their assistants and the press, all facing the deputies across the floor of the House. Glaring down on proceedings from the front wall was Ilya Repin's larger-than-life portrait of a bare-headed Nicholas II in his Preobrazhensky uniform. Diplomats and VIPs were invited to sit in galleries located between the Corinthian pillars, while a single gallery with space for about one hundred people was provided for the public.

If Nicholas thought his display of imperial pomp at the Winter Palace would humble the Duma, he was mistaken; he had simply

---

i Also known as the Taurida Palace and the Tavricheskiy Palace succeeded in making the deputies even more militant. They were determined to make their mark despite the straight-jacket into which the Fundamental Laws had placed them. One of the founders of the Kadet Party, Professor Sergey Muromtsev, a fifty-six-year-old nobleman and lawyer, had the honour of taking the dais as the Duma's first President. His job was to maintain order while pursuing a constitutional agenda with an anti-autocratic theme.

The Kadet Ivan Petrunkevich, a former exile himself, called on the delegates 'to devote our first thought to those who have sacrificed their own freedom for the liberation of our dear Russia. The prisons are full and Free Russia demands the liberation of all political prisoners'. Facing the ministers in their box, the deputies chanted, 'Amnesty! Amnesty!' Robert Wilton summed up in *The Times*: 'The events of today show that the long-hoped-for reconciliation between the Tsar and his people is far from being an accomplished fact.'[10]

The overwhelming majority of deputies were opposed to the Tsar and his Ministers - Ivan Petrunkevich, for example, was a member of the Zemstvo of Tver which had so infuriated Nicholas – and the ill-will was reciprocated. When the government sent the Duma its first two bills for approval, one was for a new laundry and the other for a greenhouse. The insult was hardly subtle: the ministers were determined to prevent these dangerous political novices from debating anything important.

To damage the Duma's image in the minds of the public, the reactionary press routinely referred to 'the Jewish Duma', blithely ignoring the fact that 75 per cent of its members were Greek Orthodox. The other religions were very much in a minority: 14 per cent were Catholic, 3.3 per cent Protestant and Muslim, and only 2.7 per cent Jewish.[11]

The leftwing majority of the Duma issued an Address to the Throne proposing the abolition of capital punishment, an amnesty for political prisoners, equal rights for Jews, dissenters, members of religious sects and minorities, recognition of trade unions and the introduction of wide-reaching land reform. When the new Prime Minister, Ivan Goremykin, an absent-minded sixty-seven-year-old, criticised the Duma's radicalism, V. D. Nabokov dashed to the podium and threw down an even more revolutionary challenge: 'Let the executive power bow before the legislative.' He then moved a vote of censure in the government, which was passed to riotous applause.[12]

Nicholas rejected the Duma's reforms out of hand and, to prevent further embarrassment to the throne, dissolved the assembly on 8 July after just seventy-two days. Soldiers were stationed in front of the Tauride Palace, the front door was locked and the imperial proclamation was pasted to the walls. 'The Duma members refused to be a mere machine to register the bureaucratic will,' *The Times* reported. 'By that independence, even although it often asserted itself in strange and uncouth ways, the Duma rendered incalculable and permanent service to the national cause. Because it loved freedom, much, much licence is forgiven.'[13]

President Muromtsev proposed that the deputies should continue their work in the Grand Duchy of Finland, whose constitution guaranteed a measure of independence from Tsarist interference. From the Belvedere Hotel in Vyborg, the Kadets issued the Vyborg Manifesto, a radical appeal drafted by Paul Miliukov and calling for a campaign of civil disobedience. Russian citizens were urged to withhold the payment of taxes and to veto the draft of military conscripts ('not a kopek to the treasury, not a soldier to the army') until the Duma was permitted to ratify the state budget. As direct taxation provided only a tiny fraction of government revenue and the next army draft wasn't due until November, this was ineffectual. A further suggestion that drinkers should give up vodka voluntarily was laughed out of court. Not surprisingly, the public greeted the Vyborg Manifesto with indifference.

Nicholas appointed Peter Stolypin, the Minister of the Interior, as Prime Minister and, to strengthen his hand, left him in charge of the police and the Gendarme Corps. The Tsar then authorised the election of the Second Duma but only after more than one hundred Kadet signatories to the Vyborg Manifesto had been imprisoned and banned from standing in future Duma elections. Paul Miliukov, the man most responsible for the debacle, escaped punishment – he had written the document but he wasn't a member of the Duma, so he hadn't been able to sign it.[14]

Despite the Tsar's refusal to grant a general amnesty, many 'politicals' who had not been charged with any offence were quietly released from captivity. Among them were Alexander Kerensky and Sergei Vasiliev. Kerensky, however, had been banned from living in Saint Petersburg, a punishment that would have seriously destabilised his life. He appealed to Senator Zvolyansky, the Director of the Police Department, and it was agreed that he would leave the capital until the autumn.[15]

For Olga, this was a mixed blessing. 'When Alexander was released, we went to Tashkent to see his father,' she says. 'He wished all his family to be present at the annual memorial service for Nadezhda.' Unfortunately, Fyodor Kerensky assumed that Olga was the instigator of his son's downfall and 'she was treated badly and was glad to return to Saint Petersburg'.[16]

The family moved into a four-room flat on the fifth floor of a building without a lift in Perekupnoy Alley, Nepeyilok. 'Alexander's brother Fyodor came to study law at the University of Saint Petersburg.' Olga says. 'He lived with us through his student years.' Fedya's letters home to Tashkent helped to heal the rift between Fyodor Mikhailovich and his elder son and, in time, they were reconciled.

Assassinations were running at record levels: between October 1905 and September 1906 3600 Tsarist officials were murdered. All the revolutionary parties and their breakaway factions had turned to gangsterism to fund their homicidal activities, which now included the use of suicide bombers. Stolypin was almost one of the victims. On Saturday 12 August 1906 he was receiving petitioners at his dacha on Aptekarsky Island in the Neva when three suicide bombers entered the room and blew themselves up. Twenty-seven people were killed and seventy, including two of his young children, were injured. Bleeding from a facial wound, Stolypin carried his wounded daughter out of the wreckage. A faction calling itself the Union of Socialist Revolutionary Maximalists claimed responsibility for the atrocity.[17]

Nicholas invited the Prime Minister to move his family into the Winter Palace and gave him carte blanche to crush the regime's enemies. Sidestepping the courts, he introduced martial law which denied defendants most of their legal rights. 'General Pavlov, the chief military prosecutor, was a merciless man,' Kerensky says. 'He expected the judges to fulfil their "duty" without paying any attention to the arguments of the defence. Expecting attempts on his life, he lived in an apartment in the military court building. The apartment had a garden surrounded by a high fence and that is where he was assassinated.'[18]

During Stolypin's reign of terror more than 2500 revolutionary suspects were hanged, many of them convicted at drumhead courts-martial, while a further 60,000 were imprisoned or exiled. The hangman's noose became known in Fyodor Rodichev's chilling phrase as 'Stolypin's necktie'. This description so offended the Prime Minister that he challenged Rodichev, a pacifist, to a duel. To avoid bloodshed, Rodichev apologised but the phrase stuck to its target.[ii]

In the midst of this turmoil Kerensky finally got his chance to become a political advocate. Nikolai Sokolov, a prominent Social Democrat barrister, explained in a telephone call at the end of October that he had to drop a case in order to defend the Socialist Revolutionary activist Ilya Fondaminsky, who had been charged with inciting Kronstadt sailors to mutiny.

'This is your chance to take a brief in an important political trial,' Sokolov said.

'When?' Kerensky asked. 'Where?'

The case involved a group Estonian peasants accused of looting and destroying a foreign-owned baronial estate. The trial was due to open in Reval in a few days' time.

'But that's impossible,' Kerensky said. 'I've never handled a political case.'

'Well, it's up to you,' Sokolov said. 'This is your big chance. Take it or leave it.'

Kerensky packed a bag and after picking up the brief from Sokolov's office caught the midnight train to Reval. Drinking black coffee through the night, he studied the witness statements, police allegations, medical reports and the depositions of the accused. The files made grim reading. 'The position of the Baltic peasants was particularly difficult,' Kerensky says. 'They had not been given land after the Liberation but had become the tenants of the local landowners, mostly German barons.'[19]

During the current troubles the landowners had been given special powers to mount punitive expeditions against rebellious peasants. After the castle of an unpopular landlord had been attacked, these vigilantes shot dead many peasants in that area. Twenty scapegoats were then selected at random, flogged and dragged before the judges' bench, while the real culprits had either been killed or had run away.

[ii] The exact phrase used by Rodichev in the Duma on 17 November 1907 was 'Stolypin's efficient black Monday necktie'.

On 30 October the case opened in the Reval District Court before a presiding judge named Muromtsev. While the defendants had hired a number of local attorneys, including I. I. Poska, a future president of the Estonian Republic, everybody expected that an experienced counsel from Saint Petersburg would lead the defence. Instead, they had been given a twenty-five-year-old barrister whose only political cases had been the ones he had studied for his Bar exams. 'I asked Poska to take over the lead,' Kerensky says, 'but he amiably declined the offer and I was on my own.'

For four days Kerensky listened to the evidence and then rose to make the concluding address. Defence advocates enjoyed freedom of speech in Russian courts and he took full advantage of it. Deciding that attack was the best form of defence, he made an impassioned speech that pointed an accusing finger at the landowners who had not only instigated violent reprisals against local peasants but had actually taken part in them.

Who were the real victims here, he asked, the landowners or the defendants who were being scapegoated? After he finished his speech, there was a moment of silence and then the local people who had been following the case with intense interest broke into tumultuous applause. Judge Muromtsev threatened to clear the court.

Some of the charges were dismissed outright and seven defendants were acquitted of all charges; none of the accused was imprisoned for more than three years, the Tsarist equivalent of a rap over the knuckles. 'After the verdicts were read out, the lawyers and the relatives of the accused crowded around me to shake my hand,' Kerensky says. 'Poska couldn't believe it was my first case.'

Back in Saint Petersburg, Kerensky was feted when he visited the Lawyers' Division, a meeting place of the court establishment.

'Remarkable, indeed,' said one lawyer.

'Congratulations,' said another.

Kerensky was perplexed about the comments until one of the members explained, 'We've had telephone calls and read the reports in the press about your summing-up in Reval.'

The peasants' case had made Kerensky famous. Fame was not money, however, and Olga's long training in frugality kept the family afloat. Cases poured in, giving Kerensky the chance to represent peasants, factory workers and 'politicals' in many parts of the country in exchange for a second-class return ticket and a daily allowance of just ten roubles. 'It was not a remunerative practice,' one contemporary recalled, 'and Kerensky lived in very modest circumstances.'[20]

Olga had taken a job at the Cooperative Society which enabled the family to move into a four-room flat in Basseynaya Street in the eastern half of the left bank of the Neva for one hundred roubles a month. The flat consisted of two bedrooms, living room and kitchen, and was on the third floor above a funeral parlour. Their second son, Gleb, was born there on 25 November 1907. Olga gave up paid work but her political commitment never slackened. During the day she gave freely of her time as a receptionist at the Legal Advice Centre in the People's House and she visited political prisoners with gifts and messages as a member of the Political Red Cross.[21]

Meanwhile, at Tsarskoe Selo, Rasputin was dropping in uninvited for tea with Nicholas, Alexandra and their four daughters. As well as relieving the Tsarevich's suffering he also treated Alexandra's neurosis with his mystical drivel. 'It is an unspeakable joy that You, our beloved, were here with us,' she wrote to him on 7 February 1907. 'How can we thank You enough for everything? I wish only for one thing: to fall asleep on Your shoulder... I love You and I believe in You.... I kiss You warmly. Bless and forgive me – I am your Child.'[22]

Alexandra's infatuation made it easy for Rasputin to insinuate himself into the very heart of the family. She instructed her daughters to call him 'Father Grigory', to pray with him and to trust him with their innermost secrets. As a fourteen-year-old, Olga had developed a crush on a young guardsmen in the royal entourage. She wrote to Rasputin, 'It's hard without him. I have no one to turn to. Nikolai is driving me crazy. My whole body shakes. I love him. I want to fling myself at him. You advise me to be cautious but how can I be when I cannot control myself?'

Rasputin had not only penetrated the children's nursery but was known to have visited Olga and Tatiana's bedroom, giving rise to rumours among the Tsar's household staff that he had deflowered both girls. He shrugged off such suggestions with one of his peasant sayings, 'Nobody fouls where they eat.' According to Pierre Gilliard, 'The children never mentioned Rasputin's name to me and in my presence even avoided the slightest allusion to his existence. I realised that in so doing they were acting on their mother's instructions.' He finally came face to face with the *starets* in an anteroom at the palace:

> He was very tall, his face was emaciated, and he had piercing grey-blue eyes under thick bushy eyebrows. His hair was long, and he had a long beard like a peasant. He was wearing a Russian smock of blue silk drawn in at the waist, baggy black trousers, and high boots. This was our one and only meeting, but it left me with a very uncomfortable feeling. During the few moments in which our looks met I had a distinct impression that I was in the presence of a sinister and evil being.

Nicholas was aware of the danger and deliberately ignored it. When Peter Stolypin presented him with a dossier of secret police reports on Rasputin's misdeeds, the Tsar reproached him. 'Perhaps everything you say is true,' he said. 'But I ask you never again to speak to me about Rasputin. There is in any case nothing I can do.'[23]

Despite the electoral ban on the Vyborg Kadets, the Second Duma opened on 20 February 1907 with another leftwing majority. The Kadets (again without Miliukov, who had failed the property qualification but with the addition of the former Marxist Peter Struve to their ranks) found themselves outnumbered two-to-one after the Social Democrats and the Socialist Revolutionaries abandoned their electoral boycott and fielded candidates.

The youngest member of the Duma was Irakli Tsereteli, a tall, handsome Georgian Menshevik with what was described as 'a pale El Greco-like face', the result of a form of haemophilia. At twenty-five, the minimum age for membership, he was already a veteran of the revolutionary movement. While studying law at the University of Moscow, he had been exiled to Eastern Siberia for five years for taking part in a student demonstration. From the Duma rostrum, his fiery speeches attracted the admiration of his fellow radicals and the loathing of the conservatives.

On 1 June Stolypin accused the Social Democrats of preparing an armed uprising and demanded that the Duma exclude fifty-five Social Democrats from the Duma and strip sixteen of their parliamentary immunity so that they could be charged.[iii] When the President of the Duma, Fyodor Aleksandrovich Golovin, demanded to see the evidence against them, Nicholas closed down the Duma. Irakli Tsereteli was

---

iii The 'plot' was later revealed to be the work of provocateurs working for the Okhrana.

charged with conspiracy to overthrow the government and sentenced to five years' imprisonment, with the added punishment after his release of exile in Eastern Siberia.

The Second Duma had lasted only 103 days during which the Opposition had been a constant thorn in the government's side. The Tsar had no intention of allowing this to happen again. He ordered Stolypin to draft changes to the electoral law which would guarantee an autocracy-friendly lower house. Stolypin handed this odious task to his assistant, Sergei Kryzhanovsky, a monarchist who could be relied on to do his duty.

There are many examples of the Tsar's inability to play fair, such as the enactment of the Fundamental Laws shortly before the opening of the First Duma, but few things were more indicative of his character than his manifesto of 3 June 1907 which was nothing short of a coup d'état. The new electoral law reduced the franchise to such an extent that the Third Duma would be dominated by members of the gentry, the landowners and businessmen.

The bombs used in the attack on Peter Stolypin's family had been made in a laboratory at the home of Leonid Krasin, an engineer from Kurgan in the Tobolsk region of Siberia. Krasin, a lofty, well-built, highly intelligent young man, was an early convert to revolutionary politics. Arrested towards the end of the 1890s, he was exiled to Eastern Siberia, where he worked as a draughtsman on the Trans-Siberian Railway. Released in 1900, he moved to Baku, where he met Josef Stalin, who was making a name for himself as one of the most active Social Democrats in the Caucasus.

During the 1905 Revolution Krasin was put in charge of raising money for the Bolsheviks' war-chest. His biggest coup was the 1907 raid on a bank stagecoach transporting money between the post office and the Tiflis branch of the State Bank of the Russian Empire in Erivansky Square (now Freedom Square). Bolshevik gangsters attacked police and soldiers with bombs and gunfire, killing forty people and wounding fifty. The Bolsheviks got away with today's equivalent of US$3.96 million but found they were unable to use most of the largest denomination banknotes because their serial numbers were known to the police and were circulated to banks and other institutions throughout the Empire.

When the Third Duma convened on 7 November that year, Stolypin's new electoral laws had produced the desired conservative majority, with the Octobrist Party, a collection of businessmen, industrialists and landowners named after the October Manifesto, taking one-third of the seats at the expense of the socialists and nationalists. Stolypin knew from experience that repression alone would not stem the revolutionary tide, so he introduced a number of agrarian reforms to induce the peasants to remain loyal to the Crown.

Under the new laws a peasant could leave his *mir* and become the permanent owner of his own farm, with the assistance of a new financial institution, the Peasant Bank. The reforms proved extremely popular: more than one-fifth of the heads of peasant households successfully applied to withdraw from the village commune and become individual owners of their agrarian holdings. The Stolypin reforms had thus created a new class of landowner, the *kulak*.

There was nothing to stop the 'Duma of the Lords and Lackeys' lasting the full five-year term. By the time it was dissolved on 9 June 1912, it had passed 200 pieces of legislation and voted on 2500 bills. The dead hand of the autocracy was never far away. Speakers were forbidden to refer to the dissolution of the Second Duma, to the funeral of the Tsar's enemy Leo Tolstoy, or to the treachery of Evno Azev, who had fled to Germany in 1909 after being unmasked as an Okhrana spy.

The most effective opposition to Stolypin came from feminists like Countess Sofia Panina, Ariadna Tyrkova, Anna Miliukova and Elena Stasova. Under the leadership of the suffragette-physician Poliksena Shishkina-Iavein, the League for Women's Equal Rights lobbied the Duma in favour of sexual equality. They subjected every bill to gender scrutiny and compelled the conservatives to debate bills on divorce, separate spousal homes and the rights of women lawyers, even though these measures had no chance of becoming law.[24]

It was an open secret that an assassin was hunting Stolypin but the Okhrana was unable to establish his or her identity until Dmitri Bogrov, an anarchist who had been acting as an Okhrana agent for the past five years, offered to help. The assassin, he said, would make an attempt on the Prime Minister's life at an imperial performance of Rimsky-Korsakov's *The Tale of Tsar Saltan* at the Kiev Opera House on 1 September 1911. He offered to point out the villain and was permitted to enter the theatre along with ninety police officers who were placed among the audience.

After the second act, Stolypin was standing in the parterre facing Nicholas and his daughters Olga and Tatiana in the Royal Box when Dmitri Bogdov strolled up to him, fired two shots and then ran away. Stolypin removed his gloves and unbuttoned his jacket, exposing a blood-soaked waistcoat. He made a gesture as though telling the Tsar to go back and then collapsed. He had been shot in the chest and died four days later. Bogrov got as far as one of the exits before being apprehended. Despite a plea by Stolypin's widow for the court to spare his life, he was sentenced to death and hanged on 11 September.

Meanwhile, Artem Sergeyev was 9000 miles away living as a free man in Brisbane, the semi-tropical capital of Queensland. Distance, however, had not released him from bitter memories. Sweating through the humid nights, his subconscious took him back to rotting Tsarist prison cells and the soul-destroying labour camps of Eastern Siberia. In a letter to a friend, he recalled 'waking in a cold sweat after enduring again in my dreams the terrors of the past. Images of abuse of the human body and soul are too deeply imprinted in my mind, and it will be many years before they fade'.[25]

Part of him did not want to forget. Every day the memories of those grim years fanned the flames of revolution in his heart. Suffering great hardship, he had escaped from Siberia in 1910 and made his way across Manchuria to Harbin and thence to Korea, where he crossed the Yellow Sea to Shanghai. Large steamers anchored at the Woosung bar of the Yangtze River and passengers were ferried up its tributary, the Huangpu, to the Customs jetty. The river was packed with fast tea clippers, slow barges, big junks and little sampans, while the gunboats of the occupying Western nations bobbed at anchor in midstream. Closer inshore were the hulks of two ancient sailing vessels that had been converted into storehouses for imported opium.[26]

The signs of colonialism were all too obvious: skinny Chinese 'coolies' hauled rickshaws containing European men in white linen suits, while their women sheltered under colourful parasols. Walking along The Bund, Sergeyev would have come to the exclusively white 'public' gardens opposite the British Consulate and, crossing Garden Bridge, he would have seen the Astor House Hotel, the magnificent

'Waldorf-Astoria of the East' beside Soochow Creek, where thousands of poor Chinese families lived in a floating slum.[27]

China, he decided, was ripe for revolution. Indeed, a few months hence the Xinhai, or Double Tenth, Revolution of 10 October 1911 - hailed by Lenin as the 'awakening of Asia' – would create a democratic republic and trigger other movements for reform and self-determination in the region.

Sergeyev found himself labouring as a 'coolie' on the Shanghai docks, humping great loads on his broad shoulders from the barges to the godowns of Hongkew to scrape together enough money to buy his passage to Australia. Why Australia? He had met up with five other Russian refugees who had heard stories about the 'Great Southland', where men were free and work was plentiful. He decided to join them on their southern odyssey.

Sailing down the Queensland coast, they arrived at the tidal estuary of the Brisbane River in Moreton Bay on 14 June 1911. Their ship followed the route of the brig *Amity* which had negotiated the sandbanks and mudflats in 1825 and sailed upstream to deposit the first British settlers - thirty convicts and twenty troopers - at North Quay on the present site of the City of Brisbane. Reaching the same spot, Artem Sergeyev was looking at the fine buildings that the convicts and the first free settlers had fashioned out of blocks of stone quarried from the cliffs rising above the mangroves on the river's edge at Kangaroo Point. There was no doubting the subtropical beauty of the place. Come spring, jacarandas would turn whole blocks into avenues of purple blossom, and bougainvillaea and hibiscus flowered everywhere.[28]

Sergeyev told himself that this was just a stopover on his roundabout journey back to his revolutionary work in Russia, 'an asylum for me, a refuge for the insane. I will soon vanish from here.'[29] After a few weeks, however, he started to change his mind. 'I don't think I could find such a beautiful sanatorium for my nerves and muscles anywhere in the world,' he wrote in a letter home on 30 July 1911. 'As for the country I have landed in, there's one thing I can say, it's among the best countries for the working man. Here a worker has everything available for him, and if he isn't able to win a solid position for himself he will have only himself to blame.'[30]

The Queensland political scene was an inflammatory mixture of Irish republicanism and British conservatism. Socialists were proud of the fact that the very first Labour government anywhere in the world had been elected there in 1899, three years before the states became one nation. Sergeyev worked as a railway ganger, bricklayer, waterside worker (docker) and farm labourer in and around Brisbane. His hard work and easy comradeship earned him the respect of his fellow workers, who gave him the title of 'Big Tom'. Once established, he set about finding out how his Bolshevik skills might be best employed.

By the end of 1911 a mixed bag of 800 Russians ranging from Marxist intellectuals to anarchists and Bolsheviks were living in the tenements, boarding houses and rundown cottages of the migrant ghetto along Stanley Street, South Brisbane. In December Sergeyev was one of the founders of the Union of Russian Emigrants, an organisation designed to help Russian émigrés settle down in their new home. Within a matter of months, he had transformed that moderate body into the confrontational Union of Russian Workers with the aim of winning the class war against 'the bosses'. He made a point of fraternising with radical politicians and union leaders at the Brisbane Trades Hall. When the union opened a clubhouse in Merivale Street, South Brisbane, it received many messages of solidarity. Queensland's militant timber workers pledged: 'It is our hearts' desire to see you prosper in the grand work of working-class emancipation.'[31]

Unbeknown to the Brisbanites on the north side of the river, strange conspiracies involving the words 'proletariat' and 'soviet' were being hatched in 'Little Russia'. Lenin had great plans for Australia – he saw it as a 'social laboratory' in which the incubus of revolution might be successfully bred. Sergeyev was up for the fight. In his letters home he attacked the hypocrisy of the Brisbane bourgeoisie 'who proclaim democracy on every street corner while oppressing the workers'. But to his fellow workers he remained 'Big Tom' and, fearing police spies, he did not enlighten them about his past or the world-changing plans of his comrades Lenin, Stalin and Trotsky.[32]

9

The Kerensky Ascent

By eight years' hard work, Alexander Kerensky climbed to the summit of the legal profession as defence counsel in high-profile political and terrorist cases. There was no better example of his expertise than his appearance before a special Senate Court in Saint Petersburg in January 1912. Donning his advocate's frockcoat, he defended members of the Armenian intelligentsia – writers, physicians, lawyers, bankers and merchants – who had been accused of acts of terrorism targeting high-ranking officials of the Caucasian administration.[1]

The defendants were Armenian Dashnaks who had joined the revolutionary Dashnaktsutyun Party to protect themselves from marauding Turks. They turned against Russia in 1903 when the Governor-General of Transcaucasia, Prince Grigory Golitsyn, enforced the Russification of the Armenian education system. As a reprisal for terrorist attacks, Golitsyn seized property belonging to the Armenian Church. As religion would be one of the issues raised in court, the trial would take place behind closed doors, with even relatives of the 159 accused barred from hearing the evidence. There was to be no press coverage.

The proceedings began sensationally when Kerensky intervened after the presiding judge, Senator Krivtsov, asked for an incriminating pre-trial deposition to be read out. Kerensky rose from his seat and requested the judge to appoint an expert witness to examine the testimony 'because I know it contains perjured evidence'. The judge warned Kerensky that if he were mistaken he would face a severe penalty from the court. Nevertheless, he persisted. The deposition was examined and it was discovered that the magistrate had altered the words of Kerensky's client from 'cannot recognise' to 'and also recognises', and from 'unlike' to 'very like'.[2]

Further challenges followed and much of the evidence was found to be false. 'Whenever I rose to object, the judge would raise his hand and mutter, "Request granted, Counsellor".' Such was the drama surrounding the case that even while the court was sitting other suspect documents mysteriously disappeared. Ninety-four of the defendants were acquitted, while the others were imprisoned or exiled to Siberia for six years or less. After the trial, Kerensky and his fellow counsellors exposed the scandal to the press. The examining magistrate behind the falsifications was charged with perjury but a panel of psychiatrists certified him insane and he quietly disappeared.

'My grandfather discovered in a precise legal way exactly what the faults of the judicial system were,' says Stephen Kerensky. 'He knew how to speak to people, hence the somewhat overemotional style of some of his speeches.' According to Jonathan Daly, Professor of History at the University of Illinois, Kerensky was simply following the most successful defence advocates of the period who 'melded together logical argumentation, verbal eloquence and theatrics'.[3]

Vladimir Stankevich, secretary of the Trudovik Group in the Duma, met Kerensky at different meetings, sometimes legal, sometimes semi-legal and sometimes decidedly illegal. 'I remember vividly that whatever kind of meeting it was, however many people were present, as soon as Kerensky appeared all eyes and attention were turned to him,' he says. 'He was only a very young barrister [but] many of us felt that his real mission would be the Duma.' Events taking place in the Siberian *taiga* in the spring of 1912 would indeed provide Kerensky with the opportunity to turn his legal expertise into a political career in the upcoming Fourth Duma.[4]

The Lena Goldfields in Eastern Siberia were the main source of the Empire's bullion. Working conditions in the mines were harsh, with miners contracted to work up to sixteen hours a day in temperatures as low as minus 60 Centigrade. For every thousand workers, there were 700 accidents each year. Part of their meagre salaries was often withheld to pay fines; the remainder was given as coupons to be spent on necessities in company-owned stores.

The Nadezhda Mine on the upper reaches of the Lena was no exception to this iniquitous system of slavery. In March 1912 its miners went on strike over low pay, atrocious food – rotten horsemeat posing as beef – and exceptionally dangerous working conditions. On

3 March they presented the Lena Gold Mining Company (Lenzoto from its Russian initials) with a list of demands including an eight-hour day, a thirty per cent wage rise, the elimination of fines and a vastly improved food supply.

Lenzoto had been formed by the brothers Alexander and Alfred Ginzburg in 1908 to acquire seventy per cent of the shares in the alluvial gold deposits owned by the Russian Mining Corporation in Irkutsk Province. At the time of the strike, however, sixty-six per cent of Lenzoto was owned by Lena Goldfields Limited, a company registered in London and traded on the London, Paris and Saint Petersburg exchanges.[5]

The largest shareholder in Lena Goldfields was Grigory Benenson, a Jewish industrialist who had made his fortune as one of the pioneers of the Baku oil industry. Moving his family into the Admiralty Quarter of Saint Petersburg, Benenson built up his business interests to include platinum mines, sugar refineries and two million square feet of prime property on Nevsky Prospekt.

His partner in Lena Goldfields was Herbert Guedalla, a British accountant, with whom he had founded the Russian and English Bank as a means of bringing British capital into the Russian economy. After a blessing from the Archpriest of the Kazan Cathedral, the bank opened its first branch in Nevsky Prospekt on 15 November 1911. Its investors included the Boulton Brothers, bankers, of Old Broad Street, London EC1, and the Imperial and Foreign Corporation, one of Britain's most distinguished overseas investment funds.

The extent of Benenson's influence can be gauged from his contacts in British and Russian society. The Russian and English board contained four Russian princes, including a future Prime Minister, Prince Nikolai Golitsyn, an elderly Prussian-born aristocrat who was deputy chairman of one of the Tsarina's favourite charities. As a director of Imperial and Foreign himself, Benenson rubbed shoulders with such British political luminaries as Lord Balfour of Burleigh, the corporation's chairman, and fellow board members Austen Chamberlain and Sir John Harmood-Banner.

'Father was the Lena gold mine's anonymous absentee proprietor with faithful local agents to control operations,' his daughter Flora Benenson (later Flora Solomon) says. 'The miners were also watched over by government officials and detachments of police. It was almost a secret operation, part of the great silence in which so much of Russia was entombed.'[6]

The ruler of the 'faithful local agents' was I. I. Belozerov, the chief manager of Lenzoto, whose brief was to extract the maximum profit from the mine at the cheapest possible cost. Between 1908 and 1912 his tyrannical methods generated huge profits for the owners and earned him the undying hatred of the workforce. By 1912 Belozerov was a millionaire who could afford to spend three-quarters of the year in the fleshpots of the Riviera and the West End of London, returning to the Lenzoto township for the final quarter to squeeze the miners even harder and, to their disgust, exercise droit du seigneur over of the prettiest women.[7]

When the Governor of Irkutsk Province, F. A. Bantysh, attempted to resolve the miners' strike, Belozerov remained intransigent. As a result, the dispute spread until more than 6000 workers in all parts of the goldfields had downed tools. This serious situation cried out for the intervention of a higher authority but such was the ineptitude of the Russian Government that no one dared to interfere.[8]

On the night of 3-4 April 1912, by order of the local police commander, Captain N. V. Treschenkov, eleven members of the miners' strike committee were arrested and placed in custody. Treschenkov had staked his reputation on ending the strike, boasting to his Lenzoto colleagues that he had suppressed eight previous stoppages. He also let slip, should anyone doubt his resolve, that he had been one of the marksmen who had fired on the Bloody Sunday marchers in 1905.[9]

Word of the arrests spread around the mining community and on Wednesday 4 April 2500 men and women marched from their bleak quarters to the company settlement on a tributary of the Lena, with the intention of delivering a petition to the provincial prosecutor asking for the release of the prisoners.

As they arrived in the township, the marchers – dressed in their best clothes and carrying no weapons - were confronted by more than one hundred soldiers who, on the orders of Captain Treschenkov, opened fire. Volley after volley of bullets ripped into the miners' ranks, and then, as the survivors scrambled for safety, the soldiers picked out individual targets to kill or maim. Kerensky later wrote, 'They left behind 200 dead and no fewer wounded. Just as the great famine of 1892 under Alexander III had roused the public from its stupor; just as the insane slaughter of the workmen on 9 January had brought about the Revolution of 1905; so the Lena massacre on 4 April 1912 was the signal for a new burst of public activity and revolutionary agitation.'[10]

News of the Lena atrocity reached all corners of the globe. In faraway Australia, the *Bendigo Advertiser*, the newspaper of the Bendigo goldfields, reported under the headline 'Dreadful massacre in Russia':

> Not since the massacre of workmen in the streets of Saint Petersburg in January 1905, has an event caused such excitement among all classes of the vast Russian Empire, and particularly among the working classes, as the similar massacre of miners at the Lena Goldfields, Siberia. Everywhere, from north to south of the country, the workmen are ceasing to work in protest. Wholesale arrests are being made everywhere, but this has not had the slightest deterrent effect. In Saint Petersburg this morning about 60,000 workmen were idle. In some of the factory yards the work people sang hymns in memory of the Lena victims, but were dispersed by the police.[11]

The Minister of Commerce and Industry, S. I. Timashev, informed the Duma that Lenzoto had systematically violated the law regarding the conditions of labour on the goldfields. His ministry had repeatedly censored the mine's management but there had been little improvement. In fact, these violations had been the starting point of the current labour disputes.[12]

Nothing infuriated radical opinion more than the statement of the Minister of the Interior, Alexander Makarov. 'When a crowd which has lost its reason under the influence of malicious agitators throws itself on troops, they have no other resort but to shoot,' he said. 'Thus it has been and thus it will always be.'[13] Public outrage over this blatant falsification of the facts (and particularly the minister's use of the phrase 'thus it will always be') forced the government to send a commission of inquiry to investigate the massacre. At the head of the commission was Senator Sergei Manukhin, a former Minister of Justice and a respected figure in Tsarist circles. Fearing a cover-up, the Opposition parties in the Duma hired three lawyers to mount their own investigation. One of them was Alexander Kerensky.

Explaining the massacre to Flora and her younger sister Fira, Grigory Benenson claimed that the police commander had lost his head when the miners' demonstration had got out of hand and had given the order to fire. The sisters, serious young women with inquiring minds, were unhappy with that explanation. 'The agitation was directed against our father who reaped wealth on the backs of the workers,' Flora says. 'We had to do something.'

She confronted her father. 'You ought to go to Lena and explain to the workers that you knew nothing about their conditions,' she told him. 'Let them understand that everything will be better from now on.'

'It's out of my hands,' Benenson replied. 'We had the wrong people in charge; these things happen all the time in Russia. The liberals in the Duma have started an inquiry of their own. They're sending Kerensky and if I know that man we shall be cast as the villains.' It was the first time Flora had heard that name.[14]

The Nadezhda Mine was located along the shores of the Lena River twenty-eight miles northeast of Bodaibo, which was 1200 miles to the northeast of Irkutsk. Kerensky's arrival coincided with the spring thaw and the river ice was breaking up with ear-splitting creaks and groans. The *taiga's* great snow-bound forests of spruce, fir and pine were shedding their white winter coats and the wolf and the Arctic fox had emerged from their lairs. 'We travelled by train, by troika, by steamboat and by rowing boat,' he says. 'The beauty that surrounded us on the Lena River would be hard to describe. We saw human habitation on one bank and bears on the other. With the rising of the sun we saw whole families of bears which came to drink.'[15]

All the way down the Lena, political exiles came out of their hovels to greet Kerensky and his colleagues. His most memorable meeting was with Catherine Breshko-Breshkovskaya, one of the founders of the Party of Socialist Revolutionaries. Born of noble Polish parents in 1844, 'Babushka' had witnessed the course of Russian history since Sevastopol. Now almost seventy, she had spent nearly four decades in prison and exile for peaceful opposition to Tsarism. Kerensky says, 'The government was so frightened [of Babushka] as to keep her in the wilds of Siberia under the guard of two Yakuts armed with wooden clubs.'[16]

Reaching the Lenzoto township, the Duma trio established their headquarters in a house opposite Senator Manukhin's official commission. Witnesses, including survivors of the massacre, went from one house to the other to give their evidence. Kerensky cabled progress reports to the Duma and the Saint Petersburg press, while the Senator kept the Tsar and the Ministry of Commerce and Industry in touch with developments.[17]

'As a result of an open investigation, the monopoly position of the company was liquidated and its administration completely reorganised,' Kerensky says. 'Slums, where the workers and their families lived, were destroyed and in their place new houses were built. Wages were increased significantly and working conditions improved.'

Captain Treschenkov, the true villain of the piece, was dismissed from the Gendarmerie and demoted to the ranks under an assumed name. Lenzoto also dispensed with the services of the brutish Belozerov. The reforms, however, came too late for many of the miners, who had moved on and found work elsewhere before they came into effect.

The Lena Massacre reignited the revolutionary spirit in Russian society to root out the corruption and mendacity of the Romanov regime. It also generated a desire to punish capitalist greed for squeezing profits out of a demoralised and underpaid workforce. Josef Stalin, a better descriptive writer than either Lenin or Trotsky, declared in the Bolshevik weekly *Zvezda*, 'The Lena shots broke the ice of silence and the river of popular resentment is flowing again. The ice has broken. It has started!'[18]

In 1912 Artem Sergeyev, Stalin's future comrade-in-arms, became a British citizen in Brisbane and helped to launch the Russian-language newspaper *Australiiskoye Ekho (Australian Echo)*. Cyrillic printing fonts were purchased from the United States and shipped to Queensland. Sergeyev served as editor until the authorities, tipped off about the paper's revolutionary content, closed it down on the grounds that it was an unregistered publication.

Sergeyev's chance to collaborate with other unionists came in January 1912 when a local dispute over union recognition on the city's privately-owned tramways escalated into Australia's first general strike. The Russian unionists formed a strike committee and collected funds for the strikers. A Russian tramdriver named Dorf was elected to the official strike committee. In a speech at the Trades Hall in Turbot Street, Sergeyev urged the unions to show solidarity and warned of the dangers of 'scab' labour being brought in to run the trams.

As part of their campaign, the strikers and their Trades Union supporters set off on Friday 2 February 1912 on a peaceful march through the city centre to see the Queensland Premier, Digby Denham, a conservative Englishman, at Parliament House. The Irish-born Police Commissioner, Major William G. Cahill, ordered a huge force of mounted troopers, police armed with rifles and fixed bayonets, and a unit of truncheon-wielding special constables – 'a fine, athletic-looking body', according to the *Brisbane Courier* - to block the route to Parliament House. In the ensuing melee, many people, including onlookers, were brutally battered in what became known as 'Baton Friday'.[19]

To Artem Sergeyev, it seemed like a re-run of Saint Petersburg 1905. At the head of several hundred women marchers was his friend, seventy-three-year-old Emma Miller, the daughter of an English Chartist and an indefatigable battler for women's rights. Confronting the demonstrators in Albert Street, Major Cahill led a mounted baton charge to disperse them but he had reckoned without 'Mother Miller'. Although frail and only five feet two inches tall, she drew her hatpin and stabbed the Commissioner in the thigh. His horse reared up and threw him to the ground.[20]

Chief Inspector Charles Urquhart, another Englishman with a 'vindictive and tyrannical nature', then led a second cavalry charge to clear the streets.[21] The Russians among the strikers noted that the baton-wielding riders behaved 'just like Cossacks'. 'Never before was a more disgraceful display of brute force witnessed,' *The Worker* reported. The Brisbane correspondent of the Sydney *Catholic Press*, who saw the beatings, commented, 'It is the saddest of all reflections in connection with this matter that out here in our free and enlightened Australia, where we all enjoy equal rights and privileges, that hitherto peaceful citizens should be subjected to the fearful experience of being chased like fugitives in their own streets and relentlessly struck down if they happened to be within reach of a policeman's baton.'

Premier Denham was appalled at this outbreak of union militancy in his city. He backed Cahill and Urquhart to the hilt. A German warship was moored in the Brisbane River on a goodwill visit and the Premier took the extraordinary step of threatening to land German marines to deal with the troublemakers. The strike crumbled. 'Australia has just experienced an unprecedented event,' Artem Sergeyev wrote to friends abroad. 'In a country where all institutions, all past experience appears to have destroyed the very thought of a revolution [there is] a general strike.'[22]

As a result of his work in the Lena Massacre, Alexander Kerensky was offered the chance to seek election as a deputy in the Fourth Duma. 'I had never given much thought to the future and I had no political plans,' he says. He was taken by surprise when two senior members of the Trudovik Group invited him to stand as one of their candidates. 'The Trudovik faction in the Duma was to be expanded with the inclusion of other Populist groups,' he says. 'I had always sympathised with the Populist movement, so I accepted the offer without hesitation.[23]

The government was determined to ensure that it enjoyed a loyal majority in the new parliament. Thousands of Orthodox priests were drafted in to tell their congregations how to vote. Candidates were excluded, voters intimidated. 'The voting public has been replaced by 7200 priests,' said Fyodor Rodichev, the outspoken barrister from Tver. 'It's the same as cranking up 7200 gramophones and saying that it is the voice of the people.'[24]

Kerensky was given a difficult seat to contest in the Volga region, not his home town of Simbirsk but a constituency in the neighbouring Saratov Province. After submitting his report on the Lena Massacre to the Opposition, he left for Volsk, the district capital of Saratov, to start his electoral campaign. His first step was the purchase of a small house to fulfil an electoral requirement of property ownership. His son Gleb later wrote, 'Some kind of fictitious ownership was arranged and presumably my father saw the house in Volsk during his election campaign. His wife and children never saw it!'

Deputies were elected by provincial colleges consisting of delegates from four groups: landowners, the urban population, peasants and, in urban districts, factory workers. Electoral regulations had been tightened up to prevent open discussion of any issue that would pose a threat to the autocracy. Only registered electors were permitted to attend the special preparatory assemblies whose job was to assess 'persons worthy of election'. At every one of these meetings a policeman was on hand to halt proceedings if the speaker breached the rigid electoral rules.

Volsk was 200 miles downstream from Simbirsk. Kerensky lauded 'the fierce spirit of independence of the townspeople which could be traced back to Emilian Pugachev's peasant revolts in the latter part of the eighteenth century'. Things began well on 29 August when an assortment of judges, physicians and officials turned up for his first meeting on the hustings. The candidate began his address by reviewing events since 1906 when, he said, the representatives of the people in the Duma 'stood firmly for the political freedoms promised by the October Manifesto'. But when he started to compare the policies of the different political parties contesting the election, the policeman stepped in and closed down the meeting.[25]

Kerensky learned from that experience. From then on, he used his courtroom expertise to speak freely to get his message across 'without resorting to revolutionary clichés'. The elections were held in September-October 1912. The gentry was steadily gaining ground in Saratov as a result of Stolypin's electoral law and his chances of winning would have been slim but for the fact that the urban electors of Volsk were entitled to a single uncontested nomination. They chose Kerensky. His victory as the only Trudovik from the Great Russian heartlands was announced on 21 October.

It was a matter of tremendous sorrow that his father had not lived to see it. Suffering from cancer, Fyodor Mikhailovich Kerensky, the great educator of Russian children, had spent his final months with his youngest pupils - his grandsons Oleg and Gleb - in Alexander and Olga's apartment.

On 3 December 1912 Trudovik Deputy Alexander Fydorovich Kerensky swore an oath of loyalty to 'Our Imperial Majesty, our Sovereign Emperor' and then mounted the mahogany rostrum to make his maiden speech. The Catherine Hall was now the main parliamentary lobby and the Duma's proceedings had been moved into the White Hall at the rear of the building. The layout of the chamber was almost exactly the same as before, with the deputies seated in semi-circular rows, tier on tier as in a theatre. They fell into four main groups: 150 supported the antisemitic far right, 130 Octobrists represented big business, while moderate conservatives held the centre ground, and fifty-five Kadets and twenty representatives of the national minorities were on the left. The twenty-two socialists, consisting of the thirteen surviving Social Democrats and nine Trudoviks, were labelled 'the extreme left wing'.

Flanked by two secretaries, Mikhail Rodzianko, the Duma President, was seated on a central dais above the speaker. A staunch monarchist from a Russian aristocratic family, he described himself as a democrat, 'not some kind of Black Hundred reactionary'. His huge bulk, glistening bald head and sweaty neck made him an easy target for ridicule among the leftwing deputies. Indeed, he had once introduced himself to the Tsarevich as 'the biggest and fattest man in Russia'.

Equipped with a bell rather than a gavel, Rodzianko acted as chairman and called to order any speaker who breached the rules of engagement. The speeches were taken down verbatim by stenographers seated at a table between the rostrum and the first semicircle of deputies. If any speaker spoke out of turn, the President would censure the official record before it was released to the public.

Pale and beardless, Kerensky stood mutely for a moment while the light poured through the glass roof on to his short-cropped head and Ilya Repin's huge portrait of the Tsar stared down on him from the chamber wall. He looked younger than his thirty-one years and his callow appearance caused a ripple of amusement. The antisemites and the Octobrists, multi-whiskered, portentous fellows, settled back in their armchairs and prepared to give this socialist upstart a blustery reception. Kerensky did not disappoint them. Clasping the lapels of his morning coat, he launched into a scarcely veiled attack on Stolypin's restricted franchise.

'For as long as the Duma exists in its present form,' he said, 'there will not be an hour in Russia when people will not die on the gallows or be destroyed in forced labour'.[26]

Several narcoleptic bodies suddenly jerked into life and sat bolt upright in their chairs.

Drawing attention to the mindless cruelty of the autocracy was reckless at the best of times; it would bring the wrath of the Tsar down on their heads. Rightwing members tried to laugh it off as an indiscretion of naïve youth. 'For those to whom life is precious...'

Kerensky was saying, but the rest of the sentence was drowned by noisy interruptions. When the stenographers resumed their work, he said, 'I say to those who laugh at this moment: I am happy because there can be no communication between you and us: it is either you or us.'

The President called him to order but Kerensky carried on.

'In a country ruled by violence, where the masses in their millions are excluded from legislation, where at any moment any police inspector – to say nothing of the governors – can arrest any citizen and throw him into jail, there can be no strong people, there can be no national security.'

Uproar! The President rang his bell for order.

Kerensky had crossed the line and was now officially an extremist in the eyes of the parliamentary elite.

Nor was he finished.

'….but,' he was saying, 'I believe that Russia will turn to a better life, and not by those methods indicated by Messrs Octobrists here.'

Kerensky's comrades on the extreme left were delighted with the speech; others were nonplussed. 'Very soon,' Vladimir Stankevich says, 'I noticed that everyone in the Duma were looking around the benches trying to see whether Kerensky was there.' One immediate outcome was that Kerensky was invited to join the Masons. Since the dissolution of the Second Duma, Freemasonry had enjoyed a new lease of life as a clandestine society in which men could trust one another with their political secrets. 'After serious contemplation, I came to the conclusion that my own objectives coincided with the goals of the society,' Kerensky says. 'I accepted the offer.'

He took his Masonic duties seriously, attended meetings in the Duma-based lodges and eventually rose to the post of Secretary-General of the Supreme Council of the Grand Orient of the Peoples of Russia. A strong Masonic bond developed between Kerensky and two of the leading Kadets, Nikolai Nekrasov, Vice Chairman of the Duma, and the industrialist Alexander Konovalov.[27]

South of the Equator, dissent was still simmering in Brisbane over 'Baton Friday' when Jean Haslewood Turner returned to the city of her birth in March 1912 after spending five years abroad. At twenty-one, she had recently become engaged to Robert Hamilton

Bruce Lockhart, a dashing Scottish diplomat whom she had met at a dance at Eagle House, the Sandhurst school of which his father was headmaster. For Lockhart, it was love at first sight. 'I succumbed at once,' he wrote in his memoirs. 'I had only a fortnight in which to press my suit. In ten days we were engaged.' He later admitted that he was hopelessly impulsive, while Jean would reflect that the engagement was the biggest mistake of her life.[28]

Over tea at the Cecil Hotel in George Street, however, she excitedly told friends from Somerville House, her former school, that her fiancé had been posted to Russia and, following their wedding, they would be living among the Consular Corps in Moscow.[i] Jean had been born in Brisbane on 29 August 1891. Her grandfather, the banker and property owner T. Sargent Turner MLC, was probably the wealthiest man in Queensland. His home 'Kinellan', a Colonial-style mansion on the river at New Farm, was one of the centres of the city's social and business life.

Jean knew South Brisbane well – Somerville House was built on a rocky headland overlooking the migrant ghetto and she passed through it every day on her way to school. At fourteen, she was a star pupil who had won prizes for music and French when tragedy struck the family. On the morning of 5 February 1906 her father, Major Leonard Turner, heir to his father's estate and a wealthy accountant in his own right, was found dead with his service revolver in his hand and a bullet wound in his head. Dressed in pyjamas, he had left 'Wangerao', his house in Moray Street, New Farm, in the middle of the night and committed suicide on a vacant allotment next door.

The grief of his widow Annie and their three children was made immeasurably worse when his suicide was reported in graphic detail in the local scandal sheet, *Truth*. In November 1907 Annie sold the house and all its contents and with the proceeds took Jean overseas to complete her studies in Europe. She bought a house in Switzerland and began to rebuild her life. Having been married to an unbalanced man herself, she was more than a little concerned at Jean's choice of husband.

Bruce Lockhart boasted there wasn't a single drop of English blood in his veins. He had been born at Anstruther in the County of Fife on 2 September 1887. After studying at Fettes in Edinburgh, he completed

---
i The Brisbane High School for Girls was known as Somerville House after 1920.

his education in Berlin and Paris, and then, for three years from 1908 to 1910, worked as a rubber planter in Malaya.

Jean wasn't the first beautiful young woman to fall for the charms of this flawed Young Lochinvar. While a rubber planter, he had seduced the daughter of a Malay prince, ignoring the fact that she was betrothed to another Malay prince. Breaking every local taboo, he installed Princess Amai in his bungalow, provoking outrage among the local population. The bungalow was besieged by angry villagers and lynching was a distinct possibility until Lockhart was bitten by an anopheles mosquito and contracted malaria. His family had him smuggled out of the country and the Princess was abandoned to her fate.[29]

After recuperating in his native Scotland, Lockhart joined the British Consular Service. His boss in Whitehall, J. D. 'Don' Gregory, admired a collection of short stories he had written about life in Malaya and took him under his wing. His first posting was to Moscow as deputy to the British Consul-General, Montgomery Grove. He learned Russian and worked hard during the day but after a few nights on the strictly proper consular social circuit he discovered gipsy nightclubs. Gipsy music, he decided, was 'more intoxicating, more dangerous, than opium, or women, or drink'. He was quickly addicted. His carousing endeared him to like-minded Muscovites who called him 'Roman Romanovich Lokkart'. It was this self-described 'broken-nosed chancer with a squat, stumpy figure and ridiculous gait' who would save Alexander Kerensky's life not once but twice.[30]

On 3 May 1913, thirteen months after the outrage had been committed, the Duma got its first chance to debate the Lena Massacre. Kerensky opened the attack on behalf of the miners. 'They searched for God's truth everywhere; the Tsar's truth was not to be found!' he said. 'When Manukhin went there, the workers said, "Look, the Tsar's messenger is coming, he will tell the truth, he will punish the murderers of our brothers." But Manukhin came, Manukhin went and the murderers were not punished. And the workers at the mines know that the truth they sought is not to be found on earth.'[31]

Kerensky named Timashev, the Minister of Trade and Industry, Baron G. E. Ginzburg, one of Lenzoto's shareholders, and the manager Belozerov as the guilty parties in the atrocity. His speech ended in uproar when, with a searching gaze around the chamber, he declared, 'There are people sitting even here who have got blood on their hands.'

As Lenzoto and Lena Goldfields had separate boards of directors, Grigory Benenson and his British investors escaped censure. Alexander Makarov responded to Kerensky's allegations with an attack on the Jewish character of both companies. 'We are dismayed that in our state, which is under the virtuous administration of the All-Russian Autocrat, signs are beginning to be observed which are characteristic of parliamentary countries, of countries ruled by the Yiddish *kahal*, and of republics, especially democratic ones.'[ii]

He failed to mention that two of the Lenzoto investors were the Tsar and the Dowager Empress, Maria Fyodorovna. Nicholas, however, judged his handling of the Lena Goldfields Affair so inept that he was dismissed. Meanwhile, Kerensky's humanitarian endeavours attracted international attention. According to *L'Humanité*, the French socialist newspaper founded and edited by Jean Jaurès, he was 'the greatest lawyer in Russia despite his youth'.

> He folds his arms and glares in the most disconcerting fashion at an opposing witness, at the judge who ventures to correct him, at a lawyer with whom he is battling. The transfer of that stare to the Duma has had the most prodigious effect. Kerensky in the Duma launches a torrent of words swiftly yet each distinct and telling. At the height of the deluge it ceases. He folds his arms and gazes about him in that tense, strained, alert fashion. A pin could be heard to fall. Then he fires his terrific shot – an epigram it may be, or a charge of ineptitude or a crushing citation of what Peter the Great or what Pushkin said – and the sensation that ensues is immense.

The complexion of the Duma turned a deeper shade of red when the Bolsheviki were victorious in six of the nine labour curias in the 1912 elections. Four of the Bolsheviks, Roman Malinovsky, Grigory Petrovsky, Matvei Muranov and Alexei Badayev, were metal workers, while the other two, N. R. Shagov and F. N. Samoylov, worked in textile factories. Lenin greatly admired the hard-hitting oratory of Malinovsky, a Polish lathe operator who had been elected to the Bolshevik Central Committee.

---

ii The kahal or qahal was a theocratic organisational structure in ancient Israelite society.

Malinovsky was placed at the head of the Bolshevik deputies in order to emphasise the difference between them and the seven Mensheviks among the Duma's Social Democrats. His powerful rhetoric compared more than favourably with the dull, mumbling delivery of Nikolai 'Karlo' Cheidze, the Freemason who led the Menshevik group. No one had any idea that Lenin's protégé was an Okhrana agent who had already helped to send Josef Stalin, Yakov Svedlov and Stalin's one-time friend, Grigory 'Sergo' Ordzhonikidze, into Siberian exile.

In June 1913 Alexander Kerensky was in Moscow to campaign for higher wages and improved conditions for clerks and shop assistants. In a rare alliance with the Bolsheviks, he was elected chairman of the Fourth All-Russian Conference of Employees of Trade and Industry, describing the appointment as 'the greatest honour of my life'.[32]

When the first session of the Fourth Duma closed on 25 June 1913, the Kerensky family travelled to Kainki for a holiday. During one of their rambles around the farm Olga photographed Alexander, Oleg and Gleb sitting on a ploughshare. There is no doubting the closeness of father and sons or the intensity of their embrace. Oleg wears a blouse outside short pants, long black stockings and high-top shoes. Gleb, bare-legged and shirtless, is in short pants fastened by braces. The boys worship their father and he cherishes them.

The photograph was a memento of a time that was quickly passing. Even on holiday in the country, Kerensky wears jacket, shirt and tie as though he might be called on at any moment to make a speech. As a civil rights lawyer-*cum*-leftwing politician, there was no shortage of judicial battles to be fought. In the most sensational case of the period, the Tsar tried to frame an innocent Jewish father, Mendel Beilis, for the 'ritualistic' murder of a Christian boy in Ukraine.

Nicholas's new Minister of the Interior, Nikolai Maklakov, and his Minister of Justice, Ivan Shcheglovitov, ordered the local authorities to find a Jewish suspect to support the Tsar's theory of ritual murder. Beilis was arrested simply because he was Jewish and worked as a salesman for a brick factory near the scene of the crime.[iii]

---

iii The previous Minister of the Interior, Alexander Makarov, resigned in December 1912 in the aftermath of the Lena Massacre and over disagreements about the regulation of the press involving false claims of a sexual connection between Rasputin and the Tsarina.

Two policemen, however, established beyond doubt that the real killers were members of a criminal gang which had carried out a series of robberies in Kiev. The boy, Andrei Yustshinsky, was stabbed to death on 12 March 1911 after he discovered their secret cache and threatened to tell the police. To cover up this embarrassing flaw in the prosecution case, the policemen were sacked and the District Attorney suppressed their findings. Even though the Tsar was informed of Mendel Beilis's innocence, he insisted the trial should proceed. He summoned the judge, gave him a gold watch and promised him a promotion if the prosecution won the case.[33]

By the time the trial began in September 1913, the identity of the real murderers was an open secret. The defence team, which included Vasily Maklakov, brother of the reactionary Tsarist minister Nikolai Maklakov, discredited every prosecution witness to take the stand, including a psychiatrist who swore on oath that Andrei's murder was 'typical of the ritual killings regularly carried out by Jews'. One of the gang committed perjury by testifying she had actually seen Beilis kidnap the boy.

The jury consisted of seven peasants, three middle-class citizens and two minor officials. Six returned a guilty verdict but the other six shunned pressure from the authorities and found the defendant not guilty. As there was no casting vote, the judge had to acquit Mendel Beilis, who left court a free man.[34]

In the Duma, Kerensky denounced the rightwing deputies and Orthodox priests who had signed a petition demanding that the government bring the non-existent criminal sect of Jews to justice. That evening, at the annual general meeting of the Saint Petersburg Bar, Kerensky and Nikolai Sokolov sponsored a motion describing the Beilis Case as 'a slanderous attack on the Jewish people launched within the framework of judicial order to propagate racial hatred and national hostility'. For this act of defiance, Kerensky and Sokolov were charged with defaming the judiciary and sentenced to eight months' imprisonment. They were released pending an appeal. The Beilis Affair - the 'Russian Dreyfus Case' – placed Nicholas in a special category of regal villain, proving yet again that he would resort to criminal methods to destroy the Jews.[35]

Bruce Lockhart and Jean Turner were married at All Saints Church in London's West End on 29 January 1913 (NS). After a short honeymoon, the clock went back thirteen days and Jean found herself in Moscow, an ancient, snow-encrusted city which seemed dirty, frightening and disturbingly alien after the fashionable quarters of London and Geneva. 'My wife was used to a life of luxury and to ask a girl who had been brought up in this way to share with me a life of poverty in a semi-barbarous town like Moscow was an effrontery for which there is no excuse,' Lockhart says. 'It is a tribute to her courage that she was able to adapt herself so quickly to a situation which imposed so many hardships upon her.'[36]

Jean's arrival in Moscow coincided with the three-hundredth anniversary of Romanov rule. Following the defeat of the Polish invaders, it was there, in the old imperial capital, that Mikhail, the first Romanov Tsar, had been crowned in February 1613. And it was to Moscow in May 1913 that Nicholas brought the Tsarina and the Tsarevich Alexei for a massive celebration to honour his own name.

Alexei was then nine and a half and rather tall for his age. He was a good-looking boy with auburn hair and large blue-grey eyes like his mother's. Huge crowds wielding flags, crosses and icons turned out to watch the Tsar ride a white horse at the head of his Cossack escort from the Alexandrovsky Station to the Kremlin. Reaching Red Square, the 'Anointed One' dismounted and walked through the massed ranks of chanting priests to the Cathedral of the Assumption to acknowledge his special relationship with his God.

Alexandra and Alexei were supposed to walk together into the cathedral but the boy had been struck down by a haemophilic attack and was barely able to stand. The Romanov tragedy was encapsulated in the sight of the heir apparent being carried in the arms of his gigantic Cossack bodyguard. 'Now you can see for yourself what cowards those State Ministers are,' the Empress Alexandra told a lady-in-waiting. 'They are constantly frightening the Emperor with threats of revolution and here - you see it for yourself - we need merely to show ourselves and at once their hearts are ours.'[37]

But Alexandra was deluded. Dr Eugene Botkin, the Imperial Family's doctor, treated her ailments and neuroses with cocaine, opium, morphine and opiate-based barbiturates. Drug addiction exacerbated her hysteria and made her completely vulnerable to Rasputin's wiles. 'My poor daughter-in-law does not perceive that she is ruining both the dynasty and herself,' the Dowager Empress told the Prime Minister, Vadimir Kokovtsov. 'She sincerely believes in the holiness of an adventurer and we're powerless to ward off the misfortune which is sure to come.'[38]

During an audience with Nicholas, Mikhail Rodzianko insisted on describing Rasputin's debauchery in lurid detail. 'The Tsar was evidently struggling to overcome his emotions,' he says. 'He nervously lit one cigarette after another, then threw them down again. Finally, he said, "Rasputin is a simple peasant who can relieve the sufferings of my son by a strange power. The Tsarina's reliance upon him is a matter for the family, and I will allow no one to meddle in my affairs".'[39]

One of the most astute observers of the fading Romanov tableau was Maurice Paléologue. 'Nicholas II does not enjoy the exercise of power,' he noted. 'If he jealously upholds his autocratic prerogatives, it is solely on mystical grounds. He never forgets that he has received his power from God Himself, and is always reminding himself that he will have to account for it in the Valley of Josaphat.'[40]

The chances of Nicholas completing his reign successfully and dying peacefully in bed had always been slim. By 1913 the forces that would destroy him were gathering strength inside and outside the imperial boundaries. Within a matter of months the arms race, the Balkans and the revolutionary threat would coalesce to create a perfect storm that would sweep the Romanovs into history.

Alexander Kerensky, Minister of War, June 1917.
(Kerensky Family Papers)

Alexander 'Sasha' Kerensky (right) and three of his siblings (from left) Fyodor 'Fedya', Elena 'Lyolya', and Nadezhda 'Nadya' circa 1900. Fyodor was shot by the Bolsheviks in 1919 and Elena was executed in the Stalinist Purges of the 1930s. *(Kerensky Family Papers)*

Alexander Kerensky's parents: Nadezhda (née Adler) and Fyodor Kerensky in the 1890s when Fyodor was the inspector of schools for Tashkent.
(Kerensky Family Papers)

Mrs Olga Kerenskaya (née Baranovskaya), Alexander Kerensky's first wife, on a visit to her Baranovsky relatives in Paris circa 1925. The Kerenskys had two sons but separated in 1917 following Kerensky's affair with her cousin, Elena 'Lilya' Baranovskaya. *(Kerensky Family Papers)*

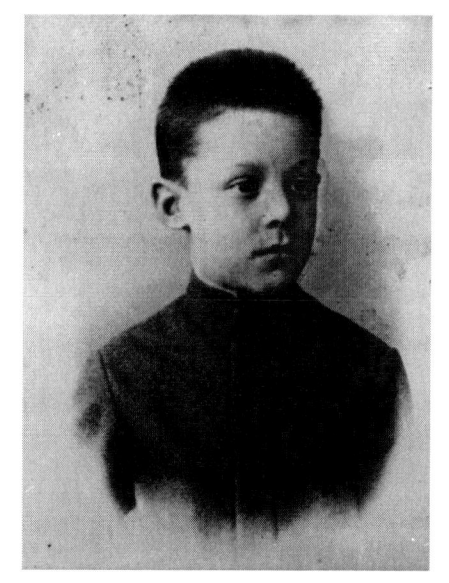

Left: Olga and Elena Baranovskaya. Elena (Lilya) became Alexander Kerensky's lover and the mother of his daughter, Irina.
Right: Vladimir Baranovsky, the girls' brother, who escaped to America in 1917. *(Kerensky Family Papers)*

Alexander Kerensky, 'persuader-in-chief', at the front June 1917.
(Kerensky Family Papers)

Flanked by two aide-de-camps, Alexander Kerensky, Russia's Minister-President, sits at his desk in the library of the Winter Palace, Petrograd, in summer 1917. *(Kerensky Family Papers)*

Top row: Vladimir Lenin in disguise July 1917 and as he really looked.
Lower row: Josef Stalin and (right) his mortal enemy Leon Trotsky.

(PA Images)

Alexander Kerensky with his sons Oleg (left) and Gleb (right) on their last summer holiday at the Baranovsky estate at Kainki, Kazan Province, before the February Revolution of 1917.
(Kerensky Family Papers)

Olga Kerenskaya with her sons Oleg (left) and Gleb (right) in March 1916 before the start of their ordeal. The Bolsheviks locked them up in the Lubianka and they were lucky to survive. *(Kerensky Family Papers)*

The document identifying Olga Kerenskaya as Olga Peterson, an Estonian national, that enabled Olga and her sons Oleg and Gleb to escape from Petrograd to London in 1920. *(Kerensky Family Papers)*

PART II
REVOLUTION
(1914-1917)

10

The Damn Fool Thing

The Great Powers had been at peace in Europe since the Franco-Prussian War of 1871, the longest period of harmony since the Roman Empire. It was very much a dynastic achievement - no fewer than seven of Queen Victoria's direct descendants and two of her Coburg relatives occupied European thrones. It was unthinkable that two bullets fired through the haze of a Balkan summer's day would trigger the greatest dynastic cataclysm of all time.

Britain had ended her 'splendid isolation' from European entanglements after finding herself friendless in the South African War of 1899–1902. The Entente Cordiale with France was signed in April 1904 following the settlement of colonial differences between the two powers over their interests in Africa and Asia. Three years later, in September 1907, Britain joined the Franco-Russian Alliance to create the Triple Entente after reaching agreement with Saint Petersburg on their respective spheres of influence in Persia.

The Triple Entente was a military pact and its primary aim was to neutralise the Triple Alliance of Germany, Austria-Hungary and Italy. As Edward VII was instrumental in promoting both the Entente Cordiale and the Triple Entente, the German press labelled him 'Edward the Encircler', and his nephew the Kaiser exploded, 'He's a Satan! You can hardly believe what a Satan he is!'[1]

Sir Arthur Nicolson, who, as Ambassador to Saint Petersburg, had been closely involved in the rapprochement between Britain and Russia, recalled that he had 'not seen such calm waters' since joining the diplomatic service in August 1870. Some of Britain's gilded youth, however, were unhappy. Joyce Cary, an Anglo-Irish Oxford graduate, expressed a view common to a generation raised on the military glories of Wellington and Nelson. 'I wanted the experience of war,' he says. 'I thought there would be no more wars.'[2]

He was in luck. Since the end of the Russo-Japanese War in 1905, Nicholas's foreign policy had swung away from Asia to the tinder-dry powderkeg of the Balkan Peninsula.[i] Tensions rose in 1908-09 when Austria-Hungary, to the fury of little Serbia, annexed the Slavic provinces of Bosnia and Herzegovina. As the Slavs' protector, Russia opposed the annexation but Nicholas shied away from taking his country into another war so soon after the Japanese debacle. His army was in the process of reorganisation and would not be battle-ready until 1917. To Serbia's dismay, her big brother swallowed his pride and allowed the annexation to go ahead unchallenged.

Peace, however, did not last long in that troubled region. In the First Balkan War of 1912-1913 Serbia, Greece, Montenegro and Bulgaria joined forces to attack the Ottoman Turks. Joyce Cary headed for Montenegro as fast as the antiquated transport system would allow. As a Red Cross stretcher-bearer on the battlefields he discovered that military glory was, in Lincoln's words, 'that attractive rainbow that rises in showers of blood - that serpent's eye that charms to destroy'.[ii]

Having inflicted a humiliating defeat on the Turks, the Balkan brotherhood then fought one another over the spoils, with Serbia emerging the biggest territorial winner. To the annoyance of her neighbours, her size doubled and her population jumped from 2.9 million to 4.4 million. Serbia, a Christian kingdom, then invaded Albania and Kosovo and massacred hundreds of their Muslim citizens. On 17 October 1913 Austria-Hungary, which had guaranteed Albanian independence, gave Serbia eight days to withdraw her forces or face the military consequences. Once again conflict was avoided. Nicholas persuaded the Serbs to retreat and Kaiser Wilhelm advised the Austrians to take no further action. It would, however, prove to be a temporary reprieve.

By 1914 Britain had won the shipbuilding battle against Germany and the Chancellor of the Exchequer, David Lloyd George, believed that swelling the Royal Navy's strength any further 'would wantonly

---

i Nations and provinces in the Balkan region in 1914 included Hungary, Romania, Bulgaria, Croatia, Bosnia-Herzegovina, Serbia, Dalmatia, Montenegro, Macedonia, Albania and Greece

ii Joyce Cary became a successful author with novels such as The Horse's Mouth. His Balkan experiences are recounted in his 1965 autobiographical Memoir of the Bobotes.

provoke other nations'. His efforts to trim the naval budget of £54 million (£6.12 billion today) brought a furious reaction from his friend, the First Lord of the Admiralty, Winston Churchill, the Tory turncoat who, as champion of the Admiralty's Blue Water strategy, was committed to building bigger, faster, wider-ranging, more lethal, oil-fuelled dreadnoughts.[3]

The Balkan crises, however, precipitated an arms race on land between Franco-Russian and Austro-German allies that would prove even more threatening to peace than the naval race. Bismarck had claimed that the next war between the great European powers would explode from 'some damned foolish thing in the Balkans'. His prophesy was about to come true.[4]

In February 1914 the Tsar ordered Peter Durnovo (who had retired from the Interior Ministry after the Dowager Empress complained to her son that he was reading her mail) to provide an analysis of the consequences of Russia becoming involved in a great European war. In his Memorandum, Durnovo wrote that the central factor in current world history was the conflicting interests of England and Germany.

> This rivalry must inevitably lead to an armed struggle between them, the issue of which will, in all probability, prove fatal to the vanquished side. The interests of these two powers are far too incompatible, and their simultaneous existence as world powers will sooner or later prove impossible. On the one hand, there is an insular State, whose world importance rests upon its domination of the sea, its world trade, and its innumerable colonies. On the other, there is a powerful continental empire, whose limited territory is insufficient for an increased population. It has therefore openly and candidly declared that its future is on the seas. It has, with fabulous speed, developed an enormous world commerce, built for its protection a formidable navy, and, with its famous trademark, 'Made in Germany', created a mortal danger to the industrial and economic prosperity of its rival. Naturally, England cannot yield without a fight, and between her and Germany a struggle for life or death is inevitable.

Two months later the Duma passed 'the Big Military Programme for 1914-1916', a secret agreement with France under which the balance of military strength along the Russo-German frontier and in the Baltic would be radically altered in Russia's favour. 'It was obvious that Germany, who was well-informed about this plan, would take counter-measures,' Alexander Kerensky says. 'The programme was passed as a military secret and there was no knowledge of the approaching danger in democratic circles.'[5]

The really frightening thing from a Russian point of view was that when General Vladimir Sukhomlinov, the Minister of War, met with select Duma members behind closed doors, he revealed a total ignorance of the new master plan. According to Paul Miliukov, 'he knew as much about the reform he was supposed to explain to us as the man in the moon'.

On 8 May the Duma was rocked when Rodzianko announced that Lenin's star recruit Roman Malinovsky had handed in his resignation. Speculation was rife until an official leak disclosed that the Bolshevik deputy was an Okhrana spy and provocateur. His incendiary, anti-Tsarist speeches, which were intended to cover up his treachery, had created such a stir among the Council of Ministers that his police handlers were forced to pay him off and send him to Germany on a one-way ticket.

Lenin refused to believe in Malinovsky's guilt until the Ministry of the Interior's files were opened in 1917 and his treachery was proved beyond doubt. 'What a scoundrel!' Lenin raged. 'He tricked the lot of us. Traitor! Shooting's too good for him!'[6]

Given the jingoistic nature of the times, the odds on war breaking out shortened dramatically on 15/28 June when Gavrilo Princip, a nineteen-year-old Bosnian Serb, assassinated Archduke Franz Ferdinand, heir to the Habsburg throne, in the Bosnian capital of Sarajevo. Franz Ferdinand, the fifty-year-old nephew of the Austro-Hungarian monarch Franz Josef (Emperor in Austria, King in Hungary), was an easy target in the six-car motorcade that drove slowly through Sarajevo that morning. He was dressed in a sky blue tunic with gold collar and wore a helmet adorned with green peacock feathers. Moreover, he had refused a squad of bodyguards to protect him and his morganatic wife, the Duchess Sophie, during their progress through the crowded streets in a Gräf & Stift open touring car.[7]

Outside Moritz Schiller's delicatessen on Franz Josef Street, Princip fired two shots, fatally wounding the royal couple. By 11.30 a.m. both were dead, the first victims of the First World War. The assassin had obtained the murder weapon – a 9-mm Belgium-made Browning pistol - from the Black Hand, a secret military society which regarded Bosnia-Herzegovina's large ethnic Serb minority as a part of 'Greater Serbia' incorporating all Serbs on the Balkan Peninsula.

Many people, including senior Austrian politicians, did not regard Franz Ferdinand's death as a great loss to humanity. While he was a moderating influence on the warmongers, he could also be sharp-tongued and short-tempered, with an extravagant lifestyle and an unpleasant desire to slaughter game. One historian described him as a 'suspicious, morose and violent man who saw enemies everywhere'.[8] Indeed, the Hungarian co-rulers of the Empire regarded Franz Josef's heir with fear and loathing. As a sign of contempt, he drew the blinds of his carriage whenever the royal train passed through Hungarian territory. Politically, he advocated reducing the size of their country and limiting their power inside the Dual Monarchy. There were many important people in Budapest who thought his life was not worth a drop of Magyar blood.

The position of the Austro-Hungarian Empire, a hotchpotch of more than a dozen countries and provinces, five major religions and a dozen languages, was threatened as never before. The Kaiser, unimpressed with the Dual Monarchy's meddling in the Balkan Wars, was thinking of making another friendly approach to Nicholas. Sarajevo provided the Austro-Hungarians with an opportunity to crush Serbia and reinforce their alliance with Berlin.[iii]

The Foreign Minister, Leopold, Count Berchtold, had no proof of Serbian complicity in the assassination but he was a friend of Franz Ferdinand's and he was determined to crush Serbia. All that was required was Germany's support. The Kaiser had also been a friend of Franz Ferdinand's - they had recently participated in the mass slaughter of wildlife on the Archduke's estate - and Wilhelm was furious about his murder. He told the German Chancellor, Theobald von Bethmann Hollweg, 'This cowardly, detestable crime has shaken me to the depths of my soul.' Two days after the killing, he scribbled on a report from the German Ambassador in Vienna, Baron Heinrich von Tschirschky und Bögendorff, that 'the Serbs must be disposed of, <u>and</u> that right <u>soon</u>!'[9]

---

iii The Empire consisted of Austria, Hungary, the Czech Republic, Slovakia, Slovenia, Bosnia, Croatia and parts of present-day Poland, Romania, Italy, Ukraine, Moldova, Serbia and Montenegro.

Count Berchtold's first obstacle was the Hungarian Prime Minister, István Tisza, who argued that any military chastisement of Serbia would bring the Russian hordes storming across their western border into Hungary.[iv] Nevertheless, on Sunday 5 July the Austrian Ambassador to Berlin, Count Laszlo Szogyenyi, presented the Kaiser with two documents: a memorandum in which Austria held Serbia responsible for the assassination and a letter in which Emperor Franz Josef, now in his eighty-fourth year, denounced Belgrade's policy of uniting all Southern Slavs: 'The bloody deed was not the work of a single individual but a well organised plot whose threads extend to Belgrade. Although it may be impossible to establish the complicity of the Serbian Government, no one can doubt that its policy of uniting all Southern Slavs under the Serbian flag encourages such crimes and that the continuation of this situation is a chronic peril for my House and my territories. Serbia must be eliminated as a political factor in the Balkans.'[10]

So the real casus belli was not the loss of the unloved Franz Ferdinand but Serbia's very existence. After receiving an assurance from his Minister of War, General Erich von Falkenhayn, that the German army could handle any military eventuality, the Kaiser warned German business leaders to consider selling their foreign securities. Then, believing that Little Nicky lacked the will to risk war, he decided to give Franz Josef a blank cheque of unconditional German backing. He told Ambassador Szogyenyi that Austria-Hungary must march into Serbia with Germany's support, even if it resulted in war with Russia.[11]

The next day Chancellor Bethmann confirmed the Kaiser's pledge and urged the Austrians to send an ultimatum to Serbia, followed by an immediate declaration of war. 'Whatever our decision turned out to be,' Szogyenyi informed Vienna, 'we could be confident that Germany as our ally and a friend of the Monarchy would stand behind us.'[12]

Leaving the next move up to Austria, the Kaiser embarked on

---

iv It was later revealed that the Serbian Prime Minister, Nicholas Pasic, had sent a telegram to the Serbian legation in Vienna warning of a plot against Franz Ferdinand. The legation passed a message to the Austro-Hungarian Finance Minister saying only that the Archduke's visit could end in tragedy. The warning was so vague that no action was taken.

his annual cruise to the Norwegian fjords in the royal yacht *Hohenzollern II*, while his ministers went on holiday (or, in one case, on honeymoon).[v] The Austrians took the Germans at their word. On Tuesday 7 July the Austro-Hungarian Council of Ministers decided to send an ultimatum to Serbia that was so forceful as to 'make a refusal almost certain, so that the road to military action should be opened'.

Then there was a delay while Tisza was persuaded that failure to avenge Franz Ferdinand's assassination would send a signal to Hungary's enemies in Romania that they could employ the same destabilising tactics in the disputed province of Transylvania. Despite his doubts, Tisza finally relented and on 14 July the Hungarians joined the Dual Monarchy's war party. The Habsburgs then had to decide what to do with Serbia after the invasion. Five days later on 19 July they secretly agreed to divide most of her territory among Bulgaria, Albania and Greece, while retaining the remainder for themselves. Serbia - 'the nest of vipers' - would cease to exist as an independent state.[13]

The following day the stoutly anti-German French President, Raymond Poincaré, and the French Prime Minister, René Viviani, arrived in Saint Petersburg on a goodwill visit to their ally, the Tsar. Count Berchtold feared that if the ultimatum were served on Serbia during that visit the French statesmen might persuade the Tsar to take joint action against Austria-Hungary. Ironically, Pioncaré assured his host that, in his opinion, 'the Emperor Wilhelm is too cautious to launch his country on some wild adventure and the Emperor Franz Josef's only wish is to die in peace'.[14]

By 10/23 July the French leaders were heading back to Paris and the Kaiser, a creature of habit, was still pottering around his favourite spots on the Norwegian coast when Serbia was presented with the Austrians' swingeing terms. The Note alleged that Princip and his fellow Bosnian-Serb conspirators had conceived their plot in the Serbian capital of Belgrade and that the Serbian authorities had supplied the weapons and helped them cross the border back into Bosnia. It also contained specific demands aimed at suppressing anti-

---

v Wilhelm's sadism was never more apparent than on his yacht, where he ordered elderly guests to do sit-ups, push-ups and knee-bends to the point of exhaustion while roaring with laughter at their agonies. He had photographs taken of himself pushing them over on their backs and sitting on their stomachs.

Habsburg propaganda; removing activists from the Serbian Military; arresting everyone involved in the assassination plot; permitting Habsburg officials to visit Serbia to ensure these measures were being carried out; and entitling Habsburg officials to take part in a Serbian judicial inquiry into the whole affair.[15]

To make things even more difficult for the Serbian Government, the Austrians demanded a reply within forty-eight hours. According to Berchtold's wife Nadine, her husband had spent a sleepless night adding ever-tougher clauses to the ultimatum because he feared the Serbs might accept it.[16]

Alexander Kerensky spent the spring and early summer months of 1914 travelling across Russia with a group of friends in his campaign to bring down the autocracy, or, as he put it, 'marshalling the political forces of the country for the expected joint offensive of all bourgeois, proletarian and peasant parties and organisations against Tsarism'.

At Ekaterinburg, a town at the foot of the Ural Mountains that was destined to be stained in Tsarist blood, he attended a secret gathering of teachers in a forest clearing. 'When the discussions were at their fiercest, we heard rustling noises on all sides,' he says. 'Next, we discerned the snorting of horses, the beating of hooves. We were surrounded. All names and addresses were taken and droves of prisoners were led under guard to the police station. 'As a member of the Duma, I could not be arrested and continued on my tour to Samara on the Volga, where I made revolutionary speeches in a theatre to audiences thousands strong. The Chief of Police himself sat in the front row and merely shrugged his shoulders, being powerless to arrest me.'[17]

News of the Austrian ultimatum reached Kerensky as he was preparing to board a paddle-steamer on the Samara quayside for the trip to Saratov, the leading city in his Duma constituency. 'Suddenly, a group of newsboys came running towards the gangplank crying, "Austria ultimatum to Serbia". In that moment our mood underwent a sharp change. In the cries of the newsboys, we sensed at once the first breath of the historic hurricane.'[18]

Kerensky decided to cancel his trip and return to Saint Petersburg to discuss the implications with his Duma colleagues. 'Quite intuitively, I perceived that Tsarism would not survive the war and that on the fields of battle Russia's liberty would be born,' he said. 'On the steamer I expressed the same thought to none other than the sister of Nicolai Lenin. After exchanging a few reminiscences of our childhood days, the conversation turned upon Lenin himself, who had been living for many years as a political exile in Western Europe. "But don't worry," I said. "You will soon see him again. There will be war and it will open to him the road to Russia".'[19]

Kerensky admits he was only half serious but, considering the consequences to his country and himself, his prediction about Lenin's imminent return must rank as one of the most calamitous self-fulfilling prophecies of all time.

In Belgrade, the Serbian Prime Minister, Nicholas Pasic, was inclined to avoid hostilities. His government accepted everything in the ultimatum except the demand for Austrian involvement in a judicial inquiry inside Serbia. Even then, it suggested this question should be referred to the International Court at The Hague or left to the Great Powers to decide.

Nevertheless, Vienna immediately broke off diplomatic relations with Belgrade and prepared for war. Four days before the assassination of Franz Ferdinand, the sickly King Peter of Serbia had transferred his royal prerogatives to his son, Crown Prince Alexander. It was Alexander who turned to Russia for help. Nicholas had no stomach for war but, having given in to Austria over the Bosnian annexation, he knew that turning his back on Serbia a second time would be fatal to Russia's reputation in the Balkans.

'As long as there remains the faintest hope of avoiding bloodshed,' he told Prince Alexander, 'all my efforts will tend in that direction. If we fail to attain this object, in spite of our sincere desire for peace, Your Royal Highness may rest assured that Russia will in no case remain indifferent to the fate of Serbia.'[20]

The British Government was conflicted. According to Churchill, 'at least three-quarters [of the cabinet] were determined not to be drawn into a European quarrel, unless Great Britain herself were attacked'. Some cabinet members felt that autocratic Russia was an inappropriate ally for Liberal Britain, while others sought to establish better relations with Germany.[21] There was, however, an unbreakable linkage between Britain's foreign policy and her naval strength. For this reason, the Foreign Secretary, Sir Edward Grey, had preached for years that Britain should focus on Germany's expansionist threat to the British Empire. He thought the Kaiser dangerously unstable, once describing him in a naval metaphor as being 'like a battleship with steam up and screws going, but with no rudder, and he will run into something some day and cause a catastrophe'. Others thought Russia's ambitions towards India posed a greater menace to Britain than the German High Seas Fleet.

Russia also had serious doubts about her British ally. 'We do not travel the same road as England; she should be left to go her own way, and we must not quarrel on her account with Germany,' Peter Durnovo had advised the Tsar in his February Memo. 'The Triple Entente is an artificial combination, without a basis of real interest. It has nothing to look forward to. The future belongs to a close and incomparably more vital rapprochement of Russia, Germany, France and Japan.'

The deciding factor on the path to war lay in the different forms of governance among the powers. In Britain and France, foreign policy was debated in the Houses of Parliament and the National Assembly respectively. In Russia, Germany and Austria-Hungary – the three nations at the heart of the crisis – executive power rested with their Emperors, the first of whom was unstable, the second insane and the third geriatric. Leaving Franz Josef out of the equation, it was the ineptness of Nicholas and the folly of Wilhelm that would ignite hostilities and drag Britain and France into the abyss.[22]

Even at this late stage, a firm British declaration of her commitment to fight alongside France and Russia might have pulled Germany back from the brink but the cabinet was divided and the Prime Minister, Herbert Henry Asquith, had other things on his mind. Preoccupied with the prospect of civil war in Ireland over Home Rule (and with writing love letters to his daughter's best friend, Venetia Stanley, twenty-five to his sixty), he left the European crisis in the hands of his Foreign Secretary.[23]

Sir Eyre Crowe, Assistant Under-Secretary at the Foreign Office - half-German, German-educated and married to a German wife - knew the Teutonic mentality better than his colleagues. He warned Edward Grey that the war would not be about Serbia at all; instead, it would be a contest 'between Germany aiming at a political dictatorship in Europe and the Powers who desire to retain individual freedom'.[24]

Few British politicians were less warlike than Grey, a mild-mannered pacifist who treated diplomacy with the same saintly patience he devoted to fly-fishing and bird-watching. Having made only one trip abroad (to Paris with Edward VII), one of his blind spots was that he regarded alliances with foreign powers as a commitment to war rather than a guarantee of peace.[25]

On Saturday 25 July he made a gaffe that would take events to a dangerous new level. Early that morning Count Alexander Benckendorff, the Russian Ambassador, advised him that if Austria were to mobilise against Serbia, the Tsar would probably put the Russian army on a war footing prior to mobilisation. Grey was regarded at the Foreign Office as the master of cryptic remarks that could interpreted in several ways. On this occasion, he replied that such a move would be a 'perfectly natural response'. Reading Benckendorff's telegram on the conversation, Russia's pro-Serbian Foreign Minister, Serge Sazonov, took the remark to mean Britain would condone Russia's war preparations.[26]

The Tsar went ahead and approved the partial mobilisation of his forces in the four military districts nearest the Austro-Hungarian borders. As Russia had a total of fifteen military districts, it was intended to be a limited operation. He was unaware that the Chief of the General Staff, General Nikolai Yanushkevich, had made things so complicated that there was in practice no distinction between 'partial mobilisation' and 'general mobilisation'.[27]

Later that same day Grey left London for a spot of fishing at his cottage on the banks of the River Itchen in Hampshire, leaving Sir Arthur Nicolson, the former Ambassador to Russia who was now his Permanent Undersecretary, in charge of the Foreign Office. The two men had discussed the possibility of inviting the belligerent nations to a conference in London to discuss the crisis. On Sunday the twenty-sixth Nicolson went ahead and sent invitations to Berlin, Paris, Saint Petersburg, Vienna and Rome (though not to Belgrade).

Returning to London, Grey approved Nicolson's action but saw little chance of success. He believed Germany's preparations for war were well advanced and that Berlin would resist any delay that would give France and Russia time to catch up.[28]

Meanwhile, the Kaiser had learned about the strident tone of Austria's ultimatum in one of the many telegrams he had received from Berlin during his holiday cruise. He panicked – if Austria cashed his cheque, he would be blamed for prompting the rush to war. Early that Sunday, he sailed from Norway for home.

Fearing that the Kaiser might lose his nerve, the hawkish Bethmann rejected the British invitation without consulting him. Grey was tempted to tell Berlin that if war came the responsibility would rest with Germany. Instead, in typical cryptic fashion, he warned Bethmann not to count on Britain's neutrality in the event of war and then he advised the French and the Russians not to count on her support.[29]

At Buckingham Palace King George, who had been 'inexpressibly shocked' at the murder of Franz Ferdinand, was anxious to keep Britain out of any European conflict. Tsar Nicholas, Tsarina Alexandra and Kaiser Wilhelm were his first cousins and he regarded the very thought of Britain joining in a war involving his relatives as an abomination. However, he unintentionally assisted the German hawks when, on 26 July, he gave Wilhelm's brother, Prince Heinrich of Prussia, who was visiting London, the impression that 'England would remain neutral if war broke out between the Continental powers'.

This news was immediately flashed to Bethmann, who used it to crank up the pressure in favour of war. He briefed his Ambassadors in London, Paris and Saint Petersburg to blame Russia for the deteriorating situation.[30] By the time Wilhelm arrived back at Potsdam on 28 July, he was too late to do anything – Austria declared war on Serbia at 11 a.m. that day and on the twenty-ninth Austrian gunboats on the Danube shelled Belgrade. Austrian reservists living in Germany were summoned to join the colours and the leave of all German officers and other ranks was cancelled.

All eyes turned to Russia. How would she respond? The British Ambassador in Saint Petersburg, Sir George Buchanan, a tall, slim, erect Old Etonian who spoke no Russian, wrote in his memoirs, 'On 30 July Russia mobilised in support of her Slav brother, or tried to, but the Herculean task of clothing, feeding, arming and transporting eighteen million men was beyond the powers of the Tsar's bureaucrats and the inadequate Russian railway system, much of which was still single-track.'

Buchanan was wrong about most things and this was one of them. Russian mobilisation was no longer the snail's pace procedure it had been at the time of the Russo-Japanese War. Between 1900 and 1914, railway mileage across the Empire had almost doubled, giving Russia more track than any nation except the United States and halving the time it would take to mobilise her huge army in time of war from forty days to fewer than twenty.

New double-tracked lines now connected Moscow, Saint Petersburg and the Polish capital of Warsaw. Only the previous year a French loan of $500 million had been invested in roads and railways in the Austro-Hungarian theatre, depriving the enemy of their historic logistical advantage in moving troops, guns, munitions and other supplies to the Galician border region of southern Poland and northern Hungary.[31]

On Friday 31 July Asquith told the House of Commons, 'We have heard, not from Saint Petersburg, but from Germany, that Russia has proclaimed a general mobilisation of her army and her fleet; and that, in consequence of this, martial law was to be proclaimed in Germany. We understand this to mean mobilisation will follow in Germany...'[32]

For the previous forty-eight hours there had been a frantic exchange of telegrams, in English, between Cousin Nicky in his summer palace at Peterhof and Cousin Willy at Potsdam. The mise-en-scène could perhaps be likened to a family squabble being decided by a tennis match at Osborne House, with Nicky and Willy exchanging shots over the net while a perplexed Cousin Georgie watched from the umpire's chair and the spectre of Grandmamma haunted the Pavilion. Willy's first telegram, dispatched late on 15/28 July after Austria had declared war on Serbia but before the first shots had been fired, said:

> It is with the gravest concern that I hear of the impression which the action of Austria against Serbia is creating in your country. The unscrupulous agitation that has been going on in Serbia for years has resulted in the outrageous crime to which Archduke Franz Ferdinand fell victim. You will doubtless agree with me that we both, you and I, have a common interest, as well as all Sovereigns, to insist that all the persons morally responsible for this dastardly murder should receive their deserved punishment. In this, politics play no part at all.
>
> On the other hand, I fully understand how difficult it is for you and your government to face the drift of public opinion. Therefore, with regard to the hearty and tender friendship which binds us both from long ago with firm ties, I am exerting my utmost influence to induce the Austrians to deal straightly (*sic*) to arrive at a satisfactory understanding with you. I confidently hope you will help me in my

efforts to smooth over difficulties that may still arise. Your very sincere and devoted friend and cousin.
Willy

Willy's telegram crossed with one from Nicky:

Am glad you are back. In this most serious moment I appeal to you to help me. An ignoble war has been declared on a weak country. The indignation in Russia, shared fully by me, is enormous. I foresee that very soon I shall be overwhelmed by pressure brought upon me, and forced to take extreme measures which will lead to war. To try and avoid such a calamity as a European war, I beg you in the name of our old friendship to do what you can to stop your allies from going too far.
Nicky

Willy replied on 16/29 July:

It would be quite possible for Russia to remain a spectator of the Austro-Serbian conflict, without involving Europe in the most horrible war she ever witnessed. I think a direct understanding between your government and Vienna possible and desirable and as I already telegraphed you, my government is continuing its exertions to promote it. Of course, military measures on the part of Russia which would be looked upon by Austria as threatening, would precipitate a calamity we both wish to avoid, and jeopardise my position as mediator which I readily accepted on your appeal to my friendship and help.
Willy

Nicky then suggested a way out of the crisis:

I thank you for your conciliatory and friendly telegram, whereas the communications of your Ambassador [Count von Pourtalès] to my Minister [Sazonov] today have been in a very different tone. Please clear up this divergence! It would be right to turn the Austro-Serbian problem over to the Hague Conference. I trust in your wisdom and friendship.
Your loving Nicky

Nicky then ordered General Sukhomlinov to cancel the mobilisation. 'I won't be responsible for a monstrous slaughter,' he said. Sukhomlinov was horrified. 'Mobilisation is not a mechanical process which one can stop at will,' he said. Nevertheless, Nicholas was adamant. Then, on 30 July, he informed Willy about the partial mobilisation against Austria.

> The military measures which have now come into force were decided five days ago for reasons of defence on account of Austria's preparations. I hope with all my heart that these measures won't interfere with your part as mediator which I greatly value. We need your strong pressure on Austria to come to an understanding with us.
> Nicky

Willy was outraged. 'The Tsar's been mobilising behind my back,' he fumed to his Ministers. 'He's been lying to me.' That afternoon Sazonov told the Tsar, 'I don't think Your Majesty can postpone the order for general mobilisation.' Nicky vacillated. He wanted to believe his cousin's emotional assurances that he truly desired peace. He replied, 'Think of the responsibility you are advising me to take. Remember, it would mean sending hundreds of thousands of Russian people to their deaths.'[33]

Sazonov declared that everything possible had been done to avoid war but Germany and Austria were 'determined to enslave our natural allies in the Balkans, destroy our influence there, and reduce Russia to a pitiful dependence on the arbitrary will of the Central Powers.' The hours passed. Nicky smoked. The bags under his eyes were swollen and he looked exhausted. Finally, he reached a decision. 'You are right,' he told Sazonov. 'There is nothing left for us to do but get ready for an attack upon us. Give my order for general mobilisation.'[34]

At midnight on 18/31 July Ambassador Pourtalès presented Sazonov with an ultimatum to cancel the mobilisation within twelve hours. When Russia failed to reply by noon on Saturday 1 August, Willy ordered general mobilisation. 'The sword,' he declared melodramatically, 'has been forced into our hands.'

Posterity had handed Willy and Nicky one of the most vital tasks in human history – to avoid the long-predicted clash of arms between the Slavs and the Teutons – and they had failed to do so. 'The Tsar certainly desired peace,' Sir Edward Grey wrote in his memoirs. 'No one can doubt that his suggestion to the German Emperor for a settlement by use of the machinery of the Hague Tribunal was genuine, nor can the Russian mobilisation be fairly construed as evidence of a desire of war.'[35]

Asquith's dinner guest at 10 Downing Street that night was Count Benckendorff. The atmosphere was so tense that Asquith's wife, the former Margot Tennant, informed the visitor that she was glad Britain could act independently of Russia. She then quipped, 'Britons never, *never* will be Slavs.'[36]

Germany demanded that France declare her neutrality within eighteen hours or face the consequences. President Poincaré was intent on reclaiming the provinces of Alsace-Lorraine lost to Germany in the Franco-Prussian War. He had already given Russia a blank cheque of his own and, instead of acquiescing to German demands, France mobilised in support of her Russian ally on 20 July/2 August. An hour later Germany declared war on France. It was harvest time in rural France and church bells summoned the men from the fields to exchange their working clothes for uniforms.[vi]

Nicholas returned to Saint Petersburg with his family in the royal yacht *Standardt*. In Palace Square, 100,000 people knelt and prayed in front of the Winter Palace. There was a surge of patriotism among the Russian people. During President Pioncaré's visit 150,000 workers had been on strike demanding political reforms. All that was about to change. When Nicholas stepped on to the palace's red-draped balcony overlooking the square, the noise was deafening. At his side was the Tsarina, dressed all in white. In a rare of treat for the crowd, she turned up the brim of her picture hat so that they could see her face.[37]

'All at once not a trace was left of the revolutionary movement,' Kerensky says. 'The workmen returned to their factories. They took part in their thousands in patriotic demonstrations before the Allied embassies and missions. The mobilisation proceeded in the most exemplary manner all over Russia.'[38] In the same patriotic mood, the Kadets dropped their opposition to the government and urged their followers to forget about internal dissension and 'let the union of the Tsar and the people grow ever stronger'.[39]

Germany was well prepared for war against both Russia and France. Goaded by the Franco-Russian alliance, Count Alfred von Schlieffen,

---

vi Prussia had annexed all of Alsace and one-third of Lorraine. Pioncaré had been born in Lorraine and loathed the German occupation of his birthplace.

the former Chief of the German General Staff, had devised an apparently foolproof strategy for his country to fight a war against France and Russia simultaneously using Germany's superb railway system. Eleven thousand trains would carry four million men to their posts within a matter of days. Most these soldiers – 'the hammer' - would sweep through neutral Belgium to avoid the strong defences on the Franco-German border and attack France, while the remainder – 'the anvil' - blocked the French Army from advancing into Germany through Alsace-Lorraine.

The Chief of the German General Staff was Helmuth von Moltke the Younger, nephew of Helmuth von Moltke of Franco-Prussian War fame. Now sixty-six, he had succeeded Schlieffen in 1906. 'It is not pleasant to begin the war by violating the neutrality of a neighbouring state,' he mused. 'But it is necessary because it is our only chance for quick success.'[40] Moving into France en masse, German troops would encircle Paris and, in six weeks, defeat the French forces in a pincer movement. The capital would be bombarded from all sides and the French would surrender rather than face its complete destruction. Once the Channel ports had been secured to fend off Britain, the full weight of German arms would then travel east by rail to join Austro-Hungarian forces in crushing the more slowly mobilising Russians. This, the Kaiser was assured, would bring victory in a matter of months.[41]

General Moltke, however, was in poor health – he had suffered a stroke shortly before the outbreak of war - and he lacked the nerve of his distinguished uncle. Indeed, he had written to Chancellor Bethmann that the conflict would turn into a 'world war' in which the great powers would 'tear each other apart'. 'The culture of almost all of Europe,' he predicted, 'will be destroyed for decades to come.'[42]

British cabinet ministers had learned about the 'Schlieffen Movement of German Troops' four years earlier when Sir Henry Wilson, Director of Military Operations, gave them a secret briefing based on surprisingly accurate military intelligence. British agents were now reporting that German armies were massing, as predicted, in those same border areas.[43]

The drawback with the Schlieffen Plan was that once it had been activated any sudden changes would create chaos. And yet, as the mobilisation order was being signed in Wilhelm's Berlin palace,

Chancellor Bethmann dashed into the room bearing a telegram from Prince Lichnowsky in London. The cable reported (mistakenly, as it turned out) that the British Government had guaranteed that France would remain neutral in the event of war.[44]

'Champagne,' roared the Kaiser, 'We must halt the march to the west.'

He then insisted that the mobilisation process must be switched from France to Russia. Moltke knew that this change of direction would throw a spanner into the works of his well-oiled machine. 'If I cannot march against France,' he exploded, 'I cannot take responsibility for the war.'[45]

Wilhelm backed down and the Schlieffen Plan proceeded more or less as planned. Ten years earlier the Kaiser's wicked Uncle Bertie had foreseen this sort of catastrophic outcome with astonishing prescience. 'Through his unbelievable vanity, my nephew falls in with all the nationalistic toadies of his entourage who continually assure him that he is the greatest sovereign in the world,' he said. 'But because his cowardice is even greater than his vanity, he will cower before [the] pressure of the General Staff. When they dare him to draw the sword, he will not have the courage to bring them to reason. Abjectly he will be dominated by them. He will unleash war not through his own initiative and not with militant élan, but through weakness.'[46]

On Sunday 2 August, Prince Lichnowsky ('a sincere and honest man with a peevish voice and bad manners with servants') had the following exchange with Margot Asquith when she called at his residence in Carlton House Terrace:

> Prince Lichnowsky: But I do not understand what has happened! What is it all about?
> Margot Asquith: I can only imagine the evil genius of your Kaiser…
> Prince Lichnowsky (interrupting): He is ill-informed – impulsive, and must be *mad*! He never listens, or believes one word of what I say; he answers none of my telegrams.[47]

Once the trains were rolling towards the Belgium border, the German Foreign Office spread the fabrication through its embassies abroad that Germany had 'indisputable proof' that France and Britain were about to take over that country. The German nation had already been primed for war with false reports that French soldiers dressed in German uniforms had been shot while trying to blow up a German railway tunnel; that French aviators had dropped bombs on Nuremburg; and that French saboteurs had infected German waters supplies with cholera.[48]

On Monday 3 August the Belgian Government notified the German Minister it would not permit German troops to pass through Belgium to attack France and would resist with force. 'I rule a kingdom not a road,' King Albert of the Belgians reminded the Germans. Meanwhile, in Paris, the German Ambassador delivered the declaration of war to Premier Viviani. At his home in West Sussex, the anti-imperialist Wilfrid Scawen Blunt wrote in his diary that night:

August 3 1914
Things are marching fast. The Germans have begun their campaign against France by seizing Luxemburg, and seem to be already in Belgium. The spectacle of England at this crisis of the world's history without a single statesman of any real power is depressing. Winston perhaps I ought to except as he at least has energy but Asquith and all of them are old women, quite unable to deal with a situation demanding virility. How can they be expected to meet all Europe in arms when they are incapable of keeping their wild women in order at home, or coming to any decision about Ireland, or even keeping their fingers out of each other's pockets on the Stock Exchange?[49]

On 28 July, the Grand Fleet was ordered to steam 'at high speed and without lights' through the English Channel to its war stations at Scapa Flow in the Orkneys. The result was that the Royal Navy had taken control of the North Sea and the Channel, a manoeuvre that would enable the British Army, slimmed down and modernised by the great reformer Lord Haldane, to reach France unmolested and prevent the German High Seas Fleet from attacking France's Channel ports.

As First Lord, Churchill has been credited with this decision but he was away from his office that critical weekend (25-27 July), so the First Sea Lord, Prince Louis of Battenberg, prepared the order on his own initiative. Churchill merely endorsed it on his return. It was ironic that a man born in Austria and raised in Italy and Germany should have struck the first blow against the Triple Alliance.[vii][50]

[vii] Churchill acknowledged Battenberg's role when accepting his resignation four months later. Battenberg stepped down as First Sea Lord after being vilified in

Under the 1839 Treaty of London, Britain had guaranteed the perpetual neutrality of Belgium, though the treaty did not state what action she was bound to take in order to protect that neutrality. C. P. Scott, the pacifist editor-proprietor of the *Manchester Guardian*, suspected 'an organised conspiracy to drag us into the war'. Britain, he said, was not honour-bound to support the French or the Belgians – indeed, 'if we decide differently then we violate dozens of promises made to our own people, promises to seek peace, to protect the poor, to husband the resources of the country, to promote peaceful progress'.

When King Albert made a direct appeal to Britain and France for assistance, Sir Edward Grey argued that not confronting the German threat in Belgium would be more dangerous than doing so. For once, he received overwhelming support from his cabinet colleagues. That evening, watching the lamplighters in the street below his window in Horse Guards Parade, he solemnly intoned, 'The lamps are going out all over Europe; we shall not see them lit again in our lifetime.'[51]

About 9.30 p.m. on Tuesday 4 August German troops marched into Belgium and advanced toward Liège. Grey sent an ultimatum through the British Embassy in Berlin to the German Government demanding their immediate withdrawal. Late that night he joined the Prime Minister, Margot Asquith and Churchill in the Cabinet Room at 10 Downing Street. They smoked in silence while awaiting Germany's answer. When the ultimatum expired at 11 p.m. Greenwich Mean Time (midnight in Berlin), no answer had been received and Britain and her Commonwealth were at war with Germany. As Big Ben tolled the hour, a crowd outside in the street sang 'God Save the King'. Moments later the Admiralty flashed the signal to every Royal Navy ship: 'Commence hostilities against Germany.'[52]

Grey had assured the Commons in arguing for intervention over Belgium that 'if we are engaged in war, we shall suffer but little more than we shall suffer even if we stand aside'. He had no conception that Britain would become embroiled in a long, land-based war of attrition requiring the conscription of millions of his fellow countrymen. Indeed, most Britons imagined that the war would be decided by a

---

the British press over his German origins. He was replaced by Admiral of the Fleet Lord 'Jacky' Fisher, seventy-four, whose motto was 'Fear God and Dread Nought'. In 1917, at the request of George V, Battenberg anglicised the family name to Mountbatten.

titanic clash between the British and German fleets in the North Sea and would be all over by Christmas. Edward Grey later confessed that the failure of diplomacy to head off the four-year apocalypse kept him awake for years.[viii][53]

The patriotic spirit reached the far corners of the British Empire, none more so than Australia, a country of 4.5 million people which offered her navy and 20,000 troops to Britain even before she had declared war. In a quote that rankled with every Australian republican, the Scots-born Prime Minister, Andrew Fisher, pledged that 'Australians will stand beside our own to help and defend her to our last man and our last shilling.'

That spirit extended into the front room of 'Elderslie', a large timber house in the Clayfield suburb of Brisbane, where fourteen-year-old Lydia Ellen Tritton, known as Nell, roped her Australian cousins, brothers and servants into presenting a tableau for the neighbours. Her father was chief curtain-raiser, her uncle operated the lighting and even the family cat was given a role as the Lion of England in a scene called 'Rule Britannia' in which Nell draped herself in the Union Jack and posed as Britannia.

Not everybody was in favour of supporting Britain. Artem Sergeyev and his little band of Brisbane Bolsheviks opposed the war because it was an imperialist conflict that had nothing to do with the aspirations of the working class. They argued that the best thing that could happen to the Russian people would be the defeat of the Tsar's armies. Revolution would then break out in Russia and spread like wildfire across Europe.[54]

---

viii Grey was elevated to the peerage in July 1916 as Viscount Grey of Fallodon and he resigned as Foreign Secretary in December 1916.

11

The Iron Hurricane

The Kaiser refused to accept any responsibility for the catastrophe that had befallen Europe. He had thousands of postcards printed with his picture and the caption, 'Before God and History, I did not want this War!' The chief culprits, he said, were his cousins Nicky and Georgie. 'To think that Nicky and Georgie should have played me false!' he confided to friends. 'If my Grandmother had been alive, she would never have allowed it.'[1]

Willy - 'Kaiser Bill' to British troops - divested himself of his honorary British titles of Admiral of the Fleet and Field Marshal of the British Army. In common with his generals, he did not rate Britain as a serious military force and felt so confident of victory that he sneered at the 100,000-strong British Expeditionary Force as 'a contemptibly little army', a description that the Tommies proudly adopted in their nickname, 'the Old Contemptibles'.[2]

Austria-Hungary, which had been responsible for accelerating the rush to war, entered the fray against the Triple Entente on 6 August (NS). Italy, a member of the Triple Alliance, initially opted for neutrality and then, on 23 May 1915, abandoned Germany and Austria-Hungary altogether and joined the Allies in what Emperor Franz Josef described as 'perfidy of which history knows not the like'.[3]

Had he lived, Franz Ferdinand would have been Commander in Chief of the Austro-Hungarian Army. As things were, the Austrian commander was Field Marshal Franz Conrad von Hoetzendorf, a sixty-two-year-old chancer whose only combat experience had been as a captain attached to an infantry battalion in Bosnia thirty-six years earlier. On the eve of Franz Ferdinand's assassination, he had scribbled a note to his mistress, Gina, predicting that war was coming and that Austria-Hungary would not survive it. Russia and Serbia would be 'the coffin nails of the monarchy'. Through rash decision-making, it would be Conrad who hammered those nails in. After the assassination, his hatred of Serbia took control of his senses and he described his policy in three words: 'War! War! War!'[4]

Count Laszlo Szogyenyi saw the war as an opportunity to stir up a Jewish revolt in the Pale of Settlement. In most undiplomatic language, he urged the shtetls, 'Russian Jews! Rise Up! Seize weapons! Freedom comes from Europe! Organise yourselves! And send trustworthy men to German and Austro-Hungarian commanders!'[5]

The Austrian narrative on the war was that Russia, a corrupt and backward country, had delusions of enslaving millions of Germans and Austro-Hungarians as the central aim of a pan-Slav crusade to save the Romanov Dynasty from the ravages of revolution. This moonshine appealed enormously to one Russian living peacefully in Poronin, a hamlet at the foot of the Tatra Mountains in Austrian Galicia, a province straddling the modern-day border between Poland and Ukraine.[6]

Vladimir Lenin was working night and day in this provincial backwater on his campaign not to enslave Austria but to destroy the Tsar. As his Bolshevik friend and chief cheerleader Grigory Zinoviev, the curly-haired son of a Jewish dairyman, lived nearby with his second wife Zina, Lenin referred to Poronin as 'the Foreign Bureau of the Bolshevik Central Committee'. On 7 August (NS) the Austrian police searched his house, found a loaded Browning pistol and arrested him as an enemy spy. His revolutionary exploits could so easily have ended in front of an Austrian firing squad.[7]

That same day advance parties of the British Expeditionary Force sailed for France, with the main bodies following a week later. Four infantry divisions and one cavalry division were transported to Le Havre, Boulogne and Rouen without the loss of a single man. The Royal Navy escorted the troopships across the Channel and there was no sign of German warships.

News of the outbreak of war reached Grishka Rasputin in Tyumen, where he was recovering from a stab wound. ('Some bitch poked me with a knife'). The assailant, Khionia Guseva, was a disciple of one of his rivals, a defrocked monk named Sergei Trufanov Iliodor, who regarded him as a false prophet. Guseva accosted the *starets* as he walked down a street in Pokrovskoe and stabbed him in the stomach.[8]

Rasputin was not quite on first-name terms with the Nicholas and Alexandra - he called them 'Papa and Mama' - so from his hospital bed he cabled the Tsar, 'A terrible storm hangs over Russia. Disaster, grief, murky darkness and no light ... Let Papa not make war, for war will mean the end of Russia and yourselves.'

Nicholas ignored the warning. 'You can't imagine how glad I am the uncertainty is over,' he told his son's Swiss tutor, Pierre Gilliard. 'I've never been through so terrible a time.' One of his first actions was to change the name of his capital from the German-sounding Saint Petersburg (actually of Dutch origin) to the unmistakably Slavonic Petrograd. He also ordered the government to prohibit the sale of vodka during the mobilisation in order to guarantee the maximum turnout and then made it permanent.

The vodka ban brought protests that the rich could still drink as much wine, brandy and whisky as they liked, so the government imposed a general prohibition, driving liquor sales into a thriving black market. The ban inconvenienced the diplomatic corps but little. They poured their liquor from teapots instead bottles and even that pretence was dropped after a while.[9]

On 26 July the Tsar convened an emergency sitting of the Duma to debate the war. The Trudoviks and Social Democrats were due to make a joint statement expressing the determination of the people to defend Russia against the Central Powers. Cheidze, 'a rather simple-minded, sympathetic Georgian spouting the catchword patter of Marxism', approached Kerensky in the Catherine Hall. He had received a telegram, he said, stating that the Social Democrats in Germany had organised a demonstration against the war and that he had to support them.

'I objected it could not be true - the Germans were far too pigheaded to do that,' Kerensky says. Cheidze, however, withdrew from the pact and Kerensky went ahead and read out the statement on behalf of the Trudoviks:

> Firm as a rock in our faith that the mighty democracy of Russia, in harmony with the other forces of the Empire, will repel the assailant and defend the soil that bore it... We hope that the fraternal feeling which unites all the peoples of Russia will further deepen in the common sufferings of the battlefield, and will create an iron determination that, in the end, will also free our land from internal fetters. Steel your

hearts, peasants, workmen and all who burn for Russia's prosperity and progress. Steel them for days of adversity and trial. Muster the strength which is in you, that you may be the liberators of the land you have defended.[10]

Kerensky wasn't surprised when the anti-war rebellion in Germany failed to materialise – in fact, the German Social Democrats rallied behind the Kaiser in support of the war and earned Lenin's undying enmity.[11] Alexandra Kollontai, a Menshevik comrade of Leon Trotsky's, was in the Reichstag when the turncoats, some dressed in army uniforms, approved the Kaiser's military budget. 'I could not believe it,' she wrote in her diary that evening. 'I was convinced that either they had all gone mad, or else I had lost my mind.'

To the Bolsheviks' intense annoyance, Russian peasants and workers responded to Kerensky's heart-felt plea and lined up behind the war effort. It would require, one Communist historian noted sourly, 'painstaking work' to correct and eliminate 'the patriotic feelings of the revolutionary masses'.[12]

According to the Bolshevik deputy Alexei Badayev, Lenin's imprisonment in Austria had thrown the Bolsheviks into confusion. 'It was two months before we could satisfactorily reestablish communications with the Bolshevik Centre abroad,' he says. 'Our chief work was antiwar propaganda which, under war conditions, rendered every member who was caught liable to trial by court-martial and almost certain death.'[13]

Lenin was released from prison on 6 August once the Austrians accepted that he represented a far greater threat to the Tsar than to their Emperor. Nevertheless, he had to find somewhere safe in which to continue his work. Switzerland offered such a refuge and he and Nadezhda moved first to Berne and then to Zurich. Despite the risk to his comrades' lives, he launched a campaign of 'revolutionary defeatism' which insisted that the 'imperialist war' must be converted into a civil war against the Bolsheviks' class enemies. 'He who accepts the class struggle,' he said in his most quoted utterance on the subject, 'cannot fail to accept civil wars, which in every class society are the natural, and under certain conditions inevitable, continuation, development and intensification of the class struggle…'[14]

In Lenin's opinion Russia was 'a semi-colonial appendage of

western European finance-capital'. This might be so but his theory that a Russian defeat would bring about the collapse of the Romanovs and lead to revolution was problematical. In fact defeat would probably see Russian Poland, the Baltic provinces and Finland incorporated in a Greater Germany and lead to the occupation of European Russia. It would also stifle the revolutionary movement in Germany, perhaps indefinitely.[15]

The defection of many German Social Democrats had so shaken Alexandra Kollontai that she applauded Lenin's defeatist position. Half-Finnish, half-Ukrainian, she was described as an emotional woman 'prone to fall in love with young men and Utopian ideas'. She would become the most influential woman in Bolshevik ranks, sharing the opposition of male Bolsheviks to any campaign addressed specifically to the interests of women.[16]

Despite Lenin's contention that the Russian Army 'voted for peace with its feet', Russia's military contribution to the Triple Entente's war effort was far greater and much more successful than Allied politicians would admit. Serious military defeats undermined her troops' morale and desertion was widespread but over the next three years she would virtually knock Austria-Hungary and Turkey out of the war and lead one senior German commander to remark that the Russian Army remained, 'to the end, a redoubtable adversary'. Indeed, Russian troops on the Western Front were still fighting Germans when the guns fell silent on 11 November 1918.[17]

The outbreak of war had presented the Tsar with the chance to make peace with his people in the name of their common love for Russia. At the Duma's one-day sitting, Alexander Kerensky urged such a reconciliation in the interests of national defence. 'I felt,' he says, 'that the battle we had been waging against the remnants of absolutism could now be postponed.'

Perversely, Nicholas chose this moment of national emergency to take an aggressive course. He prorogued the Duma after just one day and, instead of uniting the nation, he and his ministers replied to the people's patriotic outpouring by redoubling the pressure of the autocracy. The war became a pretext for the Prime Minister, Ivan Goremykin, the Minister of the Interior, Nikolai Maklakov, and the Minister of War, General Sukhomlinov, to suppress all opposition.

Labour organisations and the entire labour press of Petrograd were closed down. Hundreds of thousands of 'disloyal' citizens were sent to Siberia. Poles, Jews, Finns and other non-Russian nationalities were persecuted.[18]

Goremykin likened himself to an old fur coat that had been taken out of mothballs and would one day be returned to the cupboard. It was a suitable epithet for a politician who was only too willing to do the Tsar's dirty work.

Immediately after the outbreak of hostilities one of Peter Durnovo's predictions in his February Memo came true: 'The main burden of the war will undoubtedly fall on us, since England is hardly capable of taking a considerable part in a Continental war, while France, poor in manpower, will probably adhere to strictly defensive tactics. The part of a battering ram, making a breach in the very thick of the German defence, will be ours, with many factors against us to which we shall have to devote great effort and attention.'

Nicholas received a desperate plea from his French allies. 'The French Army will have to withstand the terrible assault of twenty-five German corps,' Ambassador Paléologue, told him. 'I beg Your Majesty to order your troops to begin their offensive immediately. Otherwise the French Army is in danger of being crushed.'

The Russian General Staff, located in the west wing of the massive General Staff Building on Palace Square, had planned to attack the weaker Austrians while holding the Germans at bay but the rapid advance of the German armies on the Western Front made it imperative for Russia to create a diversion in the East. Nicholas ordered Grand Duke Nicholas Nikolaievich, Supreme Commander of the Russian Armed Forces, 'to open up the way to Berlin at whatever cost and as quickly as possible. We must aim at the destruction of the German Army'.[i][19]

Grand Duke Nicholas, a mediocre strategist at best, had been appointed to his vital post at the last minute. He had played no part in formulating military plans for the three sections of the Eastern Front: Northern, Western (or Central) and South-Western. Nevertheless, he was invested with unlimited powers over civilians under the 'Rules for the Administration of the Army in the Field'. No one except the

---

i The Foreign Ministry and the Ministry of Finance were in the east wing of the General Staff Building.

Tsar could challenge the authority of military commanders in the territories where the army was deployed, whether in the theatres of war or in Petrograd itself.

When Rasputin, who had returned to the capital, telegraphed the Stavka - the Russian Army's General Headquarters - for permission to bless the troops at the front, the Supreme Commander unhesitatingly replied, 'Do come! I will hang you.'[ii]

Two Russian armies, partially mobilised and lacking guns and ammunition, marched into East Prussia. The campaign started promisingly when General Paul von Rennenkampf's First Army defeated the Germans under General Max von Prittwitz at Gumbinnen, while General Alexander Samsonov's Second Army threatened the German rear. Samsonov, however, had only four-fifths of his infantry and only part of his cavalry reconnaissance force, while his logistical echelon struggled to catch up with him.[20]

For the first ten days operations were so successful that it seemed the whole province – bristling with the estates of the German officer corps east of the River Elbe - would soon be at the Russians' mercy, a quality that proved to be in short supply. Indeed, the invaders looted and burned down many towns and villages and nearly 1500 East Prussian civilians lost their lives in mindless atrocities.[21]

Facing a catastrophe that would derail the Schlieffen Plan, Moltke recalled sixty-seven-year-old General Paul von Hindenburg from retirement and placed him in command of the German Eighth Army on the Eastern Front, with a sour-faced technocrat, General Erich Ludendorff, as his Chief of Staff. 'The Duo', as they became known, formed what Hindenburg described as 'a happy marriage'.[22]

On arrival at the front they discovered that a General Staff officer, Colonel Max Hoffmann, had already shifted many Eighth Army units into position using fast rail movements to mount a counterattack against Samsonov's Second Army near the medieval battle site of Tannenberg. The eavesdroppers of German Intelligence then gave them a huge advantage when the Russians, lacking reliable military ciphers, revealed their movements by transmitting radio messages en

---

ii At the beginning of the war the Stavka was based in railway carriages at Baranovitchi, a Polish town on the line between Minsk and Brest-Litovsk, well placed behind the centre of the Russian front. In 1915 German advances forced it to move to Mogilev in eastern Belarus.

clair.[iii] German aircraft and airships hovering over the battlefield also provided vital information about the Russian dispositions.[23]

When two extra German corps arrived from the West, Samsonov was surrounded with surprising speed in a double envelopment and his two central corps had to lay down their arms. After telling his staff, 'The Emperor trusted me. How can I face him again?' the Russian commander committed suicide. A week later Rennenkampf's First Army was defeated at the First Battle of the Masurian Lakes. The Russians were driven out of the province with the loss of 250,000 men, all of their artillery and vast quantities of shells, which they could ill afford to lose. The civilian death toll was also horrific. Thousands of ethnic Germans, Poles, Latvians and Lithuanians were caught up in the fighting and an unspecified number were killed and wounded.

The Tsar, Grand Duke Nicholas and General Sukhomlinov were convinced that Russia's defeats were down to pro-German civilians, especially the large Jewish population, spying on Russian units and reporting their positions to the enemy. Indeed, newspapers and leaflets found in German trenches contained enemy propaganda aimed at undermining Russian authority by creating the impression that German and Habsburg forces would liberate the Jews from the Tsarist yoke. The Stavka issued orders making it legal to deport civilians and, if necessary, take them hostage. Alexander Kerensky says, 'The High Command caused veritable chaos within the country by forcibly evicting every Jewish member of the population from the area near the front.'[24]

News of the defeats in East Prussia triggered waves of discontent that never really ceased. Anti-German feeling was so strong in Russian towns and cities that civilians attacked anything visibly German. In two days of rioting in Moscow, 475 shops, offices and factories whose owners had German or German-sounding names were looted, 700 'Germans' were beaten up, sometimes fatally, and 207 apartments were ransacked.[25]

Meanwhile, the Tsarina's belief in Rasputin's mystical powers gave the *starets* and his clique of pro-German aristocrats, criminals, opportunists, incompetents and black marketeers a licence to drive the country towards physical and spiritual bankruptcy. Despite her

---

iii German radio operators were also guilty of sending messages *en clair* due to lack of time to encode them but the effect was less damaging to the Germany army.

fragile health, Alexandra dressed herself and her elder daughters in nurses' uniforms to care for wounded soldiers at Tsarskoe Selo, while Rasputin held sway over Petrograd society in her name. His influence in state policy-making was greatly exaggerated but his ability to secure appointments in exchange for money and sexual favours had become highly offensive to members of the political and aristocratic elites.

Alexander Kerensky became progressively disenchanted. Russia's overriding problem, as he saw it, was that the Romanov regime was 'enmeshed in Rasputin's web'. He blamed the *starets* for transforming Alexandra into 'an afflicted, unbalanced, passionately hysterical woman who thought only of her son and the power he would wield on becoming Tsar. His malign influence weakened the Romanovs and their government so critically that the whole regime became vulnerable'.[26]

It was necessary to remove the destroyers from power and, at the same time, to protect the army and the administrative apparatus from collapse. 'I am quite convinced that, but for the war, the revolution would have come not later than the spring of 1915, perhaps even the end of 1914,' he said. 'The war interrupted the crusade for liberty and the nation – under the leadership of men like Rasputin, Sukhomlinov and their ilk – was doomed.'[27]

Vladimir Sukhomlinov's career was symptomatic of the autocracy's malaise. Plump, greedy and obsequious, he was a relic of the Russo-Turkish War of 1877-78 in which he had won the Cross of Saint George as a cavalry officer. By 1914 he had more decorations than a Christmas tree, giving rise to the 'Sukhomlinov Effect' that an Army may travel on its stomach but defeat rides on its epaulets.

The Minister of War's fourth wife, Catherine, an attractive young widow, revelled in her new position. She ordered the latest couturier fashions from Paris, dined in expensive restaurants and threw lavish parties for her friends. To fund these extravagances, her husband fiddled his expenses, gambled on the stock market and creamed off a tidy profit from defence contracts.[28]

Now aged sixty-six, he deplored the phrase 'modern warfare' and boasted that he had not read a military manual for twenty-five years. He opposed training innovations that would have placed the emphasis on infantry firepower instead of sabres, lances and bayonets. Young officers who challenged his stupidity found themselves posted to remote regions of the Empire.[29] The Tsar indulged this elderly has-been because he was one of Rasputin's acolytes and because he found his buffoonish antics at Court amusing. According to Serge Sazonov, 'It was difficult to make him work but to get him to tell the truth was well-nigh impossible.'[30]

To cover up his inadequacies, Sukhomlinov had appointed as Chief of the General Staff a man who would pose no threat to his own position: Nikolai Yanushkevich, a clerk in the Ministry of War who had never held a field commission. Sir Alfred Knox, the Russian-speaking British liaison officer with the Russian Army, said Yanushkevich had found favour with the Tsar while serving as a captain in the palace guard.[31]

Sukhomlinov's dishonesty about the true state of Russia's armaments and Yanushkevich's incompetence would cost thousands of valiant Russian soldiers their lives. Once the troop trains started returning from the front with the sick, the wounded and the dying, it was impossible to hide the scale of the disaster that had befallen the Russian Army.

Two voluntary organisations, the Union of Zemstvos[iv] and the Union of Towns, had been permitted to offer assistance to the soldiers at the state's expense. Word soon leaked out through these bodies that the army had been starved of munitions and other essential war matériel. As Sukhomlinov insisted on dealing with the Duma through emissaries, outraged deputies, including Kerensky and Alexander Guchkov, the Octobrist leader who had visited the front and seen the misery for himself, grilled his surrogates about what had gone wrong. By the time the truth was wrung out of them, the damage had been done.

Russia's losses in East Prussia were counterbalanced to some extent in August-September 1914 by the brilliant victories of General Nikolai Ivanov, an unmissable figure with his massive shovel-shaped beard, against the Austrians in the south of Poland. The campaign was planned by his Chief of Staff, General Mikhail Alekseyev, a veteran of the Turkish and Japanese wars. The Central Powers suffered 130,000 casualties and most of their forces were driven out of Galicia. It was

---

iv The Local Government Association

just as well that Lenin had moved to Switzerland - had he fallen into Russian hands Ivanov would surely have hanged him as a traitor.[32]

Lemberg (Lvov, now Lviv in Ukraine), the capital of Galicia, had been captured early in September and, in November, Przemysl, the most important Galician stronghold consisting of thirty-five forts housing barracks, storehouses and magazines, was invested. The Austrians regarded Galicia as so important that its fall, according to the Austrian Official History, 'would undermine the spirit of the army and the people'.[33]

Galicia was indeed a major victory for Russia and it could have been so much better. At the onset of hostilities Conrad had foolishly split his forces into three, deploying one section to invade Serbia, another to hold Galicia against the Russians and the third to swing between those two theatres. The third section was heading south to attack Serbia when Conrad recalled it to stave off the Russian assault. As a result, the Serbian offensive failed for lack of strength and the reinforcements arrived too late to save Galicia.

Conrad's reckless gamble could have been the end of his army. Complete disaster was averted because Yanushkevich had assigned too few troops to either the Austrian or the German fronts. Had the Russians stuck to their original plan and thrown the bulk of their forces into Galicia, they would have destroyed Austria's forces on the Eastern Front as early as the autumn of 1914.[34]

The Germans also had a narrow escape from a crushing defeat east of Lodz in November when the Russians surrounded several divisions. In driving snow, the enemy troops fought their way back to their lines and reinforcements arrived just in time to turn the tide of battle. By the middle of December, 'General Winter' had brought the Russians' southern offensive to an end.[35]

The distressing thing for the Triple Entente was that Russia's sacrifices in East Prussia had failed to save the French Army from disastrous reverses in the West. Following the quasi-Napoleonic strategy of offensive à outrance (offensive to excess), the Supreme Commander, General Joseph 'Papa' Joffre, had sent the First, Second and Third French Armies storming north-eastwards into Lorraine, while the Fifth Army remained in France to cover the Belgian frontier.[36]

The German High Command[v] had anticipated the French attack and ordered its forces in Lorraine to dig in with the result that heavy machinegun fire cut the French infantry to pieces. In the Battle of the Frontiers between 14 August and 25 August, the French Army was defeated at a cost of 300,000 men, almost 25 per cent of the combatants in those engagements.[37]

By this time seven German armies totalling 1.5 million men were swinging west through Belgium in a huge enveloping move to drive the Allies back on either side of Paris and then roll them up against German armies approaching from the east. Anticipating the fall of the French capital, the Kaiser opined that it was '*ein frischer und fröhlicher Krieg* (a bright and cheery war)'. The German General Staff were so certain of victory that they had already struck a commemorative medal showing the Arc de Triomphe surmounted by the dates 1871 and 1914.[38]

Further north at Mons, entrenched in a dismal Belgian coal-mining area, the four infantry divisions of the British Expeditionary Force clashed with six divisions of General Alexander von Kluck's First Army. After six hours of intense fighting on 23 August, casualties on both sides were heavy. The British troops swept the battlefield with aimed fire from their ten-shot Lee-Enfield rifles at the rate of fifteen rounds per minute per man, leading the Germans to believe they were facing a machinegun battalion.

As darkness enclosed the battlefield, Lieutenant Edward Spears, the British liaison officer with the French Fifth Army, arrived breathless at the headquarters of the BEF's Commander in Chief, Field Marshal Sir John French, with the news that General Charles Lanrezac had ordered his forces to pull back. As French was relying on Lanrezac to cover his right flank, the British were in danger of encirclement.[vi] Cursing Lanrezac for 'abandoning the field', French ordered that most difficult of military manoeuvres, the fighting withdrawal. For ten gruelling days and nights, the 'Retreat from Mons' took place with the two forces locked in combat until the Germans were stopped at the River Marne. By then the situation was critical: the BEF had

---

v Oberste Heeresleitung (OHL), the Army Supreme Command. The Eastern Command was known as Ober Ost.

vi Lanrezac was demoted by Joffre 'for not living up to the hopes placed in him'. Overall, one hundred French generals were relieved of their commands.

sustained 12,000 casualties, Paris was threatened with invasion and the French Government had fled to Bordeaux.[39]

But despite the Kaiser's euphoria, the Germans got no further. At first light on 6 September 100,000 British troops, including a newly arrived fifth infantry division, joined a million French soldiers to attack the 750,000-strong German right wing on a front of 150 miles between Paris and the border fortress of Verdun on the River Meuse in northeastern France. Two thousand Parisian taxis were requisitioned to rush a division of Zouaves, recently arrived from Tunisia, to the frontline in the Marne Valley.[40]

Within a week, the Battle of the Marne had driven the Germans back sixty miles to the River Aisne, which crossed Picardy from east to west, and the Schlieffen Plan had hit the buffers. General von Moltke, in a state of nervous collapse, told the Kaiser, 'Your Majesty, we have lost the war.' He was instantly replaced as Chief of the General Staff with Wilhelm's favourite officer, General Falkenhayn. Germany's master plan had failed to deliver victory partly because Moltke tinkered with the numbers and partly because of Russia's campaign in East Prussia. The French and British commanders counted their lucky stars: Schlieffen called for a seven-to-one superiority between the hammer and the anvil on the Western Front; Moltke had reduced this superiority to three-to-one. The overriding consequence was that Germany would be forced to fight a war on two fronts for the next two years.

As the first winter set in, the Kaiser found himself having to contend with a rift between Falkenhayn, who argued in favour of the Western Front, and Hindenburg, who had been elevated to Commander in Chief of all German Forces on the Eastern Front following the victories at Tannenberg and the Mausurian Lakes. The East-versus-West dispute and the inherent weakness of his Austro-Hungarian allies would prove Wilhelm's undoing.

Back in London, the lovesick Prime Minister, Herbert Asquith, with a stupefying disregard for national security, sent a copy of a secret telegram giving precise details of the BEF's defensive positions on the Marne to his epistolary lover, Venetia Stanley. In an accompanying note, he wrote, 'I wish we had something like a code that we could use by the telegraph. This morning for instance I longed to let you know before anyone else what had happened & was happening.'[41]

His correspondence with Venetia Stanley flowed at the rate of three letters a day until her collection totalled 560 items. Had a single letter gone astray, the consequences could have been appalling for the British war effort. Asquith's infatuation with Miss Stanley showed in endearments such as: 'Think of me & love me & *write*. Every day I bless & love you more.' His most alarming act was committed in a letter marked 'Most Secret' and dated 24 October 1914 in which he informed Venetia of Allied plans for a naval and seaplane raid on the Zeppelin sheds in the Kiel Canal. '*Nobody* knows of this except W [Winston] & myself,' he wrote like a boastful schoolboy.

Meanwhile, the opposing forces on the Western Front were participating in a frantic 'Race to the Sea'. The First Battle of Ypres, fought in Flanders from 19 October to 11 November, prevented the Germans from seizing the Channel ports of Calais and Dunkirk but at huge cost to the BEF, which was literally decimated. By the end of the year, the conflict in the West had settled into its static phase of trench warfare stretching from the flooded coast of Belgium to the Swiss border. Attrition became the watchword on land and at sea, where British warships hunted German raiders and laid down a blockade to prevent supplies reaching Germany through Dutch and Scandinavian ports.

The Eastern Front, stretching 700 miles from Riga on the Gulf of Finland to the Romanian border, would remain more mobile until the Great Russian Retreat of April 1915. 'In the West, the armies were too big for the land,' Churchill observed. 'In the East, the land was too big for the armies.'[42] Commanders on both fronts were unable to land the knockout blow despite being equipped with the means to kill one another on an industrial scale.

The artillery bombardments of World War I – 'the iron hurricane' in Solzhenitsyn's mournful phrase – will rank with the greatest crimes against humanity of all time. Shellfire, in which a million exploding metal shells ripped through human flesh, caused seventy-five per cent of casualties on the battlefields. These powerful new weapons had new types of ammunition – for example, every exploding shell of the German Field Shrapnel 96 fired 300 lead bullets into enemy lines - while improvements in artillery tactics such as the creeping barrage, counter-battery work and aerial reconnaissance maximised the carnage.

Machineguns capable of firing 400 rounds a minute, hand grenades, poison gas (first used by Germany near Ypres in 1915 and, in the same year, at Bolimov in eastern Poland), iron tanks on caterpillar tracks, vastly improved rifles and the bayonet, as well as infection and disease, accounted for the other casualties. 'Victory,' Churchill said, 'was to be bought so dear as to be almost indistinguishable from defeat.'

Despite the BEF's modest numbers and the proficiency of its riflemen, it took the quartermasters some time to provide them with the same firepower as the enemy. When the shooting started, each infantry battalion had only two machineguns. British gunners also lacked heavy guns, mortars and howitzers for attacking entrenched positions. Moreover, they received less than one-fifth of the ammunition required to hold their own in counter-battery work.[43]

Nevertheless, the numbers being fed into the meat grinder on the Eastern and Western Fronts every day were so astronomical that it seemed impossible for the slaughter to continue. On a single day - 22 August 1914 - 27,000 French soldiers were killed, making it the bloodiest date in French military history. In the first six months up to the end of January 1915, British, French and German deaths totalled 102,196, with another 528,000 French soldiers permanently incapacitated. Russia's losses were even more horrific: in the first five months, she lost nearly two million men dead, wounded, captured and missing.

During the winter of 1914-15, the toll on the battlefield, coupled with shortages of food and fuel in Petrograd, Moscow, Kiev and other major cities heightened opposition to the war. Count Witte openly declared that Russia ought to make peace. England, he said, was determined to fight to the last drop of Russian blood.[44] 'Witte's condemnation of the war gave his enemies the opportunity to call him pro-German,' says Alexander Kerensky. 'In reality, it was simply that Witte fully realised that Russia had everything to lose in the war with hardly anything to gain.'[45]

After Witte's death, his widow, Matilda, Countess Witte, vehemently denied he was pro-German. 'The legend is entirely without foundation,' she said. 'When the war began he said, "Let the armies fight, since they have already started that madness, but let the diplomats immediately begin their work of making peace.".'[46]

Nicholas disagreed with Witte – and Durnovo – that Russia had nothing to gain from an Allied victory. As usual, his mind was on Byzantium. As soon as Turkey joined the Central Powers in October with the objective of recovering the Transcaucasian territories lost to Russia in the Russo-Turkish War of 1877-78, he became obsessed with the prospect of retrieving Constantinople as his share of the spoils. Russian occupation of the capital of the Byzantine Empire would guarantee his place in Paradise.

In November that year he issued a manifesto calling for 'the fulfilment of Russia's historic mission on the shores of the Bosphorus'. His mission had the unqualified support of Cousin Georgie, who whispered to Count Benckendorff, 'As to Constantinople, it is clear it must be yours.' The British Government duly obliged by secretly promising the Tsar that Russia would indeed possess the prize when Turkey and her allies were defeated.[47]

The pact illustrated Britain's concerns that Russia would abandon the Entente and make a separate peace with Germany. Sir Edward Grey described the promise in a secret message to the Russian Government as 'the greatest proof of friendship that it is in our power to give'. Berlin had the same idea. Sir Esmé Howard, British Minister at Stockholm – which had become the wartime crossroads for spies posing as diplomats - reported that Wilhelm had approached the Tsar with an offer to divide Constantinople equally between their two countries.

Meanwhile, General Sukhomlinov had managed to conceal the shortfall in shells and rifles until the New Year when the Budget Commission of the Duma discovered the truth. Even then, he claimed the army was in fine fettle and that there was no crisis. When the Duma deputies tried to test his assertions, they found themselves blocked by GHQ's wartime powers. The Minister of War and his incompetent Chief of Staff were untouchable.[48]

In November a new front opened in the Caucasus when the Turkish Minister of War Enver Pasha took personal command of the Ottoman forces and occupied two frontier towns. The Sultan, Mehmed V, in his capacity as Caliph, declared a *jihad* urging all Muslims in Russian-held territories to rise up against the infidel. The commander of the Caucasian Army, General Nikolai Yudenich, came under tremendous pressure as the Turks advanced into Adzharia with the aim of cutting off Russian access to oil-rich Baku on the Caspian.

Enver Pasha rated himself a great strategist but fundamental errors in his plan of attack confirmed the opinion of his German military adviser, Liman von Sanders, that he was dangerously incompetent. The Turks were dressed in summer uniform and suffered huge losses with the onset of winter in the mountainous terrain. As nearly half of Yudenich's force had been sent to East Prussia, he relied on volunteers from Armenia, the landlocked country on the dividing line between the Christian and Muslim worlds, to drive the Turks back over the border. Enver Pasha blamed his defeat in the Battle of Sarikamish – Turkey's greatest defeat of the war - on these volunteers and in the near future the Russian victory would serve as a prelude to the Armenian Genocide.[49]

To relieve pressure in the Caucasus, Nicholas requested the Allies to stage a diversionary attack on Constantinople. Members of the British War Council (Asquith, Lloyd George, Grey, Churchill and the Minister of War, Lord Kitchener) responded positively. On 15 January 1915 (NS) it was decided that 'the Admiralty should prepare for a naval expedition in February to bombard and take the Gallipoli Peninsula, with Constantinople as its objective'.

The idea had emanated from Lieutenant Colonel Maurice Hankey, Secretary of the Committee of Imperial Defence. Churchill, a brilliant but erratic amateur strategist, saw it as an opportunity for the Royal Navy to turn the Central Powers' eastern flank. Protruding from the Turkish mainland like a jagged tooth, the Gallipoli Peninsula commanded the Dardanelle Straits leading from the Aegean to Constantinople and the Black Sea. During the Crimean War it had served as a major encampment for British and French troops on their way to and from the Russian battlefields.

The Gallipoli Campaign exceeded the Tsar's wildest expectations. It would secure Constantinople during the war rather than after it and provide an ice-free route for Russia to export her grain and oil through Black Sea ports and to receive sorely needed Allied supplies and munitions from the Mediterranean. The original plan was that British battleships would force a passage through the Dardanelles, demolishing Turkish forts on the way. This plan had to be abandoned when 'the soft underbelly of Europe' proved to be heavily defended. Sir Ian Hamilton was then entrusted with the awesome task of capturing the Gallipoli Peninsula through amphibious landings virtually under the muzzles of Turkish machineguns.

Meanwhile, the Central Committee of the RSDLP held a conference near Petrograd on 17 November 1914 to discuss Lenin's 'War Theses', which had arrived by courier from his new base in Switzerland. An Okhrana spy alerted the police and the five Bolshevik deputies, Petrovsky, Muranov, Shagov, Samoylov and Badayev, were arrested, along with Trotsky's brother-in-law, Lev Kamenev, who had returned from exile abroad and was living legally in Petrograd.

All six were in custody awaiting trial when the Duma reconvened in January 1915, leaving only the Trudoviks and Mensheviks to shatter the illusion that the war was going well. Kerensky led the Opposition charge. He asserted that the allegations against the Bolshevik deputies were 'a slander against our comrades'. Rodzianko hastily cut his remarks from the Duma record but the Tsar seized on them to prorogue the session on 29 January.[50]

Kerensky revised his opinions about his Bolshevik 'comrades' after acting as defence counsel at their trial. The court heard that during their interrogation the accused had claimed that the event at which they had been arrested was a wedding or a birthday party and had nothing to do with Lenin's organisation in Switzerland.[51]

'I have seldom had to deal with such pusillanimous defendants in a political case,' Kerensky says. 'Kamenev distinguished himself. He not only repudiated Lenin's maxims; he produced a witness [to clear his name]. In fact, all the defendants, though defeatists, stoutly denied in court that they had any wish to see the Russian Army beaten.'[52]

Kamenev's witness, a well-known Social Democratic journalist, had published an article in a Marxist periodical under the heading 'Let There Be Victory'. He told the judges that the author of this patriotic headline was none other than Lev Kamenev. The defendants were all found guilty of belonging to an organisation dedicated to the overthrow of the state and exiled to Siberia for life.

'Few workers knew the contents of Lenin's Theses – they only knew that their spokesmen in the Duma had been thrown out,' Kerensky says. 'The Bolsheviks were delighted to have gained five martyrs and the fate of "the Five" became the dominant theme in the destructive operations carried out by Lenin's followers among the workers.'[53]

12

The Great Retreat

When the fighting resumed on the Eastern Front in February 1915, the Russians captured the great fortress of Przemysl after a four-month siege at a cost to its Austro-Hungarian defenders of 800,000 dead, wounded and missing. Advancing to within a few miles of Cracow, they broke through the passes of the Carpathians, the mountain range that forms a thousand-mile barrier across Central and Eastern Europe, and descended on to the Hungarian plain. Tsar Nicholas celebrated the capture of Galicia with a tour of inspection of the occupied territory. Here was the proof that he was right to demand a victorious conclusion to the war: Galicia today, Constantinople tomorrow.

Jews had lived in Przemysl for half a millennium but that was about to change. In Tsarist hands 17,000 Jewish men, women and children were rounded up and deported. Saratov on the Volga became the destination for many of these tragic convoys, while others were sent as far as Siberia.[1] Nicholas's imperial vision of assimilating the Austro-Hungarian province into the Crown was short-lived, however. 'There is only one possibility of victory,' the brilliant German strategist Colonel Hoffmann decided on 3 April. 'The centre of gravity of the war must be shifted to the East.' Germany transferred thousands of troops from France and Belgium and placed Field Marshal August von Mackensen in command of Austro-German forces to beat off the Russian challenge.[2]

The Tsar's attention switched to Gallipoli where, in the pre-dawn hush of 12/25 April, British, French, Australian and New Zealand troops (the Anzacs) arrived in rowing boats beneath the scrub-covered cliffs.[i] General Hamilton assigned the British 29th Division to the

---

i The Anzacs comprised one Australian division and one mixed Australian and New Zealand division; both were commanded by Lieutenant-General William Birdwood, an Indian Army officer of outstanding merit.

main landing beaches at Cape Helles, while the Anzacs would attack fifteen miles up the west coast at Gaba Tepe in an attempt to prevent Turkish reinforcements from reaching the southern battlefield. The French Corps Expéditionnaire d'Orient would make a diversionary landing on the Asiatic shore.

Gallipoli, however, was a military disaster. Four Turkish divisions had dug in on the peninsula and there were another two divisions on Turkey's Asiatic shore. The Anzacs gained a tactical advantage by landing without a preliminary bombardment but as they moved inland casualties mounted in battles against the crack Turkish 19th Division under the command of Mustafa Kemal Bey, the future Kemal Atatürk.

Within a matter of weeks, Gallipoli had lapsed into the same blood-stained stasis as the Western Front. It would eventually cost the lives of 40,000 troops among the 250,000 Allied casualties, nearly half of whom were victims of contagious diseases. Turkish losses were roughly the same. The campaign spelled the end of Churchill's influence in the direction of the war.[ii] Above all, it reinforced the view of British and French commanders that the Western Front was the only place in which the war could be decided.[3]

Allied reverses continued in May when Mackensen attacked the Russian salient in Galicia with a terrific bombardment that the Russian gunners had no means of answering. Having captured 1000 Austrian guns, a chronic shortage of shells denied them the chance to fight back. Enemy troops then smashed through the Russian line between Gorlice-Tarnow, near Cracow, and surged eastwards. The Russians were forced into headlong retreat.

As their hard-won conquests were lost one after another, Russia's military chiefs ordered civil administrators to evacuate their towns and villages. The rearguard then destroyed buildings, bridges, military stores and food supplies in a deliberate 'scorched earth' policy which in many places descended into criminal pillaging. Given no time to pack, Jewish families were driven by Cossack whips on to badly made roads heading east. Children and old people who became separated from their families died on the way.[iii]

---

ii In 1916 Churchill commanded a battalion on the Western Front but rejoined the government as Minister of Munitions in July 1917, serving in that post until he was appointed Minister of War in January 1919.

iii From 1914 to 1916 at least 189 Jewish communities in the Russian Empire, Galicia and Bukovina were cleared out.

Mackensen seemed unstoppable. 'The shortage in rifles was so great,' says Sir George Buchanan, 'that a considerable percentage of the Russians had to wait unarmed till they could pick up the rifles of their fallen comrades.' The German forces recaptured most of Eastern Galicia following the fall of Przemysl and Lemberg, while Warsaw, Novogeorgievsk, Kovno, Grodno and Brest-Litovsk surrendered in quick succession. Brest-Litovsk, the Polish border town which had seen savage fighting, was reduced to a smoking ruin.

Florence Farmborough, an English nurse with the retreating Tenth Field Surgical Unit, worked in a small dressing station in the village of Frishtak, south of the Vistula. 'Still the wounded came,' she wrote in her diary. 'They came in groups, singly, on stretchers, in vans, battered and mutilated. We cared for them as best we could; God knows that our hearts were in our work, for we felt their agony, endured their despair and shared their misery.'[4] The dead were buried in shallow graves scraped in the forest floor and marked with two pieces of wood nailed together in the shape of the cross, or wrapped in sheets and lowered into a common grave.

The thunder of big guns drew ever closer and shrapnel crackled overhead. From time to time, tremendous explosions rent the air as the sappers blew up another bridge. The horizon was tinged red with the glow of many fires as villages and towns were put to the torch. At Yaroslav, west of Lemberg, the defenders held the enemy at bay for three days 'without shells and cartridges'. 'Ours fought like devils,' one of the exhausted survivors said, 'with clubs and rifle butts – even with fists when all else failed and we came face to face.'[5]

It later emerged that General Sukhomlinov and his Chief of Staff Yanushkevich had squandered the arms budget on fortifying old fortresses while starving artillery regiments of the latest field-guns and ammunition. Each of the 114 infantry divisions had just forty-eight field-guns and the entire army could call upon only 450 light howitzers and only 84 modern heavy guns. Grand Duke Nicholas's inept leadership and the collapse of the Russian railway network - clogged with wounded soldiers and civilian deportees – ensured a calamity.[6]

Meanwhile, the Gallipoli disaster, Britain's own shell shortage (for which Lord Kitchener was largely to blame) and a bizarre altercation between Churchill and the First Sea Lord, Lord 'Jackie' Fisher, created a political upheaval in Westminster. Asquith was in poor shape to handle it – in addition to writing to Venetia Stanley, his daily routine included an afternoon visit to his Pall Mall club and games of bridge in the evening. He was also drinking heavily, giving rise to his nickname, 'Squiffy'.

On 12 May 1915, he received the shattering news that Venetia was engaged to be married and that their correspondence would have to cease. To make matters worse, her fiancé was none other than his Jewish Parliamentary Private Secretary, Edwin Montagu.[iv][7] His response on 25 May was to change direction and form a national coalition with Unionist members (Law, Balfour, Curzon and Carson) and the Leader of the Labour Party, Arthur Henderson. Churchill and Haldane were jettisoned and Jackie Fisher was allowed to resign. The Chancellor, Lloyd George, was put in charge of a newly created Ministry of Munitions and the shell problem was solved, though not in time for the 1915 campaigns.[8]

Russia's shortfall in munitions was no greater than any other country's and yet the effect on the battlefield had been far greater on the Eastern Front. The Octobrist deputy Alexander Guchkov, an industrialist himself, initiated the All-Russian War Industries Committees to mobilise the manufacturers of ammunition and military equipment for a prolonged war. Despite great claims about its efficiency, the committees' main contribution was to enrich their leading members.[9] V. D. Nabokov was outraged over the mismanagement of the war. 'It was clear that to support Sukhomlinov, Maklakov and Shcheglovitov meant to lead Russia knowingly to defeat and catastrophe,' he said.[10]

Sukhomlinov was the first to go. When General Joffre wrote to him to express his concern about Russia's shell and artillery supplies, the compulsive liar replied, 'There is nothing to worry about'. Joffre, however, had his doubts. He referred Sukhomlinov's letter to Ambassador Paléologue, who showed it to Serge Sazonov. The Foreign Minister was aghast at this bald-faced untruth and handed the letter to the Tsar. On 11 June 1915 Nicholas presided over a joint meeting of the Stavka and his ministers to discuss the issue. The

---

iv At Montagu's request Venetia agreed to convert to Judaism. She also laid down some conditions of her own: she would have sex with him only when she felt like it and she would have the right to extramarital affairs.

following day Sukhomlinov's scandalous reign came to an end. His replacement at the Ministry of War was General Alexei Polivanov, a seasoned campaigner whose liberal inclinations had thus far retarded his advancement.[11]

When Nicholas reconvened the Duma on 19 July, even moderate deputies called for the dismissal of Ivan Goremykin. They also asked the Tsar to take the Duma into a real partnership with the Crown. The Prime Minister was one of Rasputin's stooges and the Tsar refused to dismiss him. Instead, he sacked three of the most hated figures in the government, Shcheglovitov, Nikolai Maklakov and the Procurator of the Holy Synod, V. K. Sabler, former deputy to the grand inquisitor, Konstantin Pobedonostsev.

On 21 August roughly half the deputies banded together to form the Progressive Bloc under the leadership of Paul Miliukov, Alexander Konovalov, Nikolai Shidlovsky, Vasily Shulgin and the head of the Union of Zemstvos, Prince Georgi Lvov, with the sole purpose of democratising the governing of the country. They called on Nicholas to appoint a 'ministry of national confidence' headed by the Duma President, Mikhail Rodzianko, and including the Kadet and Octobrist leaders Miliukov and Guchkov, plus the most honest Tsarist bureaucrats, Krivoshein, General Polivanov and Count Ignatiev.[12]

Contrary to the advice of a majority of his ministers, the Tsar turned down this bold offer of power-sharing. Having sacked four ministers, he believed that any further concessions would be seen as weakness. He agreed, however, to the formation of emergency consultative committees on defence, transport, fuel and food in all ministries concerned with the conduct of the war. They were to include representatives of the Duma, the State Council, the Union of Zemstvos and the Union of Towns.[v] [13]

The most important casualty of the Great Retreat was the Russian Commander in Chief. Grand Duke Nicholas Nikolaievich had survived the military defeats and the scandal over the displacement of millions of civilians, many of whom had been brutalised, but he could not survive the Tsarina's animosity. When he joined Duma politicians in calling for the dismissal of conservative ministers and urging the Tsar to make concessions to public opinion, she encouraged Rasputin to spread the rumour that his prestige was eclipsing that of his Sov-

---

v The two unions were merged under the name Zemgor.

ereign. 'The evil spirit has returned,' the Dowager Empress Maria Fyodorovna wrote in her diary, meaning Rasputin, 'and Alix wishes that Nicky should assume the Supreme Command instead of [Grand Duke] Nicholas. She is mad if she actually wants it....'[14]

Following a visit from Nicky to the Elagin Palace, her summer residence at the mouth of the Neva, the Dowager continued in the same vein: 'Nicky came and started the conversation himself. I was so horrified that I nearly had a stroke. I told him all that was on my mind. I insisted it would be the biggest mistake. I entreated him not to do so. Everybody would regard it as being Rasputin's orders. I think this impressed him because his face went very red. He does not understand the misfortune he may bring down upon the country and upon ourselves.'[15]

Alexandra, however, was so insistent that Nicholas ignored his mother's advice and on 23 August 1915 he assumed Supreme Command of his armies, making him the first Tsar since Peter the Great to do so. Grand Duke Nicholas was sent off to the Caucasus as Viceroy, taking Yanushkevich with him. As his Chief of Staff with free rein to conduct operational matters, the Tsar appointed the dependable General Alekseyev, a much better strategist than either the Tsar or Grand Duke Nicholas.[16]

'Everyone was against the Tsar becoming Supreme Commander,' Kerensky says, 'but still the decision was taken for it had been approved by "Our Friend".' From then on, Nicholas spent most of his time at Mogilev, 400 miles south of Petrograd, or visiting the troops in the field even further away from home. As he was absent for long periods from Tsarskoe Selo and Peterhof (renamed Petrodvorets), he was unable to keep in touch with his ministers.

On 3 September the Duma was prorogued. Bruce Lockhart noted in his diary, 'The Progressists and Social Democrats left the room during the reading of the Tsar's ukase (decree). Kerensky, the Trudovik deputy, is said to have cried, "Down with the Government" and even to have raised his voice against the Emperor.'[17]

The day-to-day running of the country fell increasingly into the hands of Alexandra and Rasputin. 'I have no patience with ministers who try to prevent [my husband] doing his duty,' the Tsarina told Sir George Buchanan. 'The situation requires firmness. The Emperor, unfortunately, is weak, but I am not and I intend to be firm.'[18]

Suspicions among the populace that Alexandra's German heritage made her an enemy spy was a constant source of disquiet. 'The Tsarina's blind faith in Rasputin led her to seek his counsel not only in personal matters but also on questions of state policy,' Kerensky says. 'General Alekseyev tried to talk to the Tsarina about Rasputin but only succeeded in making an implacable enemy of her. Alekseyev told me later about his profound concern on learning that a secret map of military operations had found its way into the Tsarina's hands. But like many others, he was powerless to take any action.'

According to Kerensky, the Tsarina's most intimate conversations with Rasputin took place in 'Annie's little house' – the villa of her friend Anna Vyrubova, a key member of the Court camarilla, close to the gates of Tsarskoe Selo. He subscribed to the conspiracy theory that German agents collected secret information via the camarilla. 'Rasputin was a godsend for any intelligence service,' he says. 'The German Government would have been mad not to exploit him.' While it had never been established that Rasputin was a paid enemy agent, Kerensky insisted there was no doubt 'he was a pawn in the hands of people who were agents of the German General Staff'.[19]

The antisemitic Sir George Buchanan was convinced that Russia's real enemies were pro-German Jewish bankers based in Petrograd. 'Rasputin was not in direct communication with Berlin and he did not receive money directly from the Germans but he was largely financed by certain Jewish bankers, who were, to all intents and purposes, German agents,' he said. 'As he was in the habit of repeating to these Jewish friends of his all that he had heard at Tsarskoe Selo, and as the Empress consulted him on both military and political questions, much useful information reached the Germans through this indirect channel.'[20]

What Buchanan had failed to grasp was that Grishka Rasputin exploited rich Jewish businessmen as readily as everyone else. When he wanted to publish his own newspaper, he summoned Grigory Benenson to his apartment on the third floor of a block of flats in unfashionable Gorokhovaya Street. 'He told me that all the newspapers were corrupt and that the peasants were not being fairly treated in them,' Benenson says. 'They had nowhere to express their point of view, so he was going to fill the breach. He had writers, printers, everything ready, and I had been given the privilege of paying for it.

Could I turn my back and tell him to go to hell? I am a Jew; the man could finish me.'[21]

Buchanan lamented it was his melancholy task 'to follow in the Emperor's footsteps and to watch him, with his inbred fatalism, deliberately choosing a path that was to lead him and his [family] to their doom'. The Ambassador thought Nicholas 'a lovable man possessed of many good qualities, a true and loyal ally, having, in spite of all appearances to the contrary, his country's true interests at heart'.

Sergie Witte, a sterner critic than the Ambassador, had written his memoirs with the intention of having them published posthumously. Word reached Nicholas that they contained seriously embarrassing material about himself. When Witte died earlier that year - on 28 February - the Tsar had ordered the study of his house to be sealed and all his papers confiscated. But Witte knew his man. He had written the book during his holidays in Biarritz and had then placed the manuscript in a Paris bank under his wife's name for safe-keeping.

Matilda took the added precaution of moving the manuscript to another bank in Bayonne under a friend's name. It was just as well. 'The Chief of the General Staff came to me in the Emperor's name and said that His Majesty, having perused the table of contents of my husband's memoirs, had become interested in them and wished to read them,' she said. 'I replied that to my regret I was unable to present them to His Majesty because they were kept abroad.'[22]

Despite the pressing emergencies of the time, the military attaché was sent from the Russian Embassy in Paris to search the Wittes' villa at Biarritz. He came away empty-handed. The memoirs were eventually published in New York in 1921, too late to do any damage to Nicholas but nevertheless providing a fascinating view of Nicholas's character and lack of judgment.[vi]

According to Witte, the Tsar surrounded himself with incompetents because he would not tolerate having anybody around him who was more intelligent than himself, or anybody 'with opinions differing from those of the Court camarilla'. 'The extent of Alexandra's influ-

---

[vi] Witte was right to believe that the Tsar would have destroyed his memoirs if he had found them. Nicholas had not only torn up the diary of a former minister because it contained critical remarks about him but he blamed the diary's loss on an innocent officer who had been charged with sorting out the man's papers.

ence upon her husband can hardly be exaggerated,' he warned. 'In many cases she actually directs his actions as the head of the Empire. She might have been harmless even as the Empress of Russia were it not for the lamentable fact that His Majesty has no will power at all. On one occasion, I recall, Nicholas referred to Her Majesty as "a person in whom I have absolute faith". The fate of many millions of human beings is actually in the hands of that woman.'[23]

Sir George Buchanan agreed that the Tsar's main weakness was his wife. 'The Empress, though a good woman actuated by the best of motives, was instrumental in bringing about the final catastrophe,' he said. 'Her fatal misconception of the meaning of the crisis through which Russia was passing made her impose on the Emperor ministers who had no other recommendation than that they were prepared to carry out her reactionary policy.'[24]

The German advance ground to a halt in late September 1915 after starvation, disease and Russian counter-attacks had taken their toll on the invading forces. Battle casualties were high on both sides. The Russians, however, consolidated a new front running from the Baltic Sea through the Belarusian forests and Pripet Marshes to the Romanian border. This line would remain intact until September 1916.

Meanwhile, the home front was becoming dangerously unstable. It had become painfully obvious that misrule at the highest levels was creating chronic shortages in the cities. The railways were overstretched and river transport, which carried much of the grain, oil and timber to market, was also breaking down. The long queues that formed overnight outside breadshops would become an outward symbol of the looming crisis.

Staple foodstuffs like flour, cheese and sugar were hard to find. Indeed, the families of many officers relied on parcels that their husbands were able to send from military stores at the front. Even Mikhail Rodzianko's Guardsman son brought him packets of sugar whenever he came home on leave.[25]

'If there has ever been a government that richly deserved a revolution,' Colonel Knox wrote in a report at this time, 'it is the present one in Russia. If it escapes, it will only be because the members of the Duma are too patriotic to agitate in this time of crisis.' He went to see Rodzianko to discuss the shortages. 'I spoke of the preventable sufferings of the people and of my astonishment at their patience under conditions that would have very soon driven me to break windows. He only laughed and said that I had a hot head.'[26]

Vasily Shulgin was one of the first deputies to address the threat that Rasputin posed to Russia. 'No one understood when that man crossed the threshold of the Tsar's palace that a killer had arrived,' he said. 'He kills because he is two-faced. To the Tsar's family he turns his holy face, looking on which the Empress sees the Holy Spirit living in a holy man. But to Russia he turns his degenerate mug, drunken and lustful, the mug of a forest satyr from the Tobolsk *taiga*... Because of his duplicity neither side can understand the other. With their sense of resentment growing by the hour the Tsar and Russia lead one another toward the abyss.'[27]

Ivan Goremykin, the old fur coat, had lost the support of Rasputin and was about to be returned to the cupboard. At the *starets*' suggestion Nicholas replaced him with Boris Stürmer, a member of the State Council and former Master of Ceremonies at the Russian Court. Stürmer thought it would be advisable to change his German surname before assuming office but the Tsarina and Rasputin considered that unnecessary. Taking up his duties in February 1916, he regretted not doing so: leftwing deputies competed with one another to make up jokes about his German origins. Kerensky's contribution was that 'he speaks Russian with a Hohenzollern accent'.

When the fifth session of the Duma opened on 9 February 1916 the Tsar turned up in person to allay some of the hostility towards his government. His presence surprised everybody until it was whispered that he was acting on Rasputin's advice. Even the Opposition were impressed, however, when he addressed the deputies as 'representatives of the people'. This was the last that many of them would ever see of him. He left for the Stavka the following day and he would never set foot in Petrograd again.[28]

The Duma had voted by 245 to 30 in a secret session for Sukhomlinov to be prosecuted over the munitions scandal. He was arrested and incarcerated in the Peter and Paul Fortress. His wife Catherine threw herself on the mercy of Rasputin. According to the Okhrana sleuths who followed him everywhere, the *starets* paid no fewer than sixty-nine visits to her apartment. He confided to a crony, 'She has stolen my heart.'[29]

Roman Malinovsky's disappearance had removed from the Duma the only man who could rival Alexander Kerensky in appealing to the masses. Given the banishment of the other five Bolsheviks and the plodding mediocrity of the Menshevik speakers in the absence of Irakli Tsereteli, he became the undisputed spokesman of the urban proletariat. E. H. Wilcox, the London *Daily Telegraph*'s correspondent, had no doubts about his power: 'He had only to lift a finger to fill the streets of Petrograd with men and women ready for almost anything.'[30]

'What has Alexander Fyodorovich said?' or 'What will Alexander Fyodorovich say?' were the key questions in the industrial quarters on Viborg Side and the shipyards and ironworks at the mouth of the Neva. The Okhrana named him 'the chief ringleader of the present revolutionary movement'. Plain-clothes spies tracked his every move. Nikolai Sukhanov (real name: Nikolai Nikolaievich Himmer), a Left Menshevik historian and former political exile, described Kerensky sprinting out of a building and jumping on to a moving tramcar while the police jumped into their droshky and gave chase. Kerensky then abandoned that tram and jumped on to one going in the opposite direction. The Okhrana's nickname for him was 'Speedy'.[31]

Despite the later claims of Lenin and Trotsky that Kerensky had no meaningful influence whatsoever on the Revolution, the Okhrana files remove any doubt about the impact of his revolutionary activities. One read: 'The revolutionary propaganda of Kerensky has expressed itself in the watchword, "Struggle for power and for a Constituent Assembly" and led to a systematic discrediting of the government party in the eyes of the masses. For the success of these demands Kerensky has recommended the workmen to establish impromptu factory groups for the formation of soviets (councils) of workmen's and soldiers' delegates on the model of 1905, with the object of impelling the movement in a definite direction at the given moment. For the greater success of his agitation Kerensky is circulating among the workmen rumours that he is receiving from the provinces numbers of letters with the demand that he overthrow the Romanov Dynasty and take power into his own hands.'[32]

As he approached his thirty-fifth birthday, Kerensky's hyperactive lifestyle almost cost him his life. He was pale and feverish but despite health warnings he refused to slow down. The family had moved into an apartment in Tverskaya Street, next to the Tauride Gardens, to make life easier for him but its proximity to the Duma had only increased his workload.

Finally, he collapsed. On 12 February 1916 his sister Elena Kerenskaya, now a qualified physician, escorted him to a Finnish sanatorium at Bad Grankulla, a village near Helsinki. The Okhrana suspected that the purpose of the trip was to make contact with dissidents who were fighting for Finnish independence. Kerensky had no such plans and the officers sent to spy on him found themselves cooling their heels in Bad Grankulla's streets while suspicious residents kept them under surveillance.[33]

The clinic referred Kerensky to a specialist, Professor Frans Krogius, who was appalled by his condition and diagnosed a recurrence of tuberculosis. Having survived TB of the hip as a child, he now had the disease in his kidneys. This was usually a terminal condition and Professor Krogius doubted his life could be saved. On 16 March he operated and was able to save the patient at the expense of one of his kidneys. This impairment would affect Kerensky's health for the rest of his life.

On 22 April he celebrated his birthday at the Grankulla sanatorium with caviar and chocolate sent to him by men and women who identified themselves as 'Alexander Fyodorovich's admirers'. After two months' convalescence, he judged himself recovered and, against medical advice, rushed back to Petrograd, where he threw himself into political work with his customary fervour. He made twelve speeches in sixteen days, including a furious attack on a government attempt to hoodwink the peasantry with a bogus offer of equality. His single kidney could not cope with the strain. Exhausted and ailing, he returned to the sanatorium for another six weeks during which his marriage broke down.

Throwing caution to the wind, he found himself attracted to one of his visitors, Dr Elena 'Lilya' Vsevolodovna Birukova, née Baranovskaya, one of the children of Vsevolod and Lydia Baranovsky, whom he had known in his Tashkent days. Lilya had been born at Verny in 1892 and was now a beautiful twenty-three-old. She was staying with her parents in Helsinki, where General Baranovsky served in the Imperial Finnish Senate as one of the Tsar's hand-picked servants. Having reestablished contact with Kerensky, her visits to the sanatorium became quite frequent.

Casually dressed in rollneck sweater, hair trimmed in its familiar crewcut, Kerensky was at his most charismatic. He invited Lilya to join his little circle of comrades in the woods during the Midsummer Festival. He was a generous host, humorous, worldly, flirtatious. Over caviar, chocolate and sweet tea, they reminisced about Tashkent and marvelled at the coincidence that had brought them together. Not only were Lilya Birukova and Olga Kerenskaya first cousins but their mothers were sisters and their fathers were brothers. Their paternal grandfather, Stephan Ivanovich Baranovsky, had been Professor of Russian Language and Literature at the Alexander Imperial University in Helsinki and an inventor of military ordnance.

His own love affair had also begun in a health resort. Strolling through the Brunnsparken in southeastern Sweden, he noticed a young woman standing at the gate of one of the villas. Her name was Sophia Johanna Ottilla von Wittenheim, and she was a baroness from an impoverished German family. Stephan arranged an introduction through a mutual friend and they were married on 9 February 1845. Their son, Vladimir Baranovsky, founded the Baranovsky Works in Vyborg on the right bank of the Neva. One of his inventions was a light, quick-firing 2.5-inch gun on a recoilless carriage which was used by the Russian Army in the Russo-Turkish War of 1877-1878. Vladimir was killed during a test firing in 1879 when a faulty cartridge backfired and mortally wounded him.

Lilya was also married and her three-year-old son Vsevolod, nicknamed 'Olik', accompanied her on her visits to the sanatorium. Her husband, Colonel Nicholas Pavlovich Birukov, was commander of the Fourth Rifle Division - the so-called 'Iron Division'. Two awards of the Order of Saint George during a long and distinguished career placed him in a special category of heroism. While he was away with the army, Lilya had studied medicine at Bestuzhev University, the largest and most prominent women's higher education institution in Imperial Russia, and had completed her final year during her pregnancy. None of this seemed to matter to the love-struck couple. Lilya was a writer of short stories and she was attracted to Kerensky's passionate eloquence when he talked about overthrowing the Tsar and creating a socialist Utopia.

According to Kerensky's biographer, '[Lilya] had the resources to indulge in cosmetics and the trappings of femininity for which Olga had neither time, money nor interest. As the Empire crumbled, she found her way from the protection of a leading Tsarist official, her father, to that of a leading revolutionary.' It is doubtful Kerensky would have recognised Lilya from that description, which made her sound utterly superficial, calculating and cold-blooded. In his eyes, she was a desirable, intelligent woman and he thought he had found a soulmate. When he expressed his feelings to Lilya, he was overjoyed that she reciprocated them. They knew, however, there would be trouble ahead. Lilya's husband, who was nearly twenty years older than her, was devoted to her and their son, while Kerensky could hardly avoid the fact that he was not only betraying his own family but cuckolding an honourable man.[34]

Kerensky's illness had prevented him from joining members of the Duma and the State Council on a goodwill visit to Britain and France that spring. The delegation included Paul Miliukov, Andrei Shingarev and Alexander Protopopov. Welcoming the group to Buckingham Palace, King George V heaped praise on the Russian war effort:

> I can assure you, gentlemen, that the whole nation has followed with the keenest interest and the deepest admiration the marvellous feats of arms performed by the gallant Russian troops throughout this war and the brilliant achievements which, conjointly with the Russian naval forces, they have recently accomplished, in the face of formidable difficulties, in the Asiatic provinces of the Ottoman Empire.
>
> I have conveyed on various occasions to my dear cousin and ally, the Emperor, your august Sovereign, my warm congratulations on the victories of his arms, and I do not desire to let this opportunity pass by without personally expressing to you my hearty acknowledgement of the eminent services rendered to the common cause by Russian skill, courage and endurance.[35]

There were more speeches - and many glowing toasts - the following day when the Russian delegation visited the Palace of Westminster. Liveried ushers escorted them from the Prime Minister's private rooms to the Lord Chancellor's drinks party in the House of Lords Library and thence to lunch with the Speaker of the House of Commons in the

Gothic splendour of the Harcourt Room.[vii]

Protopopov, who was one of the two vice chairmen of the Duma, replied to several of the speeches on behalf of the group with a barefaced bravado that astounded his companions. Germany's only chance of escaping defeat, he declared, lay in sowing distrust among the Allies. False rumours had been spread that the differences between Russia's political parties extended to the conduct of the war. 'As a representative of the Imperial Duma, I desire to say, with all the emphasis I can command, that there is not a word of truth in these suggestions,' he said. 'The Russian people and their representatives are absolutely at one in their conviction that this war must be carried to a triumphant conclusion.'[36]

British parliamentarians cheered these bold, though demonstrably untrue, sentiments, while Miliukov and Shingarev squirmed in embarrassment. Shortly afterwards Protopopov produced 'a very strange impression' during a visit to the Russian Embassy at Chesham House in Chesham Place, Belgravia. 'From behind the mask of liberal patriotism we caught glimpses of a buffoon's grimace,' says Konstantin Nabokov, V. D. Nabokov's brother, who was Counsellor at the embassy. 'He told us the most amazing stories about the Court, the Metropolitan and Rasputin. Once or twice, however, his tongue slipped and he referred to the Duma in terms of ironical contempt.'[37]

Listening to Protopopov, Count Benckendorff muttered to Nabokov, *'C'est un imbecile.'* Indeed, Protopopov's rolling eyes, constant sweats, outbursts of foul language and disjointed conversation were symptoms of tertiary syphilis, which he was treating with liberal doses of drugs, one of which was probably cocaine.[38]

After being feted in Paris, the delegation returned home via Stockholm. While Sweden remained in a state of armed neutrality, the Swedish nobility and many Swedish politicians were decidedly pro-German. German businessmen, many of them indistinguishable from German agents, roamed freely around the capital. Protopopov let his colleagues go on ahead while he spent some time in the Swedish capital.[39] Disregarding the unity of purpose about which he had spoken so eloquently, he met the German industrialist Hugo Stinnes, the German banker Fritz M. Warburg and the Swedish Minister of Foreign Affairs, Knut Wallenberg. The Germans sensed

---

vii Later renamed the Churchill Dining Room

there was something wrong with their Russian visitor and treated him with enormous respect. They succeeded in persuading him that the prevailing British blockade could not possibly starve Germany into surrender and that Russia should negotiate a separate peace to save herself from further destruction.

Back in Petrograd there was uproar when Protopopov reported these talks to the Central Committee of the Progressive Party. The liberal-conservative coalition in the Duma disowned him for speaking to German emissaries. Maurice Paléologie wrote in his memoirs, 'Though the affair remains somewhat obscure, there is no doubt that he spoke in favour of peace. When he returned to Petrograd he made common cause with Stürmer and Rasputin, who immediately put him in touch with the Empress. He was soon taken into favour and initiated into the secret conclaves at Tsarskoe Selo. He was entitled to a place there on the strength of his proficiency in the occult sciences, principally spiritualism, the highest and most doubtful of them all.'[40]

Meanwhile, in Bad Grankulla, Kerensky's concern over how Olga would react to his affair with Lilya tugged at his emotions. He was conscious of the damaging effect that her father's betrayal had had on her as a child, and he was aware of his responsibilities towards their sons Oleg and Gleb, then aged eleven and nine. But this was an age of uncertainty in which every family with a soldier at the front walked in the shadow of death; an age in which war had twisted the traditional rules of morality. In the light of these harsh realities, Alexander and Lilya clung to the romantic notion that love was the most important thing in the world and that love would conquer all.

Olga, who had given up her job to work in a Petrograd hospital, had been sent to the Polish front to nurse the wounded, leaving the boys in the care of Maria and a servant. She found nursing therapeutic. 'When I bent down to wash the soldiers' dirty feet, or cleaned and dressed their nasty-smelling and decaying wounds, I experienced an almost religious ecstasy,' she said. 'I bowed before all these soldiers, who had given their lives for Russia. I have never felt such ecstasy.' Returning to Petrograd, Olga found out about her husband's affair by chance. 'A friend accused her of blanking her while walking down the street with Grandfather,' says Stephen Kerensky. 'Lilya was the spitting image of Olga, so she knew the woman must have been her cousin.'

The reasons behind the breakup of the Kerenskys' marriage have never been fully explained. Kerensky's other grandson, Oleg Kerensky Jr, says, 'In later life Grandfather told me that he had to leave Grandmother because she became obsessed with her sons and had no time or energy for him when he came home late and exhausted from work. When I somewhat cheekily suggested that there was no circumstances in which he would have stayed with one woman all his life, he grinned and admitted that I was probably right. He was a man of enormous vitality, physical and mental, and needed pastures new at regular intervals.'[41]

Olga added to the mystery when she told Stephen Kerensky that she had had an abortion during the marriage and had then 'closed her bedroom door' to her husband. From those two scraps of information, it seems the marriage was already in trouble when Lilya turned up in Alexander's life in the summer of 1916. He had just survived a life-threatening illness which had made him painfully aware of his mortality and it seems he was looking for a new relationship to revitalise him. None of this absolved him of blame for the distress he caused his family and he never denied that culpability.

By the summer of 1916 the killing on the Eastern and Western fronts had taken on a life of its own. The greatest slaughter had taken place on France's eastern border. The Battle of Verdun opened on 21 February 1916 with a nine-hour German artillery barrage on its forts and villages. Falkenhayn's intention was to 'bleed France white' by seizing the heights to the east of the Meuse and wiping out successive waves of French troops when they counter-attacked. Verdun was supposed to be impregnable but, unbeknown to the French public, many of its armaments had been moved in 1915 to more needy areas on the Western Front.[42]

By the end of April the French had lost 133,000 men to heavy shellfire and in hand-to-hand fighting in the Verdun salient but the Germans were 'bleeding white' in almost the same proportion as the French, with 120,000 casualties.[viii] Month-old corpses littered the battlefield and the incessant bombardment drove men mad. Lieutenant

---

viii France's Official War History, published in 1936, gave her losses in the Battle of Verdun in the ten months between February and December 1916 as 377,231, of which 162,308 were killed or missing. German losses were estimated at just under 337,000, with more than 100,000 dead or missing.

Jean Hugo, the twenty-year-old great-grandson of Victor Hugo, recorded his experiences in words and sketches. 'The entrance to our shelter opened out on a moon landscape [and] our frontlines skirted one of the vast volcano craters,' he wrote in his diary. 'The earth was pock-marked with shellholes and fountains gushed yellowish water into the mud. German bodies, dried out and black, appeared like broken umbrellas, hung out on the barbed wire. Rats abounded.'[43]

After receiving French and Italian pleas for relief from enemy pressure at Verdun and in the Tyrol, General Alekseyev made a bold move to break the stalemate of trench warfare. On 4 June 1916 he launched Alexei Brusilov, Commander in Chief of the South-Western Front, on an offensive against Austro-Hungarian forces south of the Pripet Marshes, the swamps and floodlands extending from Belarus to Ukraine.[ix] Brusilov, a debonair aristocrat whose grandfather had fought against Napoleon in 1812, distributed his attack along the entire 250-mile southwest line but concentrated his artillery fire on command posts, road networks and other strategic targets to disrupt the Austrian command. Learning from past mistakes, he ordered false military orders to be broadcast en clair, while the real orders were hand-delivered to his commanders.

The deception worked. With the benefit of an increased supply of munitions and employing new operational techniques, the Russians successfully demolished the Austrian Fourth and Seventh Armies. Germany was forced to transfer seventeen divisions from France and Belgium to counter the Russian advance. The Austro-Hungarians had little choice but to accept Hindenburg as Commander in Chief of the Central Powers' Forces on the Eastern Front.[44]

Hindenburg and Ludendorff, plus their indispensable Chief of Staff Colonel Max Hoffmann, travelled from their headquarters at Kovno (Kaunas in today's Lithuania) in a train equipped with the most advanced communications to inspect their new forces. Since the fall of Przemysl, they had been increasingly critical of *Habsburger schlamperei* - 'Habsburg sloppiness' – and were determined to impose some Teutonic iron will on their faltering allies. Space on the

---

ix Several future commanders of the White Russian armies held senior posts under Brusilov at this time. Anton Denikin was his Quartermaster-General, while Alexei Kaledin commanded the Twelfth Cavalry Division and Lavr Kornilov was in command of Forty-eighth Infantry Division.

train was limited, however, and to relieve the hot, cramped conditions Ludendorff commandeered the citadel and barracks at Brest-Litovsk, the only buildings left standing in the town. From this new base, weak points in the line were reinforced with mixed Austro-German units and German officers were put in charge of some Austro-Hungarian divisions. A network of light railways was built just behind the armies to bring up reinforcements and supplies. Nevertheless, Brusilov harassed the enemy on the South-Western Front into August, making his offensive the greatest feat of Russian arms during the war.

By the end of 1915 General Sir Douglas Haig, a personal friend of King George, had displaced Sir John French as British Commander in Chief. He had doubted French's competence in military matters even before the BEF arrived in Belgium and he had recently shared these concerns with the monarch. Haig's own prognosis was grim. He believed that 'the loss of one-tenth of the manhood of the British nation is not too great a price to pay in so great a cause'. Ten per cent of males of military age presupposed a British death toll of two million men. His first major offensive, the Battle of the Somme, did indeed send the butcher's bill soaring.

For the capture of three square miles of enemy territory, the British Army suffered greater losses on the first day of the operation - 57,470 casualties including 19,240 fatalities on 17 June/1 July 1916 - than on any other day in its history. Before the guns fell silent on 16 November three million combatants had been engaged in one of the bloodiest battles ever fought at a cost of one million killed or wounded. Haig's losses numbered 400,000 and his territorial gains were still short of his first-day objectives.[45]

Horrendous though that toll was in the West, Russian casualties on the Eastern Front in 1916 were even greater than those of Verdun and the Somme combined. Hindenburg says no one knows the true figures because 'the page on which Russian losses had been written has been torn out of the great war ledger. Five or eight millions? We, too, have no idea. All we know is that sometimes in our battles with the Russians we had to remove the mound of enemy corpses from before our trenches in order to get a clear field of fire against fresh assaulting waves'.[46]

Stanley Washburn, a Republican senator's son from Minnesota

who had witnessed 'the mangled limbs and shattered bodies that shell and shot had meted out' in the Russo-Japanese War, was now *The Times* Special Correspondent with the Russian Army:

> All this was nothing compared with the scene that one sees daily in places throughout Russia where the lists of the fallen are posted. Great crowds of women gather daily to scan these lists and it is a heart-rending sight to watch the faces of the tide going in and coming out. Peasant women with shawls over their heads jostle and crowd their sisters who have come in carriages. You see them with trembling hands turning over the huge sheets of the lists. Some who fail to read the name of husband, son or sweetheart turn away with sighs of relief; but hardly a minute passes that some poor soul does not receive the wound that spells a life of loneliness or an old age bereft of a son.[47]

France's belief in the unlimited human resources of 'the Russian steamroller' led to another plea for assistance in the shape of troops to replace her astronomical losses at Verdun. The French High Command hoped for an initial intake of 50,000 trained soldiers, with thousands more to come. Russia complied with the request but not in those numbers. Three brigades were raised, the First and Third formed the Russian Expeditionary Force (REF) for service on the Western Front, while the Second joined an Allied counter-offensive against Germany's new ally, Bulgaria, in the gruelling, malaria-infested theatre inland from the Greek port of Salonika.

The First Brigade - two regiments composed of three battalions, plus machinegun support and totalling 180 officers and 8762 soldiers - stepped ashore in Marseilles in April 1916. Accompanied by 96 French officers and 185 French soldiers, the Russians went into action on 15 July 1916 on the line defending Reims near Fort de la Pompelle and the village of Courcy. In an article headlined 'The Russians in the Trenches', the frontline correspondent of *Echo de Paris* rhapsodised, 'I have never seen soldiers so happy, so ardent in their task, so attached to their duty, so instilled with the noblesse and importance of their role! On the night of 15-16 July they raided German trenches and took prisoners who were astounded to find they had been captured by Russian troops.'[48]

By the middle of August the new Austro-German front had begun to hold against the Russian forces, although by that time Austria's fighting power had been permanently impaired. Austria-Hungary and Germany had lost 616,000 and 148,000 men respectively. Never slow in promoting himself, Brusilov claimed his offensive – which had cost Russia up to a million casualties - had relieved Verdun, rescued the Italian Army and forced Austria-Hungary to consider a separate peace. It was also one of the reasons Romania declared war on Austria-Hungary on 27 August 1916 with the invasion of the coveted Hungarian Transylvania.[x][49]

Hindenburg took this news badly. 'I laid down the receiver and thought of Verdun and Italy, of Brusilov and the Eastern Austrian front, and of the message, "Romania has declared war on us". It was a moment that required strong nerves.' Indeed, the Central Powers were on the verge of collapse owing to Falkenhayn's strategic blunders and the shattering of the Austro-Hungarian armies.[50]

On 29 August the Kaiser sacked Falkenhayn as Chief of the General Staff and replaced him with Hindenburg, who was happy to share the responsibility (and the blame) with Ludendorff. 'Never has Fate before placed so heavy a burden on human shoulders,' said Ludendorff, who was given the rank of First Quartermaster-General. 'With bowed head I prayed God the All-Knowing to give me strength for my new office. We were now faced with the difficult problem of holding both the Western and Eastern Fronts against all hostile attacks.' Ludendorff's Christianity would not survive the experience – instead of God the All-Knowing he became a pagan and on an altar at his country estate sacrificed horses to the Nordic deity Wotan.[51]

Field Marshal Prince Leopold of Bavaria replaced Hindenburg as Supreme Commander on the Eastern Front. He took command of three army groups that included both German and Austro-Hungarian troops. As Chief of Staff, he inherited Max Hoffmann, whose feats of logistical planning had been responsible for many of the Duo's successes. He was promoted to Major General and revelled in the thought that 'I shall actually become an *Excellenz*!' Hoffmann was tall and lanky – his nickname was *'der Lange'* (the Long One) – and, at forty-seven, he had developed a prodigious appetite for liquor, downing tumbler after tumbler of Cognac and the strongest Turkish coffee day and night. But he had an attribute that Napoleon had prized

---
x The other reason was the failure of an attack by Romania's neighbour Bulgaria, a German ally, on the Entente lines in Macedonia.

above all others in his generals: he was not only good he was lucky.[52]

'I cannot do more than hold on to what we have and then I shall have carried out my task,' he wrote in his diary at his headquarters in Brest-Litovsk on the night of 3 September. 'At present it is not easy. The Russians are violently attacking the army on our right and Linsingen's Group as well. We have beaten them off up till now, and I am quite confident of the issue as a whole. If things look rather bad at a particular point—well, we must just spit on our hands.'[53]

13

The Flashes of Lightning

Alexander Kerensky's successful kidney operation and the advent of Lilya Birukova in his life had given him a new spring in his step. He wore a three-piece suit with white shirt, wing collar and tie and put a snazzy straw boater on his head. He had made his decision: he would divorce Olga and marry his lover. On 5 August 1916 he poured out his feelings in a letter to Lilya, calling her 'my dearest, my loveliest'. Fate had brought them such happiness, he said, but he would have to go away on Duma business for a while and he longed for September when they would be reunited.[1]

Given his knowledge of Central Asia, the Duma had ordered Kerensky to investigate an uprising of tribesmen in Turkestan. The revolt had begun after Boris Stürmer, noting that France and Britain were using thousands of Chinese coolies to dig trenches on the Western Front, attempted to conscript 250,000 Muslims to do the same work for the Russian Army. 'The Muslim population was not even subject to military conscription, much less forced labour,' Kerensky says. 'Furthermore, the directive was put into effect just at the time when the cotton-picking season was at its peak.'[2]

If the crops were left to rot in the fields, families would starve. The Muslims were also opposed on principle to joining any military campaign against the Caliph, the Sultan of the Ottoman Empire. Arriving in Tashkent on 17 August when the fighting have been raging for five weeks, Kerensky was appalled to discover that thousands of Russians and tens of thousands of Central Asians had already been killed. His brother Fyodor, a staunch monarchist who was serving as public prosecutor, asked him caustically, 'Is this what you've planned for the rest of Russia?'[3]

Touring Samarkand, Dzhizak and Fergana, Kerensky realised that the horrors of the Eastern Front had been transplanted to Turkestan:

mass burial mounds and the smouldering wreckage of homes and crops disfigured the landscape. There had been atrocities on both sides; women had been raped, bodies mutilated. His report to the Duma discounted rightwing claims that German and Turkish agents based in Bukhara had turned the anger into rebellion. The revolt, he said, had been caused by 'the criminal activity of the government'.

He also accused the Russian Army of suppressing the uprising using barbaric methods, including summary executions, the confiscation of property and the destruction of entire villages. His report forced Stürmer to drop his demands for Muslim 'coolies' but the incident showed that the revolution had come early to Central Asia and the fighting would continue in that diverse region until at least 1926.

By the time Kerensky returned to Petrograd in the third week of September 1916, Olga had discussed his affair with his sister Elena Kerenskaya, who urged her to fight for her marriage. When her husband continued to see Lilya on his return, there were distressing scenes in the family home. The very thought of him marrying her cousin was repugnant to Olga and she refused to give him a divorce. Finally, they agreed to separate as a couple but to continue living under the same roof. He insisted that Oleg and Gleb should be told the truth about their situation, a decision that deepened the mood of unhappiness in the home.[4]

Despite all of these obstacles, Kerensky was determined to make Lilya his second wife but the revolution would intervene and disrupt their plans. The woman he would marry instead was at that time a teenager growing up on the other side of the world in Queensland, Australia. Nell Tritton, the schoolgirl who had draped herself in the Union Jack and posed as Britannia at the outbreak of the war, was born in Brisbane on 19 September 1899. She was the fourth of six children of Frederick William Tritton, a wealthy English-born furniture manufacturer, and his wife, Eliza Ellen, the daughter of a Lancashire family named Worrall.

Any thoughts of remaining in Brisbane like her siblings evaporated when she read the diaries of the Russian artist Marie Bashkirtseff. Marie was born into a noble Ukrainian family on 28 November 1858. Her descriptions of living in France with her aristocratic mother entranced the young Queenslander. The diaries became her guiding light and she became an ardent Russophile. Her destiny, Nell decided, was to write poetry and live among Russian émigrés in Paris with 'a man of great talent'.[5]

Nell identified with Marie's desire for fame, all the while fearful that her sporadic illnesses might turn out to be tuberculosis. 'Suppose I was to die quite suddenly,' Marie had written. 'Soon nothing would remain of me – nothing, nothing! It is this which has always terrified me. To live, to have so much ambition, to suffer, weep, struggle – and then oblivion! Oblivion… as if I had never been.'

Nell recognised the same vanity and ambition in herself, the same conjunction of experience, talent, energy and even the brooding presence of a lingering illness. Like two of her elder siblings, Charles and Lillian, she suffered from the long-term effects of lead poisoning after being exposed to lead-based paints at the family's old home in East Brisbane. The condition was incurable and could cause liver damage or sudden kidney failure.

The knowledge that she might not live long motivated many of Nell's decisions and formed an unbreakable bond with Marie, whose wish was to be remembered not as a diarist but as an artist. To that end she studied painting with Rodolphe Julian and Jules Bastien-Lepage and exhibited her work at the Paris Salon in the early 1880s. Just as she had feared, she died of tuberculosis aged twenty-six. *Le Journaux de Marie Bashkirtseff*, her vivid account of life as a young Russian woman living among French artists and aristocrats, was published in 1887 and brought her lasting fame. Gladstone thought her journal 'a book without a parallel'.[i]

Nell Tritton was, according to her cousin Gladys Edds, 'a feminine girl who was sympathetic to the suffering of others; vibrant, outgoing and humorous; a strong swimmer and a lover of poetry, dramatic art and the live theatre'. Her real name was Lydia Ellen but after learning from her father that one of her female ancestors was a French aristocrat who had fled the French Revolution, she reversed 'Ellen' and added an acute accent to form Nellé. When her school-friends accused her of showing off, she retorted, 'I'd rather be hated than ignored.'

After watching another of her cousins, Corporal Joseph Tritton,

---

i The English translation was published as *Marie Bashkirtseff: The Journal of a Young Artist 1860-1884*. She wrote several articles for the feminist newspaper La Citoyenne in 1881 under the nom de plume Pauline Orrel.

march down Queen Street, Brisbane's main street, on his way to Gallipoli in 1915, Nell was moved to write a poem about 'these flowers of our bravery'. Two years later, as the conflict lurched into its fourth agonising year, she penned 'Falling Tears' after hearing that Joseph, now a lieutenant commissioned in the field with the 49th Battalion in France, had been severely wounded. His battalion consisted primarily of Queensland volunteers who had been in the thick of the fighting at Gallipoli after coming ashore during the landing at Anzac Cove in the first wave. The poem speaks to families everywhere. It ends:

*A heart is the dearest sadness the good
God gave to earth,
'Tis the recompense, the punishment, the
heritage of birth,
But, oh, the sad tears are falling, falling
on the tired, sad earth.*

The literary editor of the local *Daily Mail* recalled Nell as 'a brown-eyed brunette bringing poems to me and asking me to print them; and, as there was beauty in these poems as well as in the writer of them, she rarely called in vain'. As a pupil at Jean Turner's alma mater, Somerville House in South Brisbane, Nell took a keen interest in international affairs. Every lunch hour she stood on a stump in the school playground and asked the girls to suggest a subject for a three-minute speech. 'She always found something fascinating to say,' her headmistress, Miss Constance Harker, recalled.

Meanwhile, Catherine Sukhomlinova's sexual wiles with Rasputin had achieved their purpose in freeing her husband. Alexandra wrote to Nicholas at the Stavka in September 1916, 'Our Friend has said that it is necessary to release General Sukhomlinov, lest he die in prison. He has already been in prison for six months – which is long enough (since he is no spy).' To Catherine's joy, the Tsar ignored protests from the Duma and allowed his old favourite to return to his wife under house arrest.

The Tsarina also supported the promotion of the 'imbecilic' Alexander Protopopov as Minister of the Interior. 'His appointment,' Kerensky says, 'was backed by certain financial interests in Rasputin's entourage, with a view to ending the war as quickly as possible, even at the price of a separate peace. Taking the bit between its teeth, the government rushed at full speed towards a collision with the people.'[6]

Despite Protopopov's position as the Tsar's enforcer, Kerensky was on speaking terms with him because he was also a native of Simbirsk. Visiting the minister's office to discuss a police matter, he noticed that a copy of Guido's painting of Christ's head had been placed on a easel in an unmissable position near his desk. Noting his interest, Protopopov assured Kerensky that all would go well in his new role because he was receiving divine guidance from Jesus Himself. 'I never part with Him,' he said. 'Whenever there is a decision to make, He shows me the right way.'[7]

Protopopov's former colleagues were appalled when he strutted into the Duma in the uniform of an officer in the Gendarme Corps, leaving them in no doubt where his loyalties lay. As the minister responsible for public order and food supplies at a time of acute instability and dire shortages, his brutal measures quickly made his name synonymous with the autocracy. He collaborated with General Paul Kurlov, head of the Okhrana and one of the most detested police officials of the age, to pacify Petrograd forcibly. Government agents fomented strikes in the factories which were then brutally suppressed. Protopopov even ordered the military censors to prohibit the publication in the Petrograd press of a conciliatory appeal from the labour section of the War Industries Committees, 'Comrades! Workers of Petrograd! We think it our duty to beg you to resume your work immediately. Labour, conscious of its responsibilities at this moment, must not weaken its forces by such strikes. In the interests of the working class you must return to your factories.'

Kerensky had no doubt that the official policy was to destroy any democratic organisation that stood for national defence. The unintended consequence would be to push the masses into the arms of Bolshevist agitators. Alarmed at the lurch towards anarchy, the leaders of the Progressive Bloc held a secret meeting at which they agreed to depose Nicholas and replace him with his twelve-year-old son but like so many of their schemes it came to nothing. One of the clearest warnings that Russia was on the brink of revolution was contained in a letter from Robert Wilton to the Foreign Editor of *The Times*:

> At present, in a country which is teeming with food and products of every kind, we are bereft of the most elementary necessities of life, and I think it is not an exaggeration to say that the present regime is entirely to blame for it. I hear that banners inscribed with the words 'Down with the Romanovs' have been found in the workmen's houses.[8]

Bruce Lockhart visited Petrograd to attend a gala dinner at the British Embassy, an Eighteenth Century mansion built by Catherine the Great for one of her lovers. He stayed on in the city to enjoy the hospitality of Russian friends. 'I found the atmosphere more depressing than ever,' he says.

> Champagne flowed like water. The Astoria and the Europe – the two best hotels in the capital – were thronged with officers who should have been at the front. There was no disgrace in being a 'shirker' or in finding a sinecure in the rear. I had an impression of senseless ennui and fin de siècle. And in the streets were the long queues of ill-clad men and garrulous women, waiting for the bread that never came.[9]

When the Duma reconvened on 1 November, the White Hall buzzed with excitement. Word had got around that Paul Miliukov was going to make an inflammatory speech. Alexander Kerensky was due to speak first and Mikhail Rodzianko sensed trouble. As unobtrusively as his great bulk would permit, he vacated the President's chair and handed over the session to one of his deputies, the Octobrist S. T. Varun-Sekret. Boris Stürmer also scuttled out of the ministerial box and left the palace building so that his ears would not hear the offending words.

No one was more aware of Miliukov's status as a superior being than his cheerleader, V. D. Nabokov. 'He is a master of irony and sarcasm,' he said. 'His splendid exposés, with their captivating logic and clarity, can crush an opponent.' Kerensky had been one of the targets of his sarcasm and it was his intention on that memorable autumn day to steal some of Miliukov's thunder. As the shorthand writers frantically scribbled in their notebooks, he called the ministers 'cowards' and 'hired assassins' and, even more provocatively, claimed they were 'guided by the contemptible Grishka Rasputin'. When he demanded the overthrow of the government to save the country from ruin, Varun-Sekret nervously rang his bell and ordered him to leave the rostrum. Kerensky complied; he had made his point.

Like an admiral taking the bridge, Paul Miliukov then mounted the dais and over the top of his spectacles surveyed the empty spaces in the ministerial box as though noting the names of the absentees. It was forbidden for deputies to question the honour of the Imperial Family, so Miliukov had to be careful how he introduced the subject of treason. Cleverly, he referred to 'the antechamber through which Protopopov had passed on the way to his ministerial seat'.

Cries of 'Magnificent!' 'He means Rasputin!'

The leader of the Progressive Bloc then attributed the appointment of Boris Stürmer to the people in that same antechamber. And who were these people? Quoting from an Austrian newspaper, *Neue Freie Presse*, he read in German: '*Das ist der Sieg der Hofpartei, die sich um die junge Zarin gruppiert*' ('This is the victory of the Court Party, which is grouped around the young Tsarina').[10]

Miliukov had spoken the words but they were not his words, so he could not be censured. Even so, Varun-Sekret knew no German and his bell remained silent. The speaker continued:

> 'We are telling this government, as we told it in the declaration of the [Progressive] Bloc: "We shall fight you; we shall fight with all legitimate means until you go!"'
> *Cries from the left: 'Right!', 'Correct!'*
>
> It is said [Miliukov continued] that a member of the Council of Ministers [the Minister of War Dmitri Shuvaev] on being told that the State Duma would on this occasion speak of treason, exclaimed excitedly, 'I may, perhaps, be a fool but I am not a traitor.' (Laughter) And, does it matter, gentlemen, as a practical question, whether we are, in the present case, dealing with stupidity or treason? When the Duma keeps everlastingly insisting that the rear must be organised for a successful struggle, the government persists in claiming that organising the country means organising a revolution. It deliberately prefers chaos and disorganisation. Is this stupidity or treason?
> *A voice from the left, 'Treason!'; a voice from the centre, 'Stupidity!'*[11]

Miliukov then listed one by one the government's failings under Stürmer and Protopopov - police agents provoking strikes, vicious propaganda against England, agitators inciting anarchy in the villages and threatening the food supply, agitators urging soldiers to attack officers - and answered each of them with the same question: 'Is this stupidity or treason?'

The session ended in uproar when he ended with this conclusion: 'But when the agitators put all these things together into one and say, "You are on the point of breaking with the Allies; you have no army, you have no food and therefore you must conclude peace, no matter what the consequences, then I say, "This is treason."'

Applause. Shouts of 'Bravo!'

Miliukov had managed to link the Tsarina, Rasputin, Protopopov and Stürmer in the public mind with a separate peace and call it treason. Rodzianko rejected a demand from Stürmer that Miliukov be surrendered for prosecution over his allusion to the Tsarina. Someone had to be punished for this gross insult to the Crown and the axe fell on the hapless Varun-Sekret who was ordered to step down as Vice President of the Duma.

Professor Pitirim Alexandrovich Sorokin, a twenty-eight-year-old graduate in criminology at the University of Petrograd and a Socialist Revolutionary, wrote in his diary:

> It is clear we are now entering the storm of the revolution. The authority of the Tsar, the Tsarina and all the government has terribly broken down. Defeat of Russian arms, poverty and wide discontent of the people inevitably call forth a new revolutionary clamour. The speeches of Shulgin, Miliukov and Kerensky in the Duma, and especially Miliukov's denunciation of the 'stupidity and treason of the Government', have awakened a dangerous echo throughout the country.[12]

After discussing the country's parlous state with his mother, Nicholas dismissed Stürmer and replaced him with Alexander Trepov. The appointment upset Alexandra and angered Rasputin. 'Our Friend is very grieved at his nomination as He knows [Trepov] is very against him,' Alexandra wrote to her husband. 'He is sad you didn't ask his advice.'

Trepov was an updated version of Stolypin who couldn't wait to cross swords with the socialists but first he advised the Tsar to sack the 'insane' Protopopov and send Rasputin back to Siberia. When Nicholas informed Alexandra, she replied that Protopopov was quite sane and suggested instead that Trepov should be hanged. 'You don't go and change Protopopov now, he'll be all right,' she replied. 'Give him the chance to get the food supply matter into his hands and all will go well.'

Shortly after his appointment Trepov, in the name of the Tsar, disclosed the secret agreement with Britain to hand Constantinople and the Straits to Russia at the end of the war. This was Nicholas's way of assuring Britain of Russia's loyalty to the Entente and of rallying the Russian faithful around the sacred cause. It fell completely flat. According to Kerensky, 'even the most imperialistically inclined felt uncomfortable at the pompous ministerial declaration which had so little relation to the actual state of the country'. Samuel Hoare, Mansfield Cumming's man in Russia, cabled London:

> It is probably correct to say that a very great majority of the civilian population of Russia is in favour of peace. The conditions of life have become so intolerable, the Russian casualties have been so heavy, the ages and classes subject to military service have been so widely extended, the disorganisation and untrustworthiness of the government have become so notorious that it is not a matter of surprise if the majority of ordinary people reach at any peace straw. Personally, I am convinced that Russia will never fight through another winter.[13]

Grand Duke Nicholas Mikhailovich, an elderly cousin despised by Alexandra for his liberal views, echoed the concerns of many members of the Imperial Family in a letter to the Tsar:

> You have repeatedly affirmed your intention of carrying the war to a victorious conclusion. Do you think this is possible in the present condition of the country? Do you know the real state of affairs in the border provinces and in the interior? Believe me, when I urge you to shake yourself from the web in which you are entangled, I do so only because I hope and trust that by so doing you may save your throne and our beloved country from irretrievable disaster.

He was referring to the hold that Rasputin had over the Tsarina and, through her, over the Tsar. That hold, however, was about to be broken without any effort on Nicholas's part. The man who would break it was Vladimir Purishkevich, a rightwing deputy and a founding member of the Union of the Russian People. In the Duma on 19 November he denounced the 'dark forces' that were threatening the Romanovs, ending his speech with a dramatic cry for patriotic ministers 'to go to GHQ and plead with the Sovereign to deliver Russia from Rasputin'.[14]

Shortly after that speech, he approached Vasily Shulgin in the

Catherine Hall as the latter was about to leave on a trip to Kiev.

'Listen Shulgin,' Purishkevich said, 'you're going away but I want you to know. Remember the sixteenth of December.'

Shulgin looked puzzled.

'Why?'

'On the sixteenth we are going to kill him.'

'Who?'

'Grishka!'[15]

Purishkevich had hatched a plot to murder Rasputin with the help of Prince Felix Yusupov, a wealthy transvestite who was married to the Tsar's niece, Grand Duchess Irina Alexandrovna. Three other men, the Tsar's cousin Grand Duke Dmitri Pavlovich Romanov, Lieutenant Sergei Mikhailovich Sukhotin of the Preobrazhensky Regiment and a physician, Colonel Stanislaus de Lazovert, had also joined the conspiracy.

While these plans were taking shape, Emperor Franz Josef expired on 8/21 November aged eighty-six. His own life had been beset by personal tragedy on such an epic scale that superstitious citizens believed that the Habsburgs were cursed.[ii] The Crown passed to Franz Josef's twenty-nine-year-old grandnephew, Karl. The new Emperor's main goal was to find a way of ending hostilities. 'I want to do everything to banish the horrors and sacrifices of the war as soon as possible,' he said on taking the throne, 'and to win back for my peoples the sorely missed blessings of peace.' Despite these honourable intentions, his secret diplomatic moves to negotiate a ceasefire were completely unsuccessful.[16]

On 4 December 1916 Nicholas set off for Mogilev, taking the Tsarevich with him. 'Why do people hate me?' Alexandra wrote in one of her semi-literate letters to her husband while he was still on the train. 'Because they know I have a strong will and when I am

---

ii The Emperor's estranged wife, Empress Elizabeth, had been assassinated by an anarchist; a Mexican firing squad had executed his brother, Maximillian, after he had assumed the throne of Mexico; his only son, Crown Prince Rudolf, had committed suicide in his hunting lodge at Mayerling after shooting his eighteen-year-old mistress; his brother, Archduke Karl Ludwig, had died to typhoid, and Karl Ludwig's eldest son, Franz Ferdinand, had been the victim of Sarajevo; Franz Ferdinand's younger brother, Archduke Otto, had died of natural causes in 1906, so the next-in-line was Otto's son Karl.

convinced of a thing being right (when besides blessed by Grigory) don't change my mind and that they can't bear.'

Nicholas replied, 'You are so staunch and enduring – I admire you more than I can say.' Had he been truthful, he would have added that he was fed up with hearing about the infallibility of 'Our Friend'. To humour his wife, he had eaten a crust of bread from Rasputin's table and combed his hair with his 'miraculous' comb in order to be invested with their mystical powers. Nevertheless, he had no intention of ever challenging his wife's fanatical belief in the *starets'* ability to heal their son.[17]

As Prince Yusupov and his fellow assassins completed their grisly arrangements, Rasputin visited Alexandra to oppose Trepov's plan for making concessions to the Duma. He also told her that the Prime Minister had offered him 200,000 roubles in cash to return to Siberia and abstain from political intervention. To Alexandra, this was rank treachery. 'My angel, we dined at Anna's with our Friend,' she reported to Nicholas on 13 December. 'He entreats you to be firm, to be the Master and not always to give in to Trepov.' The next passage disclosed her tenuous grip on sanity:

> I am fully convinced that great and beautiful times are coming for your reign and Russia ... we must give a strong country to Baby and dare not be weak for his sake, else he will have a yet harder reign, setting our faults right and drawing the reins in tightly which you let loose. You have to suffer for faults in the reigns of your predecessors and God knows what hardships are yours.
>
> Let our legacy be a lighter one for Alexei. He has a strong will and mind of his own, don't let things slip through your fingers and make him build all over again. Be firm ... one wants to feel your hand - how long, years, people have told me the same: 'Russia loves to feel the whip'- it's their nature - tender love and then the iron hand to punish and guide. How I wish I could pour my will into your veins.... Be Peter the Great, Ivan the Terrible, Emperor Paul - crush them all under you - now don't you laugh, naughty one.[18]

Peter the Great tortured and then murdered his son and heir, while Ivan the Terrible's cruelties towards his people - and finally his own family – helped to destroy his dynasty. Emperor Paul, Catherine the Great's half-witted son, abused the autocracy's absolute power for four years before his murder in 1801. Alexandra cared nothing for any of that; crazed with anguish over her son's illness and her husband's inability to turn the tide of war, she saw violent repression as the only answer to Russia's problems.[19]

'Loving thanks for your strong reprimanding letter,' Nicky replied the next day. 'I read it with a smile because you speak as to a child.' His plan, he explained, was to dismiss Trepov but only after he had 'done the dirty business – shut up the Duma. Let all the responsibility fall on his shoulders.' There could be no better example than this of Sergei Witte's comment that the Tsar 'always sought underhand means'. Teasingly, Nicholas signed his letter, 'Your little huzy with no will.'[20]

On 16 December - the last day of the Duma's sixth session and the day set for Rasputin's murder - Alexandra sent Anna Vyrubova to deliver an icon to the *starets* at his apartment. He boasted to Anna that he had been invited to meet the Grand Duchess Irina Yusupova at midnight. Anna thought this strange and so did the Tsarina when she heard about it. 'There must be some mistake,' she said, 'Irena is in the Crimea.' But she never interfered in Rasputin's amorous adventures and she did nothing about it.

Protopopov, however, had got wind of the plot and at 8 p.m. he also called on Rasputin. 'They will kill you,' he warned. 'Your enemies are bent on mischief.' He made his benefactor promise to stay indoors for the next few days until the danger had passed.[21]

Once the minister had departed, Rasputin ignored his advice. Driving to the Yusupov Palace on the Moika River with the Prince later that night, he chuckled over the old man's concerns. As they entered the palace through a side door, Rasputin could hear a gramophone playing 'Yankee Doodle Dandy'. Yusupov told him Irina was entertaining some friends upstairs and would join them shortly. He led Rasputin into a basement salon in which cakes containing potassium cyanide and a bottle of poisoned Madeira wine had been laid out on a table.

At first, Rasputin refused this modest repast and, when the beautiful Irina failed to materialise, he suggested going to a nightclub. While Yusupov stalled for time, his guest ate some of the cakes and drank three glasses of wine. They had no noticeable effect. About

2.30 a.m., the Prince excused himself and went upstairs, where his fellow conspirators were anxiously waiting.

Taking a revolver from Dmitri Pavlovich, he returned to the basement and, referring to a crystal and silver crucifix on top of a cabinet, told Rasputin, 'Look at the crucifix and say a prayer'. As Rasputin stumbled to his feet, the Prince shot him in the side. Blood gushed through his embroidered silk blouse from a wound in his chest.[22]

Believing him to be dead, three of the killers then drove to Rasputin's apartment, with Sukhotin wearing Rasputin's overcoat and hat in an attempt to make it look as though their owner had returned home. Back at the Moika Palace, Yusupov went down to the basement to ensure that his victim was indeed dead.

Suddenly, the *starets* rose up like a monstrous apparition, attacked the Prince and lumbered through a side door into the palace courtyard. Picking up the revolver, Purishkevich chased after him and fired two shots, one into his body and, the coup de grace, into his forehead. Weighed down with iron chains, Rasputin's body was dumped through a hole in the ice on the Malaya Nevka River near the Petrovsky Bridge.

News of his death flashed around the capital like wildfire. 'There was great rejoicing among the public,' says Maurice Paléologue. 'People kissed each other in the street and many went to burn candles in Our Lady of Kazan.' Grand Duke Dmitri was given a standing ovation at the theatre. 'Grishka Rasputin, the *starets*, stands for those "dark forces" of Russian public life of which we have heard so much lately,' the London *Observer* editorialised. 'Whether he was a mystic or a charlatan, it is certain that his death removes from Russian life a most sinister and dangerous figure.'[23]

The Tsar's daughter Olga wrote in her diary, 'Father Grigory has been missing since last night. They are looking everywhere. It is terribly hard. The four of us slept together. God help us!'[24] Then, on 19 December, Rasputin's body was recovered after two workmen noticed blood on the railing of the bridge and a boot was found on the ice. Rasputin's funeral was held on 21 December at a small church that Anna Vyrubova had been building at Tsarskoe Selo. His wife, mistress and children were not invited, although his daughters met with Nicholas and Alexandra at Vyrubova's house later that day.

Only two of the killers were punished: Prince Yusupov was banished to one of his estates and Grand Duke Dmitri was ordered to join the army in Persia. His personal rail carriage was attached to a goods train for the journey but, on reaching the Caucasus, the Viceroy, his cousin Grand Duke Nicholas, decided that the Caspian was too dangerous for crossing and detained him in Tiflis.[25]

The others got off scot-free to avoid a scandal involving the name of the Tsar's niece, Irina. The Tsarina never recovered from the loss of 'Our Friend', especially the loss of his powers to arrest Alexei's haemophilia, and she never forgave her husband for not bringing his murderers to justice.

The conspirators had hoped that once Rasputin was dead the deranged woman would be confined to a mental hospital. They were sadly disillusioned. The loss of Rasputin brought Nicholas and Alexandra together in an even closer, more tragic bond. Ignoring his duties as Supreme Commander, he spent the next two months at Tsarskoe Selo consoling her. In deference to her wishes, he sacked Alexander Trepov and replaced him with her choice, Prince Nikolai Golitsyn. Another casualty was Alexander Makarov, who had crept back into office as Minister of Justice. At the Tsar's insistence he had dragged his heels over the Rasputin case only for Alexandra to demand his head for doing so.[26]

The question of the most advisable steps to be taken in regard to the war divided the socialist parties into the 'Social Patriots' and the 'Internationalists'. 'Both factions wanted to end the war as soon as possible,' Pitirim Sorokin says, 'but the Social Patriots were against a separate peace with the German forces [while] the Internationalists were in favour of a separate peace regardless of the policies of our allies. An overwhelming majority of Bolsheviks and Left Socialist Revolutionaries took the position of the Internationalists. They wanted to replace international war with "class war". "Peace to huts and war to palaces!" was their motto.'[27]

The breakdown of the Kerenskys' marriage became painfully apparent when the family split up at Christmas and went in different directions. Alexander and Lilya took the train to Bad Grankulla, while Olga and the boys travelled to Kainki for their traditional holiday on the family's estate. Freed from the tensions of Petrograd and Olga's increasingly gloomy moods, Kerensky recaptured the joy of his first days with Lilya. For ten days they led a carefree existence in a circle of friends including Isaak Babel, Maxim Gorky's literary protégé who would achieve lasting fame as the author of *The Red Cavalry*, a book of short stories about the upcoming war between Russia and Poland.

Walking through the snow with Kerensky one day, Babel challenged him about his eyesight when he failed to recognise a skater they both knew. Was he too vain to be seen in public wearing spectacles? 'I am surrounded by wonders…,' Kerensky replied. 'Why do I need the clouds in this Finnish sky when I can see the tossing ocean above my head? Why do I need line when I have colour? The whole world is a gigantic theatre in which I am the only member of the audience without opera-glasses.'[28]

The New Year opened with the Kaiser authorising all-out submarine warfare in a desperate bid to starve Britain into surrendering within five months. The slaughter began on 1 February when German submarines attacked ships of many nationalities, including American vessels, in the 'prohibited region' around the British Isles. The German High Command figured that the Tsar's autocracy was Germany's best insurance policy against American intervention but they were willing to gamble that even if the United States did enter the war, then packs of U-boats would sink American troop transports before they could reach Europe. Tsarism was indeed anathema to President Woodrow Wilson's democratic principles and he refused to consider joining any alliance of which Russia was a member.[29]

In Petrograd police provocation increased with the arrest of almost every member of the Workers' Group of the Central War Industries Committees, including its president, Kozma Gvozdev, and its secretary, Boris Bogdanov, both Mensheviks. They were thrown into Kresty Prison on charges of plotting to form a Social Democratic republic. At the same time the government began the demobilisation of the labour sections of the provincial committees. Even though many cities and towns were on the verge of starvation, one of the regime's most spiteful acts was to cancel an independent conference whose aim was to solve the food problem.

As Miliukov had said in the Duma, the government was intent on demolishing everything that was likely to avert an uprising. The shaky hand of Protopopov could be detected in all of these repressive acts. Having read Okhrana intelligence reports on the threat of 'socialist extremism', he recruited new police officers at high rates of pay and armed them with machineguns. When trouble broke out, as it inevitably would, he planned to contain rioting crowds with this force until loyal troops could arrive from the front to suppress them.[30]

According to Kerensky, the motto of the Ministry of the Interior should be 'Through anarchy to a separate peace'. He absolved Nicholas of blame: the government's plan was to confront him with a fait accompli which would oblige him to sign a peace deal. 'I cannot say whether Alexandra Fyodorovna had anything to do with it,' Kerensky says. 'Her immediate circle was not above suspicion and German agents were hovering around her and Madame Vyrubova.'

Desertion among the armed forces had become endemic. The High Command was helpless to stem the homeward tide of peasant conscripts whose mass exit left many units in a precarious state. Special military police detachments were formed to round up deserters and rewards of from seven to twenty-five kopecks per head, depending on rank, were offered for their forcible return. Nevertheless, military discipline continued to evaporate. Quite apart from the very real risk of death or serious injury, the Russian soldier had many justifiable complaints. He was forbidden to smoke in the street, to ride in tramcars or to frequent clubs, dancehalls, restaurants or any other place where alcohol was sold. He could not attend public lectures or theatrical performances, nor receive books or newspapers without the permission of an officer. Whole companies refused to fight or to relieve their comrades in the trenches. Here and there, frontline troops fraternised with their German and Austrian enemies.[31]

The lack of military discipline was even worse in the rear, where agitators infiltrated the barracks with ease and read out revolutionary tracts to recruits. A memorandum dealing with the parlous condition of the army and the need for urgent measures was laid before the Tsar at the end of January 1917. The authors were representatives of the Duma, the State Council and various independent organisations. Andrei Shingarev, chairman of the Military and Naval Affairs Committee of the Duma, obtained an audience with Nicholas to urge him to take action to save the country. Nothing succeeded; nothing was done.

Peter Durnovo, the last Imperial Minister of the Interior to die of natural causes, expired at his villa in Petrograd at the venerable age of seventy. With unerring accuracy, he had predicted in his February 1914 Memorandum that the war would make shortages of food, fuel and medical supplies inevitable. The socialists would seize the opportunity to stir up trouble among the masses and the Army would be too weak to protect the regime. 'Russia will be flung into hopeless anarchy,' he had warned.[32]

> The trouble will start with the blaming of the government for all disasters. In the legislative institutions a bitter campaign against the government will begin, followed by revolutionary agitations throughout the country, with socialist slogans, capable of arousing and rallying the masses, beginning with the division of the land and succeeded by a division of all valuables and property.
>
> The defeated army, having lost its most dependable men, and carried away by the tide of primitive peasant desire for land, will find itself too demoralised to serve as a bulwark of law and order. The legislative institutions and the intellectual opposition parties, lacking real authority in the eyes of the people, will be powerless to stem the popular tide…

By February 1917 every word of Durnovo's prediction was coming true. The greatest and most critical problems paralysing the Home Front were disastrous food and fuel shortages, growing industrial dislocation, scandalous bureaucratic ineptitude and dismay over the insatiable demands of the war. Owing to the coal shortage, the blast furnaces of the steel mills had come to a standstill in December and the munitions factories in Petrograd were closing down. At night people knocked down wooden fences or stole wooden crosses from cemeteries to provide fuel for their fires.

Things had been allowed to drift for so long that neither the Tsar, the Tsarina's camarilla, the State Council, the Council of Ministers nor the Duma were capable of correcting them. In an unpublished letter to Printing House Square on 4/17 January, Robert Wilton wrote, 'The young Empress and her clique of women have evidently got the reins entirely into their own hands, and the Emperor is being blindly driven into acts that will sooner or later precipitate grave disorders unless a palace revolution averts a general smother. I do not think I am exaggerating the state of affairs.'[33]

Having lost the confidence of his colleagues, Asquith quit on 5 December 1916 and two days later Lloyd George kissed the King's hand to become Prime Minister. One of his first acts was to send an Allied mission to Russia to plan the 1917 military campaign. The veteran colonial administrator Lord Milner, one of the original members of his five-man War Cabinet (with Lord Curzon, Bonar Law and Arthur Henderson) would head the British section of the mission. Milner's chief military adviser would be General Sir Henry Wilson, a political intriguer described by Lloyd George as 'a man of brilliant gifts and obvious defects'.[iii][34]

The murder of Rasputin delayed the mission's departure from London for two weeks and they did not reach Murmansk until 16/29 January 1917. The port was almost 200 miles inside the Arctic Circle but thanks to the warming waters of the Gulf Stream it remained open throughout the winter months. Milner was appalled at the sight of muddy unpaved streets and shoddy buildings. Thousands of tons of war stores were stacked near the wooden jetties, with no recognisable system of distribution in operation. The port itself was congested with ships of all description and the hastily built single-track railway south to Petrograd was painfully slow and unreliable. At an average speed of eight miles per hour, it took the visitors nearly five days to cover those 800 miles.[35]

After that agonising introduction, the Tsar made sure that the mission's fifty representatives were feted like visiting royalty. They were wined and dined at sumptuous dinners and regaled with impressive speeches about the great Allied wartime alliance. At a banquet in the Alexander Palace at Tsarskoe Selo Nicholas went out of his way to speak to every one of the visitors. Knowing that if he abandoned the Allied cause he would forfeit all rights to Constantinople, he denied any possibility of Russia signing a separate peace. Milner spoke no Russian and was out of his depth but it became obvious to him that Russia's plan was to hand him a shopping list of Russia's requirements, both domestic and military, and then ask the Allies not only to send the goods but also 'to foot the bill'.[36]

Sir Henry Wilson, accompanied by a quintet of British generals,

---

[iii] As Sir Alfred Milner, he had administered the Boer territories after the South African War in which disease killed thousands of women and children in British concentration camps.

attended meetings of a four-nation military committee, which, he informed his diary, achieved absolutely nothing. This was not entirely accurate: the committee confirmed the decision made at the Allied conference at Chantilly in December that the Russian Army would begin major operations against the enemy by 1 May, 'weather permitting'. Wilson discovered that the main topic of conversation over lunch at the British Embassy was revolution, with Russian officials openly discussing the advisability of murdering the Tsar and/or the Tsarina. It was, he said, 'a murderous pity that the Emperor is so weak & so under the Empress's thumb'. He predicted that this 'extraordinary state of affairs' could only lead to 'terrible trouble'.[37]

According to Sir Samuel Hoare in his unpublished memoirs, Lord Milner 'relapsed into a state of fatalist depression, unable to understand a world so different from his own and unwilling to believe that any civilised country could be so badly governed'.[38] Despite all the evidence to the contrary, the Tsar managed to convince Milner that, politically, everything was under control. That, at any rate, was the message he relayed to Downing Street. According to Lloyd George, 'Lord Milner assured the British Cabinet that there would be no revolution in Russia during the war.'[39]

Bruce Lockhart, who had arranged the Moscow end of the British delegation's programme, summed up: 'Rarely in the history of great wars can so many important ministers and generals have left their respective countries on so useless an errand.'[40]

On 14 February the Duma opened in an atmosphere of great unrest and indecision. The majority of deputies refused to believe that the people were about to take matters into their own hands and sought some sort of conciliation with the government. On the second day of the session Kerensky threw down the gauntlet. 'There are people who assert that the ministers are at fault - not so,' he shouted from the tribune in the White Hall.

> The country now realises that the ministers are but fleeting shadows [he said]. The country can clearly see who sends them here. Have you fully understood [that] the historic task of the Russian people is the abolition of the medieval regime, immediately and at any cost? To prevent a catastrophe the Tsar himself must be removed, by terrorist methods if there is no other way. If you refuse to listen to the warning

voice, you, gentlemen, will meet facts instead of warnings. Behold the flashes of lightning that are already flaring here and there across the skies of the Russian Empire!'[41]

Following Kerensky's call for the Tsar's assassination, the authorities took steps to deprive him of his parliamentary immunity in order to prosecute him for treason. To his credit, Rodzianko refused to allow it. The Tsar had spent January and most of February with his family at Tsarskoe Selo but had solved none of the nation's problems before returning to the Stavka on Wednesday 22 February. He left Prince Golitsyn with two signed but undated decrees for the suspension or dissolution of the Duma for the Prime Minister to use if the situation deteriorated further.

During the journey to Mogilev, Nicholas received another garbled telegram from Alexandra: 'I hope that Duma man Kedrinsky *(sic)* will be hung for his horrible speeches – it is necessary (wartime law) and it will be an example. All are thirsting and beseeching that you show your firmness.' Without Rasputin's direct line to the Almighty, Alexandra felt uncertain and insecure. Thanks to her interference in state affairs, Russia had had four Prime Ministers, five Ministers of the Interior, three Foreign Ministers, three Ministers of War, three Ministers of Transport and four Ministers of Agriculture in the past seventeen months.[42]

Things had reached the point of no return. Kerensky's 'flashes of lightning' were about to ignite a conflagration. On the very eve of the revolution the Tsar wrote to his wife from his quarters in the provincial governor's mansion on the crest of a hill at Mogilev, 'My brain feels rested here, no ministers and no fidgety questions. It's so quiet in this house, no rumbling about, no excited shouts! If I'm free here I think I will turn to dominoes again.' Confident that God's will would be done, he lit a cigarette and laid out the ivory bones on the domino board. He had no idea that his two-month absence from the Stavka had sealed his fate in the minds of his own generals.[43]

14

The February Revolution

The Russian Revolution began on the afternoon of International Women's Day, Thursday 23 February 1917, when female textile workers from the Vyborg Side joined 'ladies from society, peasant women and student girls' in a march through the heart of Petrograd chanting, 'Bread! Bread!' It had been the coldest winter for years - the average January-February temperature in the capital was minus twelve degrees Centigrade – but late that morning the sun broke through the low cloud and the mercury climbed to plus eight.[1]

Suddenly, the streets were filled with working class people who, finding that the bakeries had sold out of their staple fare – big round loaves of black rye bread - gravitated towards Nevsky Prospekt to join the women's protest. 'Women and girls, mostly well dressed, were enjoying the excitement,' says Arthur Ransome, correspondent of the London *Daily News*. 'It was like a bank holiday with thunder in the air'.[2]

Alexander Kerensky saw nothing festive about 'this wave of starving women [whose] only desire is to chew on a crust of black bread'. The situation was already out of control, he told the Duma. 'For this elemental force, hunger is the only Tsar [and] it will not submit to persuasion and words anymore.' For the next seven days, the war seemed to stand still in the capital while the slow-moving avalanche of political discontent and public anger gathered pace and swept the Romanov Dynasty into oblivion. 'Hunger is the only Tsar' became one of the first catchphrases of the revolution.[3]

On that first day virtually every industrial enterprise in Petrograd from the shipyards, textile, sugar and timber mills to the Nobel, Erikson, Baranovsky and Putilov works producing dynamite and armaments, was shuttered and barred, the workers either laid off, locked out or on strike. As if on cue, thousands of workers from the Petrograd and Vyborg Districts scrambled across the ice of the frozen Neva to avoid troops guarding the Trinity and Liteiny Bridges, while the Putilov workforce and other militants in the Narva-Petergof region swarmed towards the Triumphal Arch as they had done in 1905 on their way to Palace Square.

Bakeries in the poorer quarters were besieged and looted and the Filippov patisserie on Nevsky Prospekt - among the few places still selling chocolate cakes and sweetmeats - was also sacked. A patrol of Cossacks galloped down the Nevsky but shied away from attacking protesters. From Tsarskoe Selo, Alexandra assured her husband in Mogilev, 'It's a hooligan movement, young boys and girls running about and screaming they have no bread.'[4]

The main reason for the empty shelves was that agitators, both pro-German and Bolshevik (which amounted to the same thing when it came to crippling the Russian war effort) had whipped up discontent in the bread queues. When someone started a rumour that the Minister of Agriculture, Alexander Rittikh, was about to introduce bread rationing, people started buying in bulk, thus creating the very shortage they feared.

Rittikh reported to the Duma that tremendous lines had suddenly appeared in Vyborg and demanded black bread. Having been served in one shop, the hoarders then queued up at the next shop. 'Panic was mounting,' he said. 'Everyone was trying to lay in a supply of bread to make into rusks.' Witnessing the scale of the problem, Rittikh immediately authorised bread rationing to enforce a more equitable distribution but it was too late to stop the disturbances.[5]

The agitators then claimed that the hoarding of flour for profiteering was to blame for the bread shortage and that the capitalist producers were the culprits. In many cases it was the bakers who found it more profitable to sell the flour to speculators for a high price than to bake it.[6] The finger of suspicion was pointed at the Minister of Agriculture himself. While he could not be held responsible for the heavy snowfalls that had disrupted the supply lines, or for the fact that the war took precedence over civilian needs, he had indeed bought up a greater proportion of the harvest for military and defence purposes than in previous years. The situation was so grim that, on returning to the Ministerial Pavilion adjoining the Tauride Palace that night, Rittikh, an honest patriot, burst into tears.[7]

It was an irreversible fact of life that prices of most items had almost quadrupled since 1914 and, at the same time, the rouble had been devalued. Flour was in short supply and sugar was already being rationed. Moreover, the ban on the sale of vodka had not only cost the state treasury one-third of its revenue but had also removed one of the chief incentives for trade between rural and urban areas. With no alcohol and fewer consumer goods on sale in the shops, the peasants buried their grain rather than sell it to the cities for useless money.

But the bread shortage was only the latest symptom of the malignant disease that was gnawing at the soul of Russia. There were many other grievances and topping the list was the wanton slaughter of the nation's manhood in the war. Russia had lost two million men killed and wounded, while another two million were languishing in enemy concentration camps. Seven and a half million were under arms and another two and a half million were being held in reserve depots. There had also been 1.2 million desertions, a number that was increasing every day.[8]

The effect of the war on the peasant and proletarian populations – the main sources of Russia's frontline 'cannon fodder' - was devastating. Families had been torn apart and rural life seriously dislocated through the loss of fathers and sons, brothers and cousins, and yet the farms were still expected to feed the nation while crops rotted in the field for lack of manpower to harvest them. Nor was any let-up in sight. Most of the Russian Army was still engaged at the front and Russian commanders had agreed to take part in the Allies' ambitious spring offensive.[9]

Within twenty-four hours of the women's march, 200,000 workers were on the streets demanding an end to food and fuel shortfalls, an end to the war and an end to Tsarism. Massive protests paralysed the city. Students, white-collar workers and teachers joined the demonstrations. Young thugs boarded tramcars and grabbed the driving levers without which the trams were immobile. Soon, every tramline in the city had come to a standstill and the droshky cabbies, fearing attack, headed for home.

The strikers knew they could expect fierce opposition from the police and the Gendarme Corps but the question nobody could answer was: what would the soldiers do? The Petrograd Garrison – some 150,000 men crammed into quarters designed for 22,000 – was composed of depot troops, mostly middle-aged reservists, who had no intention of fighting, and young peasants, who were being trained to replace battle casualties in their regiments. Their officers were either experienced men who had been invalided home with wounds, or inexperienced youths who were attending the military academies.[10]

The exception was the Fourth Company of the Pavlovsky Reserve Battalion, which contained trained men who were recovering from combat wounds before being returned to the front. When newly mobilised factory workers were added to their ranks, the whole company became open to agitation.

In his speech to the Duma Kerensky had demanded the immediate transfer of food distribution to elected local committees; that was not forthcoming and the public's anger increased on Friday 24 February after ministers failed to give an assurance that food supplies would be restored to acceptable levels. 'Groups of workmen and students paraded in the streets, followed by a crowd of men, women and children who had come out of curiosity to see what was going to happen,' Sir George Buchanan says. 'But for the most part it was a good-humoured crowd that made way for the Cossacks when the latter was ordered to clear some street, and even occasionally cheered them as they passed. The Cossacks, on their side, were careful not to hurt anybody and – what was of bad omen for the government – laughed and talked with those near them. It was only towards the police, with whom they had several collisions in the course of the day, that the crowd adopted a hostile attitude.'[11]

Indeed, the police intervened wherever they could to arrest looters and prevent demonstrators from invading the central business district. On Trinity Bridge leading from the northern districts to the Admiralty and Nevsky Prospekt they opened fire on the crowd and several people were killed, the first civilian casualties of the revolution.[12]

In the evening the Council of Ministers, meeting in the Marinsky Palace, heeded the wisdom of Kerensky's demand and transferred food distribution to the Petrograd City Duma. Countess Sofia Panina, who had been working at the headquarters of the municipal parliament in Nevsky Prospekt to ensure that the families of reservists were being looked after when their menfolk were called up, was appointed as a delegate to the City Duma. The food supply would soon improve but it was too late to affect the issue. When Major General Sergei

Khabalov, Commander of the Petrograd Military District, arrested known agitators in an attempt to restore order, scores of volunteers stepped forward to take their place.[13]

On Saturday the twenty-fifth, the streets were again packed with people in a state a high excitement. Nikolai Sukhanov decided he was witnessing a replay of the 1905 Moscow insurrection. 'The entire civil population felt itself to be in one camp united against the enemy – the police and the military,' he wrote in his seven-volume memoir of the Russian Revolution. 'Strangers conversed with each other, asking questions and talking about the clashes with the enemy.'[14]

Separated by half a continent from the events in Petrograd, Lenin lamented to a group of Swiss workers in Zurich, 'We older men many not live to see the decisive battles of the approaching revolution.' Krupskaya said her husband felt 'corked up, as if in a bottle'. But the revolution had actually begun. When mounted police flayed one group of protestors with whips, the crowd turned on them in fury. The Chief of Police of the Fifth District was knocked off his horse and demonstrators beat him with sticks and a piece of iron.

The Okhrana report on the incident said, 'Policemen fired into the crowd and the shots were returned from the crowd.' There were reports of individual policemen being attacked with hand grenades taken from the arms factories. The Cossacks wavered. When a policeman wounded a demonstrator with his sabre, a Cossack drew his sword and attacked the policeman. From then on, they sided with the crowd.[15]

At nine o'clock on Saturday evening the Tsar ordered General Khabalov 'to suppress, beginning tomorrow, all disorders on the streets of the capital'. Overnight, posters were pasted to the walls of buildings at intersections forbidding demonstrations and warning that all gatherings would be dispersed by force of arms. Striking workmen were warned they would be sent to the front unless they returned to work on Monday morning.

Early on Sunday morning, 26 February, commanders assembled their men and repeated Khabalov's orders: 'Save no bullets, use live ammunition. Don't use blanks or fire into the air.' The police and the military began to clear the streets with all the force at their disposal. The workers reacted violently. 'From Vyborg, the most militant district, came reports of serious action by workers against police and troops,' Sukhanov says. 'From time to time distant rifle fire was heard.[16]

The firm hand started to lose its grip when Cossack squadrons failed to break up a protest march and, in several locations, soldiers fraternised with the people. *The Times* correspondent Robert Wilton reported protesters shouting on Nevsky Prospekt, 'You are not going to fire on us, brothers! We only want bread!'

'No, we are hungry like yourselves,' the troops replied. Indeed, the bread ration for soldiers had been reduced from three pounds a day to one and three-quarter pounds.[17]

To deceive the public, Alexander Protopopov had dressed his police officers in military uniforms, giving them brown-grey overcoats instead of the regulation black and covering their heads in grey sheep-skin headwear. Some of these disguised policemen went on patrol in the streets with soldiers, who were furious at the deception. Others were placed at strategic points on the rooftops of city buildings. When they opened fire on Sunday strollers on Nevsky Prospekt, people fled down Mikhailovskaya Street. Several were killed or wounded. The Cossacks turned their guns on the police and groups of enraged demonstrators broke into the buildings and killed them.[18]

At the junction of the Nevsky and Vladimir prospekts the Semenovsky Regiment, which had supressed the Moscow insurrection in 1905, shot several marchers dead. Further along the Nevsky a training detachment of the Pavlovsky Regiment opened fire on protesters, who responded with a barrage of bricks and jagged pieces of ice. Dozens of people were killed or wounded.

The bloodiest incident took place when people attending the nonstop political meetings in Znamenskaya Square refused to disperse. A training detachment of the Volynian Regiment opened fire and killed more than fifty people in the worst atrocity since 1905. One report said the massacre happened after an officer, who had been unable to get his young troops to shoot, grabbed a rifle himself and started firing wildly into the crowd.[19]

This second 'Bloody Sunday', with its echoes of the autocracy at its most blood-thirsty, turned the industrial unrest into a revolution. That night there was violent agitation in the barracks when soldiers discussed what they would do in the morning if ordered to shoot civilians. Timofei Kirpichnikov, a twenty-five-year-old sergeant in the Volynian training detachment, told his men, 'Our fathers, mothers, sisters, brothers and brides are begging for bread. Are we going to kill them? Did you see the blood on the streets today? I say we shouldn't take up positions tomorrow. I myself refuse to go.' The soldiers cried out, 'We shall stay with you!'[20]

The first mutiny among garrison troops occurred at six o'clock that Sunday evening when the Fourth Company of the Pavlovsky Guards set out from their barracks between the Moika and Kaniushnaya Square to punish the Pavlovsky training detachment which had shot civilians on Nevsky Prospekt. The Okhrana report on this incident stated: 'The Fourth Company proceeded towards the Nevsky under the command of a non-commissioned officer with the intention of removing the training detachment from their posts. However, in the vicinity of the Church of the Saviour on the Spilled Blood, they met a mounted patrol of ten policemen. The soldiers abused the policemen, calling them "pharaohs" and firing several volleys which killed one policeman and wounded another.'[21]

Later that evening a detachment of the Preobrazhensky Guards surrounded the mutineers and, after ordering them to lay down their arms, escorted them back to barracks. To defuse this explosive situation, Colonel Alexander Eksten promised the mutineers that their street patrols would be halted. After addressing them, he stepped out into Konyushennaya Square, where a group of demonstrators attacked him. One grabbed his sabre, slashed off three fingers and then decapitated him.[22]

As President of the Duma, Mikhail Rodzianko regarded himself as the second most important personage in the Russian Empire. He had never been a revolutionary and, at fifty-eight, he had no intention of becoming one. According to his friend, the historian Sir Bernard Pares, 'his views were those of English country Toryism'. Indeed, he and his political allies in the Duma 'were as fearful of the unrestrained actions of the masses as they were opposed to the regime of Nicholas II'.[23]

The previous day Rodzianko had telephoned the Tsar's brother Misha, the Grand Duke Michael Alexandrovich, 'informing him of what was happening and telling him that he should immediately come to the capital'. Michael, the childhood bear killer, was now Inspector-General of Cavalry based at Gatchina. Unlike his brother, Michael had distinct democratic leanings and had pleaded with him to permit constitutional reforms before it was too late. He listened attentively to Rodzianko, who told him, 'You are the only person who can save the situation and you only have until tonight.' Michael agreed to a face-to-face meeting but said the earliest he could make the trip to Petrograd was Monday afternoon.[24]

Rodzianko also spoke to the President of the State Council, Ivan Shcheglovitov, who assured him there was nothing to worry about. Despite that denial, Rodzianko was convinced the disturbances were out of control. One of the phone calls to his office in the Duma that Sunday was from a resident living at 128 Nevsky Prospekt who reported that fifteen police officers had been executed one by one outside his house.

Determined to use his position to protect the monarchy, Rodzianko prepared a telegram to be sent to the Tsar. It read: 'The situation is serious. There is anarchy in the capital. The government is paralysed. General discontent is growing. There is desultory firing in the streets. One portion of the troops is firing on the other. It is absolutely necessary to appoint someone possessing the confidence of the country to form a new government. Delay will be fatal. I pray God that a share of the responsibility may not fall upon the Monarch.'

Nicholas tossed this message on to his desk and lit a cigarette. Turning to Count Fredericks, he snorted, 'That fat Rodzianko has written me all sorts of nonsense, to which I will not even reply.' He ordered the prorogation of the Duma and decided to return to Tsarskoe Selo. Two of his daughter had measles and Alexei had also come down with the illness. His place was at home with his family.[25]

Knowing Nicholas to be a devious man, Rodzianko took the precaution of sending copies of his telegram to General Alekseyev, General Aleksei Brusilov, General Nikolai Ruzsky and other frontline commanders. This one simple action would have profound consequences for the dynasty.

Between six and seven p.m. that Sunday evening the Socialist Information Bureau attended one of their regular meetings in Kerensky's apartment. Those present included his Socialist Revolutionary comrade Vladimir Zenzinov, his Social Democrat friend Nikolai Sokolov, the Bundist Henryk Ehrlich, Alexander Shliapnikov, a member of the

Bolshevik Central Committee (and the lover of Alexandra Kollontai), and his comrade Konstantin Yurenev. The debate centred on the events in the streets over the past four days. 'There is no revolution and there will be no revolution,' Shliapnikov declared. 'We have to prepare for a long period of reaction.' Yurenev strongly supported this view.

The general view was that the revolutionary movement was losing its impetus; the demonstrations were unorganised and without purpose or direction. According to Kerensky, 'Men who a few days later would become the most uncompromising revolutionaries said we should concentrate our efforts on propaganda to prepare for a serious revolutionary movement later on.'[26]

Meanwhile, several deputies had approached Rodzianko in the presidential suite, Room 5 on the lefthand side of the Tauride Palace, and urged him to summon a meeting of the Council of Elders for midday the following day to discuss the crisis. The results of the Elders' deliberations should then be reported to an informal 'private' meeting of Duma deputies. Rodzianko agreed to both suggestions.[i]

He was about to retire at eleven o'clock that night when he received an urgent invitation to visit Prince Golitsyn at his apartment in Mokhovaya Street. As soon as he began protesting about the shooting of demonstrators, the Prime Minister handed him the Tsar's pre-signed decree proroguing the Duma. Despite the late hour, Rodzianko telephoned his deputy, Nikolai Nekrasov, to inform him that Nicholas had declared war on the people's representatives.

Far away at GHQ in peaceful Mogilev, the Tsar was scribbling in his diary: 'At ten o'clock I went to Mass. The reports were on time. There were many people at breakfast, including all the foreigners. Wrote to Alix and went for a walk near the chapel by the Bobrisky road. The weather was fine and frosty. After tea I read and talked with Senator Tregubov until dinner. Played dominoes in the evening.'

There was nothing to worry about. God was in His heaven and His will would be done. The final day of the Romanov regime's effective rule over Russia ended with its last Tsar savouring some of the moves in his favourite game.

---

i There is a great deal of disparity in books about the Revolution over which is left and right of the Tauride Palace. This work follows Kerensky and Solzhenitsyn's example of taking directions facing the palace entrance from the street.

At eight o'clock the next morning - Monday 27 February - Olga Kerenskaya shook her husband awake. As usual, he had worked until three or four a.m. and it was difficult to rouse him. Kerensky recalls his wife shouting, 'Get up! Nekrasov is on the telephone. He says the Duma has been dissolved, the Volynian Regiment has mutinied and is leaving its barracks. You are wanted at the Duma at once.'[27]

Kerensky came to with a jolt. 'I perceived, or rather felt, that the decisive hour had struck,' he says. Dressing quickly, he forgot about breakfast and headed for the door. 'My husband left the house immediately,' Olga recalls. 'He never came back there to live with us again.'

As he hurried down Tverskaya Street and crossed the mist-shrouded English garden of the Tauride Palace, Kerensky's first thought was to keep the Duma in session and to establish close contact with the troops and the people. Entering the palace through a side door into the library, he threw off his hat and overcoat and ran down the long, deserted corridor in search of information.

As no one had bothered to lock the palace gates, deputies started showing up to find out what was happening. Vasily Shulgin and Andrei Shingarev, who lived in the same apartment block on the Petrograd Side, arrived together after driving through a rebellious crowd to the well-guarded Trinity Bridge, where they were recognised and allowed to pass through the military cordon. Reaching the Tauride Palace, they joined the tide of frockcoated deputies ebbing and flowing through the grand Cupola Hall into the meeting rooms or mounting the stairs to the cafeteria.[28]

Kerensky found his Masonic friend Nekrasov talking to Ivan Efremov, President of the Progressive Bloc, and a Trudovik deputy, Vasily Vershinin, in the chandeliered Catherine Hall. The morning sun crept through the curved Venetian windows and gleamed off the freshly beeswaxed parquet floors. Kerensky's comrades informed him that the Duma had been prorogued at midnight on the Tsar's orders. There among the white Corinthian columns Kerensky made his first decision: if the Duma were to play any role in the revolution it was absolutely vital for the deputies to defy the imperial decree and remain in session.[ii]

[ii] Prorogation meant the session was discontinued. Dissolution would have meant an election.

Meanwhile, Mikhail Rodzianko, having received no reply to his first telegram, dispatched a second telegram to Mogilev through the Tauride Palace's own telegraph office, telling the Tsar that he must take immediate steps to save the country and the Romanov Dynasty because 'by tomorrow it may be too late'. He then barricaded himself behind the stout oak door of the presidential suite, while deputies prowled down dark corridors in search of authority, any authority, and could find none.[29]

The thing that was missing in Petrograd that day was leadership. 'There were no authoritative leaders on the spot in any of the parties,' Nikolai Sukhanov says. 'They were all in exile, in prison, or abroad.' Vladimir Lenin (Bolshevik) and Julius Martov (Menshevik) were in Zurich, Viktor Chernov (Socialist Revolutionary) in Paris and Leon Trotsky (still a Menshevik) in New York, while Stalin (Bolshevik), Irakli Tsereteli (Menshevik), Fyodor Dan (Menshevik) and Avram Gotz (Socialist Revolutionary) were in Siberia.[30]

H. G. Wells thought the power vacuum was deliberate. 'For generations the chief energies of Tsarism had been directed to destroying any possibility of an alternative government,' he later wrote. 'It had subsisted on that one fact that, bad as it was, there was nothing else to put in its place.' Indeed, Rodzianko, Miliukov, Guchkov and their Duma cohorts had devoted their energies to criticising the government but had failed to prepare themselves for power.[31]

Only Alexander Kerensky seemed to have a purpose. He saw the chaos as an opportunity to bring down the Old Order and he buzzed around planning a revolution in his head. He and his comrades had set up a rudimentary but effective newsgathering service in many quarters of Petrograd, including an observation post in the City Duma. Every few minutes telephone messages were handed to them with the latest reports. Mutinies had broken out in the Preobrazhensky, Volynian and Lithuanian Regiments located between the Tauride Palace and Liteiny Prospekt. Three companies of the Preobrazhensky Guards had shot their senior officer, Colonel Bogdanovich, when he refused to distribute rifles and cartridges and had then looted the regimental arsenals.

True to their word, the Volynian training detachment had refused to shoot any more civilians; instead, they had killed one of their officers, Captain Ivan Lashkevich, and marched out of their barracks towards

Liteiny Prospekt. The Lithuanians heard the ruckus in their adjacent compound and joined the revolt as soon as the rebels appeared outside their gates shouting slogans and firing blanks.[32]

The *New York Times* reported, 'The people's cry for food reached the hearts of the soldiers and one by one the regiments rebelled until finally those troops which had for a time stood loyal to the Government gathered up their arms and marched into the ranks of the revolutionists.' Driven by elation and terror, the rolling insurrection reached the Sixth Sapper Battalion in Kirochnaya Street, where the engineers shot their commander and several other officers and marched out of their barracks to the stirring strains of their band.[33]

Heavy snow had fallen in Liteiny Prospekt. Revolutionaries had set fire to the District Court and blocked the street with barricades. Armed civilians lurked in the shadow of buildings and on dark corners. Suddenly, loyal Tsarist troops commanded by Colonel Alexander Kutepov opened fire. People scattered; several fell to the ground. 'As we turned into Liteiny, the crowd grew larger and the shooting became louder,' Pitirim Sorokin says. 'The frantic efforts of the police to disperse the crowd were utterly without effect. "Ah-h, Pharaohs! Your end is coming!" howled the mob. Advancing cautiously, we came upon fresh bloodstains and saw two dead bodies on the pavement.'[34]

Another mob had broken into Okhrana headquarters on the Fontanka Embankment and seized its archives. 'News was brought to us of skirmishes with the police,' Kerensky says. 'Government machineguns were firing on the people from roofs and belfries. It was quite clear that the government intended to take advantage of the growing anarchy for its own dark purposes. The hunger riots of the preceding days, the military disintegration, the alleged need to dissolve the "disloyal" Duma were intended to serve as proof that it had become impossible to continue the war. This was the path along which the government was moving and this was clearly its aim - a separate peace.'[35]

Kerensky realised that the rebellion would become a revolution only if the soldiers came to the Duma in search of leadership. 'I rushed to the telephone and urged some friends to go to the barracks of the insurgent regiments and direct the troops to the Duma,' he says. 'The deputies were rapidly filling the lobbies and there was an atmosphere of increasing tension.'

Unbeknown to Kerensky, the leaders of the Progressive Bloc were about to make a fatal tactical error. As Rodzianko was in his office with the door firmly closed, Miliukov, Shidlovsky and Shulgin met with other non-revolutionary liberal deputies around a green baize table in Room 11. They were committed to the bourgeois model of establishing a 'ministry of confidence' responsible to parliament. Failing that, their preferred option was for the Tsar to abdicate in favour of the Tsarevich, with the Grand Duke Michael Alexandorvich serving as regent in a constitutional monarchy.[36]

The Progressive Bloc had no intention of abandoning the Romanov Dynasty to revolutionary forces but were agreed on one thing: that the Duma had no mandate to intervene in the events taking place all over the city. Shulgin summed up their position: 'In my opinion, gentlemen, our Bloc has ceased to exist.' Instead of exploiting the situation, they would stand on the sidelines and observe what happened.[37]

Over on Palace Square Sir George Buchanan and Maurice Paléologue had made their usual Monday morning visit to the Ministry of Foreign Affairs in the east wing of the General Staff Building. Colonel Knox reached Buchanan there by telephone to inform him that the Petrograd Garrison had mutinied and mutineers were in control of Liteiny Prospekt. Buchanan repeated this message to Nikolai Pokrovsky, the Foreign Minister, and added, 'Protopopov can congratulate himself on bringing Russia face to face with revolution.'

Pokrovsky said that loyalist troops would be brought from the front to restore order. As for the Duma, it would be suspended until April. Buchanan replied this was madness – the only way to prevent the insurrection from spreading to Moscow and other towns was through concession and reconciliation.[38]

Kerensky's on-the-spot reporters supplied him with a steady stream of news. Finland Station had fallen. The Vyborg Side was in the hands of rebels. Another mob was crossing the Champ de Mars and heading for the Winter Palace. The Munitions Works had fallen. One band of revolutionaries had invaded the House of Preliminary Detention in Shpalernaya Street and freed 958 prisoners, many of them criminals, while another band liberated Gvozdev, Bogdanov and other members of the Workers' Group from Kresty Prison.

The Peter and Paul Fortress surrendered after revolutionaries threatened to attack it with artillery. All the 'political' cells were found to be empty and the only prisoners inside the fortress were nineteen soldiers who had been arrested in the recent troubles. The medieval Kronwerk Arsenal, a central storehouse of arms, was opened and its revolvers, rifles and ammunition distributed to the revolutionaries.

Deputies of the right and moderate parties bombarded Kerensky with questions about what was happening and what would become of them. He replied that a revolution was taking place, that the troops were on their way to the Duma and that it was their duty, as the democratic representatives of the people, to bond with the mutineers and the revolutionaries. Indeed, most deputies were increasingly conscious of the fact that the Duma, as an elected body, could be the only centre of authority commanding public respect and that it was essential for them, in Kerensky's words, 'to save Russia from ruin'.

At midday Rodzianko opened his door and the Duma's party leaders – the Council of Elders – filed in. Sitting on the red silk-covered benches in his office, they listened as he informed them of the steps he had taken in the past forty-eight hours. He read the telegrams he had sent to the Tsar and told the deputies of his conversations with ministers. The deputies pressed him: What should they do? What was the Government doing, if anything? Neither Rodzianko nor Miliukov had any answers. The leaders of the Opposition - Kerensky, Nekrasov, Efremov and Cheidze - demanded they ignore the Tsar's dissolution decree. Kerensky urged Rodzianko to ring the electric bells and summon the deputies to an immediate session of the Duma in the White Hall.

'The majority did not agree with us,' he says. 'Argument, persuasion and passionate appeals were in vain. The problem was that the majority still believed in the past. The crimes and follies of the Government had not yet succeeded in rooting this faith out of their souls. The meeting rejected our proposal and decided that the Duma would convene in "unofficial" session.' This decision would have immense ramifications for the Duma and the country. At a stroke it removed the Duma's already leaky umbrella of legality, as well as stripping the deputies of their immunity from prosecution.[39]

Instead of representing their constituencies, they had become a collection of individuals attending a private meeting and, as such, would have no legal right to claim national recognition. The majority decision had placed the Duma on the same level as any other self-appointed organisation, including the Petrograd Soviet of Worker' Deputies, which was about to make a dramatic reappearance. Even now, Gvozdev, Bogdanov and other members of the Workers' Group were heading for the Duma with their liberators to reconstitute that body as the nerve centre of the strike movement.[40]

Without a murmur of protest, the Duma died on 27 February, the day when its strength and influence were at their highest. 'This refusal to continue in session formally was perhaps the greatest mistake the Duma ever made,' Kerensky says. 'It meant committing suicide at the very moment when its authority was supreme and it might have played a decisive and fruitful part had it acted officially.'

Just after midday a panicky General Khabalov cabled the Stavka from his base in the office of the City Governor, Major General Alexander Balk,[iii] requesting that a huge force of loyal troops be sent from the front to Petrograd as quickly as possible. He assured General Alekseyev that, in the meantime, he would take 'all measures necessary to suppress the rebellion'. He then ordered the commanders of loyal regiments in the Petrograd Garrison to assemble their troops in Palace Square.

An hour later, however, Alekseyev received a telegram from the Minister of War, General Mikhail Beliaev, which presented a very different picture. 'The disturbances which began in some army units from the morning are vigorously and energetically being suppressed by companies and battalions remaining faithful to their duty,' Beliaev claimed. 'It has not been successful so far to suppress the rebellion, but I am firmly convinced of the rapid approach of tranquillity, the achievement for which merciless measures are being taken. The government is maintaining complete calm.'[41]

Beliaev, a jug-eared sycophant in the Sukhomlinov mould, was too craven to admit that 25,000 soldiers in the Volynian, Preobrazhensky, Lithuanian, Litovsky and Finlandsky Regiments were already in open revolt and that soldiers in one military unit after another were joining them. The astonishing thing was that this had happened without any centralised command or unified strategy. The historian William Henry Chamberlin called it 'one of the most leaderless, spontaneous,

---

iii The City Governor was in charge of the Petrograd police, with military rank. After his arrest on 27 February, Balk claimed Khabalov had given the order to strafe civilians with machineguns.

anonymous revolutions of all time'. Indeed, the pleading and cajoling of civilians in the streets seemed to have had as much effect on the soldiers as the agitation of SR, Menshevik and Bolshevik activists in the barracks. Meanwhile, the conflicting telegrams from Khabalov and Beliaev had delayed the Stavka in organising a counter-offensive. Engulfed in clouds of nervous smoke, the Tsar waited in vain for a clarifying message from his Minister of the Interior. Where was Protopopov and why had he fallen silent?[42]

Kerensky knew that everything depended on whether the soldiers, the workers and their civilian supporters would come to the Duma and accept it as the centre of the Revolution. Otherwise, this explosion of people power could easily turn into a destructive anarchic force that would tear the country apart. The barracks of thousands of soldiers were only a few hundred yards from the Tauride Palace and yet another hour passed and there was still no sign of them. 'Hoping from moment to moment for the arrival of the Guards, I sent messenger after messenger down the street to see if they were coming,' he says. '"Where are your troops?" demanded my colleagues on all sides. Why the troops were mine, nobody knew; but all felt it was so. The Revolution wanted it so.'

At half past one panic rippled through the Catherine Hall like an electric current. A uniformed Duma official called to Kerensky, 'The soldiers are coming!' Members of a dozen different factions grabbed one another in Pavlovian fear. The barbarians who were shooting people in authority were at the palace gates. 'I flew to a window to convince myself that it was actually so,' Kerensky says. 'I had no thought of what I would do next. From the window I saw soldiers, surrounded by a throng of civilians, lining up on the opposite side of the street. They were forming their ranks rather undecidedly, evidently finding it difficult without the guidance of their regular officers.'

Overjoyed, Kerensky shouted to his colleagues, 'May I tell them that the State Duma is with them, that it assumes all responsibility, that it will stand at the head of the movement?' Getting no coherent answer, he dashed to the colonnaded entrance. Men from the Volynian and Lithuanian Regiments were streaming through the gates into the courtyard. The miracle had become fact: the army had defied its sacred oath to the Tsar and sent its representatives to the representatives of the people. This was surely the point of departure from the Old Order, or, as Kerensky would put it in his memoirs, the moment when the Tsarist autocracy retired forever into history.

Outside the Tauride Palace startled attendants stood on the porch not knowing what to do. The crowd numbered no more than a few hundred but it was increasing all the time. Kerensky gazed at the scene for a moment. The vast majority were rank-and-file soldiers without any obvious leadership; nor was there any sign of red flags or red banners. Bareheaded and dressed only in his black jacket, he ran out to greet them. 'Citizen soldiers,' he cried, 'on you falls the great honour of guarding the State Duma…. I declare you to be the First Revolutionary Guard!'

He had committed the Duma to the Revolution.

The soldiers rushed towards him and surrounded him in an excited mass. At that moment other leftwing deputies joined in and Cheidze also spoke some words of greeting. Kerensky then asked a group of Volynian soldiers to follow him into the palace to replace the Tsarist guards and take over the defence of the building. 'The whole throng pushed after me towards the main entrance,' he says. 'Somehow the soldiers separated themselves and, drawing up in disciplined form, followed me.'

Kerensky had gone out to meet the troops as a mere deputy; he returned to the palace a few minutes later the bearer of revolutionary authority. 'Those around me realised this before I did,' he says. He led the troops towards the Guardroom on the lefthand side of the palace. As he brushed past other deputies, he wondered whether there would be any resistance. Some of the palace guards had fled, others wisely joined the Revolution. The only casualty was the Commander of the Guard, Ensign Medvedev, who was shot in the hand and slashed with a sabre when a violent gang of revolutionaries burst into the Guardroom through a side entrance.[43]

Kerensky explained to a non-commissioned officer where the sentries should be placed and left them to it. 'Returning from the Guardroom, I addressed the crowd which remained outside the palace entrance,' he says. 'They were in no doubt that we were in the middle of a revolution and asked me how they should deal with the representatives of the old regime.' Kerensky ordered them to arrest the Tsarist ministers and bring them to the Tauride Palace. Bloodshed should be avoided. He then retired to a desk in the vestibule, where other units reported to him for duty. These were sent to guard the palace's telephone system and telegraph office, and to occupy the water tower across the street to ensure an uninterrupted supply of water. His biggest coup was to send a squad of troops to the Armoured Car Division on Znamenskaya Street. They returned with ninety-seven machineguns and sixteen armoured cars which were parked in the courtyard next to other commandeered vehicles.

Vasily Shulgin was the first man to acknowledge Kerensky's central role in these events. 'He grew every minute,' he says. 'There were people who obeyed him. To be more precise I should say there were armed people who obeyed him. For in a revolution only those who hold a rifle in their hands are people.'[44] Kerensky's force was minute – it consisted of a couple of hastily appointed adjutants and a handful of soldiers - but it proved effective. 'They weren't good for anything big but they gave at least some illusion of power,' Shulgin says. 'For Kerensky, with his actor's nature, with his inflammatory and self-confident nature, it was enough.'

At 2.30 p.m. the deputies met in their unofficial capacity. As the meeting had no legal standing, it was not held in the White Hall but in the adjoining Polutsirkulnyi Hall, a semi-circular chamber overlooking Tauride Gardens. After two hours of discussion, the meeting decided that the Council of Elders should appoint a 'Temporary Committee' of Duma members. It was also agreed that Rodzianko and other members of the Duma Presidium should meet with Grand Duke Michael that evening to discuss the crisis. The Tsar's brother had arrived in his private train at Warsaw Station that afternoon with his English secretary, Brian Johnson, and had been driven to the Marinsky Palace, where the Council of Ministers planned to meet later that day.

Alexander Kerensky's home telephone number – 119-60 – was known to a bewildering number of people ranging from strikers at the Putilov Iron Works (who would call asking for 'Citizen Deputy Kerensky') to reporters on the Petrograd newspapers and the foreign correspondents and diplomats of many nationalities. Ever since he had left the apartment that morning, the phone had rung virtually nonstop with questions that Olga Kerenskaya could not answer.

Around three o'clock in the afternoon she had had enough. She decided to see for herself what was happening at the Tauride Palace.

Leaving Oleg and Gleb in the care of their servant, she put on her overcoat and boots and walked out into the street. It was a fine, frosty afternoon and all along Tverskaya Street bright sunlight sparkled off the crisp white snow. At that moment, tingling with the thrill of expectation, she knew that her life was about to change but she had no inkling of how dramatic that change would be.[45]

At the end of the street she caught up with a detachment of soldiers who were marching in formation without the assistance of an officer. Their faces glowed with an inner joy and they were singing.

'Where are you going, little brother,' she asked one.

'To the Duma!' he replied confidently, as though all the answers to their problems were to be found among the people's representatives.

As the group approached Shpalernaya Street, Olga saw that the palace courtyard was already packed with people. Civilians sat on fences and ledges listening to impromptu speakers; soldiers were jammed together like a football crowd, all eyes focussed on the front entrance. Olga recognised the noble, bespectacled head of a leading Socialist Revolutionary, Herman Lopatin, the man who, in a previous incarnation, had organised the People's Will from 1867 to 1884. A friend of Marx and Engels (and translator *Das Kapital* into Russian), he had survived nineteen years of solitary confinement in the Shlisselburg Fortress. Now in his seventies, he had walked all the way from his home on the outskirts of the city to witness the Revolution.

'Mrs. Kerensky,' he said, 'today I can say the *Nunc dimittis* (Lord now lettest thou thy servant depart in peace). This is the day I have been waiting for all my life. I wish I could die today.'[iv] Olga's breast filled with an inner contentment. Celebratory bonfires were burning in the streets and she walked home a happy woman.

By mid-afternoon several thousand men from infantry and cavalry units, as well as foot police and mounted police had responded to General Khabalov's order to assemble in Palace Square. There were two Preobrazhensky companies from their so-far-loyal barracks in Millionnaya Street near the Winter Palace, a Pavlovsky battalion, three Ismailovsky companies, a company of the Third Rifle Regiment, three companies of the Eger Regiment, a company of the First Reserve Machine Gun Regiment and two artillery batteries.

---

iv Herman Lopatin died of cancer in December 1918

Leaving the Preobrazhensky Guards standing in formation on Palace Square as a sign of imperial strength, Khabalov deployed the rest of the force in an area bounded by the Winter Palace, the General Staff Building, the Admiralty and the Petrograd *gradonachalstvo*, the administrative centre that controlled the Okhrana, the police force and the gendarmerie. His strategy was to avoid further contact with the enemy in the hope that reinforcements would arrive in time to save him. Meanwhile, he sought courage in a bottle of Cognac.

Back in the Tauride Palace Kerensky received a request from the organisers the Soviet of Workmen's Deputies to arrange quarters for its members. With Rodzianko's consent, he led the delegates to Room 12, the former home of the Budget Commission, on the righthand side of the palace. The Soviet's first action was to revive their newspaper, *Izvestia*. A special edition was rushed on to the streets calling on workers to send delegates to the palace for the Soviet's first plenary session at seven o'clock that very evening. Delegates should be chosen on the basis of one delegate for every thousand workers or, for the soldiers, one for every company. Factories with fewer than a thousand workers were asked to elect one deputy from each factory.[46]

Meanwhile, the Tauride Palace was undergoing an extraordinary transformation. Outside, soldiers had set up bivouacs in the courtyard and the gardens. Small groups were singing the 'Marseillaise' around campfires; bayonets glistened in the firelight. Inside, a nest of machineguns had been set up in the vestibule and the corridors were packed with soldiers of all ranks. Stocks of food and ammunition 'liberated' from quartermasters' stores were piled high wherever space could be found. And everywhere the shells of sunflower seeds attested to the fact that the palace was now a proletarian citadel.

In true revolutionary spirit every room overflowed with delegations of civilians and soldiers addressing their concerns to handfuls of flustered deputies. Meetings were taking place in the White Hall and the Catherine Hall, though who was in charge and what they hoped to achieve was anybody's guess.

Mikhail Rodzianko was the last man who should have been in charge of a situation which required initiative and daring. As he admitted to anyone who would listen, 'I do not want to rebel. I am not a rebel. I have made no revolution and I do not wish to. If it has happened, it is precisely because people did not obey us. But I am not a revolutionary. I will not go against the supreme authority.'

When he asked Vasily Shulgin what he should do, Shulgin replied, 'Take power, Mikhail Vladimirovich. Take power as a loyal subject.'

Shulgin found the whole thing deeply offensive. At lunchtime he had joined hundreds of people in a queue shuffling into the cafeteria on the first floor in the hope of being fed. 'They all had the same faces: vilely and beastly stupid or vilely and devilishly evil. God, how disgusting it was!' By the time he got to the counter, not a morsel of food remained and the manager was complaining that all the silver spoons had been stolen. 'I wasn't the only one who felt that way,' he says, 'that is, who felt that this was the end, who felt a deep hatred for the revolution from its very first day.'[47]

At 5.30 p.m. Kerensky and Shulgin were in Rodzianko's room for another meeting of the Council of Elders to discuss the composition of the Temporary Committee when a messenger dashed in to announce that Ivan Shcheglovitov had been brought in. The news caused great excitement among the deputies. Shcheglovitov, the President of the State Council, the former Minister of Justice responsible for the Beilis Case, the man Kerensky had once called 'a crocodile without tears', was under arrest!

The moderates urged Rodzianko to intervene. 'We must let him go,' they insisted. 'We cannot arrest the President of the State Council in the very halls of the Duma. What about the immunity of members of legislative bodies?'

They turned to Kerensky.

'I will not release Scheglovitov,' he said.

'You want to turn the Duma into a prison?'

This was a valid objection but to release Shcheglovitov would have meant handing him over to a lynch mob. Kerensky, Rodzianko and some of the deputies hurried towards the entrance, where they found Shcheglovitov surrounded by a group of angry soldiers. According to Kerensky, Rodzianko greeted him amicably and invited him into his rooms as his guest. Stepping between the two men, Kerensky said, 'No, Mikhail Vladimirovich, Mr Shcheglovitov is not a guest here and I refuse to have him released.'

He then asked the President of the Imperial Council, 'Are you Ivan Grigorievich Shcheglovitov?'

'Yes.'

'I must request you to follow me. You are a prisoner. Have no fear. I guarantee your safety. The State Duma does not spill blood.' Everyone obeyed and fell back. Rodzianko and his friends, somewhat confused, returned to his rooms, while Kerensky led Scheglovitov to the Ministerial Pavilion, a separate building connected to the White Hall by a glass-roofed passage. Ministers stayed there in well-appointed rooms whenever they were due to appear before the despised Duma. As the Pavilion was under the control of the government, deputies had no unrestricted right of entry in normal times but these were anything but normal times. By occupying the building with revolutionary troops, Kerensky turned it into a temporary prison and thus avoided degrading the Duma.

Vasily Shulgin, who witnessed Kerensky's treatment of Shcheglovitov, was impressed. 'This revealed the total Kerensky – an actor to the marrow but a man with an honest aversion to blood.'[48]

A few minutes before seven o'clock that evening the Reserve First Infantry Regiment of more than 200 officers and 12,000 troops marched up to the Duma in full military formation to join the Revolution. Kerensky realised that in order to coordinate the activities of this huge force he would need a command post inside the palace. Without consulting anybody, he formed the Duma Military Commission in Room 42. 'I had to set this whole enterprise up: to dispatch the guard, to decide on the movement of forces against the enemy, to send automobiles with machineguns and so on,' he says.[49]

Meanwhile, a group of newspaper correspondents whose job was to cover the Duma had decided to produce their own newspaper, *The Journal of Petrograd Journalists*. First, they needed a permit. One of them approached Kerensky.

'Alexander Fyodorovich,' he said, 'will you please sign an order permitting us to publish a revolutionary newspaper?'

Kerensky was astonished.

'Why do you address your request to me?' he queried.

'Don't you realise,' said the journalist, 'what power you now wield in Russia?'

Kerensky laughed and signed the order.

15

The End of Tsarism

Sunset was shortly after five o'clock that evening and darkness had fallen when Mikhail Rodzianko and his Duma colleagues Nikolai Nekrasov, Ivan Dmitriukov and Nikanor Savich set off in two motorcars to meet Grand Duke Michael at the Marinsky Palace. Not trusting the Duma President, several self-appointed bodyguards were keeping an eye on him. As the presidential limousine moved off, soldiers with fixed bayonets jumped on to the running boards and lay down on the fenders with bayonets pointing forward like spears.

After the comparative security of the Tauride Palace, the four-mile journey along the embankments to Saint Isaac's Square was a nerve-wracking experience. The Battle of Petrograd between Tsarist forces and revolutionaries reached its climax that night and one wrong turning could have proved fatal. No one knows for sure how many people were killed and wounded in the capital during the February Days – one estimate gives a figure of 'up to 1500 killed and 6000 wounded' - but near the top of the list were the hated pharaohs. Dozens of police stations were incinerated and their occupants hunted down like wild animals and slaughtered with whatever weapons came to hand.

In the absence of a functioning police force, the mobs raided private homes, restaurants, shops, public buildings looking for loot or their Tsarist enemies. The District Court, the Alexander Nevsky Police Station and the Okhrana building were on fire and their crimson glow reddened the night sky. Nowhere was safe for anyone of rank - even a Tsarist war hero was butchered.

Around the Liteiny and Trinity Bridges the 'revolutionary zone' bristled with mutinous soldiers and armed civilians. Rodzianko's bodyguards had attached a red flag to the leading vehicle and the Duma delegation got through impromptu checkpoints without any bother. Once they reached the 'government zone', however, the soldiers thought better of it and vanished into the darkness.¹ Travelling west along the Neva, the Duma men could hear the sound of shooting in all directions and from time to time the telltale rat-a-tat-tat of a machinegun rent the chill night air. They passed the British Embassy at 4 Palace Embankment, where Sir George Buchanan had forbidden his family and staff from leaving the building. His daughter Meriel says she spent the evening listening to the chatter of the machineguns.

Despite these audible signs of battle, the resistance of the Tsarist forces under General Khabalov was disintegrating. During the day his callous disregard of the men's welfare had led to a steady stream of desertions. There was no food for them to eat and no fodder for the horses. The Pavlovsky battalion deserted in disgust and every patrol defected to the insurgents.² Khabalov had also kept the two Preobrazhensky companies standing in Palace Square for hours on end. It was a very cold day and, having received no orders, their officers sent the troops back to their barracks in Millionnaya Street to be fed. Khabalov reported to the Stavka that he was unable to restore order because his units 'had sustained heavy casualties'. He did not think it necessary to elaborate on what had happened to them.

Just before dinnertime at Mogilev, the Tsar ordered General Ivanov, hero of the Austrian front, to travel to the capital with a large force of frontline troops, including a battalion of the Knights of Saint George, to suppress the revolution. As Khabalov had failed in his duty to the Crown, he also ordered Ivanov to replace him as Military Dictator of Petrograd.

Inside the solid baroque walls of the Marinsky Palace, a liveried usher led the Duma delegation from an anteroom into the dimly lit Rotunda, the white-pillared chamber at the very heart of the Romanov regime's legislative powers. This was the location of the State Council's grand ceremonial occasions at which medals, sashes, gold braid and all the other paraphernalia of high office were de rigueur. It was also the scene of the tottering deliberations of the Tsarist ministers who had brought the country to the brink of destruction.

A bronze-embossed door at the far end was flung open and the visitors were admitted to the office of one of the palace's former residents, Duke Maximilian de Beauharnais, grandson of the Empress Josephine Bonaparte. Rodzianko realised that this was now the private quarters of Kerensky's prisoner, Ivan Shcheglovitov. To his great relief another door opened and they found themselves in the office of the Secretary to the State Council. Grand Duke Michael, a handsome man as tall as his father but with an easy-going disposition, was waiting to greet them. It was almost eight o'clock when they took their places around a conference table and got down to business.

After a preamble in which he repeated that his primary purpose was to protect the hereditary monarchy, Rodzianko suggested the only way to save the country was to transfer power to the State Duma. This should be done today because, as he had said in his telegram to the Tsar, tomorrow would be too late. Michael politely informed Rodzianko that he had no power to sanction such a transfer. He then led them upstairs, where the Council of Ministers was meeting in their private quarters. They found the Tsar's hand-picked defenders slumped in burgundy velvet armchairs around an immense table littered with ashtrays, plates and glasses. The only absentee was Protopopov.

Rodzianko wasted no time in demanding the resignation of the entire cabinet and the transfer of power to the Duma Committee. Prince Golitsyn, a distant relative of Rodzianko's, explained that he had already telegraphed his resignation to the Tsar but, as no minister could lay down his burden without royal permission, he was waiting to hear whether it had been accepted. Some of the ministers loathed the Duma President and they expressed their feelings in no uncertain terms. According to Nekrasov, the most belligerent was the State Secretary, Sergei Kryzhanovsky. 'They knew about Shcheglovitov's arrest,' he says. 'Kryzhanovsky made it clear that he suspected the arrest was made on Rodzianko's orders. The hostility toward us was quite pronounced.'[3]

Several ministers, such as the normally judicious Nikolai Pokrovsky, were in favour of the violent suppression of the revolutionaries. General Beliaev, who had informed the Tsar some hours earlier that the disorder in military units was being dealt with 'vigorously and energetically', insisted that the government was on solid ground and that the broad measures he was taking would pacify the rebels. 'So where is Protopopov?' Rodzianko wondered out loud. Golitsyn mumbled that he was no longer a minister; indeed, the Minister of the Interior had offered to commit suicide 'if that would help' but the ministers had ignored the offer. Instead, he had submitted his resignation and since then had been wandering through the palace's gilded halls like a lost soul.

Returning to the State Secretary's office, Rodzianko demanded that Grand Duke Michael get in touch with his brother via direct wire 'and tell him that he is falling into the abyss - unless, tomorrow, Alexandra Fyodorovna is expelled to the Crimea and he allows an announcement in the Duma that a responsible government is to be promulgated'.[4]

Michael's democratic leanings did not extend to telling the Tsar what to do, especially in relation to the Tsarina, but he agreed to speak to his brother about the crisis. Arrangements were made for him to use the telegraphic equipment at Beliaev's home for that purpose and the Minister of War agreed to report the results of the conversation to Rodzianko. By then it was ten o'clock and the Duma delegation headed back to the Tauride Palace. 'There were no longer any zones,' Nekrasov says. 'It was all one continuous revolutionary wave - revolution had taken everything over.'

Hearing from Nekrasov that the Tsar's ministers were in the Marinsky Palace, Kerensky ordered a detachment of soldiers to fight their way through and arrest them. Meanwhile, Grand Duke Michael and Brian Johnson accompanied General Beliaev across Saint Isaac's Square to the General's apartment in the Ministry of War's mansion at 67 Moika to make contact with the Tsar using his Hughes Telegraphic Apparatus, a rudimentary form of telex machine connected by direct wire to the Stavka at Mogilev.

Missing the Tsarina's comforting arms, Nicholas had retired for the night determined to be reunited with her and the children at Tsarskoe Selo as soon as possible. When General Alekseyev informed him that Grand Duke Michael wanted to converse with him from Petrograd, he knew instinctively that his brother was in the hands of the Duma malcontents. Tapping a cigarette on his jewelled case and lighting up, he ordered Alekseyev to go to the telegraph office and find out what he wanted.

The first proposal that clicked out of the tape machine one word at a time was that the Tsar dismiss the Council of Ministers in order to calm things down. 'In view of the extremely serious situation,' Michael added, 'would not Your Imperial Majesty deign to delegate me immediately to announce [the Zemstvos leader] Prince Georgie

Lvov as Prime Minister of a new government responsible only to you?'

Alekseyev replied: I will report to His Imperial Majesty the telegram of Your Imperial Highness. Tomorrow His Majesty the Emperor leaves for Tsarskoe Selo.

Michael: I request you report to His Imperial Majesty that, according to my conviction, it perhaps would be desirable to postpone his arrival at Tsarskoe Selo for several days.

Alekseyev delivered these messages to Nicholas and returned some time later with his replies: 'His Majesty the Emperor ordered me to thank Your Imperial Highness on his behalf and to report to you the following: First, in view of the exceptional circumstances, His Majesty the Emperor does not consider it possible to postpone his departure and he will leave tomorrow at half-past two in the afternoon. Second, His Imperial Majesty will postpone until his arrival in Tsarskoe Selo all measures which concern changes in personnel. Third, tomorrow, General Ivanov is proceeding to Petrograd as Commander in Chief of the Petrograd District, having at his disposal a reliable battalion. Fourth, tomorrow four infantry and four cavalry regiments from the most reliable units of the Northern and Western Fronts will start for Petrograd.'[5]

There was no doubting the Tsar's determination to defend his throne but Nikolai Ivanov was now an ailing sixty-five-year-old and he would have little chance of controlling thousands of troops, mostly peasants whose only interest was in acquiring land and whose sympathies lay with the Socialist Revolutionaries. Indeed, he had so misread the enormity of his mission that he packed luxury items in his kit to give to friends in the capital.[6]

Meanwhile, General Khabalov had abandoned the City Governor's Offices and moved his headquarters and his shrinking force into a deserted section of the massive Admiralty Building. The only area of the city under his control now was the narrow strip of land between the Admiralty on the Neva and the Marinsky Palace. When the Council of Ministers demanded he supply troops to strengthen their guard, he replied that if they wanted protection they should come to the Admiralty.[7]

Back in the Tauride Palace Kerensky received a report that his troops had been fired on by machineguns and had not been able to reach the Marinsky Palace. He sent the armoured cars in and within an hour the revolutionaries had broken through the defences on the Blue Bridge over the Moika and were fighting their way towards the palace. Kryzhanovsky feared that Protopopov's presence would place the other ministers in danger of attack, so he arranged for him to spend the night at the nearby State Control building. When the Council of Ministers' meeting adjourned, Nikolai Pokrovsky was going through the front entrance at the same time as Protopopov when they bumped into a group of soldiers with fixed bayonets.

'Where is Protopopov?' one shouted.

'He's over there somewhere,' Pokrovsky replied, pointing vaguely behind him. The soldiers ran past them into the palace and Pokrovsky and Protopopov got away.[8]

A few of the ministers were still upstairs when the soldiers burst into their room. Some headed for the nearest exit but one hid under a table. Fortunately, the soldiers did not recognise any of them and in the confusion they escaped. There was no sign of Prince Golitsyn. At 11.25 p.m. he had received a telegram from Nicholas refusing to accept his resignation and 'personally bestowing upon you all necessary powers for civil rule'. Golitsyn had read the message, sighed and had then gone home.[9]

Meanwhile, Mikhail Rodzianko joined the Council of Elders in electing a Temporary Committee with powers to issue orders to the armed forces and the general public. *Izvestia* listed the members of this self-appointed body in this order: A. F. Kerensky, N. S. Cheidze, V. V. Shulgin, P. N. Miliukov, N. V. Nekrasov, M. A. Karaulov, A. I. Konovalov, I. I. Dmitriukov, V. A. Rjevsky, S. I. Shidlovsky, Vladimir Lvov and Colonel Boris Engelhardt. Other deputies were appointed commissars to take charge of all ministries and central government offices. Every party was represented in these appointments except the extreme right and the Government Nationalists, whose members had suddenly disappeared from the palace. According to Kerensky, 'These outcasts of the nation – some of them paid government agents - melted away like wax in the sun.' After a great deal of vacillation, Rodzianko agreed to become chairman of the Temporary Committee.[10]

Colonel Engelhardt, a conservative member of the Duma, took over Kerensky's Military Commission with the rank of Commander of the Revolutionary Petrograd Garrison. He supplied a squad of troops to assist a Progressive deputy, Alexander Bublikov, in taking over the Ministry of Transport, whose railway-telegraph system gave the Duma control of the entire railway network and enabled Bublikov to spread the news to every railway station in the country that the Duma's Temporary Committee had taken the formation of a new government into its own hands.[11]

Bublikov, an engineer by profession, was appointed Commissar of Transport with the power to delay or dispatch trains. Vikzhel, the railway workers' union, accepted the Revolution enthusiastically and it was due to the efforts of its members that military trains were kept rolling and the general traffic suffered few interruptions. Jubilant telegrams were also dispatched to frontline soldiers. 'The army in the field recognised and welcomed the Revolution,' Kerensky says. 'They realised more clearly than anyone else that Russia stood on the brink of catastrophe.'

Mikhail Karaulov, a moderate deputy representing the Cossacks of the Tersk region, was appointed Commandant of the Tauride Palace. He warned the public that many criminals who had been freed from the prisons were now on the loose in Petrograd. 'Murderers, thieves and burglars, disguising themselves in uniforms of the lower military ranks, are brazenly bursting into private residences, carrying out illegal searches, robbing, raping and bring terror,' he said. 'I order that all such persons must be detained and dealt with severely to the point of being shot in the event of resistance.'[12]

Then there was a complication: the Petrograd Soviet had elected its own Executive Committee (the *Ispolkom* or Excom), with Nikolai Cheidze as chairman and Matvei Skobelev and Kerensky as vice chairmen. So many soldiers were packed into Room 12 and such was their enthusiasm for the Revolution that the Executive Committee established its own Military Commission and voted to change the Soviet's name to the Soviet of Workers' and Soldiers' Deputies. 'The Temporary Committee of the Duma could claim no better right than the Executive Committee of the Soviet, which also began issuing orders to the garrison,' Kerensky says. 'So two centres of authority, each with its own committee, had been established on the very first day of the Revolution. This division would lead to the decay of all authority and to the anarchy of Bolshevism.'

By the morning of the twenty-eighth, the Tsar had given up hope of getting any sleep and at five a.m. had set off for Tsarskoe Selo in the Royal Train. The shortest route from Mogilev to Tsarskoye Selo was through Orsha, Vitebsk and Dno, a trip of fourteen to sixteen hours. In order to leave the main line clear for Ivanov's forces the train driver was ordered to take an indirect route eastwards via Smolensk, Viazma, Bologoye and Malaya Vishera. This totally unnecessary detour, which added 200 miles and nine hours to the Tsar's journey, would seal the fate of his dynasty.

At 8.25 a.m. General Khabalov reported to the Stavka that the number of loyal troops at the Admiralty had declined to 600 infantrymen and 500 cavalrymen, with no more than fifteen machineguns and twelve artillery pieces. 'The situation,' he said, 'is extremely difficult.' It became impossible when the revolutionaries sent an envoy of truce to inform him that if he did not surrender within the hour the Admiralty would be bombarded by artillery fire from the Peter and Paul Fortress. Khabalov surrendered. Having shaved off his distinctive handlebar moustache, he tried to slip away but he was recognised, arrested and taken to join the other captives in the Pavilion at the Tauride Palace.[13]

Overnight, large sections of the palace had been used as a dosshouse. People snoozed in armchairs in the White Hall or slept in the corridors like bundles of rags. The Catherine Hall, its parquet floor covered in a sheen of melted snow and mud, was as slippery as a skating rink. The soldiers had stacked their rifles muzzle-to-muzzle in orderly circles and laid down beside them. Having heard on the grapevine that 'the Duma does not spill blood', dozens of policemen in civilian clothes had queued up outside to be arrested.[14]

Elated young officer-cadets from the Mikhailovsky Artillery School sought out Kerensky and lifted him on to their shoulders. He spoke to them of the free men and women who had been born in the new, free Russia; of the great deeds that lay ahead of them; of how they must carry the War and the Revolution on their shoulders. He spoke of the heroic revolutionaries who had died unflinchingly for the liberty of future generations. 'Representatives of all classes have perished for this cause and all classes must now trust each other,' he said. 'I call for generous, heroic sacrifices in the name of our reborn Motherland.'

Pockets of resistance still existed. During the day shots were fired at a regimental parade from the roof of the German-owned Hotel Astoria on the eastern side of Saint Isaac's Square. Revolutionary soldiers called up three armoured cars and fired their machineguns at the roof but succeeded in shattering the hotel's windows and killing a number of guests. An armed crowd then stormed the building, wrecked the plush foyer, looted the pantries and the cellar, and shot or bayoneted several dozen monarchist officers who were sheltering there.[15]

By sunset most of Petrograd was in the hands of revolutionary troops and any further military attempt to save the dynasty was doomed to failure. Everywhere, the Old Order was crumbling. Ivan Goremykin, an even more exalted personage than Shcheglovitov, sought refuge in Rodzianko's office. Kerensky found the former Prime Minister sitting in a corner, his miserable little figure reflected in the huge mirror that almost covered an entire wall. 'He wore a fur coat and looked like a gnome,' he says. 'Deputies, priests, peasants, officials stood around him. They could not take their eyes off the famous Goremykin with his chain of the Order of Saint Andrew the Apostle. At my request he got up, his chain jingling mournfully, and I led him to the Pavilion.'

Shortly afterwards, he discovered Alexander Protopopov skulking outside the door of the office he had occupied during his time as vice chairman of the Duma. The aging lunatic had pulled his hat down over his face and no one had noticed him. 'Your Excellency,' he said meekly, 'I am coming to you of my own accord; do arrest me.' Kerensky told him to keep quiet and hurried him towards the Pavilion. 'I knew that if his arrival became known it would end badly for him,' he said.[16]

To keep track of the Duma's prisoners, Kerensky set up a commission in Room 34 and installed Mikhail Papadzhanov, a Kadet deputy, as chairman to receive and register each prisoner. The highest ranking category were taken to the Pavilion, while policemen, gendarmes and Tsarist officials were detained in Rooms 35, 35a, and 36.

Dawn was breaking on 1 March when the royal locomotive and its long line of blue salon cars emblazoned with the Romanov crest reached Malaya Vishera 106 miles southeast of Tsarskoe Selo. Nicholas desperately needed the comfort of his Alicky on this of all days – the anniversary of his grandfather's assassination in 1881 - but Malaya Vishera was as close as he got to his wife and family. The

Temporary Committee ordered Commissar Bublikov to block the line ahead and detain the Tsar at that station in order to negotiate with him.

Nicholas, however, was in no mood to talk to the Duma. He ordered the driver to reverse to Bologoye, a junction point halfway between Moscow and Petrograd. 'So we ordered the railway to be cut at Bologoye,' Kerensky says. 'For the first time the Tsar and his suite found they could no longer go where they wished.' Unable to reach Petrograd or Moscow, the train turned west to Dno and then proceeded to Pskov, the headquarters of General N. V. Ruzsky, Commander in Chief of the Northern Front, arriving there around seven o'clock that evening. 'Shame and dishonour,' wrote Nicholas. 'Impossible to get to Tsarskoe. How difficult it must be for poor Alix.'

Meanwhile, General Ivanov, the Saviour of Tsarism, and the Knights of Saint George had reached Tsarskoe Selo on the direct line to find that the mutiny had spread to the Imperial Guards and that General Alekseyev had cancelled his orders to attack the revolutionaries and to return to Mogilev. The worst violence was at the Kronstadt Naval Base, where brutalised trainees murdered thirty-nine of their officers and hacked the base commander, Admiral Robert Viren, to death with bayonets. Another 500 people, including more than two hundred officers, were imprisoned in the base's dungeons. The Revolution had even spread to the dancers of the Bolshoi Ballet, who had gone on strike that day after placing a sign outside the theatre reading: 'No rehearsal on account of Revolution.'[17]

News of these disorders provoked Rodzianko into making a decision that would have a direct bearing on the fate of his country. Fearing that mutinous soldiers might threaten the Temporary Committee, he issued an order through the Military Commission that troops must return to their barracks and obey their officers. The soldiers regarded this instruction with deep suspicion - back in the barracks they would face punishment at the hands of their old commanders. Sukhanov watched as Nikolai Sokolov, Kerensky's friend at the Bar, sat a table in Room 13 surrounded by soldiers 'standing, sitting, and leaning on the table, half-dictating and half-suggesting to Sokolov what he should write ... When the work was finished, they put a heading on the sheet: "Order No. 1"'.

A few minutes later the order was read out to the soldiers in the dimly lit Catherine Hall. It was passed to thunderous applause and was published in *Izvestia* the following day as the Soviet's first legislative act. The poor strategic decisions of Grand Duke Nicholas and his Tsarist cadre had already undermined the morale of the Russian Army and Order Number 1 would destroy its discipline.[18]

The order instructed soldiers and sailors of the Petrograd Garrison to obey their officers only if their orders did not contradict the decrees of the Petrograd Soviet. It also called on units to elect a soldiers' committee which would run each unit and balance the authority of the officers. All weapons were to be handed over to these committees 'and shall by no means be issued to the officers, not even at their insistence'. Soldiers of all ranks were to be addressed formally as '*vy*' instead of the disrespectful '*tyi*'.

The order also allowed soldiers to dispense with standing to attention and saluting when off duty, although while on duty strict military discipline was to be maintained. The honorific titles of the officers, such as 'Your Excellency' and 'Your Honour', which the peasant soldiers, in particular, resented as a remnant of serfdom, were to be replaced by new forms of address, such as 'Mister General' or 'Mister Colonel'. The Soviet hastened to emphasise that Order Number 1 applied only to the Petrograd Garrison but the cat was out of the bag. Mutinous soldiers at Tsarskoe Selo broadcast the order over the country's most powerful transmitter to the front as though it applied to the whole of the Russian Army and the resulting havoc in the trenches dealt the army a blow from which it never recovered.

At 10.30 that night Sukhomlinov, the soldiers' bête noire, was marched into the Tauride Palace by an ensign and two sailors who had arrested him at his house. 'The soldiers surrounded the repulsive old man and seemed ready to tear him to pieces,' Kerensky says. Hearing that one group were on the way from the Catherine Hall to skewer him with their bayonets, Mikhail Papadzhanov intercepted them and promised that if they desisted he would hand them the general's gold-entwined epaulets.

The disgraced Minister of War was hustled into Room 4 next to Rodzianko's presidential suite. 'His eyes were filled with horror; he did not quite grasp what was happening around him,' says Peter Gerasimov, a Kadet deputy who witnessed the scene. 'He was put in a chair and at that very moment, Papadzhanov flew into the room and jumped on him, hysterically screaming, "Epaulets, epaulets!"'

Several soldiers and civilians watched gleefully while Papadzhanov cut the epaulets off Sukhomlinov's uniform. He took them outside the room and showed them to the troops. 'You see? Epaulets!' he shouted. Sukhomlinov then took a penknife out of his pocket and slowly cut the shoulder boards off his greatcoat and handed them over.[19]

Kerensky led the guard that took him away. 'We had to walk through the ranks of the enraged soldiers in the Catherine Hall,' he says. 'The narrow corridor between Catherine Hall and the White Hall was almost deserted but there were more soldiers near the door of the Pavilion. It was there that we passed the most terrible moments.' As soldiers lunged towards Sukhomlinov, Kerensky stepped in front of him and shouted that he would not allow them to disgrace the Revolution. 'I declared that they would lay hands on Sukhomlinov over my dead body,' he says. The crowd hesitated and the guards were able to push Sukhomlinov through the Pavilion door and slam it shut.

At midnight on 1 March a Soviet delegation comprising Nikolai Sukhanov, Nikolai Cheidze, Nikolai Sokolov and Yuri Steklov-Nakhamkes marched into the Temporary Committee's meeting room to negotiate the formation of an emergency government. 'There was not the same chaos and confusion here as with us,' Sukhanov says, 'but the room nevertheless gave an impression of disorder: it was smoke-filled and dirty, and cigarette butts, bottles and dirty glasses were scattered about. There were also innumerable plates, both empty and holding foods of all kinds, which made our eyes glitter and our mouths water.'[20]

It had been a long day and Rodzianko was exhausted. While Miliukov did most of the talking, he sat quietly at a table drinking soda-water. 'The Soviet representatives took the position that the distribution of ministerial portfolios was not their affair,' Kerensky says. 'They would not join the Provisional Government. The organisation of authority was entirely in the hands of the Duma Committee. It was already organised, whereas the Soviet was still searching for its policies.'[21]

This was not the case with the Bolshevik wing of the RSDLP, which had published its internationalist priorities in *Izvestia* that very day. 'The immediate and urgent task of the provisional revolutionary government,' it said, 'is to come into contact with the proletariat of the belligerent countries in order to wage a struggle of the peoples of all countries against their oppressors and enslavers, against tsarist governments and capitalist cliques and for immediate cessation of the bloody human butchery which has been thrust on the enthralled people.' The Bolshevik challenge fell on deaf ears. The first priority of the emergency government being formed that night was not to end the war but to end the autocracy.[22]

On the morning of Thursday 2 March Rodzianko contacted General Alekseyev to gauge his reaction to the idea of abdication. Unaware of Order Number 1, Alekseyev assured him that all the frontline commanders, including General Brusilov, agreed that Nicholas must step down to prevent the army from further collapse. That afternoon Guchkov and Shulgin, both monarchists, set off for Pskov in a train consisting of a locomotive and a parlour car to secure the abdication and to ensure the succession of Alexei as Tsar, with Grand Duke Michael as Regent.[23] Meanwhile, the Romanov crisis was causing palpitations throughout the royal world: in Buckingham Palace King George wrote in his diary that night, 'I fear Alicky is the cause of it all and Nicky has been weak. I am in despair.'[i]

Alexander Kerensky had been rushing about the Duma for seventy-two hours and was on the verge of a breakdown. V. D. Nabokov watched in amazement as he 'grabbed the upturned corners of the starched collar on his black jacket and ripped them off, achieving a deliberately proletarian look'. Sometimes he passed out for fifteen or twenty minutes until Olga or Lilya, who had turned up to serve food and drink, made him take some sustenance. 'While I was there,' Nabokov says, 'he nearly fainted and Count Orlov-Davidov [one of Kerensky's Masonic allies] gave him something to inhale or to drink.'[24]

By ten o'clock it was unanimously agreed between the Temporary Committee and the Soviet that a government should be formed of the best available men, whether they were members of the Duma or not,

---

i King George V, following the advice of his Private Secretary Baron Stamfordham, changed his family's surname from the Germanic 'Saxe-Coburg-Gotha' to the irrefutably English 'Windsor', prompting the Kaiser's best crack of the war. Shakespeare's play, he suggested, should be renamed *The Merry Wives of Saxe-Coburg-Gotha*.

to see the country through the national emergency. This 'Provisional Government' would be the sole sovereign power until a new system of government could be established but there was profound disagreement over what type of government that should be. Miliukov insisted on retaining the monarchy because in his opinion only the monarchy could legitimise the transfer of power, while Kerensky and Cheidze argued for a people's republic. It was agreed to leave this decision to a nationwide Constituent Assembly to be elected as soon as possible. A manifesto containing the Soviet's conditions for supporting the government was published setting out the following policies:

1. An immediate amnesty for all political prisoners.
2. The immediate granting of freedom of speech, press and assembly.
3. The immediate abolition of all restrictions based on class, religion and nationality.
4. Immediate preparations for the convocation of a Constituent Assembly, elected by universal, direct, secret and equal suffrage to determine the form of government and the constitution of the country.
5. The abolition of all police bodies and, in their place, the creation of a people's militia with elected officers responsible to the organs of local self-government.
6. Elections to these organs on the four-fold suffrage principle described above.
7. A guarantee that Petrograd military units which had part in the revolution would neither be disarmed nor sent to the front.
8. Recognition of full civil rights for off-duty soldiers.

The manifesto avoided any mention of peace and the land, the two basic issues on which there were bound to be differing views. When the cabinet of the Provisional Government was named later that day, it was virtually a list of the leaders of the Progressive Bloc, the very bourgeois coterie that had declared itself impotent to act in the crisis. The exceptions were Kerensky and Cheidze. Because the Soviet had declined to participate in the new government, the latter immediately rejected his portfolio, leaving Kerensky as the only leftwinger in the cabinet. For that reason, he was also given the title of Deputy Prime

Minister. The Prime Minister would be Prince Georgi Lvov, the man Grand Duke Michael had suggested to the Tsar for that position:

- Minister-President (Prime Minister) and Minister of the Interior, Prince G. E. Lvov (No Party)
- Minister of Foreign Affairs, P. N. Miliukov (Kadet)
- Minister of War and Navy, A. I. Guchkov (Octobrist)
- Minister of Justice, A. F. Kerensky (Socialist Revolutionary)
- Minister of Labour, N. S. Cheidze (Menshevik)
- Minister of Transport N. V. Nekrasov (Kadet)
- Minister of Trade and Industry A. I. Konovalov (Kadet)
- Minister of Finance M. I. Tereshenko (No Party)
- Minister of Education A. A. Manuilov (Kadet)
- Ober-Procurator of the Holy Synod, V. N. Lvov (Octobrist)
- Minister of Agriculture A. I. Shingarev (Kadet)

Later that morning Paul Miliukov was deputed to announce the formation of the government to a packed Catherine Hall. As he read out the names, someone shouted, 'Who elected you?' Miliukov calmly replied, 'Nobody elected us - we were elected by the Russian Revolution'. This was a bold statement but one that was seriously at odds with his own pro-monarchist views. Indeed, howls of outrage greeted his next announcement that Nicholas was expected to abdicate in favour of his son, with Grand Duke Michael as Regent.

The crowd demanded that the Romanovs had to go completely and there were angry shouts to know whether the government concurred. The meeting broke up in disorder. To defuse this explosive situation, Miliukov was forced to admit later that day that he had merely expressed a personal opinion. The damage to the new government's reputation had been done, however, and it would never enjoy the full confidence of the Soviet or the masses.[25]

Cheidze's rejection of his portfolio had left Kerensky in an awkward position. Should he accept the Soviet veto and walk away or should he defy the Soviet and accept the position? This conflict brought him close to collapse and he was fortunate that Olga was at his side. As if in a trance, he was persuaded him to accompany her home for a rest. 'For two or three hours I lay in a semi-conscious, semi-delirious state,' he says. 'Then suddenly I sprang up and telephoned my acceptance of the post. I'd decided to fight it out not with the Executive Committee of the Soviet but with the Soviet itself. Let the Soviet decide between the Executive Committee and myself! My weariness disappeared and I returned to the Duma.'

Reaching the Tauride Palace, Kerensky discovered that a plenary session of the entire Soviet was in session. He could hear Yuri Steklov-Nakhamkes, a pro-Bolshevik member of the Excom, reporting on the Soviet's talks with the Temporary Committee on the formation of the new government. When he had finished, Cheidze, the chairman, was told that Kerensky wanted to speak and he was granted the floor. Climbing on to a table, he launched his speech with a question.

'Comrades! Do you trust me?' he asked.

'We do, we do!' the delegates shouted.

'I speak, comrades, from the bottom of my heart and if you do not trust me then I am ready to die.'

The delegates' wild applause told Kerensky he was winning.

'I appear before you as Minister of Justice in the Provisional Government. Revolutionary democracy must be represented so that the government might be in close touch with the will of the people. I must now ask for your vote of confidence. Do I have it?'

The answer was another explosive ovation. Kerensky descended from the table and was hoisted on to the shoulders of Soviet delegates who carried him to the door of the Temporary Committee's room. Describing himself as a 'hostage to democracy', he took his seat in cabinet not only as the Minister of Justice but also as Deputy Prime Minister and vice chairman of the Soviet of Workmen's and Soldiers' Deputies. He was the formal representative of the working class in the Provisional Government.

'There is only one man who can save the country,' Colonel Alfred Knox told his diary, 'and that is Kerensky, for this little half-Jew lawyer has still the confidence of the over-articulate Petrograd mob, who, being armed, are masters of the situation. The remaining members of the government may represent the people of Russia outside the Petrograd mob, but the people of Russia, being unarmed and inarticulate, do not count. The Provisional Government could not exist in Petrograd if it were not for Kerensky.'[26]

Grand Duke Michael was staying in the apartment of his friend, Princess Olga Putiatina, at 12 Millionnaya Street next to the Hermitage. Rodzianko wrote to him there early on Wednesday evening that the Tsar had abdicated in favour of his son and had named Michael as Regent. According to the Grand Duke's executive secretary, A. S. Matveev, this was the first Michael had heard of the events at Pskov.[27]

Meanwhile, Nicholas had changed his mind after hearing from the Court physician that the Tsarevich's illness was terminal and that his life could be cut short at any time. When Guchkov and Shulgin arrived in Pskov at ten o'clock that evening, he handed them a prepared statement in which he renounced the throne in favour of his brother. As he had no right to deprive his underage son of the throne, this was an illegal act which neither Guchkov nor Shulgin was competent to challenge.

At 3 a.m. on 3 March the Provisional Government received the long-awaited communication from Pskov: 'Abdication has taken place but in favour of Michael Alexandrovich who is already proclaimed Emperor.' The ministers looked at one another in bewilderment. 'We could not understand it,' Kerensky said. 'What had happened? Who had inspired this move? Who was backing the new Emperor? What had our envoys done about it? Michael as Emperor! It was impossible, preposterous!'[28]

The first problem was to prevent this news from being made public. Rodzianko rushed to the Ministry of War to communicate with General Alekseyev at the Stavka. As Grand Duke Michael was still in Petrograd, the question could be decided quickly: either the ministers must take an oath of loyalty to him or they must compel him to abdicate. A majority of ministers favoured abdication, which would make the Provisional Government the supreme power in the land. But Miliukov refused to submit and Andrei Shingarev gave him half-hearted support. For hour after hour Miliukov defended his position with great tenacity. 'He seemed to misunderstand the situation completely,' Kerensky says. 'He thought we were losing our heads.'

Shortly before dawn Kerensky telephoned Princess Putiatina's apartment and arranged for the ministers to call on Grand Duke Michael. Guchkov and Shulgin had been delayed on their return journey from Pskov, so at 9.30 a.m. Kerensky, Nekrasov, Rodzianko, Miliukov and Prince Lvov filed into the Princess's apartment. Michael met them in the drawing room. 'He thought the members of the Provisional Government were coming to report on the regency,' Matveev says. 'He therefore was thinking over the appropriate reply expressing his consent.'[29]

Michael was astonished and then perplexed to learn that he was now 'the Emperor Michael'. He had no time to consider his options before Lvov and Rodzianko informed him of the majority opinion that he should step down. It was Kerensky who explained the reasons to him. 'You will not save Russia by accepting the throne.' he said.

> On the contrary, I know the sentiment of the mass of the soldiers and workers. Bitter dissatisfaction is now directed against the monarchy. Just this question will be the cause of bloody confusion. And this at a time when Russia needs complete unity. Therefore, I appeal to Your Highness as a Russian to a Russian. I implore you in the name of Russia to make this sacrifice - if it is a sacrifice, because I haven't the right to conceal the perils to which you will be personally exposed should you decide to accept the throne. I cannot vouch for the life of Your Highness.[30]

Then it was Miliukov's turn. According to W. H. Chamberlin, he was 'pale from sleepless nights, his voice hoarse and broken from endless speeches'. Nevertheless, he launched into a veritable lecture, speaking coldly and calmly. It seemed to him, he told Michael, that his colleagues had 'fallen under the influence of the mob' and had lost control of themselves. 'If you decline, Your Highness, there will be ruin,' he croaked. 'Because Russia will lose its axis. The Monarch is the axis, the sole axis of the country. Around what will the Russian masses rally? If you refuse, there will be anarchy, chaos, bloodshed....' He declared that if Michael refused to take the Crown he would resign as Minister of Foreign Affairs.

Miliukov had spoken for more than an hour in the hope that Guchkov and Shulgin would turn up and, indeed, they walked in just as he was about to conclude. There was a short recess while Guchkov and Shulgin reported on what had happened at Pskov. As Miliukov had hoped, Guchkov decided he must support the monarchy. He declared that should Michael side with the majority of the Provisional Government he would also resign his ministry. Not being constitutional lawyers, no one had twigged that the Tsar had no legal right to transfer the Crown to anyone and that it would be illegal for his brother to accept it.[31]

Michael, however, had sensed danger. After a private talk with Prince Lvov and Rodzianko, he announced that he had decided not to take on the burdens of government. He asked the delegation to draft the instrument of abdication. It was then 1 p.m. and the abdication crisis was over. 'We shook hands and from that moment we were on good terms,' Kerensky says. Rodzianko went on the record describing the Grand Duke as 'one of the noblest, most honest and incorruptible people in the world'. V. D. Nabokov, a constitutional lawyer par excellence, was called to the apartment to draft the instrument of abdication.

Life in Petrograd had become so unpredictable that people woke up every morning without the faintest idea of how the day might end. On 3 March the guards were withdrawn from the Winter Palace and its doors were opened to the public. Wooden carvings of the double-headed eagle crest and every other symbol of Tsarism were torn down and thrown on to fires. The old regime was going up in smoke.

The Provisional Government's legality depended on the document drafted by Nabokov and signed by Grand Duke Michael, which entrusted it with 'plenary powers' to promulgate laws until the Constituent Assembly was convened. The government's most obvious flaw in the eyes of the masses was the elitism of its ministers: Prince Lvov was an aristocrat, Miliukov an imperialist, Guchkov an industrialist and Tereshenko the heir to a huge sugar-beet fortune. Given its bourgeois character, only Kerensky's rapport with the soldiers and the workers provided it with a figleaf of credibility. As things turned out, his slender shoulders would not be strong enough to bear such a load for long.[32]

Kerensky dictated his first order as Minister of Justice to a young man who happened to be standing beside him in the TaBauride Palace, a serious, clean-shaven figure in clerical black with a white wing-collar. 'Please send a telegram to the wardens of prisons throughout Russia to liberate all their political prisoners,' he said. When the young man, Pitirim Sorokin, presented him with the written telegram, he signed it 'Minister of Justice, Citizen Kerensky'.[33]

A similar telegram was sent to public prosecutors regarding political prisoner facing trial or awaiting appeal, while the commandants of Siberian and Caucasian labour camps were ordered to release their 'politicals', including Kerensky's friend Catherine Breshko-Breshkovskaya, the Menshevik leader Irakli Tsereteli, the Bolsheviks Josef Stalin and Lev Kamenev and the five Bolshevik deputies - Petrovsky, Muranov, Shagov, Samoylov and Badayev - who had been condemned to life-long exile.[34]

Professor Sorokin had come to the Duma from the University of Petrograd to offer his services to the Revolution. Invited to join the Soviet, he declined the offer but instead gravitated towards Kerensky. 'He was exhausted and a little theatrical,' he wrote in his diary soon after that first meeting. 'I am not sure how strong his mediating powers will prove, and I fear that this dual rule by the Provisional Government and by the extremists of the Soviet cannot last long. One will certainly swallow the other. Which? Certainly the Soviet.'[35]

Indeed, Yuri Steklov-Nakhamkes enjoyed goading Prince Lvov at meetings of the Liaison Commission, which had been set up to monitor the Provisional Government's activities on behalf of the Petrograd Soviet.[ii] 'You know perfectly well that we could take power into our hands,' he told the Prime Minister. 'We have only to wish it and you will no longer exist.' Sorokin thought Steklov 'a dirty person, dirty both physically and mentally'. His commitment to the Revolution was quite recent - only two years earlier he had petitioned the Tsar to preface his surname Nakhamkes with the more aristocratic Steklov.[36]

According to Professor Sorokin, the Soviet Excom 'directed its energy towards obstructing the government, preaching socialism and doing nothing at all to reeducate or reorganise society. Its proclamations were addressed "to the Whole World" and the speeches and demeanour of its leaders were absurdly pompous'.[37]

Alexander Solzhenitsyn called the Excom 'a narrow, closed committee hiding behind the many thousands of noisy members of the larger scale Soviet, a committee not taking responsibility for anything and propelling everything to ruin'.[iii] He named no names but concluded, 'In those days there shone forth neither heroes nor

---

ii Also known as the Contact Commission, the Liaison Commission's original membership was Skobelev, Steklov- Nakhamkes, Sukhanov, Filipovsky and Cheidze.

iii Researching his 'Red Wheel' series, Solzhenitsyn visited the Hoover Institution Library and Archives at Stanford. His studies there changed his perception of the February Revolution.

great deeds. From the very first days everything began to sink into the quicksand of anarchy, with an amplitude that grew ever more deadly, while the most educated people, who up to that point were so bitterly opposed to arbitrary rule, now turned cowardly and fell silent or lied. And then for a period of eight months everything fell deeper and deeper into decay and death.'[38]

None of this was forseeable when, on Saturday 4 March, the Provisional Government packed up and prepared to vacate the Tauride Palace to put some distance between themselves and the Soviet. The Duma's political prisoners - Scheglovitov, Sukhomlinov, Kurlov, Protopopov, Goremykin, Stepan Beletsky, the Okhrana chief, and Nikolai Maklakov – were transferred from the Ministers' Pavilion to the Peter and Paul Fortress. Rodzianko and other members of the Duma not included in the government would continue to share the Tauride Palace with the Soviet in order 'to warn of the menacing dangers and to point to the correct course'. They would have little prestige and no power.[39]

Kerensky paused for a few moments in the White Hall, the scene of innumerable political dramas leading up to the fall of the autocracy. One thing was missing: Repin's huge portrait of Nicholas was no longer facing the chamber from its place of honour on the wall behind the chairman's dais. Early one morning two soldiers had climbed up the elaborate woodwork, cut the canvas free with their bayonets and then torn it from the frame. They rolled the portrait up and took it away.

After leaving the palace, the Provisional Government spent three days in temporary accommodation at the Ministry of the Interior in Aleksandrovsky Square and then occupied the ministerial chambers of the Marinsky Palace. Kerensky attended the closed sessions of the government in the Rotunda but otherwise lived and worked in the Ministry of Justice. Olga, Oleg and Gleb were regular visitors but once Lilya moved in he asked his wife and children to make an appointment to see him.

His name was known to practically everybody in the country and his photograph was published in hundreds of newspapers and magazines. 'We loved Kerensky,' Zinaida Hippius says. 'There was something alive, something bird-like and childish in him.' This was the beginning of the Kerensky cult. He symbolised the people's hopes and dreams. He was 'the poet of freedom', 'the heart of the nation', 'the first love of the revolution'. Harold Williams, whom Bruce Lockhart rated as 'the greatest and most modest of all British experts on Russia', interviewed him in his office on 6 March:

> Kerensky is a young man in his early thirties, of medium height, with a slight stoop, and a quick, alert movement, with brownish hair brushed straight up, a broad forehead already lined, a sharp nose, and bright, keen eyes, with a certain puffiness in the lids due to want of sleep, and a pale, nervous face tapering sharply to the chin. His whole bearing was that of a man who could control masses.
>
> He was dressed in a grey, rather worn suit, with a pencil sticking out of his breast pocket. He greeted us with a very pleasant smile and his manner was simplicity itself. He led us into his study and there we talked for an hour. We discussed the situation thoroughly and I got the impression that Kerensky was not only a convinced and enthusiastic democrat ready to sacrifice his life if need be for democracy - that I already knew from previous acquaintance - but that he had a clear, broad perception of the difficulties and dangers of the situation, and was preparing to meet them.[40]

The 'difficulties and dangers of the situation' ranged from the elitist composition of the cabinet and the shortage of food to the fate of the former Tsar, the state of the Russian Army and the explosive question of 'war aims'. The Provisional Government was pledged to continue fighting on the Allied side but there was no unanimity over the reasons why. The Tsar's secret treaties, which had been discovered among the official archives at the Marinsky Palace, had created increasingly militant demands from the proletariat, the peasantry and the army rank-and-file for the Zimmerwald peace formula of 'no annexations or indemnities and the right of national self-determination'.[iv]

No sooner had news of the abdication reached Petrograd than the Soviet demanded the arrest of Nicholas and his family, and their incarceration with the Tsarist ministers in the Peter and Paul Fortress. Some advocated that 'Nicholas the Bloody' should be executed for crimes against the people. The Soviet demanded that the Provisional

---

iv Zimmerwald, a Swiss village, hosted three anti-war international socialist conferences during World War I.

Government carry out the arrests and warned if this request were refused the Soviet might take the law into its own hands.[41]

Bowing to Soviet pressure, the Provisional Government ordered Nicholas to be taken under armed escort from Mogilev to rejoin his family at Tsarskoe Selo. At the station, he said goodbye to his mother and then climbed into the train. 'One of the most awful days in my life,' wrote Minnie, 'separated from my beloved Nicky!' As the train steamed away, Nicky stood at the window smiling with 'an expression of infinite sadness' on his haggard face. Minnie made the sign of the Cross and prayed, 'May God hold His hands over him.' She never saw him again.[42]

16

The Return of the Exiles

Living in a shoemaker's house at Spiegelgasse 14, Zurich, Nikolai Lenin, as the Bolshevik leader signed his editorial contributions, could only shout from the sidelines. Having waited twenty years for this moment, his frustration was palpable in the letter he wrote on 3 March 1917 to Alexandra Kollontai in Norway. 'The workers have been fighting in bloody battles for a week, yet Miliukov plus Guchkov plus Kerensky are in power!' he wrote. 'The same 'old' European pattern... Well, what of it! The "first stage of the revolution" bred by the war will be neither final nor confined to Russia. We, of course, retain our opposition to the defence of the fatherland, to the imperialist slaughter directed by Shingarev plus the Kerenskys and Co.'[i]

The truth that Lenin could not stomach was that while he was conjecturing about what was happening in Petrograd, it was Alexander Kerensky who was making history: it was Kerensky who had demanded that the deputies defy the Tsar's decree to suspend the Duma; Kerensky who had made the compact among the Duma, the soldiers and the people; Kerensky who had persuaded Grand Duke Michael to stand aside; and it was Kerensky who was bridging the gap between the Provisional Cabinet and the Soviet. As the only socialist in power, he saw it as his duty to protect the Revolution from the conservative forces trying to steer Russia away from the republican path. 'From the moment of the collapse of the monarchy, I found myself in the centre of events,' he says. 'I was, in fact, their focal point, the centre of the vortex of human passion and conflicting ambitions which raged around me.'[1]

Lenin singled Kerensky out as the Bolsheviks' main target. Using his real surname, he sent a telegram to the Bolsheviks' Central

---

[i] Evidently Lenin was referring to Shingarev's former position as chairman of the Military and Naval Affairs Committee of the Duma

Committee in Petrograd: 'Our tactics: no trust in and no support of the new government; Kerensky is especially suspect; arming of the proletariat is the only guarantee; immediate elections to the Petrograd City Duma; no rapprochement with other parties. Ulyanov.'

In Lenin's vocabulary 'suspect' was high praise indeed and it did seem in those early months that the Minister of Justice was involved in just about everything: in Reval he addressed a mass gathering of soldiers and sailors on the aims of the Revolution and averted a mutiny... in Moscow he turned down Soviet demands for the execution of the Tsar. ('Nicholas is in my hands, the hands of the Attorney-General, and I say to you, comrades, the Russian Revolution took place bloodlessly and I won't permit, it to be stained. I will never be the Marat of the Russian Revolution.')[ii] At outdoor rallies and in concert halls his acting ability, quick wit and penetrating baritone voice made him the star turn – an 'impressionist-politician', as Sukhanov and Chernov put it - because he could catch the mood of an audience and reflect it back to them in improvised speeches. Josef Gessen, a Kadet newspaper editor, called him 'the axle of the revolution' because 'the revolution revolved around him'.[2]

Elation and terror were now mixed with fatigue, passion and pain. During his trip to Reval he had been mobbed by hundreds of soldiers and sailors who wanted to slap him on the back and shake his hand. As a result, the hand was bruised and scratched. One of the scratches turned septic and he returned to Petrograd with his arm in a sling. From time to time he also suffered excruciating pain from his kidney operation and needed morphine injections to keep going.[iii] [3]

The 'difficulties and dangers' multiplied after his amnesty decree became law on 6 March and Russian émigré committees sprang up all over the world to repatriate exiled Russians. Paris, Rome and Berne sent as many applicants as possible to London to join the convoys of steamers travelling to Scandinavian ports under Royal Navy escort. Konstantin Nabokov, who had been promoted to chargé d'affaires at

---

[ii] Neither the February Revolution nor the October Revolution was 'bloodless' despite many claims to the contrary.

[iii] Kerensky's lover Flora Solomon recalled that the hand 'bore a scar from his time at the front greeting his troops'. Despite these references, historians would later write that there was no record of his arm ever having been hurt. He was accused of a deliberate attempt to suggest that he had been wounded like a soldier.

the Russian Embassy following the death of Count Benckendorff, had to deal with hundreds of individuals ranging from the Socialist Revolutionary leaders Nikolai Avksentiev and Viktor Chernov ('a grey-haired, sulky, repulsive individual' in Nabokov's opinion) to a trio of SR terrorists, Ilya Fondaminsky, Boris Moiseenko and Boris Savinkov.

However, it was the Bolshevik exiles who would represent the biggest threat to the stability of the Provisional Government. Nabokov reported to Paul Miliukov that Georgi Chicherin and Maxim Litvinov, the two most prominent anti-war campaigners, were straining every nerve to get as many defeatists as possible back to Russia. He warned the minister, 'If you continue to allow all this immigration without any discrimination whatsoever you will cut the branch upon which you are sitting.' There was no reply from Miliukov and the Foreign Office took no preventative action. When the matter was raised in cabinet, Prince Lvov and Alexander Guchkov, the Minister of War, admitted that they did not possess the means to prevent people crossing the frontier.[4]

Nor did Kerensky, as Minister of Justice, have any intention of placing legal restrictions on returnees. Stephen Kerensky says, '[People ask] "Why was this man so stupid? Did he not realise that if he invited these people back there would be trouble?" But the point is you're either a Tsarist or you're not. You either imprison people without a trial or you don't. And if they haven't done anything wrong there's no reason to put them in prison. On the contrary, there is every reason not to do so because to do so is counter-revolutionary and the Revolution will roll on past you.'[5]

Georgi Chicherin, the son of a noble Tsarist diplomat, had fled Russia prior to the 1905 Revolution. Since then he had used his inherited wealth to fund the Bolshevik wing of the RSDLP abroad. His brusque style cut no ice with Jacob Gavronsky, a Socialist Revolutionary who was also an eminent London physician. 'Dr Gavronsky saw the danger of this mass penetration of Bolsheviks into Russia,' says Nabokov, 'and had the courage to raise his voice in the committee against Chicherin.'[6]

Jacob Osipovich Gavronsky conceded nothing to Chicherin in terms of wealth or credibility: on his mother's side, he was a Wissotsky, the ultra-wealthy tea merchants of Moscow, and he had been sentenced to twenty years' exile in Siberia for crimes against the Tsarist state. Escaping to the West, he studied medicine at the universities of Berlin, Heidelberg and Halle, and, in May 1911, was admitted to the Royal College of Surgeons. He conducted medical research at the London Hospital in a laboratory endowed with his own money.[7]

The arguments with Chicherin became so heated that Gavronsky resigned from the committee and travelled to Petrograd on one of the steamers to report the situation to the Foreign Office in person. While he was away, the British Government stepped in and ordered Chicherin's arrest for his anti-war activities. After a spell in Brixton Prison, he was deported to Russia and Maxim Litvinov, Lenin's former arms procurer, took over as the Bolshevik emissary to London.[8]

'For over fifteen years I was intimately connected with all the leaders of the Socialist Revolutionary Party,' Gavronsky later wrote. 'Avksentiev, Savinkov, Gotz and Fondaminsky were all my intimate friends. I was connected with them during my revolutionary activities; I lived in their midst while in Petrograd at the time of my sojourn there in the months of August and September 1917.'[9]

Gavronsky's friends had spent their exile enjoying the liberties of the Third Republic in Paris. Savinkov, who was under sentence of death for the assassinations of Pleve and Grand Duke Sergei, was a regular among the bohemians at La Rotonde in Montparnasse. Having retired as a professional assassin, he passed the time seducing women and writing novels, such as the semi-autobiographical *The Pale Horse* (1909), a collaboration with Zinaida Hippius which depicted the revolutionary as a violent, self-seeking outsider. The Bolshevik author Ilya Ehrenburg knew Savinkov in those days as 'a dapper little gentleman in spats and bowler'. Back in Russia he would become as dangerous to the fledgling Russian democracy as the Bolsheviks, while exuding an aura of ruthless aptitude to the Entente's ambassadors and military attachés.

Lenin was determined to reach Russia as quickly as possible but the journey from Switzerland was problematic. He persuaded the Swiss Socialist Fritz Platten to pitch the idea to Gisbert von Romberg, the German Consul in Berne, that he and his comrades should be given permission to cross Germany on their way back to Russia. Romberg relayed the plan to his Foreign Ministry, which immediately agreed.

The German High Command were consulted and Hindenburg and Ludendorff reacted enthusiastically; they saw Lenin as the ideal carrier of the Bolshevik plague and were happy to grant him 'extra-territorial status' to plant it in the middle of the Revolution.[10]

According to the security specialist Christopher Andrew, there was nothing new about Germany's attempts to subvert the Russian war effort. Two years earlier the Imperial Treasury had approved grants totalling seven million marks 'for the support of Russian revolutionary propaganda'. German money was passed to the Bolsheviks through Alexander Helphand, a corrupt businessman who used the nom de guerre Alexander Parvus in his dealings with Lenin.[11]

Over the next two weeks Lenin composed a series of 'Letters from Afar' to his comrades in which he plotted the replacement of democracy in Russia with a one-party state. 'Lenin,' says Kerensky, 'had no moral or spiritual objection to promoting the defeat of his own country. His chief aim was to overthrow the Provisional Government as an essential step toward the signing of a separate place with Germany.' The first two letters were sent to Alexandra Kollontai, who smuggled them into Russia in her corset. Travelling through Sweden and Finland, she dressed in her most fashionable outfit to pass for a member of the bourgeoisie.

Leon Trotsky was even further away from Petrograd than Lenin. Having been expelled from France as an anti-war campaigner, he was living with his wife Natalya and sons Lev and Sergei in the Bronx, New York. Emma Goldman, the Russian-born anarchist, described him then as 'a man of medium height, with haggard cheeks, reddish hair and a straggling red beard'.[iv] As soon as he read about the amnesty for political exiles, he obtained a visa from the Russian Consulate in New York and booked passage to Europe.[12]

Josef Stalin was already in Petrograd. On 12 March he took a tram to the dingy *Pravda* offices on the Moika, where the editor Vyacheslav Mikhailovich Molotov, a serious Marxist student, had taken a hard anti-government line in his editorials.[v] Judging it too

---

iv Bruce Lockhart, who met Trotsky in Petrograd in February 1918 and saw him several times in the flesh, said he had 'great masses of black, waving hair'. (British Agent, p. 226)

v Established in 1912 with financial help from Maxim Gorky among others, *Pravda* had the largest circulation of all the socialist press, with about 40,000 copies bought, and read by many more, every day.

early for the Bolsheviks to make their bid for power, Stalin removed Molotov and shared the editing duties with Lev Kamenev. When Alexandra Kollontai delivered the first two 'Letters from Afar', she was outraged to discover that they had formed an alliance with the Menshevik majority in the Petrograd Soviet to cooperate with the government.

Lenin's plan was to turn the Petrograd Soviet into a weapon of state power in partnership with the Bolshevik Party. 'The Soviet of Workers' and Soldiers' Deputies is a workers' government in embryo, a representative of the interests of all the poorest masses of the population, i.e., of nine-tenths of the population which is striving for peace, bread and liberty,' he wrote. 'The government of the Octobrists and Kadets, of the Guchkovs and Miliukovs, could give neither peace, nor bread, nor freedom, even if it were sincere in its desire to do so.'[13]

To Lenin's fury, Stalin and Kamenev deleted key passages from both letters, including a section calling for a boycott of the Provisional Government. Stalin rightly judged that the Petrograd Soviet had no desire to take over the awesome task of governing the country. Instead, it issued on 14 March an 'Appeal to the Peoples of All the World': 'Throw off the yoke of your semi-autocratic rule, as the Russian people have cast off the Tsar's autocracy; refuse to serve as an instrument of conquest and violence in the hands of kings, landowners and bankers - and then, by our united efforts, we will stop the horrible butchery that is a stain on humanity and is darkening the great days of the birth of Russian freedom.'[14]

Paul Miliukov saw the declaration – correctly - as a threat to Russia occupying Constantinople and taking control of the Straits. Having already angered the Soviet over his 'personal opinion' that Russia should remain a monarchy, he now dug his heels in to save Nicholas's grandiose Byzantine dream. On 23 March he gave a newspaper interview in which he stated, 'The possession of the Straits is the protection of "the doors to our home" and it is understandable that this protection should belong to us.'[15]

Miliukov's comments caused a sensation. The espousal of annexationist motives was not only contrary to President Wilson's pledge to the American people on joining the belligerents but entirely hostile to the Soviet's peace formula. Says V. D. Nabokov, 'He considered it would be simply criminal of us to renounce the "greatest prize of the war" (as Grey called Constantinople and the Straits) in the name of the humanitarian and cosmopolitan ideas of international socialism. But most importantly, he believed that this prize had not really slipped from our grasp.'[16]

There was uproar at the Tauride Palace, where representatives of the Petrograd Soviet and the Duma met in permanent session. Through the Liaison Commission, the Soviet demanded that the government renounce the minister's annexationist views. Overriding Miliukov's objections, it published its Declaration of War Aims in line with the Petrograd Soviet's peace formula: 'The Provisional Government considers it to be its right and its duty to declare at this time that the aim of free Russia is not domination over other nations, or seizure of their national possessions, or forcible occupation of foreign territories, but the establishment of a stable peace on the basis of the self-determination of peoples. The Russian people does not intend to increase its world power at the expense of other nations. It has no desire to enslave or degrade anyone.'

The declaration was issued on 27 March in the name of Prince Lvov, Minister-President, as a domestic document addressed to Russian citizens. It was not intended as a diplomatic Note until Soviet leaders insisted that it should be presented to the Allies as a statement of Russia's official foreign policy.[17] Once again Miliukov dug his heels in. He would disseminate the document to foreign powers only if he could attach a disclaimer stating his own position. Prince Lvov agreed to this and Miliukov set about composing his response.[18]

For months Miliukov, Rodzianko and Guchkov had been searching for a latter-day General Skobelev to take control of the army.[vi] It was at this point that they found their champion in General Lavr Kornilov, the officer who had made his name with a daring intelligence mission into Afghanistan in the 1890s. Kornilov had been captured during the Battle of Przemysl in March 1915 but had made a daring escape. Returning to Petrograd, he received a hero's welcome and Guchkov appointed him Commander of the Petrograd Military District.

Lavr Georgievich Kornilov was an intriguing combination of

---

vi General Mikhail Dmitriyevich Skobelev (1843-1882) was famous for his conquest of Central Asia and his heroics in the Russo-Turkish War. Dressed in white uniform and mounted on a white horse in the thick of the fray, he was known to his soldiers as the 'White General'.

truculence and recklessness, deeply patriotic but politically naïve. 'I am General Kornilov, peasant, son of a Cossack,' he liked to proclaim. He was born on 18 August 1870 at Karkaralinsk in Western Siberia (today Qargaraly, Kazakhstan). According to General Brusilov, he was 'a man with the heart of a lion and the brains of a sheep' but he saw himself in an entirely different light. While a prisoner of the Austrians, he had read the life of Napoleon and had come to believe that he was destined to save Russia from anarchy and defeat.[19]

As his propagandist, he appointed Vasily Zavoiko, a Ukrainian nobleman who had founded the Society for the Economic Regeneration of Russia with Aleksei Putilov, a director of the Russo-Asiatic Bank, and other financiers. They saw Kornilov as a potential dictator whose seizure of power would destroy the Soviets and place them in a position to enrich themselves.[vii] Zavoiko, a tall stout man with streaks of grey in his dark hair, was given the misleading title of 'orderly' in Kornilov's entourage. 'He wields the pen with perfection,' the General said. 'I therefore entrusted him with the drafting of those orders and documents that required a particularly vigorous and artistic style.'[20]

Meanwhile, Kerensky had appointed a Special Commission of Inquiry to investigate his suspicions about Rasputin's anti-war activities and the Court camarilla's possible dealings with Germany, including the role played by Anna Vyrubova, who was rumoured to be Rasputin's mistress, or perhaps Alexandra's lesbian lover (neither of which was true).

At two o'clock on the afternoon of Tuesday 21 March Kerensky arrived at the Alexander Palace in the imperial Rolls-Royce for his first meeting with Citizen Romanov. He entered the palace through the kitchen door with fifteen soldiers and his aide-de-camps. 'He was dressed in a blue shirt buttoned to the neck, with no cuffs or collar, big boots, and he affected the air of a workman in his Sunday clothes,' Count Paul Benckendorff, formerly Grand Marshal of the Court, says. 'His manner was abrupt and nervous.'[21]

Kerensky ordered the Guard to fall in in the passage outside the kitchen and then harangued them on the aims of the Revolution. The royal servants were also treated to the news that they no longer served

---

vii Aleksei Putilov was the greatnephew of Nikolai Putilov, founder of the Putilov Company.

their old imperial masters but were beholden to 'the people' for their livelihood. After searching many of the palace's private rooms, Kerensky found Anna Vyrubova in her sickroom with Alexandra's friend, Lili Alexandrovna Dehn. 'She had foolishly kept all her papers until the last moment, which she was at that moment burning in the fireplace,' Benckendorff says. 'This did her a lot of harm.'[22]

Kerensky ordered Anna to change out of her nightdress and to pack a bag; she was under arrest and would be returning to Petrograd with him. A liveried footman then ushered him into the royal apartments, where he found the former Emperor, Empress and Tsarevich sitting at a table in the children's schoolroom. Three of the daughters were seated nearby, while Maria was still bedridden with measles.

'A small man in uniform moved forward to meet me, hesitating and smiling weakly,' Kerensky says. 'He stopped as if uncertain what to do next. He did not know what my attitude would be. Was he to receive me as a host or should he wait until I spoke to him? Should he hold out his hand or wait for me to greet him first? I sensed his embarrassment, as well as the confusion of the whole family left alone with a terrible revolutionary.'[23]

It seemed incredible that this slow-moving man, who looked as if he were dressed in someone else's clothes, had ruled over an immense empire for twenty-three years. Kerensky had no intention of treating him harshly. He walked up to Nicholas, held out his hand and said, 'Kerensky'. Smiling, Nicholas shook his hand and introduced him to his wife and son. Alexandra Fyodorovna extended her hand so reluctantly that their palms barely touched. A few weeks earlier she had urged her husband to have him hanged. 'This was typical of the difference in character and temperament between the husband and wife,' Kerensky says. 'He did not wish to fight for power and it simply fell from his hands. Alexandra Fyodorovna, though broken and angry, was still a clever woman with a strong will.'

Count Benckendorff had followed Kerensky into the room. 'Kerensky was in a state of feverish agitation; he could not stand still, touched all the objects which were on the table and seemed like a madman,' he says. Kerensky informed Nicholas that he had appointed a new Palace Commandant, Colonel Paul Korovichenko, a military jurist and veteran of the Japanese and European Wars. The Colonel was called into the room and was introduced to his former monarch.

Kerensky then asked Nicholas to accompany him into the next room so they could speak privately. There, he informed Nicholas that his ministers had referred in their evidence before the Commission of Inquiry to orders from the Supreme Command of which there was no trace in the Archives of the Ministry of War. He asked Nicholas to provide an explanation. He also raised the question of his wife's possible involvement in the matters being investigated.

'When I told him that Alexandra Fyodorovna might have to be tried, he did not turn a hair and merely remarked, "Well, I don't think Alicky had anything to do with it. Have you any proof?" To which I replied: "I don't know yet".'

The meeting ended soon afterwards. Nicholas wrote in his diary that night: 'This afternoon Kerensky, the current Minister of Justice, came quite unexpectedly. Walked through all the rooms, wanted to see us, spoke with me for about five minutes, introduced the new commandant of the palace and then left. He ordered poor Anna put under arrest and taken to town along with Lili Dehn.'[24]

Two days later everything stopped in Petrograd for the burial of the victims of the Revolution. 'What a moving spectacle!' Pitirim Sorokin wrote. 'Hundreds of thousands of people moved behind red and black banners emblazoned with the words, "Glory to Thou Who Perished for Liberty".' There were about 200 coffins and as each one was lowered into the grave on the Champ de Mars a salute was fired from the Peter and Paul Fortress. No priests officiated.[25]

Leon Trotsky and his family set sail for Europe with other émigrés in the SS *Kristianiafford* on 14/27 March. The voyage proceeded in a spirit of hearty comradeship until the ship berthed at Halifax, Nova Scotia, to pick up more passengers. After an exchange of telegrams between Ottawa and London, British naval police came on board and arrested Trotsky and seven other émigrés.

Resisting violently, Trotsky was dragged ashore, stripped and searched. He was then driven ninety miles to Amhurst and incarcerated in a prisoner-of-war camp with 800 German submariners, while Natalya and his sons remained in Halifax at the Prince George Hotel. When news of the émigrés' detention reached Petrograd, the Mensheviks in the Petrograd Soviet demanded their release. 'The revolutionary democracy of Russia impatiently awaits the return of its fighters for freedom,' the Soviet declared.[26]

Under pressure from the Mensheviks, Paul Miliukov protested to Sir George Buchanan about Trotsky's detention. The Ambassador had no alternative but to ask the British Government to allow him to proceed to Russia. Two days later Miliukov begged Buchanan to cancel that request; the Provisional Government wanted him detained in Canada until further information could be obtained about him. Buchanan pointed out to Miliukov that it was now the Provisional Government who was responsible for Trotsky's detention.[27]

At Amhurst, Trotsky took advantage of his incarceration to spread antiwar propaganda among his captive audience. He explained Zimmerwaldism to the German POWs and told them that revolutionaries were already fighting against the Kaiser inside Germany. When German officers protested to the camp commandant about the effect these speeches were having on their men, they were terminated. 'Thus,' Trotsky jeered, 'the English colonel sided with Hohenzollern patriotism.'[28]

By early April, 'Free Russia', as Kerensky called it, was a place of marked contrasts in which war and peace, danger and reprieve, harmony and distress walked hand in hand. He recorded instances of bureaucrats being thrown out of their offices, many of them suffering injuries and, in some cases, death; workers grabbing unpopular managers and trundling them out of their factories in wheelbarrows; peasants chasing away their landlords and seizing the land for themselves.[29]

Dashing from one tricky situation to another, Kerensky was the nearest thing the Revolution had in its chaotic first months to a national figure. Removing his arm from the sling, he revived his schoolboy habit of placing his right hand inside his jacket. When photographs were published, this teenage affectation was read as Bonapartist. 'Grandfather kept his arm in his jacket to rest it without looking like an invalid, not because he admired Napoleon.' Stephen Kerensky says. 'Napoleon wasn't all that popular in post-1812 Russia and "Bonapartist" did not fit in with his republican principles.' Indeed, Kerensky was quick to distance himself from Napoleon. 'How did 1792 end in France?' he asked the Soviet at one point. 'It ended in the fall of the republic and the rise of a dictator.'[30]

Inside the cabinet his bitterest opponent was Paul Miliukov, who referred to him sarcastically as the 'comely figure of the young man with a bandaged arm'. The bad feeling burst into the open at a closed session in the Marinsky Palace when Miliukov remarked that German money had played a role in the downfall of the Tsar. Kerensky, who was working night and day to produce some sort of amity between the Soviet and the government, took Miliukov's suggestion personally.

'What did you say? Repeat it!'

Miliukov repeated what he had said. According to V. D. Nabokov, who had been appointed chief secretary to the cabinet, Kerensky slammed his briefcase on the table, accused Miliukov of slandering 'the sacred cause of the Great Russian Revolution' and stormed out of the chamber.[31]

Nabokov disliked everything about him. A smart dresser in Savile Row's finest suits himself, he was scathing about the younger man's 'dandified appearance' (though Harold Williams thought him 'anything but a dandy - his boots sadly need a polish'). He derided his 'actor's clean-shaven face', his 'constant squint' (from myopia) and his 'unpleasant smile' (from false teeth). He accused him of 'abnormal pride and conceit' and a 'love of posing, ostentation and pomp'.[32] Nevertheless, he took his seventeen-year-old son Vladimir to hear one of his speeches.[viii] Sitting in the front row of the auditorium, the young Nabokov experienced Kerensky at his emotive best, flaying the audience with florid words and startling images. 'He spoke very well, with his hand in his bosom like Napoleon,' he said, 'because it had almost been broken by handshakes.'[33]

Then, gasping for air, Kerensky fainted. He was sufficiently revived to pull off one last dramatic flourish. As he uttered the words, 'I swear on the heads of my sons....', Oleg and Gleb bounded out of the wings and Kerensky placed his hands on their heads as he completed the vow.

'There was something theatrical about him,' young Nabokov said. 'Pleasingly theatrical apparently.' In later life he referred to Kerensky with a hint of sarcasm as 'my eminent friend Kerensky'. His father, however, thought that Kerensky 'must have realised that all the admiration and idolisation was nothing but crowd psychosis, for he had neither the merits nor the intellectual or moral qualities to justify them'. It never occurred to him that Kerensky's passion for the Revolution might be real.[34]

---

viii Vladimir Vladimirovich Nabokov was born on 10/22 April 1899 in his family's townhouse at 47 Bolshaya Morskaya, Saint Petersburg.

On Wednesday 29 March Kerensky returned to the White Hall of the Tauride Palace for the All-Russian Conference of Soviets. The 479 delegates occupied the Duma's former seats and were surrounded by workers, soldiers and sailors, while hundreds more were packed into the galleries between the soaring pillars. The blank wooden frame that had held Repin's portrait of the Tsar bore witness to his downfall. Suddenly, the massed ranks exploded in what Nabokov would have described as 'an outbreak of crowd psychosis' when Kerensky walked into the chamber with Catherine Breshko-Breshkovskaya on his arm.

'Babushka' had been brought straight to the palace from the railway station on her return from Siberia. Kerensky looked ill and trembled with excitement. As he launched into an impassioned speech, she 'stroked his head like a mother calming the enthusiasm of an already overstrained child'. A respectful silence then fell over the great hall as 'the Grandmother of the Revolution' started to speak. In quiet measured tones she supported the Provisional Government's desire to continue the war against Germany. It was the Soviets' duty, she said, to prevent the Hohenzollerns from conquering what the people had been taken from the Romanovs. Hearing this cry to arms, the soldiers and sailors could restrain themselves no longer. Shouting with joy, they rushed to the tribune and surrounded the tiny figure. 'We have brought you from Siberia to Petrograd,' one cried. 'Shall we not guard you?' 'We have won freedom,' another shouted. 'We will keep it.'[35]

The Allies had sent a delegation of British and French Socialists to the conference to urge the Soviets to defy the Bolsheviks and keep Russia in the war. Two members of the British contingent were the trade union MPs Will Thorne and James O'Grady. They were singularly unimpressed with the lawyers, journalists and professional revolutionaries on the Petrograd Soviet Excom. 'Look at their hands!' O'Grady whispered to Thorne. 'Not one of them has done an honest day's work in his life!'[36]

Irakli Tsereteli, a Zimmerwaldian who had returned from Siberian exile eleven days earlier, had come to accept that in certain circumstances socialists could support a defensive war. He called this policy 'revolutionary defencism' and hoped it might provide a bridge between the Soviet leaders and the government liberals on the question of war aims. Arguing in favour of continuing the war, he said the revolutionaries should fight the foreign enemy with the same courage they had shown in defeating their Tsarist foes. The conference voted 325 to 57 in favour of his resolution to strengthen the front against the enemy and to defend the Revolution in the rear.

Meanwhile, the German strategy aimed at reducing Russia to revolutionary chaos had reached the point of execution. The Germans insisted that Lenin give a guarantee that he and his fellow revolutionaries were 'partisans of an immediate peace'. This assurance was given and the plan went ahead. According to Christopher Andrew, it had 'the strong personal support of the Kaiser who joked that Lenin and his Bolshevik comrades should be given copies of his speeches to take with them on their train journey'.[37]

Leaving Zurich on 27 March/9 April the group of thirty-two adults and two children took a local rail service to the frontier post of Gottmadingen, where they boarded their 'extra-territorial train' for the journey across Germany to the Baltic ferry port of Sassnitz. Among the adults were nineteen Bolsheviks, six members of the Bund and three Mensheviks. Lenin travelled with his wife Nadezhda Krupskaya and his mistress Inessa Armand.

At forty-six, he was a stocky, balding redhead of medium height, with a great domed head, a short beard and hazel eyes. The joke among his acolytes was that his brain was so enormous it had pushed the hair out of the top of his head. In adulthood, he had survived typhoid and influenza, and had learned to live with migraine headaches, blackouts, abdominal pain, insomnia and erysipelas, known as 'holy fire', a severely contagious skin infection.[38]

The Bolshevik Express consisted of a locomotive and a single green wooden carriage with three second-class and five third-class compartments, two toilets and a baggage room. Two German guards travelled in the rear of the carriage, with a chalk line serving as the border between 'Russia' and 'Germany'.[39]

The carriage was supposedly sealed on Lenin's orders so he could say, hand on heart, that he had never set foot on German soil and therefore could not have been infected by German propaganda. In fact, only three of the four doors on the platform side of the carriage were locked after the passengers had boarded and during the journey some of Lenin's entourage left the train at various stations to buy refreshments, while everyone spent one night in a hotel.[40]

The myth of the 'sealed train' persisted despite a speech to the Petrograd Soviet by one of the Bolshevik passengers, Grigory Zinoviev:

> What a howl there was about the celebrated 'sealed carriage'. As a matter of fact, Lenin entertained towards the German imperialism a hatred as fierce as towards the other imperialisms. At the beginning of the war the Austrian Government had arrested Lenin, and he spent two weeks in a Galician arrest-house. When a prominent member of Scheidemann's party wanted to enter our carriage (which, as a matter of fact, was not sealed) in order to welcome us, the gentleman was told purposely by Lenin that we had no inclination to talk with traitors, and would give him a thrashing if he came to us.[41]

At Sassnitz, Lenin's group took a boat to Trelleborg then travelled by train across Sweden to the Finnish border. The eight-day journey from Switzerland to the customs house at Tornio, the cross-border river port on the Russian side of the frontier between Sweden and Finland, turned all the fables surrounding Lenin's persona into hard reality. Day and night he worked to expand the five 'Letters from Afar' into an 'April Theses' aimed at seizing power by armed rebellion. Lenin contended that Russian workers had no interest in an Allied victory and that the conflict should become an international civil war between the proletariat and the bourgeoisie.[42]

'In sending Lenin to Russia,' General Ludendorff wrote in his memoirs, 'our government took upon itself a very great responsibility. This journey was justified from the military point of view: it was necessary that Russia should collapse.' Kerensky had no doubts that an alliance existed between German imperialism and extreme Marxism. 'Each hated the other,' he says, 'and yet they had the same aim – to destroy the Russian front and to destroy the Russian Government.' But although the Germans had enabled Lenin to return to Russia, Kerensky did not believe he was a German agent.[43]

Lenin arrived at the Finland Station in Petrograd on 3 April, one week before his forty-seventh birthday. In the splendour of the imperial waiting room Nikolai Cheidze greeted him on behalf of the Petrograd Soviet with the hope that he would 'join in the defence of our Revolution against attacks from without or within'. Hearing the cheering of Bolshevik supporters outside, Lenin brushed past the guard of honour, walked out of the station and was lifted on to the body of an armoured car.⁴⁴

From this warlike podium he told the pro-Bolshevik crowd that the enemy wasn't Germany but capitalism, and that 'the robbers' imperialist war is the beginning of civil war in all Europe'. He denounced the Petrograd Soviet's support of the Provisional Government and shouted, 'Long live the worldwide socialist revolution'. From that moment on, Lenin projected himself as the leading representative of 'the people's will' against a counter-revolutionary bourgeois legislature.⁴⁵

The British Embassy faced the Art Nouveau mansion of Nicholas II's former lover Matilda Kshesinskaya on Kronverksky Prospekt across the Trinity Bridge on the Petrograd Side.[ix] The ballerina had fled to Paris during the February Days and the hoisting of a red flag outside her massive red-and-grey granite complex indicated that it was now the headquarters of the Bolshevik Party. For protection, the Bolsheviks shared these luxurious premises with a reserve armoured-car squadron, while the barracks of the Bolshevised First Machine Gun Regiment were close at hand.⁴⁶

Stepping on to a balcony overlooking the street, Lenin made another short speech advocating a transfer of power to the Soviets. 'All Power to the Soviets', a slogan he had coined in the April Theses, became the Bolsheviks' war-cry. Retreating into Matilda's neoclassical drawing room, he laid down the law regarding non-cooperation with the Provisional Government to a gathering of 300 party members. In bold, uncompromising language he explained that this policy was a necessary prelude to a complete Bolshevik takeover of the state.

Suddenly, the Bolsheviks were awash with money. The Kshesinskaya mansion was turned into a revolutionary production line inciting violence and anarchy. Bolshevik agitators churned out propaganda texts on typewriters and duplicators, while new printing presses produced *Pravda* and a new offering, *Soldatskaia Pravda*, which aimed at politicising the troops. Frank Golder, a Russian-born American historian who was living with a Russian family, described the situation in the capital as 'most pitiful and heartbreaking'.

---

ix Matilda Kschesinskaya married one of the Tsar's cousins, Grand Duke Andrei Vladimirovich. She died in Paris in December 1971, just eight months short of her one-hundredth birthday.

> German agents with pockets full of money have been working among the soldiers to disorganise the army and they have had good success. Under the cloak of socialism they preach all damnable doctrines – incite lawlessness, plunder, strikes – until no one knows what tomorrow may bring forth. No one knows whether we have an army or a mob. Here in Petrograd we have no army but a lot of lazy, good-for-nothing soldiers who obey orders when it pleases them to do so.[47]

The Kshesinskaya mansion had a garden with a circular gazebo from which speakers addressed large groups of people gathered on the pavement. William Gerhardie, the Russian-speaking aide of Colonel Alfred Knox, heard Lenin promising bread, peace and land to the crowd from this pulpit. He noted there was 'nothing in the man's speech or looks to give an inkling of his future career' - he was short, balding and couldn't pronounce the Russian 'r'.[48]

Oliver Locker-Lampson, the Old Etonian Unionist MP commanding the Royal Naval Armoured Car Division, remembered seeing 'a short, bearded man enter a house, open a window and speak to the multitude. I heard this man, who was Lenin, preach anarchy and murder and treachery. I went straight to the ministers and asked them why they did not lock up this crazy incendiary. The answer was that Lenin was a negligible nonentity to whom nobody would pay the slightest attention'.[49]

Professor Sorokin adjudged Lenin a poor speaker but thought he would succeed in his mission 'because he is ready to encourage all the violence, all the criminality which the mob is straining to let loose'. He recorded Lenin's words to his diary:

> Comrade workers, take the factories from your exploiters! Comrade peasants, take the land from your enemies, the landlords! Comrade soldiers, stop the war, go home! Make peace with the Germans and declare war on the rich! Poor wretches, you are starving while all around you are plutocrats and bankers. Why do you not seize all this wealth? Steal what has been stolen! Pitilessly destroy this whole capitalistic society! Down with it! Down with the Government! Down with all war! Long life to the social revolution! Long life to class war! Long life to the dictatorship of the proletariat!'

David Soskice had returned to Petrograd as one of two correspondents of the *Manchester Guardian* and was working with Piritim Sorokin in Kerensky's secretariat. When Constance Garnett learned that Lenin was in Petrograd, she wrote to Soskice, 'I feel certain Lenin will capture power. I wish we knew what he will do with it.'[50]

A despairing Konstantin Nabokov blamed 'the weakness and folly' of the Provisional Government for permitting this situation to develop. 'The fact that Lenin was allowed to cross the border and to live in Petrograd unmolested contributed more to the loss of prestige in London of the Russian Government than any other of their errors,' he said.[51]

Grigory Zenoviev had followed Lenin on to the balcony of the Kshesinskaya mansion. 'What a disgusting creature, this Zinoviev,' Sorokin told his diary. 'In his high womanish voice, his face, his fat figure, there is something hideous and obscene, an extraordinary moral and mental degenerate.' Back in his office on the other side of Trinity Bridge, Sorokin was filled with foreboding. 'If I were the government, I would arrest these men without hesitation,' he says. 'If necessary I would execute them to prevent the horrible catastrophe into which they plan to plunge this country.'[52]

Meanwhile, Trotsky was still languishing behind barbed wire. The incitement against British citizens in Soviet newspapers had become so serious that the lives of British factory owners were endangered. After a further protest from Miliukov, Trotsky was released on 12/25 April. He left Amhurst to the cheers of the German POWs and the stirring strains of 'The Internationale'. He and his family sailed for Europe in a Norwegian ship, the SS *Hellig Olaf*.

Despite the disruption and rancour, the 'powerless' Provisional Government nevertheless managed in those critical early months to overcome many of the abuses of Tsarist misrule. 'Everything that generations of the Russian people had dreamed about during their century-long struggle for freedom was given to them at one stroke,' Kerensky says. Sometimes, however, the all-male cabinet needed a hefty push. When the League for Women's Equal Rights discovered that the legislative programme did not include a bill on women's suffrage they staged a rally in which 40,000 women of all ages and from every class gathered in Nevsky Prospekt to register their dissatisfaction. They also sent a deputation to visit Prince Lvov at his office in the Marinsky Palace. The Prime Minister surrendered without a fight. 'Why shouldn't women vote?' he said. 'I don't see the problem. Surely, with universal suffrage there can be no reason to exclude women.'ˣ [53]

Alexandra Kollontai, however, dismissed the campaigners as 'bourgeois little ladies'. Their demands for equality posed a threat to working-class solidarity, she said, and had nothing to do with the needs of the impoverished female masses. As Lenin was promising the proletariat total freedom in a Communist Utopia, the Bolsheviks saw no need for elections. 'Women's suffrage' was therefore an irrelevance. Nevertheless, the government hastily passed an electoral law that granted women full civil and political rights. All women over the age of twenty were given the vote and the right to run for public office. Sofia Panina became the first woman to be given a ministerial post when she was appointed Assistant Minister of Social Welfare.[54]

The list of reforms was truly impressive. The government granted a full amnesty to political prisoners and abolished capital punishment; eliminated all extraordinary courts, making trial by jury the only form of justice for both criminal and political offences; eradicated all religious, national and class limitations and proclaimed full liberty of conscience; restored the independence of the Orthodox Church from the State; introduced equal rights for women; set up a commission to draft the electoral laws for the Constituent Assembly; abolished punishment by exile; permitted absolute liberty of the press and unions, and total freedom of assembly.

It abrogated all measures which infringed on the independence of the judiciary; drafted new standing orders for the election of urban and rural authorities; did away with all political and economic discriminatory measures against the peasantry; extended the rural self-government principal down to the *volost* (the smallest administrative unit); reestablished the constitution of Finland; proclaimed the independence of Poland; appointed a commission for the introduction of self-government in Lithuania and Ukraine; reformed the administration of Turkestan and the Caucasus; introduced the eight-hour day

---

x The deputation included Poliksena Shishkina-Iavein, Ariadna Tyrkova, the feminist writer who was married to Harold Williams, the paediatrician Anna Shabanova, the physician Maria Pokrovskaia, Anna Miliukova, a leading Kadet in her own right, and the philanthropist Countess Panina.

at all offices and factories; established works committees; introduced industrial arbitration; established a grain monopoly and fixed prices for essential commodities; and revised the entire military code.[55]

For a time, Russia was the freest, most democratic country on the planet. Colossal as these reforms were, however, the government ignored popular demands for peace and failed to break up the landed estates. These shortcomings enabled Lenin and the Bolsheviks to advocate an end to the war, the seizure of land by the peasants and control of industry by the workers. Bolshevism, 'red in tooth, claw and flag', was on the march.[56]

Bruce Lockhart met Alexander Kerensky at the Ministry of Justice. 'His face has a sallow and almost deathly pallor,' he says. 'His eyes, narrow and Mongolian, are tired. He looks as if he were in pain, but the mouth is firm, and the hair, cropped close and worn en brosse, gives a general impression of energy.' Dressed in a dark suit worn over a workers' black blouse, Kerensky led Lockhart into his private apartment. Lunch was served at a long table with almost thirty places. Lilya Birukova sat beside Catherine Breshko-Breshkovskaya and a great brawny-armed sailor from the Baltic Fleet. People drifted in and out at will.[57]

Despite prohibition there was wine on the table but Lockhart noted that Kerensky drank nothing stronger than milk. And all the while he talked. He resented the pressure that the Allies were putting on him through their ambassadors, he said, and he asked his guest, 'How would Lloyd George like it if a Russian were to tell him how to manage the English people? We are only doing what you have done centuries ago, but we are trying to do it better – without the Napoleon and without the Cromwell. People call me a mad idealist, but thank God for the idealists in this world.'[58]

Republican America saw the Provisional Government as a positive step towards to a true democracy and on 7/20 March became the first country to recognise it as the legitimate ruler of Russia. Britain, France and Italy quickly followed suit. The Revolution had removed President Woodrow Wilson's objection to joining Russia in a military alliance and two weeks later Congress declared war on Germany.[xi]

---

xi Following a series of attacks on American ships, the American public were further outraged to learn of the Zimmermann Telegram, a secret diplomatic

Wilson told Congress that Germany was engaged in 'nothing less than war against the government and people of the United States'. He requested a military draft to raise an army and an increase in taxes to pay for it. 'We have no selfish ends to serve,' he said. 'We desire no conquest, no dominion… no material compensation for the sacrifices we shall freely make. We are but one of the champions of the rights of mankind. We shall be satisfied when those rights have been made as secure as the faith and freedom of the nations can make them.'

Wilson refused to be lumped in with 'imperialist' Britain and France, so the United States was described as 'an associate power' rather than 'an ally'. As the US Army totalled a mere 100,000 troops, it would take many months for the men to be recruited, equipped and trained for the European battlefields.

Russia celebrated May Day on 18 April to fit in with the rest of Europe. Huge crowds carrying red banners gathered in the capital to denounce the war and demand Miliukov's resignation from the Foreign Office. Every socialist party and trade union in Russia were represented, as well as every nationality of the former Empire. 'The First of May celebration,' Morgan Philips Price, the other *Manchester Guardian* correspondent in Petrograd, wrote in his memoirs, 'was really a huge religious festival in which the whole human race was invited to commemorate the brotherhood of man.'[59]

Kerensky, his arm back in a sling to avoid handshakes, was photographed marching with the celebrated General Kornilov and his comrade Albert Thomas, the French Minister of Munitions. Bruce Lockhart described Thomas as 'a jovial bearded man with a sense of humour and a healthy bourgeois appetite'. He had been sent to Russia to recall Ambassador Paléologue, who was considered too sympathetic towards the Romanovs. Thomas gave wholehearted support to Kerensky in his battles with rightwing members of the cabinet, so much so that Miliukov claimed the Frenchman's authority 'seemed beyond dispute to our inexperienced politicians'. He also blamed Thomas for the Soviet's adoption of the Zimmerwald peace formula.[60]

The Miliukov Note did nothing to allay the Soviet's fears. 'While

---

communication from the German Foreign Secretary which sought to persuade Mexico to take part in a war against the United States in exchange for Texas, Arizona and New Mexico.

continuing to have complete confidence in the victorious conclusion of the present war,' he had written, 'the Provisional Government is quite certain also that the questions raised by the war will be solved by the creation of a solid foundation for a lasting peace, and that imbued with similar aspirations, the leading democracies will find a way to establish those guarantees and sanctions which are required to prevent new bloody encounters in the future.'[61]

References to a 'victorious conclusion' and 'guarantees and sanctions' convinced Miliukov's enemies that he still favoured the original Tsarist objectives. Large demonstrations for and against this proposition broke out in Petrograd. Anti-Miliukov soldiers from the Moscow and Pavlovsky Regiments descended on the Tauride Palace, while his Kadet supporters picketed the Marinsky Palace. Several people were killed in brawls when the rival groups clashed in Nevsky Prospekt. Protesters attacked Miliukov's car with their fists while he was in it. General Kornilov sought permission to suppress the disorders by force but Prince Lvov turned him down. The Soviet Excom then ruled that, as a precaution against such extremism, all military measures must receive their endorsement.[62]

The government and the Petrograd Soviet were agreed about one thing: unless order was restored the Revolution would collapse into anarchy and bloodshed. Civil war, Lenin's preferred option, was a very real threat. The Soviet took control of the Petrograd Garrison and prohibited further demonstrations. The following day a joint statement was issued condemning the Miliukov Note, a compromise that ended the 'April Crisis' but which revealed yet again the inadequacies of the dual-power system.

On 4 May, one month after Lenin, Trotsky was travelling across Finland by train on the final leg of his journey to the Russian capital. The Bolshevik Central Committee greeted him at Finland Station and supporters draped in red flags carried him along the platform on their shoulders. Bruce Lockhart summed up the 'Trotsky Incident': 'He was treated as a criminal. Then, having roused his bitter hate, we allowed him to return to Russia. The outraged Trotsky came back to Russia and threw in his lot with the Bolsheviks.'[63]

Trotsky loathed the fact that Kerensky, 'a pseudo-popular patriot', had risen to such exalted heights. 'Kerensky entered the government somewhat in the character of a plenipotentiary ambassador,' he wrote. 'His connection with the revolution, however, was that of a provincial lawyer who had defended political cases. Kerensky was not a revolutionist; he merely hung around the revolution. Arriving in the fourth Duma thanks to his legal position, Kerensky became the president of a grey and characterless faction, the Trudoviks, anaemic fruit of a crossbreeding between liberalism and *narodnikism*. He had no theoretical preparation, no political schooling, no ability to think, no political will.'[64]

The tempo of Bolshevik activism quickened when Trotsky, theatrical in appearance and Jacobin in spirit, joined forces with Lenin (though he would not become a member of the Bolshevik Party until 10 July). Adjacent to the Kshesinskaya mansion on Petrograd Side was the Cirque Moderne, an auditorium that could hold 10,000 people. Trotsky was the most popular speaker there. Favouring a well-cut three-piece suit and glaring angrily through his pince-nez glasses, he galvanised the roaring Soviet crowds in support of a violent socialist revolution.

'I tell you heads must roll, blood must flow,' he informed the Kronstadt sailors in a speech at their main assembly place, Anchor Square. 'The strength of the French Revolution was in the machine that made the enemies of the people shorter by a head. This is a fine device. We must have it in every city.' Delirious multitudes bore him aloft and carried him triumphantly from the halls. The Red sans-culottes had found their Marat.[65]

17

The Poison Chalice

On 25 April Prince Lvov described the government as 'an authority without power' and the Soviet as 'a power without authority'. Ending this gridlock meant finding a way of enticing the Soviet into sharing responsibility for governing the country. Prince Lvov discussed the problem with Irakli Tsereteli, the leader of the Menshevik majority in the Soviet. During their talks, Lvov floated the idea of a coalition government in which a sizable number of Soviet representatives would serve as ministers. Tsereteli reacted positively. He thought the idea would appeal to workers and soldiers alike: workers would regard it as a means of extracting higher wages from their bosses; soldiers would see it as the path to a separate peace.

Prince Lvov appealed to all progressive elements in the country to support the coalition project. 'There is a sombre and grievous course in history,' he warned, 'leading from freedom through civil war and anarchy to reaction and the return of despotism. This course must not be the course of the Russian people.'[1]

Two days later, however, the Soviet Excom voted against its members joining any cabinet that contained Miliukov and his ally Guchkov, both of whom were seen as imperialist warmongers. The deadlock broke on 1 May when Guchkov, who suffered from a heart condition, resigned as Minister of War.[2] Prince Lvov had never rated Guchkov and was glad to see him go. He promised Tsereteli that he would also force Miliukov out of the cabinet. As a result, the Soviet Excom voted 44 to 19, with two abstentions, in favour of permitting socialists to accept ministerial posts.

Miliukov followed Guchkov into the wilderness on 4 May after a majority of his cabinet colleagues urged him to relinquish the Foreign Affairs portfolio for the sake of amity and move to the less inflammatory post of Education for which he was eminently qualified. The following day the new coalition was announced, with socialists taking six out of the sixteen portfolios. For a brief interval, the political climate brightened up and the government appeared stronger. Liberals and socialists even agreed on the need to cooperate in defence of the country – at the front against the Central Powers and in the rear against the increasing strength of the Bolshevik Party.[3]

Kerensky, the pacifist father who had broken his son's toy sword, replaced Guchkov as Minister of War, while Mikhail Tereschenko, the twenty-nine-year-old Ukrainian-born Minister of Finance, took over at the Foreign Office. Kerensky was a strange choice. Eminently qualified as Minister of Justice, he had no military training or expertise in logistics or ordnance. Nor did he have any illusions about the magnitude of his task. 'What was required was a buffer between the commanding corps and the rank and file,' he says. 'It became my fate to be the buffer, with all the inevitable consequences confronting anyone who puts his head between the hammer and the anvil.'[4] While he favoured the Soviet peace formula, he was determined that any settlement with the Central Powers must take account of the nation's sacrifice and, until that day came, Russia must support the Entente.

Kerensky's appointment was made at a critical time for the Allies. Field Marshal Douglas Haig was reluctant to accept that advances in modern weaponry had rendered his beloved cavalry redundant. He repeatedly launched frontal assaults that cost his forces huge losses for little reward in captured territory or German casualties. After his failure to break the German Army on the Somme in 1916, the task became even harder when the Germans shortened their line and employed systems of defence in depth in which successive lines of trenches and barbed wire were reinforced by concrete pillboxes housing machineguns.[i][5]

The French Commander in Chief, General Robert Nivelle, who had replaced the aged Marshal Joffre in December, concocted an ambitious plan to breach the Hindenburg Line at the Chemin des Dames, literally the 'Ladies' Path', a twenty-mile stretch of countryside that ran along a ridge between the valleys of the rivers Aisne and Ailette. Paying

---

[i] Under Operation Alberich, the retreating Germans turned 579 square miles of French territory around Arras and San Quentin into a wasteland of destroyed towns, villages and orchards, blown-up bridges, roads and railways, booby-trapped buildings and poisoned waterholes.

no heed to the Revolution, Nivelle informed General Alekseyev, now Supreme Commander, that his Spring Offensive would begin on 26 March/8 April and he expected Russia to launch her own attack around that time. 'It is essential that our joint operation be begun within a few days of each other,' Nivelle said. 'Otherwise the enemy will be free to utilise their reserves, which are large enough to enable them to halt the offensive at the very outset.'[6]

Alekseyev, however, knew it was impossible for Russia to follow this timetable. Sixty per cent of Central Power forces were located on the Eastern Front and his army was in turmoil. The political upheaval had also destabilised his reserve units in the rear and the entire army was short of vehicles and horses. Thanks to the Soviet manifesto, not a single soldier could be transferred from the Petrograd Garrison, now numbering 250,000 men, to the front.[ii] The result was that thirty other towns and cities had to shoulder the burden of providing replacements for the fallen, a casualty figure that had reached 400,000 per month at the height of the fighting.

In a memorandum to Nivelle dated 13 March, Alekseyev stated that his army could not attack before June or July, and he urged the French supremo to delay his plans for a general offensive until then. Nivelle decided to start without the Russians. After three postponements enforced by bad weather, the offensive went ahead on 3/16 April.[7] 'All I care for is to win the war this year,' Nivelle told Edward Spears, the British liaison officer with the French forces. But the Nivelle Offensive was a disaster. By the time it was called off on 26 April/9 May, French losses totalled 271,000, a catastrophic failure that triggered mutinies in many divisions in the spring and summer of 1917 during which 20,000 soldiers deserted to the Germans. When fifty divisions, almost half the French Army's strength, refused to return to the attack, Nivelle was dismissed and Marshal Philippe Pétain, the 'Hero of Verdun', took his place.[8]

Moving into the Ministry of War's apartment at 67 Moika with Lilya, Kerensky tackled his new job with his customary gusto. He appointed a young adjutant, Lieutenant Nicholas Vinner, and recalled his brother-in-law, Colonel Vladimir Baranovsky, from the front to act as his eyes

---

[ii] The troops had successfully argued that their mutiny in February had 'made the revolution' and they claimed the right to remain in Petrograd to defend it from 'counter-revolutionaries'.

and ears in military matters as head of his personal secretariat (chef de cabinet). As head of the Petrograd Military District, he replaced General Kornilov with General Peter Polovtsev. Kornilov requested a return to the front and was given command of the Eighth Army.[9]

Kerensky had serious reservations about the army's chances of success. Since the advent of Order Number 1 antiwar propaganda had shattered its morale, crippled its fighting capacity and played into the German High Command's hands. In the opinion of Boris Engelhardt, the situation could only be saved 'if the government were willing to wallow in blood, and this government will not do that'. Furthermore, Kerensky believed that Nivelle's recklessness 'had not only destroyed all chance of a combined attack from east and west but had also deprived the Entente powers of almost all hope of ending the war in 1917'.[10]

Kerensky had one advantage over his predecessor: he was popular with the rank-and-file of the armed forces. Guchkov had refused to sign a Declaration of Soldiers' Rights restating many of the reforms of Order Number 1, as well as allowing servicemen to belong to political organisations. One of Kerensky's first acts was to add two clauses in favour of discipline and then sign it into law. The first clause confirmed the right of commanders to nominate and remove officers, while the second empowered officers to use force against mutinous troops in combat. To neutralise the Bolsheviks' antiwar propaganda, he appointed commissars, mainly Soviet-oriented 'defencists', to mediate between officers and the soldiers' committees.[11]

The exception was Boris Savinkov, a Freemason whom Kerensky was soon describing as 'my protégé'. The SR political assassin loathed the Soviet – he called it the 'Council of Rats', Dogs' and Chickens' Deputies' – and he was more rightwing than Kerensky would have wished. Nevertheless, he appointed him commissar to the Seventh Army on the South-Western Front. Now thirty-eight, Savinkov was as duplicitous and self-serving as ever, but he looked the part in his well-cut French uniform, with a new hairpiece disguising his baldness. He was soon in trouble with the South-Western commander, General Alexei Gutor. When Gutor failed to punish the ringleaders of a mutiny, Savinkov protested to the Ministry of War and was told that his remit as commissar did not include questioning the orders of a senior commander.[12]

This incident convinced Savinkov that an iron-fisted martinet would have to take control of the army to restore its fighting fitness. Everybody knew Lavr Kornilov's name from his much-publicised escape from the Austrians but it was Maximilian Filonenko, a commissar with Kornilov's Eighth Army, who alerted Savinkov to his potential. Savinkov discovered he had much in common with the Cossack general: they both wanted to reintroduce the death penalty at the front, disband the soldiers' committees and ban all Bolshevik newspapers from the trenches. They also revered Napoleon as their guiding star. At five feet six inches tall, Savinkov was an inch shorter than his hero but he had starred as the lead character in a play he had written himself in which Bonaparte won the Battle of Waterloo and restored his rule over France.

Nivelle's failure had made it imperative that Russia mount an offensive as soon as possible to prevent the mass transfer of German troops to the Western Front. With the French army in disarray, an injection of fresh enemy troops could have proved catastrophic to the Allied cause. Indeed, there was a growing belief in Petrograd that Russia must support its Allies with more than words. 'The blood of the Allies is shed on the Western Front for the liberty of the French and of the Russian democracies,' the moderate newspaper *The Day (Den')* declared in an editorial on 30 April, 'but it is impossible to hoist on the shoulders of England and France the whole burden of the struggle. From the standpoint of the treaties, we must actively support our Allies by an offensive.'[13]

On 9 May Miliukov's Kadets ramped up the pressure for action. 'Only in that way can we bring an end to the war closer; only in that way can we guarantee a quick and, at the same time, not shameful peace,' the Kadets stated in a resolution at their party congress. 'The present standing in one place at best only prolongs the war indefinitely and, at worst, may bring us to an irreparable catastrophe.' Even the Petrograd Soviet endorsed the principle of an offensive, with the proviso that it be authorised by the First All-Russian Congress of Soviets' and Workers' Deputies.[14]

Publicly, Kerensky advocated fighting the war to a finish, though he deprecated the idea of conquest. The government, he told Sir George Buchanan, favoured a war of defence but a military offensive might be necessary to secure that objective. 'We prosecute the war in order to end it,' he said, 'and to end it quickly it is necessary to prosecute it vigorously.'[15]

The planning of an offensive presented the Stavka with few problems: General Alekseyev had drawn up the orders for such an operation in the Tsar's time and all that was required was the Minister of War's approval. Having no knowledge of strategy, Kerensky did not challenge Alekseyev's assumptions; instead, he concentrated on galvanising frontline regiments into action by appealing to their patriotism.[16] As he put it, 'The Bolsheviks spoke to them in simple language and played on the deep-rooted instinct of self-preservation. The gist of Bolshevik propaganda can be summed up in Lenin's words, "We appeal to you not to die for others, but to destroy your class enemies on the home front." My words to the soldiers were, "It's easy to appeal to exhausted men to throw down their arms and go home. But I summon you to battle, to feats of heroism – I summon you to sacrifice yourselves to save your country".'

'Kerensky has begun by telling the army that he is going to reestablish the strictest discipline, to insist on his orders being obeyed, and to punish all recalcitrants,' Sir George Buchanan noted in his diary. 'He is the only man who can do it if it can be done, but his task will be a difficult one. He has been going around the barracks today [7 May], and tomorrow he leaves for the front.'

Uninvited, Kerensky fronted up to the barracks of the pro-Bolshevik regiments among the Petrograd Garrison, including the Finland Guards who had torn up General Kornilov's personal standard a few days earlier. Expecting a rough reception, it had gone very well indeed: the soldiers of the pro-Bolshevik 180th Regiment listened attentively to his speech and then surrounded him, lifted him up on their hands and chaired him to his car.[17]

On 8 May Kerensky left Petrograd in his own train for a three-week tour of the country's defences from Finland to the Crimea. His entourage at various times included his Trudovik comrade, Colonel Vladimir Stankevich, now a 'defencist' member of the Petrograd Excom, his Masonic friend, Nikolai Sokolov, author of the notorious Order Number 1, and his French ally, Albert Thomas. Sokolov had volunteered to join the mission because he wanted to make amends for the damage Order Number 1 had done to relations between officers and men.[18]

On 12 May Kerensky met the Commander in Chief of the South-Western Front, General Aleksei Brusilov, at his headquarters in the Ukrainian town of Kamenets-Podolsk just inside the pre-war Austrian border. The offensive would be launched on this front with the aim of retaking Eastern Galicia and seizing the oilfields around Drohobych. Brusilov's forces would have the help of 120 spotter planes, some flown by French and British pilots, to pinpoint enemy dispositions, while in the absence of tanks Locker-Lampson's squadron of armoured cars would add weight to the attack.[iii] The main thrust in the Southwest would be supported by blows on the Western and Northern Fronts.[19]

Many regiments, however, reported for duty complete with Bolshevik agitators in their ranks and the frontline had become a fertile breeding ground for Bolshevism. Colonel Knox witnessed one incident at Kamenets-Podolsk which showed the inherent weakness of General Brusilov's command. 'I waited with many Russian generals in his ante-room while he reasoned for four hours with an ensign who had arrested his divisional commander,' he says. 'The General told me next day that this particular division recognised no one, neither the Provisional Government nor the Soviet, and its only programme was to leave the front and to avoid fighting.'[20]

On 13 May Kerensky's entourage was near the frontline at Podgaytsy in Western Ukraine. Thousands of troops gathered on a hillside outside the town to hear him speak. As he stepped from his staff car, they greeted him with a great roar and the noise followed him all the way on to a platform on the hilltop. Florence Farmborough, the British nurse with the Russian troops, was unimpressed. Was this small, insignificant figure in a darkish uniform really the man she had heard so much about? Was this the Minister of War whose reforms were intended to create a closer relationship between officers and men but were having the opposite effect?[21]

'For a while he stood in silence; then he began to speak, slowly at first and very clearly,' she says. 'His eloquence literally hypnotised us. He spoke for about twenty minutes but time seemed to stand still.'

Kerensky promised the soldiers that the offensive would not be

---

[iii] The RNACD originally consisted of 500 men, fifty officers, forty-five armoured cars, fifteen lorries and fifty motorcycles. It had fought in the Caucasus in 1916 and then Romania 1916-1917 before heading into Galicia.

delayed and assured them that they would be armed with new batteries of heavy artillery and would have plenty of ammunition. His words were interrupted by enthusiastic shouts and wild applause.[22]

'You will fight to a victorious end!'

'We will!'

'You will drive the enemy off Russian soil!'

'We will!'

'You, free men of a Free Country, you will fight for Russia, your Mother-Country!'

'We are free men! We will follow you into battle. Let us go now!'

When he descended from the platform, Kerensky was hoisted aloft and carried on young shoulders to his car. They kissed him and shook his newly recovered hand until it was bruised, then fell to their knees in prayer. Many were weeping.

At another point 10,000 soldiers ran after their car for nearly two miles, stretching out their hands to be pressed. Weeping with joy, some actually leaped on board, flung their arms around Kerensky and kissed him.

At the headquarters of the 113th Division, which had been withdrawn for refusing to go into the trenches, Kerensky addressed 40,000 men. 'Is it true, as the German thinks, that Russian troops cannot fight without a Tsar?' he asked. 'Is it true that what the Russian soldier needs is not freedom but a whip, because without that he remains inactive while Wilhelm takes away his best regiments from our front and sends them against the freest of all nations, France?' To this challenge the soldiers shouted back: 'It is not true. Lead us to the attack.'

Mounting the speaker's platform, one of the men shouted, 'For the first time for three years we have heard a kind word. It has been spoken to us by our War Minister, Comrade Kerensky. Did you hear what he said, comrades? You will not forget his words. The Provisional Government demands that we should die for freedom's sake. We will die but we will never surrender our freedom.'[23]

Both the commanders of the Seventh and the Eleventh Armies reported to Brusilov that Kerensky's visits to their troops had been favourably received. However, the commander of the Seventh Army stressed that 'the Bolsheviks exist [and] there is no doubt that on the ignorant masses their influence continues to be harmful and struggle against it is difficult'.[24]

Based on his own experiences, Brusilov's view of the men's 'war aims' was even more negative. 'The soldiers wanted only one thing - peace,' he said, 'so that they could go home, rob the landowners, and live freely without paying any taxes or recognizing any authority. They veered towards Bolshevism because they believed that this was its programme. They did not have the slightest understanding of what either Communism, or the Internationale, or the division into workers and peasants, actually meant, but they imagined themselves at home living without laws or landowners. This anarchistic freedom is what they called "Bolshevism"'.[25]

Indeed, 'war aims' had become the most important political issue of the conflict. On 10 May the Petrograd Soviet appealed to socialists in all countries to send representatives to an International Socialist Conference in Stockholm for the purpose of securing a general peace on the acceptable formula of no annexations or indemnities. The British Labour Party Leader, Arthur Henderson, a member of Lloyd George's War Cabinet, who visited Petrograd that month, strongly supported Kerensky's efforts to keep Russia in the war. He believed the Stockholm conference would strengthen the Provincial Government against the Bolsheviks. Furthermore, he thought that Labour Party participation would strengthen Kerensky's position.[26]

Henderson's rightwing colleagues in the War Cabinet, however, were appalled by the suggestion. He was told to wait outside the Cabinet Room like an errant schoolboy while his position was discussed – the infamous 'doormat incident' after which he angrily resigned from the coalition government.[iv]

By rights, the summer offensive should have been named after General Alekseyev, just as the Brusilov Offensive in August 1916 had been named after its military commander. However, on 22 May Kerensky complicated matters by replacing Alekseyev with Brusilov and in so doing inherited the poison chalice himself.[v] 'I needed men who believed that the Russian army was not ruined,' Kerensky says.

---

iv The Stockholm Conference was doomed to failure after the British Government joined other Entente Governments in blocking Socialists who wished to travel to Stockholm.
v General Alekseyev was given the new post of military adviser to the Provisional Government.

'I needed men who had lived through the utter folly of the years of war under the old regime and who fully understood the upheaval that had occurred.'

The Kerensky Offensive would pit the Russian Seventh, Eighth and Eleventh Armies against the Austro-German South Army and the Austrian Second and Third Armies. Russian forces would advance on either side of Berezhany towards Lemberg. Crossing the Zlota Lipa, the Seventh Army would take Lemberg from the south, while the Eleventh Army struck from the north. General Kornilov, commanding the Eighth Army on the Romanian Front, would defend the Seventh Army's left flank.[27]

The Russian forces were better equipped than in previous battles. There was no shortage of armaments because of increased factory production and the vast quantities of war matériel, paid for by Russia's gold on deposit in the Bank of England, that had been shipped from Britain to Murmansk.[vi] Thanks to the arrival of British artillery pieces, their gunners would enjoy a two-to-one superiority in the South-Western theatre, with plentiful supplies of ammunition, while overall the Russian commanders had a significant numerical advantage of three-to-one, with 900,000 Russian troops attacking a third of that number of defenders.[28]

The only thing that would guarantee success, however, would be the infantry's willingness to obey orders and advance. There was ample evidence that the 'Kerensky Effect' had a limited lifespan in that regard. 'The exultation of the troops on the South-Western Front has gradually weakened,' Florence Farmborough noted in her diary in late May. 'Had orders to start the offensive come at once, the soldiers would have risen to the occasion; they were all afire to go. But the weeks passed and no orders had come.'[29]

The First Congress of Soviets, which would have the final say on whether the Kerensky Offensive went ahead, was finally convened on the evening of 3 June.[vii] The following day Kerensky and Lenin locked

---

vi Between 1914 and 1917 about one-third of Imperial Russia's gold reserves were shipped to the UK and Canada for 'temporary storage'. This bullion was used as collateral for British loans to purchase military equipment.

vii A total of 777 delegates declared allegiance to a political party: these included 285 Socialist Revolutionaries, 248 Mensheviks, 105 Bolsheviks and 25 Menshevik Internationalists.

horns in public for the first and only time. Lenin arrived in the Hall of the Naval Cadet Corps on the banks of the Neva with Nadezhda Krupskaya. 'We passed through a long corridor; the classrooms had been turned into dormitories for the delegates,' she wrote in *Memories of Lenin*. 'The hall was crowded. The Bolsheviks sat in a small group at the back.' Three of Lenin's key lieutenants, Lev Kamenev, Grigory Zinoviev and Anatoli Lunacharsky, were seated in that section. In the Presidium Group were his Menshevik opponents Matvei Skobelev, Nikolai Cheidze, Georgi Plekhanov and Irakli Tsereteli.

As one of the 'fraction' speakers for the opposition, Lenin was invited to speak first. 'The hostile crowd looked on him as a wild beast,' Nikolai Sukhanov reported. 'Lenin clearly felt himself insignificant and had no special success. He wouldn't have been allowed to speak at all except for the enormous curiosity every one of the provincial Mamelukes felt for this notorious figure.'[30]

Given the fifteen minutes allotted to fraction speakers, Lenin launched a savage attack on bankers, imperialists and capitalists. He didn't seem to care that his own three-piece suit and bourgeois paunch gave him the look of a moderately well-off provincial tax inspector. 'Arrest them,' he shouted, his defective 'r' delivered with an alien Gallic burr, 'expose their tricks, uncover their intrigues!' Rocking on the heels of his boots and stabbing the air with a finger, he continued, 'The citizen Minister of Posts and Telegraphs (Tsereteli) has declared that there is no political party in Russia that would agree to take the entire power on itself. I answer: "There is." No party can refuse to do this; all parties are contending and must contend for the power, and our party will not refuse it. *It is ready at any moment to take over the Government* (Sukhanov's italics).'

The delegates sat up a little straighter in their seats. This was the first time Lenin had stated in public that 'All Power to the Soviets' actually meant a one-party dictatorship rather than any sort of power-sharing coalition. 'When we seize power we shall curb the capitalists, then the war will be *entirely* different from the one now waged – for the nature of a war is determined by the class that conducts it, and not by what is written on scraps of paper. But as long as the capitalist class has a majority in the government, the war will remain an imperialist war, no matter what you write, no matter how eloquent you are, no matter how many near-socialist ministers you have.'[31]

In attacking imperialism Lenin was on safe ground. Nadezhda Krupskaya says, 'Although only the Bolsheviks applauded Lenin, there was no doubt about the strong impression his speech created.' Kerensky later wrote about the experience of listening to his Bolshevik opponent. 'It was our only encounter and it has remained indelible in my memory,' he says.

> Lenin was advocating the deposition and arrest of the ministers, myself included. 'Down with the capitalist ministers and everything will be splendid!' he cried. Everyone present roared with laughter. My speech followed his and, addressing myself to the Bolsheviks in general and to Lenin in particular, I said, 'Be careful! Out of this chaos, like a phoenix out of the ashes, there will come a dictator – and it will not be me… You are recommending childish prescriptions: arrest, kill, destroy! Who are you? Socialists or police of the old regime?'
>
> It was clear to me already then that Lenin's only interest was the assumption of dictatorial powers and I did not forget the record of the Bolsheviks under the Tsarist regime when their members worked hand in glove with the dreaded Okhrana.[viii] Several members of their Central Committee were in fact agents of the secret police and they used their special powers freely to arrest, suppress and destroy the liberals, leftists, socialists and other progressive-minded people who were not allied to the Bolsheviks.
>
> Lenin's 'April Theses' and his book *State and Revolution*, both produced in 1917, clearly showed the workings of his mind. Even members of his own Bolshevik Party were at that time aghast at the destructive, anarchistic streak in his writing and called them 'the ravings of a madman'.[32]

The Provisional Government's archive recorded for posterity the full flavour of Kerensky's speech to the congress:

> Comrades!
> You have been told of 1792 and of 1905. How did 1792 end in France? It ended in the fall of the republic and the rise of a dictator. How did 1905 end? With the triumph of reaction. And now, in 1917, we are doing that which we could have done earlier. The problem of the Russian socialist parties and of the Russian democracy is to prevent such an end as in France – to hold on to the revolutionary conquests already made; to see to it that our comrades who have been released

---

viii Kerensky was referring to Lenin's friend Roman Malinovsky among others.

from prison do not return there; that Comrade Lenin, who has been abroad, may have the opportunity to speak here again, and not be obliged to flee back to Switzerland.

Applause

We must see to it that the historic mistakes do not repeat themselves; that we do not bring on a situation that would make possible the return of the reaction, the victory of force over democracy. Certain methods of fighting have been indicated to us. We have been told that we should not fight with words, not talk of annexation, but should show by deeds that we are fighting against capitalism. What means are recommended for this fight? To arrest Russian capitalists.

Laughter

Comrades, I am not a Social Democrat. I am not a Marxist, but I have the highest respect for Marx, his teaching and his disciples. But Marxism has never taught such childlike and primitive means. I suspect that Citizen Lenin has forgotten what Marxism is. He cannot call himself a socialist, because socialism nowhere recommends the settling of questions of economic war, of the war of classes in their economic relations, the question of the economic reorganisation of the state, by arresting people, as is done by Asiatic despots… Every Marxist who knows his socialism would say that capitalism is international, that the arrest of a few capitalists in a certain state would not affect the iron law of the economic development of a given period… You Bolsheviks recommend childish prescriptions – 'arrest, kill, destroy'. What are you – socialists or the police of the old regime?

Uproar. Lenin: You should call him to order.

This gathering of the flower of Russian democracy understands its problems. Such prescriptions do not excite it, but among the masses such words will be taken seriously. We do not cater for the mob; we are not demagogues. What we say now, we said ten years ago: You [Bolsheviks] recommend that we follow the road of the French Revolution of 1792. You recommend that way of further disorganisation of the country… when you, in alliance with reaction, shall destroy our power, then you will have a real dictator. It is our duty, the duty of the Russian democracy, to say: Don't repeat history's mistakes. You are asked to follow the road that was once followed by France, and that will lead Russia to a new reaction, to a new shedding of democratic blood.[33]

Kerensky says he was still speaking when Lenin picked up his briefcase and stalked out of the auditorium.[ix] Two days later the Petrograd Soviet urged Kerensky to issue orders regarding the offensive prior to the congress's decision. Then, on 12 June, congress resolved that the army should be prepared for both offensive and defensive action, with the decision whether to attack being decided on purely military and strategic grounds.[34] Kerensky took this resolution to the Stavka in Mogilev and ordered the offensive that now bore his name to go ahead.

On 16 June the Kerensky Offensive began with a two-day artillery bombardment of enemy positions along a thirty-mile sector of the South-Western Front. Kerensky took the train to Tarnopol to confer with General Brusilov. The Supreme Commander warned him 'trench Bolshevism' was rampant and that mutinies had broken out among some units. 'He paid not the slightest attention to my words,' Brusilov later complained, 'and from that moment on, I realised that my own authority was quite irrelevant.'

Nevertheless, Brusilov had at his disposal 50,000 specialist troops and 175,000 'bayonets' in twenty-three and a half divisions, a superiority of three to one over the enemy. Alfred Knox reported that the cavalry and artillery were sound but that every division had one unreliable regiment. The downside was that the Kerensky Offensive had been so widely advertised that Ludendorff had had plenty of time to transfer six divisions of crack German troops from the Western Front to prepare General Hoffmann's forces for a counter-attack.[35]

Kerensky took the train with General Gutor to the forward positions of the Seventh Army. He spent the next day addressing frontline regiments in the hope of recapturing the spirit of May. Gutor's battle plan relied heavily on soldiers who had been relatively untouched by Bolshevik influence, including Finnish, Siberian and Trans-Amur divisions, plus the Czechoslovak Rifle Brigade, consisting of 3580 Czechs, Slovaks, exiles and former prisoners of war who had defected to the Russians. They wore the Russian uniform with red-and-white ribbons on the bands of their service caps, a lion cockade and the letters 'Ch' and 'S' on their shoulder-boards.

At 9 a.m. on Sunday 18 June Kerensky and Gutor were at the main

---

ix The concluding act of the Soviets' June Congress was to replace the Petrograd Excom with the 300-strong All-Russian Central Executive Committee (VTsIK).

observation point seven miles from the enemy trenches near the village of Kozova on the edge of an oak forest south-east of Berezhany. 'The battlefield lay before us like a huge, deserted chessboard,' he says. 'We looked at our watches. The strain was unbearable. Suddenly, there was a deathly hush. For a second we were gripped by a terrible fear that the soldiers might refuse to fight. Then we saw the first lines of infantry, with their rifles at the ready, charging toward the front lines of German trenches.'

Advancing behind a creeping barrage of artillery fire, General Leonid Belkovich's Seventh Army streamed forward under their new red battle standards to attack the Austro-German South Army. 'Almost in the very centre appear the English armoured cars,' Kerensky says. 'The German artillery begins to pound them. Our artillery is now silent. Many of the guns sent to us by the Allies have failed to withstand two days' work. Apparently our Allies acted according to the old Russian saying: "Take, oh God, what is of no use to us".'[36]

Nevertheless, the VII Siberian Corps, including a composite division of units that had previously mutinied, drove Austrian and German defenders out of their fortified trenches and established themselves on high ground commanding the Zlota Lipa Valley. At the same time, the Third Trans-Amur and 74th Infantry divisions succeeded in occupying the slopes of Mount Lysonia.[37]

Further north, the Eleventh Army, commanded by General Ivan Erdeli, attacked the Austro-Hungarian Second Army, with two of its corps swarming up the slopes of an elevated feature known as the Mogila, or the Graveyard. They blew a huge gap in the Austrian line and one of the three Czech regiments gained the heights and held them against a nighttime counter-attack.[38] Erdeli's forces virtually destroyed two Austrian divisions, taking 10,000 prisoners, many of them Czechs who willingly surrendered to their compatriots, for the loss of 2500 soldiers killed and 10,000 injured. Kerensky cabled Prince Lvov that the Russian units taking part in the first day's action should be awarded revolutionary banners emblazoned 'Regiment of the 18th of June'[39]

Florence Farmborough watched the advance from a vantage point on a hill near Podgaytsy. 'By midday, the wounded had reached us and our hands and our minds were kept busy,' she says. 'The offensive was more successful than one had hoped. Three lines of trenches had already been captured and hundreds of prisoners taken. We worked until 2 a.m. without ceasing and slowly the gunfire became more distant as our troops advanced into enemy territory.' Max Hoffmann wrote in his diary that night, 'The Russians are attacking us in Galicia. I hope they will keep it up for eight or ten days, so that we can give them a proper dressing- down.'[40]

During the night the Germans staged a savage counter-attack to dislodge the Russians on Mount Lysonia. Unable to get their artillery into position in time to respond to the enemy bombardment, the Third Trans-Amur and 74th Infantry divisions suffered heavy casualties and were driven off the mountain.[41] As night fell on the second day, these two divisions were back at their starting points and were ignoring repeated orders from General Brusilov to renew the attack. Instead, their committees voted to be replaced regardless of the consequences to their comrades in the Russian line.

Nevertheless, the Russians had forced a sixteen-mile gap in the enemy's defences and, in the first two days, had advanced up to twenty miles on the South-Western Front. Hoffmann was impressed. He said the attack was being carried out 'with such fury and with such concentration of troops as we have never seen in the East'. The Kerensky Offensive appeared to be on the verge of a great victory, so much so that on 20 June - the third day of combat when things looked promising - the Petrograd Soviet approved the operation by 472 votes to 271.[42]

'Our offensive began brilliantly and at once the spirit of the people was immensely uplifted,' Professor Sorokin wrote in his diary. 'Patriotic demonstrations filled the streets of Petrograd and Kerensky's popularity was widely acclaimed. The Bolsheviki, for the moment, suffered a complete eclipse. Oh, if this would only last!' In Nevsky Prospekt four agitators who spoke against the offensive were beaten up and then arrested as German spies.[43]

Kerensky, however, knew that his forces had sustained heavy losses - the Seventh Army had inflicted 12,500 casualties on the enemy but had lost 15,000 killed, wounded and captured themselves – and that morale, always fragile, was in danger of breaking down. General Erdeli reported that 'despite our gains on June 18 and 19, which ought to have raised the spirits of the men and encouraged them to press on, no such spirit was noticeable in the majority of regiments, while in some there was a predominant feeling that they had done their stint and there was no point in going on with the advance.'[44]

Meanwhile, Nikolai Sokolov's desire to reverse the damaging effects of Order Number 1 backfired badly on 21 June when he visited troublesome units of the Tenth Army on General Anton Denikin's Western Front. He was urging the mutinous infantrymen of the 703rd Suramsky Regiment to move into position when a Bolshevik soldier shouted, 'I know him! He's a *pomeshchik* (landlord) I used to work for!'[45]

This was a lie but other Bolsheviks among the 4000-strong gathering took up the cry. Soldiers surged forward and attacked Sokolov and his companions. Semi-conscious and bleeding from his wounds, Sokolov was held prisoner while the mob debated whether to shoot him, hang him, or just throw him on to a barbed wire entanglement.

Fortunately, the officers and men of the 704th Regiment standing nearby intervened. They threatened to shoot the rebels unless they released their hostage and Sokolov, although badly beaten, staggered to freedom. Denikin intended to disarm the mutinous regiment and send it to the rear but the mutiny spread to three other divisions, with the result that 'I had to deprive myself at one stroke without a shot being fired of 30,000 men'.[46]

Meanwhile, on 23 June, General Kornilov's Eighth Army was ordered into battle. As the spearhead, he sent in his Shock Regiment, consisting of volunteer units including a company of Czech riflemen. Kornilov drove through the Habsburg Third Army and threatened the Drohobych oilfields. Kerensky met him at Stanislav (Ivano-Frankivsk) on the Dniester River. As the commander approached his car, he was holding a red flag in either hand. 'Under these red flags,' he declared, 'the army will carry out its duty… Long live the people's leader, Kerensky.' From Stanislav, Kornilov advanced along the Dniester and captured the ancient town of Halich, and then pushed on towards Kalush in the foothills of the Carpathians.[47]

On 24 June, however, Kerensky wrote a confidential report to the Ministry of War in which he admitted that the offensive would not be a political or military success. 'The operation is developing significantly less successfully than one might have hoped in view of the strength of the preliminary bombardment and the numbers of soldiers concentrated [at the front],' he wrote. He could have added that defeatist Bolshevik propaganda had taken a higher toll of Russian forces than enemy machineguns.

Four days later, however, the Russian Army experienced its greatest triumph since the Brusilov Offensive when the Eighth Army's right column under General Vladimir Cheremisov exploited a thirty-mile gap in the Austro-Hungarian Third Army's line. Two Caucasian cavalry divisions galloped forward to capture Kalush, twenty-five miles from the front, and then drove on to take Galich. Thousands of Austrian prisoners were seized in the Bukovina region before German reinforcements and torrential rain bogged down both sides. Hoffmann was furious with his Austrian Allies. 'Not content with running away, they lie and send false reports, and with it all they are quite unashamed,' he said. 'I should like to go to war with *them*.'[48]

From ecstatic reports in the pro-government newspapers, Bruce Lockhart started to believe that Kerensky was winning his improbable battle. 'For a few weeks,' he says, 'it seemed that his oratory might work a miracle.' When Kerensky returned from the front, Lockhart heard him address an audience from the stage of the Bolshoi Theatre in Moscow:

> He was the first politician to speak from that famous stage which has given to the world Chaliapin, Sobinov, Geltzer, Mordkin and scores of other famous dancers and singers. The huge amphitheatre was packed from top to bottom. Generals, high officials, bankers, great industrialists, merchants, accompanied by their wives, occupied the parterre and first balcony boxes. On the stage were the representatives of the Soldiers' Soviets.
>
> A small pulpit had been erected in the foreground of the stage just above the prompter's trapdoor. Then the buzz of conversation gave place to a burst of clapping, and from the wings the pale figure of the War Minister made its way to the central dais. The audience rose to him. Kerensky held up his hand and plunged straight into his speech. He looked ill and tired. He drew himself up to his full height, as if calling up his last reserves of energy. Then, with an ever-increasing flow of words, he began to expound his gospel of suffering.
>
> Nothing that was worth having could be achieved without suffering. Man himself was born into this world in suffering. The greatest of all revolutions in history had begun on the Cross of Calvary. Was it to be supposed that their own revolution was to be consolidated without suffering? They had a legacy of appalling difficulties left to them by

the Tsarist regime: disorganised transport, lack of bread, lack of fuel. Yet the Russian people knew how to suffer. He had just returned from the trenches. He had seen men who had been living for months on end with mud and water up to their knees. Lice crawled over them. For days they had had nothing but a crust of black bread for sustenance. They were without the proper equipment for their self-defence. They had not seen their women-folk for months. Yet they made no complaint. They had promised to do their duty to the end. It was only in Petrograd and in Moscow that he heard grumbling. And from whom? From the rich, from those who, in their silks and ornaments of gold, came here today to listen to him in comfort.

He raised his eyes to the balcony boxes, while with fierce staccato sentences he lashed himself into a passion. Were they to bring Russia down in ruins, to be guilty of the most shameful betrayal in history, while the poor and the humble, who had every reason to complain, were still holding out? He was ashamed at the apathy of the big cities. What had they done to be tired? Could they not watch a little longer? He had come to Moscow for a message for the men in the trenches. Was he to go back and say that their effort was in vain because 'the heart of Russia' was now peopled by men of little faith?

As he finished his peroration, he sank back exhausted into the arms of his aide-de-camp. In the limelight his face had the pallor of death. Soldiers assisted him off the stage, while in a frenzy of hysteria the whole audience rose and cheered itself hoarse. The man with one kidney - the man who had only six weeks to live - would save Russia yet. A millionaire's wife threw her pearl necklace on to the stage. Every woman present followed her example and a hail of jewellery descended from every tier of the huge house.

In the box next to me, a general who had served the Tsar all his life and who hated the revolution wept like a child. It was an epic performance - more impressive in its emotional reactions than any speech I have ever heard. The speech had lasted for two hours. Its effect on Moscow and on the rest of Russia lasted exactly two days.[49]

Indeed, jewels and oratory could not save the Kerensky Offensive. In the days that followed, frontline Russian troops camped in enemy trenches and waited for reinforcements that never arrived. The second wave simply refused to go forward in many places. Some soldiers shot their commanding officers rather than attack the enemy. Whole units fled the battlefield but not before inflicting serious damage on local civilians. In Kalush, Russian troops took part in a pogrom in which

Jewish and Ukrainian women were raped and their homes looted. The assailants were not deserters but soldiers acting under the direction of their antisemitic officers.[50]

Military setbacks at the front were mirrored in the collapse of the Soviet leaders' compact with the bourgeoisie in the rear. A split had been inevitable ever since the Kadets had swung to the right and taken up the defence of property rights, the imposition of military discipline and other law-and-order issues. Despite the efforts of Prince Lvov to limit the damage, the socialists on one side and the liberal-conservative majority on the other were slowly tearing the coalition apart. The Kadets saw the land policy of the Minister of Agriculture, Viktor Chernov, as sanctioning a peasant revolution by giving the land committees temporary control of the estates. It did not help the cause of unity that Prince Lvov, a landowner himself, branded the policy as 'a Bolshevik programme of organised confiscation'.

On 20 June the First Machine Gun Regiment was ordered to transfer 500 machineguns and their crews to the front, an order that broke the Petrograd Soviet's pledge that the 'guardians of the Revolution' were exempt from doing any actual fighting. The soldiers' committee informed the Ministry of War that the regiment would comply 'only when the war shall have a revolutionary character'. This was tantamount to mutiny but Kerensky lacked the arms in Petrograd to do anything about it.[51]

Having intensified their propaganda in barracks and factories, the Bolsheviks chose this moment to tighten the screw on the government. The Bolshevik Military Committee, the party's fighting group, proposed an armed uprising to topple the government. Support, however, was by no means unanimous. Lenin had declared in his speech to the Soviet Congress that the Bolshevik Party 'is ready at any moment to take power in its entirety'; now, the Bolshevik Central Committee hung back and Lenin claimed that such a drastic move should be delayed until the Kerensky Offensive was over and the Bolsheviks had won a majority in the Soviet. 'One wrong move on our part can wreck everything,' he said. 'If we were now able to seize power, it is naive to think that we would be able to hold it.'[52]

Nevertheless, the machinegunners declared the Coalition Government 'counter-revolutionary' and on 21 June resolved to overthrow it. The Bolshevik Military Committee enjoyed close links with the Petrograd Garrison and the Baltic Fleet. It made plans for the capture of the capital using Red Guard brigades (workers' militias), the Kronstadt sailors, the Machine Gun Regiment and other Bolshevised troops.[53]

Complaining of deteriorating health, headaches and insomnia, Lenin accepted an invitation from his secretary, Vladimir Bonch-Bruevich, to join him and his wife at their dacha in the Finnish countryside. On 29 June he travelled to the village of Neivola, twelve miles northwest of Terijoki on the Gulf of Finland. Lenin was nowhere to be seen when the Military Committee launched the Bolsheviks' first armed attempt to overthrow the government.[54]

18

The Bolshevik Rising

During the night of 2-3 July Alexander Kerensky was in the Rotunda of the Marinsky Palace when four rightwing ministers resigned their portfolios in a dispute over Ukrainian self-rule. The Kadet Party wanted to keep the Empire intact pending the realisation of its impossible dream – the restoration of the monarchy. It opposed giving anything more than cultural freedom to 'Little Russia' and argued that even that decision could only be taken by the Constituent Assembly.

Having defended Ukrainian rights in the Duma, Kerensky was identified with pro-Ukrainian sympathies. He had visited Kiev with Tsereteli and Tereschenko to placate the rebellious Ukrainian Rada,[i] and was in no mood for party politics. He had learned that day that 1200 officers and 37,500 men had been listed as killed, wounded or missing in the June offensive. Compared with the Somme or Chemin des Dames, these were relatively modest losses but they deeply affected him. As the defectors – three Kadets and one Octobrist - left the chamber, he shouted, 'The blood be on your heads. Tens of thousands of men are giving their lives for the Motherland and you desert your posts.'[1]

Prince Lvov was furious with both sides in the dispute. He wrote despairingly to his aged parents:

Sweet Father and Mother,
Without a doubt the country is heading for a general slaughter, famine, the collapse of the front, where half the soldiers will perish, and the ruin of the urban population. The cultural inheritance of the nation, its people and civilisation, will be destroyed. Armies of migrants, then small groups, and then maybe no more than individual people, will

---
[i] The Central Rada, the Ukrainian parliament, was founded in Kiev on 4/17 March 1917.

roam around the country fighting each other with rifles and then with no more than clubs. I will not live to see it, and, I hope, neither will you.[2]

The Provisional Government was ill-equipped to deal with emergencies. Its defence was in the hands of the factory militias and the Petrograd Garrison, the very sources of the insurgency which began at six o'clock that evening when thousands of soldiers and workers, all bearing arms, spilled on to the streets of the capital. Some of the protesters were servicemen over forty who just wanted to go home but there was also a hard core of activists.[3]

'The rioters seized all the automobiles on the streets,' says Colonel Knox, who had returned to Petrograd, 'and armed them with machineguns, men with fixed bayonets as usual lying along the splashboards to impress onlookers.' These 'hedgehog' vehicles combed the city looking for Kerensky or drove to the barracks of other regiments to urge them to join the insurrection. They had no luck with the Preobrazhensky, Semenovsky and Ismailovsky, all of which decided to remain neutral.[4]

At the Tauride Palace pro-Bolshevik deputies stacked a meeting of the Workers' Section of the Petrograd Soviet and forced through a resolution calling on the coalition to hand over power to the Soviets. This was too much for the Mensheviks and Socialist Revolutionaries, who stormed out of the White Hall and summoned a joint meeting of Workers', Soldiers' and Peasants' deputies with the intention of overruling the rebels.[ii] The All-Russian Soviet Excom then issued a stern proclamation addressed to all soldiers and workers in the capital warning them against joining the rebellion.[5]

Across the city in the Kshesinskaya mansion the Bolshevik Central Committee met to decide how to react to the sudden crisis. Lev Kamenev and Grigory Zinoviev urged caution and Trotsky, though not yet a Bolshevik, agreed with them. By early evening, however, reports reached them that a noisy procession of Putilov factory workers waving banners inscribed 'Down with the Capitalist Ministers' and three regiments of soldiers - the First Machine Gun, Moscow and Grenadier regiments – was heading for the city centre.

---

ii Sorokin had been elected to the Peasants' Excom. The peasants' deputies met separately from the workers' and soldiers' deputies but the two groups came together in joint sessions in the White Hall to discuss matters of mutual importance.

Realising that a coup d'état was going ahead with or without their permission, the Central Committee changed tack and urged workers' and soldiers' committees to organise 'peaceful' demonstrations in support of Soviet power. An urgent message was sent to Lenin that he should return to Petrograd as soon as possible. The first real test of strength between the coalition and the Soviet Excom on the one hand and the Bolshevik Central Committee and its military organisation on the other was under way.[6]

Professor Sorokin was heading along Liteiny Prospekt towards the Tauride Palace to take part in the joint Soviet session when the demonstration escalated into violence. Soldiers in the midst of the march suddenly opened fire and gunned down innocent passers-by. Not to be outdone, a group of Red Guards set up a machinegun in Nevsky Prospekt and terrified Petersburgers with reckless gunfire. At the City Duma further along the Nevsky gunfights broke out between troops, hooligans, anarchists and loyalist forces. 'The Revolution was hungry again,' Sorokin says, 'and was calling for human sacrifice.'[7]

At 7.30 p.m., having learned that Kerensky was leaving for the front, one of the 'hedgehogs', bristling with gun barrels and bayonets, pulled up outside Warsaw Station. Bearing a red flag inscribed 'The first bullet for Kerensky', soldiers dashed on to the platform but Kerensky's train had already pulled out of the station.[8] By then a heaving mass of demonstrators had reached the virtually unguarded Tauride Palace and was calling on the Soviet leaders to take power from the ministers. The mob also demanded the arrest of Nikolai Cheidze, the Soviet chairman, for 'surrendering to the landlords and the bourgeoisie'.[9]

'Here and there cannon and machineguns pointed at the palace,' Sorokin says. 'Red banners floated everywhere and there was the sound of incessant firing. It was like a madhouse. Here was the mob demanding "All Power to the Soviets" while at the same time threatening them with extinction.' Some soldiers pushed their way into the White Hall and could have arrested everyone there but instead, in the absence of firm orders from Lenin, they sat down on the floor and listened to the debate.[10]

At 10 p.m. the coup became even more farcical when another detachment of troops arrived at the Minister-President's house in Teatralnaya Street, where Tsereteli, Chernov and Nekrasov were discussing the political crisis with Prince Lvov. Bursting into the lobby, the soldiers announced to the hall porter that they had come to arrest the ministers. When Tsereteli offered to discuss their grievances, they thought better of it and drove away, taking his ministerial motorcar with them but leaving other vehicles untouched.[11]

Chernov gave Tsereteli a lift back to the Tauride Palace for the joint session of the Soviet during which the Georgian told the rebels, 'We are here for the very purpose of realising the will of Russian democracy. Our duty is to defend the unity and integrity of the Revolution. He who thinks that he is on our side when he steps out armed into the street has been deluded.' The debate dragged on until 5 a.m. on Tuesday 4 July when the Soviet Excom dispatched representatives to factories and barracks to reinforce their injunction against taking part in the illegal uprising.[12]

By then, however, the Bolshevik Military Committee had taken command of the insurgents and things had spiralled out of control. Armoured cars seized the bridges and a company of mutinous soldiers took over the low granite bastions of the Peter and Paul Fortress, giving them access to the adjoining Kronwerk Arsenal. As thunder clouds rolled over the capital, the first craft in an armada of warships, tugboats and barges moored on the Nicholas Embankment on Vasilevskii Island, bringing thousands of armed sailors from the Kronstadt Naval Base to join the revolt. Heading for the Kshesinskaya mansion, they joined a noisy mob of striking Putilov workers and rebellious soldiers in demanding orders from the Central Committee. The sailors' leader, Fyodor Raskolnikov, shouted that his men were ready 'to turn the demonstration into an armed uprising'.[13]

Lenin arrived at the mansion in the middle of these chaotic scenes. Gone was the bold revolutionary who had declared that the Bolsheviks were ready to take power at a moment's notice. Nervous, indecisive and sickly, he was all too aware that any miscalculation on his part would almost certainly mean the end of the Bolshevik Party. All the key points in the city - the telephone exchange, the post offices, the banks and the railway stations - were wide open. A word from Lenin would have sent thousands of armed insurgents stampeding through the city to occupy them. Instead, he stayed his hand.

Stepping on to the balcony, he made a short speech which he later described thus: 'First, an apology for confining myself to only a few words on account of illness; second, a greeting to the revolutionary Kronstadtians in the name of the Petrograd workers; third, an expression of confidence that our slogan "All Power to the Soviets" must, and will, conquer, despite all the zigzags of the path of history; and fourth, an appeal for "firmness, steadfastness and vigilance".'[14]

This wasn't what the mob wanted to hear. Now numbering six thousand, the Kronstadtians surged across the Trinity Bridge with the intention of joining the siege of the Taumore Palace. Watching this 'monster procession' pass by the British Embassy, Sir George Buchanan noted, 'The position of the government on that afternoon was a very critical one and had not the Cossacks and a few loyal regiments come in time to save them they would have had to capitulate.'[15]

As the marchers turned into the Liteiny, Cossack snipers and cadets from the military academies opened fire from upper-story windows and rooftops. The sailors fired back and stray bullets killed and wounded dozens of their comrades. The gunfire turned the march into a riot, with soldiers firing wildly into the windows of houses, beating up passers-by and looting shops. 'The Cossacks charged the Kronstadt sailors and sent them flying for their lives,' Buchanan says. 'They then rode back along the quay, but a little higher up they got caught in a crossfire. We saw several riderless horses returning at full gallop.'[16]

Bodies and dead horses littered the square adjoining the Embassy and the sounds of gunfire, breaking glass and screams echoed along the Nevsky. At 5 o'clock, the storm which had been threatening all day burst over the capital and torrential rain soaked the demonstrators outside the Taumore Palace. One of the soldiers dropped a hand-grenade which exploded, killing several people. Thinking themselves under attack from government forces, some of the insurgents opened fire on the building, creating panic among civilians in the crowd. Dozens were crushed in the stampede to find shelter from the rain and the bullets.[17]

Darkness had fallen and the rain had eased off when the Soviet leaders asked Viktor Chernov to use his influence to placate the crowd. As soon as he appeared on the porch, however, the sailors surged forward and seized him. One shouted, 'Take power, you son of a bitch, when it's handed to you.' Chernov was bundled into the back seat of an open touring car parked in the courtyard. Armed men prowled around him and he was in danger of being murdered when an unmistakable, wild-haired figure pushed his way through the mob and climbed on to the bonnet of the car.

Leon Trotsky had made his way to the palace to support the rioters. He had no love of Chernov but realised that the public assassination of a government minister would turn civilians against the insurrection. 'Comrade Kronstadtians, pride and glory of the Russian Revolution,' he shouted, 'you've come to declare your will and show the Soviet that the working class no longer wants to see the bourgeoisie in power. But why hurt your own cause by petty acts of violence against casual individuals? Individuals are not worthy of your attention.' He then ordered the sailors to release their hostage. The sailors shouted angrily at Trotsky but obeyed him and Chernov limped back into the palace.

Meanwhile, Kerensky was visiting troops at Molodechno, northwest of Minsk, when he received an urgent telegram alerting him to the uprising. He replied that 'traitorous actions must be decisively suppressed, insurgent units disarmed, and all instigators of insurrections and mutineers brought to trial'. These remarks were addressed to General Polovtsev, the Commander of the Petrograd Military District. Kerensky expected him to organise a force of loyal troops and put down the insurgency. Polovtsev, however, was short of loyal troops in Petrograd itself and would have to summon reinforcements from encampments outside the city boundaries. This would take time and, as time was running out, something else was needed…

Since April Kerensky, Nekrasov and Tereschenko had been gathering evidence of Bolshevik treachery through a counter-espionage bureau attached to the Petrograd Military District. Although the investigation was incomplete, the Minister of Justice, Paul Pereverzev, rightly surmised that releasing some of the details that evening would generate an anti-Bolshevik mood in the barracks. Therefore, representatives of 'neutral' regiments were summoned to General Staff Headquarters and briefed on the most serious allegations. Armed with this information, they returned to their barracks to report on what they had heard.[18]

Meanwhile, the joint session of the Soviet Excoms had reconvened in the White Hall. The debate dragged on for hours, with the soldiers and sailors becoming increasingly belligerent towards the non-Bolshevik deputies. At one point a large number of armed Putilovites stormed into the hall. The deputies feared the worst when their leader jumped on to the rostrum beside the chairman's seat and, shaking his rifle in the air, shouted:

> Comrades! How long must we workers put up with treachery? You're all here debating and making deals with the bourgeoisie and the landlords ... You're busy betraying the working class. Well, just understand that the working class won't put up with it! There are 30,000 of us all told here from Putilov. We're going to have our way. All power to the Soviets!

Nikolai Cheidze remained unflappable. Calmly, he handed the man a newly printed manifesto which told demonstrators to return to their homes or be condemned as traitors to the Revolution. 'Please take this, Comrade,' Cheidze said. 'It says here what you and your Putilov comrades should do. Please read it carefully and don't interrupt our business.' Not sure how to react, the worker took the manifesto and meekly led the Putilovites out of the hall.

Towards midnight, according to Pitirim Sorokin, the door of the chamber was flung open again and three officers, their uniforms white with dust and caked with mud, marched into the hall and advanced on Cheidze. Identifying himself as the commander of the Third Cyclist Battalion, the ranking officer saluted the chairman and then addressed the Bolshevised soldiers, 'Instead of fighting like men against the invading enemy you have been murdering peaceful citizens, organising riots, encouraging the enemy, and meeting us, the soldiers of the great Russian Army, with machineguns and cannon. What infamy! But your treachery is in vain. Your rioters are dispersed. Your machineguns are in my hands. Your fighters have fled like the cowards they are. And I tell you that those who make the first attempt to repeat this uprising will be shot down like dogs.'[19]

This tirade was greeted with wild applause by most of the Soviet deputies. Accompanied by Trotsky, Zinoviev and Sukhanov, the insurgents were filing out of the hall when the stirring sounds of the 'Marseillaise' echoed around the chamber and, in full battledress, the Ismailovsky Regiment swung through the gates to join the cycle-mounted troops in putting down the coup. The soldiers and sailors in the courtyard scattered for their lives.

Overnight, the capital was seized by anti-Bolshevik hysteria when Pereverzev's 'evidence' was printed in a rightwing newspaper. Convinced that Lenin was either a German provocateur or a secret agent, other newspapers then published as fact allegations that the uprising was being carried out at the behest of the German High Command. Even Georgi Plekhanov, editor of *Edinstvo*, charged that if the government claims were true 'the riots cannot be treated as if they were the regrettable result of tactical confusion [but] were an integral part of a plan formulated by the foreign enemy to destroy Russia'.[20]

While there was no doubt that German money had financed the Bolshevik Party, there was no conclusive proof that Lenin was actually a German agent (even though he must have been aware that he was acting on Germany's behalf). Nevertheless, on 6 July Colonel A. I. Kuzmin, a commander in the Petrograd Military District, led a task force of loyalist troops, complete with armoured cars and heavy artillery, in an attack on the Kshesinskaya mansion. The beautiful Art Deco building had been turned into a filthy barracks housing dozens of armed Bolsheviks. Discretion being the better part of valour, they surrendered without firing a shot, as did the insurgents in the Peter and Paul Fortress.[21]

That morning Lenin was at the *Pravda* office working on an article rebutting the government's 'spy' claims when one of his informants in the Ministry of Justice warned him that he was going to be arrested on a charge of high treason. 'Now they are going to shoot us,' he told Leon Trotsky. He shaved off his beard, donned a wig and a worker's cap, and went into hiding with Grigory Zinoviev in the flat of a Bolshevik sympathiser. Minutes after he had left *Pravda* a detachment of military cadets raided the building. They searched the premises for incriminating documents, beat up staff members, wrecked furniture and dumped bales of the newspaper into the canal.[22]

At six o'clock that evening Kerensky arrived at Tsarskoe Selo station. His first act was to dismiss General Polovtsev. 'I asked for his resignation over his failure to obey my demands for extreme measures against the traitors,' he says. From the station, he drove through cheering crowds to the General Staff Headquarters, where the Provisional Government was in session. 'I ordered the staff officers to prepare a list of the Bolsheviki subject to arrest, to submit it to me for approval and to begin at once the search for the leaders of the mutiny.'[23]

Earlier that day, however, the All-Russian Excom had passed a resolution declaring that the arrest of the Bolshevik leaders would be premature until the allegations against them had been investigated and confirmed. 'Indeed, on entering Prince Lvov's office,' says Kerensky, 'I found a number of prominent Soviet members "maintaining contact" with the government in an effort to prevent the arrests. I said nothing concerning the order I had just given, knowing that the Staff officers would make the necessary arrests as quickly as possible.'[24]

At midnight Kerensky received a telegram from the South-Western Front informing him that the enemy had launched a massive counter-offensive against the Eleventh Army in the direction of Tarnopol. Eleven divisions, nine of them German, were driving back the Russians and exposing the flanks of the Seventh and Eighth armies. The Russian soldiers' committees had voted not to defend their ground and were fleeing eastwards in a panicky retreat. 'With the telegram in my hands I returned to the Provisional Government's meeting,' Kerensky says. 'The Soviet representatives were also present. Controlling myself with difficulty, I read aloud the entire telegram and, turning to the Soviet delegates, I asked them, "I trust that now you will no longer object to the arrests?" There was no reply.'

Later that night the Excom drew up a new legislative programme demanding that the government proclaim a republic, introduce Chernov's radical land reforms and dissolve the State Duma (which was still meeting in the Tauride Palace 'to warn of the menacing dangers and to point to the correct course'). When these demands were presented to Prince Lvov on 7 July, he resigned as Minister-President. The entire programme was unacceptable to him, he said, 'because it would usurp the supreme rights of the Constituent Assembly'. The real reason, however, was that the mild-mannered aristocrat could no longer endure the conflict in his hopelessly polarised cabinet.

Lvov nominated Kerensky, whom he saw as the proverbial axle around which the Revolution revolved, as his successor. 'He was terribly depressed and had waited for my arrival to quit the government,' Kerensky says. The cabinet endorsed his appointment as Minister-President and agreed that he should also retain the post of Minister of War and the Navy. Explaining his decision, Lvov said, 'At this, the most dangerous moment of the Revolution, the elements needed to bring about a strong government are embodied in the person of Kerensky. He possesses real power and among the socialists he is perhaps the only man of action.' What did this mean exactly? Lvov confided to a friend, 'To save the situation it was necessary to dissolve the Soviets and fire at the people. I could not do it but Kerensky can.'[25]

When the new government published its programme on 8 July, however, there was no mention of any of the policies that had so offended him. At a meeting of ministers Nekrasov agreed to take over as Acting Prime Minister for two weeks to enable Kerensky to return to the front that afternoon. Nekrasov and Tereschenko were so indignant about the premature disclosure of the charges against the Bolsheviks that Pereverzev was forced to resign as Minister of Justice.

Meanwhile, Kerensky had promoted Boris Savinkov to Chief Commissar of the South-Western Front, a position that made him immune to Soviet threats. He used this position to mount a vendetta against General Gutor and to advance the cause of his champion, General Kornilov. For days he bombarded Kerensky with telegrams about command failures and Bolshevik penetration on Gutor's front. Kerensky responded on 8 July. He ordered General Brusilov to dismiss Gutor and, at Savinkov's urging, replace him with Kornilov. Savinkov had thus achieved the first objective in his plan to bring Kerensky and Kornilov together in a united assault against the Soviets and the Bolsheviks.[26]

Returning to General Denikin's sector, Kerensky joined the Second Caucasian Grenadiers, a division that had been badly affected by Bolshevik propaganda. 'It was getting dark, the artillery preparation had started and shells were flying overhead,' he says. 'The men told me that they had rid themselves of all the traitors in their midst and now wanted to be the first to go over the top. Never before had I felt so ashamed of not doing myself what I was asking others to do.'[27]

General Hoffmann had removed four divisions from General Denikin's sector in order to maximise his attack against the armies further south. This handed Denikin an overwhelming majority. After a three-day barrage, his Tenth Army attacked on 9 July with marked success. In the first thirty minutes the shock troops of I Siberian Corps overran the three lines of enemy trenches and, in the words of their commander, 'crushed their artillery, took 1400 captives and seized many artillery pieces and machineguns'.[28]

As night was falling, the First Russian Women's Battalion of Death, commanded by Lieutenant Maria Bochkareva, went into action near the Belarusian town of Smorgon. Watching the women advance with fixed bayonets, two battalions of male conscripts were shamed into joining the attack. This mixed force captured the first two lines of German trenches in their sector and then came under heavy fire. While most of the men jumped into the nearest trench, the women continued to advance and took the third line of defences for the loss of about half their number.

The men, meanwhile, had found a large supply of liquor and were drinking themselves into a stupor. When Bochkareva discovered one of her women having sex with a soldier in a shell-hole, she ran her through with a bayonet. Bochkareva had been wounded herself and with most of her troops hors de combat and no reinforcements in sight she withdrew the surviving members of her battalion from the battlefield.[29]

Thousands of Russian troops had deserted and many others, like the French in the Nivelle Offensive, had simply refused to budge. Fresh German troops stopped the breakthrough on Denikin's front and rebuffed a limited counterattack by the Russian Fourth Army and some Romanian contingents in the south. Meeting little resistance, the German counter-offensive advanced as far as the Zbruch River in Ukraine, while the Russian retreat degenerated into an orgy of crime. Drunk and disorganised troops ran riot in towns and villages, looting houses and stores, raping peasant children and murdering Jews.

No sooner was Kornilov in his new post than he sent an angry telegram, written in Vasily Zavoiko's lurid purple prose, to the Ministry of War demanding the return of courts-martial with the power to pronounce the death sentence:

> An army of maddened, benighted people whom the authorities have done nothing to protect against systematic disintegration and debauchery and who have lost all traces of human dignity is in full retreat. The fields, which we dare not even call battlefields, are the scene of unrelieved horror, shame and humiliation the like of which the Russian Army has never known before in its entire history. The extreme leniency of the government's measures has undermined discipline and is responsible for the uncontrolled anarchic cruelty of the masses... The

death penalty will save many innocent lives at the cost of those of a few cowards and traitors.

General Kornilov went unpunished for this faux pas, Kerensky says, because the Provisional Government thought it excusable for a military man at the front to lose his mental and moral equilibrium. 'I personally liked General Kornilov's impulsive gesture,' he says. 'We had already had plenty of experience with the revolutionary "wild men" on the left who were properly tamed as soon as they were led into the harness of government and given responsibility. I believed that General Kornilov would likewise be tamed.'

By 10 July the Russians had been driven out of Galicia and Bukovina, and in addition had surrendered all the territory gained in earlier campaigns. Tarnopol was abandoned on 11 July despite General Brusilov's order that it must be defended at all costs. Before boarding east-bound trains Russian soldiers raped women and children, plundered houses and stores and then, to deny the Germans food and shelter, set fire to the city. 'I should like a few more prisoners,' Hoffmann wrote in his diary. 'The fellows ran away so frantically that we could not catch any of them. Only 6000 up to date, and only 70 guns.'[30]

Kerensky was appalled by the descent into depravity. 'The retreat from Galicia was not as terrible as were the pogroms in Kalush, Tarnopol and other towns,' he said. General Kornilov ordered the assailants to be hanged at crossroads with details of their crimes pinned to their chests. On 12 July the coalition, with the support of the socialist ministers, voted in favour of Kerensky's decree to restore the death penalty for desertion at the front, or for failing to obey orders in battle. Furthermore, as Kornilov had also demanded, justice would be administered through new field 'revolutionary courts'.

Five days later Kornilov forbade meetings of any kind in the theatre of military operations on his front. He also gave orders 'to shoot without trial all those who rob, use force on, or kill peaceful citizens, and all those who refuse to carry out military orders'. 'I will stop at nothing,' he declared, 'to save the country from destruction due to the despicable behaviour of traitors, betrayers and cowards.'[31]

The Russians had retreated 150 miles and the Germans were now advancing on Riga, the Baltic port within striking distance of

Petrograd. 'Ludendorff has sent me a number of very good Divisions, which helped us to win the battle in a style I could have scarcely dreamed of,' Hoffmann said. 'We are going forward well, and the Russians are on the run as far south as the Carpathian Front.' Even so, Germany was losing the war on the home front, where the failure of unrestricted submarine warfare to bring Britain to her knees within six months had created a political crisis. Food and coal were in short supply and the workforce was exhausted.

In the Reichstag, Matthias Erzberger of the Catholic Centre Party demanded that Chancellor Bethmann Hollweg explain why 'the wonderful work of our U-boats cannot make it possible for a single ship to reach us, while 90 per cent of ships arrive in England'. On 6/19 July deputies of the Centre, Social Democrat and Progressive parties passed a peace resolution which rejected the 'acquisition of territories by force' and instead advocated 'a peace of understanding'. The 'Peace Resolution' might have salved troubled consciences but it proved utterly useless in ending the war. Despite a growing number of strikes in favour of peace, the Reichstag approved huge new credits to keep the German war machine rolling along as before.[32]

There were also few signs that resolve was weakening in either Britain or France. As far as the British and French High Commands were concerned, the Kerensky Offensive had served a valuable purpose. Thousands of German troops had been removed from the Western Front and French commanders had been given time to pacify and reshape their mutinous regiments. The positive effects on the British could be judged from an entry for 15/28 July in Field Marshal Haig's diary. When his intelligence chief, Brigadier General John Charteris, reported that the presence of four more German divisons on the Eastern Front indicated that Germany was making a strong effort to knock Russia out of the war, Haig commented, 'This is all in favour of our operations here.'

As Prime Minister, Kerensky's biggest single mistake was to stick with the Allies. In a cable to Lloyd George he promised the Entente, 'Russia will devote all her efforts to carry on the war to a finish which will insure to all peoples the blessings of a durable peace as well as the triumph of the great democratic principles of justice and liberty.' These lofty sentiments failed to acknowledge the simple truth that Russians in every strata of society, and almost unanimously among the proletariat and the peasantry, wanted peace at any price.

'The Prime Minister's task is one of immense difficulty in face of the indiscipline in the Army, the agrarian question, and the crisis in financial, economic, transport, and food matters,' *The Times* correspondent noted. 'The work requires a Colossus, for not only has the work to be done, but the implements wherewith to do it have to be forged.'[33]

Given his affair with Olga's cousin, it was inevitable that Kerensky's private life would become a national scandal. False stories were published about him: one of the most preposterous was that he had secretly married a young actress at the Alexandra Theatre named Yelizaveta Timé. Olga received phone calls expressing sympathy for her plight. 'I could not understand why people were being so solicitous,' she says, 'but then it turned out that there was some story in the leftwing press that Kerensky had left his wife and had run off with an actress.'

Timé (and her husband) both denied these reports but had the truth emerged it would have been even more damaging to Kerensky's reputation. Lilya was carrying his child while her husband, General Nicholas Birukov was fighting for his country. As a graduate of the General Staff Academy and a lecturer at the Pavlovsk Military Institute in Petrograd, Birukov was a popular figure among the officer class. The General Staff at Mogilev was traditionally hostile towards civilian ministers and they turned on the man who had cuckolded one of their own with a particular venom.

On 15 July Kerensky swore on the heads of the dead Cossacks that 'any attempts to create anarchy and disorder will be mercilessly suppressed in the name of the blood of these innocent victims'. Arriving at Mogilev the following day to hold an autopsy on the June offensive, the antipathy of the Stavka towards him was evident from the very beginning. Brusilov was 'too busy' to meet him at the station and Kerensky had only just recovered from that slight when the Supreme Commander announced in front of Savinkov, Filonenko, Alekseyev, Ruzsky and other members of the General Staff that the government was letting him down. Kerensky must insist, he said, that Russian troops obeyed the orders of their officers. 'At present there is nothing to be done with them,' he said. 'After every order, there are twenty-four-hour meetings and, as a result, a refusal to follow instructions.'

Anton Denikin then accused Kerensky of trampling the Russian Army's glorious banners into the dirt. Authority had been abolished and the officers humiliated, he said, and officers up to and including the Supreme Commander (Alekseyev) had been expelled like servants. He demanded the abolition of every change in the army's organisation since the outbreak of the Revolution, with the disbanding of the soldiers' committees at the top of the list. 'Lead Russia to truth and brightness under the red banner of freedom,' he urged the Prime Minister, 'but give us the opportunity to lead our troops under the old banners that have been winnowed with victories.'[34]

Kerensky listened to Denikin's outburst hunched over a table with his head in his hands. Relief, however, was at hand. General Kornilov had been unable to attend the meeting, so he had sent his views in a telegram. Savinkov had advised him to make only moderate demands and to stress the role of the commissars in checking the power of the soldiers' committees. The ploy worked. After Savinkov had read out Kornilov's proposals, Kerensky left the conference in a much better frame of mind and invited Savinkov and Filonenko to accompany him back to Petrograd in his train.

During the journey Savinkov seized the opportunity to argue that all of the matters raised at the conference could be resolved if he and Kornilov were given the power to take decisive action against the malcontents. Kerensky responded favourably and Savinkov arrived in the capital convinced that in a matter of days Kornilov would be appointed Supreme Commander and that he would be elevated to Minister of War.[35]

Kerensky, however, was having second thoughts. Savinkov might be a fellow Freemason and a senior commissar but he was also a renegade, a subversive and a killer, hardly suitable attributes for a position of ministerial trust in a democratic government. On 18 July he recommended to the Provisional Government that the 'defeatist' Brusilov be removed from office and that Kornilov should take his place. Regarding Savinkov, he recommended that he become his assistant at the Ministry of War. Both appointments were duly authorised. As Savinkov had expected to be running the ministry, he considered his demotion to the lowly status of assistant a betrayal of his agreement with Kerensky.[36]

While Kerensky had been in Mogilev, the Coalition Government and its bureaucratic arm had moved into the Winter Palace, which provided spacious rooms, a ready-made guardhouse, an efficient telephone system, a functioning kitchen and a well-trained staff of servants. But the move provoked cries of grandiosity, especially when it leaked out that the Minister-President had taken Alexander III's suite on the third floor for himself. He slept in Alexander's blue-and-gold bed, worked at a Tsarist desk and was driven around in a Tsarist Rolls-Royce. His reception room was the Tsar's library, a great mahogany chamber lined with heavy Gothic bookcases, and his desk was next door in the Tsar's rosewood-panelled billiard room. As he had once imagined, he could stand on the Tsar's balcony and watch the Neva flowing under Palace Bridge, or stroll down the storied corridors singing arias.[37]

'He worked twenty hours a day trying to save Russia from surrender and total economic collapse, and the palace made perfect sense as a base,' Stephen Kerensky says. 'Catherine Breshko-Breshkovskaya was also living there and she became the nurse who gave him morphine injections to ease the pain from his kidney operation. This was the source of the untrue stories about him being a drug addict.'[38]

Drug addiction was just one of the slings and arrows aimed at Kerensky's head. His enemies on the right and left spread wild rumours that he was enriching himself at the expense of the state (unproven); that he was often drunk (he rarely drank); that he was a Jew (untrue); and that he liked dressing up in women's clothes (also untrue). Kerensky's health, however, became an international issue. 'Those who have seen the brilliant Russian leader in the last few weeks describe his face as being haggard and drawn, his figure emaciated, his voice still strong and vibrant but speech marred by frequent coughing, and his eyes brilliant but not with the brilliance of ruddy health,' the *New York Times* reported. 'The Premier's whole appearance unmistakably shows the effect of the enormous work required of him and the heavy responsibility and constant drain on his slender physical resources. "If Kerensky can only hold out", is the phrase more and more frequently heard among his friends and admirers, indicating their dread of his physical collapse and what it would mean to the destinies of free Russia.'[39]

The first test of his prime ministership came in an uncoded telegram signed by Kornilov but written by Vasily Zavoiko informing the

Provisional Government that he accepted Supreme Command on the following conditions:

1. That he was responsible only to his conscience and to the Russian people as a whole.
2. That there would be no interference with his operational orders or his appointment of senior commanders,
3. That the restoration of the death penalty would apply to army reserves in the rear.[40]

'Reporting Kornilov's ultimatum to the Provisional Government, I suggested his immediate dismissal and prosecution,' Kerensky says. 'Savinkov tried to convince me that General Kornilov simply did not understand the meaning of the telegram. In consequence, I withdrew my proposal and Kornilov remained Supreme Commander.' Kerensky later confessed his error. 'I plead guilty,' he said, 'for not having insisted on Kornilov's dismissal but those were such terrible times that there was a sore need of a strong personality at the front.'

For two weeks Kerensky haggled with the Kadets and the Socialists over the composition of the new coalition government but each side was so entrenched that he was unable to reach agreement. Given the circumstances, the combatants could be likened to a group of villagers squabbling over the seating plan for the mayor's banquet while a pack of wolves could be heard howling in the forest. It seemed no one apart from Kornilov and Savinkov was prepared to hunt down the beasts and kill them. On 21 July Kerensky resigned. While he and Lilya headed for Tsarskoe Selo on their way to spend some time at Bad Grankulla, Nekrasov and Tereschenko summoned the ministers, the two Soviet Excoms and the Duma Committee to a joint meeting in the Malachite Hall on the second floor of the Winter Palace.

Horrified at the prospect of having to form a government themselves, the Kadets and the Socialists retreated from their partisan positions and voted to give Kerensky free rein to appoint the cabinet of his choosing. Had Kerensky been gifted with clairvoyance, he would have declined the offer and stayed in Finland. Instead, a sense of duty, misguided perhaps but central to his character, took him back to the encroaching twilight of Petrograd. He named a new coalition with a more national character than the previous one, with six socialists and eight non-socialist members, including five Kadets. Only three members of the original Provisional Government survived: Tereschenko, Nekrasov and himself.

As he retained the post of Minister of War, he appointed Boris Savinkov and Vladimir Lebedev as his deputies for the Army and Navy. Nikolai Avksentiev, one of the strongest opponents of Bolshevism, became Minister of the Interior with the power to tackle the Bolshevik threat. Kerensky also brought in some new blood in the shape of Professor Fyodor Kokoshkin, a moderate Kadet (Minister of Social Welfare), and Ivan Maisky, a returning Menshevik exile (Deputy Minister of Labour). Vladimir Lvov, Minister of Religious Affairs (previously Procurator of the Holy Synod) was dismissed in favour of Anton Kartashev, a respected religious philosopher and professor of Church history.

By accepting the prime ministership, Kerensky had ceased to be the link between the government and the Soviet. For that reason Irakli Tsereteli had decided to remain outside the cabinet in order to take over the role. 'If Kerensky has the support of all parties with a real desire to save Russia from her accumulating ills, his efforts should meet with success,' *The Times* commented. 'If he fails, democracy in Russia will receive a blow from which it will be difficult to recover.'

The most controversial appointment was Boris Savinkov's. Sir George Buchanan commented to the Foreign Office, 'We have come to a curious pass in this country when one welcomes the appointment of a terrorist who was one of the chief organisers of the murders of the Grand Duke Sergie and of Pleve in the hope that his energy and strength of character may yet save the army.'[41]

Bruce Lockhart found Savinkov odious and untrustworthy. 'For some reason which I have never been able to understand, he has always been regarded by Englishmen as a man of action and therefore as a hero,' he says. 'He was a schemer - a man who could sit up all night drinking brandy and discussing what he was going to do the next day. And, when the morrow came, he left the action to others.[42] Colonel Knox was completely taken in. 'Savinkov makes a good impression as a fearless and honest man,' he said. 'He was in complete agreement with Kornilov, and states that as long as he remained in the government I could be assured that Kornilov would have a free hand.'[43]

The appointment that would cause the greatest ructions appeared quite innocuous at the time. Vladimir Lvov, an annoying busybody with delusions of grandeur, had performed poorly in reforming the administration of the Orthodox Church. His dismissal in favour of Professor Kartashev caused barely a ripple but it incensed Lvov (no relation to Prince Lvov). He told Tereschenko, *'Kerensky, c'est mon ennemi mortel.'*[44]

On 1 August Kerensky supervised Nicholas's departure from Tsarskoe Selo after deciding it was no longer safe for him to remain close to Petrograd. 'The Bolsheviks are after me,' he explained, 'and then they will be after you.' Nicholas had hoped to retire to the Crimea to devote himself to Alexei's education. Kerensky, however, had decided to send the Romanovs to Tobolsk in Siberia, a bizarre choice considering its associations with Rasputin but far enough away from revolutionary Petrograd to be relatively safe. Tobolsk was 1800 miles east of Saint Petersburg in the Siberian vastness beyond the Ural Mountains. Under the guise of a 'Red Cross mission', the seven Romanovs were to take the train to Tiumen, the nearest railway station, and then board a river steamer for the final 155-miles leg of the journey. They would travel with an entourage of thirty-nine servants, their doctor, Eugene Botkin, the children's tutor, Pierre Gilliard, and a 300-strong armed escort.

The family packed their own trunks, hiding a fortune in jewels among books, letters and diaries. They had been instructed to include warm clothes, while the servants were told to take hampers containing enough food for five days.[45] As the hour of departure neared, Kerensky watched Alexandra sobbing in a corner and for the first time saw her 'simply as a mother, anxious and weeping'. She had written to Anna Vyrubova, who had just been released from prison, 'Our Friend has eased the road to Tobolsk and calls us there.' At 5.15 a.m. the family boarded their train and Kerensky shouted, 'They can go!'[46]

Meanwhile, the Soviets had been transferred from the Tauride Palace to the Smolny Institute for Girls of the Nobility. This three-storey Palladium building beside the Neva became the new home not only of the Soviet Excoms and the Petrograd Soviet but also of the Bolshevik Central Committee. One by one, returning Bolsheviks filed past the Red Guards keeping watch at the entrance and reported for duty. Revolutionaries hurried along the school corridors from the former 'Ladies Classroom Number 4' to the 'Teachers' Bureau', or queued up in the downstairs Refectory for cabbage soup, chunks of meat and piles of *kasha* (boiled grain) served with thick slices of black bread.[47]

One of the returnees was the Brisbane Bolshevik Artem Sergeyev, who had travelled by ship to Japan and Vladivostok and had then taken the Trans-Siberian Railway to Petrograd. Now thirty-four, he was 'aflame with emotions' to be back in Russia. Known for his ability as an organiser – 'I cannot stand the sight of unorganised masses' - he was elected to the Bolsheviks' Central Committee at the Sixth Party Congress which was held in secret at the Smolny between 26 July and 3 August.[iii] 'The membership of this Central Committee should be well noted,' Trotsky later wrote. 'Under its leadership the October Revolution was achieved.'[48]

The defiant air inside the assembly room showed that the premature release of the anti-Bolshevik documents had taken the sting out of Kerensky's anti-Bolshevik campaign. The cadets who had raided the *Pravda* offices were ordered to evacuate the premises and replace all documents, while the Kronstadt sailors who had been disarmed were freed and sent back to base. Nevertheless, as he had ordered, Alexandra Kollontai, Lev Kamenev, Anatoli Lunacharsky, Nikolai Krylenko and many other Bolsheviks had been arrested. They included Vladimir Antonov-Ovsienko and Paul Dybenko, two young men who would play prominent roles in the events to come. Trotsky's name had not been on the list but on 23 July he was taken to Kresty Prison after sending an indignant message to the government that he should be placed on the same level as Lenin, Zinoviev and Kamenev.

When word leaked out that the Bolshevik congress was being held in the Smolny, Kerensky's friends and political allies urged him to strike. Tereschenko warned him that unless he acted with greater vigour he would resign as Foreign Minister. It was necessary, in his opinion, to militarise the whole country, to repress all disorders and to invite Kornilov to join the government. Kerensky claimed his hands

---

iii The members of the Bolshevik Central Committee in August 1917 were: Ia. A. Berzin, Andrei Bubnov, Nikolai Bukharin, Felix Dzerzhinsky, Lev Kamenev, Alexandra Kollontai, Nikolai Krestinsky, Vladimir Lenin, V. P. Miliutin, M. K. Muranov, V. P. Nogin, A. I. Rykov, Fyodor Sergeyev, S. G. Shaumian, I. T. Smilga, G. Ia. Sokolnikov, Josef Stalin (still known as Koba), Y. M. Sverdlov, Leon Trotsky, Moisie Uritsky and Grigory Zinoviev.

were tied because socialist ministers would not agree to repressive measures.

'Sometimes I feel sympathy, sometimes rage with Kerensky,' Pitirim Sorokin wrote in his diary. 'As a man he is honest, sincere and ready to give his life for the country's good. But he is inconsistent, weak-willed and without mental direction. He knows nothing about governing and imagines he is doing great things when he makes paper plans. Force, coercion and cruelty are abhorrent to him – he believes that it is entirely possible to rule by kind words and lofty sentiments.'[49]

Almost daily Sorokin was reading telegraphic reports of strikes among the workers, riots among the soldiers and outbreaks of anarchy among the peasants. At the front, units murdered their officers and commissars with bayonets and rifle butts, and were then beaten into submission by Cossack whips or bombarded by artillery until they surrendered.

Conscious of his lack of power, the factional conflicts within his cabinet and the constant interference of his enemies in the Soviet, Kerensky prevaricated. Hippius wrote in her diary, 'Kerensky is afraid. Of what? Of Whom?' His cabinet was hopelessly split, with the Kadets supporting Kornilov and Chernov demanding his dismissal. His description of himself as a 'hostage to democracy' no longer applied. 'Kerensky was a prisoner of his mediocre companions and of his own past,' V. D. Nabokov stated. 'He was incapable by nature of acting directly or boldly, and despite his conceit and vanity, he did not have that calm and inexorable self-confidence which is characteristic of really strong men.' Prince Lvov's belief that he would have the cold-blooded resolve to 'dissolve the Soviets and fire at the people' had been wide of the mark.[50]

David Soskice recalls the scene at the Winter Palace when Catherine Brezhkovskaya confronted him about his inaction:

> Suddenly without answering his arguments the grey-haired woman bowed to the ground before Kerensky and repeated several times in solemn imploring tones, 'I beg thee, Alexander Fyodorovich, suppress the conference, suppress the Bolsheviki. I beg thee do this, or else they will bring ruin on our country and the revolution.' I looked at Kerensky. His pale face grew still whiter. His eyes reflected the terrible struggle that was proceeding within him. He was silent for long, and at last he said in a low voice, 'How can I do it?' 'Do it,

Alexander Fyodorovich, I beseech thee' and again Babushka bowed to the ground. Kerensky could stand it no longer. He sprang to his feet and seized the telephone.[51]

Kerensky rang Avksentiev with the intention of ordering the Bolsheviks' arrest but the Minister of the Interior was not in his office. He put down the phone and took no further action. 'He made no attempt to find and arrest Lenin,' says Sir George Buchanan, 'and he contented himself with issuing proclamations ordering the workmen to deliver up their arms, instead of allowing the military authorities to disarm them forcibly… He had his chances and he never seized them; he was always going to strike and he never struck; he thought more of saving the revolution than of saving the country; and he ended up by losing both.'[52]

Lenin directed the work of the Smolny congress through a shuttle service of couriers who travelled between Petrograd and his hiding place in the village of Razliv, twenty miles northwest of the capital. He told the delegates that it was time to end the 'All Power to the Soviets' strategy. By collaborating with the bourgeoisie, he said, the Soviets had shown they no longer represented the true interests of the proletariat. It was not a question of abandoning support for Soviets in general but rather of combating the treachery of the Soviet Excoms. In a new manifesto 'to all workers, soldiers and peasants of Russia', the party issued a call to arms. 'The hour of death for the old world is approaching,' it said. 'Prepare for new battles, our fighting comrades! Steadfastly, courageously and calmly, not giving in to provocation, collect your strength and form fighting columns! Proletarians and soldiers, gather under the banner of the party! Oppressed villages, gather under our banner!'

Lenin's new strategy was to overthrow of the Provisional Government. Never in his wildest dreams could he have anticipated that his greatest ally in the coming battle would be the rightwing Supreme Commander of the Russian Army, General Lavr Kornilov.

On 3 August, the final day of the Bolshevik congress, Kornilov arrived in Petrograd to report to the government. He handed Kerensky a list of reforms that included the abolition of the soldiers' committees, the banning of soldiers' meetings at the front and the disbanding of revolutionary regiments. When Kerensky objected that these measures were too radical, it was agreed that Savinkov and Filonenko would work out a revised programme which he could present to the cabinet. Kerensky warned Kornilov against flirting with the idea of a military dictatorship. Any attempt to do so would lead to a general strike and the deaths of officers at the hands of the rank-and-file. 'I foresee that possibility,' Kornilov replied, his Kalmyk eyes boring into his adversary's skull, 'but at least those who are left alive will have the soldiers in hand.'[53]

There was no mistaking his meaning: he was prepared to shed as much Russian blood as required to achieve his objective. Returning to Mogilev, he ordered his Chief of Staff, General Alexander Lukomsky, to move the Third Cavalry Division, consisting of the Savage Division of Muslim tribesmen and two divisions of Cossacks, from the Romanian front to Velikie Luki, 300 miles south of Petrograd.[54]

When Lukomsky queried the order, Kornilov claimed that a new Bolshevik uprising was planned for 28 or 29 August and that the 'spineless weaklings' of the Provisional Government would allow the Bolsheviks to go unpunished once again through the connivance of such men as Viktor Chernov'. 'It is time to put an end to all of this,' he said. 'It is time to hang the German agents and spies led by Lenin, to break up the Soviet, and break it up in such a way that it will never meet again anywhere.' When the uprising occurred, the Cavalry Corps would move into Petrograd 'to deal with the traitors appropriately'.

Meanwhile, Kerensky assured the Soviet Excoms, 'As long as I stand at the head of the new government, I shall not permit any attempts at a restoration, or a return to autocracy or monarchy.' This pledge infuriated Savinkov, who wanted to see the entire Soviet system disbanded. While flattering Kerensky to his face about his 'noble nature', he described him to Ilya Ehrenburg as 'our narcissistic women's premier'. He also cultivated Kerensky's enemy Alexander Guchkov, who declared him 'a man worth ten Kerenskys'.[55]

Savinkov opened his own office in the Winter Palace and recruited a chef, a valet and a dozen or so male and female adjutants. His personal tailor dressed him in the uniform of a British officer. According to Vladimir Lebedev, his folie de grandeur increased with his rank: he informed Zinaida Hippius that he was planning to set up a three-man directorate of Kornilov, Kerensky and himself to rule Russia.[56]

Savinkov encountered his first stumbling block when Kerensky refused to sign a draft decree to reestablish the death penalty for soldiers in the rear. In a fit of pique he resigned his post and summoned Kornilov to Petrograd to confront the Prime Minister. Kornilov arrived at the Winter Palace on 10 August with an armed escort and an even more draconian list of demands: the imposition of martial law throughout the country, the restoration of the death penalty, and the militarisation of the railways and ordnance factories. Kerensky recognised this as the manifesto for a military dictatorship and refused to even discuss it. The two men fell into a shouting match that echoed down the palace corridors.[57]

When Mikhail Rodzianko, who had accompanied Kornilov to the palace, was permitted to enter Kerensky's office, he roared at the Prime Minister, 'The blood of the country will be on your head.' Kornilov and Rodzianko then adjourned for lunch at the Duma President's home during which Kornilov stated that if Kerensky dismissed him or refused to pass his reforms he would use the Savage Division to oust him.[58]

For months Kerensky had been hearing rumblings that reactionary forces were planning to overthrow the Provisional Government and dissolve the Soviet. The chief suspects were rightwing members of the Union of Officers at GHQ and Vasily Zavoiko's cabal of bankers and industrialists. Indeed, on 8 August the Foreign Office alerted Sir George Buchanan to the fact that Zavoiko's plans for a coup d'état were well advanced.[59]

Kerensky's remedy for the growing threat was to summon 2400 of the nation's defenders and decision-makers to a State Conference in Moscow from 12-15 August in an effort to unify the country 'in its hour of deadly danger'. On the eve of the conference he summoned Savinkov to his office in the Winter Palace and accused him of disloyalty. 'You are a Lenin but of the other side!' he said. 'You're a terrorist! Well then, come and kill me.' The Lenin comparison stung Savinkov deeply and he later lamented it was a pity that Kerensky's name had not been on the Battle Group's hit-list in the pre-Revolution days. Nevertheless, the description was broadly true. Lenin plotted to destroy the government and replace it with a dictatorship of the proletariat; Savinkov plotted to destroy the Soviet and introduce a dictatorship of the military. In both cases the outcome would be civil war.[60]

Kerensky and Savinkov were at loggerheads when the Minister of Social Welfare, Professor Fyodor Kokoshkin, walked in and handed the Prime Minister the resignations of the Kadet ministers. They would return to the coalition, he said, only if Kerensky agreed to the militarisation of the railways, the introduction of ironclad discipline in the army, the limitation of Soviet interference and, if necessary, the dispersal of the Soviet and the establishment of a dictatorship.[61]

After Kokoshkin and Savinkov had departed, Kerensky told Pitirim Sorokin, 'They think I am ambitious for power. Fools! If I could only resign, get away from all this and retire to some quiet village, I would be the happiest man in the world. But to whom could I resign my office? Where is the man? I know they are plotting against the government. This same scheme was proposed to me by Savinkov, then by Kornilov, and now Kokoshkin proposes it. God knows, if I could see any possibility of its realisation I would welcome it with all my heart. But I know it would result in new and more terrible riots.'

'It may be,' Sorokin suggested, 'that if we abandon the war, give the land to the peasants and make all possible concessions to the working class we might avoid catastrophe.'

Kerensky shook his head.

'A separate peace would be shameful,' he said. 'No, no - better to perish with honour than with infamy.'[62]

Later that evening Kerensky boarded the train for Moscow, alighting at the Kremlin Palace at 10 a.m. the following morning. He had chosen the Bolshoi Theatre as the venue for the State Conference because it was thought Moscow was relatively free of Petrograd's revolutionary extremes. It made little difference. Only a matter of weeks after their name had been trampled in the mud, the Bolsheviks were back. Not only were they boycotting the conference but, to register their contempt, they had called a twenty-four-hour strike. On the opening day of the conference no trams would be running, no factories would be working and all restaurants and cafes would be closed.[63]

The Bolshevik Central Committee gather on the courtyard balcony of their headquarters in the Kshesinskaya mansion, Petrograd, in the summer of 1917. Lenin is the man in a hat and Stalin is in a white blouse.
(Kerensky Family Papers)

Four of the children of Frederick Tritton and his wife, Eliza 'Leila' Tritton, née Worrall: (from left) Lillian, Lydia Ellen 'Nellé', Charles Frederick and Ivy Jane. *(Tritton Family Album)*

Photographer Viktor Bulla, later executed by the Bolsheviks, captured Vladimir Lenin with delegates to the Second Congress of the Third Communist International (the Comintern) on 17 July 1920 to plan world revolution. (Second from left in hat) Lev Karakhan, 'the Bolshevik Adonis', (third, smoking) Karl Radek, (fifth) Nikolai Bukharin, 'the darling of the party', (seventh, in uniform) Mikhail Lashevich, (behind the column) Maxim Peshkov, Maxim Gorky's son, (ninth, shaved head) Maxim Gorky, an observer, (tenth, hands in pockets) Vladimir Lenin, (eleventh, in hat) Sergei Zorin, (thirteenth, hands behind his back), Grigory Zinoviev, (white shirt and tie) Charles Shipman (Jesus Ramirez), (coat and tie), M. N. Roy, (nineteen, white blouse) Maria Ulyanova, Lenin's sister, (with beard) Nicola Bombacci, (in light hat) Abram Belenky, and (top right, bald-headed) Fyodor 'Artem' Sergeyev, the Brisbane Bolshevik.

Lydia 'Nellé' Tritton, known as Nell, who made her debut at the Mayoral Victory Ball in Brisbane on 26 April 1919.
(Tritton Family Album, courtesy of Lavinia Tritton)

Nell Tritton on the day of her disastrous marriage to Nicholas Nadejine, a White Russian opera singer, at Saint Philip's Russian Orthodox Church, London, on 9 February 1927.
(Tritton Family Album, courtesy of Lavinia Tritton)

Left: Nell Tritton at the time of her wedding to Alexander Kerensky in August 1939. Right: Alexander Kerensky, wearing his gold monocle, at the time of the wedding.

Alexander and Nell Kerensky leave Sydney for Brisbane on 13 November 1945. Nell saved Kerensky's life by getting him out of France in June 1940. She died of chronic nephritis in Brisbane on 10 April 1946.

Lydia 'Nellé' Tritton as a young socialite-journalist-poet in Brisbane circa 1922. *(Tritton Family Album, courtesy of Lavinia Tritton)*

Alexander Kerensky (right) watches a game of boules at the Ménard-Dorian family home, 'Mas de Fourques', at Lunel in the Hérault, in 1924. On the left is Kerensky's friend, the artist Jean Hugo, while the players are Jean Hugo's first wife Valentine (Gross), a German friend Gerda von Gerlach and the composer Georges Auric.
(Jean Hugo Archive, courtesy of Jean Baptiste Hugo)

Alexander Kerensky (right) with his friend Aline Ménard-Dorian (centre), Jean Hugo (left), Marguerite Hugo and Gerda von Gerlach at 'Mas de Font Fougassière', another family home a few miles north of Lunel.
(Jean Hugo Archive, courtesy of Jean Baptiste Hugo)

The last photograph: Nicholas II and his five children on the greenhouse roof of their house in Tobolsk after Alexander Kerensky evacuated them from the Alexander Palace. Alexandra rarely left went outside. The family were executed at Ekaterinburg on 17 July 1918. *(PA Images)*

PART III
RETRIBUTION
(1917-1924)

19

The Kornilov Revolt

Moscow was a tense, divided city on the afternoon of Saturday 12 August 1917 when delegates arrived at the Bolshoi Theatre for the opening of the State Conference. 'The atmosphere on the streets was electric,' says Morgan Philips Price. 'One instinctively felt that unseen powers were at work, one acting from the right and the other from the left.' The English journalist had to pass through a triple cordon of soldiers and military cadets which was keeping a mob of 10,000 Muscovites at bay. 'The crowd met the delegates with considerable reserve,' *Izvestia* reported. 'For the most part, the attitude was hostile; whistles were heard but there was no disorder.'[1]

Inside the building delegates discovered that even the staff of the theatre's buffet were on strike and they had to brew their own tea. Kerensky and his ministers took centre-stage. 'My seat was precisely in the middle,' he says. 'On my left were the Democratic-Socialist ministers; on my right were the ministers from the bourgeoisie. The Provisional Government was the only centre uniting both Russias and I was the mathematical point of unity.'[2]

Back in June this very stage had been the scene of one of his greatest oratorical triumphs; today the vast amphitheatre was filled with doubt, anger and suspicion. Mikhail Rodzianko, Paul Miliukov, Alexander Guchkov, 'arisen as if from the dead' like hundreds of other deputies of all four Dumas, filled the right side of the stalls along with members of the Kadet and Octobrist parties and the Union of the Landed Nobility (tactically renamed the Union of Landowners). Industrialists, bankers and members of the *zemstvos* and cooperatives occupied the middle ground, while the Mensheviks and Socialist Revolutionaries sat with rank-and-file soldiers on the left. The High Command, the Soviet Excoms and the Diplomatic Corps were given pride of place in the opera boxes.[3]

'Morning coats, frockcoats and starched shirts dominated over workers' blouses,' the *Izvestia* reporter noted. 'One gains the general impression that the representatives of the so-called bourgeois world overshadowed the democratic elements.' Indeed, the lodgings of the Soviet representatives were so far afield that many seats in their box were vacant when Kerensky strode to the tribune at two o'clock that afternoon and, with an adjutant standing on either side of him, announced the conference open.

'The Coalition Government expects that this will be the centre from which our country will receive new inspiration in accomplishing its heavy task,' he said. 'All who truly love their country expect that the State Conference will find a way to unite all the healthy elements in Russia.' Turning to the left, Kerensky evoked Bismarck to warn pro-Bolshevik delegates that any further attempt to raise arms against the people's government would be stopped 'with blood and iron'. Turning to the right, he warned the Union of Officers and other pro-Kornilov groups that his government would not tolerate any attempt to usurp its authority and that rebels would have to contend with 'the will of the supreme power and myself as its head'.

But the conference was, in the opinion of Nikolai Sukhanov, 'foredoomed'; in fact, it never had a chance of achieving Kerensky's objective. 'Not only was he walking a tightrope in a gale,' says Stephen Kerensky, 'but his opponents in London, Paris, Berlin and Petrograd were shaking the rope.'

One short passage demonstrated the irreconcilable differences between left and right. 'While Minister of Justice I introduced the abolition of capital punishment. (*Applause. Cries: 'Bravo'.*) And as Minister of War I introduced partial restoration of capital punishment. (*Cries: 'Right!' Boisterous applause, suddenly interrupted.*) 'Who dares applaud? Don't you know that at that moment, at that hour, a part of our human heart was killed?' The applause faded and the hall fell silent. According to Harold Williams, Kerensky's ninety-minute speech was 'an aggressive assertion of authority [but] in effect it was almost a plaintive appeal for support'.[4]

The conference did not sit on Sunday the thirteenth. Rightwing political groups joined the Union of Officers, the Council of Cossacks and the Union of the Knights of Saint George to dance attendance on Lavr Kornilov when he arrived at the Alexandrovsky Station at two o'clock that afternoon. Travelling with him was General Alexander Krymov, the ultraconservative Commander of the Third Cavalry Corps, who had been briefed during the journey on the objectives of his Petrograd operation. While Krymov passed unnoticed, Kornilov was showered with flowers and carried from the platform on the shoulders of jubilant Cossacks to an open touring car. Surrounded by mounted cavalry, he thrilled the Muscovite crowds by driving through the streets to worship at the feet of the Madonna in the Iberian Chapel near the Kremlin.

Back at the station later that day Kornilov's visitors to his saloon carriage included the Kadet members of the Duma Miliukov, Vasily Maklakov and Fyodor Rodichev, and a returnee named Alexis Aladin, who had been a brilliant Trudovik orator in the First Duma. Ignoring all protocols, Rodichev called on the General to 'save Russia and a thankful people will crown you'. Miliukov later claimed he had warned Kornilov against attempting a military coup; on the contrary, said Maklakov, their adulation and promises of support had provoked that very thing.[5]

As far as Kornilov was concerned, the most useful of the Duma deputies was Alexis Aladin, who had joined the British Army while in London and had turned up in Moscow wearing the uniform of a British Army translator. By way of introduction, he handed Kornilov a letter, supposedly written by Lord Milner, which gave his blessing to the anti-Soviet movement and approved of a military dictatorship. 'It is not improbable,' Kerensky says, 'that this message was the deciding factor in the destiny of that unsuccessful Russian Napoleon.'[i][6]

On Monday 14 August Kornilov made an even more theatrical entrance at the State Conference, driving to the Bolshoi with the duplicitous Boris Savinkov at his side in the open touring car. As the General swept into the hall at the head of his red-robed, scimitar-wielding Turkoman bodyguards, the righthand side of the chamber

---

[i] At a meeting in London on 7 September 1933 Kerensky asked Lloyd George why his government had systematically encouraged a conspiracy aimed at overthrowing him and establishing a military dictatorship. Lloyd George affected astonishment. He claimed he knew nothing about any such conspiracy and, if it were true, 'then the British Ministry of Supply and the War Office must have been conducting their own private war'. Kerensky recalls this meeting in Russia's Turning Point (p. 493). Turning Point was written in 1965 and, as the Ministry of Supply was not formed until 1939, Kerensky has clearly misremembered. Perhaps Lloyd George said the Ministry of Munitions.

– in other words, all the Kornilovist elements who wished to see Kerensky overthrown – leaped to their feet and gave him a rowdy ovation, while the Soviets remained stoically anchored to their seats. Having warned Kornilov to restrict his comments to military matters, Kerensky called on him to speak.

'Upon the tribune rose a wiry little man with strong Tatar features,' says Morgan Philips Price. 'He wore a general's full-dress uniform with a sword and red-striped trousers. His speech was begun in a blunt soldierly manner by a declaration that he had nothing to do with politics. He had come there, he said, to tell the truth about the condition of the Russian Army. Discipline had simply ceased to exist. The army was becoming nothing more than a rabble. Soldiers stole the property, not only of the state, but also of private citizens, and scoured the country plundering and terrorising. The Russian Army was becoming a greater danger to the peaceful population of the western provinces than any invading German army could be.'[7]

Kornilov had stuck to the politically correct guidelines but had still managed to highlight the Prime Minister's powerlessness. Kerensky admitted as much in his closing speech. 'I will not dream any more,' he said. 'I will try to have less faith. Since it must be, so let it be. Let my heart turn to stone, let all the chords of my faith in man die away, let all the flowers of my dreams for man wither and die…'

After this rambling diatribe, he lost his way and the delegates began to murmur uncomfortably. When he halted for breath, they burst into applause and started leaving their seats. The conference ended with Kerensky fainting into his chair.[8]

'There is only one name that unites everyone,' Zinaida Hippius had written in the halcyon days of early March, 'and that is the name of Kerensky.' Now, less than six months later, she described him in her diary on 14 August as 'a railway car that has come off the tracks. He wobbles and sways painfully and without the slightest conviction. He is a man near the end; and it looks like his end will be without honour.' Sir George Buchanan reported to the Foreign Office, 'He made a distinctly bad impression by the way in which he presided over the conference and by the autocratic tone of his speeches.'[9]

No one was more aware of the disaster than Kerensky himself. Kornilov had returned to Mogilev triumphant and his supporters in Petrograd and Moscow were baying for blood. 'After the Moscow conference,' Kerensky said, 'it was clear to me that the next attempt at a blow would come from the right and not from the left.'[10]

Back in Petrograd on 17 August the Kadet members of his cabinet urged him to reinstate Savinkov to the Ministry of War. Kerensky reluctantly agreed. Savinkov said he would return only on condition that the Prime Minister restored the death penalty in the rear. He then reminded Kerensky of his offensive remarks at their previous meeting when he had described him as 'the Lenin of the other side'. 'I have forgotten everything,' Kerensky replied. 'I am a sick man. No, not quite. I have died, I am no more. At the conference I died. I cannot offend anyone and no one can offend me.'[11]

After their meeting, Savinkov signalled Filonenko at Mogilev to inform Kornilov that Kerensky had agreed to his terms and that he was working on a decree that would introduce their most stringent reforms.

Not since the Gunpowder Plot has a botched conspiracy had such shattering consequences. The Kornilov Revolt would fail completely and yet it would change Russia's history. Given Kornilov's sheep's brain, it was not surprising that his plan did not follow a logical, or indeed rational, trajectory; nor was it surprising that the Kornilovist cabal included a number of crackpots and dilettantes without whose contributions the story might well have unfolded along very different lines.[12]

The misunderstandings and downright lies that led to the debacle began on 20 August when Savinkov informed Kerensky that he had completed his draft of the decree for military reforms, including the restoration of the death penalty in the rear. Kerensky prevaricated. According to Savinkov, the Prime Minister said he was concerned that publication of the decree would trigger violent riots among the Petrograd Garrison. He had decided to put Petrograd under martial law and he asked Savinkov to go to GHQ to instruct Kornilov to send him a force of loyal troops capable of enforcing it.

Kerensky disputed this version: Savinkov must have misunderstood. As the front was now only 250 miles from Petrograd, he wanted to place the Petrograd Military District, with the exception of the city itself, under the Supreme Command. He also denied he had asked for troops to be sent into Petrograd – he wanted them not *in* but *near* the city. This sort of hair-splitting was bound to lead to confusion.[13]

The next day the enemy's forward divisions swept into Riga, bringing the threat of invasion to Petrograd for the first time in the war. Kornilov blamed this humiliating defeat on the Russian defenders who, he alleged, had abandoned their posts and fled in disorder. According to Kerensky, this was untrue. 'The Russian soldiers fought stubbornly under a hail of heavy artillery and in a cloud of yellow cross [poisonous] gas,' he says. Nevertheless, the publication of Kornilov's allegations in rightwing newspapers caused a wave of ill-feeling against the rank-and-file. His motive was to reinforce the points he had made in Moscow – that the army was ill disciplined and unreliable – and thus apply pressure on Kerensky to sign off on his proposals. He also wired the government demanding that the Petrograd Garrison be placed under his command.[14]

The Battle of Riga effectively brought the fighting between the Russian Army and the Central Powers to an end. Hindenburg says in his memoirs that the Germans halted their advance because of supply problems, 'thanks to the destruction of the railway stations by the retreating Russians'. The German High Command also feared that any further penetration ran the risk of reviving the patriotism of the Russian masses and thus undoing the work of the Bolsheviks in undermining it. The respite on the frontline, however, was not reflected elsewhere. Finland and Ukraine had declared independence; factories were on strike; the railways were disrupted; peasants were attacking landlords; and the crime rate was soaring in the cities.[15]

It was at this point that Alexis Aladin and Vasily Zavoiko brought the military, political and financial conspirators together for their strike against democracy. Aladin saw himself as Foreign Minister in a Kornilov dictatorship, while Zavoiko had reserved the Ministry of Finance for himself. Through Prince Lvov, Aladin tried to set up a meeting with Kerensky to hand over an ultimatum demanding his support for the new regime. Kerensky, however, refused to see him. Casting around for an alternative messenger, Aladin and Zavoiko settled on the other Lvov, the former Minister of Religious Affairs, Vladimir Lvov.

During the Moscow conference the conspirators had met this wealthy conservative landowner when a mutual friend, a Knight of Saint George named I. A. Dobrinsky, brought him to their base in the National Hotel. According to Kerensky, Lvov was not in favour of a

Kornilov dictatorship but he had been initiated into the conspiracy and had expressed a willingness to help. He saw himself as Minister of the Interior in the new regime, with a private army at his disposal to suppress dissent.[16]

Lvov is often described as 'a self-appointed mediator' between Kerensky and Kornilov but a more accurate description would be agent-provocateur. He became involved because he saw a chance to get even with Kerensky for removing him from his cherished position in the Holy Synod. Zavoiko had returned to Mogilev with Kornilov, so Aladin and Dobrinsky met Lvov at the National Hotel on 21 August and briefed him on his duties, the first of which was to deliver a note to Paul Miliukov warning him of the impending coup. Lvov took the overnight train to Petrograd and, in the morning, he tried but failed to contact the Kadet leader. Discovering that he was away from the city, he arranged to meet V. D. Nabokov at his apartment in Morskaya Street in the Admiralty Quarter at six o'clock that evening.

Nabokov was no longer chief secretary to the cabinet - he was working on the electoral laws for the Constituent Assembly - but he was still a senior member of the Kadet Party. He regarded Lvov as a bit of a clown. 'He always spoke with great fervour and animation and invariably evoked amusement,' he says. He was astonished to be handed the note intended for Miliukov which said, 'The general who sat across the table from you requests you to warn the Kadet ministers to resign on 27 August with the object of creating new difficulties for the government and in the interests of their own safety.' Unbeknown to Nabokov, the general in question was Kornilov's Chief of Staff, Alexander Lukomsky, who had joined the conspirators and was privy to their plans. The note made no sense to Nabokov, so he questioned Lvov as to its meaning.[17]

'When I leave you, I am going to see Kerensky,' he said, 'and I am taking him an ultimatum; a coup d'état is being planned, and a programme for a new government with dictatorial powers has been established. It will be proposed that Kerensky accept this programme. If he refuses, that will be the final rupture, and it will only remain for me, a person close to Kerensky and well-disposed toward him, to try to save his life.' Far from being well-disposed towards Kerensky, Lvov was executing a plan to destroy him. Further questioning left Nabokov in no doubt that the ultimatum had originated from the Stavka.

After his visitor had departed, Nabokov reflected that entrusting this mission to a man like Lvov 'attested to the fact that the initiators of the coup were very bad judges of human character and had acted exceedingly thoughtlessly'. Indeed, the American Ambassador, David Francis, described Lvov as a 'meddlesome rattle-brain'. Kerensky knew the frivolities of Lvov's twisted mind and he also knew that he bore a grudge. Despite these reservations, he admitted him to his study at the Winter Palace later that evening.[18]

Kerensky says Lvov made no mention of Kornilov's supposed ultimatum but instead tried to persuade him that he had no support anywhere because he was now 'hated by the right' and had 'lost his influence' with the left. His reliance on the Soviets had placed him in a precarious, even dangerous, position vis-à-vis the Bolsheviks. 'Influential circles', however, were prepared to support him provided he agreed to accept some changes in the cabinet.[19]

When Kerensky demanded to know on whose behalf Lvov was speaking, he replied, 'I have no right to tell you. I am only authorised to ask whether you are willing to enter into discussion.' He let slip, however, that his people were backed 'by a considerable force which nobody could afford to ignore'. He then asked whether he could report back that Kerensky had agreed to talk to them. 'Of course you may,' Kerensky replied. 'You know I am interested in forming a solidly-based government, not in hanging on to power myself.'[20] Lvov then made his excuses and left but not before telling Kerensky that he would see him again. 'I gave him no instructions and no power [to negotiate on my behalf],' Kerensky says.[21]

Boris Savinkov, accompanied by Vladimir Baranovsky, met Kornilov at the Stavka the next day - Wednesday 23 August – to discuss having loyal troops on hand in the event of another Bolshevik uprising in the capital. Not trusting Savinkov, Kerensky had wanted his brother-in-law to witness these conversations but Savinkov insisted on speaking to Kornilov in private. After Baranovsky, Filonenko and Zavoiko had left the room, the general heaped invective on Kerensky – 'weak, vacillating, incompetent' – but he calmed down when Savinkov promised that the death penalty would be introduced within a matter of days. The two men then agreed that the Third Cavalry should proceed to Petrograd in case of trouble with the Bolsheviks. If the Soviets interfered, they would be forcibly suppressed. Savinkov, however, insisted that the wild men of the Savage Division should be excluded from the force and that the 'bloodthirsty' General Krymov should be replaced with a more acceptable commander.[22]

Word about the projected military coup d'état reached Sir George Buchanan that same day from one of Kornilov's principal backers, the banker Aleksei Putilov. He told the Ambassador that a group of financiers and industrialists planned to arrest the ministers with Kornilov's help and then dissolve the Soviet Excoms. He asked Buchanan to put the British armoured car division at Kornilov's disposal. Buchanan was outraged. He told his visitor it was 'very naïve to ask an Ambassador to conspire against the Government to which he was accredited'. He promised, however, that he would not betray the conspirators' confidence.[23]

The fact remains that two responsible people, Nabokov and Buchanan, had been warned on consecutive days that Kerensky faced a military rebellion and yet they said nothing to the Prime Minister or any of his ministers. Meanwhile, in London, Colonel Knox urged the Imperial War Cabinet to back General Kornilov in the coming struggle as the only way of reviving the Russian Army as an effective fighting force. 'The conflict between Kornilov and Kerensky was inevitable from the first,' he said, 'for the two men were of very different character and stood for diametrically opposed principles.' He saw Kornilov as 'a hard-headed soldier of strong will and great courage, without a spark of personal ambition', whereas Kerensky was nothing but a jumped-up backwoods socialist lawyer.[ii][24]

Arriving at Mogilev on 24 August shortly after Savinkov and Baranovsky's departure, Vladimir Lvov presented himself to Kornilov as an emissary from the Prime Minister. He carried no letter of authorisation and the general made no attempt to verify his position. Nor did he find it strange that Kerensky would send another emissary to see him when he had just said goodbye to two others. Kornilov, however, was too busy to speak to Lvov that night and their meeting was put off until the following morning when Lvov offered him his choice of three proposals which, he inferred, were from Kerensky but which emanated from his discussions at the National Hotel in

---

ii 'The exact details and motivations of the Kornilov Affair are unconfirmed due to the general confusion of all parties involved,' Wikipedia warns. 'Many historians have pieced together varied historical accounts as a result.'

Moscow:

1. That Kerensky should assume dictatorial powers.
2. That a Directory should be formed, with Kornilov as a member.
3. That Kornilov should become dictator, with Kerensky and Savinkov serving in ministerial positions.

Not unnaturally, Kornilov opted for the third choice but, according to Lvov, said he would work under Kerensky if necessary. He asked Lvov to invite Kerensky to come to Mogilev to talk about it. After Lvov's departure, Kornilov – despite his agreement with Savinkov - ordered General Krymov to occupy Petrograd with the Third Cavalry Corps, including the Savage Division. He was to disperse the Soviets and disarm the garrison to avert a Bolshevik uprising. He told General Denikin and the other commanders in his circle that he was acting on behalf of the Provisional Government. If the socialist ministers resisted, they would be arrested and he would form a military dictatorship. Kerensky could either support him or take the consequences.[25]

Meanwhile, Lvov returned to the Winter Palace around six o'clock on the evening of 26 August to complete his mischief-making mission. Kerensky noticed that his manner had completely changed and that he was highly agitated. Boldly, he told the Prime Minister that the Supreme Commander was demanding dictatorial powers and had issued an ultimatum to the Prime Minister. This was indeed a sensational development - it was the first time Kornilov's name had been mentioned in their conversations. Lvov then enunciated the three points in Kornilov's ultimatum. Kerensky was dumbfounded. 'Neither Lvov nor Kornilov had ever been mentioned in the reports I had received of the military conspiracy,' Kerensky says. 'I asked him to write down the three points. As soon as he began to write my last doubt disappeared. I had only one desire: to check the madness at the outset.'[26]

Lvov had written:

General Kornilov proposes:
1. That martial law shall be proclaimed in Petrograd.
2. That all military and civil authority shall be placed in the hands of the Supreme Commander.

3. That all ministers, including the Prime Minister, shall resign and that the temporary executive power shall be transferred to the assistant ministers till the formation of a cabinet by the Supreme Commander.
V. Lvov, Petrograd 26 August 1917.[27]

Lvov then told Kerensky that he and Savinkov should travel to GHQ that very night to assume their portfolios in the new cabinet – Kerensky as Minister of Justice and Savinkov as Minister of War. 'Certainly not,' Kerensky said. 'Do you think that I can be Minister of Justice under Kornilov?'

Lvov sprang to his feet.

'You are right! Don't go there. A trap is set for you. He will arrest you. Go away – somewhere far away; but you must get out of Petrograd. They hate you.'[28]

At 8.30 o'clock that night Kerensky contacted Kornilov on the Hughes Apparatus in the Minister of War's apartment on the Moika Canal and asked for a clear statement of his intentions. Impersonating Lvov, Kerensky told the General that Kerensky 'is hesitating to give his full confidence without your personal confirmation'. Kornilov appeared to confirm that a military coup was indeed imminent and that Kerensky should proceed to Mogilev to be out of harm's way. 'Not only did the General confirm that he had authorised Vladimir Lvov to speak on his behalf,' Kerensky claimed, 'but he went even further in corroborating every statement made by Lvov.'[29]

Returning to the Winter Palace, Kerensky ordered Lvov's arrest and then told Boris Savinkov, 'Your hand is in this, Boris Viktorovich.' Savinkov denied any knowledge of Lvov or his proposals, and insisted that the ultimatum must be the result of a misunderstanding. 'I am profoundly convinced that General Kornilov did not take part in the plot,' he said. 'I am no less convinced that General Lukomsky and the other principal instigators tried to influence him.' He challenged Kerensky to put him on trial or authorise him to organise the defence of the city. Kerensky promptly appointed him Governor-General of Petrograd.[30]

Armed with Lvov's written ultimatum and the tape of his conversation with Kornilov, Kerensky presented the evidence to a midnight cabinet meeting in the Malachite Hall. Taking his seat at the green baize table, he demanded a free hand to deal with the emergency. Two Kadet ministers resigned on the spot and Viktor Chernov, who thought it was Kerensky who should resign, was expelled from the meeting. The other ministers handed the Prime Minister dictatorial powers and, in a telegram early the next morning, he dismissed Kornilov as Supreme Commander and ordered him to report to Petrograd.[31]

Savinkov had a direct telephone line to the Stavka and he spent the next few hours talking to Kornilov and Filonenko to establish what was happening there. He pleaded with Kornilov to relinquish his command because, he said, his present course spelled disaster for all they had worked for in reforming the army.[32]

Kornilov disputed almost every detail of Kerensky's version. He said he believed that Lvov had indeed been acting on Kerensky's behalf and after hearing 'Kerensky's' three proposals, he had declared his profound conviction that 'the only way to solve Russia's predicament would be to establish a dictatorship and proclaim an immediate state of martial law'. He had added that he did not seek personal power and was willing to subordinate himself to anyone holding a dictatorial mandate. Then, having apparently reached agreement with the Prime Minister over the Hughes Apparatus, he was astonished to be dismissed a few hours later in a telegram signed simply 'Kerensky'.[33]

As only the full cabinet had the authority to dismiss him, Kornilov assumed there had been a Bolshevik coup in Petrograd and that the Prime Minister was being held captive. He refused to step down or to report to Kerensky in Petrograd; instead, he ordered General Krymov to advance on Petrograd with the Third Cavalry Corps and place the city under martial law. He had seen it as his duty, he said, to put down the Bolsheviks.

This was mutiny and Kerensky had no difficulty persuading the Soviet Excoms to join him in making plans to defeat the mutineers. His first move was to send out a circular telegram branding Kornilov a traitor to the Revolution and calling on all loyal Russians to sabotage the rebellion. Responding to this plea, the All-Russian Railway Union (Vikzhel) ordered its members to stop the Third Cavalry in its tracks at Luga, eighty miles from Petrograd, and agitators fraternised with Krymov's troops in their carriages to persuade them to abandon their mission.

The pendulum then swung in favour of the Bolsheviks. Disregarding Savinkov's position as Governor-General, the Bolshevik Military Committee took the opportunity to turn the Smolny Institute into a command centre directing operations against the 'counter-revolution'. Red Guards were issued with rifles and ammunition and instructed to guard the city. Lenin, who was still hiding in Finland, urged the Bolsheviks to fight Kornilov but without building up Kerensky. 'We shall now show everybody his weakness,' he said. Kerensky further strengthened the Bolsheviks' hand by ordering the release of Leon Trotsky, Alexandra Kollontai, Lev Kamenev, Vladimir Antonov-Ovsienko and Paul Dybenko.[34]

The Russian Army emerged from the crisis more fractured than ever. On 29 August, at General Alekseyev's suggestion, Kerensky appointed himself Supreme Commander, with Alekseyev as his Chief of Staff. The following day General Krymov agreed to travel to Petrograd with a government escort. He met Kerensky at the Winter Palace on 31 August. Krymov tried to explain that he was bringing his troops to Petrograd in order to defend the government from the Bolsheviks but Kerensky would have none of it. He ordered him to be tried by a military court on a charge of high treason. Leaving the palace in despair, Alexander Krymov went to a friend's apartment and shot himself.

On 1 September Alekseyev took control of the Stavka and ordered Kornilov's arrest. Instead of riding down Nevsky Prospekt on a white horse to the cheers of grateful Petersburgers, he was imprisoned at the Bykhov Monastery, ten miles south of Mogilev, with General Denikin, General Lukomsky and other officers suspected of having been involved in the 'counter-revolution'. Hundreds of Kornilovist officers in the army and navy were arrested by their men and some were executed without trial. This internecine bloodshed was exactly what Kerensky had been trying to prevent. He sent telegrams to the naval bases: 'I demand that all atrocious acts of violence shall cease immediately. Crews committing these crimes, under pretext of saving the Revolution, are traitors to the country.'[35]

The Kornilov Affair seriously damaged the Provisional Government and weakened Kerensky's personal standing in London, Paris and Rome. Lloyd George told his confidant, the newspaper proprietor Lord Riddell, that Kerensky's policies had brought only indecision and inefficiency to Russia and that Kornilov's failure to seize power was 'a serious blow for the Allies'. Kerensky had already lost the confidence of the officer corps, many of whom had backed Kornilov, and now he lost the respect of the Soviets, who suspected he had been part of the conspiracy and had then changed his mind.[36]

Chernov wrote in his party's newspaper *The People's Cause (Delo Naroda)* that he 'could not make out where Kornilov ends and where Filonenko and Savinkov begin, where Savinkov ends and where begins the Provisional Government as such'. Lenin was the big winner. 'General Kornilov had obligingly presented him with the opportunity of seizing power much sooner than he had planned,' Kerensky says, 'and, even more important, of doing so under the slogan "All Power to the Soviets", which he had dropped after the July fiasco.'[37]

Kerensky was tense and suspicious; he no longer knew who to trust. Nikolai Nekrasov had been acting as his deputy since July but their friendship ended when he discovered that his fellow Freemason had secretly sided with his critics during the Kornilov debacle.[38] He appointed a Directory of four socialists and one non-party affiliate, though in practice, three men - Kerensky, Tereschenko and the Minister of Post and Telegraph, A. M. Nikitin - would rule the country until a new coalition could be assembled. The other two members of the Directory, Minister of War General A. I. Verkhovsky, and Minister of the Navy Admiral D. N. Verderevsky, would concentrate on military issues. In defeating a dictator, Kerensky had become a virtual dictator himself.[iii]

Pushing Savinkov's reforms on to the back burner, his first act was to issue a proclamation that was dear to his heart: he declared Russia a republic. 'The word that for decades had been forbidden has been pronounced,' cheered the *Volia Naroda (The People's Will)*. 'The Provisional Government proclaimed a republic and thus separated the old order from the new. No matter what evils might befall the Russian revolution in the future, this "little paper" cannot be destroyed.'[39]

As well as Nakrasov, Kerensky also lost another friend in Bruce Lockhart, whose support had remained constant. Lockhart's marriage had been under strain ever since Jean had almost died giving birth to their daughter on 20 June 1914. It was an instruments delivery and the

---

iii Nikitin, a Moscow lawyer, had been a member of Kerensky's investigating team on the Lena Goldfields in 1912. General Verkhovsky, in the words of V. D. Nabokov, was 'a sort of psychopath undeserving of any trust'.

baby did not survive. When Jean found out he was having an affair with Madame Vermelle, the highly strung wife of a wealthy French diplomat, she complained to her novelist friend Hugh Walpole. As the head of the Anglo-Russian Propaganda Bureau, Walpole felt it was his duty to alert Sir George Buchanan. To avoid a scandal, the Ambassador ordered Lockhart home to England on 'sick leave'. Taking Jean with him, he 'slunk out of Moscow in early September as a culprit rather than as a martyr'.[40]

Meanwhile, the odds against Kerensky surviving as Prime Minister were shortening all the time. The British Foreign Office believed rumours that David Soskice was a German agent and that Kerensky was about to conclude a separate peace with Germany. Such were the contradictions of British policy that while Lloyd George and his War Cabinet were anxious to depose Kerensky in favour of a rightwing alternative, Mansfield Smith-Cumming, the head of the Secret Intelligence Service, was more alert to the Bolshevik menace than his Prime Minister and had decided that everything possible should be done to keep him in power.

Smith-Cumming supplied Sir William Wiseman, his man in New York, with $75,000 ($1.6 million today) to be smuggled into Russia to fund the Provisional Government. A similar sum was received from the Americans. The agent chosen by Wiseman to carry the first tranche of $21,000 into Russia and hand it over to Kerensky was Somerset Maugham. The author (codename: 'Somerville') was 'staggered' by the proposition. 'The long and short of it,' he says, 'was that I should go to Russia and keep the Russians in the war.'[41]

Carrying the cash in a money-belt, Maugham arrived in Petrograd via Vladivostok and the Trans-Siberian Railway at the end of August. He booked into the Hotel Europe and contacted his former Russian mistress, Alexandra 'Sasha' Kropotkin, daughter of the anarchist Prince Kropotkin. Sasha was a Kerensky supporter and she introduced the two men at the Winter Palace. Maugham spoke fluent Russian so they were able to converse without the help of a translator. 'What struck me most was his colour,' Maugham says. 'One often reads of people being green in the face with fright and I had always thought it an invention of novelists. But that is exactly what he was. He seemed fearfully on edge.'[42]

Maugham gave the money to Kerensky and later entertained him to dinner at Medved, the best French restaurant in Petrograd. 'I think Kerensky must have supposed that I was more important than I really was,' Maugham wrote in his memoirs, *Looking Back*, 'for he came to Sasha's apartment on several occasions and, walking up and down the room, harangued me as though I was at a public meeting for two hours at a time.'[43]

Kerensky's problems multiplied in September when the Bolsheviks expunged the shame of the July Days and scored victories in key Soviet elections, including the Petrograd Soviet. Then, on 14 September, Cheidze and Avksentiev convened a Democratic Conference on behalf of the Soviets to decide whether Russia should be ruled by a coalition or by a purely socialist government. The conference ended in confusion without expressing a clear opinion on this vital issue but it agreed to establish a Council of the Russian Republic, a 'Preparliament' that would give the republic a semblance of legitimacy prior to the setting-up of the Constituent Assembly.

According to V. D. Nabokov, the parties involved in the coalition – mainly the Kadets and the socialists – agreed in advance that it was the chief task of the newly constituted council to reinforce the government in its struggle with Bolshevism. Teresteli, however, had resigned from the Soviet Excom and his replacement, Fyodor Dan, refused to honour this commitment. He told Nabokov that his support was contingent on the government's 'mode of action' and that he 'could not take the position that Bolshevism must be fought above all else regardless of the outcome'.

At the Preparliament's first meeting in the Marinsky Palace, Leon Trotsky, revitalised by his time in Kresty Prison, set out to sabotage it. He accused Kerensky of planning to abandon Petrograd to Wilhelm's troops and turn Moscow into a stronghold of counter-revolution. 'Only the people can save themselves and the country,' he said. 'We address the people: Long live an immediate, honest, democratic peace. All power to the Soviets, all land to the people. Long live the Constituent Assembly.' As Trotsky and the other Bolsheviks stalked out of the chamber, someone shouted, 'Go to your German trains!'[44]

On 25 September Kerensky went ahead and announced his new government, a coalition consisting of the five members of the Directory plus a handful of non-Korvilovist Kadets and the chairman of the Moscow Stock Exchange. As Deputy Prime Minister, the untrustworthy Freemason Nikolai Nekrasov was replaced by a trustworthy Freemason, Alexander Konovalov. Nikolai Kishkin, a high-ranking Kadet, was appointed Minister of the Interior.

Meanwhile, the Bolsheviks had taken over four of the seven seats on the Central Executive Committee of the Petrograd Soviet, 'the parent of all the other Soviets'. Leon Trotsky replaced Nikolai Cheidze as chairman. One of the new members was Artem Sergeyev, who had been elected by the Soviet of Peasant Deputies for Petrograd Province. In the days ahead he would stand out as one of Lenin's strongest supporters on the Excom in demanding the immediate overthrow of the government. 'Since the April Days the Soviet had gone against the revolution and been the mainstay of the bourgeoisie,' Sukanov says. 'It was now Trotsky's guard, ready at a sign from him to storm the Coalition, the Winter Palace and all the bourgeois citadels.'[45]

On 26 September the French, British and Italian Ambassadors strode into the Winter Palace to express the Entente's misgivings about Russia's ability to carry on fighting the war. Sir George Buchanan read out a joint Note in English (with Tereshenko providing Kerensky with a Russian translation), warning that the Allies would cut off military supplies unless order was restored in the army. Kerensky was furious. The Allies had hesitated in supplying ammunition to the Russian gunners, he said, and the results of that hesitation were being felt at the front two or three months later. Russia would continue the struggle against the Central Powers 'whatever the international tensions would be'. He then dismissed the Ambassadors with a reminder that despite their criticisms Russia was still a great power.[iv][46]

As news of these events reached Lenin in his Helsinki pied-à-terre, he became convinced that the Bolsheviks must stage a preemptive strike to bring down the Provisional Government *before* the Second All-Russian Congress of Soviets opened at the Smolny on 25 October. The Bolsheviks needed the benediction of the Soviet Congress to legitimise their seizure of power; otherwise, as with the July Rising and the Kornilov Revolt, the insurgents could find themselves at odds with pro-Soviet soldiers, workers and peasants defending the government. Assuming the Bolsheviks could arrest Kerensky and his

---

iv Tereschenko sent a telegram to the US Secretary of State Robert Lansing in Washington thanking him for the American Ambassador's abstention from the démarche.

ministers by the time the congress opened, their socialist opponents would find it very difficult to dislodge them.

During the night of 7 October Lenin slipped into Petrograd disguised as a Finnish pastor of his mother's old church, the Lutherans. He stayed with Margarita Fofanova, a young Bolshevik agronomist, in Serdobolskaya Street in the Vyborg District. Three days later he risked arrest to attend the meeting of the Bolshevik Central Committee that would decide Russia's fate. The venue was the apartment of Nikolai Sukhanov at 32 Karpovka Embankment on the Petrograd Side. Sukhnanov, however, had not been invited. His wife, Galina Flaxerman, was an ardent Bolshevik and she had pointedly advised him to spend that night at the Smolny. 'For such a cardinal session not only did people come from Moscow but the Lord of Hosts himself, with his henchmen, crept out of the underground,' Sukhanov says. 'Lenin appeared in a wig but without his beard. Zinoviev appeared with a beard but without his shock of hair.'[47]

Besides Lenin, eleven of the twenty-one committee members attended the meeting, including Alexandra Kollontai, Josef Stalin, Grigory Zinoviev, Lev Kamenev, Leon Trotsky, Felix Dzerzhinsky and Moisei Uritsky.[v] The talking went on until three o'clock in the morning and ended with the committee voting by ten to two, with Zinoviev and Kamenev dissenting, in favour of Trotsky's resolution that the Bolsheviks would seize power in the name of the Second Congress of Soviet in the coming days. It was agreed that the uprising would be planned by Trotsky through a new Military Revolutionary Committee (MRC), but the date of the coup was left open.[48]

Kerensky placed the guilt for what was about to happen at the feet of the belligerents. 'For the sake of her victory, Germany sent us Lenin and helped to poison Russia with Bolshevism,' he said. 'For the sake of Allied victory, and with equal zeal, some of the Allies undermined the Provisional Government. The Germans believed that all was permissible in war, while the Allies acted on the supposition that they could do anything they liked in Russia after the disappearance of the Tsarist Government.'[49]

---

[v] The others were Andrei Bubnov, a trade unionist, Georgy Lomov, the Bolshevik chief in Moscow, Grigory Sokolnikov, joint editor of Pravda, and Yakov Sverdlov, one of the original Bolsheviks.

20

The October Coup

Alexander Kerensky entered Red October in a surprisingly bullish mood. He talked to deputations from the Eastern Front, the Caucasus and Siberia, received Allied ambassadors and argued with reactionary priests over the separation of Church and State. Despite his workload he made time to sit for two artists: Ilya Repin and his star pupil Isaak Brodsky. Guardsmen snapped to attention when he passed, flunkeys lowered the Red Flag whenever he left the Winter Palace and raised it when he returned. Rumours of an impending Bolshevik rising did not bother him. 'I would be prepared to offer prayers to produce this uprising,' he told V. D. Nabokov. 'I have greater forces than necessary. They will be utterly crushed.'

In mid-October three American journalists, John Reed, his wife Louise Bryant and Albert Rhys Williams, all Marxists, were admitted to his office. Kerensky shook hands with them, studying each face in turn, and then sat them down at the big mahogany table. 'His whole face was greyish in colour, puffed out unhealthily, with deep pouches under the eyes,' John Reed later wrote in the magazine *The Liberator*.[1]

> He looked at one shrewdly, humorously, squinting as if the light hurt. The long fingers of his hands twisted nervously tight around each other once or twice, and then he laid them on the table, and they were quiet. His whole attitude was quizzically friendly, as if receiving reporters was an amusing relaxation. When he picked up a paper with questions on it, I noticed that he put it within an inch of his eyes, as if he were terribly near-sighted.[2]

'What do you consider your job here?' John Reed asked him. Kerensky laughed, as though amused.

'Just to free Russia,' he answered drily and smiled as if it were a good joke.

'What do you think will be the solution of the present struggle between the extreme radicals and the extreme reactionaries?'

'That I won't answer,' he shot back swiftly. 'What's the next?'

'What have you to say to the democratic masses of the United States?'

'Well …' he rubbed his chin and grinned. 'Let them understand the Russian democracy and help it to fight reaction – everywhere in the world. Let them understand the soul of Russia, the real spirit of the Russian people. That's all I have to say to them.'

'What lesson do you draw from the Russian Revolution for the revolutionary democratic elements of the world?'

'Ah-hah.'

The Prime Minister turned that one over in his mind and gave Reed a sharp look. 'Do you think the Revolution in Russia is over, then? It would be very short-sighted for me to draw any lesson from the Revolution.' He jerked his head in emphasis and spoke vehemently. 'Let the masses of the Russian people in action teach their own lesson. Draw the lesson yourself, comrade – you can see it before your eyes!'

He stopped and then began abruptly:

'This is not a political revolution. It is not like the French Revolution. It is an economic revolution, and there will be necessary in Russia a profound revaluation of classes. And it is also a complicated process for the many different nationalities of Russia. Remember that the French Revolution took five years; that France was inhabited by one people, and that France is only the size of three of our provincial districts. No, the Russian revolution is not over – it is just beginning!'[3]

Standing up, Kerensky shook hands with the reporters and, even before they were out the room, he had seated himself at his desk and started to write.

On 16 October the Petrograd Soviet, now comprising a breakaway faction of radical Socialist Revolutionaries known as Left SRs, launched the Military Revolutionary Committee.[i] The ostensible purpose of this group was to defend the capital from a counter-revolutionary attack but, in reality, it had been formed to overthrow the government. The MRC had Bolshevik and Left SR members, with

---

i The split in the PSR was not completed before the Consitiuent Assembly elections in November 1917.

Paul Lazimir, a Left SR, as the nominal chairman. Its real leaders were Leon Trotsky and his lieutenants Vladimir Antonov-Ovsienko, Nikolai Podvoisky and Paul Dybenko. Trotsky knew it was vital to trick the soldiers and the factory militias who would be doing the fighting into believing that the MRC was a Soviet organisation; otherwise, there was a risk they would refuse to obey orders and might even turn on the Bolsheviks.

Antonov-Ovsienko, party alias Bayonet, was a Ukrainian-born former officer-cadet who had been expelled from college in 1901 for refusing to take the oath of loyalty to Nicholas II. Trotsky described him as 'politically shaky but personally courageous - impulsive and disorderly but capable of initiative'. Podvoisky was a street-fighting veteran who was itching 'to carry the affair to its conclusion'. Dybenko, a huge black-bearded Baltic sailor, was the current lover of Alexandra Kollontai (and soon to be her husband). He boasted that he had once thrown Kerensky over the side of a warship, an event that no one else seems to remember.[4]

As the self-described 'mathematical point of unity', the Prime Minister's position at the centre of the coalition was more vulnerable than ever. Yeats had yet to write 'The Second Coming' but his poem would have made a suitable epitaph for the Provisional Government:

> *Things fall apart; the centre cannot hold;*
> *Mere anarchy is loosed upon the world…*
> *The best lack all conviction, while the worst*
> *Are full of passionate intensity….*[ii]

Over the past 200 days no one had done more for the New Russia than Alexander Kerensky but he was nearing the limits of his endurance. His indecisiveness was also driving Alexander Konovalov to despair. 'So this is how it will be, Alexander Fyodorovich,' the Deputy Premier would say, 'it is now firm, the decision is final, there will be no change?' Konovalov would receive a categoric assurance that this was so. A few hours later he would discover that an entirely different measure had already been implemented. 'And so it is day after day,' he sighed to V. D. Nabokov. 'There is really no end to it.'[5]

Buffeted by events outside his control as well as those of his own

---

ii 'The Second Coming' was inspired by the 1916 Easter Rising in Dublin.

making, Kerensky's popularity was falling like the autumn leaves. 'I have studied too many people not to know the real value of popular love and hatred,' he says. 'When I was at my height and the crowd bowed before me, I quietly said to my friends, "Wait, they will come and smite me".' He was exhausted and frequently collapsed on the divan in his office. He burst into tears easily. An existential dread replaced his bullish confidence.[6]

Lilya, now six months' pregnant, had moved out of the palace and was living with her brother, Vladimir Baranovsky, and his actress wife, Maria, known as Moussia, at their home, Apartment 10, 59 Bolshaya Pushkarshkaya. To see her, Kerensky drove through the city streets in his open touring car, returning the salutes of soldiers as though nothing was wrong. His condition, however, worried his family. 'Day by day he seemed to grow weaker but he never stopped working or took care of himself,' Moussia says. 'He would come to our house, where he knew he would be safe, throw himself on a couch and snatch a few hours' sleep.'[7]

Kerensky realised he had a crisis on his hands when his attempt to transfer local regiments to the Northern Front to defend the capital triggered a mutiny in the Petrograd Garrison. The majority of the soldiers refused to obey the orders of General Georgi Polkovnikov, the latest commander of the Petrograd Military District, and switched their allegiance to the MRC, which replaced senior officers with Bolshevik commissars.[8]

The main source of dissent was, of course, the war. All the efforts of Kerensky and Tereschenko to persuade the Allies to discuss the principle of altering their war aims had failed miserably. Irakli Tsereteli's Zimmerwald argument that the conflict had resulted from the imperialism of the Triple Alliance and the Triple Entente was anathema to Britain and France, who considered themselves victims of premeditated Austro-German aggression.[9]

'The British hatred of the Provisional Government was founded on its reforms, such as votes for women, and its federal system of government,' says Stephen Kerensky, 'but worst of all was my grandfather's view that there should be no reparations and no land-grabbing.'

When Kerensky heard that Somerset Maugham was leaving Petrograd for London, he tried one last throw of the dice. On 17

October he summoned the spy to the palace and asked him to take a message to Lloyd George urging him to offer peace to Germany but a peace without annexations or indemnities. The Germans were bound to reject it but the very fact that the belligerents were discussing peace would have a positive effect on the Russian Army. 'I must make the Russian soldiers understand what they are fighting for,' he explained to Maugham. He also appealed for guns and ammunition, boots and food. Without that help, he said, 'I don't see how we can go on. Of course, I don't say that to the people. I always say to the people that we shall continue whatever happens, but unless I have something to tell my army it's impossible.'[10]

The message was so sensitive that Kerensky would not let Maugham write it down and nor could he cable it to London because Sir George Buchanan had forbidden him to use the Embassy's encryption facilities. He would have to rely on his memory. That night he left Petrograd for Oslo, where a Royal Navy destroyer would take him to Scotland.

On Friday 20 October General Verkhovsky, the Minister of War, declared that the Russian Army was unfit to fight. He recommended 'raising at once the question of concluding peace' as a means of saving it from annihilation. Kerensky had done all he could in that regard without bringing down the government. Anyway, it was too late to prevent the MRC from proclaiming itself the ruling authority of the Petrograd Garrison.

Deciding that attack was the best form of defence, he released Verkhovsky from his duties and ordered an infantry brigade, a cavalry regiment and an artillery battery to be dispatched from the Northern Front to the capital with the aim of crushing the Bolsheviks. In the meantime there was nothing to stop the 'All Power to the Soviets' campaign from gaining traction. The beauty of Trotsky's battle plan – the cherry on the top – was the unwitting collaboration of the vast majority of Soviet members in launching Lenin's coup. 'It is clear that an uprising against the coalition, and its destruction, were incumbent on the Petersburg proletariat and garrison,' Nikolai Sukhanov explained. 'Hence the official agency of the uprising was the Petrograd Soviet. The political and technical work had to proceed from there.'[11]

On Sunday 22 October Leon Trotsky, Alexandra Kollontai, Lev

Kamenev, Nikolai Krylenko and other popular Bolshevik speakers stirred up the masses at political rallies in factories and halls throughout the city. Speaking as chairman of the Soviet Excom to a huge meeting at the House of the People on the right bank of the Neva, Trotsky, curly hair flying and eyes blazing, could have been a hot gospeller whipping up religious frenzy in the American Bible Belt. The government proposed by the Second Congress of Soviets would, he claimed, start a revolutionary fire of such intensity that it would engulf not only Russia but the entire world. When he urged the faithful to show their support for the Soviet, a thousand hands shot into the air. 'Let this vote of yours be your vow,' he said, 'with all your strength and at any sacrifice to support the Soviet that has taken on itself the glorious burden of bringing the victory of the revolution to a conclusion and of giving land, bread, and peace!'

The people swooned at the very thought of it. 'All around me was a mood bordering on ecstasy,' Sukhanov says. 'It seemed as if the crowd, spontaneously and of its own accord, would break into some religious hymn.'[12]

Very few of those who heard Trotsky's speech would have realised that supporting the transfer of power to the Soviets actually meant installing a Bolshevik government. His plan was to forcibly disperse the Preparliament and then arrest Kerensky and his ministers at the Winter Palace. If all went well, the Bolsheviks would be in charge of Petrograd in time for Lenin to present the seizure of power as a fait accompli to the opening session of the Soviet Congress in just three days' time. He knew that the Mensheviks, who were still waiting for a bourgeois revolution to legitimise a full-blooded socialist revolution, and the Socialist Revolutionaries, who were divided over every issue except land, would protest but by then the Bolsheviks would be the new masters of Russia.

The very next day – Monday 23 October - Trotsky persuaded the defenders of the Peter and Paul Fortress to join the Soviet bandwagon and hand over the keys to the Kronwerk Arsenal, which held enough weapons to equip a small army. Controlling the fortress also gave the Bolsheviks use of the cannon overlooking the Winter Palace, a psychological rather than a military advantage because the guns were actually defective.

At the Smolny Institute that night Vladimir Antonov-Ovsienko explained the moves that the MRC was making 'to protect the revolution, the Congress of Soviets and the Constituent Assembly'. The Petrograd Soviet then voted overwhelmingly in support of a Bolshevik-sponsored resolution endorsing these defensive measures and giving the MRC carte blanche to take whatever further steps were necessary. It was this vote that signed the Provisional Government's death warrant: Kerensky could be overthrown in defence of the Revolution.

Meanwhile, the cabinet had agreed to charge members of the MRC with sedition for circulating appeals for civil disobedience and indulging in activity against the lawful government. They also resolved to imprison Trotsky and other Bolsheviks for conducting anti-government agitation while on bail. Their first measure, however, was to shut down two pro-Bolshevik newspapers, *Workers' Road (Rabochy Put)* and *Soldier (Soldat)*, and to prosecute their rabble-rousing editors and inflammatory authors.

General Iakov Bagratuni, Chief of Staff of the Petrograd Military District, ordered cadets from the Petrograd military schools and the officers' training academies at Peterhof and Gatchina, a battery of horse artillery from Pavlovsk, a rifle regiment from Tsarskoe Selo, and the First Petrograd Women's Shock Battalion from Levashova to report for duty on Palace Square. At 5 a.m. on Tuesday 24 October a detachment of cadets and loyal militiamen raided the printing plant of both newspapers and shut them down. Several thousand copies were seized and the printing plates were destroyed.[13]

News of the attack on the newspapers and the action to be taken against the MRC reached Trotsky at the Smolny Institute. He was also alerted to Kerensky's attempt to bring in anti-Bolshevik troops from outside the capital. Panicking, he summoned his comrades to a meeting at which he issued Directive Number 1: 'The Petrograd Soviet is in direct danger; counter-revolutionary conspirators have attempted to bring cadets and shock battalions from the suburbs to Petrograd during the night. The newspapers *Soldat* and *Rabochy Put* have been closed. You are hereby directed to bring your regiment to battle readiness [and to] await further instructions. Any procrastination or interference in executing this order will be considered a betrayal of the revolution.'[14]

Kerensky had defended the Revolution from the Bolsheviks in

July and from General Kornilov in August. Branding him a 'counter-revolutionary conspirator' for opposing yet another illegal attempt to seize power ranks as one of the greatest mockeries of Red October. When David Soskice arrived at Kerensky's office that morning, however, he found his friend unconcerned: General Polkovnikov had assured him that there was no threat to the government. 'I watched from Kerensky's windows how loyal troops were taking possession of the bridges across the Neva, leaving one bridge open for the passage of the crowds,' Soskice says. 'We saw the Women's Battalion regulating the movements of the crowd and arresting anyone who showed resistance.'

During the morning Kerensky received further reports by telephone that indicated the Bolsheviks, as in the July Days, were heading for another embarrassing defeat which would justify the government taking strong measures against them. A fresh warrant was issued for Lenin's arrest and, once captured, he would finally be tried for high treason. With his chief lieutenants in prison, the Bolshevik threat would be curtailed for a very long time.[15]

At midday Kerensky informed the Council of the Republic at the Marinsky Palace that a Bolshevik coup was underway and that 'all possible measures' were being taken to defeat it. Waving an intercepted MRC order to the garrison, he accused the Bolsheviks of 'treason and betrayal of the Russian state'. When the Mensheviks and SR Internationalists protested, he snapped, 'Yes, yes, listen, because at the present time, when the state is imperilled by deliberate or unwitting treason and is at the brink of ruin, the Provisional Government, myself included, prefers to be killed and destroyed rather than to betray the life, the honour and the independence of the state.'[16]

He requested a vote of confidence in the coalition and walked out of the chamber to a standing ovation. Driving to the General Staff Building to consult with General Polkovnikov, he was convinced that the support he had requested would be forthcoming. Later that afternoon the telephone lines to the Smolny were cut, destroying Lenin's easy access to his high command, and the order was given to keep the bridges raised to separate the inner city from working-class districts. David Soskice left the Winter Palace that evening believing the uprising had misfired.

Questioned by reporters in his red-carpeted office at the Smolny,

Trotsky denied that a Bolshevik insurgency was imminent and he made a point of stressing to his commanders the need for discipline and patience. The hours dragged most heavily on Lenin, who feared that his party was in danger of missing its opportunity. At six p.m. he sent Margarita Fofanova to the Smolny with a desperate appeal to Trotsky to launch an attack in the next few hours. 'The government is tottering,' he wrote. 'It must be *given the death-blow* at all costs. To delay action is fatal.'

Unaware of the drama unfolding around them, Petersburgers took part in the evening cavalcade along Nevsky Prospekt and it was business as usual in the restaurants, theatres and bordellos. Hearing nothing by ten o'clock, Lenin donned his wig and a worker's cap and, wrapping a bandage around his head for extra effect, set off for the Smolny with a Finnish comrade, Eino Rakhia. They rode through the Vyborg District in an empty streetcar as far as the Finland Station and then continued the journey on foot.

By then Kerensky had returned to the Winter Palace to await news of the Preparliament's vote of confidence. Three members of the council - the socialists Fyodor Dan, Avram Gotz and an embarrassed Nikolai Avksentiev - turned up in his study to deliver the verdict. Dan informed him that the Council of the Republic had questioned his ability to restore order impartially and had declined to support him. After a testy debate, the Preparliament had passed a resolution – 'interminably long and hopelessly muddled' in Kerensky's words - recommending the establishment of a democratic government committed to peace and radical reforms.

'I told Dan somewhat curtly that the resolution was unacceptable,' he says. 'Dan replied calmly to my heated words. I shall never forget what he said. In his opinion I was exaggerating the danger under the influence of my "reactionary staff". On the other hand, he continued, the Bolsheviki themselves had expressed their readiness to "subordinate themselves to the will of the Soviet majority" and were willing, beginning tomorrow, to undertake all measures to stop the uprising, "which had begun against their wish and without their sanction".' Given this unlikely scenario, Kerensky informed the delegation that the government would take the necessary action without their approval.[17]

He had no way of knowing that a few minutes earlier, near the

Tauride Palace, a government patrol had stopped Lenin and Rakhia but taking Lenin for a hopeless drunk had waved them on. It was almost midnight when the vast, blazing silhouette of the Smolny Institute, almost a block long and with a façade resembling a Greek temple, reared up in front of them. Outside the gates, Red Guards had set up bivouacs and their bonfires crackled in the freezing night air. Lenin had no pass but he slipped past the sentries in the midst of a small group.[18]

Once inside the building he stormed into Room 36, the location of the Central Committee caucus, and at a hastily convened meeting with his startled comrades insisted that the Winter Palace must be taken the following day – Wednesday 25 October – in time for him to present his coup to the delegates at the Second Soviet Congress. Finally, the doubts of Zinoviev, Kamenev and other waverers, who had questioned the reliability of popular support and thought the Constituent Assembly represented a stronger base of operations, were overcome and the order was given for the insurrection to begin at once. Trotsky laid out a map of the city and explained the main lines of attack to Lenin, Podvoisky, Antonov-Ovsienko and the other Bolshevik members of the MRC.[19]

At 2 a.m. Bolshevik forces moved into the city centre. Red Guards replaced government troops holding the bridges and Bolshevik armoured cars patrolled the streets. One thing led to another. The Mensheviks and Socialist Revolutionaries had their own military assets but failed to mobilise them. In the absence of any opposition, the Bolsheviks took control of the railway stations, the post and telegraph offices, the State Bank, the Central Telephone Exchange and the main electricity station. They also reopened all but two of the bridges to facilitate troop movements around the city. All this happened in the space of a few hours without a shot being fired.[20]

Kerensky was holding a cabinet meeting in the Malachite Hall when reports began flooding in about the seizures. The meeting ended on a despondent note and most of the ministers went home. Kerensky was discussing the rapidly deteriorating situation with Alexander Konovalov and the Minister of the Interior, Nikolai Kishkin, when General Polkovnikov appeared in the room and urged Kerensky to authorise a fantastic plan to capture of Smolny Institute. 'During this conversation I followed with more and more interest his ambiguous behaviour,' Kerensky says. 'It became evident that all his reports of the past ten to twelve days concerning the preparedness of his staff for a decisive struggle with the Bolsheviki had no basis in fact.'[21]

At the Moscow conference Kerensky had promised to suppress the next Bolshevik rebellion with 'blood and iron' but during the night every regiment in the capital rallied around a Bolshevik allegation that he was about to surrender Petrograd to the Germans 'so as to exterminate the revolutionary garrison'. Bolshevik agitators claimed that his appointment of Kadets into key cabinet positions in the Third Coalition proved that he was defending the monarchists and the counter-revolutionaries. They also alleged that he intended to move the government to Moscow. Only a tiny minority of soldiers in each regiment took part in these critical meetings but the effect was devastating.[22]

By morning most regiments, including the Cossacks, had voted to remain passive 'for fear of shedding brotherly blood'. Even the Third Cyclist Battalion, which had rallied to the flag in July, opted out. The Bolsheviks were in control of all of Petrograd except for the central zone around the Winter Palace and the General Staff Building on Palace Square. Monarchists among the bourgeoisie abandoned the Provisional Government at the risk of allowing the Bolsheviks to assume power. 'Nobody wants the Bolsheviks,' Zinaida Hippius wrote in her diary, 'but nobody is prepared to fight for Kerensky either.'

Indeed, the rightwing strategy was to allow the Bolshevik uprising to go ahead unhindered in the belief that after the fall of the despised Provisional Government the new Bolshevik regime would collapse within a matter of weeks.

At eight a.m. the captain of the cruiser *Aurora* sailed up the Neva under orders from his Kronstadt crew and anchored beside a little chapel next to the Nikolaevsky Bridge. Sporadic bursts of gunfire echoed down the largely deserted streets but most loyalist troops had either returned to their barracks or had gone over to the Bolsheviks. Nor was there any sign of the forces Kerensky had requested from the Northern Front which had been due to arrive by rail early that morning. 'Instead of troops all we got were telegrams and telephone messages saying that the railways were being sabotaged,' he says.[23]

David Soskice arrived at the Winter Palace to learn that the government was virtually defenceless. 'Hardly a single unit in the Petrograd Garrison had executed the orders given them on Kerensky's instructions,' he says. 'The troops guarding the Arsenal joined the Bolsheviks, who got possession of all the artillery and ammunition, and enormous stocks of rifles. As the electricity and telephone services were in Bolshevik hands, the ministers had no control over their own lights or telephones.' The Bolsheviks had also stopped food supplies reaching the palace and, as a result, many of the guards had deserted their posts and gone in search of sustenance. There was no sign of the Prime Minister.[24]

At first light Kerensky had received a report from a commissar named Rogovsky that contradicted Polkovnikov's optimism in every respect. Armed with this information, he hurried across Palace Square with Konovalov to confront the commander. 'The General Staff Building was filled with officers of all ranks and ages and delegates of various military units,' he says. 'Rushing up to Polkovnikov's office on the third floor, I requested him to report on the situation again. This report convinced us that it was no longer possible to rely on him or the majority of his Staff officers.' The report confirmed Kerensky's fears that there was virtually no organised resistance and that very few units were willing to defend the ministers.

At 9 a.m. he decided his best move was to travel to Pskov, the headquarters of the Northern Front, to meet the frontline troops and lead them into the city. 'Red Guard sentries had been posted in all the streets around the Winter Palace,' he says. 'As the railway stations were in Bolshevik hands, I decided to take a risk and drive across the city in a fast car.' Leaving Konovalov to deal with Polkovnikov, Kerensky organised a small party to accompany him on his mission.

Bolshevik propaganda later claimed Kerensky escaped from the Winter Palace dressed as a woman in a car flying the American flag. In fact he was wearing his usual semi-military brown uniform with no brass buttons or epaulettes and he travelled in the back of a Pierce-Arrow open touring car with Colonel Kuzmin, a loyal member of the Military District, and two of his adjutants, Lieutenant Nicholas Vinner and Lieutenant Boris Knirsh. Lieutenant Kovanko, a third adjutant, followed closely behind in a borrowed Renault, which had been provided by the American Embassy and, because of its diplomatic status, was indeed flying the Stars and Stripes.[25]

At 11 a.m. the two cars sped through the grand arch of the General Staff Building, surprised Red Guards manning the picketlines in Bolshaya Morskaya and crossed Saint Isaac's Square in front of the Marinsky Palace. Kerensky made a point of standing up as the car shot past groups of soldiers, who were so astonished to see him that they saluted instead of shooting him. Crossing the square, he was spotted by the sergeant-at-arms at the Marinsky Palace who reported to the councillors that the Prime Minister had just gone past at speed in an open-topped car and was heading in the direction of Voznesenzsky Prospekt.[26]

The ministers were discussing this fascinating snippet when soldiers and sailors burst into the palace and forced them to leave the building. The Preparliament that had been so obliging to the Bolsheviks never reassembled. Senior Kadets including Paul Miliukov and V. D. Nabokov, who were in the palace on electoral business regarding the Constituent Assembly, considered themselves lucky to slip through the Bolshevik net.

At the same time a statement written by Lenin and issued in the name of the Military Revolutionary Committee was being wired to all towns and cities on the telegraphic network:

'The Provisional Government has been overthrown. State power has passed into the hands of the organ of the Petrograd Soviet of Workers' and Soldiers' Deputies, the Military Revolutionary Committee, which stands at the head of the Petrograd proletariat and garrison. The cause for which the people have struggled - the immediate proposal of a democratic peace, the elimination of landlord estates, workers' control over production, the creation of a Soviet government - the triumph of this cause has been assured. Long live the revolution of the workers, soldiers and peasants!'[27]

This was a blatant lie: the end of the Provisional Government might have been in sight but it wasn't dead yet. Lenin's statement also made it clear for the first time that power was not actually being given to the Soviets but to a Soviet organ: the Bolshevik-controlled MRC.

At midday an increasingly desperate Konovalov summoned a cabinet meeting in the Malachite Hall at which Nikolai Kishkin was appointed Governor-General of Petrograd with dictatorial powers 'to restore order to the capital'. Kishkin chose two engineers, Peter Palchinsky, a former member of the Soviet Excom, and Peter

Rutenberg, of Father Gapon notoriety, as palace commandants. Konovalov then dismissed General Polkovnikov at Military District HQ and appointed his Chief of Staff, General Bagratuni, in his place, triggering a walkout by members of the Staff. David Soskice says:

> The new commandants began to organise the defence of the palace and for that purpose I, too, went to that wing of the palace in which the offices of the palace administration were situation to obtain a plan for the immense building in order to place the guards at all possible entrances. But to my great amazement I found the vast offices absolutely deserted by the administration, and the doorkeeper informed me that none of the officials had even put in an appearance that day. Some of the old servants of the palace, who had formerly served the Tsar and were well acquainted with the building, volunteered to serve as guides. 'You will find no traitor among us,' they said to me.[28]

In the absence of a map, one of the side-doors was left unguarded and Bolshevik spies and journalists were able to enter freely. Colonel Alfred Knox, whose tireless efforts to undermine the democratic government were now bearing the wrong kind of fruit, observed the weakening of the government's last line of defence:

> The garrison of the Winter Palace originally consisted of about 2000 all told, including detachments from *junker*[iii] and ensign schools, three squadrons of Cossacks, a company of volunteers and a company from the Women's Battalion. The garrison had dwindled owing to desertions, for there were no provisions and it had been practically starved for two days. There was no strong man to take command and to enforce discipline. No one had any stomach for fighting; some of the ensigns even borrowed greatcoats of soldier pattern from the women to enable them to escape unobserved. The greater part of the *junkers* of the Mikhail Artillery School returned to their school, taking with them four out of their six guns. Then the Cossacks left, declaring themselves opposed to bloodshed! [They also registered their objection to the idea of fighting alongside 'women with guns'].[29]

During the afternoon John Reed was one of several foreign journalists who slipped into the palace and entered one of its large ornate rooms.

---

iii From the German *Juncherre* (*jung* and *Herr*) meaning young nobleman but used in Russia to signify an officer-cadet.

He wrote: 'On both sides of the parquet floor lay rows of dirty mattresses and blankets, upon which occasional soldiers were stretched out; everywhere was a litter of cigarette butts, bits of bread, cloth, and empty bottles with expensive French labels. More and more soldiers with the red shoulder straps of the *junker* schools moved about in a stale atmosphere of tobacco-smoke and unwashed humanity. One had a bottle of white Burgundy, evidently filched from the cellars of the palace. They looked at us in astonishment.'[30]

At 3 p.m., while the ministers were still barricaded inside the Winter Palace, Lenin chose a session of the Petrograd Soviet to make his first public appearance. Dressed in baggy clothes, he had discarded his wig and the shadow of a beard could be seen on his bristly chin. He claimed the Provisional Government had indeed been overthrown and that the old state machine was being broken up and replaced by a new order. Things then started to go wrong. The Kronstadt sailors were hours late arriving at their designated positions in the capital and it was discovered that the cannon overlooking the Winter Palace were incapable of firing. It took several hours to bring field-guns to the fortress and install them in front of its walls.[31]

At 6.50 p.m. the MRC delivered an ultimatum to the palace demanding the surrender of the ministers. Gambling that the Bolsheviks would be widely condemned if they used force, Konovalov turned down the ultimatum and the ministers went upstairs to Kerensky's dining room. For several hours nothing happened. Lenin found the tension almost unbearable. Nikolai Podvoisky recalls that he 'paced around a small room in the Smolny like a lion in a cage'.[32]

At 9.40 p.m., the ministers had just finished their dinner of borscht, fish and artichoke when the *Aurora*, so ill-equipped for battle that it had no live ammunition on board, fired a blank round. The sound of the blast reverberated around the dining room and echoed down the corridors. Ministers dived for cover under the table and the women from the Battalion of Death were led to a safer room at the back.[33]

After a short pause to allow people to evacuate the palace, the gunners at the Peter and Paul Fortress opened fire. Their aim was dreadful and apart from a couple of broken windows most of the thirty-five shells landed harmlessly in the Neva. The most serious damage was caused to the front of the building by machinegun and rifle fire from Red Guards and soldiers in Palace Square.

The question all sides wanted answered was: where was Kerensky?

In the early afternoon a naval officer had brought Olga Kerenskaya a message that her husband had left the capital and was driving to the front to recruit loyal regiments to suppress the Bolshevik revolt. The hours passed without any further word. 'By the evening I decided to go and see for myself what was happening in the streets,' she says. Vasily Somov, a family friend from Kerensky's Tashkent days, offered to come with her. Before leaving the flat he put a revolver in his hip pocket.

The Bolsheviks had posted proclamations all over Petrograd announcing that the Provisional Government had been overthrown and that henceforth all power belonged to the Soviets. Olga was in a belligerent mood and started tearing the placards off walls and lampposts. 'Somov begged me to stop behaving in such a silly and even dangerous way,' she says. 'I took no notice. I went on methodically tearing down the placards.'

They reached Mikhailovsky Street leading into Nevsky Prospekt at the Town Hall, the very centre of the city. Crowds of people were milling about but Olga could not resist destroying another placard.

'What are you doing?' a man demanded.

'Tearing down Bolshevik placards. They don't like the Provisional Government and I don't like the Bolsheviks or their placards.'

A crowd gathered around, angry, threatening.

Someone said she and Somov should be taken to the Commandant's office further along the street. Someone else shouted that they should be searched. With horror, Olga remembered Vasily Somov's revolver. If they found that, they would definitely be arrested. She stopped arguing and announced haughtily that she had no wish to talk to them any longer. She remained silent until they reached the Commandant's building and then she stepped inside. 'You should have seen the consternation on his face when I told him I was Kerensky's wife,' Olga says. 'I could see that the situation was beyond him. The city might be in the hands of a belligerent mob but Kerensky could still return with some troops.'

The Commandant told Olga and Vasily Somov that he would keep them for a short while until the crowd dispersed and then he would let them go. After waiting for some time, the Commandant ordered a soldier to take them out into the street. No sooner had the soldier half-opened the heavy gate than they heard angry shouts. Some of the crowd were still there. 'There they are!' someone shouted. 'He set them free, comrades. Let's take them to the Pavlovsky Barracks. They'll teach her not to tear our placards down.'

The threat terrified Olga. She had heard that several middle-class women had been dragged into different barracks and gang-raped. The soldier quickly shut the gate, locked and chained it, and took them back to the Commandant. 'He was quite upset,' Olga says. 'He did not wish to burden himself with my fate. He was an officer of the Tsarist regime and he had no sympathy for me.'

The Commandant said with barely suppressed anger, 'I do not know what to do with you but I do know I can't keep you here. This place is for arrested military men only.' Someone suggested that he should phone the Town Hall. He made the call and a car was sent to pick up the prisoners. Under armed escort Olga and Somov were driven to the Town Hall. 'Everybody there was so busy discussing the day's events that nobody paid any attention to us,' Olga says. 'We stayed there for two or three hours. Then we left quietly and headed for home. My poor mother had waited up for us but the children were asleep.'[34]

The Soviet Congress was supposed to have opened at 2 p.m. but the Bolsheviks had arranged a postponement to suit Lenin's timetable. When Fyodor Dan finally rang the bell in the Great Hall to call the 650 delegates to order it was 10.40. Dan reported that, contrary to Lenin's proclamation, the Provisional Government, including its socialist ministers, were at that moment 'under fire at the Winter Palace'. This caused uproar and the Bolsheviks were accused of 'a criminal political venture' and 'a purely military plot'.[35]

In the ensuing melee the Mensheviks and Socialist Revolutionaries committed political suicide. Instead of staying to fight the Bolsheviks they withdrew en masse from the congress in protest against their underhand methods. Trotsky taunted them, 'You are miserable bankrupts, your role is played out; go where you ought to go; into the dustbin of history!'[36]

The Menshevik Internationalists also headed for the exit after Julius Martov failed in an attempt to form a broadly based socialist government. This meant that the only group remaining in the chamber with the 338 Bolsheviks were the Left Socialist Revolutionaries, led by Maria Spiridonova,[iv] a situation that pleased Lenin because of their huge base among the peasants.[37] Nikolai Sukhanov, a Menshevik Internationalist himself, saw the walkout as a tragic mistake:

> We completely untied the Bolsheviks' hands, making them masters of the entire situation and yielding to them the whole arena of the revolution. A struggle at the Congress for a united democratic front might have had some success. ... By quitting the Congress ... we gave the Bolsheviks with our own hands a monopoly of the Soviet, of the masses, and of the revolution. By our own irrational decision, we ensured the victory of Lenin's whole 'line'!

Meanwhile, Kerensky had reached Pskov at nine o'clock that evening. Fearing that the insurgency might have spread to the Staff officers, he drove to the home of his brother-in-law, Quartermaster-General Vladimir Baranovsky. His instincts proved correct. The Staff had turned their backs on the Provisional Government and were collaborating with the local Military Revolutionary Committee. Through V. S. Voytinsky, the Chief Commissar of the Northern Front, Kerensky established that General Vladimir Cheremisov, the Commander in Chief, had cancelled his orders for troops to be sent to Petrograd on the grounds that 'this was a political matter that had nothing to do with him'.[38]

Kerensky summoned Cheremisov to the house and 'a very unpleasant conversation followed'. 'The general had no intention of binding his fate to that of the "doomed" government,' Kerensky says. 'There was an order for my arrest signed by Lieutenant Krylenko and the sailor Dybenko, and he declared that he could not guarantee my safety.'

The only officer who expressed any desire to tackle the Bolsheviks was General Peter Krasnov, the new commander of the remnants of the Third Cavalry Corps, the very force that Kornilov had chosen to occupy the capital in August and whose 'demoralised' units had been dispersed by Kerensky. They hated Kerensky but they hated 'the

---

iv Maria Spiridonova had served eleven years in Siberian prisons over the 1906 assassination of a Tsarist security chief in Tambov Province. Her wavy brown hair was parted in the middle and draped over her temples to hide the scars of torture at the hands of Cossack assailants.

Reds' even more. 'Krasnov held back much that he would have liked to say to me,' Kerensky says, 'but he was ready to do all he could to crush the Bolshevist mutiny.'

By midnight the ministers had moved from the dining room to a more compact office on the second floor. Most of the cadets had abandoned the palace, leaving their fate in the hands of the ensigns from the Engineering School and the company of women. With the clocks showing 2.10 on the morning of the twenty-sixth, resistance finally crumbled. Shouting was heard outside the chamber and shots rang out as the remaining cadets were disarmed. Vladimir Antonov-Ovsienko, 'a wide-brimmed hat askew on his head, eyeglasses balanced uncertainly on his nose', entered the room at the head of an angry mob and declared that the eighteen ministers and their senior assistants were under arrest.

Although the prisoners included three socialist ministers (Nikitin, Maliantovich and Gvozdev), some of Antonov-Ovsienko's squad favoured murdering them on the spot but he summoned twenty-five Red Guards to escort his prisoners across Trinity Bridge to the Peter and Paul Fortress. On the way soldiers tried to strike them and someone shouted, 'Death to them! Shoot them!', but the leader of the Red Guards cried out, 'Do not stain the proletarian victory!'[39]

As dawn was breaking over the Neva, many of the invaders headed down into the palace cellars and raided the Tsar's liquor supply. 'Broken bottles littered the square, cries, shrieks, groans, obscenities, filled the clean morning,' Pitirim Sorokin says. 'Many of those who entered the cellars could not get out owing to the press of those who madly pushed forward to get in. The cellars swam in wine from broken casks and men were actually drowned in the flood of it.'[40]

At the first sign of trouble thousands of soldiers in the Petrograd Garrison had fled to their homes in the country and would take no further part in the Revolution but many of the remainder went on a drunken binge. Throughout 26 October mobs rampaged through the city, looting shops and liquor stores. Residents of the more salubrious districts had to contend with gangs of sailors and soldiers robbing their apartments. Some people were reported to have been killed for sport. The Military Revolutionary Committee declared martial law to deal with the disorders but most garrisons ignored the summons. The Bolshevik grip on the capital began to loosen.[41]

The most determined resistance to the Bolshevik takeover occurred in Moscow after the local MRC proclaimed the seizure of power at 10 p.m. on 25 October. The Kremlin become the centre of an intense struggle when the Bolsheviks captured it from the government on the twenty-sixth with the help of sympathisers among its defenders. The anti-Bolshevik forces then rallied around a Committee of Public Safety created by the Moscow City Duma. The Duma's leader, V. V. Rudnev, the socialist Mayor of Moscow, cajoled Colonel K. I. Riabtsev, the weak-willed commander of the Moscow Military District into sealing off all entrances to the Kremlin and mounting an assault.[42]

Loyalist officers and cadets showed great spirit in driving out the Bolshevik force the following day. The MRC then rallied thousands of Red Guards and fighting broke out in Red Square during which the Bolshevik forces were pushed back into the industrial suburbs until the Bolsheviks were able to roll out artillery pieces on to the surrounding hillsides and fire at targets in the centre of the city.[43]

Meanwhile, Lenin had read out his decree on peace to congress calling for an immediate ceasefire on all fronts. His 'Proclamation to the Peoples of All the Belligerent Nations' proposed a just and democratic peace on the Soviet formula of no annexations or indemnities. John Reed joined the delegates in jumping to their feet and belting out 'The Internationale'. 'A grizzled old soldier was sobbing like a child,' he says. 'Alexandra Kollontai rapidly winked the tears back. The immense sound rolled through the hall, burst windows and doors, and soared into the quiet sky. "The war is ended! The war is ended!" said a young workman near me, his face shining.'[44]

But that day was some way off. On Friday 27 October, the final day of the congress, a representative of the Executive Committee of Vikzhel, the railway workers' union, interrupted proceedings. Having been closely involved in derailing the Kornilov revolt, Vikzhel knew a power grab when they saw one and they were determined to stop it. The railwaymen's emissary denounced the Bolshevik seizure of power and insisted that Lenin agree to an all-Soviet government. Otherwise, he said, his comrades would shut down the railways and reduce Petrograd to starvation. This threat made no difference. The

Left SRs were unwilling to join a government that did not include representatives of the other socialist parties, so the first Soviet cabinet – the Council of People's Commissars (the Sovnarkom) – was made up entirely of Bolsheviks, with Lenin as chairman.[v][45]

Petrograd was no longer safe for anyone connected to the Prime Minister. *Izvestia* had declared that morning, 'Any help or assistance given to Kerensky is punishable as high treason and the penalty is death'. Lilya intended to wait in the apartment for Kerensky to return but Vladimir and Moussia Baranovsky set off that day on the Trans-Siberian Railway to Vladivostok on their way to America. Lilya's actress sisters Vera and Olga were in Moscow pursuing their stage careers and she sent her son Olik south with her parents, Vsevolod and Lydia Baranovsky, to Ekaterinodar (today's Krasnodar) in the Kuban region of the Black Sea Cossacks. As a former Tsarist general, Vsevolod was a marked man in his own right and the fact that he was the father of Kerensky's lover increased the danger to him and his wife.

During the day Kerensky had arrived at Gatchina, twenty-five miles southwest of Petrograd, with General Krasnov and his Cossacks. 'The town was filled with Bolsheviks - local infantry, artillery, Kronstadt sailors, armoured cars from Petrograd, etcetera,' he says. 'Despite the enemy's overwhelming numerical superiority, we unloaded our troops from their train and almost without firing a shot captured the town. The "revolutionary" troops fled in all directions or surrendered their rifles, guns and hand grenades.'[46]

Kerensky moved into the Great Gatchina Palace and at four p.m. appointed General Krasnov as Commander of all the Armed Forces of the Petrograd District. It was decided to attack the Bolsheviks at Tsarskoe Selo, seventeen miles to the north, early the next morning. Kerensky wired many military commands demanding reinforcements. 'We were particularly in need of infantry,' he said, 'as it was difficult to develop our operations with only cavalry and artillery at our disposal.'

Olga had been persuaded to leave the family's apartment in Tverskaya Street next to the Tauride Gardens because it was known as Kerensky's home. She and her sons were staying with the Somovs when Kerensky telephoned from Gatchina that night and told her that

---

v This was the Soviet cabinet, the supreme executive of the Congress of Soviets.

he would be in Petrograd with loyal troops tomorrow. She went to bed 'reassured and joyful'.[47]

Lenin gave an interview on the Bolsheviks' victory to *Le Matin* which was published in Paris on 28 October/10 November. He devoted one section to attacking Kerensky. 'We must always in the end prove the stronger, because boldness is on our side, whereas Kerensky' – here Lenin shrugged his shoulders disdainfully – 'is nobody. He has always hesitated. He has never done anything and he is always vacillating. He was a partisan of Kornilov and had him arrested. He was an opponent of Trotsky and allowed him his liberty. As he has not dared to defend himself, I firmly believe he did not dare to attack us.'

As French readers were digesting these words, General Krasnov's force had arrived in Tsarskoe Selo in an armoured train equipped with light quick-firing field pieces. The train had turned up in Gatchina overnight despite the efforts of railway and telegraph workers to hinder troop trains going in that direction. Kerensky intended to watch the battle through field glasses from the dome of the Pulkovo Astronomical Observatory on the Pulkovo Heights, a chain of hills outside Tsarskoe Selo, but after a short barrage everything stopped. Driving up to Krasnov's headquarters in the Pierce-Arrow, Kerensky learned from the General that the Bolshevik defences were more thorough than he had expected and it would be difficult to defeat them with his insignificant force.

Kerensky then noticed that several members of the rightwing Council of Cossacks had joined Krasnov and were interfering with his command. When he objected to the delay, Krasnov asked him to leave the battlefield. No sooner had he returned to the Observatory than Boris Savinkov strode into the room. Having been dropped from the government and expelled from the Socialist Revolutionary Party, he was one of the last people Kerensky wanted to see. Savinkov informed him that he was now a delegate of the Council of Cossacks and his purpose was to continue the struggle against the Bolsheviks.[48]

Kerensky was suspicious. According to Savinkov's biographer, he accused Savinkov and his Cossack cronies of being counter-revolutionaries. Savinkov replied that if Kerensky wanted to defeat the Bolsheviks he should lead his troops from the front instead of sheltering in a palace at the rear. He then walked out. His real purpose was to use Kerensky as a bargaining chip in persuading the Bolsheviks to allow the Cossacks to retreat fully armed to their homeland in South Russia.[49]

Fortunately, the army commissar Vladimir Stankevich had also arrived from Petrograd and, at his urging, Krasnov decided to go ahead and occupy Tsarskoye Selo. 'Our detachment entered the town about midnight without any difficulty,' Kerensky says. 'This could have been achieved with equal success twelve hours earlier.' Petrograd was still twelve miles away and instead of sweeping down Nevsky Prospekt in triumph he returned to Gatchina in a mood of utmost dejection. According to the pile of telegrams awaiting him there, no fewer than fifty military trains were supposedly making their way to Gatchina but he had no way of discovering whether these trains were phantoms or the real thing.

Anticipating Kerensky's arrival at the head of a victorious army on Sunday 29 October, a few hundred officers and cadets launched a counter-attack on Bolshevik positions in Petrograd with the aid of the SR-led Committee for the Salvation of the Motherland and the Revolution. This tiny loyalist force took over the Central Telephone Exchange, the Hotel Astoria, the State Bank and, for a time, even the Smolny Institute. Vladimir Antonov-Ovsienko, now Commissar of the Army, had been making a tour of inspection of the Telephone Exchange and was taken captive.[50]

The cadets' successes were short-lived. The previous evening a copy of their detailed battle plan had fallen into the hands of a Bolshevik patrol with the arrest of a Socialist Revolutionary. It was a simple matter for the MRC to use squads of Red Guards and Kronstadt sailors to attack individual strongpoints, including the military schools. W. H. Chamberlin claims that enraged Red Guards threw some of the cadets from the roofs of houses.[51]

The leaders of Vikzhel issued an ultimatum to both sides demanding a ceasefire. The workers at the Obukhov Factory threatened to 'knock the heads of all the party leaders together' if they failed to reach agreement. There was no truce and by the end of the day the revolt had been extinguished with the loss of two hundred dead or wounded on both sides.[52]

At Gatchina, the entire day had been devoted to preparations for the Cossacks' decisive battle with the Bolshevik forces due to begin on the Pulkovo Heights at dawn on Monday. According to Krasnov's scouts, the Bolshevik forces numbered 12,000 to 15,000, while he had 700 Cossacks, a limited quantity of artillery, an armoured train and a regiment of infantry which had arrived from Luga. As soon as Krasnov ordered his artillery to open fire, large numbers of Bolshevik troops deserted their positions but the heights were held by well-trained Kronstadt sailors and the right flank held fast.[53]

The scouts had failed to notice that the battlefield contained a patch of marshy ground which proved impassable and by late afternoon Krasnov's advance was bogged down. Short of ammunition, the Cossacks were now in danger of being outflanked. General Krasnov ordered a withdrawal and at eight o'clock that evening he led his weary troops back through the gates of Gatchina Palace. 'The fight at Pulkovo was concluded successfully for us,' Kerensky says, 'but we could not follow up this "success" by pursuit or consolidate it because of our insignificant numbers.'[54]

The following message - the first in the history of radio propaganda - was broadcast that evening by the powerful transmitter at Tsarskoe Selo with the intention of reaching revolutionaries all over Europe: 'The All-Russian Congress of Soviets has formed a new Soviet Government. The Government of Kerensky has been overthrown and arrested. Kerensky himself has fled. All official institutions are in the hands of the Soviet Government.' This time it was true.

In the morning Kerensky held a war council with, among others, General Krasnov, Captain Kuzmin, Boris Savinkov and Vladimir Stankevich. 'Only two opinions - Savinkov's and mine - were in favour of unconditional refusal of any negotiations,' Kerensky says. 'It was decided that Stankevich would go to Petrograd to inform the Committee for Salvation of my conditions for an armistice: first, the immediate laying down of arms by the Bolsheviki and their promise to obey the Provisional Government and, second, the reorganisation of the government by agreement with representatives of all political parties.'

Shortly after the war council meeting had broken up, Savinkov sidled up to Kerensky bearing a piece of paper. 'Please sign this paper, Alexander Fyodorovich,' he said. 'I want to leave.' The paper stated that the bearer, Boris Savinkov, was commissioned by the Supreme Commander to travel to General Headquarters to facilitate the dispatch of reinforcements to Gatchina. 'Go ahead,' Kerensky replied. He signed the paper even though he knew Savinkov was running away. 'Both of us understood the purpose of his departure and it would have been useless to discuss it,' he says.[55]

At ten o'clock that night Kerensky was shaken awake to be told by a loyalist soldier that Paul Dybenko, newly promoted to Commissar of the Navy, had arrived with a deputation and was negotiating with members of the Cossack Soviet to hand him over to the Bolsheviks. 'The bargaining for my head was in progress downstairs,' Kerensky says. Escape would be difficult - the palace grounds had only one exit which was guarded by both Cossacks and Kronstadt sailors.

At three o'clock the next afternoon, the same soldier who had brought the news of Dybenko's arrival came running in. His face was ashen. The bargain had been concluded, he said, and the Cossacks had bought their freedom to return to their homes for the price of Kerensky's head. He would be turned over to the Bolsheviks and put on trial.[56]

'Lieutenant Vinner and I were determined not to give ourselves up alive,' Kerensky says. 'Our plan was that while they were searching for us in the front rooms of the palace, we would use our revolvers in the rear chambers.'

Suddenly, another soldier and a sailor that Kerensky had never seen before entered the room.

'There is no time to lose,' the sailor said. 'Put this on.'

He handed Kerensky a sailor's cloak, a sailor's hat and a pair of driving goggles. The cloak was too short, the hat too small and the goggles looked suspicious but he donned the outfit and accompanied the sailor, whom he called Vanya in his memoirs, out of the front door of the palace and past the guards at the gates. The soldier was waiting for them in a car.

Kerensky was driven to the edge of a forest outside Gatchina. Alighting from the car, Vanya led him into the forest. They tramped through the wilderness for what seemed like hours until they reached a cottage in the middle of a clearing. This was the home of Vanya's uncle. Kerensky would spend the next forty days there while the Bolsheviks tried to track him down. 'I had boundless faith in these strangers who were risking their lives to save me,' he says.[57]

Meanwhile, the Bolshevik counter-attack in Moscow was causing carnage. The artillery barrage had damaged many buildings and started fires. Government strongholds such as the National Hotel were stormed after being mercilessly shelled. The former Supreme Commander General Brusilov was severely wounded in the foot by a shell fragment that hit his bathroom. On 3 November the fighting ended abruptly with a ceasefire arranged through the Vikzhel intervention.[58]

Meanwhile, David Soskice had used his British passport to get through Soviet lines and reach Stockholm. He blamed the Vikzhel ultimatum for Kerensky's defeat at Gatchina. 'They threatened to proclaim a general strike unless fighting immediately stopped,' he said. 'Kerensky thereupon declared his willingness to negotiate and sent representatives to Petrograd. The railwaymen's refusal to transport troops was directed formally against both sides but in fact only Kerensky, who had to obtain his reinforcements from the front, was hit. The Bolsheviki had breathing space to organise their forces in Petrograd and when the fighting restarted they had obtained the upper hand.'[59]

Olga had moved Oleg and Gleb to another flat under a false name but the police found them there with the help of their servant, a Bolshevik spy. At three o'clock in the morning the doorbell rang and Olga opened the door to find several soldiers and the concierge on the landing.

'Resist and I'll shoot you,' said a very short officer, pointing his revolver at her chest.

Olga could be recklessly brave.

'Shoot if you like. I am not afraid.'

The Bolshevik turned to the concierge. 'She's a real fighting cock, that one,' he said.

The hall and the passage to the kitchen filled with soldiers and the servant had admitted a second detachment through the back door. Olga knew that Alexander was hiding on a farm in a forest near Gatchina but she was so angry that she told the soldiers to be sure to look under the beds. They found nothing and the civilian demanded she sign a piece of paper recording the details of the search. She refused to do so and they trooped out of the flat without another word. 'I understood then that it was useless to live in hiding.' Olga says. 'I became ill with pleurisy and went to live with my mother.'

By then many other towns and cities as far away as Tashkent in Central Asia had declared for Soviet rule. Sir George Macartney, the British Consul-General at Kashgar in Chinese Turkestan, led a four-man mission to make contact with the Tashkent Soviet. 'The gang of adventurers who had seized power were all local men from the lower ranks of official life,' he says. 'With the help of soldiers and workmen, they murdered officials of the old regime.' The surviving bureaucrats were imprisoned while their fate was decided. Among the captives was the public prosecutor, Fyodor 'Fedya' Kerensky.[60]

Despite the intense hatred that the rank-and-file felt for General Kornilov and his accomplices, General Dukhonin, the Acting Supreme Commander at the Stavka, allowed them to escape from the Bykhov Monastery on 19 November. Dukhonin was already in trouble with Lenin for refusing to engage in peace negotiations with the German military at the frontline. In a conversation on the Hughes Apparatus he had made the perfectly reasonable point that the Germans would only listen to the central government. Lenin dismissed him and appointed Krylenko as Supreme Commander.

The following day trainloads of Red Guards and Baltic sailors pulled into Mogilev station to take over General Headquarters with the intention of instructing the soldiers to engage their German enemies in peace talks. Dukhonin went to meet Krylenko in his railway carriage. Angry soldiers and sailors seized him and, on the orders of Paul Dybenko, beat him senseless, shot him and defaced his body.[61]

Meanwhile, Somerset Maugham had landed in the north of Scotland. Twenty-four hours later he saw Lloyd George at 10 Downing Street. By then it was much too late to make any difference. Afraid that his stammer might prevent him from quoting Kerensky correctly, Maugham had written down the message. After reading it, Lloyd George said, 'I can't do that. I'm afraid I must bring this conversation to an end. I have a cabinet meeting I must go to.'

By turning a deaf ear to Kerensky's pleading for a revision of war aims, Bruce Lockhart says, Britain and France must take their share of responsibility for the triumph of Bolshevism.[62]

> There was only one way to save Russia from going Bolshevik [he said]. That was to allow her to make peace. It was because he would not make peace that Kerensky went under. It was solely because he

promised to stop the war that Lenin came to the top. It will be objected that Kerensky ought to have shot both Lenin and Trotsky. The soldiers who argue in this way always ignore the psychological premises. The old regime having broken down, the type of leader (i.e., a Kerensky) whom the first revolution threw up was bound to be a man who would not shoot his opponents. It was the first state of a natural process. Secondly, even if Kerensky had shot Lenin and Trotsky, some other anti-war leader would have taken their place and would have won through on his anti-war programme.[63]

The extraordinary thing about the October Revolution was that it was the Bolsheviks' sworn enemies – the pro-Kornilov officers, the Cossacks and the moderate socialists – who enabled Lenin to destroy the Provisional Government and sweep the winnings off the table. Without their active opposition or submissive neutrality Kerensky would probably have prevailed. Contrary to Eisenstein's 1927 film *October*, casualties in the taking of the Winter Palace were light – five sailors and one soldier were killed and several wounded, while no fatalities were recorded among the defenders. The blood flowed a few days later in the battles around Petrograd and Moscow that heralded the start of a civil war costing seven million lives.[64]

21

The Death of Freedom

Within the first few months of its existence the Bolshevik regime made no secret of the fact that Bolshevism was an ideology that demanded the elimination of the 'enemies of the people'. Truth and morality were replaced by the higher truth of Marxist-Leninism. The population was divided into 'revolutionaries' and 'counter-revolutionaries'. As only Bolsheviks could be true revolutionaries, all the others – including Mensheviks and Socialist Revolutionaries, irrespective of their roots – must be counter-revolutionaries. Thousands of lives depended on the hair-trigger judgment of the leaders of the Bolshevik squads that hunted down these 'enemies of the people'. Summary executions were commonplace.

Lenin saw civil war as the quickest, surest method of eliminating his class enemies. 'An imperialist war cannot end otherwise than in an imperialist peace unless it is transformed into a civil war of the proletariat against the bourgeoisie for socialism,' he had written in November 1916. Like Marx, he viewed the world as a battleground between the cosmic forces of good (the proletariat) and evil (the bourgeoisie). Thus the Russian Civil War would be a Manichaean struggle between the Reds and the Whites.[1]

Lenin's first chance to win popular support was in the elections for the Constituent Assembly. The All-Russian Electoral Commission containing sixteen representatives from six political parties, with N. N. Avinov at its head and V. D. Nabokov as its deputy, announced that the poll would be held over several days in November on the basis of universal and equal suffrage. The commission, which continued to hold daily meetings in the Marinsky Palace, refused to recognise the Council of Commissars or to disband voluntarily.[2]

Lacking support in the countryside to suppress the election there, Lenin allowed it to go ahead. Fifty million votes were cast and the results were a huge disappointment for him. The Bolsheviks won only 25 per cent of the popular vote, mostly in urban areas, compared with the PSR's 40 per cent, the Kadets' 5 per cent and the Mensheviks' 3 per cent. 'Had the Bolsheviki received a majority, we would have submitted,' says Pitirim Sorokin, who was elected as an SR candidate in Vologda Province, 'but the votes of the people declared them an illegal government.'

The Bolsheviks achieved majorities in the armies of the Northern and Western Fronts and the Baltic Fleet but fell behind the PSR and the Ukrainian nationalist parties on the Southern Fronts and in the Black Sea Fleet. The Socialist Revolutionaries' victory rested firmly on its popularity among the peasants. The extreme left would have improved its share of the vote if the electoral lists had been drawn up after the Left Socialist Revolutionaries had split from the PSR.[3]

Lenin maintained that the Bolsheviks had never claimed to represent the population as a whole but had taken power in the name of the working class. The dictatorship of the proletariat and the authority of the Soviet were 'the only form of democracy'.[4] The Constituent Assembly was due to convene at the Tauride Palace on 28 November and as that date approached he became truculent. On 23 November he ordered the arrest of the All-Russian Electoral Commission over their refusal to recognise the Sovnarkom. Twelve members of the commission, including the chairman Avinov, his deputy Nabokov and Mark Vishniak, the Constituent Assembly's secretary, were seized and carted off to the Smolny, where they were locked in a narrow little room.[5]

'The first day we were not very well off,' Nabokov says. 'In the room were wooden benches, chairs, two scanty beds and nothing more. I slept on a narrow wooden bench. We were not given linen or mattresses and, on the first day, food or even tea was out of the question.' Fortunately, friends heard about their plight and were given permission to take a meal to them. They were then interrogated by Peter Krasikov, a Bolshevik member of the Soviet Excom, to establish that they did indeed refuse to recognise the Bolshevik takeover. After that, conditions improved and they were given bedding and allowed to eat in the communal dining room.

On 26 November, the Sovnarkom postponed the assembly's opening indefinitely and issued a decree that it could only be opened by a person 'empowered by the Sovnarkom to do so'. The following day thousands of Petrograd's citizens swarmed around the locked gates of the Tauride Palace bearing placards declaring, 'Long Life to the Constituent Assembly, the Master of Russia'. As deputies from the socialist and Kadet parties approached, the crowd greeted them with deafening cheers. The Latvian mercenaries hired by the Bolsheviks to shut down the palace stood mutely by.[6]

'Something had to be done,' Pitirim Sorokin says. He and several other deputies climbed the palace fence and unlocked the gates. Staggered by this audacity, the Latvians hesitated and the crowd rushed in filling the courtyard. Sorokin thanked the Latvians for guarding the venue and embraced their commanding officer. In the White Hall 172 deputies resolved that the Constituent Assembly should overcome every obstacle placed in its path and open on 5 January 1918 despite the regime's opposition.

The Bolsheviks responded to this challenge by reorganising the All-Russian Electoral Commission and placing Moisei Uritsky in charge. The defiant commissioners who had refused to recognise the Sovnarkom were freed from the Smolny and then dismissed. Uritsky informed the deputies that they must receive new credentials from the commission in order to attend the opening of the assembly, which would indeed take place on 5 January but only if at least 400 registered members turned up.[7]

The Sovnarkom outlawed the Kadet Party as 'enemies of the people' and ordered the arrest of four members of its Central Committee: Countess Sofia Panina, F. F. Kokoshkin, A. I. Shingarev and Prince Paul Dolgorukov. All four were seized during a committee meeting at Sofia Panina's house at 23 Sergievskaia Street in the Liteiny District and taken to the Smolny. Panina, who had served as Deputy Minister of Education in Kerensky's Third Coalition, was charged with criminal sabotage. Judging the new government to be illegal, she had refused to hand over 93,000 roubles in cash and securities belonging to the Ministry of Education.[8]

The armistice on the Eastern Front came into force on 2/15 December 1917. One week later the Bolshevik delegation turned up at General Hoffmann's headquarters at Brest-Litovsk for the peace conference. All four Central Powers - Germany, Austria-Hungary, Bulgaria and the Ottoman Empire - were represented. They were anxious to agree a treaty as quickly as possible to give them access to Caucasian oil and Ukrainian wheat, and to enable Ludendorff to transfer dozens of German divisions to the West. Conversely, the Russian delegation was determined to keep talking for as long as possible in the hope that the peoples of France and Germany would rise up and demand an end to hostilities without annexations or indemnities.[9]

Lenin's chief negotiator, Adolph Joffé, was stunned when the Central Powers demanded that eighteen Russian provinces, including Russian Poland, Estonia, Latvia and Lithuania, should be granted self-determination. The breaking of Russia's hold over her non-Russian vassal peoples had been one of Germany's earliest war aims. Her plan was to draw these occupied territories into the *Kaiserreich*'s orbit and restore their German minorities to power. Joffé requested a twelve-day recess to report back to the Sovnarkom.[10]

The British War Cabinet was anxious to keep track of the Bolsheviks' peace manoeuvres to ascertain the chances of reviving the Eastern Front. On 21 December 1917 Bruce Lockhart was invited to Downing Street. Having read his reports on the Revolution, the Prime Minister was expecting a much older man and he listened with rapt attention as the former vice-consul in Moscow regaled him with his impressions of the new Russian rulers. Two weeks later Lockhart was appointed head of a secret mission to Russia to establish informal relations with the Bolsheviks and to offer them financial aid to keep Russia in the war.

He was perplexed. The chief of MI1c in Petrograd, Lieutenant Ernest Boyce, was to play no part in the mission, so Lockhart was responsible for its success or failure but lacked the authority to make it work. He consulted his friend Rex Leeper, a thirty-year-old Foreign Office *wunderkind*. Leeper was learning Russian from Theodore Rothstein, a Bolshevik, who, despite his extreme political views (and the fact that Lenin had often stayed in his house on Clapton Square), was employed as a translator at the War Office in Whitehall.[i] [11]

Leeper arranged to meet Rothstein for lunch at a Lyons Corner House next to Charing Cross Station in the Strand. As agreed, his

---

i Sir Reginald 'Rex' Leeper was born in Sydney in 1888 and educated at Melbourne Grammar School, Trinity College, Melbourne, and New College, Oxford. He had a distinguished career as a British diplomat and was the architect of the British Council.

guest turned up with his friend, the Bolsheviks' London emissary Maxim Litvinov. The purpose of the lunch was to inform the Russians about Lockhart's mission and to obtain a letter of introduction from Litvinov to Trotsky who, it was hoped, would be more amenable to the Prime Minister's offer than Lenin.[12]

The Russians were both middle-aged: Rothstein, short with dark, darting eyes and a sharp intellect; Litvinov, heavier in build and more ponderous but still scholarly. Through his marriage to Ivy Low, the daughter of a Bloomsbury literary family, he was on friendly terms with George Bernard Shaw, H. G. Wells and Sidney and Beatrice Webb. At the end of the lunch, Litvinov took up pen and paper and wrote a short personal letter to Trotsky:

> The bearer of this, Mr Lockhart, is going to Russia with an official mission with the exact character of which I am not acquainted. I know him as a thoroughly honest man who understands our position and sympathises with us. I should consider his sojourn in Russia useful from the point of view of our interests.[13]

Sofia Panina's trial before the Revolutionary Tribunal of the Petrograd Soviet on 10 December made her the first defendant to be tried under the Bolsheviks' new system of justice, a pale imitation of French Revolutionary law. The seven judges on the tribunal consisted of two soldiers and five workers, six of whom were Bolsheviks. The concept of an independent judiciary made no sense to the regime. It was assumed that the defendant's wealth and social position would make a guilty verdict automatic: 'proletarian consciousness' would make it so.

But the Countess's philanthropic work at the Ligovsky People's House was known far and wide and things did not go according to plan. She appeared in the dock in a modest black dress and close-fitting black turban, nothing like the popular image of an aristocratic socialite.

When the chairman, Ivan Zhukov, called for someone to act as prosecutor, no one stepped forward. Sofia's defender Jacob Gurevich took the opportunity to argue that there were no longer any universally recognised laws in Russia, so the trial must be politically motivated. He identified the funds in question as a donation to the Ministry of

Education for charitable purposes. 'You must not, before the entire world, return evil for good and violence for love,' he said, a sentiment that received a rousing ovation from the packed courtroom.[14]

Unexpectedly, a factory worker, N. I. Ivanov, stepped forward and gave an emotional account of how he had learned to read and write at the Ligovsky People's House. His testimony also received a round of applause. Zhukov then invited a worker called Naumov to speak for the prosecution. He merely identified Sofia as member of the nobility and suggested that this was enough to determine her guilt, whatever her good deeds might have been in the past.

Sofia's enemy Isak Borisovich Rogalsky of the Bolsheviks' Commissariat for Education then took the stand. He claimed that the funds were unpaid wages owed to ministry workers who had been called up for military service. This was untrue and in her concluding statement Panina denied the allegation. She was safeguarding the funds for the benefit of the people, she said, and would hand them over to the democratically elected Constituent Assembly.

After deliberating for an hour, the tribunal found her guilty of 'opposition to the people's authority' but ruled that if she handed the money over to the commissariat there would be no punishment other than 'public censure'. Panina still refused to release the money and was put back in prison until her friends paid the 93,000 roubles themselves.[15]

Evading Bolshevik justice, Lavr Kornilov and his fellow escapees from the Bykhov Monastery made their way 550 miles southeast to Novocherkassk, upstream from Rostov at the base of the Don River. General Alexie Kaledin, the Ataman (Chieftain) of the Don Cossack Host, had invited General Alekseyev to use his capital as a base for operations against the Bolsheviks. In December Alekseyev formed the Volunteer Army with Kornilov, Denikin, Lukomsky and other anti-Bolshevik officers. Kornilov, who was named as Commander in Chief, declared that in order to defeat the Bolsheviks he was willing 'to set fire to half the country and shed the blood of three-quarters of all Russians'.

When the peace conference reconvened at Brest-Litovsk on 27 December, Lenin replaced Joffé with Leon Trotsky as his chief negotiator. Determined to spread the revolutionary gospel to the enemy, Karl Radek, the Polish Bolshevik leader, handed out revolutionary pamphlets to German soldiers at Brest-Litovsk railway station. Trotsky's strategy was to interrupt the war and demobilise the Russian Army but avoid signing a treaty. His slogan was 'No war, no peace'.

By then Kerensky, unshaven and disguised, had left the farm outside Gatchina and was moving from one safe house to another in northwest Russia. From one of these hiding places, he submitted an article headlined 'Come to Your Senses!' to the SR newspaper *Delo Naroda* in which he urged the Russian people to throw off 'the violence and horror of Leninist coercion'. When the article was published, he was horrified to discover that Viktor Chernov had added a malicious preface which described it as the 'cry of the exhausted and wounded soul of a man who had played a major role in the first phase of the Russian revolution'.

On New Year's Day 1918 he came out of hiding and trudged through the frozen snow on to the platform of the Bologoye railway station to catch the overnight train to Petrograd. Bologoye was the town where the Tsar had lost his cat-and-mouse game with the Provisional Government ten months earlier. Kerensky was then the first love of the Revolution; now, he was posing as a Swedish doctor, a shaggy-haired, bearded figure in blue spectacles, who was playing his own game of cat-and-mouse with the Bolsheviks.

Lenin had replaced the Military Revolutionary Committee with a secret police organisation, the Cheka, and its head, Felix Dzerzhinsky, regarded catching Kerensky as a personal challenge.[16]

The Constituent Assembly was due to meet at the Tauride Palace on 5 January to agree a new constitution. Having been elected to the assembly by five districts in the November elections, Kerensky was determined to take his seat. 'The situation was quite absurd,' he says. 'It was impossible for a truly elected Constituent Assembly to coexist with a dictatorship that rejected the very idea of popular sovereignty.' The answer, as he saw it, was to exert the assembly's authority over the Sovnarkom, even at the risk of bloodshed.[17]

Kerensky's journey to Petrograd in a third-class carriage passed without incident but earlier that night an attempt had been made on Lenin's life when two disgruntled army officers, who wished to protect the Constituent Assembly from Bolshevik sabotage, fired at his car near the Simeon Bridge over the Fontanka. Lenin's luck held - he was unhurt – but the attack gave him the opportunity to accuse the Socialist Revolutionaries and the Mensheviks of conspiring to murder him.[18]

Pitirim Sorokin and Andrei Argunov, one of the PSR founders, were among the first to be arrested. They were taken to the Peter and Paul Fortress on 2 January and incarcerated in the Trubetskoi Ravelin. There were no chairs or beds in the cold and dirty cell, and the walls were covered with streaks of half-frozen water. The two men huddled together on a damp straw mat on the floor in an attempt to get some rest. Water dripped from the walls and to add to their discomfort, the chimes rang every hour with 'How Glorious is our God'.

Kerensky was driven from Nikolaevsky Station to his mother-in-law Maria Baranovskaya's apartment for an emotional reunion with Olga and his sons. They greeted him warmly. Money was tight and his estranged wife had struggled to make ends meet. 'Many people in Petrograd were sorry for me and would gladly have given me a job in their offices,' she says, 'but they were already terrorised and realised that to give Mrs Kerensky a job might bring upon them their complete destruction. Mother and I were at our wits' end.'

Neither woman knew anything about the tobacco business but ready-made cigarettes were in short supply and they hit on the idea of making them at home. They bought cigarette papers and tobacco products, made up their own mixture and hand-rolled it into cigarettes on the dining room table. Orders flooded in. Many of them came from people who wanted to be helpful but at the same time there was a gap in the market.

Kerensky joined the family for a frugal meal and he spent time talking to the boys, who found his disguise bewildering but at least recognised his voice. All the while his mind was on Lilya. On 30 December she had given birth to a daughter named Irina at her brother's apartment. Kerensky knew the building would be under Cheka surveillance, so he resisted the temptation to dash to her side. Instead, he was driven to the digs of a revolutionary student across the Neva in the Petrograd District.[19]

Vladimir Zenzinov, who had also been elected, visited him there late that night. He was horrified when his friend demanded a ticket to the opening of the assembly. If Kerensky showed up, he said, there would be violence and that must be avoided at all costs. The SR leaders had even called off an armed demonstration that its followers were planning to hold outside the Tauride Palace.[20]

Kerensky replied that his life was his own business and it was his duty as an elected member to attend to assembly.

'It will be the end of all of us,' Zenzinov groaned.

'No, it won't,' Kerensky countered. 'I'll be the target and you will remain unnoticed.'

He then told Zenzinov that he intended to show himself to the Bolshevik gunmen. If they shot him, so be it; he was willing to martyr himself. Such an act would have achieved nothing but it was an indication of Kerensky's desperation: he was willing to sacrifice his life in order to make some sort of impact on events. 'He must have thought my plan was absolutely mad,' Kerensky says, 'but he was moved to tears, shook my hand and said, "I'll talk it over with the others".'[21]

The following morning Zenzinov returned to Kerensky's hiding place with a firm rejection of his plan. His SR comrades repeated their ruling that there must be no violence; instead, the Union for the Defence of the Constituent Assembly was organising a peaceful march to the Tauride Palace to demonstrate their widespread support among the population. Even more maddening for Kerensky, Viktor Chernov would be proposed as chairman of the assembly.

That evening, carrying false papers, he turned up at Bolshaya Puskarshkaya and met his daughter, 'Irinouchka', who gazed at this strange hairy creature with uncomprehending eyes. Lilya had been waiting anxiously for news of her lover and the reunion was an extremely emotional affair. Even as they were talking, Vladimir and Moussia Baranovsky were docking in San Francisco in the steamship *Ecuador*. In an interview with an American news agency Vladimir said he was confident that Kerensky would return to power. 'He is a strong man,' he said. 'He stood out as long as he could and then fled. It is known in Russia that Lenin and Trotsky are paid German agents and their fall is certain. When it comes, Kerensky's star will once more be in the ascendancy.'[22]

January the fifth 1918 was a freezing day in Petrograd, with an icy wind and snow flurries whipping across the frozen grey waters of the Neva. Red Guards patrolled the city streets rounding up 'counter-revolutionaries', while sailors from the *Aurora* and the *Republic* guarded the Tauride Palace. Despite the cold and a ban on demonstrations, 40,000 people, including many moderate members of the Constituent Assembly, gathered in the Champ de Mars at midday to join the march to the palace. Bearing banners declaring 'All Power to the Assembly' and 'Down with Political Terror' – direct challenges to Bolshevik authority – the marchers set off to the strains of the 'Marseillaise'.

As they reached Liteiny Prospekt, Red Guard snipers on the rooftops opened fire, killing ten people and wounded about seventy. The marchers fled in terror. Reaching the Tauride Palace, they discovered that the Kronstadt sailors and Latvian Riflemen under the control of Vladimir Bonch-Bruevich had surrounded the building. The approaches were effectively cordoned off and only deputies with registration papers were allowed to enter.[23]

Even as the deputies were filing into the palace, Lenin taunted them. 'Since we made the mistake of promising the world that this talk shop would meet, we have to open it up today,' he said, 'but history has not yet said a word about when we will shut it down.'[24]

Despite all the threats and obstacles, Russia's first freely elected parliament opened in the White Hall at 4 o'clock that afternoon when 410 deputies took their seats. The Bolsheviks (with 110 to 120 seats) and their new coalition partners, the Left Socialist Revolutionary (30 to 35), were easily outnumbered by the right and moderate Socialist Revolutionaries (at least 237 seats), the Nationalists (86) and the Mensheviks (16). There were no Kadet deputies – they had either been imprisoned or were in hiding – and the Ukrainians stayed way following the formation of the Ukrainian National Republic at the end of December.

The Bolsheviks and the Left SRs took the lefthand side of the chamber, while all other SRs, joined the Mensheviks and representatives of other groups in the centre or on the righthand side. Ten female deputies – the Bolsheviks Alexandra Kollontai, Evgenia Bosh, Elena Rozmirovich and Varvara Iakovleva, and the Socialist Revolutionaries Catherine Breshko-Breshkovskaya, Vera Figner, Maria Spiridonova, M. D. Perveeva, O. A. Matveevskaia and Anastasia Sletova (the wife of Viktor Chernov) - sat among their male comrades.[25]

Some foreign diplomats and 400 ticket-holding members of the public were admitted to the upstairs galleries. Entering the building through a back door, Lenin walked up to the mezzanine floor and took his seat in a box offering a panoramic view of the chamber.

Repeating a fake-news story in the Bolshevik press, the *New York Times* reported that 'Sorokin and other Socialist Revolutionary members who had been arrested were escorted under guard from their prison to the Tauride Palace to take part in the meeting'. Argunov, Avksentiev and Sorokin, however, remained firmly locked up in the Peter and Paul Fortress and never had a chance to make the speeches that were credited to them in the press.[26]

Yakov Sverdlov, chairman of the All-Russian Central Executive Committee (VTsIK), had been given the honour of opening the assembly. When he failed to show up on time, an elderly SR deputy stepped into the breach but the Bolsheviks and Left SRs made so much noise banging on desks and stamping their feet that no one could hear what he was saying. Then Sverdlov arrived. Roughly pushing the old man aside, he read out the 'Declaration of the Rights of the Working and Exploited People' and urged the assembly to acknowledge the authority of the Sovnarkom. This attempt to hijack proceedings was unsuccessful. To reinforce the point, the deputies elected Viktor Chernov as chairman with 244 votes to Maria Spiridonova's 151.

Chernov then made a long denunciation of the October coup d'état which was partially drowned by a noisy rendition of 'The Internationale'. One SR deputy, N. P. Oganovsky, noted in his diary, 'The chairman's speech got us in such a deep mess that we will never get out of it.' During the speeches Mark Vishniak, the assembly's secretary, watched Lenin in his box 'sink back in his chair apathetically', while armed bodyguards kept watch over him in case of another assassination attempt.[27]

Irakli Tsereteli, though seriously ill, joined Chernov in defending the assembly as the sole body empowered to legitimise the revolutionary government. He denounced the Bolsheviks over their destructive use of force and the suppression of all anti-Bolshevik views. 'Let's suppose Kerensky was worse than you are, but that doesn't prove you are better than the Constituent Assembly,' he said. 'At the present time you are fighting neither Kerensky nor Tsereteli but the expressed will of the entire population.'

Lenin looked bored. Many of the Red Guards were drunk and interrupted the speakers with jeers and catcalls. One sighted Chernov along the barrel of his rifle as though preparing to shoot him. The Bolsheviks hissed when Socialist Revolutionaries cheered the proposal 'All Power to the Constituent Assembly'. Nikolai Bukharin, a young Bolshevik theoretician who had worked closely with Lenin and Trotsky in exile, joined the fray with an accusation that Chernov and Tsereteli were impeding the march of history. 'The dictatorship [of the proletariat] is laying the foundations for the life of mankind for a thousand years,' he declared.[28]

Fyodor Raskolnikov, the leader of the Kronstadt sailors, attempted to proclaim Russia the 'Republic of Soviets'. To Bolshevik shouts of 'Judas!' and 'Traitors!', this move was rejected by 237 votes to 146. When the assembly went ahead with the SRs' agenda on the vital questions of peace and land, the Bolshevik deputies declared the assembly to be in the hands of counter-revolutionaries and stormed out of the hall. A recess was called for tempers to cool down but it achieved nothing. By the time the deputies returned to the chamber at 11.30 p.m., the Bolshevik members had left the palace.[29]

A majority of the assembly then voted to express regret to the Allied powers that the Bolsheviks' negotiations with Germany were heading towards a separate peace. They called for the setting up of an international socialist conference 'for the purpose of realising a general democratic peace', and they voted to adopt a new name for the Russian Empire: the Russian Democratic Federative Republic.

Lenin had heard enough. At 1 a.m. on 6 January he roused himself and gave the order to close down the assembly. Then he left for the Smolny. At 4 a.m. the Left SRs decided to support the Bolsheviks and announced their departure from the assembly. As they trooped out, Paul Dybenko who was now married to Alexandra Kollontai, ordered the Red Guards to clear the chamber. Their commander, an anarchist sailor named Anatoly Zhelezniakov, walked up to Chernov on the podium and tapped him on the shoulder.

'Everybody here should leave the chamber now,' he said. 'The Guards are tired.'

Chernov bravely stood his ground.

'We are also tired,' he said, 'but that cannot interrupt our work.'

And he reminded the sailor, 'All Russia is watching.'

Swaggering drunkenly around the chamber, the Guards abused the deputies and started turning out the lights. Chernov hastened to finish the reading of a decree on land reform, the most important issue of all as far as the SRs' supporters in rural Russia were concerned. He succeeded in putting the decree to the vote and it was carried without opposition. It mattered little: the assembly had lost the quorum on which its powers depended.[30]

'The sailors and Red Guards then lost their restraint,' Mark Vishniak says. 'They leapt into the boxes and pushed deputies towards the exits with their rifle-butts, and swirled up into the balconies where the public was close to panic. The deputies meanwhile remained stationary in their seats, tragically silent. We had been isolated from the world, just as the Tauride Palace had been isolated from Petrograd and Petrograd from the rest of the world.'[31]

At 4.40 a.m. the deputies gave up the struggle. Chernov declared the sitting closed and they filed out of the hall. As they left the palace, the gates were locked behind them. The Constituent Assembly had lasted a mere twelve hours. Kerensky had survived; it was democracy that had died. 'The forcible dissolution of the assembly,' he says, 'destroyed the last hope that the nation would regain by peaceful means the freedom it had won on 27 February.'[32]

Trotsky agreed. 'The simple, open, brutal breaking-up of the Constituent Assembly dealt formal democracy a blow from which it never recovered,' he wrote. Later that day the Soviet Excom and the Sovnarkom formally approved the permanent dissolution of the Constituent Assembly on the grounds that it was a bourgeois body intent on overthrowing the Soviets. 'The people wanted the Constituent Assembly to be convened and we convened it,' Lenin told the meeting. 'But now it can see what this notorious assembly really is. So now we have fulfilled the will of the people, a will which calls for "all power to the Soviets".'[33]

Pravda, edited by Nikolai Bukharin, published false reports about what had happened in Petrograd over the previous twenty-four hours. Reflecting Lenin's contempt for his opponents, the paper claimed the march in favour of the Constituent Assembly had been organised by the bourgeoisie and that the marchers were shopkeepers and bankers. Such a profoundly dishonest statement outraged Maxim Gorky. '*Pravda* knows that workers from the Obukhov, Patronny and other plants took part in the demonstration,' he wrote in his newspaper *Novaya Zhizn*, 'that it was the workers from the Vasilevsky Island, Vyborg and other districts who marched beneath the red banners of the Russian Social Democratic Party to the Tauride Palace. And these were the workers who were shot down; no matter how many lies *Pravda* tells, it cannot hide the bitter truth.'[34]

Lenin's rationale behind the scourging of the assembly - 'Democracy is a bourgeois state-form upheld only by those who are traitors to true socialism - could be used to justify just about anything. A few hours later sailors from the Baltic Fleet cruiser *Seagull* entered the Marinsky Hospital and murdered Andrei Shingarev and Fyodor Kokoshkin, who had been moved there from the Peter and Paul Fortress for treatment. They were strangled in their beds and then shot and/or bayoneted.[35]

The cold-blooded executions of respected men – one a physician, the other a professor of law – brought another furious reaction from Maxim Gorky. He asked his friend Fyodor Chaliapin to accompany him to the old Ministry of Justice building to lodge a protest. 'Pale with emotion,' Chaliapin recalls, 'Gorky declared that it was abominable to treat human beings as these men had been treated. "I insist on the immediate release of the members of the Provisional Government," he told Isaak Steinberg, the People's Commissar of Justice. "If you refuse, they will probably be murdered like Shingarev and Kokoshkin. It will be a blot on the Revolution."'[36]

Steinberg, a Left SR in the shaky coalition, was anxious to do the right thing. He identified the killers and insisted to Lenin that they should be arrested. 'This was murder, not political terror,' he said. 'Really?' Lenin replied. 'I don't think the people are interested in such matters.' Lenin's perception of what 'the people's will' might be had become the determining factor in matters of life and death. The killers remained free.[37]

The news that a grave injustice had been committed filtered through to all levels of society. Oleg Kerensky's schoolmate Dmitri Shostakovich, a bespectacled twelve-year-old musical prodigy, wrote a funeral march in memory of the murdered ministers.

After the debacle of 5 January, Kerensky found the atmosphere of Petrograd oppressive. The SR Central Committee wanted him to move abroad but he refused to abandon Russia. As a compromise, he agreed to join his friends in Helsinki and at midnight on 9 January he and his SR bodyguard Vladimir Fabrikant passed through the Bolshevik checkpoint at Finland Station. They arrived in Helsinki without incident.[38]

Finland was on the threshold of civil war herself and many young Finns were joining the anti-Bolshevik force of Baron Carl von Mannerheim, a former Tsarist general who had fought on the Austro-Hungarian and Romanian fronts during the war. 'We stayed in a small cosy apartment belonging to a young Swede,' Kerensky says. 'It was quiet and peaceful but it did not remain so for long.' Mannerheim's force had gathered in the north of Finland and their Swedish host was joining them there. Given the exodus from the capital, it would have been dangerous for Kerensky to stay in Helsinki, so the fugitives moved to a dairy farm at Abo, near the Gulf of Bothnia, and then to other safe addresses.[39]

The Bolsheviks and Left SRs were assured of an overwhelming majority in the Third Congress of Soviets, which opened in the Tauride Palace on 10 January 1918. The congress passed the Declaration of the Rights of the Working People to serve as the prototype of the first Soviet constitution. It also issued a decree that would bring the country's date into line with Europe. As of midnight on Wednesday 31 January 1918, the Georgian Calendar would be introduced, starting with the date Thursday 14 February.

Lenin paid lip service to the Soviet of Peasant Deputies, which joined the congress on 13 January, with his decree on land. Borrowing heavily from Viktor Chernov's policy passed by the Constituent Assembly, he supported the division of estates into smaller average allotments to be redistributed to the peasants. This was exactly what they wanted to hear and it seduced the Left SRs into forming a coalition with him.

Lenin's loathing of religion was given physical form in a proclamation entitled 'On the Separation of Church from State and School from Church', which forbade the Orthodox Church from owning property or organising formal religious education. Bolshevik squads raided churches and monasteries, looted their gold and silver artefacts and drank their wine.[40] Patriarch Tikhon, the newly elected head of the Church, called on the clergy to resist 'these godless rulers of darkness'. Thousands of worshippers rallied to the call and there were so many bloody confrontations outside churches that the Bolsheviks were forced to desist.

The unpalatable fact that the Bolsheviks had to face was that despite all their anti-war, anti-capitalist, anti-imperialist proselytising, no socialist revolution had broken out in any other country. According to the minutes of a meeting of the Central Committee on 11 January, Artem Sergeyev noted that every speaker agreed that the failure of the revolution in Western Europe threatened the Soviet Republic with destruction. 'Sergeyev stood for the position of Lenin – that is, for signing the peace,' Trotsky says. 'Nobody contradicted him. All three of the contending groups competed in appealing to one and the same general premise: without a world revolution we will not pull through.'[41]

Severe drought and crop failure had combined with the wartime destruction of entire towns and the displacement their populations to drag the country into a dark winter's night of starvation. Ukraine was in turmoil. Sergeyev had launched a successful military uprising in the coal-rich Donets River Basin (Donbas) in October 1917 and in December Vladimir Antonov-Ovsienko joined him in Kharkov, the main city in the region, as commander of the revolutionary forces in Ukraine and South Russia. The Ukrainian Rada refused to recognise the Bolshevik government and on 7 November established the Ukrainian People's Republic, whose first act was to marshal all Ukrainian troops in Ukrainian territory. In the ensuing battle, Kiev fell to the Bolsheviks and the Rada was ousted.

'For God's sake, use all energy and all revolutionary measures to send grain, grain and more grain!!' Lenin wrote to his commissars in Ukraine in January 1918. 'Otherwise, Petrograd may starve to death. Use special trains and special detachments. Collect and store. Escort the trains. Inform us every day. For God's sake!' 'Revolutionary measures' meant theft and, when necessary, murder. Soviet soldiers were brought in to enforce the requisition of grain from the peasants but they also seized their seed grain, which made matters immeasurably worse.[42]

Having ordered the demobilisation of the Russian Army, Lenin was confronted with threats on many fronts. On 15 January 1918 the Sovnarkom founded the Red Army of Workers and Peasants from a nucleus of Red Guard brigades in Petrograd and Moscow. The plan was that the three to four million men who had been discharged from the Russian Army with their weapons would become 'citizen soldiers'. There was also a ready-made source of officer material on hand. 'All officers in the Russian Army were told by the Bolsheviks to report for duty on pain of death and start serving again,' Gleb Kerensky wrote in *Only One Freedom*. 'Those who were determined to resist either escaped to the Whites or were shot.'

Meanwhile, Bruce Lockhart had returned to Petrograd in the middle of January on his seemingly hopeless mission to keep Russia in the war. He rented an apartment with a well-stocked cellar on Palace Quay close to the British Embassy. In Trotsky's absence at the peace talks Georgi Chicherin was running the Foreign Office and, through him, Lockhart was able to keep up with developments. After weeks of haggling, the Germans and Austrians lost patience with Trotsky's 'No war, no peace' strategy and ordered their troops to resume their advance into Russia, pushing further east in five days than they had in the previous three years.

'The Russian Army is more rotten than I had supposed,' General Hoffmann noted in his diary. 'There is no fight left in them. Yesterday one lieutenant with six men took six hundred Cossacks prisoner. Hundreds of guns, motor-cars, locomotives, trucks, and several thousand prisoners were brought in without any sort of fighting at all.'[43]

Trotsky was outraged when the delegation of the Ukrainian People's Republic unexpectedly announced their country's independence from Soviet Russia in February and declared they were willing to trade Ukrainian grain with the belligerent nations.

The 'Spanish flu' pandemic that would kill an estimated fifty million people was just starting to exert its grip on the northern hemisphere before circling the globe over the next three years. As in the Entente countries, thousands of Germany's malnourished citizens were dying from the disease. Life had become unbearable for millions and discontent was rife.[ii] Trotsky stalled for time in the hope that revolution would finally break out in Berlin. Exploiting the differences among the German, Austrian, Bulgarian and Turkish

---

ii The virus was called 'Spanish flu' because although the belligerent nations were also infected they censured that information, whereas neutral Spain allowed it to be published.

representatives, he argued every point on obscure matters of principle or delayed giving definite answers to his inquisitors.

But by the time the Russian date jumped thirteen days to 14 February, Trotsky had walked out of the peace talks and returned to Petrograd. The Germans were within one hundred miles of the capital and the Bolsheviks were about to retreat to Moscow when Lenin ordered him to sign the treaty. Bruce Lockhart met Trotsky at the Russian Foreign Office and handed over Maxim Litvinov's letter of introduction. Trotsky was still steaming over Germany's belligerence but he was also 'full of bitterness against the English'. The British War Cabinet had debated whether the United Kingdom should recognise the Bolshevik regime as the legal government of Russia. Lloyd George and Balfour supported recognition in the hope it would keep Russia in the war but the meeting ended in deadlock without a vote being taken.[44]

Trotsky was given the herculean task of organising the Red Army. He reintroduced conscription to provide him with 'bayonets', including large numbers of reluctant peasants who, having been demobilised in 1917, were suddenly called up again in 1918. When they started deserting in droves, he reintroduced the death penalty for desertion.[45]

He also had the services of some 50,000 imperial officers, now designated as 'commanders' or 'military specialists', who had gone over to the Bolsheviks, including General Vladimir Baranovsky. 'Grandma told me that he was taken to see Trotsky who threatened to shoot him unless he joined them and he agreed to do so,' Stephen Kerensky says. 'Dad saw it as a betrayal of his father and was so upset that he refused to say goodbye to him when he left Petrograd.'[46]

While new regiments were being formed, Trotsky's initial strategy was to send trainloads of trustworthy Red troops from Bolshevik strongholds in Central Russia to suppress the uprisings in Ukraine and South Russia. The 'railway war' would prove highly effective until he was able to put well-trained and well-equipped armies into the field.[47]

In the first weeks of 1918 General Vsevolod Baranovsky, Lydia and Olik, who had spent New Year's Eve with friends in Ekaterinodar near the Black Sea, found themselves in the middle of a war zone. Fighting ebbed and flowed around Ekaterinodar and Rostov. General Kaledin failed to persuade radicalised younger Cossacks who had returned from the Eastern Front to join him. Believing the military situation to be hopeless, he resigned as Ataman and on 29 January/12 February shot himself in the heart. When Ekaterinodar fell to the Soviets, General Baranovsky was forced into hiding to avoid the Soviet death squads. Lydia took Olik to safety down at Novorossisk on the Black Sea and it would be months before the family could be reunited.[48]

The day before Rostov fell to one of the railway detachments General Kornilov led his 4000 Volunteers out into the frozen steppe at the start of what would become famous as the 'Ice March'. Judging it pointless to resist superior forces, he headed south in the hope of finding a new base in the Kuban region. 'We went,' his deputy Anton Denikin says, 'from the dark night and spiritual slavery to unknown wandering – in search of the bluebird.' The soldiers carried their rifles and hauled field-guns, while thousands of civilians, many of them middle-class civilians who feared Bolshevik reprisals, followed in single file across the snow-covered terrain. The sick and the wounded were abandoned and many shot themselves rather than be captured.[iii]

While Trotsky was engaged in military matters, Grigory Sokolnikov and Georgi Chicherin were sent to Poland and, on 3 March 1918, Russia signed the Peace of Brest-Litovsk. The terms were supposedly dictated by Hindenburg and Ludendorff, though Trotsky regarded General Hoffmann, whom he recognised as 'the only element of serious reality in these negotiations', as the main architect. Russia lost Poland, Lithuania, Ukraine, the Baltic Provinces, and Transcaucasia. She gave up sixty-two million people, 1.3 million square miles of territory, including one-third of her agricultural land, three-quarters of her coal and iron, her southern oilfields and three-quarters of her industries.[49]

German and Austrian troops occupied Ukraine, chased the Red Army out of Kiev and took control of 'the bread basket', a devastating blow to the Russian economy. Artem Sergeyev was ordered by Vladimir Antonov-Ovsienko to prevent the Central Powers and the Don Cossacks from taking over the Donets-Krivoi Rog Soviet Republic, the new Bolshevik entity that Sergeyev had founded in the

---

iii Such was the ordeal that survivors of the Ice March were awarded a medal in the form of a crown of thorns pierced by a sword.

eastern provinces around Kharkov in February. Thousands of miners and factory workers were recruited into the Donets Army but they were unable to withstand superior enemy forces and Kharkov fell to the Whites. The Bolsheviks retreated 250 miles through the snow to Tsaritsyn, the revolutionary eastern city which was destined to become famous under a different name: Stalingrad.

22

The Lubianka Prisoners

Alexander Kerensky returned to Petrograd on 9 March 1918, the day on which the Bolshevik Party changed its name to the All-Russian Communist Party and the day that the Sovnarkom moved its seat of government from Petrograd to Moscow. The move precipitated a stampede of apparatchiks, camp followers and other political parties to the new capital. Emerging from Finland Station, Kerensky was swallowed up in a vast crowd carrying all manner of luggage. 'In those troubled times a pedestrian laden down with bundles or a suitcase did not seem out of place,' he says. 'It was the best way to go unnoticed.'[1]

He moved into an apartment on Vasilevsky Island as the guest of Dr Olga Maximova, a physician whose husband was serving in the army. 'She never betrayed the slightest concern about the risk she was running,' he says. 'She left home early in the morning and I remained alone in the empty apartment until late at night.' Kerensky spent his time editing and annotating a transcript of the evidence he had given to the Commission of Inquiry into the Kornilov Affair on 8 October 1917. It was his intention to publish this material as a book entitled *The Prelude to Bolshevism*.[2]

Pitirim Sorokin, who had been set free after fifty-seven days in the Peter and Paul Fortress, called on him. 'Entering his apartment,' he said, 'I was met by a long-haired, bearded man wearing thick blue spectacles; his general make-up recalled the intellectual of the 1860-1870 period. Kerensky had transformed himself and was now able to travel without being recognised. Quieter and simpler in his manner, he impressed me as someone who might fill the role of a teacher or preacher. No stranger would have believed that this was the very man who, a few months earlier, had been virtually the ruler of Russia.'[3]

The unexpected but irrefutable benefit of Brest-Litovsk to the Allies was that Trotsky's haggling over terms had caused a four-month delay in shifting thousands of German troops from East to West, a delay that would prove disastrous to Germany's chance of winning the war. Even then, as Lenin explained, a German force of one million men had to be retained in the East to appropriate Russian commodities and annex Russian territory, or, as Hindenburg put it, 'to maintain a barrier between the Bolshevik armies and the lands we had liberated'.[4]

Reinforced with forty divisions from the East, Ludendorff launched Operation Michael, Germany's last great offensive of the war, on 21 March 1918 with a series of attacks along the perimeter of the Western Front. His primary objective was to force an armistice before the overwhelming resources of the United States could be deployed on the battlefield.[i] Enjoying an advantage of 192 divisions to 173 the Germans attacked the British Fifth Army at Saint Quentin. Since Verdun, they had learned how to advance in small groups following a short, sharp artillery barrage. Armed with flamethrowers, rifle grenades and light trench mortars on mobile mounts, they overpowered strongpoints and infiltrated the rear areas.[5]

This technique proved so effective that by 25 March three British divisions had practically ceased to exist as fighting forces. The Germans were within ten miles of the vital British rail junction of Amiens on the Somme through which trains from Paris ran to northern France. Within a week, the situation was critical and, for the second time in the war, it seemed the French capital would fall.[6]

To bring terror to the population of Paris, the Germans installed a long-range, super-heavy railway cannon sixty-four kilometres away on the slopes of Mont de Joie near the village of Crépy in German-occupied territory. The Paris Gun (*Paris-Geschütz*) could fling a 106-kilogram projectile into the centre of the city. On Good Friday a single shell brought down the roof of the Saint-Gervais-et-Saint-Protais Church in the Marais, killing ninety-one members of the congregation.

As 200,000 people fled into the countryside, General Pétain dismally asserted that the war was as good as lost. While Parisians prayed to their patron saint, Saint Geneviève, more secular measures were needed. Lloyd George, Douglas Haig and the American commanders General John J. 'Black Jack' Pershing and General Tasker H. Bliss

---

i In the East, Ludendorff had a crazy scheme to depose the Bolsheviks, reinstate the Tsar and turn Russia into a vassal state.

agreed to a suggestion from the new French Prime Minister, Georges Clémenceau, that the French commander, Marshal Ferdinand Foch, should be given responsibility for coordinating the whole allied war effort on the Western Front.

Clémenceau and Foch, now styled 'Generalissimo of the Allied Forces', were a formidable team. While Foch dealt with the Spring Offensive, the Prime Minister and his enforcer Georges Mandel galvanised the Home Front, suppressing defeatists like Pétain and motivating the workforce to greater efforts. As Ludendorff prepared to launch his coup de main, things were so grim in the British sectors that on 11 April Haig issued his most famous order to the First and Second Armies: *'Every position must be held to the last man; there must be no retirement. With our backs to the wall, and believing in the justice of our cause, each one of us must fight on to the end.'* Haig would not be doing any of the fighting himself, though he would be with the troops in spirit.[7]

Meanwhile, in early April, Kerensky finished *The Prelude to Bolshevism*. He mailed the manuscript to a new anti-Bolshevik newspaper, *Vozrozhdeniye*, which was being launched in Moscow in June. In a Preface dated 3 April 1918, he described Kornilov as a man 'who in his own way loved Russia passionately [but who] was doomed by some power to bring about the victory of those who hated and despised her'.[8]

It was a timely epitaph. The Ice Marchers had reached the Kuban region and Kornilov decided to attack Ekaterinodar, the capital of the recently established North Caucasian Soviet Republic. Early on the morning of 13 April the great White hope met with a sudden end when a Soviet gunner fired a shot at his headquarters in a farmhouse on a hill outside the town. 'General Kornilov was alone in his room when an enemy shell burst through the wall by the window and struck the floor beneath his chair,' General Denikin says. 'He was apparently blown upwards by the force of the explosion and flung against the stove. Only a single shell had struck the house and he alone was killed.'[9]

Kerensky was anxious to leave Petrograd - his very presence represented a threat to his family. On one occasion he wanted to take ten-year-old Gleb to see his baby half-sister at Lilya's apartment but

Olga wouldn't allow it. After several days of agonising, he begged the PSR Central Committee for help and it was decided he should go to Moscow to do some research for the party. He could not bring himself to announce Irina's birth to Oleg until the very last moment. As he went down the stairs, he turned and stated matter-of-factly, 'You have a sister.' Thirteen-year-old Oleg hero-worshipped his father and was prepared to forgive him anything but he took the news badly.[10]

In his long-haired Swedish doctor guise, Kerensky travelled to Moscow with Vladimir Fabrikant and his brother, and moved into the apartment of Elizaveta Nelidova-Khenkina in the Arbat District near the Smolensk Market. Making contact with his former SR colleagues, he discovered that the political tide had turned and he was in the wrong place at the wrong time. The Socialist Revolutionaries realised that they had no chance of surviving in Moscow and were in the process of decamping to Samara, their political stronghold on the Volga, where they set up the Committee for the Reconvocation of the Assembly – 'Komuch' in its Russian acronym. Kerensky was anxious to join them and discussed his plan with Catherine Breshko-Breshkovskaya, who was no longer of a member of the party. 'They won't let you go', she replied, meaning the members of the Central Committee.[11]

Indeed, Kerensky was rejected, with even former colleagues like Nikolai Avksentiev failing to support him. Fortunately, there was an alternative: several political parties and anti-Bolshevik organisations had recently formed alliances that united conflicting views and contrary personalities to oppose the common enemy. One of these groups was the Union for the Regeneration of Russia, whose members included moderate socialists and Kadets dedicated to creating a national government on democratic lines and to restoring the Eastern Front against Germany in cooperation with the Allies.[ii]

Kerensky turned to this body. 'I accepted a proposal that I should go abroad and negotiate with the Allies under the terms laid down by the union,' he said. The exact nature of this proposal was never explained and its very existence has been questioned. Barred from travelling east with his former comrades, it is conceivable that he made a unilateral decision to travel west and use his political skills to persuade Britain and France to intervene in Russia.[12]

---

ii Sometimes referred to as the Union for the Resurrection of Russia or the Union for the Revival of Russia.

Vladimir Fabrikant arranged for them to join a platoon of Serbian officers who were being repatriated home. Fabrikant had a Russian passport but Kerensky needed false papers in order to leave the country. The head of the repatriation project issued him with a passport in the name of a Serbian officer, Miloutine Markavitch.[13]

Kerensky and Fabrikant were granted visas to enter France but as there was no direct route from Russia to Continental Europe they also required British visas. The last thing Oliver Wardrop, the British Consul-General in Moscow, expected was a visit from the former Russian Prime Minister and his bodyguard. When they requested permission to travel through the United Kingdom, he turned them down. Kerensky appealed to Bruce Lockhart for help and then on 25 May he and Fabrikant left Moscow in an 'extraterritorial' train reserved for the Serbian officers. The following day Lockhart sent a telegram marked 'Very Secret and Urgent' to the War Office in London.[14]

> Kerensky accompanied by a Russian subject named Vladimir Fabrikant left for Murmansk last night. A painful impression has been created by the fact that we refused a visa for his passport here after the French had already done so. As his life is now in great danger, I would beg you to send immediate instructions to Murmansk and to Archangel without revealing his identity to viser *(sic)* the following passports: Russian passport Series A No. 231 of Fabrikant and Serbian passport No. 21 in the name of Miloutine Markavitch. Kerensky is travelling as a Serbian officer and is quite unrecognisable.
>
> I quite realise the complications that may arise from Kerensky's presence in England but I hope that by the time he arrives our intervention will be so far prepared as to render further secrecy unnecessary. Whatever Kerensky's weaknesses, he has been a true friend to the Allies under circumstances of great difficulty. If through our refusing him a visa anything were to happen to him we should incur a most unpleasant responsibility. I do not know whether Kerensky will ever play a part again in Russian history [but] he represents more or less all the parties who are in favour of intervention.[iii] [15]

---

iii Unaware of Lockhart's telegram to the Foreign Office, Kerensky wrote in his memoirs, 'A British visa was issued in my name by Robert Bruce Lockhart… Lockhart granted the visa without cabling London for official approval. As he told me much later, he had had to act on his own because the visa application would have been rejected by the Foreign Office.' (Turning Point, p. 481)

Captain Hodgson of the War Office sent Lockhart's telegram to MI5, whose chief, Colonel Vernon Kell, was strongly opposed to admitting any more radical Russians to the United Kingdom. He referred the telegram to Don Gregory at the Foreign Office, with a note: 'We should be glad to have the view of the Secretary of State [Arthur Balfour] at his earliest convenience as we are uncertain as to the actual date of the sailing of the Serbian detachment from Murmansk.'

Since Lord Milner's visit in January 1917, Murmansk had become a hive of military activity. Fearing cross-border raids by German-backed White Finns, Trotsky had given approval for Allied forces to guard the stockpile of war matériel. On 6 March 130 Royal Marines, commanded by Major General Frederick Poole, came ashore and shortly afterwards three cruisers flying the flags of Britain, France and the United States dropped anchor in the harbour. Permission for further landings was quickly withdrawn in the wake of the Peace of Brest-Litovsk.[16]

One of the most serious consequences of that treaty was the mutiny on 14 May of the Czechoslovak Legion, a 60,000-strong force with the inclusion of Czech and Slovak deserters and POWs from the Austrian Army, who saw it as a sellout. Refusing to lay down their arms, they decided to continue the war against the Central Powers by taking the Trans-Siberian Railway from the Volga to Vladivostok and then sailing halfway around the globe to Europe.

On the very day that Kerensky set off for Murmansk, Trotsky declared war on the Czechs. 'All Soviets are hereby ordered to disarm the Czechoslovaks immediately,' he commanded. 'Every armed Czechoslovak found on the railway is to be shot on the spot; every troop train in which even one armed man is found shall be unloaded, and its soldiers shall be interned in a prisoner of war camp.'[17]

This order proved to be a colossal tactical blunder: within a matter of weeks the legionnaires had captured several major towns, including Samara, and replaced the local Soviets with anti-Bolshevik regimes. To rescue the Czechs, Britain and France decided to make Murmansk and its sister port Archangel the centres of Allied intervention, a decision that would fit neatly with Kerensky's scenario.

Arriving in Murmansk, he and Fabrikant were escorted by two French naval officers to the cruiser *General Hobe*. The French captain welcomed them warmly and, at Kerensky's request, a barber cut his long hair and shaved off his beard. Then there was a hitch. Balfour, the Foreign Secretary, was allergic to Bolsheviks and Socialist Revolutionaries, and the news of Kerensky's imminent arrival filled him with foreboding. The Foreign Office sent panicky telegrams to British agents at Murmansk and Archangel: 'Markavitch and Fabrikant are not to proceed to UK till further instructions dispatched to you.'[18]

The final decision of whether Kerensky lived or died rested with Balfour. The philosopher-politician was known to 'The Souls', his intimate circle of brilliant young men and women, as 'King Arthur'. He thought long and hard about the consequences of banning Kerensky and then concluded that he was not prepared to have his murder on his conscience.

On 30 May the Foreign Office informed Hodgson that 'in view of the circumstances of the case and the fact that [Kerensky] has got a French visa and his destination is France, the Secretary of State for Foreign Affairs concurs with the granting of a visa.' Hodgson wired the green light to Murmansk and a British officer came aboard the *General Hobe* with the visas. He informed Kerensky and Fabrikant that they would be leaving for England in the morning.

At first light, Kerensky was astonished to see a Secret Service trawler moored beside the cruiser. 'It looked like a toy boat,' he says, 'and we wondered what the trip through the Arctic Ocean would be like.' The trawler took almost three weeks to make the crossing and apart from a storm that tossed the little boat about for forty-eight hours it was an uneventful trip. During the first sleepless night Kerensky had an ominous feeling that he would never see Russia again.

'The thought was intolerable but it gripped me so strongly that I fell into a prolonged mood of despair,' he says. 'To awaken from this nightmare, to shake off my gloomy thoughts and pull myself together, I needed a shock and it was the storm that provided it. The fiercer the raging of waves around us, the louder the roaring of the elements, the easier it was to forget the word "forever".'[19]

Olga Kerenskaya knew nothing of her estranged husband's adventures or the fact that he was en route to Britain to rally Anglo-French opposition against the Bolsheviks. By the summer of 1918, she had saved enough money from her labours to take her sons Oleg and Gleb and her mother Maria to a healthier life in the country. The family farmhouse at Kainki would have been the preferred destination but it had been burned down during the Revolution. One of Olga's friends, a widow with three children, heard from one of her friends, the wife of an artist, that the Revolution had left much of North Russia relatively untouched. There was plenty of food there and it was said to be cheap.

The three Kerenskys, Maria Baranovskaya and the widow and her three children set off in a third-class carriage for the provincial town of Kotlas at the confluence of the Northern Dvina and Vychegda Rivers in the Archangel Oblast. With every mile of the journey, Olga hoped they were heading for somewhere safer than Petrograd. Kotlas, however, was to prove even more terrifying. The Ustyug-Kotlas district was situated between Vologda and Archangel and had become a dumping ground for military supplies. Kotlas was crammed with Red soldiers and sailors. It was under martial law and anyone suspected of counter-revolutionary sympathies was in danger of being shot.[20]

Olga's little band took a riverboat from Kotlas to the small provincial town of Ust-Sysolsk (Syktyvkar). On this leg of the journey Olga exchanged heated words with two annoying Bolshevik passengers during which they learned that she was the wife of Alexander Kerensky. This argument was to have terrible consequences for the family. From Ust-Sysolsk there was a five-mile ride in a horse-drawn cart to the village recommended by the artist's wife. They found a room in the home of a peasant identified only as 'Nicholas'. Even writing her memoirs in 1935, Olga declined to give the man's full name or to identify his village in case of repercussions from the Soviet authorities.

'Nicholas was a simple peasant, half-literate, but he had a natural intelligence and a keen mind,' she says. 'When the Revolution began he was a soldier at the front. Then the Bolsheviks started their propaganda. He heard their promises, threw away his rifle and hurried home. When I asked him how he could have done such a thing, he explained that if he hadn't made for home the land would have been divided among the other peasants and there would be nothing for him.'

Olga told Nicholas that the Bolsheviks would take his corn and his cattle, just as they had seized them from the landlords, and, in the end, they would also take his land. Blood rushed to the man's face, he clenched his fists and repeated over and over again, 'I may die but never, never will I give up my land.'

Nicholas provided the visitors with a regular supply of bread, butter and eggs, and they could buy meat if they walked the five miles to the market at Ust-Sysolsk. One day, on the way back from market, Olga was stopped by two men in a horse-drawn vehicle.

'Are you Citizen Kerensky?'

Olga admitted she was and they ordered her to get into the cart. She was taken back into the town and delivered to the Cheka, who were based at the district jail. One of the Chekists showed her a telegram which read: 'Find out where Citizen Kerensky is living, make a search, arrest her and send her to Kotlas.' The Bolsheviks on the boat had reported her presence in the area to the police. While she was shopping, the Cheka had searched her room in Nicholas's house and told her family they were going to arrest her.

'Very soon after I had been put in a cell my mother, my children and even my widowed friend and her three children came to see me,' Olga says. 'We all cried and asked each other why it had happened – why Kotlas? If the order had come from Petrograd, we could understand it, but from Kotlas …? At last my visitors were ordered from my cell but they were given permission to call every day and bring me food.'

Olga was incarcerated in the jail with no idea of how long she would be kept there or what charges she was facing. There was no bed, so she slept on a hard wooden bench. She saw little of her jailers who neither threatened nor mistreated her. Alone, she had plenty of time to reflect on the situation. Her main concern was not for herself but for her mother and her sons. The Cheka were almost certainly after information about Alexander and although she had no idea of his present whereabouts she knew they would insist that she must know something.

Early on the seventh morning, the cell door was thrown open revealing a frightening male figure with glaring eyes. He wore civilian clothes but his body was covered with weapons. A sabre dangled on a strap from one of his shoulders and knives or daggers hung from a military belt around his waist. He also had a revolver thrust through the belt and his breast pocket was stuffed with cartridges. The man asked Olga whether she had any complaints about her treatment.

'I nervously murmured that I had none and he turned on his heel and left,' she says. 'When I next saw him, he presided over my trial. It turned out that he was a doctor who was considered not quite right in the head. Before the Revolution, it was said, he had been more conservative. After the Revolution, he not only joined the Communist Party but became its local chief – all in order to prevent excesses. Goodness knows if that was true, but I came to believe it was.'

Olga's trial was held in secret with the deranged doctor presiding and three members of the Cheka on the bench. In evidence, the Cheka produced the papers they had seized from Olga's room in Nicholas's house, mostly innocent letters from friends, but she suddenly saw that the heap included letters from her brother Vladimir Baranovsky to his mother, Maria. Vladimir was employed in the War Commissariat and his letters were critical of the Communists. She had to do something to protect him.

'I do not read other people's letters,' she blurted out.

'Why? Is it your principle?' the doctor replied.

'Yes, if you want to call it that.'

'Why did you come to Ust-Sysolsk?'

'Because I was told that the cost of living was very cheap here and my children needed better food than they could get at Petrograd. My mother and I also needed a rest after working hard.'

'At what?'

'Making cigarettes.'

'Why?'

'Because I could not find any other work and the children needed food. I can type but I could not find anyone to give me office work. I am Kerensky's wife and everybody was afraid.'

The doctor jumped up from his chair, struck the table with his fist and shouted, 'Afraid? Did they tell you that? Why didn't you spit in their eyes?'

There was no answer to that, so Olga shrugged and said nothing.

'You say that you can type. Excellent. You can work in our office. We need a typist.'

Olga was bewildered.

'How can you offer me a job with the Cheka? I am here as a prisoner. You are my judges. And in any case it would be out of the question for me to work for the Cheka.'

'Why not? Is it another of your principles?'

Realising the trial had become a farce, the doctor jumped up again and addressed the other three judges.

'Do you understand why this woman was arrested? I don't. She is not guilty of anything.'

The trial was adjourned and Olga was told by a Cheka official it had been decided to send the family to Moscow. She was relieved. Compared with Kotlas, she felt that in more familiar surroundings everything would be all right.

That evening Olga, Oleg, Gleb and Maria were taken by steamer to Kotlas and escorted from the quayside by armed soldiers to a single railway carriage standing in a siding. An engine was coupled to the carriage and for a long time they crossed various railway lines before reaching the local railway station, where their carriage was coupled to a train bound for Moscow. As part of the secrecy, they were ordered not to look out of the windows.

'Our coach filled up with Communists and our soldier escort was replaced by two Tatars,' Olga says.

> During the first period of the Revolution the most faithful and reliable servants of the Bolsheviks were either Latvians or Tatars. At that time, it was not easy for the Bolsheviks to find Russians willing to be executioners or jailers. These Tatars were harsh and brutal. They shouted at my children, who looked terrified and forlorn. At last I couldn't stand it any longer. I also began to shout and told the Tartars that they had no right to treat us in this way, and that when we got to Moscow I would lodge a complaint about them. Evidently, these two Tatars were not yet quite sure of their power and their behaviour improved.

The journey took several days. Olga had been told the family would receive rations from their guards but all they were given were some rusks and bread. Reaching Moscow, they were escorted to the Lubianka, the Cheka's headquarters in an insurance building on Lubianka Square that would become synonymous with the Red Terror.

After going through the admission procedure, the Kerensky family were locked up in a communal cell with about fifty women. 'As soon as we entered, a girl rushed to greet us,' Olga says. 'She belonged to the rightwing of the Socialist Revolutionary Party and I used to see her at meetings. She told us that the news of our arrest had reached Moscow and our friends were alarmed for us. Other prisoners surrounded us and made a fuss of the children. Strangely, my mother and I sighed with relief. We were back in the centre of Russia among people like ourselves.'

One of the other prisoners was a young musichall actress, very pretty, extravagantly dressed, with a huge hat which remained on her head as though she was just making a brief social visit. She told Olga that she had dressed for a gala performance at her theatre when she was arrested. She had once lived with a member of the Social Revolutionary Party but had lost touch with him. The Cheka still pestered her with questions about him.

'That evening she was asked to sing one of her songs,' says Olga. 'She sang *Tango* very well and the words were burned on my memory. Whenever I hear that song about the heat of the Argentine, the blue skies, love and dancing, I see our dark prison and I remember those who were doomed to die…'

Sitting next to the singer was a film actress. She was young, smartly dressed and quite beautiful. These two spent their time in prison taking small mirrors from their handbags, looking at their faces, changing their hairstyle, pencilling their eyebrows, powdering and rouging their cheeks and polishing their nails as though preparing for an entrance. The film actress was soon released but the musichall singer was taken away to solitary confinement, which meant the Bolsheviks thought she could provide them with more information.

Another prisoner was the daughter of a black marketeer and the newly married wife of another black marketeer. Proudly, she told everybody what a merry and expensive wedding it had been, with food in abundance and plenty of vodka and wine. She and her husband and her 'dear daddy' were arrested the night after the wedding. Suddenly, she started beating her chest, weeping and shouting that her little brother, whom she adored, had been left alone in their empty flat. 'He will be frightened to death, and his lovely round face and little hands will become dirty because I won't be there to wash them.' She rocked herself from side to side, and cursed 'those damned spies and informers'.

There was a third actress in the cell – a student from the Moscow Art Theatre, where Vera Baranovskaya had made her name. She was so young she seemed like a child in her red knitted cardigan. Her eyes were big and frightened and she never said a word. All day long she lay in a corner on the floor with her eyes wide open. Sometimes she sobbed. No one tried to console her; she was beyond consolation.

'We were all awed by her tragic fate,' Olga says. 'We were told she was under sentence of death because she had been betrothed to a man who had already been executed for plotting against the Soviet Government. They said she had been his accomplice. Afterwards, I heard that her life had been spared. This naïf child was condemned "only" to life imprisonment. Life imprisonment for a girl of sixteen or seventeen! I still remember her eyes full of tears, her life finished before she had started to live.'

Two other prisoners, a mother and daughter, had been arrested in connection with the same plot. Like the girl's fiancé, the mother's son (an officer) had been shot. The mother and daughter never spoke to anyone. They lay on the floor clasping each other as if they were afraid of being separated even for a moment. 'Some of the other female prisoners looked like university students,' Olga says. 'I do not know why they had been arrested, but they were all quite brave and cheerful and they were very good to my sons. They played games with them and told them stories.'

At night the prisoners – streetwalkers, thieves, innocent victims – settled down in their places to sleep. Some slept on wide benches along the walls, some on top of the table at which food was eaten during the day. As newcomers, Olga, Oleg, Gleb and Maria were shown a space on the floor and given blankets and pillows, and dirty coarse sacks to use as mattresses. 'Like the girl in the red cardigan, like the mother and daughter whispering to each other and praying, I could not sleep,' Olga says. 'There was a noise in my head and my heart beat fast. Everything was as unreal as in a nightmare. From time to time the door of our cell opened and a jailer called out a name. The poor woman thus called got up and went, but where? Already that day I had heard so many tales about this prison. I heard that there was a specially made chair for torturing prisoners; that in a remote corner of the yard prisoners were shot without trial. So many tales … I do not know how many of them were true, but during that first night in Moscow I believed them all.'

There were fleas in their bedding and the food was bad. In the mornings, hot water was brought in huge tin kettles and those with a supply of tea and bread had a sort of breakfast. Those who had nothing just gulped the hot water. About noon a big pail filled with soup was brought in, along with a few tin bowls and some spoons of tin or wood. The soup was a foul-smelling and evil-looking liquid containing tainted salted herring heads. Olga could not remember seeing any vegetables in it. Their hunger was such that they devoured the soup to the last drop. In the evening, there was another ration of boiled water and a piece of rye bread.

Meanwhile, back in Petrograd, life was equally uncertain for people like Pitirim Sorokin and his wife, Dr Elena Baratynskaya. 'Every night we hear the rattle of trucks bearing new victims,' he says. 'Every night we hear the rifle fire of execution. So many arrests are made daily that cloisters and schools are being transformed into prisons. Getting up in the morning, no man or woman knows whether they will be free that night.'[21]

23

The Entente Outsider

Alexander Kerensky arrived at Thurso in Northern Scotland in the Secret Service trawler on 18 June 1918. 'There I stepped on to non-Russian soil for the first time in my life,' he says. 'We stayed overnight in the peaceful town, which the war scarcely seemed to have affected.' Speaking on behalf of the Foreign Office, a British officer impressed on him the need to remain incognito 'until you have spoken to government officials'. Kerensky accepted those terms and went to bed a relieved man. The following evening he took the train from Scotland to London. In addition to Vladimir Fabrikant, he had the company of a Royal Navy commander who had been briefed to ensure that he stuck to the Foreign Office script.[1]

Exhausted and unshaven but nevertheless full of hope that democratic Britain would support his campaign against the Bolsheviks, Kerensky arrived at King's Cross on the morning of Thursday 20 June. Jacob Gavronsky, who had returned to London as head of the press section of the Russian Embassy (a thankless task for which he declined payment), was at the station to meet him. Despite the need for secrecy, he had received a telegram from the travellers alerting him to their arrival. 'Kerensky had grown a beard and moustache on the voyage,' Gavronsky says, 'and I did not recognise him.'

Kerensky stayed with Dr Gavronsky and his wife Maria at 7 Cambridge Terrace, a Nash-designed mansion block overlooking Regent's Park. 'I only needed a day or so of wandering around the streets, looking at the shops and eating in the restaurants,' Kerensky says, 'to assure myself that despite the oppressive war Britain was still as strong, well-organised and determined as ever.' There were few outward signs of the wartime economy. The cast-iron railings around the parks had been melted down to make weapons, street lighting had disappeared and blackout curtains covered every window. Women were running many of the public services and foodstuffs, tobacco, beer, coffee and tea were strictly rationed.[2]

Among Kerensky's visitors in those early days were his old friends David and Juliet Soskice, and the not-so-friendly Russian chargé d'affaires, Konstantin Nabokov. The diplomat was extremely pessimistic about his mission and its chances of success. 'After the dismal failure of Kerensky's attempt to "capture" Petrograd, British public opinion ceased to take any interest whatsoever in his fate,' he wrote in his memoirs. 'His name appeared occasionally in press telegrams but the impression prevailed that as a statesman he had ended his career.'[3]

Nabokov's concept of 'British public opinion' had been gleaned in the salons of Belgravia and from the coverage of Russian affairs in Fleet Street newspapers. The British public had lost interest in Kerensky because no one, including the foreign correspondents in Petrograd and Moscow, had had any news about him for months.

On 23 June Philip Kerr, Lloyd George's private secretary - tall, fair-haired, 'always rumpled but never dishevelled' - called to see him at Cambridge Terrace. Kerr (pronounced 'Carr'), a grandson of the Duke of Norfolk, had the sort of aristocratic pedigree that would have guaranteed his execution in Soviet Russia. He had been a central figure in 'Milner's Kindergarten' in South Africa and it was largely through Lord Milner's influence that he had got a job at Number 10.[i] Lloyd George regarded Kerr as his most trusted adviser but he was not popular with some of the Prime Minister's colleagues. Balfour resented his role as a 'second Foreign Office' and Curzon thought him 'a most unsafe and insidious intermediary ... the chosen agent of most of his master's intrigues'.[4]

When Kerr asked Kerensky the purpose of his visit to London, Kerensky adhered to his brief to say nothing until he had met Lloyd George and declined to make any statement. Kerr departed in a huff.[5]

It was an open secret in Russia that Britain was offering political and military support to White Russian monarchists in the Civil War but, even so, Balfour had advised Lloyd George against even seeing Kerensky because such a meeting could create difficulties with the Bolsheviks. 'It is most important,' Balfour cabled the Marquess of

---

i Kerr's first job in Downing Street was as a member of the 'Garden Suburb', a privileged little group who cultivated the Prime Minister's mind at meetings in a cabin constructed in the back garden of Number 10.

Reading, the British Ambassador in Washington, 'to avoid if possible the fact of Kerensky's presence in England being twisted into proof that there is an ill-will to the Bolshevik Government.' Even France was too close for Balfour's comfort. He told the Prime Minister he hoped Kerensky would leave Britain as soon as possible for the United States, where his presence would be 'much less embarrassing to the Allied cause'.[6]

The Bolsheviks, however, required no further proof of Britain's ambiguous attitude towards them. 'Your policy towards Russia right from the beginning has been vacillating and indecisive,' Trotsky told Bruce Lockhart. 'Your Lloyd George is like a man playing roulette and scattering chips on every number.'[7]

Kerensky had no knowledge of these behind-the-scenes intrigues, or of Balfour's low opinion of him. He believed implicitly in Britain's sense of justice and he expected her Prime Minister to give him a fair hearing. He was about to discover that Britain's policy towards Red and White Russia, insofar as it could be called a policy, was a mass of ambiguity and contradiction.

At nine o'clock the following morning - 24 June 1918 – Alexander Kerensky received the first of many surprises about British political life when he arrived at 10 Downing Street with Jacob Gavronsky. The official residence of the holder of the nation's highest elected office was a modest terraced house in a nondescript little street off Whitehall. Inside its soot-blackened walls Lloyd George lived in an upstairs apartment with his wife, Margaret, while his mistress, Frances Stevenson, occupied a secretarial office next to the Cabinet Room downstairs.[ii]

The second surprise was the Prime Minister himself, not so much his appearance - 'a short, stocky man with a shock of snow-white hair, a noble brow and small, piercing yet sparkling eyes that lit up the whole of his youthful, ruddy face' – but the effusiveness of his welcome. 'He greeted me as if we had been old friends whom he had not seen in a long time'.[8]

Lloyd George listened intently to Gavronsky's translation as

---

ii Lloyd George's pet name for Frances Stevenson was 'Pussy'. She called him 'Tom Cat'. According to his son Richard, his father was 'the greatest Don Juan in the history of British politics'.

Kerensky, now minus his beard but still sporting a moustache, announced that as the leader of the Provisional Government he represented all Russians 'except the reactionaries and the Bolsheviks'. His mission was endorsed, he said, by the Executive Committee of the Constituent Assembly, the Conference of the Party Leaders of the Socialist Revolutionaries, the Social Democrats (minus the Bolsheviks) and the Kadet Party. All these parties were united in wanting Allied intervention to oust the Bolsheviks and the Germans.[9]

The Bolsheviks had seized Central Russia, he said, and were using German resources to suppress opposition there. The main resistance to them was on the Volga, where members of the Constituent Assembly had set up a democratic enclave centred on Samara and, with the assistance of the Czech Legion, were resisting the Bolsheviks. There were no Bolsheviks to speak of in Siberia and a local democratic government had been formed at Tomsk. Intervention through Siberia, he added, would be most welcome, provided it were an Allied, and not solely a Japanese, expedition, but if all the Allies took part the Japanese contingent might be as big as it liked.[10]

From this robust declaration Lloyd George correctly surmised that Kerensky's primary purpose was to secure recognition for himself and his associates as the legitimate government of Russia. Given Balfour's outright opposition to his visitor, this presented the Prime Minister with a problem, so he resorted to his legendary guile. He informed Kerensky that while the Entente would wish to stand by Russian democracy to the very end, the Bolshevik Government was apparently as hostile to the Allies as it was to Germany, and intervention would be considered an act of war and, therefore, could not be contemplated.[11]

Kerensky realised from that remark that Lloyd George had no real grasp of what was happening in Russia, while the Prime Minister must have wished he had never agreed to the meeting. As he wrote in his self-serving memoirs, 'The difficulty I found in discussing the situation with him was that I could get no clear assurance that he represented any organised force, apart from resolutions passed in secret by disgruntled Socialists. Resolutions on paper are of little value against machineguns, and in the heart of Russia it was the Bolsheviks who had the machineguns.'[12]

Ignoring Lloyd George's reticence, Kerensky ploughed on. The influence of the Bolsheviks was waning, he said, and their power in a military sense was negligible, though they were powerful enough as a police force to deal with a powerless and unorganised civilian population. Large play had been made in the West over the creation of the Red Guards, compulsory military service and so forth but in practice these measure had produced no meaningful results.

He was attempting to refute Lloyd George's misconception that Lenin was hostile towards Germany when Philip Kerr uttered a diplomatic cough and reminded his boss that it was time for him to leave for the House of Commons. The Prime Minister rose from his chair, bid Kerensky goodbye and then, apparently as an afterthought, announced that he was going to Paris for a session of the Supreme War Council at Versailles on 2 July. 'Why don't you come too?' he suggested. 'You'll be invited to Versailles.'

Considering the circumstances, this was an extraordinary thing for Lloyd George to have suggested but it was music to Kerensky's ears. An invitation to Versailles would be tantamount to recognition. He left Number 10 with the exhilarating feeling that he had been talking to somebody who really appreciated his mission. When he returned to Cambridge Terrace, he made plans to travel to Paris with Jacob Gavronsky, who had an apartment in the French capital, and Vladimir Fabricant, whose family had sought refuge there from the Bolsheviks.[13]

Lloyd George later told Lord Riddell, the press baron who acted as his liaison man with Fleet Street, that his Russian visitor was an attractive personality with the most piercing eyes he had ever seen but that he did not regard him as 'a man of action'. This annoying phrase would follow Kerensky for the rest of his life. Stephen Kerensky says, 'It suited both the rightwing establishment and the left intellectuals in Britain to lay the blame for everything on the isolated figure of Alexander Kerensky. It also suited fellow travellers such as Sidney and Beatrice Webb and George Bernard Shaw to fictionalise the Provisional Government's failings and to ignore Lenin's atrocities to prevent the very idea of revolution from falling into disrepute.'[14]

While Lloyd George's primary concern had to be the defeat of the Central Powers, he could not afford to miss an opportunity to extend British influence in Russia. He backed neither Churchill, who argued for a hard intervention against the Bolsheviks, nor Balfour, who wanted to steer clear of involvement. In the end he had one foot in and one foot out and the only thing he achieved was Soviet mistrust.

Even while he had been talking to Kerensky at Number 10 a force of 560 Australian volunteers, consisting of experienced officers and NCOs drawn from the armies fighting in France, had landed at Murmansk. The Allied intervention would develop into an Allied rescue mission to save the Czech Legion and would culminate in a campaign to defeat the Red Army with the assistance of the Czechs and anti-Bolshevik White forces. It achieved neither of these objectives.

Kerensky's visit to Number 10 had remained a secret to all but a few. On 26 June readers of *The Times* were informed that his whereabouts were a mystery. Herman Bernstein, an American author who had spent six months in Petrograd, was quoted as saying, 'I tried to find Mr Kerensky in Russia and Norway but could not get any tangible information regarding his movements.' The mystery was solved later that morning when the Labour Party Conference opened in the Central Hall at Westminster. Kerensky suddenly appeared on the platform alongside the Leader of the Labour Party, Arthur Henderson. 'He was received with tumultuous enthusiasm by the vast majority,' *The Times* reported the next day, 'but a small and noisy minority of extremists were unable to restrain their feelings of chagrin.'[15]

'I am responsible for M. Kerensky's being here,' Henderson informed the delegates. 'I learned in Russia to know and admire him. Hearing that he was in London, I remembered what is due to distinguished visitors and invited him to visit this conference.' Despite the vocal objections of Maxim Litvinov, it was agreed on a show of hands that Kerensky should say a few words to the conference and then make a speech the next afternoon.

As Gavronsky translated, he said, 'Comrades, I came straight here from Moscow and I feel it my duty as a statesman, as a man and as a politicians, my moral duty, to tell you that the Russian people and the Russian democracy are fighting against tyranny. They are going to fight to the end and I am certain that they will shortly join you in the fight for the great cause of freedom.'[16]

Kerensky was among friends: other foreign guests at the conference included the ubiquitous Albert Thomas, the Belgian statesman Émile Vandervelde and the future Swedish Prime Minister Hjalmar Branting.

The following day a thunderous burst of cheers greeted him when he stepped on to the platform to make his speech. Most of the hall broke into 'For He's a Jolly Good Fellow' at which, to Henderson's amazement, Kerensky planted a comradely kiss on his cheek. 'Seldom in the history of Labour Party Conferences,' *The Times* reported, 'has a visitor been given so rousing a welcome.'[17]

Kerensky spoke in Russian while Henderson read an English translation of his speech. Russia, he said, had gone through great trials before and always emerged with renewed strength. Bleeding now at every pore, she still opposed the enemy's invasion. 'I bear witness,' he said, 'that the Russian people will never recognise the Treaty of Brest-Litovsk, the treaty which is hurling her into the abyss of annihilation.' Russian soldiers, some armed with sticks, he said, had withstood the German onslaught for three years and had thereby saved the Western Front from collapse. The Revolution had given them new courage but it could not revive their emaciated bodies. Warnings to her Allies had gone unheeded.

The Germans called for peace, he said, and fanatics and German agents had duped Russian soldiers into accepting it. Now Russia was ruled by terror and her liberties were trampled by tyranny. 'Perhaps, abandoned by all, Russia will perish,' he concluded. 'But she will never, of her own will, submit to the humiliating and shameful treason of Brest-Litovsk. It is for you, the oldest democracies in the world, to decide whether it is, or is not, possible to remain a calm spectator of so great a tragedy.'

It was a tremendous speech. As well as striking a chord with 'disinterested' Britons, it presented a challenge to Lloyd George: how would he react? The old political vaudevillian, however, was furious with Kerensky for upstaging him. No one had fought harder than the Russian Prime Minister to keep his country in the war and yet Lloyd George had completely failed to exploit his presence in London for publicity purposes. Instead, Arthur Henderson, the man he had squeezed out of the War Cabinet, had recognised the visitor's headline-making potential and had acted accordingly.

One of Kerensky's visitors at Cambridge Terrace was Paul Painlevé, the former French Minister of War. Hearing of Kerensky's arrival in London, he had crossed the Channel to offer his support. Painlevé wanted him to know that the Kerensky Offensive had been of vital importance to France. He had tried, he said, to persuade General Nivelle to postpone his attack until the Russian Army had recovered its fighting fitness but Nivelle had refused to do so and, as a result, the French Army had been crippled. 'After Nivelle's risky venture, we could no longer dream of a decisive offensive on our front,' Painlevé said. The Kerensky Offensive, despite its ultimate failure, had given France valuable breathing space in which to regroup her forces at a most difficult time. Overcome with emotion, the Frenchman crossed the room and grabbed Kerensky in a Gallic embrace.[18]

Kerensky also received support from Harold Williams, who praised him in the *Daily Chronicle* as 'The Man Who Tried to Save Russia':

> When the Revolution broke out last year in the streets of Petrograd, Kerensky at once came to the forefront in the Duma. It was largely due to his efforts that the Duma took the lead in the movement. He was the first deputy to go out and greet the rebellious soldiers who came to the gates of the Tauride Palace.
>
> His efforts in bringing about an agreement between the two rival groups, the Duma Committee and the Soviet of Workmen's Deputies, won high praise from his former political opponents. For the first time Kerensky displayed statesmanlike instincts in addition to his strong democratic passion.
>
> Though formerly a terrorist, he was an absolute opponent of capital punishment, and he was very active in preventing any display of brutality against representatives of the old regime, including the Tsar. As Minister of Justice, he arranged for the return of all political exiles. His generosity in this respect led to his own undoing.[19]

Kerensky's enemies among White émigrés were quick to react. On Saturday 29 June 1918 General Theodore Lodijensky, a Tsarist officer, marched up to the Military Control Office in Southampton in an attempt to prevent Kerensky from travelling to France and pleading his case to the French Government. Captain H. D. Patterson reported to MI5:

> General Lodijensky avers that the sole object of Kerensky's tour is to engineer matters in such a manner that he, Kerensky, will be put at the head of the Intervention. General Lodijensky states that Kerensky is more than desirous of proceeding to America to enlist the sympathies of President Wilson. He asserts that should Kerensky be made the

nominal and 'de facto' head of the Intervention the whole cause would be ruined: that Kerensky's name bears no weight with the people whose sympathies have been laboriously enlisted. General Lodijensky is a man who strikes me as knowing what he is talking about, a man who is very much in earnest; in fact he creates quite a much better impression than Kerensky.[20]

But the General, who would end his career as an extra playing Tsarist officers in Hollywood movies, was too late. The previous night Kerensky, now clean-shaven and accompanied by Jacob Gavronsky and Vladimir Fabrikant, had passed through the Military Control Office in Southampton and taken ship to Le Havre. The Royal Navy was in charge of the Channel and they arrived safely in France, where Kerensky received a warm welcome from *L'Homme Libre*, the newspaper owned by Georges Clémenceau.

'This apostle of the Russian Revolution may be exaggerating the chances of an immediate Slav resurrection,' the paper opined, 'but we ought to listen, examine his reasons, and not allow his appeal to fall on deaf ears. Here, as in England and in America, he should find only friends and allies.'[21]

Kerensky reached Paris that same day - Sunday 30 June 1918 - to find the city under siege. The streets were uncharacteristically quiet and empty, 'more reminiscent of a Scottish country town than of the capital of the Latin races', according to the resident *Times* correspondent. The complexities of Parisian life had been reduced to a minimum to enable the city to be turned into a garrison at short notice to repel a German assault.[22]

The German Army was entrenched at Château Thierry, a town on the Marne just fifty miles northeast of Paris. The Kaiser's squadrons of Gotha G.IV twin-engine bombers had stepped up their night-time attacks. And the *Paris-Geschütz* was firing twenty shots a day, killing people indiscriminately in many parts of the capital. While Vladimir Fabrikant set off to rejoin his family, Alexander Kerensky moved into Jacob Gavronsky's apartment at 1 rue Chernovitz on the corner of rue Renoir in Passy, the main Russian district of Paris.

The following day Kerensky paid a courtesy call to the Russian Embassy in the rue de Grenelle. Vasily Maklakov, the former Kadet leader who had been appointed Russian Ambassador to France, had been sacked by Trotsky before he could be accredited to the Quai d'Orsay. Nevertheless, he continued to occupy the Embassy building, a splendid Eighteenth Century mansion with a large garden adjoining the Italian Embassy. Like Konstantin Nabokov, Maklakov had little sympathy with Kerensky's mission. His brother Nikolai Maklakov, the former Tsarist Minister of the Interior, was a Bolshevik prisoner in Russia and he had no desire to make life more difficult for him. He offered Kerensky little hope and even less support.[iii]

On Tuesday 2 July Kerensky was nowhere to be seen when Lloyd George joined the Supreme War Council at Versailles. Not surprisingly, considering his performance at the Labour Party Conference, his invitation had failed to arrive in the post. The War Council, however, had extended an invitation to another Russian - none other than General Kornilov's co-conspirator, the financier Vasily Zavoiko. This scoundrel, aided and abetted by the British Foreign Office, had escaped from Russia following Kornilov's death in April. Travelling under the alias of 'Colonel Kurbatov', he was acceptable to the Allies because, unlike Kerensky, he was in contact with the White armies who were receiving British and French aid.[23]

The most important item on the War Council's agenda was the Allied intervention in Russia, with the objective of reestablishing the Eastern Front and relieving pressure in France and Flanders. With the United States now fighting shoulder to shoulder with the Allies, the War Council approved Lloyd George's suggestion that it should appeal to Woodrow Wilson to send American troops to Russia.[24] President Wilson, heir to the Monroe Doctrine, was opposed in principle to collective intervention in another country's affairs. He was particularly opposed to an intervention that might lead to the restoration of the Tsarist autocracy.

Anglo-French forces, however, were so stretched at that moment that the War Council regarded his support as a matter of vital importance. An appeal was sent to Washington with the chilling warning that 'failure to intervene immediately must inevitably cause effects which can only be described as disastrous to the Allied cause'.[iv]

On receiving this letter, Wilson overruled State Department ob-

---

iii Nikolai Maklakov was executed in prison two months later on 5 September 1918
iv President James Monroe warned European powers in 1823 against collective intervention in the Americas, where former colonies of Spain and Portugal were struggling to assert their independence.

jections and agreed to the limited participation of American troops in the Russian adventure. The 5000-strong American North Russia Expeditionary Force (a.k.a. the 'Polar Bear Expedition') would be sent to Archangel, while another 8000 soldiers would be shipped to Vladivostok. Wilson insisted their task was 'to guard military stores which may subsequently be needed by Russian forces and to render such aid as may be acceptable to the Russians in the organisation of their own self-defence'.

Kerensky's position became even more tenuous on Saturday 6 July when Frank Lindley, the British chargé d'affaires who had been withdrawn with other foreign diplomats from Petrograd to Archangel, dispatched a cable to Balfour. Despite the fact that no fewer than five districts had voted for Kerensky in the Constituent Assembly's elections, he stated that the former Prime Minister had 'not a single friend in this country among any party [and] was universally blamed as the person principally responsible for the existing state of things'.

Lindley claimed that Kerensky's reception in Britain had produced 'the worst impression' among Russians and he urged that he should be prevented from speaking in public, or, if that were impossible, no mention of his speeches should be permitted in correspondents' telegrams being sent to Russia.[25] How Lindley was able to divine the 'universal' mindset of the Russian people from his remote northern outpost remains unclear but his outburst fitted neatly into Balfour's anti-Kerensky agenda.

Oblivious to these hostile comments, Kerensky addressed a meeting of Socialist members of the Chamber of Deputies that same day. Determined to overcome the Allied belief that Russia had reneged on her duties to the Entente, he produced a copy of a resolution passed at a secret meeting of the Constituent Assembly on 18 May 1918 denouncing the Treaty of Brest-Litovsk (and correcting his own statements on the purpose of intervention). 'Russia still considers itself at war with Germany and that the union with France and the other Allies is not broken,' he said.

> It cannot be broken by a government not recognised by the Russian people. At the same time, the Russian nation will not accept a violation of sovereignty by the Allied powers, nor the occupation of territory, nor intervention in domestic affairs. The appearance of allied troops in Russia would be consented to only for strategic reasons in the struggle

against Germany. The struggle must be led by the Russian people and assistance must come from all the Allies in common.[26]

When news of Kerensky's speech reached New York, the Inter-Party League for Restoration of Free Russia hailed him as 'the leader of Russian democracy'. 'Like you, we stand for the immediate convocation of the All-Russian Constituent Assembly as the only body which has the right to decide the fate and to define the governmental structure of Russia,' the league declared in a telegram to Paris. 'We are glad that you are again on the firing line and hope that your patriotic work, supported by the best representatives of Russian democracy, will meet with success.'

Kerensky's attempts to discuss the situation with the United States Ambassador fell on stony ground. William Graves Sharp had originally been nominated as Ambassador to Russia but the Bolsheviks objected to his appointment because, as a Congressman, he had voted to end the commercial treaty between Russia and the USA. Sharp had no intention of upsetting the Bolsheviks again. When Kerensky and Gavronsky arrived at the American Embassy at 5 rue de Chaillot, they were palmed off on the Ambassador's assistant, Lee Meriwether.

Meriwether was a fifty-six-year-old lawyer, journalist and politician from a humble Southern background. As a young man, he had travelled widely in France and had written a bestseller, *How to See Europe on 50 Cents a Day*. Meriwether knew that the State Department was firmly opposed to armed intervention in Russia and he had been briefed to scupper any notion that it might change its mind. When Kerensky informed him that intervention was the only way to restore the Eastern Front and thus save Russia, he became quite hostile.

Taking his text from the French Revolution, Meriwether reminded his visitor about what had happened when the patriots Dumouriez and Lafayette brought in 'foreign bayonets' to stop the Jacobin bloodshed. The result was to unite Frenchmen of all shades of opinion against the invaders. Dumouriez had fled to England and died in exile, while Lafayette spent years in an Austrian dungeon.[27]

Kerensky brusquely denied that the same thing would happen to him. It was only a matter of time before the Bolsheviks called in the Germans to help them retain power, he said, and the Russian people would then turn against the traitors who had betrayed their country to Germany. It would be Lenin who would play the role of Dumouriez.

The meeting was not a success. 'Kerensky speaks so little French that he refused even to try to talk in that language; he knows not a word of English,' Meriwether wrote in his diary that night.

> [He] is tall and spare rather than stout but he is by no means the delicate man living on his nerves, as many reports have described him; on the contrary, he appears physically vigorous; eyes burn like coals of fire but he keeps them half closed which gives one the impression that he is not altogether frank and candid. But once started on his hobby, the politics of Russia, he has the power to persuade and convince, although one does not understand the language in which he speaks. However, even in the heat of his argument his eyes remain half closed, his glance does not meet yours and the impression he makes is on the whole the reverse of favourable.

For a man who prided himself on his even-handedness, Meriwether's assessment was hardly fair. He had made no allowance for Kerensky's physical and mental exhaustion. He had also failed to realise that Kerensky's habit of speaking with his eyes half-closed was down to short-sightedness.[28]

Things improved on 9 July when Georges Mandel, Georges Clémenceau's righthand man, turned up at Gavronsky's apartment and invited Kerensky to visit the Prime Minister the following day. Gavronsky had returned to London, so Kerensky asked Vladimir Fabrikant to accompany him as translator. The Prime Minister, 'a thick-set man of advanced years with small, beady eyes beneath bushy eyebrows', met his visitor in the War Ministry where he was based in order to keep in touch with French commanders in the field.[29]

Clémenceau was more than 'a man of advanced years' – as the young mayor of Montmartre he had experienced the Prussian shelling of Paris in 1871. He was now in his seventy-seventh year and his portly figure and shaggy white moustache gave him the look of an illustrious old walrus.[v] He offered Kerensky his hand. 'How nice to see you,' he said. 'Take a seat and tell me what I can do for you.' This sounded promising until Kerensky made the mistake of mentioning the French Government's promise through Albert Thomas that it

---

[v] In his prime, Clemenceau had been leader of the Radical Party and, as a leading Dreyfusard, had championed the cause of Captain Dreyfus. It was Clémenceau who had published Émile Zola's famous 'J'Accuse' article on 13 January 1898 in his newspaper L'Aurore.

would support the Provisional Government. Clémenceau turned to his Foreign Minister, Stephen Pichon, and asked whether he was aware of any such promise. Pichon 'hastily mumbled a negative reply'.

There was no more spineless individual in French politics than Stephen Pichon. Serving as French Minister to China in 1900, he had earned the undying enmity of the diplomatic corps for his fatalism during the Boxer Rising when he would walk around the besieged British Legation mournfully intoning, *'Nous sommes finis; nous sommes perdus!' The Times* correspondent, George Morrison, described him as 'a craven-hearted cur'.[30]

Pausing for a moment, Clémenceau turned to Kerensky with a smile and said there had probably been some misunderstanding. He added that the French Government would, of course, assist the patriotic forces of Russia in every possible way and offered to have Kerensky's reports to his colleagues in Russia transmitted in code through the Quai d'Orsay to the French consulate in Moscow, a valuable service to Kerensky (and no doubt a useful method of eavesdropping).

After fixing a date for a second meeting, Kerensky left the War Ministry in a positive frame of mind. That evening, the Socialist Party threw a banquet in his honour at the Hotel Moderne in Saint Germain. Speaking through an interpreter, he told them:

> I'm a Socialist. I will always be a Socialist, but at this very moment, let me remind you that I am Russian, because I definitely sense that if we don't succeed in establishing the Russian State against the Prussians and those who serve them, democracy will fail, and with it the Internationale. On the contrary, if we help Russia get back on her feet, if we save democracy, the world and socialism will equally be saved.[31]

At their second meeting in the War Ministry Clémenceau handed Kerensky a cable from Washington in which President Wilson's Secretary of State, Robert Lansing, said it would be 'undesirable' for the Russian leader to visit his country. As he had no plans to visit the US (and knowing nothing of Balfour's desire that he should do so), Kerensky expressed mystification at his rejection.[32]

As proof of his statement that Russia was still at war with Germany despite the Peace of Brest-Litovsk, Kerensky could point to the existence on French soil of the Honorary Russian Legion, a battalion-sized group composed of loyal fighters from the Russian Expeditionary Force. Indeed, while Kerensky and Clémenceau were speaking, this legion was preparing to take part in one of the most significant battles of the war.

Having failed in his Spring Offensive, Ludendorff had planned an extremely ambitious gambit to destroy the British in their Flanders redoubts. His first blow was a diversionary attack along the Marne in order to draw as many Allied troops as possible away from Belgium. The Second Battle of the Marne was timed to begin at dawn on 15 July, twenty-four hours after the French celebrated Bastille Day. The Honorary Russian Legion would go into battle as a component of the First Moroccan Infantry Division.

'On 14 July there was to be a ceremonial parade past the Arc de Triomphe,' Kerensky says. 'A detachment of Allied troops had been invited to march in it. Invitations had been issued to the Russian chargé d'affaires and the military attaché for a Russian Army contingent to take part. On the eve of the parade, however, the French Chief of Staff told them that the Russians were being excluded because "Russia had become a neutral country which had concluded peace with France's enemies, and that the friends of our enemies were our enemies".'[33]

When Kerensky raised this rebuff with Clémenceau, the old walrus turned an alarming shade of scarlet and repeated, '*La Russie est un pays neuter qui a conclu la paix séparés avec nos ennemis. Les amis de nos ennemis sont nos ennemis.* Those were my words and my order.'

The Prime Minister's tone was so menacing that Stephen Pichon almost fell off his chair. Kerensky had been about to take his first report out of his briefcase for transmission to Moscow. Instead, knowing that Russian troops would be dying on the Marne in defence of France, he rose to his feet. 'In that case, M. le Premier,' he said, 'there is no point in my remaining in your office.' He bowed and stalked out.

In the next few days Raymond Poincaré, President of France, and Paul Deschanel, President of the Chamber of Deputies, met Kerensky to try to heal the breach. They acknowledged Russia's great sacrifices in the common cause and begged Kerensky to accept that Clémenceau's actions were those of a man who was under tremendous strain. But the damage was done. Lloyd George had stabbed him in the back and Clémenceau had delivered the coup de grace. Kerensky abandoned his mission to France and made plans to return to London.

News of his activities intrigued Louise Bryant, who was writing a book about her experiences in Red Russia:

> Kerensky again in the limelight! Kerensky visiting the world's capitals and hobnobbing with the world's potentates! A new Kerensky, reported to have grown a beard to hide his too apparent youth. Socialist-comrade-Kerensky now out of politics – comes thence on a special mission: to explain the revolution! Ah, well and good – the world is surely in need of explanation. But who in any country, in any language, can explain the enigmatic Kerensky?[34]

Having written him off as a dismal failure, the world's press had been following Kerensky's comeback with interest. On 28 July 1918 he returned to the row of creamy white classical mansions in Cambridge Terrace. As the father of two boys, he got along famously with the Gavronskys' sons, Lev and Asher. Many an enjoyable weekend was spent at 'Rusthall', the family's rented country house in Langton Road, Tunbridge Wells. Kerensky could be seen striding down the leafy Kentish lanes dressed like an English squire in tweed suit and brogues and humming one of his favourite Rimsky-Korsakov tunes.

He also enjoyed visiting his friends David and Juliet Soskice at 5 Woodlands Road, Barnes, a lively meeting place for writers, artists, refugees and politicians. Soskice introduced him to his former employer, C. P. Scott, a staunch Liberal who had welcomed the fall of the Romanovs in the *Manchester Guardian* as 'a wonderful and glorious event'. Scott was devoted to Lloyd George. He was also violently opposed to British military intervention in Russia to bring down the Bolshevik regime.[35]

He expressed his views forcefully to Kerensky. 'Your mission has no chance of succeeding,' he said. 'Right now, Lloyd George's Government is debating its policy toward Russia, but Russia is not even being mentioned as an ally of the Western powers.'[36]

Scott was concerned that the Entente's plans to reshape the political landscape of Europe were doomed to fail. He referred Kerensky to an open letter from Lord Lansdowne which had been published in the *Daily Telegraph* on 29 November 1917. Lansdowne, a veteran of European affairs under Gladstone and Salisbury, argued that the reconstruction of Germany and Austria should be one of the primary aims of a negotiated peace. 'To end the war honourably would be a great achievement,' he wrote. 'To prevent the same curse falling upon our children would be a greater achievement still. For, just as this war has been more dreadful than any in history, so we may be sure the next war would be even more dreadful than this.'

Kerensky understood the humane motive behind Lansdowne's letter and lamented that 'the policymakers of the world paid no heed to the warning'. Indeed, Clémenceau was determined to inflict as much harm on the Central Powers as he possibly could to make them incapable of ever threatening France again.[37]

When Kerensky learned from 'a well-informed Englishman' – possibly C. P. Scott – that the Kornilov conspirator Vasily Zavoiko had been invited to Versailles in his place, his faith in his former Allies sank to a new low. His experiences in London and Paris had made it painfully clear that his enemies were more powerful than his friends, and that the Anglo-French leaders had no genuine interest in restoring Russian democracy. 'We had imagined that somewhere beyond the far, endless Russian horizon – far from the cruel oppression of Tsarism – there were blessed lands of every democratic and humanitarian perfection,' he said. 'But the Western Europe whose image lived in the heart of the Russian intelligentsia never really existed.'[38]

24

The Dragon's Teeth

War and revolution had planted dragon's teeth all over Russia. One by one they sprang into life in the shape of Red Guard assassination squads, renegade Cossack bands, British and French secret agents, White mercenaries and the bomb-throwers of Boris Savinkov's anti-Bolshevik cells. 'Murderous gangs scoured the country at night, with and without search warrants, beating up suspected officers, looting, lynching, raping and arresting,' Gleb Kerensky wrote in *Only One Freedom*.

> Often they were just sufficiently disciplined not to indulge in any excesses, but invariably they made it clear that they had half a mind to do so. The scale of operations may be gauged from the fact that two of the people I knew personally were lynched and neither was a major 'enemy of the working classes' even within the Bolsheviks' own interpretation of those days: had they been arrested, they would have been set free. The mass rape of nurses in one of the hospitals resulted in three pregnancies. One can gauge from that the number of nurses who actually suffered violence. Russia had suffered nothing like it since the days of the Tatar Invasion.[1]

Bruce Lockhart had moved to Moscow on his new and infinitely dangerous mission. He favoured Allied intervention and was negotiating with several anti-Bolshevik groups who hoped to benefit from it. Working with him was a Secret Service agent known in the covert world as Sidney Reilly, a slight, swarthy, smartly dressed man with a long straight nose, piercing eyes, brushed-back black hair and a large mouth.[2]

Reilly had arrived in Moscow in early May 1918 with a crazy plan to bribe the Latvian Riflemen in the Kremlin Garrison into turning their guns on Lenin and his Politburo and thus bringing down the

Soviet regime. Born Sigmund Rosenblum to Jewish parents in Russian Poland on 24 March 1874, Reilly had spent the early years of the war in the United States procuring weapons for the Tsar. He had an absolute loathing of the Bolshevik hierarchy, whom he regarded as 'a collection of alien and cowardly riff-raff who had waited in safety outside Russia until the real revolutionaries had done their work'.[3]

Without consulting Lockhart, he marched up to the Kremlin gates, identified himself as an emissary of Lloyd George and demanded to see Lenin. The guards escorted him to Vladimir Bonch-Bruevich who, instead of throwing him into the Lubianka's deepest dungeon, took the trouble to ring Bruce Lockhart to check his credentials. Lockhart managed to secure his release. He was furious with Reilly for jeopardising his mission with his hare-brained scheme.

One of the subversive groups on Lockhart's list was Boris Savinkov's Union for the Defence of the Fatherland and Freedom. Savinkov had learned from the new French Ambassador, Joseph Noulens, that serious Allied military intervention in Russia was a certainty. Basing his strategy on that assurance, he planned to overthrow the Bolshevik Government and set up a military dictatorship. 'Savinkov came to see me in Moscow at a moment when a price was on his head,' Lockhart says. 'His only disguise was a pair of huge horn-rimmed spectacles with darkened glasses. His conversation was mostly recriminations against the Allies and against the Russian counter-revolutionaries, with whom he was supposed to be cooperating.'[4]

The Foreign Office warned Lockhart to keep in touch with Savinkov through a third party (i.e., Sidney Reilly) 'but not so as to destroy his credibility with the Soviets'. In other words, he was expected to back both sides in the hope that the Bolsheviks would never find out that he was working with Reilly and Savinkov towards their removal.

The arrival in Moscow of Count Wilhelm von Mirbach as German Ambassador heralded a crackdown on anti-Bolshevik forces. The Cheka's arrest of one hundred key members of Savinkov's union on 16 May forced him to abandon plans for an insurrection in the new capital and to concentrate on three locations along the Upper Volga: Yaroslavl, Rybinsk and Murom. Yaroslavl, 160 miles to the northeast, was one of the key points between the projected Allied landings in Archangel and the Kremlin. Rybinsk was selected because it contained an arsenal of weapons and munitions, especially artillery, while Murom possessed a prize target in the Red Army General Staff Offices.

In June Lenin introduced 'War Communism', a massive programme aimed at providing the supplies and war matériel essential to a Bolshevik victory in the Civil War. Its main points were the expropriation of private businesses, the nationalisation of industry and the forced requisition of grain and other food products from the peasants. When uncontrolled inflation rendered paper currency worthless, the Bolsheviks resorted to a medieval barter system for the exchange and distribution of goods and services.

Further measures were introduced at the Fifth All-Russian Congress of Soviets, which convened in the Bolshoi Theatre in Moscow on 4 July to approve the Constitution of the Russian Socialist Republic. By decree, millions of Russian merchants, clergy, former policemen, anti-Bolshevik military officers and anyone who lived off unearned income were reduced to the rank of 'former people', with no voting rights, no social services and no other state benefits.[5]

Instead of hailing this Communist milestone, however, speaker after speaker among the Left SRs' 352 delegates denounced the Peace of Brest-Litovsk and accused the Bolsheviks of turning Russia into a vassal state of the German Empire. Count Mirbach, one of the architects of the treaty, listened unmoved in the gallery. Maria Spiridonova accused the Bolsheviks of stifling the freedom of the Soviets, of betraying the peasants and of trampling on the civil liberties of ordinary citizens. 'In Lenin's philosophy, you are only dung – only manure,' she told the peasant delegates. When a motion of no confidence in the Bolsheviks was defeated, the Left SRs walked out of the congress. That evening Spiridonova and her comrades decided to murder Count Mirbach in the belief that his death would end the Bolsheviks' appeasement of Germany.[6]

On the afternoon of 6 July two of the party's Chekist members, Blumkin and Andreyev, called at the German Embassy on the pretext of discussing a spy case with the Ambassador. After a brief conversation with Mirbach in the presence of the German military attaché, Blumkin pulled out a revolver and fired five shots, all of which missed their target. Andreyev then threw a bomb which knocked down the military attaché and, as the Ambassador attempted to run out of the room, he was shot and fatally wounded.

The assassins escaped through a window and fled in a waiting car to the Pokrovsky Barracks of the Cheka Combat Detachment. This unit was commanded by an accomplice, Dmitry Popov, who turned the barracks into the command centre of the uprising. Hearing that Mirbach had been murdered by two Chekist officers, Felix Dzerzhinsky went to the Pokrovsky Barracks and demanded that Blumkin and Andreyev be turned over to him. Instead, Popov arrested the Cheka chief and the Cheka Combat Detachment declared its allegiance to the revolt. The insurgents then occupied the Cheka headquarters inside the Lubianka, placing Dzerzhinsky's deputy, the sanguinary Martin Latsis, under arrest.[7]

On the evening of the sixth there was virtually nothing to prevent the Left SRs from overthrowing the Bolsheviks and seizing power. They had 2000 well-armed troops in the capital, compared with only 700 Bolshevik loyalists. Lenin was panicking. Most of his Latvian Rifles had been celebrating Saint John's Day at Khodynka Field - scene of Nicholas's coronation disaster – and were unable to return to Moscow because of a violent storm.[8] But the Left SRs showed no inclination to press home their advantage. Their primary purpose was to force the Bolsheviks to change their policies, so instead of occupying the Kremlin their leaders returned to the congress in the Bolshoi Theatre. Even as Spiridonova was denouncing the Bolshevik regime from the tribune, the Red Guards in charge of security surrounded the building and sealed off all the exits. Bolshevik delegates were allowed to leave but the Left SRs were corralled inside and arrested.

By dawn on the seventh, the uprising was over. The Bolsheviks had recaptured the Lubianka and most of the Left SR leaders, including Maria Spiridonova, were in prison. The Combat Detachment in the Pokrovsky Barracks had also surrendered. Thirteen of its leading members were executed.[i]

Meanwhile, Boris Savinkov had launched his armed uprising in Yaroslavl. Ignoring his advice to Kerensky that a true leader always led from the front, he maintained a discreet distance between himself and danger by remaining fifty-five miles away at Rybinsk. By a twist

---

i Maria Spiridonova was released from prison but in February 1919 she was rearrested, declared insane and incarcerated in the Kremlin barracks. She managed to escape but was later re-arrested and shot.

of fate, however, Lilya Birukova was in Yaroslavl with baby Irina, her sister Olga Soumarokova and Olga's daughter Elena. Petrograd had become filthy and dangerous for the sisters and the Volga city appealed to them because its civic organisations had opposed the October Coup and Bolshevik rule was said to be weak.

On 6 July one hundred Socialist Revolutionaries, Mensheviks and monarchists, commanded by Colonel A. P. Perkhurov, seized the centre of the city with the help of the local intelligentsia, a group of monks and a number of citizens. This motley force occupied the arsenal, the post office, the telegraph office and the banks. The coup's leaders called for the establishment of an elected government that would defend political and civic freedoms. Simultaneously, they instigated a reign of terror against Communist Party members and the employees of Soviet institutions. Some were arrested and executed and eighty of the survivors were placed in a 'death barge' in the middle of the Volga from which only half emerged alive.[9]

Loyal workers and peasants took up arms with Red Army units that surrounded the city. Soviet gunners placed field-guns on the heights and for the next fourteen day shelled the city. Lilya, Olga and the children endured the horrors of a full-scale artillery bombardment in which 2000 buildings were blown to pieces or burned to the ground. Entire neighbourhoods of this beautiful medieval city were obliterated and about 600 people were killed.

By 21 July Colonel Perkhurov and his staff had fled and his troops surrendered to the Red Army. The following day, on orders from Moscow, 350 insurgents were executed without a trial. Savinkov's reliance on French assurances that the Allies would stream south from Archangel had proved fatal to his underlings. With typical chutzpah, he admitted that the revolt 'cannot be called successful but it was not useless'. It had proved that 'not all Russians were ready to submit to Bolshevik terror. Honour was saved. Glory to those who fell in battle'.[10]

General Poole's belated landing took place on 2 August when a marine detachment, a French battalion and fifty American sailors went ashore at Archangel. An anti-Bolshevik government called the 'Supreme Administration of North Russia' was established under the presidency of Nikolai Tchaikovsky, an elderly socialist who was distantly related to the composer. Bruce Lockhart had warned the

British Government 'that, in the event of intervention, the amount of support we should get from the anti-Bolshevik Russians would be in exact proportion to the number of troops we sent ourselves. As we landed in Archangel with just over a thousand men, disaster was inevitable.'[11]

In the aftermath of the Yaroslavl debacle, Lilya and Olga lived in dread. Their flat was searched and Olga was arrested by the Cheka but managed to escape back to Petrograd. Lilya remained behind with the children because Irina was sick with a strain of cholera. Her nerves had been shattered by the bombardment and she was constantly harassed. Unable to stand the pressure any longer, she hiked seventeen miles with a knapsack on her back and two children until she was well beyond the city limits. Somehow, she managed to catch a train back to Petrograd. It was just as well she had been away – in her absence a Bolshevik squad had raided Vladimir's apartment to arrest her. Petrograd was starving and Lilya had no income. She sold her possessions one by one to buy food 'but there was never enough to feed us properly'.

During these terrifying weeks the levels of fear, doubt and insecurity inside the women's cell of the Lubianka rose to the point of hysteria every time the door opened and a warder read out a list of names. Most of these prisoners were put in solitary confinement and others were transferred to another prison but some were also set free. Olga Kerenskaya froze when the warder called out her name: was it another prison, even worse than this one? Was she to be separated from her family? Not daring to hope, she could hardly believe her ears when she heard that she and her children were being released.

'Why my children and I were not liquidated or left in prison I could never understand,' she says. 'Sometimes I think we still had some well-wishers even among the Bolsheviks.' Indeed, there were good grounds for believing this was the case. Alexander Kerensky had defended Ilya Ionov, Grigory Zinoviev's brother-in-law, in court and he had been a member of the Duma at the same time as Lev Kamenev, whom he had also defended. After Kamenev and 'The Five' were exiled to Siberia in 1915, he had constantly demanded their release.

There was also another possibility. 'When Trotsky and Kamenev returned to Petrograd after the Revolution, their children went to the same school as my sons,' Olga says. 'I heard that they worried their fathers by asking them to set free Oleg and Gleb Kerensky. It may not be true but I like to believe it was.'

Returning to Petrograd, Olga moved into her brother Vladimir Baranovsky's flat and Oleg and Gleb were placed in a Soviet boarding school. 'I thought that at least if they boarded there in a Bolshevik showplace, they would be assured of fixed rations,' Olga says. 'It would mean I would only see them on Sundays and that would mean for them an eight-mile walk, but it could not be helped.'

When foreign delegations visited Petrograd, they were taken to the school to see the 'new' educational creation of the Soviet Government. One such delegation consisted of British Labour Party grandees. Before their arrival the school was thoroughly spring-cleaned and the pupils were issued with new – or rather less worn-out – uniforms which were taken back the next day. The delegation was accompanied by Alexandra Kollontai, the Commissar for Social Welfare, whose elegant dress, fur wrap and plumed hat added a distinctly bourgeois touch to such occasions.

The children stood in rows. Madame Kollontai seized a fat, red-cheeked boy and held him up to the delegates in triumph. No one had the courage to enlighten the delegation that the boy had put on weight because his father was a black marketeer who had access to plenty of food. No one dared to point out the half-starved children in the class, including Gleb Kerensky and his friend Karassev, who was soon to die of tuberculosis and malnutrition. There was one embarrassing moment for the school authorities when a delegate asked a boy near him to name his greatest desire. Unhesitatingly, the boy cried out, 'Meat!'

Olga dreaded being alone in her flat and sublet half the rooms to a young couple who said they were students. 'They brought two small attaché cases with them but they hardly ever stayed in,' she says. 'It wasn't until later, after they had gone, that I realised that they were "responsible" Communists who were supposed to watch me.'

Marx had preached that 'revolutionary terror' was the only way to prevent 'the cannibalism of counter-revolution'. This was the perfect argument to transfer the showers of blood that had drenched the battlefields to the territories of the former Russian Empire. 'We stand for organised terror - this should be frankly admitted,' Felix

Dzerzhinsky, a severe Jacobin, declared in an interview published in *Novaia Zhizn* on 14 July 1918. 'Terror is an absolute necessity during times of revolution.'[12]

At least 28,000 people on average were executed every year in the Leninist Terror between December 1917 and February 1922 (compared with about 14,000 in Tsarist Russia between 1866 and 1917).[13] In August 1918 it was the turn of the Romanovs to face the terror of revolutionary justice. Alexander Kerensky had promised the Tsar that he and his family would be repatriated to Britain in a British Navy destroyer. King George V had written to the Tsar, 'I shall always remain your true friend.' But after studying Foreign Office cables from Russia, he decided that his cousin's presence in the United Kingdom would lead to a violent uprising. Judging the risk too great, and at the urging of his private secretary Lord Stamfordham, he withdrew the Tsar's lifeline.

Exile, however, was never a possibility for the Imperial Family after the fall of the Provisional Government. Lenin was planning to hold a grand show trial in which Trotsky, as state prosecutor, would tear the Tsar to shreds and leave the world in no doubt about his crimes. The Bolsheviks would never have consented to him leaving the country.

For the past seventy-eight days, Nicholas, his family and a small entourage had been confined to Ipatiev House, a merchant's residence at Ekaterinburg in the Urals, which had been renamed 'The House of Special Purpose'. The Romanovs led a quiet, frugal existence in the company of Dr Eugene Botkin and their three servants, Anna Demidova, Aloizy Trupp and Ivan Kharitonov. Thirteen-year-old Alexei was mostly confined to a wheelchair but his sisters Olga, now twenty-two, Tatiana, twenty-one, Maria, nineteen, and Anastasia, seventeen, helped with the household chores. Nicholas shovelled snow and chopped wood; Alexandra took jewels from their hiding places and sewed them into the children's clothing.

The family's fate was sealed when the Czech Legion closed on Ekaterinburg and it seemed that they might be liberated. The local Soviet leadership was increasingly inclined to kill them and the Allied intervention provided the perfect pretext for their execution. Lenin was informed of the planned executions but the telegram in which he is thought to have given his approval has never been found.

Nicholas tried to hold fast to the belief that his life was protected by

God's angels but when the moment of reckoning arrived on 17 July 1918 no wings were beating above his head. Yakov Yurovsky, the chief executioner, reported that the Romanovs were awakened around 2 a.m. and ordered to dress. The Tsar was told that anti-Bolshevik forces were approaching Ekaterinburg and that the house might be fired on.

The family were led down into a basement at the back of the house with Dr Botkin and the three servants. In an adjoining room, the firing squad consisting of three local Bolsheviks and seven Communist soldiers from Central Europe fortified themselves with vodka. Yurovsky ordered two chairs to be brought in and when the Empress and the Tsarevich had been seated, the executioners filed into the room. Yurovsky read from a piece of paper, 'In view of the fact that your relatives continued their offensive against Soviet Russia, the Presidium of the Ural Regional Soviet has decided to sentence you to death.'

Stunned, Nicholas asked, 'What? What?'

Yurovsky repeated the order and then shot the Tsar several times in the chest. The other executioners then opened fire on his wife and family. Anastasia, Tatiana, Olga, and Maria survived the first hail of bullets. As the diamonds and other precious gems in their clothing had deflected many of the bullets, each girl was stabbed with bayonets and then shot in the head. The curse of the renegade priest Father Gapon that Nicholas and his kindred should meet gruesome deaths had been fulfilled in the most awful way. The official Soviet report on the executions concluded: 'Now Nicholas the Bloody is no more and the workers and peasants can say to their enemy, "You made your last stake upon the King. Your card lost and you received – the King's crownless, severed head".'[14]

News of the Tsar's assassination was transmitted on the official Bolshevik radio station on 21 July. The report, however, lied about the fate of the Tsarina and the Tsarevich. 'The wife and son of Romanov have been sent to a place of security,' it said. There was no mention of his daughters, Dr Botkin or the servants, all of whom had been murdered. Four days later Czech Legionnaires captured Ekaterinburg. Komuch investigators found jewellery, coins, a ripped corset and the body of a dog in a nearby mineshaft that had been used as a temporary burial ground before the Bolsheviks removed the bodies and burned them. For years, the myth persisted that one of the girls, usually Anastasia, had escaped into the forest.[ii]

Alix's sister Ella, widow of Grand Duke Sergei, had been imprisoned with five Romanov grand dukes at the Napolnaya School in the Siberian town of Alpaevsk. At 11 p.m. that same fateful day, 17 July, the prisoners were taken to a flooded mine shaft and, one by one, pushed over the edge. When the assassins heard voices in the water below, they flung hand grenades into the shaft. Even then, they fancied they could hear singing, so the shaft was filled with wood and set on fire.

The singing stopped.[15]

Meanwhile, the German attack had faltered all along the Marne. Marshal Foch ordered a counter-offensive in which the Allies were joined by five American divisions, each numbering 28,000 men. On 18 July the Allies employed new artillery techniques and improved operational methods in the Battle of Chateau-Thierry which forced the Germans into a disorderly retreat (and proved the fighting quality of the American soldiers). The Honorary Russian Legion was also involved, having gone into battle with the French XX Corps as part of the First Moroccan Division.

The Second Battle of the Marne lifted the threat to Paris and brought the war to its tipping point. From July 1918 Germany would never again be able to mount an offensive and there was worse to come. Early on the morning of 8 August Haig committed a huge force of British, Canadian, Australian, American and French troops to an attack on the German positions east of Amiens. The tragic lessons of the Somme and Passchendaele, in which thousands of young lives had been sacrificed for little or no gain, had finally been learned. Secrecy and deception protected the element of surprise and artillery, tanks and infantry were effectively coordinated. The Australian and Canadian spearheads then advanced through the fog in single file rather than fanning out across the battlefield. The assault was a total success; for the first time, German resistance collapsed. 'August 8,'

---

ii Posing as 'Anna Anderson', Franziska Schanzkowska, a Polish factory worker with a history of mental illness, claimed for years to be the Grand Duchess Anastasia despite the fact that witnesses who had met the real Anastasia insisted she was an imposter.

Ludendorff said, 'was the black day in the history of the Germany Army.'[16]

By the end of the battle, 50,000 Germans had been taken prisoner and the Allies had advanced twelve miles, which was further than the Passchendaele and Somme offensives combined. Later that month, Haig's armies broke through the multiple layers of the previously impregnable Hindenburg Line. Starved of reinforcements, enemy resistance rapidly dwindled and, just as Lenin and Trotsky had hoped, riots and social unrest broke out in Germany. The *Kaiserreich* was on the verge of a socialist revolution.

On 7 August the Czech Legion and Komuch's People's Army captured Kazan from the Bolsheviks in a two-day battle that opened the way to Moscow. The Czechs seized the Russian gold reserves deposited there and used them to finance the Komuch rebellion. Word reached Kerensky in London that Vera Baranovskaya was appearing in a play in Kazan and that her sister Lilya was with her. Unaware that Lilya was in Petrograd following her ordeal in Yaraslavl, he decided to head back to Russia.

At the end of the month he appealed to the Foreign Office for assistance in reaching the city of Ufa, 280 miles east of Kazan, 'as without such help it is at present impossible to reach that part of Russia which is freed from Bolsheviks and Germans'. As a member of the Constituent Assembly, he said, he wished to participate in the work of the Provisional All-Russian Government which had been established in Samara.

His desire to return to Russia became even more urgent on 30 August when the Bolshevik regime suddenly shifted on its axis with the shooting of Lenin. Early that day Moisei Uritsky, chairman of the Petrograd Cheka, was shot dead by Leonid Kannegiser, an officer-cadet who had been among the defenders of the Winter Palace. Kannegiser belonged to an anti-Bolshevik group led by his cousin, Maximilian Filonenko, and after gunning down Uritsky he had dashed into the British Embassy looking for him. Someone gave him an overcoat to disguise his appearance and thus attired he started to walk along Palace Embankment but was recognised and arrested.

When news of the assassination reached Moscow, Lenin dispatched Felix Dzerzhinsky to Petrograd to investigate the crime and then, despite warnings that he could be a target himself, he carried on with his busy daily schedule. At eight o'clock that night he was leaving the Hammer and Sickle, a Michelson arms factory, after warning the workers against the dangers of democracy –'Wherever "democrats" rule, you find plain, straight-forward theft,' he told them. 'Our way is superior. We have only one choice: victory or death.'

As he was about to step into his car, Fania 'Dora' Kaplan, a Socialist Revolutionary comrade of Maria Spiridonova's, called out to him. Lenin stopped and faced her. Kaplan, who had been released under the Kerensky amnesty from a sentence of 'eternal penal servitude' in Siberia, regarded him as a traitor to the Revolution for destroying the Constituent Assembly. Three shots were fired. The first bullet passed through the collar of Lenin's overcoat and hit a woman in the crowd. The other two bullets wounded him in the arm and the neck. One of these bullets lodged in his collarbone after puncturing his lung, while the other was trapped in the base of his neck.

No one saw Dora Kaplan fire the shots and there were serious doubts that she had done so – she was almost blind and, in the fading light, would have had trouble recognising Lenin, let alone hitting him with two shots out of three. Nevertheless, she was seized by the crowd, beaten up and handed over to the Cheka. Like Leonid Kannegiser, she insisted under interrogation that she had acted alone. She was executed four days later. Kannegiser followed her in October.[iii][17]

As Lenin lingered between life and death inside the Kremlin, more than five hundred political prisoners were executed in retribution for the attack and as a warning to other would-be assassins. The Tsarist Ministers Ivan Scheglovitov, Aleksei Khvostov (a former Minister of the Interior) and Stepan Beletsky were among the first to die. Alexander Protopopov and Nikolai Maklakov were killed soon afterwards.[18]

At the Fourth All-Russian Congress of Soviets back in March Lenin had boasted that the Bolsheviks had driven out 'the Kerenskys and Chernovs', torn up the secret treaties and crushed the bourgeoisie – 'badly so far, but we shall do it better'. The first official announcement of the Red Terror was published in *Izvestia* on 3 September 1918 under the headline 'Appeal to the Working Class'. It called on the workers

---

[iii] A Browning revolver was found in Dora Kaplan's handbag but there were suspicions that it might not have been the assassin's weapon.

to 'crush the hydra of counter-revolution with massive terror! Anyone who dares to spread the slightest rumour against the Soviet regime will be arrested immediately and sent to a concentration camp'.

Two days later the Cheka issued its decree 'On Red Terror' and the Bolshevik newspaper, *Krasnaya Gazeta*, warned, 'We will turn our hearts into steel, which we will temper in the fire of suffering and the blood of fighters for freedom. We will make our hearts cruel, hard, and immovable, so that no mercy will enter them, and so that they will not quiver at the sight of a sea of enemy blood. We will let loose the floodgates of that sea. Without mercy, without sparing, we will kill our enemies in scores of hundreds. Let them be thousands; let them drown themselves in their own blood. For the blood of Lenin, Uritsky and Volodarsky, let there be floods of the blood of the bourgeois - more blood, as much as possible.'[iv]

Picking up the chant, Grigory Zinoviev gave a figure of ten million dead as the target of the Red Terror, 'To overcome our enemies we must have our own socialist militarism. We must carry along with us ninety million out of the hundred million of Soviet Russia's population. As for the rest, we have nothing to say to them. They must be annihilated.'

Martin Latsis, the head of the Ukrainian secret police, was quoted in the newspaper *Red Terror* on 1 November 1918 explaining the procedure to be followed in interrogating suspects: 'We are not fighting against single individuals. We are exterminating the bourgeoisie as a class. It is not necessary during the interrogation to look for evidence proving that the accused opposed the Soviets by word or action. The first question which you should ask him is what class does he belong to, what is his origin, his education and his profession? These are the questions which will determine the fate of the accused. Such is the sense and the essence of red terror.'[19]

Deceit, cunning, brute force, state-sponsored murder – the tools of Machiavelli's princes in Sixteenth Century Italy and of Russian Tsars through the ages – were widely employed. Harold Williams lamented Russia's plunge into medieval savagery. 'I cannot tell you all the brutalities, the fierce excesses, that are ravaging Russia from end to end and more ruthlessly than any invading army,' he wrote.

---

iv Volodarsky was assassinated on 20 June 1918 by the Battle Group of the Socialist Revolutionary Party during industrial unrest at the Obukhov Works in Petrograd.

Horrors pall on us – robbery, plunder and the cruellest forms of murder are grown a part of the very atmosphere we live in… The Bolsheviks do not profess to encourage any illusions as to their real nature. They treat the bourgeoisie of all countries with equal contempt; they glory in all violence directed against the ruling classes, they despise laws and decencies that they consider effete, they trample on the arts and refinements of life. It is nothing to them if in the throes of the great upheaval the world relapses into barbarism.[20]

No British politician was more appalled at the savagery of the Bolshevik dictatorship than Winston Churchill. 'Civilisation is being completely extinguished over gigantic areas,' he declared, 'while Bolsheviks hop and caper like troops of ferocious baboons amid the ruins of cities and the corpses of their victims.'

In Petrograd, Red Guards and Cheka agents stormed the British Embassy believing they would find Boris Savinkov and Maximilian Filonenko there. Both men had indeed had dealings with the Embassy's naval attaché, Captain Francis Cromie, but neither was present that day. Thirty-six, tall and strongly built, 'Crow' Cromie was a war hero who had previously commanded a British submarine flotilla in the Baltic. When the Bolsheviks burst in, he was having afternoon tea with the Reverend Bousfield Lombard, Chaplain of the British Embassy. Hearing a noise downstairs, Cromie armed himself with a Browning pistol and left the room to investigate. When he failed to return, Lombard went into the British Military Mission, which was based in an adjacent room.[v] He recorded what happened next in his diary:

While we were talking, we heard a noise in the direction of the Chancery [on the first floor]. I left the room followed by the others, and found lots of wild-looking people rushing about with revolvers; they roared at us to go back, which we did. On looking out of the window, we could see that the Embassy was surrounded by sailors and that two destroyers had their guns trained on the house.

Presently we heard shots and a short time afterwards three excited-looking ruffians arrived and marched us to the Chancery with our hands

---

[v] Also in the British Mission that day was Victor Emile Marsden, correspondent of the London *Morning Post*, the man who would translate *The Protocols of the Elders of Zion* into English. His newspaper published many of the book's patently false claims.

above our heads. There we found the entire Consular staff assembled, and about a dozen Bolshevists armed with Service revolvers and looking very dangerous. Everyone was then examined and relieved of pocketbooks, papers etcetera, and we were then all ordered to march.

As we came down the stairs we noticed blood on the marble steps, and at the bottom the body of poor Cromie, lying very still and straight just inside the door. I wanted to stop for a moment, but they would not let me. He had often said, 'If I have to go I will bang the door behind me.' He certainly did, because before being shot himself, he apparently (from the account of the escort) shot a commissar and wounded two other men.[21]

Lombard and the embassy staff were incarcerated in the Peter and Paul Fortress. The British Government held the Soviet Government responsible for Cromie's murder and demanded immediate reparation, in addition to the punishment of the Cheka gunmen. 'By the immemorial law of all communities who have emerged from primitive barbarism, the persons and domiciles of foreign representatives are sacrosanct,' *The Times* thundered. 'The British people will regard this infamous act with the deepest horror and indignation, and require that searching and impartial investigation shall be made as to responsibility for the deed. We do not want hecatombs of the ruling party's political enemies, such as they offered to the Germans after the murder of Count Mirbach, or executions confined to insignificant underlings.'[22]

The Bolsheviks replied that the shootings of Lenin and Uritsky were part of a British conspiracy to overthrow the Soviet Government. Bruce Lockhart was denounced in *Pravda* as having plotted Lenin's assassination and he and his current mistress, Moura Benckendorff, were arrested in Moscow and taken to the Lubianka.[vi]

The Hague Conventions defined a spy as someone 'acting clandestinely or on false pretences who obtains or endeavours to obtain information in the zone of operations of a belligerent with the intention of communicating it to the hostile party'. On that definition Lockhart

---

vi Moura had been born Maria Ignatievna Zakrevskaya into a wealthy family in the Poltava region of Ukraine in March 1892. In her twenties she acquired an Estonian aristocratic husband, Djon von Benckendorff, two children and fine homes in several countries. Following his death during the Revolution, she married another member of the nobility and became Baroness Budberg. She remained serially unfaithful to her new husband and her lovers included Maxim Gorky, H. G. Wells and Alexander Kerensky.

would have been found guilty. Rex Leeper, however, arranged for him to be swapped for Maxim Litvinov, who was being held hostage in London for just such an eventuality.

Sidney Reilly, very much a law unto himself, escaped from Russia under his own steam. In a show trial in Moscow later that year Lockhart and Reilly were found guilty in absentia and sentenced to death should they ever set foot in Russia again. Jacob Peters, Felix Dzerzhinsky's deputy who interrogated Lockhart and Moura, told Arthur Ransome that Lockhart might not have been guilty but that Baroness Benckendorff was definitely a German spy.[23]

While awaiting a reply from Whitehall to his request for assistance, Kerensky became angry and frustrated. Breaking diplomatic protocol, he repeated to a journalist Clémenceau's statement that Russia had become France's enemy by signing a separate peace with Germany. Considering the fine performance of the Russian troops in the Second Battle of the Marne only weeks earlier, the timing could not have been more embarrassing for the French Prime Minister. He threatened to close down *L'Information*, the Paris newspaper that had published the disclosure, and he banned Kerensky from re-entering France.[24]

Kerensky's faux pas also went down badly in Downing Street. On 10 September he received a letter from Philip Kerr that the British Government could not transport him to Russia because Britain was determined 'not to interfere in the internal politics of Russia'. This was nonsense. At that time Allied forces were involved in clashes with the Red Army in several parts of Russia and British money and arms were sustaining the White forces of Admiral Alexander Kolchak in Siberia, General Yudenich in North Russia and General Denikin's Volunteer Army.

Kerensky had no opportunity to appeal to the Prime Minister: Lloyd George went down with a sore throat and a raging fever during a visit to Manchester. He spent the next ten days confined to bed in the Town Hall with a respirator to aid his breathing.[25]

Kerensky's dreams of a reunion with Lilya ended when Kazan fell to an 11,000-strong Red Army later that month. Vera headed west to Kharkov, which was still in White hands, and on 23 October Lilya and Olga set off from Petrograd to join her there. Crossing the border between the Red and the White armies, Lilya was strip-searched and insulted. Reunited at last, the Baranovsky family remained in Kharkov for a month, surviving a dose of Spanish flu, and then travelled down to Anapa on the northern coast of the Black Sea.[vii] The Socialist Revolutionaries, meanwhile, had reestablished the Provisional All-Russian Government, now called 'the Directory' and headed by Nikolai Avksentiev, in Ufa but time was running out - in November Kolchak deposed the SRs in a successful coup and proclaimed himself 'Supreme Ruler of All Russia'.

The failure of the Ludondorff Offensive had brought both its mastermind and his country to breaking point. On 28 September Ludendorff lost his self-control at the German High Command's Supreme Headquarters in the Belgian resort town of Spa and started ranting against the Kaiser, the Reichstag, the High Seas Fleet and the Home Front. His staff hastily closed his office door to muffle the outburst.[26]

Ludendorff refused entreaties to calm down. At 6 o'clock he stormed upstairs to Hindenburg's office and announced there was no alternative but to seek an armistice. Hindenburg agreed. The following day he invited the Kaiser, Chancellor von Hertling and the Foreign Secretary von Hintze to Headquarters, where he informed them that Germany would have to seek terms from the Allies. Knowing the Allies would never negotiate with a military dictatorship, power was handed to a constitutional government under Prince Maximilian von Baden.

The new Chancellor was answerable not to the Kaiser but to the Reichstag. Ludendorff then issued a proclamation that the enemy was demanding unconditional surrender 'which is unacceptable to us as soldiers'. Realising the ruse, Prince Max demanded his resignation and he spent the last month of the war skulking in a Berlin pension before fleeing to Sweden in disguise. Nevertheless, he had achieved his purpose: it was the civilian government and not the army that would be held responsible for Germany's capitulation.

On the night of 3-4 November the German Revolution finally erupted at the great naval base of Kiel when the crews of two battleships mutinied. Within days the entire German fleet was in uproar.

---

vii Lloyd George was so ignorant about Russian affairs that he thought Kharkov was a Russian general.

The revolt spread to Hamburg, then to Munich; it arrived in Berlin on 8 November when hundreds of thousands of citizens stampeded down the streets waving red flags, overturning vehicles, ransacking buildings, tearing badges of rank from army officers' uniforms and, in some cases, executing them. As had happened in Petrograd in February 1917, military units sent in to crush the uprising refused to fire on the people and instead joined the rebellion.[27]

With the imperial foundations in a state of collapse, the Minister of the Interior arrived at the Kaiser's château from Berlin to request his abdication. 'I won't dream of quitting my throne on account of a few hundred Jews and a thousand workers,' Wilhelm replied. 'You go and tell that to your masters in Berlin.' When he suggested he would march into the capital at the head of 'his army' to put down the revolution, his commanders curtly replied that he no longer had an army.[28]

On the afternoon of 9 November news reached Wilhelm that Chancellor Max von Baden had unilaterally announced his abdication and handed over the reins of government to the Social Democrat leader Friedrich Ebert, whose colleague Philipp Scheidemann declared in an impromptu speech from a window in the Reichstag building, 'The old and rotten, the monarchy has collapsed. The new may live. Long live the German Republic!' Having joined the ranks of unhorsed monarchs, the Kaiser ordered the royal train to convey him (and his furniture) to neutral Holland.[29]

The Armistice was signed on 11 November by members of Germany's new Socialist government in a railway dining car on Marshal Foch's train, Wagon-Lit No. 2419D, in the Compiègne Forest near the village of Rethondes on the River Aisne. The terms were agreed at 5.10 a.m., with the first term stating that fighting would end at 11 a.m. that day. Marking the spot was a stone plaque on which was inscribed in French: *Here on 11 November 1918 succumbed the criminal pride of the German Empire, vanquished by the free peoples that it sought to enslave.*

Lloyd George, who had recovered from influenza, announced to a rapturous House of Commons that an armistice had been signed with Germany, taking effect at 11 a.m. that day. Sadly, between 5.10 a.m. and 11 a.m. nearly 3000 more soldiers were killed. Since August 1914 Britain and her Empire had lost almost one million men killed, with two million wounded, placing them fifth behind Russia, Germany, France and Austria-Hungary in terms of military casualties. Overall, thirty-five million lives were snuffed out during the war.

As Ludendorff had intended, the Allies had made a fatal mistake in concluding the Armistice with the civilian government of the Weimar Republic rather than with the military dictatorship that had waged war on them. This was the origin of the 'stab in the back' myth that German civilians rather than German generals were responsible for their country's humiliation. Most Germans came to believe that their troops had not been defeated on the battlefield at all but had been betrayed by a cabal of Jewish-Bolshevik traitors at home, the same Jewish-Bolshevik conspirators who had been responsible for the triumph of Communism in Russia.[30]

At Aix-la-Chapelle on the German border, a correspondent of *The Times* watched ragged columns of German soldiers return to the Fatherland. 'Hatred of England is universal, and the idea of revenge for their defeat by England is implanted already in the hearts of tiny children,' he wrote. 'The Germans will neither forgive nor forget. They have been beaten by England, and they will live and die to smash England. England has never had a more deadly enemy than the new Germany.'[31]

The Foreign Office's retribution for Kerensky's indiscretion was swift. On the evening of 8 November 1918 it sent a telegram to B. F. Alston, the British Consul in Vladivostok:

> There is a consensus of representative Russian opinion both here and in Russia that Kerensky is entirely discredited and any active support given him by the Allies will create a very bad impression. He has consistently endeavoured to represent himself as having inspired Allied policy of intervention and as the Russian leader whom the Allies are backing. His presence here has been source of considerable embarrassment and we are very anxious to get rid of him. The French and United States Governments share our views.
>
> We have discouraged him going to Archangel, but he has now requested to go to Vladivostok for a meeting of Constituent Assembly at Omsk and we have informed him that no obstacles will be placed in his way. We are asking the United States Government to give him facilities for his passage, and he will leave as soon as he receives a reply from Avksentiev.

> Monsieur [Konstantin] Nabokov has telegraphed to Avksentiev warning him against placing too much confidence in Kerensky, and while you should do nothing to discourage him from allowing Kerensky to come, you may take an opportunity at a later date of letting him know that His Majesty's Government hold similar views.[32]

A similar telegram was sent on the same day to Colville Barclay, the British chargé d'affaires in Washington. On 14 November 1918 Barclay replied, 'After consulting Secretary of State, Mr Polk tells me that he does not want to have Mr Kerensky in the United States. I suggested that to oblige us they could make arrangements whereby he could merely pass through. Mr Polk said he regretted it would be impossible to do this and to prevent Kerensky indiscriminate speaking (sic). In view of delicate situation in Russia they really did not wish to have him here for however sort a period. He suggested that Kerensky should proceed via Canada.'

Woodrow Wilson had delivered his Fourteen Points for a stable, long-lasting peace as long ago as 8 January 1918. The Sixth Point dealt with Russia: 'The treatment accorded Russia by her sister nations in the months to come will be the acid test of their goodwill, of their comprehension of her needs as distinguished from their own interests, and of their intelligent and unselfish sympathy.' She received none of those prerequisites, least of all goodwill and sympathy. Even the President, who received a rapturous welcome on his arrival in France on 13 December, admitted he saw the various Russian factions as 'a lot of impossible folk fighting among themselves'.

By the end of 1918 there were more than 180,000 foreign soldiers on Russian soil and several White armies were receiving Allied money and guns to fight the Red Army. The Japanese, who had landed a force of 70,000 troops, had seized Vladivostok and moved westward into Siberia. The Americans were also in Siberia, so the British prevailed on Canada to supply a force to balance their numbers. Down in the south, the defeat of Turkey opened up the Black Sea to the Allies. British forces moved into the oil-rich mountains of the Caucasus and the French High Command tried their luck in the Crimea.

On 18 December 1918 French troops went ashore at Odessa but like their British, Australian and American counterparts, their numbers were insignificant. A Ukrainian nationalist Directory was in control of the port-city and, despite the opposition of the Whites, the French commander tried to negotiate with the Ukrainians. However, a groundswell of support among the local Russian and Jewish population in favour of the Reds, coupled with the fall of Kiev to the Red Army in February 1919, led to the collapse of the Directory. These reverses put the French on the back foot and they planned a quick exit.[33]

The fact that Britain had kept her troops on Russian soil at the end of the war and then offered support to the Whites meant that what had started as an anti-German campaign rapidly developed into an anti-Bolshevik intervention. Lenin had no doubt about that. He told a meeting of the Moscow Soviet that war had come to Russia once again and that the enemy this time was Anglo-French Imperialism.[34] Britain's new Secretary of State for War was Winston Churchill, who was intent on 'strangling Bolshevism in its cradle'. Lloyd George, however, feared that increased intervention would only exacerbate labour unrest in Britain, so British support for the Whites remained half-hearted with disastrous consequences for the anti-Bolshevik armies.[35]

Meanwhile, in Central Asia on 6 January 1919, a band of Red Army soldiers, dissatisfied with the autocratic behaviour of the Tashkent Soviet, tried to overthrow it. Commissars were rounded up and shot, the gates of the prison were blown open and the prisoners set free. Detachments of Red Guards, however, held out in strongpoints around the city and when they were joined by armed railway navvies, the insurrection crumbled.[36]

Bolshevik revolutionary tribunals were set up to punish everyone suspected of siding with the rebels. 'The result,' according to a Danish witness, 'was organised, wholesale murder, since these tribunals naturally recognised no other form of punishment than death.' Fyodor Kerensky had the misfortune to run into a group of Bolsheviks while escaping along a railway line. He was shot in what was described as 'a reprisal' against the rebels.[37]

25

The Suspicious Alien

On New Year's Day 1919 Lilya wrote a letter full of tenderness and hope to Kerensky from the family's latest port-of-call, Anapa. 'My only love, I wish you happiness for the New Year,' she said. 'In my thoughts I am with you all the time. I have lived through so many nightmares and horrors and when I think about them my heart freezes. We are alive and well and we are unharmed! I do not even know where you are? Where are you? Do you still belong to me? Do you love me? Remember that even if you would come back to me years from now, you will see the same love in me as a year ago when I saw you back for the first time after the birth of Irina.'[1]

As Lilya had no idea of Kerensky's current whereabouts, the letter was never sent. Meanwhile, delegates were gathering in Paris for the 1919 Peace Conference that would decide the future of the world. Kerensky's most immediate concern was to have Clémenceau's veto revoked so that he could attend. Kerensky was in a despondent mood when the Russian author M. S. Margulies called at Cambridge Terrace to interview him for his three-volume work on the Russian Revolution, *God Interventsii*. Margulies described the 'earthy colour in his face, deep lines on his forehead and screwed-up eyes. He talks immoderately loudly, with a vibrant, sonorous voice, becoming excited in discussion, then walking rapidly round the room singing something'.[2]

'I retired from politics for five months,' Kerensky told the author. 'I thought, "Something intelligent will replace Bolshevism." I waited and what now? Kolchak is marching without any political thought, without a programme. What can you expect? I think that Bolshevism is approaching its final days but there is nothing to replace it with, that's the horror.'

The veto was lifted in early January 1919 after Albert Thomas,

Émile Vandervelde and his Czech friend Edouard Beneš lobbied the American delegation in France on his behalf. Travelling to Paris, he joined what one eyewitness called the 'vast cosmopolitan caravanserai, teeming with unwonted aspects of life and turmoil, filled with curious samples of the races, tribes and tongues of four continents who came to watch and wait for the mysterious tomorrow'. He moved into Jacob Gavronsky's apartment on the Right Bank with Gavronsky's brother-in-law, the former SR terrorist Ilya Fondaminsky, and his wife, Amalia Osipovna, who was Jacob's wealthy tea-heiress sister.[3]

German spies and Bolsheviks were thought to be lurking in every hotel lobby. Sir Basil Thomson, head of the new London-based Directorate of Intelligence, staffed the Hôtel Majestic with British chambermaids, valets, chefs and barmen to look after his country's delegates. He could not, however, avoid a very English scandal. As there was no place for wives at the Majestic, Edwin Montagu's wife, Venetia Stanley, moved into Lord Beaverbrook's suite at the Ritz. 'It's a disgusting case,' Lady Diana Manners wrote to her fiancé Duff Cooper. 'Her face lights up when that animated little deformity so much as turns to her. They are living in open sin at the Ritz in a tall silk suite with a common bath and unlocked doors between while poor Ted is sardined into the Majestic.'[4]

When the Peace Conference opened in the Salle d'Horloge at the Quai d'Orsay on 18 January 1919, the most notable absentee was Russia. Revelling in his new title of 'Père la Victoire', Clémenceau made it clear to all and sundry that Russia had betrayed the Allied cause and, therefore, had no right to join the 'peacemakers'. He chose to ignore the fact that Germany had been forced to renounce the Treaty of Brest-Litovsk during the Armistice negotiations and that Russia could still have been regarded as a member of the Triple Entente. Indeed, Russian troops had not only fought to the very end of the war on the Western Front but some were still fighting with the Allies against the Bolsheviks in the Baltic Provinces.[5]

Not that 'les Russes' were in short supply: in addition to ethnic Russians, representatives of nationalist causes from Finland to the Caucasus were in Paris hoping to carve up the Old Empire. Clinging to the wreckage of the Provisional Government, Kerensky bridled at the very thought. 'We are all representatives of Russian democracy and not of the individual nationalities comprising Russia,' he told the press. 'We cannot betray the tradition of Russian democracy and conduct negotiations in the name of Great Russia with other nationalities.'[6]

Prince Lvov, the former Foreign Minister Serge Sazonov, the uncredited ambassador Vasily Maklakov and Nikolai Tchaikovsky (representing the Provisional Government of the North) invited him to join a body called the Russian Political Conference, which had been formed to lobby the 'peacemakers' on Russia's behalf. He turned down the offer because the conference also included supporters of Bessarabian nationalism and the Kolchak dictatorship.

Kolchak's 'accredited agent' in Paris was Boris Savinkov. Winston Churchill, the snub-nosed grandson of the Duke of Marlborough, had a morbid fascination with the killer of grand dukes and politicians. 'How do you get on with Savinkov?' he asked Serge Sazonov during a visit to his apartment. The elderly monarchist made a deprecating gesture. 'He is an assassin,' he replied. 'I am astonished to be working with him. But what is one to do? He is a man most competent, full of resource and resolution. No one is so good.'[7]

Kerensky had not seen Savinkov since those dark days at Gatchina and he refused to speak to him. Having decided to go it alone, he argued that he should be recognised as the last legal head of the Russian state and allowed to take part in discussions about his country. The 'peacemakers' turned him down. That the Bolsheviks had repudiated Russia's foreign debt at a cost of billions to French and British banks made them even more hostile towards Russia.

On 19 February 1919 the peace talks were thrown into confusion when Clémenceau was shot and wounded by an anarchist after leaving his house in rue Benjamin-Franklin. He was out of action until 1 March. Lloyd George, who had set up house with Philip Kerr and Frances Stevenson in a luxurious apartment at 23 rue Nitot, seized the opportunity to suggest that the original unwieldy council of ten should be reduced to just four, Britain, France, the United States and Italy. From then on, Clémenceau, Lloyd George, Woodrow Wilson and President Vittorio Orlando would decide Germany's fate.[8]

In April, Kerensky was invited to the National Congress of the French Socialist Party, where he heard his friend Hjalmar Branting make a swingeing attack on Bolshevism. 'Sweden has been in a position to judge the Bolshevik experiment better than any of her neighbours, for she has been able to see its results in Finland and in great towns like Petrograd,' he said. 'Under the Bolshevik regime production is interrupted. It is the death of all activity; it is absolute economic decomposition, with its frightful consequences of misery and famine. Bolshevism is not an image of socialism and still less is it a triumph of socialism. It is only its negation. The dictatorship of the proletariat is nothing but a caricature of socialism, which, above all, is the continuation of democracy.[9]

The spring thaw in Russia enabled the White Armies to launch attacks from Ukraine to Siberia. By mid-April General Denikin, Admiral Kolchak and the other anti-Bolshevik commanders had pushed the Soviet regime out of 300,000 square kilometres of territory. More civilians were killed in the fighting than soldiers; atrocities abounded on all sides. Prisoners were dismembered or burned alive, or were released after having their ears and noses cut off as a warning to others. The Whites were particularly harsh on Jews – Cossacks enjoyed pogroms and their officers encouraged them in orgies of rape, mutilation and slaughter.[10]

'The noble and gallant Admiral Kolchak is recognised as the uncrowned head by all decent Russians,' one White supporter wrote to *The Times* on 22 May, 'and the time draws near when his Government will be recognised by the Allies.' The very next day the Allies extended partial recognition to the Kolchak regime. To Kerensky, Kolchak was one of the worst rightwing butchers mutilating Russia and he stirred up such a commotion in Paris over this decision that on 24 May he was invited to express his objections to Colonel Edward M. House, President Wilson's chief political adviser. Considering the State Department's hostility towards him, this was an extraordinary offer.[11]

Kerensky explained to the influential Texan over tea in his suite at the Hôtel de Crillon that, with Allied help, the Bolsheviks could be defeated in the next few months. His greatest fear was that Kolchak would replace them with a dictatorship hardly less repressive than that of Lenin and Trotsky. The Allies, he suggested, should insist that, in return for financial and military aid, Kolchak would have to agree to restore Russian democracy. Ideally, civil liberties would be reinstated and a coalition cabinet set up. The peasants would retain their land and the workers would be given the right to strike. Then, at the appropriate time, a democratic Constituent Assembly would take control of the country.[12]

When the Big Four convened a fortnight later, Woodrow Wilson put Kerensky's terms to the other three leaders after first making the point that they 'happened to tally with information he received elsewhere'. Lloyd George, who had come close to recognising the Bolshevik regime only weeks earlier, nodded sagely. Clémenceau remained mute. It was agreed, however, that a dispatch should be sent to Siberia seeking assurances that democratic institutions would be introduced. By the time Kolchak replied with a rather garbled acceptance of the terms it was too late - Red armies were already breaking through his centre and he was forced to order a retreat.[13]

Even so, Boris Savinkov and Nikolai Tchaikovsky tried to persuade the Union for the Regeneration of Russia to back Kolchak, a move that convinced Kerensky it was time to make a diplomatic retreat himself. He asked Vasily Maklakov to apply to the British Embassy in Paris for a visa authorising his return to the UK. Maklakov was only too happy to oblige – it meant getting rid of the Russian Conference's chief critic.[14]

The British Ambassador, Lord Derby, had had a bellyful of troublesome Russians. Taking no chances, he referred Kerensky's request to Whitehall. Sir Ronald Graham, Curzon's Under-Secretary for Foreign Affairs, asked the Director of Military Intelligence, Sir William Thwaites, for his opinion and on 23 May Thwaites passed the buck back to Graham with the comment that there was no military objection to granting Kerensky a visa 'provided the visit was considered desirable on political grounds'.

Surprisingly, the Foreign Office raised no objection and thus turned down the chance to be free of Kerensky forever. A visa was duly granted. The task of keeping track of Kerensky fell to Rafael Farina, chief of the Russian Section at MI5 headquarters at 73-74 Queen's Gate, South Kensington. Born to a British mother and Italian father in Switzerland in 1877, Farina had been trained as a mining engineer at Camborne School of Mines. Having worked in Siberia prior to World War I, he spoke Russian and was looking forward to locking horns with this controversial émigré.[15]

On 29 May 1919 Farina's office sent an urgent alert to passport control at Southampton, Dover and Folkestone: 'Kerensky, the well-known Russian demagogue, is at present in Paris and we want to know when he comes to this country.'[16] As the weeks slipped by, there was no word of Kerensky's whereabouts and Farina was quietly panicking: his quarry seemed to have disappeared into thin air.

Meanwhile, the Allies presented Germany with the 'Treaty of Peace between the Allied and Associated Powers and Germany'. Clémenceau had insisted that the Palace of Versailles should be the setting for the signing ceremony. 'In the Hall of Mirrors the German Empire had been proclaimed in 1871,' he said. 'The cradle of the Empire should be its grave.' The German Foreign Minister, who had been denied any direct role in the discussions, refused to sign the treaty, so two minor German officials reluctantly put their signatures to it on 28 June 1919, the fifth anniversary of the assassination of Franz Ferdinand.[17]

Clémenceau had succeeded in avenging the destruction of his homeland and reducing Germany to penury. All Germany's colonies were forfeited, her armed forces disbanded and Allied troops occupied the industrial Rhineland. Under Article 231, the 'War Guilt' clause, Germany accepted full responsibility for the war and was required to pay punitive reparations. The Allies also continued to enforce the naval blockade on German ports, resulting in life-threatening food shortages and pushing the country closer to revolution.[18]

The treaty created nine new nation-states. Poland regained her independence under Józef Pilsudski, the first President, and celebrated 11 November as her National Independence Day. Finland and the three Baltic provinces, Estonia, Latvia and Lithuania, also won their freedom. Newly created Czechoslovakia celebrated 28 October 1918 as her day of liberation from the Habsburg Empire. Tomas Masaryk, son of a Slovak father and a Czech mother, became the country's founding father. The Dual Monarchy ended with Austria and Hungary becoming separate nations. And the Slavonic dream came true with the founding of Yugoslavia among the Balkan states.

Germany lost thirteen per cent of her territory, with millions of Germans ending up in Poland, Czechoslovakia, Yugoslavia and Danzig, a free city on the Baltic nominally under the control of the newly formed League of Nations. The Rhineland was set up as a demilitarized buffer zone between France and Germany. Friedrich Engels was exaggerating only slightly in his prediction of 1887 that 'dozens of crowns will roll in the streets and no one will want to pick them up'. *The Times* editorialised:

> We are living in one of the immense upheavals of the world. There has been no change comparable to it among the States of Europe since the downfall of the Roman Empire. All the old military Monarchies are gone. The crowns of the Hapsburgs, the Hohenzollerns and the Romanovs are in the dust. The whole system of Central and Eastern Europe has perished by the sword in which it trusted. In its place old nations are reviving and new are struggling to life. Poland is restored; the Czecho-Slovaks are an independent people; from the Baltic to the Black Sea race units claim self-determination and sovereignty. How will changes so vast, so far-reaching, and so sudden work out?

Germany and Austria-Hungary had lost vast swathes of territory but so too had Russia. Grievances over Versailles would lead to one of its most devastating consequences: a dangerous alliance between the Bolsheviks and the German military that would rock the very foundations of peace. The chances of maintaining the New Europe in a state of harmony plummeted when Woodrow Wilson failed to impose American ideals on his European colleagues. He reminded Ben Hecht of 'a virgin in a brothel sturdily calling for a glass of lemonade'. The League of Nations was the only thing he managed to salvage at Versailles and then his own country declined to join it. The League's powers were so limited that it could only advise on sanctions against transgressors and then only by a unanimous vote of member states.[19]

Marshal Foch, Herbert Hoover and John Maynard Keynes were among the many leading figures who disowned Versailles. 'This is not a peace,' Foch said. 'It is an armistice for twenty years.' General Archibald Wavell called it 'the Peace to end Peace' and Kerensky branded it 'punitive and unrealistic'. Clémenceau and Lloyd George were later portrayed as the draughtsmen, if not the actual architects, of the rise of Nazism and the onset of the Second World War.

Article 227 of the treaty specifically provided for the trial of Kaiser Wilhelm by a tribunal of five Allied judges 'for a supreme offence against international morality and the sanctity of treaties'. The Dutch Government, however, refused to extradite him to France and Willy got off scot-free. He spent the rest of his life at Huis Doorn, a manor house at Doorn in the Netherlands, where he chopped down so many of the estate's trees that he deforested the local landscape. Now, instead of counting the number of animals he had slaughtered, the All Highest counted the number of trees he had chopped down - twenty thousand in the first eleven years of exile. His best effort was an astonishing 2590 in a single week.[20]

Meanwhile, in March 1919, the Bolsheviks had launched a reign of terror against the Cossacks in the Don-Kuban area with the aim of exterminating the leadership and disarming every Cossack under pain of death. In retaliation, the Cossacks mustered 30,000 troops against a Red Army force consisting of 39,800 infantry, 5570 cavalry, sixty-two field-guns and 341 machineguns. Many of the Bolshevik troops were conscripted peasants who refused to attack the Cossacks and one regiment from Saratov Province even defected to the other side.[21]

The Red Army's failure to defeat the Cossacks enabled the Volunteer Army to break through the southern front. After capturing the Donbas and Kharkov in June 1919 General Denikin advanced towards Moscow in early July with 40,000 men to deliver the coup de grace to the Bolshevik regime.

Kerensky was still missing. Thanks to Vernon Kell's wartime work catching German spies operating in Britain, MI5 enjoyed close relations with many of the Chief Constables. On 3 September 1919, Rafael Farina wrote to Captain M. L. Sant, Chief Constable of the Surrey County Constabulary in Guildford, 'Mr Kerensky: We do not know the present whereabouts of the above-named, but we have heard that he may be in Dorking. Would you kindly report if this is a fact and also [provide] his address.'

Captain Sant made inquiries and discovered that Kerensky had indeed visited Dorking. He had stayed at South Holmwood Vicarage, an ivy-covered redbrick residence, as a guest of the vicar. That, however, was eight months earlier in December the previous year.

The search for Kerensky then switched to Germany after a report from Copenhagen that he was actually in Berlin. The antisemitic White Russian correspondent who reported this 'fact' to the Secret Service also claimed that Kerensky had dispatched a letter via courier from Paris to a group of Jewish businessmen in the Danish capital. 'It is quite obvious that Russian Jews have become afraid for their skins realising that their position in a future monarchist Russia will not have been improved by the actions of their co-religionist Bolshevik leaders. Kerensky has more or less sold his soul to the Jews and the Germans, and the former now look to him as their saviour.'

This report proved as baseless as many others that would find their way into the British security network. Meanwhile, Farina had caught up with the fact that Kerensky sometimes stayed in Tunbridge Wells with Jacob Gavronsky's family. On 13 October Charles Prior, Chief Constable of Tunbridge Wells Borough Police, informed him: 'I beg to acknowledge the receipt of your letter of the 9th instant, P.F.R.52/M.I.5.G4, and to acquaint you that Dr Gavronsky resides at "Rusthall", Langton Road, Tunbridge Wells, which is on the border of this Borough but in the Kent County Constabulary district. The Superintendent of the Tonbridge Division, Kent Constabulary, states that M. Kerensky does not reside at "Rusthall" but visits there at weekends.'

Kerensky had actually slipped back into England soon after his visa was granted back in May. Having survived the best efforts of the Okhrana and the Cheka to curtail his activities, he was skilled at covering his tracks, protecting his contacts and giving away very little in his phone calls, letters or telegrams. His main method of communication was through personal contact or using couriers to deliver mail.

On 25 October 1919 Farina received confirmation that Kerensky was not only back in England but was staying at 'Rusthall'. He leapt on the new lead. 'Kerensky seems to have come to UK without attracting anyone's notice,' he wrote in a memorandum to Vernon Kell in requesting permission for a Home Office Warrant to intercept Kerensky's mail. 'The rumour current in Russian circles here to the effect that Kerensky is not to be trusted is confirmed by the recent reports on him, namely that he has been in Berlin and was negotiating with the Germans.'

On the strength of this misinformation Farina was authorised to submit an I.P. Form G3 on Kerensky, which was signed by the Home Secretary and sent to the Postmaster-General:

> I hereby authorise and require you to detain, open and produce for my inspection all postal and telegrams addressed to Alexander Kerensky,

'Rusthall', Langton Road, Tunbridge Wells, or to any name at that or any other address if there is reasonable ground to believe that they are intended for the said Alexander Kerensky, and for so doing this shall be your sufficient warrant. Reason: Has been recently in Berlin and is now reported to be in league with the Germans to the detriment of Allied interests, and to influence Russian public opinion against Admiral Kolchak's Government.

Farina's indictment was a gross distortion of the facts, though he was right about Kerensky's hostility towards Kolchak. In December, he added Kerensky's mail arriving at 7 Cambridge Terrace, Regents Park to the intercept order. The early fare at both addresses was far from promising. There was an invitation to address the Educational Department of the Equitable Pioneer Society in Rochdale and an inquiry from the London branch of the Union of Siberian Cooperatives about what kind of imperial or social government was to be adopted in Siberia and which elements 'must be put down in founding the new regime'.

Having taken Kiev in August and Kursk in September, General Denikin's forces swept into Orel, barely 200 miles from Moscow, with one aim in sight: to seize the Kremlin. Denikin, however, followed the White movement's policy of 'Russia, One and Indivisible' and refused to make an alliance with Ukrainian nationalists; indeed, he antagonised them to such an extent that partisans attacked his supply lines. The most decisive date in the Russian Civil War was 20 October 1919 when he was driven out of Orel and began a long retreat that ended at the sea. On that same day General Yudenich's campaign ground to a halt after penetrating the very suburbs of Petrograd. Shorly afterwards Admiral Kolchak fell into Bolshevik hands at Irkutsk and was shot as an 'enemy of the people'.[22]

The Bolsheviks' position was now secure and Britain's War Council decided it was time to call it quits. On Saturday 8 November, Lloyd George sprang one of his surprises by abruptly ending Britain's role in the Civil War. He chose the Lord Mayor's banquet at the Guildhall rather than the Dispatch Box to announce a dramatic shift in government policy, throwing over Kolchak, Denikin, Yudenich and all the other anti-Bolshevik forces in order to secure a peace-making trade deal with Lenin.

Having told his audience that Britain had already spent £100 million (£1.5 billion today) funding her efforts in Russia, he continued, 'We cannot afford to continue so costly an intervention in an interminable civil war. Our troops are out of Russia – frankly, I am glad. Russia is a quicksand. Victories are easily won in Russia but you sink in victories and great armies and great empires in the past have been overwhelmed in the sands of barren victories. Russia is a dangerous land to intervene in.'[23] *The Times* rebuked the Prime Minister for his latest volte face: 'Consistency can hardly be charged to the present Government in their support and their withdrawal of support of anti-Bolshevik forces at Archangel and in Siberia, and far less in the field of diplomacy.'[24]

Many false reports about Kerensky flowed into London. The most common lie was that he was either a Bolshevik or was secretly aiding the Bolshevik cause. One SIS report sent to London from Constantinople on 6 January 1920 and distributed to MI5 and the Special Branch, claimed, 'Kerensky has been accorded a warm welcome in Georgia. Apart from meeting many of his old party friends, the Georgians as a whole are inclined to be very favourably disposed towards him, owing to his openly hostile attitude with regard to the Volunteer Army. Kerensky's idea is to inflict a defeat on Denikin's rear and with this aim in view he is looking round for supporters. In Georgia he finds these among the numerous deserters from the Volunteer Army, as well as among the Bolsheviks who survived the Vladikavkaz defeat.'

Rafael Farina thought this report unlikely. Remembering the Dorking fiasco, he checked Kerensky's whereabouts with Chief Constable Prior in Tunbridge Wells. Prior made inquiries with the Divisional Superintendent at Tonbridge and on 12 February replied that Kerensky was in residence at 'Rusthall', though 'he is in London today but is expected home tonight'.

Four days later Farina asked the SIS station in Constantinople, 'Can you please say between what dates Kerensky was in Georgia? He is now and has been for the past two or three months in London.' But Farina had been misled. It was left to Detective Constable W. Austin of the Kent County Constabulary to inform him that the Gavronskys had left 'Rusthall' permanently on 28 January that year. 'There are no Aliens at "Rusthall" now,' he wrote. 'It is understood that Mr Kerensky left this district two days or so before the permanent removal of the Gavronsky family. As far as the police know, none of them have visited this district since.'

Indeed, Kerensky was in London on 29 January when he gave an interview to *Manchester Guardian* clarifying his policy on Allied intervention. 'If the Allies had sent an army of 100,000 men and had supplied artillery and munitions, the Russian people would have continued the war and Bolshevism would have been overthrown,' he said. 'But since the Armistice I have been opposed to intervention which has become intervention in Russia's internal affairs.'[25]

One of Kerensky's most vocal accusers was General Alexander Lukomsky, General Kornilov's Chief of Staff in the abortive revolt of August 1917. When the White armies retreated from Russian soil, Lukomsky ended up among the anti-Soviet diaspora in Constantinople. So many Russians were there that it seemed to him 'the ancient Russian dream had come true, and Tsargrad had become a Russian city'. Lukomsky blamed Kerensky for the betrayal of Kornilov and the Bolshevik takeover of his country. He was only too willing to feed the 'Red Peril' perceptions that dominated British foreign policy-making in the 1920s.

In July 1920 Lukomsky handed a report compiled by 'a member of the Russian Secret Service' to the Turkish office of the Secret Intelligence Service. The Russian agent, who had recently been in Paris, claimed that Kerensky 'is now taking an active part in helping the Bolsheviks to carry out their sinister designs. He is reported to be assisted in this by a certain Jewess, with whom he is on terms of great intimacy. This woman, whose name, unfortunately, it has not been possible to verify, has travelled frequently to Paris and there had interviews with Rutenberg and other Socialist leaders.'

Kerensky was also believed to be in close touch with 'Margulis, the London representative of the Paris Union Bank – a Jewish concern, which is reported to be financing the Left groups in France. Kerensky's conversion to Bolshevism is regarded as being due to disappointment with the French and English Socialist and Labour parties, whom he describes as "the mute slaves of Imperialism"'.[26]

That the former head of the Russian Government was now a Bolshevik agent committed to world revolution would have been a matter of some importance if it were true. But Kerensky had heard it all before. He routinely denounced accusations that he was pro-Bolshevik as 'outrageous libels and hellish lies'. 'You may deny the news about any reconciliation between me and the Soviet government absolutely and in the most drastic manner possible,' he said after one such claim. 'Under no circumstances at the present or in the future in this life or in the life hereafter would I ever think of such a reconciliation.'[27]

Nevertheless, the Secret Service sent the Constantinople report, with its heavily antisemitic overtones, to Basil Thomson's Directorate of Intelligence at Scotland House opposite Scotland Yard in Westminster. Their inquiries revealed there was no such bank in London as the Paris Union Bank and no banker named 'Margulis'. The Secret Service sleuths, however, easily identified 'Rutenberg' as Peter Rutenberg, the Socialist Revolutionary who had been involved in the lynching of Father Gapon. The non-existent banker 'Margulis' was almost certainly the author M. S. Margulies, who had interviewed Kerensky in London.

Two of the victims of the influenza pandemic were Nell Tritton's siblings Charles and Lillian, who contracted influenza in 1919. Their weakened kidneys could not cope with the virus. Lillian died on 19 September, Charles on Christmas Eve.[28] Their deaths had a profound effect on Nell, who knew that she was living on borrowed time herself. Like Marie Bashkirtseff, she was determined to leave her mark on society with whatever time remained. On leaving school she had trained as a journalist on the *Daily Mail* and in 1920 the newspaper published her greeting to a royal visitor, the Prince of Wales (later Edward VIII), with a poem, 'Our Prince':

> *All loyal hearts make holiday to greet*
> *our future king;*
> *O let us show our love for him and England*
> *far across the sea.*
> *And with our songs of gladness, let the skies*
> *of sunshine ring.*

At the Governor's Ball in his honour, the Prince danced with the young poet twice. Later that year she published a book of poetry which was reviewed in *The Triad*, a Sydney-based monthly arts magazine. The anonymous reviewer wrote, 'Miss Tritton is a rather strikingly handsome Queensland girl. She has a good memory of many moonlit evenings, and with that a certain plunging sincerity that is oddly attractive. She loves nature, and there is some natural strain of music in her heart. She makes the mistake that so many young girls make, the mistake of writing love verses addressed to women. Better by far for the rapt aspiring girl to sing of her love for something in trousers.'[29]

Nell was not short of male admirers. According to a family member, one of her beaux was Tommy Lawton, a Rhodes Scholar who captained the Australian Rugby Union team that beat the All Blacks three times in one season. She had no intention of settling down, however, and in 1923 she moved to Sydney. Bowling up to *The Triad* office, she reminded the editor, Charles Nalder Baeyertz, 'a big blond man with eyes a'dance with merriment', and asked for a job. Nell's poetry-writing and her light touch with a feature article were tailor-made for *The Triad* and he was happy to publish her work. The pay was poor and the magazine was struggling, so she also wrote for the *Sydney Guardian*, a daily newspaper founded by Frank Packer's father and on which young Frank was earning his spurs as a cadet journalist.[30] The events that would shape Nell's life, however, were taking place in South Russia, where Lilya Birukova was experiencing the unremitting cruelties of the Civil War: hunger, terror and death.

26

The Hungry Years

While Alexander Kerensky had no idea of Lilya's whereabouts during his difficult months in Paris, her husband, General Nicholas Birukov, still hoped for a reconciliation with his wife. 'I want so much to have Olik close to me,' he wrote to her at Anapa from his home in Odessa on 23 March 1919. 'I also wish very much that you would come back to me. I'll give you all the freedom to live as you want, under the same roof or separately, with or without your parents. I'll acknowledge Irinouchka as my daughter with pleasure, so that her situation can be legalised.'[1]

But there was no reconciliation and Lilya remained in Anapa while the Civil War swirled around South Russia. On 6 April France suddenly withdrew her forces from the Odessa bridgehead, creating panic among civilians who dreaded the arrival of the victorious Red Army. The next letter Lilya received from Nicholas – dated 28 June that year - shocked her to the core:

> I am writing to you anticipating that in a few days' time, or maybe even within a few hours, I will be shot. They arrested me on 11 May with a camera in my hands in a street close to the Cheka. They accused me of espionage but when that was refuted they decided to condemn me to death anyhow because I had been a general. I have not been notified of any accusation and they have not even interrogated me. They held me at the Cheka for a week and then transferred me to Odessa Prison.
>
> I am asking Zinaida Stepanovna [a friend] to forward this letter to you, together with some personal items and money. I ask you specially to instil in my son, in spite of everything, the love for the whole of the Russian people and that he will not harbour any hate or feelings of vengeance towards those who have executed me without any reason. I believe in a justice supreme. God is their judge.

By the time Lilya received the letter Nicholas was already dead. Leaving Olik and Irina with her parents and her sister Olga, she set off for Odessa to retrieve her husband's body and give him a Christian burial. Locating the body in a makeshift grave, she had it disinterred and then reburied after a funeral service at a church near Odessa. Her troubles were far from over. After the funeral, she was struck down with typhus and spent six weeks in hospital. By then she was trapped in Odessa and she would have to endure two years of hardship before she could evade the Bolsheviks and be reunited with her children.

Rafael Farina thought he had struck gold when the latest intercepts of Kerensky's mail informed him that his quarry's mysterious female accomplice was staying at Claridge's Hotel in the Champs Élysées and there were strong indications that she was possibly his mistress. To identify her, Farina enlisted the help of Major Kendall, a Paris-based Secret Service agent. 'She signs all her letters "I"', he told Kendall. 'Can you possibly find out who she is and whether her activities are of special interest?'

It was a simple matter for Kendall to elicit the woman's name from the guest register at Claridge's. In a report dated 28 January 1920 and headed 'Counter Bolshevism', he wrote, 'It is strongly suspected that the woman "I" is no other than Rabinovitch, Nina, born at Petrograd on 22.5.94; no profession; usual domicile Petrograd. She arrived at Claridge's Hotel Paris on 10.10.19, travelling from London.' But this promising lead, like so many others, ended in a dead end and Farina was no closer to trapping his quarry.[2]

Lloyd George's plans for an Anglo-Soviet Trade Agreement moved a step closer with the arrival in London on 27 May 1920 of Leonid Krasin, the bomb-making bank robber. Four days later he met Lloyd George at Downing Street and, against diehard Conservative criticism, began negotiations with the President of the Board of Trade, Sir Robert Horne. On 16 March 1921 the Anglo-Soviet Trade Agreement was signed by Krasin for the Government of the Russian Socialist Federal Soviet Republic and by Horne, now elevated to Chancellor of the Exchequer, on behalf of His Britannic Majesty's Government. It was the first time Horne had exchanged pleasantries with a bank robber.[3]

H. G. Wells met Lenin in the Kremlin in September 1920. He

described him as 'a little figure at a great desk in a well-lit room that looked out on palatial spaces'. Wells, who was a short, plump man himself, noted that Lenin, at five feet five inches tall, was so short that 'his feet scarcely touch the ground as he sits on the edge of his chair'. His domed head reminded him of Arthur Balfour's. 'Lenin has a pleasant, quick-changing, brownish face, with a lively smile and a habit (perhaps due to some defect of focussing) of screwing up one eye as he pauses in his talk,' he said.

'Even now,' Lenin told him, 'all the agricultural production of Russia is not peasant production. We have, in places, large-scale agriculture. The Government is already running big estates with workers instead of peasants, where conditions are favourable. That can spread. It can be extended first to one province, then another. The peasants in the other provinces, selfish and illiterate, will not know what is happening until their turn comes....'

Despite Lenin's confidence, Russia was heading for a breakdown and famine. War Communism, his belligerent response to the rigours of the Civil War, had proved a colossal failure. Large areas of Russia remained outside Bolshevik control and peasant rebellions had broken out in many places. Food requisitioning in the province of Tambov triggered the Antonov Mutiny, named after the renegade Socialist Revolutionary Alexander Antonov, which began with armed resistance to the confiscation of grain and developed into guerrilla warfare against the Red Army, the Cheka and the Soviet authorities.

The Red Army used chemical weapons against the peasants and 100,000 people were arrested and 15,000 shot dead before the uprising was crushed. Resistance in Ukraine and Siberia reduced food supplies to the cities to such an extent that industrial workers, already alienated from the dictatorship of the proletariat, called strikes which were ruthlessly suppressed.[i][4]

'The utter disregard for human life that was a key feature of the ruling style of the Bolshevik leaders was to a significant degree an echo of the massacre of millions of soldiers on the orders of their political leaders and military commanders in the First World War,' the historian Kees Boterbloem wrote in *A History of Russia and its Empire*. 'The survival of the dictatorship at any price replaced the

---

[i] Alexander Antonov was killed in a firefight with Chekist gunmen on 24 June 1922.

Marxist goal of the creation of a society of equals whose human rights and freedoms were meticulously protected.'[5]

During the war Petrograd had lost seventy per cent of its population. There was no traffic because there was no petrol and no trams were running because the horses had been slaughtered for food. Olga Kerenskaya likened people trudging through the snow during the winter of 1919-1920 to 'doomed shadows'. They shuffled past huge placards proclaiming the glory of the Soviets, one of which said in huge red letters, 'We will make the whole world like a blossoming garden.' Until that happened, the vast majority of the population was condemned to a life of starvation and misery.

Olga was offered a job as an organiser in charge of the printing department at Centrosoyus, the Central Cooperative Union, after one of its executives heard that Alexander Kerensky's family was starving. 'I told him frankly that I had no talent for organisation,' she says. 'He told me I would soon learn. In fact, there was nothing for me to do - I was the head of a fictitious department. Instead of doing nothing I offered to help with the typing and I still received my organiser's salary.'

Shortly afterwards a Bolshevik official arrived from Moscow to reorganise the cooperative. He dismissed the heads of all bogus departments but kept Olga on as a typist – at typists' pay. 'I was very happy to stay,' she says.

As there were no trams, she had to leave her flat early in the morning to reach the office in time and when she got back it was already dark. The front doors and front staircases of all apartment buildings were boarded up, so she crept in via the back stairs. There was no electricity or any other lighting on the staircase and the flat was in complete darkness.

As she could not afford candles, she turned to the Russian proverb that 'Poverty is the best teacher' and made a tiny paraffin lamp out of an ointment jar and a cork, with twisted threads as a wick. The lamp provided just enough light to show the way from the kitchen to the single room in which she was living. 'Every day one heard of robberies and murders,' she says. 'I had always been an extremely nervous child, always afraid of the dark. In this unlit flat I was terrified.'

Having ascertained that Olga represented no threat to the regime, her Communist lodgers were rarely there, so she spent many nights sitting on a kitchen chair too afraid to make the short walk to her bedroom. One night she arrived home to find the lock on the front door broken and the door ajar. She fled down the stairs to the flat of the head of the House Committee. Armed with a revolver and carrying a lantern, the man returned with her. The thieves had fled but the flat had been ransacked. They had made off with a gold watch which had belonged to Kerensky's father and a length of cloth which co-op employees were allowed to buy at cost and which she had hoped to exchange for food.

'I went to my mother's flat that night and the next day she moved back with me,' she says. 'We knew at last that everything was ashes and ruin. We knew it was no use any more even trying to save our possessions. All that was left to us was to stay alive because our end would be the end of my sons.'

Their diet consisted mostly of dirty half-rotten potatoes, washed in cold water and boiled on a tiny stove fed by chips of wood, old newspapers and torn-up books. The stove could heat water and boil food but it gave out no heat and their hands were stiff with cold. Weak from hunger, their only thoughts were of food, light and warmth. 'We were living in darkness not only physical but spiritual,' Olga says. 'At night we curled up on a sofa and tried to get warm. The water pipes were frozen solid and I had to wait until I got to the office to wash.'

Darkness, cold, dirt, hunger – those were Olga's memories of those winter months. The only working tap was in the basement washhouse. The steps leading to it had no handrails and were covered in ice from splashed water. Going down them with a bucket was dangerous enough but coming up with a pail full of water was like walking up an ice flow. When she got home in the evening, the water had frozen in the pail and had to be heated on the tiny stove.

'My belly became swollen with hunger,' she says. 'Sometimes we would get a two-ounce ration of soggy bread, or, on lucky days, a quarter pound. When there was no bread we were issued with oats. But on some days there would be no rations at all, just those slimy, half-black potatoes and occasionally a few putrid herrings.'

One of the stories in the Kerensky family's legend is how, in the midst of this desolation, Oleg bought his mother a proper stove –

a real solid cast-iron stove. 'Uncle Oleg gave up some of his daily food ration to buy the stove from a woman at his boarding school,' says Stephen Kerensky. 'When the last payment had been made, he borrowed a sledge from the school and he and Gleb started to drag the stove home. My father was ill and weak, so he sat on the stove for most of the journey and Oleg pulled him along, too.'[6]

The boys arrived home exhausted but happy to have got a stove for their mother. Olga applied for a permit to buy firewood from the government wood store on the banks of the Neva. By good luck, she was given several logs which she hauled home on a sledge made from an old ironing board. 'I was panting like an exhausted horse when at last I brought the logs into our yard,' she says. 'We still had to chop them up, but from we were never cold again.'

By the end of that winter, though, Gleb was dangerously weak from starvation. He often felt giddy and one day he fell down the school stairs and broke his arm. The school called a doctor who set the arm and said that he was suffering from anaemia and needed a more nourishing diet. This infuriated Olga. 'Where could I find extra food for him?' she says. 'When he was at home, he would lie listlessly on the divan.'

Gleb was so ill that he told his grandmother, 'Grannie, don't tell mother – she will cry even more - but I believe I shall never be well again and will die soon.'

Once again Oleg came to the rescue. 'My brother bartered bread for cabbage stalks, which were more filling than bread and the peasants did not as yet value them highly,' Gleb wrote in *Only One Freedom*. 'We ate acorns and potato peelings until people stopped peeling potatoes, made "soup" from tree sap and burned wooden houses and mahogany furniture for fuel. We lost an aunt, a cousin and numerous acquaintances from "starvation diseases" and one acquaintance died of hunger. Those who do not understand famine conditions would suppose that they would lead to further revolts and troubles. Quite the contrary is the case. There is nothing more docile than a hungry man if his hunger has been developing gradually and if there are scraps of food to be had by odd jobs, barter, wangling, toadying and thieving. And so the Soviet machine creaked on.'[7]

Meanwhile, the Volunteer Army and the Don Cossacks, fighting as the 50,000-strong Armed Forces of South Russia (AFSR), had captured vast areas of Soviet territory outside Central Russia. Kharkov had fallen to the Volunteers, Saratov was on the verge of surrender and General Peter Wrangel had finally occupied Tsaritsyn, the 'Red Verdun'.[8] All of these gains, however, merely delayed the inevitable result. Commanding an army of almost five million men, Leon Trotsky was no longer the wild-haired demagogue of the past but a daunting figure in Red Army cap and shapeless military overcoat, the pince-nez long since replaced by metal-framed spectacles. He travelled the length and breadth of the battlefields in his armoured train, driving the Whites back to the Black Sea, the Baltic and the Pacific.

Meanwhile, Stalin had recalled Artem Sergeyev from Ukraine to Moscow.[ii] Under Stalin's patronage he was appointed secretary of the Central Committee of the Moscow branch of the party and in July 1920 he attended the Second Congress of the Third Communist International (the Comintern) to plan world revolution. Sergeyev was one of twenty-seven delegates who were photographed by Viktor Bulla outside the Tauride Palace on 17 July. Aware he was in the presence of greatness, he discreetly placed himself at the very back of the group, while Lenin, Lev Karakhan ('the Bolshevik Adonis'), Karl Radek, Nikolai Bukharin ('the darling of the party') and Grigory Zinoviev were at the front.[iii]

The congress formulated the 'Twenty-one Conditions' for Comintern membership and, according to the historian E. H. Carr, it marked 'the moment when the Russian Revolution seemed most certainly on the point of transforming itself into a European revolution'. Lenin nursed a particular hatred of the Leader of the British Independent Labour Party, Ramsay MacDonald, and he used the congress to take him to task over his book, *Parliament and Revolution*:

> MacDonald remains a thorough-paced bourgeois pacifist and compromiser, a petty bourgeois who dreams of a government that stands above classes. Like all bourgeois liars, sophists and pedants, MacDonald recognises the class struggle merely as a 'descriptive fact'. He

---

[ii] When he was summoned to Moscow, Sergeyev was head of the Executive Committee of Donets Gubernia, as well as a member of the Central Committee of the Communist Party of Ukraine and of the All-Ukrainian Central Executive Committee.

[iii] Viktor Bulla was executed on 30 October 1938 after being forced to confess to false espionage charges.

ignores the experience of Kerensky, the Mensheviks and the Socialist Revolutionaries of Russia, the similar experience of Hungary, Germany, etc., in regard to creating a 'democratic' government allegedly standing above classes. MacDonald lulls his party and those workers who have the misfortune to regard this bourgeois as a Socialist, this philistine as a leader, with the words: 'We know that all this [i.e., the revolutionary crisis, the revolutionary ferment] will pass ... settle down.' The war, he says, inevitably provoked the crisis, but after the war it will all 'settle down', even if not at once![9]

Meanwhile, back in Petrograd in the spring of 1920, Olga Kerenskaya knew that only a miracle could save Gleb's life. 'No one could help me. Vladimir (Baranovsky), my brother in Moscow, had a family and his life was always in danger. My sister-in-law Elena (Lyolya) was fighting for her own existence because she was Kerensky's sister. My own sister Elena (Tarchova) had always had an unhappy life – it was I who had to help her, not the other way round. Only my mother never left me during those dreadful years.'

In a roundabout way Olga received a message that Boris Sokolov, a Socialist Revolutionary who was about to leave Russia, was willing to take a letter to her husband. Born in 1889, Boris Theodore Sokolov had graduated in 1913 from the University of Saint Petersburg and received his MD from the Second Medical School, Petrograd, in 1917. He served as a captain in the Russian Army Medical Corps on the South-Western Front and was decorated with the Order of Saint Vladimir. He had been one of Kerensky's staunchest supporters.[10]

When Olga met Sokolov to hand over her letter, she described the kind of life she and her family were leading. Sokolov listened in silence and then said, 'Why don't you escape abroad, too?' Olga explained that there was no chance of that: she had no money to pay for a secret escape and, anyway, one of her sons was seriously ill. Sokolov said nothing but when he met Olga for a second time he handed her a piece of paper. 'It was part of a list showing the names of people living in a certain apartment house in Pushkinskaya,' she says. 'One of the names was Olga Peterson, the widow of an Estonian subject, who had two sons. I never found out how he obtained that piece of paper and inserted our names.'

Sokolov told Olga that a party of Estonians was leaving Petrograd in a week's time and that she and her sons should join them. On that day, however. Olga's little niece, Galia, the only child of Elena Tarchova, died after a short illness. 'She had been sent from school to hospital with dysentery,' Olga says. 'Even now, I can see her yellowish face, her deep-sunk eyes, the smile on her bloodless lips, and can hear her voice growing weaker. Even now, I can see the big hospital ward, the rows of white beds, and the small figures lying on them, their yellow faces already stamped with the seal of death.'

The doctors and nurses fought heroically to save the children but they were too worn out from months of privation to survive the disease. Elena was numb with grief over her daughter's death and Olga dared not leave her. 'She could not bear the thought that Galia would be buried into a communal grave,' Olga says, 'and we were obliged to go to several places before we could get a permit to buy a small coffin. By the time we had done that, it was too late for my appointment with the Estonians.'

Sokolov, however, turned up at Olga's flat with another date for their departure but before then Gleb went down with an attack of jaundice. Olga called a doctor and asked him whether the boy could make a journey in his condition. 'I pretended that we were going to Moscow to see my brother,' she says. 'The doctor was emphatic: Gleb must not be moved. I went to Sokolov and told him our plan was off – and again, there was a miracle.'

Sokolov told her that the departure of the first batch of Estonians had been postponed for a week. If Gleb had recovered enough by then, the Kerenskys should go to the railway station. It was not an easy decision for her to make. 'Except for my sons, I was leaving behind in Russia everyone and everything that was dear to me,' she says. 'I was going without money to I knew not where.'

Oleg, now fifteen, did not want to leave at all – he had made firm friendships at school and although he and his friends were half-starved he felt he would be deserting them. Conversely, he knew that escape was the only thing that could save his brother's life. 'It was not easy for him to accept my decision to go but he did accept it,' Olga says. 'He had been my moral support during the dark years. It was him who got me a blonde wig to make me look more like an Estonian woman when the time came for us to leave.

'Even now, I cannot understand how the Cheka overlooked a non-existent family on the list of Estonian subjects sent to them for checking and final approval. But there again I was unexpectedly helped. I went to an office with my "passport" and was recognised by a woman whom I knew by sight. 'Mrs. Kerensky,' she said, 'what are you doing here?'

Olga thought everything was lost but, realising it was useless to lie, she told the woman about the false documents and her son's illness, and how the documents had to be approved before they could escape. 'Leave these papers with me and go away quickly,' the woman said. 'I will put them among other people's documents and they will pass unnoticed.' And that is exactly what happened.

On the day of departure Gleb's jaundice had improved, so Olga decided to risk it. 'My mother and sister and a friend came to the station to see us off,' she says. 'Between us we carried Gleb and our three cases to the Baltic Station.' Sitting on the platform waiting for the train, Olga felt utterly miserable. She whispered to Maria and Elena that they would soon be together again. 'I tried to give them hope but there was no hope in my heart,' she says. 'The train came in. I hugged them for the last time. I never saw my sister again. She died under anaesthetic during a minor operation.'

The train began to move. 'I could not see anything – tears were blinding me. I did not know where I was going but I knew that my past life was left behind forever. It was a farewell to Russia, a farewell to everything.'

The danger was not over, however. Stephen Kerensky says, 'Grandma told me that a ticket inspector asked her to sign some sort of official paper. She took Grandfather's pen from her handbag – it was a gold pen given to him for some aspect of his work – and after she had signed the document the inspector took the pen from her and put it in his top pocket. When she demanded it back, he replied, "Forget about the pen, Mrs Kerensky".'

The train took the Kerenskys to Tallinn (previously Reval) and from there they crossed over to Sweden. 'My father told me he had his first proper meal there,' Stephen Kerensky says. 'It was a pasta dish and he loved pasta for the rest of his life.'

The Secret Service were alerted to the Kerensky family's imminent arrival in London when, on 2 October 1920, Basil Thomson informed Rafael Farina, 'It may be of interest to you to know that Alexander Kerensky arrived at Dover on 23 September [1920] en route to

7 Cambridge Terrace, Regent's Park. He was travelling on a diplomatic passport [actually a Nansen passport which described him as stateless].'[11]

Kerensky was standing on the dock in Harwich when his family arrived by sea from Sweden. It was an uncomfortable reunion. The boys were exhausted after the trip and they could sense the tension between their parents. Olga would always support her husband's battle for the liberation of Russia but she could not overlook his affair with Lilya Birukova or the existence of their daughter. 'I knew our life together was finished; destroyed,' she says. 'He had other family ties now.'

The Kerenskys moved in with the Gavronskys at Cambridge Terrace and Kerensky was reconciled with his sons but he did not stay long - on 11 October the Directorate of Intelligence reported that Kerensky had left Dover for Calais. Hoping for evidence that he and his wife were involved in some sort of revolutionary conspiracy, Farina started opening Olga's mail from Russia but it produced only family news and local gossip.

Meanwhile, in Anapa, Kerensky's 'other family ties' started to unravel when General Vsevolod Baranovsky decided it was too dangerous to wait any longer to hear from Lilya. 'We must think of the children,' he said. Despite his wife's protestations, he moved the family to Novorossick on the Black Sea, marched them down to the docks and took ship to Turkey. Arriving in Constantinople, they found shelter with scores of other Russian families in a deserted palace, each family hanging sheets on cords to mark out their living space in the large halls.

While Lilya lived in hope that she would find them again, her greatest fear was that Irina would have forgotten her. In August 1920 she was well enough to leave Odessa but it took another six or seven months to make her way to Vera's home in Kharkov. Vera told her that the family had gone to Constantinople and that the Turkish authorities had recently moved them to an abandoned Greek monastery on Antigone (Burgazada), one of the Princes' Islands in the Sea of Marmara. Their brother Sviatoslav (Tossie), who had been repatriated with one of the White Armies, had joined them there.

Lilya packed her suitcase and set off once again. Heading south, she crossed the border into Romania, where the French Military

Mission helped her find passage to Constantinople. Hoping for a joyous reunion with her family, she was heartbroken to discover that her father had died of pneumonia just three days earlier.

During 1920 General Denikin had shipped his entire force from Novorossick to the Crimea. Resigning his post, he spent the rest of his life in exile, first in France and then in the United States. General Wrangel, who replaced him, held the Crimea until November 1920 when he accomplished the immense task of evacuating 150,000 Whites to Turkey.[12]

The Communists had been victorious in the Civil War but they were in an economic tailspin of crippling famine, falling production and rising debt. The demobilisation of the Red Army only increased the problems. Lenin had promised the soldiers a Communist Utopia in exchange for their sacrifices but instead of equality, justice and food they had got conscription, starvation and the Gulag.

Outright rebellion against the Kremlin came from a most unlikely quarter. The sailors of 'Red Kronstadt', heroes of the October Revolution, had become disillusioned with the limitations of the one-party state and the enforcement of War Communism. On 28 February they rose in revolt and arrested the local commissars on Kotlin Island. Mass meetings of 15,000 sailors and soldiers demanded that the Soviets elect new members by secret ballot; that freedom of speech be restored to all leftwing socialist parties; that trade unions and peasant organisations be granted freedom of assembly; that Communist political agencies be abolished in the army and navy; that all grain-requisitioning squads be withdrawn, and that the peasants be permitted to sell their produce in a free market.

Lenin denounced the Kronstadt Uprising as a White Russian plot but it was much broader than that: the rebels represented genuine concerns among the Russian masses and highlighted the failure of the Soviet system. At first news of the rebellion Kerensky dashed from Paris to Prague to raise funds in support of the sailors. Through contacts in the Czech Government, he secured a pledge of three million francs a month, which would be routed through Edouard Beneš to Tallinn and taken by courier across the Gulf of Finland to Kronstadt.

On 6 March, Trotsky, his Van Dyke whiskers bristling with fury, told the men he had once called the 'the pride and glory of the

Revolution', 'I order all those who have raised a hand against the Socialist Fatherland immediately to lay down their weapons. Those who resist will be disarmed and put at the disposal of the Soviet Command. The arrested commissars and other representatives of the Government must be freed immediately. Only those who surrender unconditionally will be able to count on the clemency of the Soviet Republic.'

When this uncompromising statement failed to break the deadlock, Trotsky ordered the Red Army to attack Kronstadt. As artillery shells rained down from the night skies, thousands of sailors fled across the ice into Finland but hundreds were shot on the spot and another 2103 were arrested, put on trial for mutiny and executed.[13] Maxim Gorky held Grigory Zinoviev responsible for the brutal treatment of the sailors. He based his play *The Plodder Slovotekov* on his experiences of dealing with Lenin's chief braggart. It opened on 18 June 1921 but was closed down after only three performances.

The Kronstadt mutineers had been right about War Communism; it had brought the economy to the brink of collapse and led to starvation in many parts of the country. Lenin realised that instead of exporting revolution abroad his first priority must be to protect the Revolution at home. Accordingly, the Tenth Communist Party Congress, which opened in Petrograd on 8 March during the Kronstadt Uprising, introduced the New Economic Policy (NEP), a partial reversion to state capitalism.

The free market was revived and the retail trade and some light industry were returned to private ownership. The peasants were permitted to keep the land they had acquired during the revolution, provided they supplied grain to the state and paid taxes. They were also permitted to sell some of their produce at the market price.

But no sooner had the NEP been introduced in spring than crop failure in the Volga basin for the second year running produced a famine affecting at least twenty million people. The famine forced the Bolsheviks to reestablish ties with capitalist nations in the West, from which food aid poured in, most notably from the American Relief Administration (ARA) directed by the future American President, Herbert Hoover. Over the next two years, the ARA supplied food and medical assistance to ten million people. Nevertheless, an estimated five million people died from starvation, cholera and typhus.

Following the Red Army's victory in the Civil War, new emigrant communities were springing up in many parts of Europe, Asia Minor and China. Berlin, Paris and Prague were the preferred European destinations, while thousands of White Russians remained in Turkey and others took the Trans-Siberian Railway to Vladivostok and made their way down to Harbin and Shanghai. Many of those who had chosen the French capital moved to Berlin or Prague after 1921 when prices in France rose astronomically. When Alexander Kerensky and his supporters joined them, the officers of the Sûreté and the Deuxième Bureau heaved a sigh of relief – the fewer Russian revolutionaries in their midst the better.

The mass exile of Russian intelligentsia also brought many of the Soviet's finest authors, poets and philosophers to Berlin, creating what was described as 'a cultural supernova' in 'Little Moscow', the proletarian neighbourhoods of Wedding and Moabit. At least one theatre showed nothing but Russian plays, no fewer than eight newspapers reported Russian news and views, and seventeen publishing houses churned out Russian books and magazines. According to the poet Ilya Ehrenburg, Russians were everywhere, 'with balalaikas and zurnas, with gipsies, pancakes, shashliks and, naturally, heartbreak'.[14]

On 4 May 1921 Kerensky celebrated his fortieth birthday during a visit to Prague. He seemed happy and was surprisingly positive but his finances were as perilous as ever. The Czechs gave generously to the Russian refugees in their midst and he was visiting Prague to see Viktor Chernov and Vladimir Zenzinov, who were publishing a Czech-funded anti-Bolshevik newspaper called *Golos Rossii* both there and in Berlin. Kerensky was also reunited with Bruce Lockhart, who was serving as commercial secretary at the British Legation in Prague. They found themselves reliving the revolutionary events in Petrograd. 'As far as Russia was concerned,' Lockhart says, 'I felt that we both belonged irrevocably to the past.'[15]

Prague was an entrepôt of intrigue and no intrigue was complete without Boris Savinkov. Poland had fought Russia in a bloody conflict during the summer of 1920. Polish troops advanced as far east as Kiev but were driven back 300 miles to the outskirts of Warsaw. Only a desperate surprise attack by Pilsudski into the rear of the Russian forces – the Miracle on Vistula – routed the enemy.[16] When the war ground to a halt, Polish authorities asked Savinkov to leave the country for an extended period as a sign of good faith to the Soviets. Placing a trademark white gardenia in the buttonhole of his well-cut suit, he moved to Prague and joined forces with another snappy dresser, Sidney Reilly, to raise funds from the Czechs to finance a revolt among Russian peasants.

Lockhart noted that Reilly, who had always been in awe of Savinkov, had now taken the lead in their conspiracies. 'Savinkov himself was a bundle of nerves,' he wrote. 'Sometimes, under the influence of brandy, the old fire would come into his eyes, and he could summon up some of the old energy but his spirit was broken.'[17]

Kerensky studiously avoided Savinkov but had several meetings with Sidney Reilly, another Freemason, during which the spy tried to involve him in his counter-revolutionary activities. Kerensky dropped him after hearing that he had discussed their talks with Vladimir Zenzinov. Affecting injured pride, Reilly wrote to him on 21 July 1921:

> I was glad that I met you quite by chance today and to have heard the reason why you did not reply to my letter of yesterday. You accused me of indiscretion. In the interest of our work, please tell me what was the reason of this accusation? I should be very distressed if, as a result of this innocent conversation, you were to refrain from finding a means to accomplish the plan I suggested. I shall contact you on my return from Warsaw and if you wish to see me, I shall be happy to do so. I hope you will understand the motive of this letter.
> Yours very sincerely,
> Sidney Reilly [18]

Kerensky understood Reilly's motives all too clearly and continued to avoid him as well as Savinkov. Acting in character, Savinkov persuaded the Czechs to stop funding the Socialist Revolutionaries' activities and to divert the money to him instead. Thanks to Savinkov's dog-in-the-manger attitude, the SRs' newspaper was forced to cease publication and, in August, Kerensky gave up the unequal struggle and returned to Berlin.[19]

Meanwhile, Artem Sergeyev had fallen in love with Elizaveta Lvovna Repelskaya. They had sealed their union in a civil ceremony in Moscow and, on 5 March 1921, Elizaveta gave birth to a son, Tomik

Fyodorovich Sergeyev, known as 'Artyom' (the Russian for Artem). Shortly afterwards Sergeyev's abilities and Stalin's patronage took him back to the Donbas in the vital role of Commissar of Mines. 'A mark of his importance [to the Communists],' the Australian historians Thomas Poole and Eric Fried wrote, 'was his election on five separate occasions to Lenin's Central Committee when this elite body comprised only a score or more of Bolsheviks.'[20]

On 24 July Sergeyev was back in Moscow for the Third Congress of the Communist International. During that visit he was among a group of twenty-two Communists who were invited to take a trial run in an experimental train called 'The Aerowagon'. Invented by the Latvian engineer Valerian Abakovsky, this extraordinary Heath Robinson contraption was driven by a propeller powered by an aircraft engine. It was capable of speeds up to ninety miles per hour.

The outward journey to Tula, an industrial centre 120 miles south of Moscow, passed without incident but on the return trip the Aerowagon hit some rocks which had been placed on the line. The little train was derailed and the engine exploded, killing six of the passengers, including Sergeyev, the inventor Abakovsky and Paul Freeman, an American-Australian Communist. A seventh man later died of his injuries. Paddy Lamb, a Communist member of the Miners' Union of Broken Hill, escaped from the wreckage unhurt. As a member of Lenin's inner circle, Sergeyev was granted the supreme honour of being buried in the Kremlin Wall Necropolis in Red Square.[21]

Following his father's death, Artyom's mother Elizaveta became seriously ill with depression and Lenin entrusted Stalin to look after her and to raise Artyom, then four months old, as a Communist. He became Stalin's adopted son and was brought up alongside Vasily, Stalin's son with his second wife, Nadezhda 'Nadya' Alliluyeva.

'We were friends from childhood and trusted each other,' says Vasily, who was born nineteen days before his adopted brother in the same hospital. 'My father loved Artyom and set him up as an example to me.' The boys spent much of the week receiving a Communist education among orphans and street urchins at a children's home, returning each evening to Stalin's quarters in the Kremlin.

Two weeks after Sergeyev's death, Lenin complained of insomnia and terrible headaches. He wrote to Maxim Gorky on 9 August 1921, 'I am so tired that I am unable to do a thing.' In the next two years he would suffer three strokes. In the meantime he was well enough to instigate a purge to exterminate all political opposition. Lenin had never concealed his belief that the new world could be built only with the aid of physical violence. In March 1922 he wrote to Kamenev, 'It is the biggest mistake to think that NEP has put an end to the terror. We shall yet return to the terrorism, and it will be an economic terrorism.'

The Central Committee of the Communist Party decided to prosecute the leaders of the Socialist Revolutionary Party for its past crimes, the most serious of which was said to be Dora Kaplan's attack on Lenin. Dzerzhinsky, Kamenev and Stalin were ordered to choose the moment to release the information about this purge to the wider world. The Bolsheviks also subjected the Orthodox Church to its greatest torment since the Golden Horde had descended from the East. Persecution of theistic faiths had begun almost immediately after Red October in order to save the Russian people from what Marx called 'the sigh of the oppressed creature... the opium of the people'. Cardinals were crucified upside down and churches were turned into social clubs and labour camps.

Using the famine as a pretext, the Soviet authorities now demanded once again that the Church hand over all its gold, silver and other precious ornaments. Metropolitan Benjamin replied that the Church was indeed willing to help the starving but wished to distribute the food themselves, or through the American Relief Organisation. This enraged the Government. When Chekist soldiers attempted to take these objects by force, crowds of believers blocked the entrances to their churches. 'Twice the Chekists attacked the Kazan Cathedral and the Alexander Nevsky Church in Petrograd and twice unarmed masses drove the soldiers back,' Pitirim Sorokin says. 'The third time they tried to do it they were mowed down by machineguns and the churches were sacked. Thousands of priests and people were arrested for this show of "counter-revolution".'[22]

Lenin's first stroke took place at his dacha - an Empire-style manor house at Gorky in the woods outside Moscow[iv] - on the night of 25-26 May 1922. It caused paralysis down his right side and loss of speech but, with a superhuman effort, he learned to speak again and to write with his left hand. He could do nothing about his loss of memory and

---

iv Vladimir Putin's grandfather, Spiridon Putin, was one of Lenin's cooks at Gorky.

some cognitive functions. He was told that, with time, they might come back.

European doctors were consulted. They offered several diagnoses: nervous exhaustion, chronic lead intoxication from the two bullets lodged in his body, progressive arterio-scelerosis of the brain (the thickening and hardening of the arteries, leading to a restriction of the blood flow through the body) and endarteritis luetica (a reference to meningovascular syphilis). Lenin's Wassermann test proved negative but nevertheless he was treated with injections of an arsenic solution, the prevailing remedy for syphilis.[23]

Metropolitan Benjamin and ten other defendants were tried by the Petrograd Revolutionary Tribunal in the former Nobles' Club from 10 June to 5 July 1922. As the prisoners entered the courtroom, the Communist spectators shouted abuse and hissed these 'poisoners of the people's minds'.

'Peace be upon you,' the Metropolitan said and blessed them.

Given a chance to address the Tribunal, Benjamin took the blame for the priests' resistance. 'I and only I, as head of the Church, am responsible for the actions which you call criminal, but which I look upon as fulfilment of duty,' he said. 'These priests and believers are but executors of my commands and they must be acquitted. Judge me as you will and I will accept your verdict.'[24]

To great applause, the defendants were found guilty and condemned to death (though six were later reprieved). On 13 August Benjamin was shot in the Kovalevsky Forest. His hair had been shorn and he was dressed in rags so that his executioners would not recognise him.

Meanwhile, in Moscow on 8 June 1922, the show trial of the Socialist Revolutionaries began before the Supreme Tribunal. The main defendant was Avram Gotz, who had thought Kerensky was exaggerating the threat of a Bolshevik takeover in October 1917 and who had later tried to organise armed resistance to the Bolshevik regime. Four socialist lawyers from abroad, including Émile Vandervelde, acted for the defence but they might as well have stayed at home. At the outset it was announced that 'the court does not intend to handle the case from a dispassionate, objective point of view but will be guided solely by the interests of the Soviet Government'.[25]

The trial concluded with preordained death sentences for the twelve leading SRs and acquittal for those who had given evidence against them. The sentences, however, were commuted to long terms of imprisonment on the basis of an agreement with international socialists, who had threatened to boycott the Comintern's proposed 'united front' if they were carried out.[26]

Purges of one kind or another were conducted against anti-Bolshevik émigrés around the world. For Kerensky, there was danger from both Red and White assassins. To the Whites, he was guilty of bringing down the Tsar and thus bore a heavy responsibility for the Communists' destruction of the whole edifice of the ancien regime. 'The reactionaries and imperialists who once fawned on him have no good word to say of Kerensky,' Bruce Lockhart says. 'More even than the Bolsheviks, he was made the scapegoat of their shortcomings.' According to Gleb Kerensky, 'many Russian émigrés who had welcomed the Revolution were more hostile to him than to Lenin on the principle that if a mad dog bites you, you do not blame the dog so much as the man who failed to shoot the dog.'[27]

Among the exiled ministers none suffered more than the family of V. D. Nabokov, who had fled with his wife Elena and their five children in 1919. The Nabokovs settled briefly in England while young Vladimir, who spoke fluent English, was enrolled at Trinity College, Cambridge ('this little provincial English town, where, like a great soul in a small body, an ancient university lives its proud life'). He started reading Zoology and later switched to Slavic and Romance languages. While at Trinity, he translated *Alice in Wonderland* into Russian. His younger brother, Sergey, was enrolled at Oxford but remained for only a few months. The following year their parents took the three younger children to Berlin where, on 15 November, V. D. launched a liberal Russian-language daily newspaper, *The Rudder (Rul)*.[28]

On the evening of 28 March 1922 the Kadets hired the Berlin Philharmonic Hall for a political rally. The main speaker was to be Paul Miliukov, who now edited the Paris-based Kadet newspaper, *The Latest News* (*Poslednie Novosty*), and who had recently returned from a visit to the United States. V. D. Nabokov belonged to the right wing of the Kadet Party, which refused to compromise with the Russian left, while Miliukov openly courted socialists who refused to toe the Bolshevik line. Despite their conflicting views, V. D. had invited Miliukov to address the audience of 1500 on the subject of 'America and the Restoration of Russia'.[29]

V. D. was sitting in a chair on the stage when Peter Shabelsky-Bork, a fanatical Russian monarchist, rose from his seat singing the Imperial Anthem, 'God Save the Tsar'. As he approached Miliukov, he opened fire with a pistol. Someone in the crowd shouted, 'For the Tsar's family and Russia!' As we have seen, Miliukov was a monarchist himself but his 'stupidity or treason?' speech in the Duma in 1917 had infuriated many loyalists. Jumping down from the stage, Nabokov wrestled the gunman to the floor but a second assassin, Sergei Taboritsky, stepped forward and shot him dead. Miliukov was unhurt. At the Nabokov home at 1 Egerstrasse, Vladimir was reading a poem about the wonders of Florence to his mother when a phone call informed them of V. D.'s death. The killers were sentenced to long terms of imprisonment but were released shortly afterwards.

Simultaneous with the rise of Nazism, Soviet agents and Soviet-sponsored newspapers sought to increase Communist influence among Russian emigrant communities. To counteract Red propaganda, Kerensky launched his own newspaper, *Days* (*Dni*), in Berlin on 29 October 1922 with the help of Czech money. Subtitled 'a Russian daily for politics, economics and literature', the paper would also publish news reports of Soviet life which had been smuggled into Germany.

Kerensky promised his readers that *Days* would not countenance extremism of the right or the left, 'neither a return to monarchy nor, even less, cooperation with the tyranny of Russia's present rulers'. Once again he was 'Speedy' Kerensky and the experience of dodging the Okhrana and then the Cheka kept him one step ahead of his enemies. He went everywhere with a bodyguard at his side, usually Colonel Nicholas Poradyelov, who varied his daily routine to avoid ambushes. A password was required to gain entry to his newspaper office and visitors were closely vetted. The *New York Times* reported there was a price of 50,000 gold roubles on his head but if that were the case he would never have survived.[30]

Among the new arrivals in Berlin was Nina Berberova, a writer with dark hair and even darker flashing eyes. Her lover, the poet Vladislav Khodasevich, introduced her to Kerensky with the words, 'This is Kerensky. He screams terribly. He has one kidney.' Nina soon learned that 'the screaming' was actually Kerensky dictating his editorials in a loud voice to a member of the *Days* staff.

Kerensky scored a notable scoop when three German foremen called at the *Days* editorial offices. They had just returned from working at a gas and explosives plant which had been financed by the Germans near Samara on the Volga. This secret project proved that the Soviet Government had granted extraterritorial rights to their former enemy to enable the Reichswehr, Germany's tiny authorised army, to evade the punitive terms of the Versailles Treaty that limited Germany's armed forces to 100,000 men and prevented the construction of a modern navy and air force.[31]

Lloyd George had warned in a confidential memorandum to the French, Italian and American delegations at the Paris Peace Talks, 'The greatest danger that I see in the present situation is that Germany may throw in her lot with Bolshevism and place her resources, her brains, her vast organising power at the disposal of the revolutionary fanatics whose dream is to conquer the world for Bolshevism by arms.' Indeed, that danger was now becoming a reality on an ever-increasing scale to subvert the aims of the Versailles 'peacemakers'.[32]

German and Soviet military experts worked together on manoeuvres in Ukraine and, most importantly in view of the later blitzkrieg innovations, operated an armoured-warfare training school. They also collaborated on developing the latest destructive weapons and were provided with an artillery range near Lipetsk in Tambov Province on which to test them. Nothing was too much trouble: an airfield was set aside for training German pilots and a factory was built to manufacture a small number of bombers and fighter aircraft.[33]

The collaboration between the Bolsheviks and the embryonic Nazis, would eventually play an important part in bringing the two countries together in an armed alliance. Further proof of their intimacy was the signing on 16 April 1922 of the Treaty of Rapallo under which the German and Soviet governments renounced all territorial and financial claims against the other as laid down at Brest-Litovsk and Versailles.[34]

The most celebrated new arrivals in Berlin were two hundred anti-Soviet intellectuals who were expelled from Russia in two 'philosophers' ships' in September 1922. The most famous figure in the group was the Christian-existentialist philosopher Nikolai Berdyaev, a former Marxist and ex-member of the Union of Liberation, who had bravely opposed the Bolsheviks. 'The Russian revolution,' he wrote, 'has turned to be a consistent application of Russian nihilism, atheism and materialism – a vast experiment based on the denial of all absolute spiritual elements in personal and social life.'

When Felix Dzerzhinsky interrogated him, he refused to recant – quite the opposite: according to Solzhenitsyn, he gave the Cheka boss a dressing down on the deficiencies of the Bolshevik ideology. Trotsky, however, justified the expulsions with unshakable Bolshevik logic:

> These elements we send away and will send away in future are nothing in a political sense. But they are a potential weapon in the hands of our enemies. In case of new military conflicts that cannot be excluded in spite of our peaceful policies, these irreconcilable dissident elements will be military-political agents of the enemy. In that case, we will have to shoot them in accordance with the rules of war. This is why we prefer to deport them now, beforehand in the quiet period. I hope you will not refuse to recognise our prudent humanity.

Having survived four years of the Bolsheviks' 'prudent humanity', Pitirim Sorokin and his wife, Dr Elena Baratynskaya, joined the exiles to avoid the threat of further incarceration. None of the exiles was left destitute or homeless. Alexander Kerensky arranged lodgings for many of them and was happy to publish their work in his newspaper.[35]

Kerensky paid several visits to England to see his family. He had been unable to make contact with Lilya Birukova but in case their lives should coincide at some point he wanted to be free to marry her. When he asked Olga for a divorce, she exploded. 'The time when I was ready to give you a divorce without posing any conditions has passed,' she told him angrily. She demanded a settlement large enough to pay for their sons' education. As Kerensky had no money, this was out of the question and he returned to Berlin.[36]

From Regent's Park Olga, Oleg and Gleb had moved into a rented room in Bloomsbury, London's literary and artistic bohemia. 'When the Bloomsbury intellectuals heard that the Kerenskys were there,' Stephen Kerensky says, 'they couldn't wait tell grandma what a genius Lenin was and how the Soviet Union was the brilliant new civilisation.'

Olga was anxious that her sons should not be beaten at school and with the help of a Czech subsidy paid through Catherine Breshko-

Breshkovskaya in Prague she was able to send them to Oakfield, a small private boarding school at Crouch End. Instead of being beaten, they were introduced to the arcane mysteries of cricket.

On 22 December 1922 Russia joined with Belarus, Ukraine and Transcaucasia to create the Union of Soviet Socialist Republics (USSR), a one-party state ruled by the Communists. Kerensky's dream of a popular republican regeneration was as far away as ever. 'I cannot accept and I won't accept that I am an émigré,' he wrote to his comrades in Berlin. 'Alas, you often have to do what you don't want to do.'

The Baranovsky family would have agreed with him. Life on Antigone was anything but a pastoral idyll. The monastery was hot in summer, cold in winter. With her husband's military insignia pinned to the collar of her jacket, Lydia Baranovskaya had taken over as head of the family. Every day Tossie, Lilya and Olga took the ferry to the Turkish mainland and worked in restaurants and hospitals. By December 1922 they could afford to move out of the monastery and return to a better life in Constantinople. Lilya's fears that Irina would have forgotten her had proved baseless. She vowed that she would never be separated from her children again.[37]

PART IV
REDEMPTION
(1924-1970)

27

The French Connection

Adolf Hitler's emergence on the international scene on 8-9 November 1923 was a military failure but it made his reputation for violence. Partly funded by Henry Ford and supported by Erich Ludendorff, the 'Beer Hall Putsch' was an attempt to overthrow the German Government. The Nazi leader marched on Munich with 3000 supporters, sixteen of whom were killed in a gunfight with soldiers and police. Hitler was convicted of high treason but instead of spending years in prison the anti-Weimar judiciary released him after nine months. 'Germany needed such a man,' Vasily Grossman wrote in his epic novel *Stalingrad*. 'After being defeated in 1918, Germany was looking for Hitler, and she found him.'

> The only means at his disposal was violence. Violence towards states and nations; violence in the education of children, violence towards thought and labour, with regard to art, science and every emotion. Violence – the violence of one man over another, of one nation over another, of one race over another – was declared a deity.[1]

Kerensky recognised the danger in the rise of Fascism and described it in his newspaper as 'a sick, a very sick phenomenon'. He attacked Hitler personally as 'the leader of the Bavarian monarchists'. While Nazi Stormtroopers fought pitched battles with the Red Banner Fighters of the Communist Party in the streets of Berlin, Kerensky and his friends within the émigré community fought a losing battle against rising costs and galloping inflation.

By the summer of 1923 thousands of Russians had been driven from Berlin to Paris, which had shaken off its postwar gloom and immersed itself in les années folles ('the crazy years'). With the franc enjoying a rare period of stability, the country was edging warily towards a hard-won prosperity. Kerensky moved the *Days* editorial operations into an apartment at 9 rue de Vineuse beside the Tracadéro. He employed Vladimir Zenzinov as office manager and Mark Aldanov, an exiled Russian author, as literary editor. David Soskice and Jacob Gavronsky made regular trips across the Channel to read proofs and to revive Kerensky's flagging spirits. There was so little money that the staff considered themselves fortunate if they were paid at all.

Among the contributors was Nina Berberova, who had moved to Paris with Vladislav Khodasevich. It was Nina's dream to study at the Sorbonne but she had no money and in common with other stateless refugees was forbidden from taking a job. Instead, she eked out an existence doing menial piecework, such as cross-stitching embroidery or stringing beads together, and submitting short stories and poems to Mark Aldanov for publication in *Days*.[2]

Her lover Khodasevich was tall and painfully thin, with a mop of lank black hair and pince-nez glasses. He was also suicidal. Nina could not leave him for more than an hour for fear that he would jump out of a window or turn on the gas. When he wasn't slumped in melancholy, he earned a few francs as the poetry editor of *Days*.

Giving up hope of ever returning to Russia, Lilya's family had arrived in Paris from Constantinople, via Marseilles, in the autumn of 1923. Kerensky's hopes soared that he would be reunited with his lover when she and her two children joined them there. In the meantime, he was living in the *Days* office with Sonia Martyanova, a petite, dark-haired Russian. Judging Kerensky's chances of material success to be slim, she exchanged him for a more likely prospect, a Russian monarchist.[3]

His relationship with Lilya had an even more pitiful ending. During her escape from Russia, she had promised Kerensky, 'Remember that even if you would come back to me years from now, you will see the same love in me as a year ago when I saw you back for the first time after the birth of Irina.' By the time she arrived in Paris in the spring of 1924, the murder of her husband at the hands of the Bolsheviks had extinguished that love. In a eulogy published in a pro-White newspaper in Odessa, she had publicly transferred Irina's paternity to Nicholas Birukov: 'The deceased leaves behind a wife and two infant children without any means of subsistence.' When Kerensky met her at the Baranovskys' tiny flat in Rue Mouffetard on the Left Bank, he was rebuffed. Her family says she refused to have anything to do with him.[4]

Despite years of deprivation, Lilya at thirty-two was still a beautiful woman and she attracted the eye of a prosperous Russian émigré, Georgy Alexandrovich Stern. Plump and bald, 'Georgik' (Little George) had moved to France before the Revolution and founded a successful business. He located a much bigger apartment for the family in rue du Faubourg Saint Honoré and, as Lilya was unable to practice as a doctor, he helped her find work as a nurse in a hospital.

Meanwhile, the Kremlin hierarchy was experiencing a convulsion that would determine Russia's path for the next thirty years. In January 1923 Lenin's relationship with Stalin broke down completely when he learned that Stalin had verbally abused Nadezhda Krupskaya in a telephone call. He was so angry that he amended the text of his 'Testament' – a series of observations and recommendations to be released to the Communist Party after his death - to suggest that Stalin should be replaced as the party's General Secretary, the position he had created for him the previous year and which had become the source of his power.[5]

Trotsky claimed, 'Krupskaya said to me in the presence of Zinoviev and Kamenev, "Volodya (so Lenin was called) said of Stalin, 'He lacks the most elementary sense of honour.'" And she continued, "Do you understand? The simplest human decency".'[6]

On the night of 9-10 March, Lenin suffered a second stroke that shattered all hope of recovery. According to his neurologist, the haemorrhage resulted in 'complete loss of speech and complete paralysis of the right extremities'.[7] Stepping into the leadership void, Stalin sent a note to the Politburo that effectively terminated Lenin's leadership:

> On Saturday, March 17th in the strictest secrecy Comrade Krupskaya told me of 'Vladimir Ilyich's request to Stalin', namely that I, Stalin, should take the responsibility for finding and administering to Lenin a dose of potassium cyanide. I felt it impossible to refuse him, and declared, 'I would like Vladimir Ilyich to be reassured and to believe that when it is necessary I will fulfil his demand without hesitation.[8]

Stalin maintained that he 'did not have the strength to carry out V. Ilyich's request and I have to decline this mission, however humane and necessary it might be, and I therefore report this to the members of the Politburo'.[9]

That summer Lenin was photographed with his younger sister, Maria Ulyanova, while sitting in a wheelchair wearing one of his leather caps and staring at the camera through wild, startled eyes. There was no resemblance between this cruelly reduced figure and the cocky victor of October 1917. It was the portrait of a human being in terminal decline. Only Stalin among his Soviet comrades could have allowed such a demeaning photograph to be published.

At 6.50 on the evening of 21 January 1924, immobile, speechless and powerless to prevent Stalin's rise to power, Vladimir Ilyich Lenin suffered a final massive stroke in his dacha outside Moscow. He was fifty-three, a year younger than his father had been when he died of a cerebral haemorrhage. A few hours before his death he experienced a series of convulsions, an unusual occurrence in a stroke victim. Dr Lev Lurie, a Russian historian, speculated that poison was the most likely cause of death and that Stalin was the most likely perpetrator. An autopsy was performed but even though his doctors knew about his request to Stalin for poison, no one thought it necessary to carry out a toxicology test.

The autopsy revealed that the arteries leading to Lenin's brain were almost totally obstructed. It was thought he had inherited a tendency towards high cholesterol levels, causing the blockage that had led to the fatal stroke.[10]

Kerensky was unforgiving in his assessment of his greatest enemy:

> Lenin was never a humanitarian or a lover of freedom. He was cruel; the meaning of compassion or love was alien to him. Once he assumed power in October 1917 he continued to apply the methods he had developed in the underground: dictatorial control, terror and destruction. Intolerant of any opposition, he put to death over a thousand people in the first few months of his regime.
>
> He took personal direction of the Terror, scribbling note after note to Dzerzhinsky – the first head of the Cheka – naming the persons he selected to have put out of the way. Dora Kaplan's assassination attempt, the Green Revolution [in Ukraine] and the Kronstadt Revolt led Lenin to even greater excesses of terror and in 1921, at the Tenth Congress, he introduced the principle of a monolithic Communist Party which would harbour no factions or dissent.
>
> The period of War Communism (1917-1921) was a reign of terror, disorganisation and destruction of all institutions and liberties. Above

all, Lenin had no sense of statesmanship, nor could he have. He did not care for Russia. Russia was but a stepping-stone on his path to world revolution. Under his aegis, the Treaty of Brest-Litovsk with the Kaiser's Germany reduced Russia to a minor power. It remained for others to undo the havoc perpetrated on the Russian land and peoples.[11]

Stalin lost no time launching the cult of Leninism. He had the body embalmed, draped in a flag of the Paris Commune and put on show to the masses in the Hall of Columns in the former Nobles' Club. For four days, half a million Muscovites queued outside in temperatures of minus 35 degrees for the privilege of filing past the body of their saviour in its crimson coffin. Lenin was later placed in a pyramid-shaped mausoleum under the faded rose-red walls of the Kremlin in Red Square. Petrograd was renamed Leningrad in his honour, while the citizens of his home town, Simbirsk, had to make do with Ulyanovsk. Statues in his honour proliferated like spring flowers.

At the time of Lenin's death Trotsky, the heir presumptive, was travelling through Georgia on his way to the Black Sea resort of Sukhumi to recover from a dose of paratyphoid fever. He failed to make it back to Moscow in time for the lying-in-state or for the funeral on Red Square on Sunday 27 January. The pro-Stalin press made sure the public knew all about his 'disrespect' for their deceased leader.[12]

On 22 January 1924 - the day following Lenin's death - Ramsay MacDonald, the man he'd described as 'a petty bourgeois, a liar, sophist, pedant and philistine', formed the Labour Party's first government at Westminster. While *Izvestia* tut-tutted that the Labour Party included such undesirables as 'persons professing religious convictions, Anglicans, Catholics and members of various other sects', one of the new British Government's first acts was to recognise the Soviet Union and offer it a loan to help solve its financial problems.[13]

On 9 April a Russian delegation arrived in London to discuss the terms of the loan. Don Gregory, now head of the Northern Department of the Foreign Office, met the visitors at Victoria Station. Despite his anti-Bolshevik views, he took a shine to the Soviet missionaries, especially Christian Rakovsky, Yevgeni Preobrazhensky and Grigory Sokolnikov (none of whom would survive the Stalinist purges). 'They were a very agreeable and easy-going party,' he says, 'and they lived in a hotel that no one had ever heard of before in Lancaster Gate.' After six months of intense negotiations, an agreement of sorts was cobbled together and, once the mandatory Soviet veto had been withdrawn, it was signed by both parties.[14]

Back in Moscow Nadezhda Krupskaya handed Lenin's Testament to the Central Committee Secretariat. He had wanted it to be made available to delegates at the Thirteenth Communist Party Congress in May 1924. 'Comrade Stalin,' he had dictated, 'having become General Secretary, has concentrated unlimited authority in his hands, and I am not sure whether he will always be capable of using that authority with sufficient caution.'[15]

In a postscript, he added, 'Stalin is too rude, and this defect, although quite tolerable in our midst and in dealing among us Communists, becomes intolerable in a General Secretary.' He suggested that Stalin be replaced in that post by someone 'more patient, more loyal, more courteous and more considerate of his comrades'.

Instead of being read aloud to the congress, as Lenin had wished, his Testament was read in small group sessions and Trotsky, in an effort to appease his rival, voted with the majority that it should never be made public.[i] Trotsky needed the party's support for his plan to use Russia as a base for world revolution. In his opinion, 'the Russia of icons and cockroaches' was too backward for anything else. Stalin, on the other hand, agreed with Nikolai Bukharin that socialism could be built in a single country, even one as underdeveloped as Russia.[16]

Most of the party's higher echelon agreed with Stalin. Even the cautious Lev Kamenev (Trotsky's brother-in-law) and Grigory Zinoviev (leader of the Comintern) joined forces with him to prevent Trotsky from taking power. The other three members of the Politburo - Alexei Rykov, Mikhail Yefremov (a.k.a. Mikhail Tomsky) and Bukharin - wavered for a time and then threw their weight behind him. They would live to regret it. As Churchill observed, the worst misfortune ever to befall the Russian people was Lenin's birth and the next worst was his death.

Heartbroken over the loss of Lilya, Kerensky moved out of the *Days* office into a pokey flat at 1b Avenue de la Villa de la Réunion. He could easily have taken a downward slide into the perdition that destroyed

---

i Lenin's Testament was published in the Soviet Union after Stalin's death in 1953.

many émigrés. Instead, he had the good fortune to find a French patron who connected him with the leftwing literary and political mainstream of the Third Republic. Aline Ménard-Dorian was reputed to be Proust's inspirations for Madame Verdurin, the salonniere in *À la recherche du temps perdu*. Kerensky was introduced to her by Albert Thomas, who had tutored her grandson, the war hero Jean Hugo, and was a regular visitor to her salon at 89 rue de la Faisanderie, Passy.[17] Jean Hugo's younger son, Jean Baptiste Hugo, told this author:

> My great-grandmother was a staunch anti-clerical socialist. She was always on the lookout for politicians with a human touch and she invited Kerensky to join her salon. She was in her seventies then but she had lost none of her radical spirit and many of Europe's leading leftwing political figures still visited her. Her house was packed with artworks and Kerensky would have conversed with them beneath a Rodin sculpture or Manet's portrait of his wife.

Aline was born Louise-Aline Dorian in 1850. Her father, Pierre-Frédéric Dorian, was a steel magnate and radical Republican leader who had served as Minister of Public Works during the Siege of Paris in the Franco-Prussian War. In 1869 - the year before war broke out – she had married Paul Ménard, son of a wealthy Protestant family from the Midi. As a mark of respect for her family, he added 'Dorian' to his own surname. 'She befriended my great-great grandfather Victor Hugo when he returned to France from exile on Guernsey after Louis Napoleon's fall from power in 1870,' says Jean Baptiste Hugo. 'She accompanied him to Guernsey during his convalescence in 1878 and she was at his bedside in Paris when he died in 1885. Her daughter, Pauline Ménard-Dorian, married Victor's grandson, Georges Hugo, and they had two children, my father Jean Hugo and my aunt Marguerite. Both children became Kerensky's friends.'[18]

Aline Ménard-Dorian's interest in the fate of the Russian people dated from the failure of the 1905 Revolution when she and her husband Paul, a member of the Radical Party, formed the Society of the Friends of the Russian People with Anatole France, Émile Zola and Kerensky's friend, Paul Painlevé. Many Russian émigrés joined her circle then but returned to Russia in 1917 under Kerensky's amnesty. It was typical of Aline's practical idealism that some of the new democracies created at Versailles in 1919 owed a debt to her patronage. She had given hope and inspiration to the young Thomas Masaryk, first President of the Czechoslovak Republic, and to his successor, Edouard Beneš. According to Jean Hugo, 'Politics was more necessary to her than bread.'[19]

At rue de la Faisanderie Kerensky met his old socialist friends Hjalmar Branting and Émile Vandervelde. According to Vandervelde, visitors to Aline's salon consisted of English Labour MPs, exiled Bulgarian agrarians, Irish Fenians, members of the International League for Human Rights,[ii] and some American passers-by who had come to Europe to investigate what was going on. One of Aline's favourite political writers, Geneviève Tabouis, recalls her at this time:

> From the tip of the high tortoise-shell comb which surmounted her fluffy white hair, to the soles of her little slippers, she was very much the grande-dame. Dressed in black lace, with suede gloves covering her exquisite arms and hands, bowing and smiling she received all the advanced democratic spirits of the day in her handsome house which, with its library, its paintings, bronzes and engravings, was a perfect museum of the history of the Republic from 1870 to 1914.[20]

Kerensky owed a great deal to Aline Ménard-Dorian's friendship. In the summer of 1924 he travelled south to stay at the family home, 'Mas de Fourques', at Lunel near Montpellier in the Hérault. Georges Hugo had inherited his grandfather's creative talent, which came into full flower in his son Jean Hugo, a brilliant artist, illustrator, theatre designer and author. Born in Paris in November 1894, Jean had been honoured for his valour in World War I with the Croix de Guerre, the Distinguished Service Cross and the Légion d'Honneur. His friends included Jean Cocteau, Pablo Picasso and Georges Auric, and Kerensky was welcomed into their leftwing milieu.[iii]

'There is a place in the garden that my father called "La Tribune de

---

ii Aline Ménard-Dorian, a passionate Dreyfusard, served as Vice President of the League of Human Rights *(Ligue des droits de l'homme,* LDH), the organisation founded in 1898 to correct the miscarriage of justice visited upon Alfred Dreyfus. The LDH would become the model for all future European human rights entities.

iii Jean Hugo also served as interpreter to Major George C. Marshall when the United States Army arrived in France in 1918. Marshall would become America's Chief of Staff in World War II and he was the instigator of the Marshall Plan, which did much to revive Western Europe after the war.

Kerensky"',' says Jean Baptiste. 'He told me Kerensky used to stand there speaking in Russian as though addressing a public meeting. One of the photographs in my father's album shows Kerensky playing boules on our lawn with my father and his first wife, the artist Valentine Gross, a German friend Gerda von Gerlach[iv] and the composer Georges Auric.'

A common love of music brought Kerensky closer to Georges Auric, a musical prodigy described by the head of the Soviet Conservatorium as 'a servile titillator of snobbish bourgeois tastes'. His works included the scores of many films, including *The Lavender Hill Mob, The Good Die Young, Moulin Rouge, Roman Holiday* and *Bonjour Tristesse*.

Meanwhile, the Kremlin was dissatisfied with the lack of progress being made towards world revolution. At the Fifth World Congress of the Comintern, held in Moscow from 17 June to 8 July 1924, Grigory Zinoviev harangued the delegates for five hours about their shortcomings. He complained that comrades in Britain - 'the most important section of the Communist International' – were opposed to infiltrating the Labour Party and would do so only under considerable pressure. Two or three months ago, he said, he had written a letter to the Communist Party of Great Britain in which he pointed out its grave mistakes.

> I think the situation is similar to that which existed in Russia during the Kerensky regime. No one dared to speak a word against Kerensky. Criticism had to be applied by insinuation. One had to repeat for an hour or so that certainly Kerensky was a fine fellow, a great man, but perhaps, after all, he was capable of making mistakes.
>
> The situation in Britain is very similar. The workers are still attached to MacDonald, they are still full of illusions, and, moreover, he has the advantage of not possessing a majority in the House. Matters are therefore not so simple as they seem. MacDonald's Government is in the ascendant, but if we wait till the policy he represents is overthrown, we do not need a Communist Party.
>
> We all know that the Social Democrats are doomed to a political

---

iv Gerda von Gerlach was related to Helmuth von Gerlach, a German pacifist who became chairman of the German Human Rights League in 1926. He escaped from the Nazis in 1933 and died in Paris two years later.

death, but we exist to quicken the process. Therefore, our party in Britain must fight MacDonald in order that the working masses, when they realise his meanness, should understand that we, the Communists, were the first to estimate him at his true value.

Our task in Great Britain is to create a mass party, edit a daily paper, mingle with the inner life of the trade unions, devote more attention to British youth, tackle the question of the Colonies, oppose all tendencies towards the right and conduct revolutionary propaganda at all costs.'

On 8 October 1924 the British Government lost a vote of no confidence and Ramsay MacDonald called an election for 29 October. Four days before polling day the *Daily Mail* published the 'Zinoviev Letter', allegedly written by Grigory Zinoviev to the Communist Party of Great Britain in which the head of the Comintern urged the party to 'strain every nerve' to have the Soviet trade treaty ratified by the MacDonald Government. Echoing the critical tone of Zinoviev's speech to the Comintern Congress in July, it also scolded his British comrades for their failure to radicalise the British armed forces in advance of the coming British revolution.[21]

That evening Winston Churchill took to the hustings and launched a broadside against MacDonald and the Russians:

While Mr MacDonald has been tampering and tinkering with the Bolsheviks, these foul, filthy butchers of Moscow have not been idle. They write from their Presidium to order that germ cells shall be established in our regiments and on our ships, that propaganda shall be made for bloody revolt to be started and for civil war, flames and carnage to defile our streets. They write to order these things in this country at the very moment when they are here discussing with the British Government a treaty for a loan asking for more of our money. I say such a thing has never occurred in the history of this country.

You all know the story of Kerensky, how he stood there like Mr MacDonald pretending that he meant to do the best he could for his country and all the time apologising behind the scenes to the wild, dark, deadly forces which had him in their grip. You see the same thing here, but luckily this country is not Russia. We are capable of managing our own affairs without the interference of foreign nations.[22]

Much of the election campaign was devoted to jousting between members of all parties over the Communist threat to Britain. Lloyd

George also attacked the Bolshevik dictatorship:

> There is an idea in the minds of our Labour friends that there is a great democratic Government in Russia. But there is not. The Russian Government represents a few hundred thousand of the workmen of Russia. Ninety per cent of the Russian population work on the soil. They have no voice in the government of Russia. The Bolsheviks, by sheer force, overthrew the Kerensky Government, which represented the whole of Russia, and seized power, and have governed ever since by sheer terror.[23]

The Zinoviev Letter outraged Leon Trotsky. He asserted in *Pravda*:

> How a document so nonsensical, so politically meaningless, a document which cries aloud that it is a forgery, could become the focus of attention of the leading political parties of the oldest civilised country in the world, a country of centuries of world supremacy and of parliamentary regime – that is what is truly incomprehensible.

The Zinoviev Letter was written in English and dated 15 September 1924. The original has never been found and there is no evidence that Zinoviev wrote it, or that it was ever sent to his British comrades. Zinoviev, Radovsky and Maxim Litvinov, now Deputy Commissar for Foreign Affairs, all denounced it as a forgery.

So who was to blame? Anybody who had read the *Izvestia* report of Zinoviev's speech to the Comintern less than three months earlier would have known that he had indeed written a letter of complaint to British Communists. Using the text of that speech, he or she could easily have manufactured the Zinoviev Letter. The most likely suspect was Ivan Pokrovsky, a former Tsarist officer connected to a forgery ring in Berlin. He is thought to have leaked the letter to the Secret Intelligence Service in London via Kerensky's former bloodhound, Rafael Farina, who had been appointed head of the SIS's Riga Station in the cover role of British Passport Control Officer.[24]

Farina transmitted the letter in a telegram from the Latvian capital to London. It was decoded at the Government Code and Cypher School in Queen's Gate, South Kensington, and the text was sent from SIS headquarters to the Foreign Office in Whitehall. A copy was also sent to Ramsay MacDonald, who was on the campaign trail in Scotland. He demanded proof of the letter's authenticity but before that could be obtained – indeed, it was never obtained - the Foreign Office mandarins delivered a formal protest, signed by Don Gregory in MacDonald's absence, to Christian Rakovsky, the Soviet chargé d'affaires in London. Someone leaked copies of the letter to Thomas Marlowe, editor of the *Daily Mail*, and to Stanley Baldwin's Conservative Party. 'The publication of the precious document over my humble signature was the signal for nearly everyone to go stark staring mad,' Gregory recalled in his memoirs.

On polling day the Labour vote actually rose by more than a million compared with the 1923 election but the party lost forty seats because the Liberal vote collapsed, sweeping the Conservatives into power. One of the new Government's first acts was to disown the Anglo-Soviet agreement that Don Gregory had laboured to produce. The Zinoviev Letter had achieved its most likely objectives: to embarrass the Kremlin and destroy the Labour Government.[25]

Meanwhile, Nell Tritton had become the beneficiary of a family trust fund on her twenty-fifth birthday on 19 September 1924, giving her the financial independence to explore the wider world. A trip to Europe was one of the rites of passage for young Australians and in April 1925 she sailed for England with the English novelist Francis Brett Young and his wife Jessie, who were visiting Australia to promote Brett Young's Mercian novels. Nell's intention, she told a reporter, was 'to study abroad and gather material for a novel' but there was more to it than that. Secretly, she would be looking for 'a Russian of great talent' to make her romantic dreams come true. She had no idea she would marry not one Russian but two.

London in the Roaring Twenties was exciting, promiscuous. There was no shortage of material to inspire a young writer. The Bright Young People were indispensable fodder for the Fleet Street gossip columns. Mayfair was their playground. They drank gin at the Embassy Club in Bond Street and took cocaine around the corner at the Ambassador in Conduit Street.

Nell met her Tritton and Worrall relatives and immersed herself in the arts. Francis Brett Young introduced her to George Bernard Shaw (another admirer of Maria Bashkirtseff), the sculptor Jacob Epstein and the poet Sir Henry Newbolt. It should have been a tremendous start for a young journalist but apart from mentioning these luminaries in her letters home she appears to have done nothing with them in her work.[v]

At Easter 1926 Nell went on holiday with the Brett Youngs and her younger brother Roy Tritton to Capri, the 'Island of Pleasure' which D. H. Lawrence described as 'a gossipy, villa-stricken, two-humped chunk of limestone'. Even London hadn't prepared her for the lifestyle there. She was swept up in a whirl of drunken parties, cocaine sniffing and ether cocktails, nude bathing and easy sex. Fortunately, she was in safe hands with the Brett Youngs. 'No one here has a shred of reputation,' wrote Hugh Walpole, 'except the Brett Youngs, and they are unpopular because they are so moral!'[26]

Nell spent the days swimming and taking walks along the steep paths. A press photographer snapped her on one of the rocky coves dressed in a one-piece swimsuit and waving an open parasol. Charles Baeyertz, her former boss on *The Triad*, was now editor of the *Sunday Times* in Sydney. He published the photo on 16 May 1926 under the headline: 'Young Australian writer in festive moment'. Pursuing her French dream, Nell now called herself 'Thérèse Nellé Tritton'.

Brett Young introduced her to the author Compton Mackenzie and his wife, Faith, who lived in 'La Solitaria', a luxurious villa clinging precariously to the rockface. Faith described the island's social life as 'first-class bacchanalia' and she took full advantage of it. While her husband was completing *Vestal Fire*, his novel about the infatuation of two American lesbians for a drug-addicted French pederast, she had taken a lover. Nicholas Alexandrovich Nadejine was a burly thirty-eight-year-old White Russian with a fine baritone voice who was trying to make a career for himself in opera.

Nell became quite friendly with Nadejine. As he told it, he had been exiled to Siberia in 1910 for taking part in a student disturbance at the University of Moscow. After three years of 'not such bad fun' (possibly because of his father's position as a general in the Tsar's army), he escaped in a small boat down the Angara River and then travelled overland through Austria and France to Italy.[27]

---

v Ironically, Bernard Shaw, one of Lenin's 'useful idiots' among European socialists, was involved in a war of words with Grigory Zinoviev. Through the pages of *Izvestia*, he advised the Soviet Government to dissociate itself from the Comintern leader's 'schoolboy nonsense' posing as socialism. Zinoviev replied sourly that Shaw was 'a fossilised Chauvinist and a self-satisfied Englishman', a slur that cut the Irish playwright to the quick.

Settling in Rome, he received a pardon for his youthful indiscretions and was given a job at the Russian Embassy, only to lose it after the October Revolution. Father and son had both joined the Russian exodus to Paris, where General Nadejine was employed as a taxi driver. Nell sensed that Nicholas's bravado masked a touching vulnerability and she returned to London wondering whether this might be her 'Russian of great talent'.

Following France's recognition of the Communist regime in October 1924, Stalin had appointed Leonid Krasin, as the first Soviet Ambassador to France. After seven years' occupancy, Vasily Maklakov was forced to move out of the Russian Embassy. He took with him sixteen boxes containing the Okhrana files on all the leading Bolshevik revolutionaries – Lenin, Trotsky, Stalin, Molotov – that had been compiled in Paris over many years. At great personal risk he shipped this huge trove of anti-Communist material to Stanford University in California. Any announcement of its existence would have placed his life in danger, so the boxes remained sealed until his death in Switzerland in July 1957.[28]

Kerensky was well-placed in the volatile world of French politics through his friendships with Albert Thomas and Paul Painlevé, who served as Prime Minister until November 1925 and then became Minister of War in Aristide Briand's new government. Kerensky also reconnected with Marius Moutet, a Socialist senator whom he had met in May 1917 when Moutet travelled to Petrograd to persuade Russia to continue the war as part of the Entente. Since the October Coup he had become an unfailing supporter of Russian exiles.

Sitting behind a cluttered desk in his newspaper office in Passy, Kerensky told Georges Suarez of *Le Temps* that the workers and democrats of Europe were now convinced that Russia was not a 'socialist paradise'; in fact, the Soviet state was not in the process of evolution, or even revolution, but of liquidation. He advocated a renewal of economic relations between Western nations and his homeland 'so that the latter may take more quickly her place among civilised nations'. The Kremlin agreed. Stalin transferred Leonid Krasin from Paris to London to open the door to a new trade deal. The Conservative Prime Minister Stanley Baldwin and his Foreign Secretary Austen Chamberlain had no intention of cooperating in that strategy. Krasin struggled with a non-responsive Whitehall until November 1926 when he succumbed to a long-standing blood disease.[29]

Don Gregory attended his lying-in-state - 'the Godless equivalent of a memorial service'- at the Russian Embassy in Belgravia. Chesham House was arrayed for a vast reception, complete with orchestra, waiters, red carpets and a cloakroom but, Gregory reported to the Foreign Office, no more than a dozen visitors turned up to pay their respects.[30]

Meanwhile, Nell Tritton had taken the boat-train across the Channel to follow in the footsteps of Marie Bashkirtseff. 'At last I have found what I longed for without knowing what it was!' Marie had written in her diary. 'Life, that is Paris! Paris, that is life! How happy it makes one to know what one desires.' Nell, like her heroine, moved into Montparnasse. From a modest apartment a short walk from the Luxembourg Gardens, she made the pilgrimage to Marie's tomb at Passy Cemetery. It was an extraordinary sight: a large Gothic mausoleum topped with a dome and a stylised metal crucifix. Inside, there was a full-sized artist's studio containing a copy of Marie's bust sculpted by her friend René de Saint Marceaux. One of her last paintings, 'Women Saints', was also on display.

Nell had no difficulty fitting into the Parisian scene. She wore the bobbed hair and shorter, knee-length skirts of the garçonne (as the French flapper was called) but she also favoured the stylish, flowing outfits of the Right Bank couturiers. As a fluent French-speaker, Paris was an easy place in which to meet new people. She was soon contributing articles to New York magazines under a variety of pennames, one of which was 'An American Girl in Paris'.

One of her new friends was John Brownlee, a farmer's son from Geelong who was making a name for himself as an operatic baritone. He had been studying in Paris ever since Dame Nellie Melba heard him singing Handel's *Messiah* in Melbourne and urged him to go overseas for further tuition. By the time Nell arrived three years later, he was singing operatic roles at the Trianon Lyrique in Montmartre.

Nell reconnected with Nicholas Nadejine, who sometimes sang at La Rotonde to make a few francs. He was delighted to see the young Australian heiress again and lost no time letting her know of his interest. Nadejine had sung some of Massenet's *Thaïs* and Puccini's *Tosca* with the great Canadian soprano Louise Edvina. She thought him sufficiently talented to introduce him to Harry Higgins, chairman of the Grand Opera Syndicate which leased the Covent Garden Theatre in London's West End. After nearly thirty years as adjudicator, Higgins did not think Nadejine measured up to the required standard and turned him down. Nadejine was desolated; he became moody and drowned his sorrows in vodka.[vi][31]

Meanwhile, the Communists had won their battle of wits with Boris Savinkov and Sidney Reilly. Savinkov had left Paris in August 1924 on a secret mission to Russia after being duped into joining yet another hare-brained scheme. *Izvestia* reported that he had been arrested, tried and condemned to death. A later report said his sentence had been commuted to ten years' imprisonment. Finally, the OGPU announced he had been released and was living in a comfortable house in Lubianka Square (a Soviet joke – the political prison of that name was in a narrow street leading into the square).

Reilly received a letter from Savinkov saying he had changed his views of the Bolsheviks. 'How many illusions and fairytales have I buried here in the Lubianka!' he said. 'I have met men in the GPU whom I have known and trusted from my youth up and who are nearer to me than the chatterboxes of the foreign delegation of the Socialist Revolutionaries.'[vii]

Reilly said the letter was a forgery and that his friend was already dead. 'Savinkov was killed when attempting to cross the Russian frontier,' he said, 'and a mock trial, with one of their own agents as chief actor, was staged by the OGPU in Moscow behind closed doors.' Bruce Lockhart provided a mournful postscript to his extraordinary life. 'The last time I saw him was in a night-haunt in Prague in 1923,' he says. 'He was a pathetic figure for whom one could not help feeling the deepest sympathy.'

---

vi By comparison, John Brownlee's career was flourishing. When Melba heard him sing at the Trianon Lyrique, she insisted that he appear in her Covent Garden farewell on 8 June 1926. Brownlee sang Marcello in Acts 3 and 4 of *La Bohème* opposite the celebrated diva. The following year he made a sensational début at the Paris Opera House in *Thaïs*.

vii The Cheka was reformed into the GPU (the State Political Directorate) in 1922. The following year it was given additional duties and renamed the OGPU).

Ironically, Reilly also fell into an OGPU trap a few months later when a Communist front organisation called 'the Trust', which supposedly coordinated anti-Soviet activities inside the USSR, invited him to Moscow. He was duly arrested and, having been sentenced to death in 1918, was executed on 5 November 1925. Newspapers dubbed him 'the greatest spy in history' and there were claims that he had spied for at least four of the great powers. But he left behind more questions than answers about his erratic career.

28

The Incurable Romantic

Alexander Kerensky remained a mercurial figure who drifted in and out of the lives of his sons whenever he was in London. As students holidaying in Paris, they had become aware of his multiple female liaisons. 'He was not promiscuous,' Oleg Kerensky says, 'but was genuinely in love with the woman of the moment.' During his visits to London 'the woman of the moment' was his hostess, Maria Evseyevna Gavronskaya, Jacob Gavronsky's wife. Kerensky's biographer, Richard Abraham, quoted 'a privileged observer' as saying that Maria – or Mary as she liked to be called – was one of his very few 'grande passions'.

He also noted that she was the daughter of the Russian tea magnate Isaiah Kalmanovsky, who had made a fortune from plantations in Ceylon (Sri Lanka). 'Torn between the worship of a romantic hero and her admiration for Gavronsky,' Abraham wrote, 'she became more and more emotional.' Emotional or not, it seems her sense of loyalty to her husband outweighed her passion for Kerensky and the relationship was never consummated.[1]

Life for Olga Kerenskyaya, meanwhile, remained difficult. 'She lived in boarding houses while we were at Oakfield and then in rented rooms while we were engineering students at Northampton College [in Central London],' Gleb Kerensky says. 'It was a time of very real poverty. She worked as a secretary-typist in the City and when she left the office in the evening she had to do the shopping, cooking and cleaning for three. Some money was supposed to come from a charitable fund in Czechoslovakia for our education but mostly it did not arrive and she had to support us out of her salary.'[2]

Oleg and Gleb both graduated with honours in 1927 and on 3 June 1928 Oleg married Nathalie Bely, the daughter of a London-based Russian family whom he had met while she was a psychology student at King's College, London. Oleg joined the bridge department of Dorman Long and worked on designs for the Sydney Harbour Bridge. Gleb joined the English Electric Company (later GEC) in Birmingham and transferred to Rugby to specialise in hydroelectric turbines.

Back in Paris their father was attracted to Marina Tsvetaeva, one of Russia's greatest lyrical poets, who was contributing verse to *Days*. Tsvetaeva had touched his heart by presenting him with a copy of her poem 'The Tsar Maiden' ('*Tzar-Devitsa*'), which she inscribed, 'To dear Alexander Fyodorovich Kerensky - a Russian fairytale, in which nothing turns out well'.[i] She was referring to her poem but she could have been referring to his relationships with women. One of his friends recalled Tsvetaeva as 'neither eloquent nor pretty; thin, pale, almost emaciated; the oval of her face was narrow, serene, her cropped hair was still fair, but already strewn with grey. She was altogether not beautiful, but icon-like'. Her husband, Sergei Efron, had been devastated when she embarked on an affair with one of his friends while they were living in Prague. Nevertheless, she spent many hours with Kerensky and in 1926 their relationship became physical. This angered Zinaida Hippius, who disliked Tsvetaeva's Soviet sympathies. Suspecting that she was trying to draw Kerensky closer to the Kremlin, Hippius depicted her in a letter to Vladimir Khodasevich as 'a shameless harlot who uses her sexual favours for purposes of political subversion'.[3]

When Tsvetaeva wrote an admiring letter to the Soviet poet Vladimir Mayakovsky, Paul Miliukov refused to publish any more of her work in *The Latest News*. Her liaison with Kerensky ended abruptly when she abandoned Paris for a fisherman's hut at Saint-Gilles-sur-Vie, a little port in the Vendée, where she was reunited with her husband.[ii]

A much more significant relationship awaited Kerensky when the White Star liner *Olympic* docked in New York on 2 March 1927 on his first visit to America. He was met on the quayside that chilly Wednesday morning by Nicholas Vinner, his former adjutant, who was now Professor of Russian Languages at Columbia University; Simeon Strunsky, a Russian-born editor on the *New York Times*; and Kenneth Farrand Simpson, an old friend from Paris who, with his wife Helen, would become his staunchest allies.

---

i This copy of 'The Tsar Maiden' later sold at auction in Moscow for $230,000.
ii Marina Tsvetaeva and Sergei Efron later returned to Russia. Efron was executed on espionage charges in 1941 and Tsvetaeva committed suicide.

Simpson had served in France as a captain in the 302nd Field Artillery Regiment. After graduating from Harvard Law School in 1922, he returned to Paris as an attorney working with the French Government to recover artworks stolen by the German occupiers during the war. As well as befriending Kerensky, he represented Pablo Picasso, Edmund Wilson and Gertrude Stein in some of their work. He was now an Assistant United States District Attorney for the Southern District of New York City.

Kerensky's friends escorted him to his Manhattan address, the Hotel Weylin on Madison Avenue at 54th Street. His first public appearance was to be a speech commemorating the tenth anniversary of the February Revolution at the Century Theatre on Central Park West in eleven days' time. The United States had been the first great power to recognise his government in 1917 and, unlike France and Britain, Washington still refused to acknowledge the Communist regime. Assessing his role in the Revolution, the *New York Times* commented: 'His weakness is supposed to have consisted in his failure to recognise the elemental forces let loose by the revolution which overthrew Tsarism. He sought to practice reason and moderation in the midst of a hurricane, and he was brushed aside by more resolute men who were prepared to stop at nothing in trying for what they wanted. Lack of courage he has not been charged with.'[4]

Among the readers of this editorial was Grigory Benenson, the Russian oligarch of Lena Goldfields notoriety. He had bought two tickets for Kerensky's lecture and he asked his daughter, Flora Solomon, who was visiting him from London, to go with him. Flora was reluctant. 'If I thought about Kerensky at all it was with contempt for having surrendered so meekly to the Bolsheviks,' she says. But her father persisted and Flora agreed to accompany him to the event.[5]

Benenson had hit New York with his customary dynamism. On 19 December 1919, five weeks after his arrival, he paid $10 million - almost half in cash - for one of the largest office structures in the financial district, the City Investing Building at 165 Broadway. To let people know he was in town, he renamed it the Benenson Building, set up home in the Saint Regis Hotel and became a member of the New York Cotton Exchange.[6]

Around midday on Sunday 13 March Grigory Benenson and Flora Solomon arrived at the Century Theatre to find dozens of police officers attempting to control a noisy multitude of 5000 Whites, Communists, Socialist Revolutionary exiles and curious New Yorkers. Monarchists jostled with Socialists while up in the galleries the Communists belted out Red Army songs. The stage was packed with Kerensky's supporters but at two o'clock when he stood up to speak there were as many boos as cheers and the stirring strains of the imperial national anthem rang out from the orchestra seats.[7]

As the Benensons watched, Catherine Bary, a smiling young White Russian émigrée, approach Kerensky with a bouquet of red and white carnations. Instead of handing over the flowers, she struck him three times across the face with her glove. As she was led away, he addressed the Whites in the orchestra pit, 'Oh, you poor little monarchists. You have lost your manhood. Not one of your ex-officers dares to come upon this stage! Instead you send a woman.'

Flora Solomon wrote in her memoirs, 'The glove must have concealed a heavy metal object, for blood poured from his cheek. Kerensky seemed unmoved. He lifted his arm for silence and began to speak. A hush now descended on the hall. I heard for the first time the voice still spoken of as "the peal of Kremlin bells". Though shaken by what I had observed not ten feet away, I was transfixed.'[8]

Kerensky had lost none of his theatricality: pacing up and down the stage with a handkerchief clasped to his wounded cheek, his message to the faithful was that he was as willing as ever to shed his own blood for his beliefs. He denounced Lenin's treachery in betraying the Revolution and attacked the perfidy of the Western Allies for abandoning Russia in her hour of need. The Communists had stolen the Russian people's freedom, he said, and they were now held in a despotism as brutal as any the world had ever known.[9]

Later that evening Flora met Kerensky at a reception organised in his honour at the home of two of his Jewish supporters, Arthur and Judith Bookman, at 33 East 70th Street. Kerensky still spoke only a little English, so they conversed in Russian and, according to Flora, were soon oblivious to the presence of the other guests.

Explaining the assault at the theatre, Kerensky said that his attacker blamed him for the execution of her fiancé, a Tsarist officer, during the war. He understood her motivation and had refused to press charges. Kerensky felt relaxed in Flora's company and after a few minutes' conversation they slipped away from the party and took a taxi back to the Flora's hotel, the Plaza next to Central Park.[10]

In common with other American hotels the Plaza enforced strict rules relating to unmarried couples, the most puritanical of which was that no woman could entertain a man in her room alone. As they had been observed going upstairs together, the night manager was soon banging on the bedroom door. Kerensky hid himself in the bathroom while Flora dealt with the irate hotelier.

'You have brought a visitor to your room,' the man said. 'You must know that such things are not allowed.' Flora threw herself on the night manager's mercy. Her visitor, she said, was Alexander Kerensky, the former Prime Minister of Russia, and if the story leaked into the newspapers the Plaza would be involved in a scandal. The manager saw the point and retreated, leaving Flora to spend a night with her new lover. In his arms, she wrote, she experienced a joy she never knew existed.

Flora's motives in seducing Kerensky were quite straightforward: her husband, Harold Solomon, had been paralysed in a riding accident in South Africa shortly after their marriage and although she was devoted to him and their young son, Peter, she was looking for sexual fulfilment. 'I was attracted to the man with a passion which told me that hitherto my womanhood had been a hollow thing,' she says. 'Suddenly, I became aware of new aspects of my personality, so calming, so strengthening.'[iii]

Kerensky stayed in America for four months. One of the high points was a live radio broadcast from the ballroom of the Bellevue-Stratford Hotel in Philadelphia; one of the low points was another face-slapping incident at a banquet in his honour in Chicago. Back in New York, 1500 people packed the Mecca Temple to hear him speak on behalf of the USSR's political prisoners. He declared that terrorism in Russia today was worse than it had been under the Tsar; freedom of speech was throttled and the prisons and labour camps were full of political prisoners.

A Communist in the gallery demanded a definition of democracy. 'Democracy,' Kerensky replied with a smile, 'is that form of government under which a Communist might ask a question like yours without being molested.'

The biggest coup of the trip was the serialisation in the *New York Times* of his memoirs as a five-part series under the headline 'Inside

---
iii Peter Solomon, as Peter Benenson, started Amnesty International in 1961.

the Russian Revolution' in which he attacked General Kornilov and the Bolsheviks for their betrayal of Russia and the Revolution. These memoirs were expanded into a book published later that year by D. Appleton & Company of New York as *The Catastrophe: Kerensky's Own Story of the Russian Revolution*. Mourning the death of democracy under Lenin and Stalin, he had written:

> The strength of our Russian Revolution lay precisely in the fact that it triumphed over its enemies not by terror and bloodshed but by mercy, love and justice. Perhaps I dreamt all this. Perhaps this Revolution never existed, except in my imagination. But it seemed to exist then. Now everyone in Russia is dazed by blood. One hates the other to the extent of mutual annihilation. But this will pass, or if it does not pass, if the Russian people never come to understand the beauty and greatness of their first impulse, then we have been mistaken and our Revolution was not the prelude to a new life of which we had all dreamt but the epilogue of the dying culture of a people about to vanish forever into history.[11]

Kerensky returned to Paris in July 1927. Experience had taught him that his emotional attachments never lasted long but in Flora Solomon he had found not only a lover but also a benefactor. She was a wealthy woman in her own right and it was the deepest of ironies that some of her money came from her father's exploitation of the Lena Goldfields. Visiting her lover, she was appalled at the squalor of his tiny flat at 1b Avenue de la Villa de la Réunion. She rented a maisonette nearby in the rue des Belles Feuilles, which became what she called 'my bedroom paradise'. For the next decade, she helped to fund Kerensky's newspaper and to pay some of his living expenses. 'Kerensky was a true romantic,' she says, 'but he was also a man in blinkers to whom every move had to be a step towards the only goal – the liberation of Russia. Was his love equal to my own? I neither expected nor demanded it of him. And I did not punish myself with jealousy.'[12]

At the same time as Flora Solomon was conducting her affair with Kerensky on the Right Bank, Nell Tritton, the woman who would take him away from her, was beginning married life across the Seine in Montparnasse. On 9 February 1927 in a traditional Orthodox ceremony at Saint Philip's Russian Church in London, 'Lydia Ellen Thérèse

Nellé Tritton', as she described herself on the wedding certificate, had become 'Madame Nicholas de Nadejine'. The bride and groom held candles, exchanged rings and then, wearing gold crowns, circled the altar. Nell's sister and brother-in-law, Ivy and Ashley Shaw, were the only members of her family in the congregation.

Nell's marriage made headlines in Australia, where the newspapers were only too pleased to inflate the importance of her husband. 'M. Nadejine,' the Brisbane *Telegraph* solemnly reported, 'is not only a singer with a Continental reputation, particularly in Italy and France, but is a Russian poet of considerable standing. In fact, his last book of poems contains work which critics of Russian literature have said has not been surpassed since Pushkin.'

Nell paid for her husband to have professional singing lessons but despite receiving all possible artistic and financial assistance he failed to find a place at the Paris Opera House. As for his fabled talent as a poet, married life did nothing to stimulate his muse.

Since the two physical attacks in America, Kerensky had been particularly careful about security. 'He constantly received threats to his life and had once been attacked in broad daylight,' Flora Solomon says. 'I sensed danger everywhere.' Indeed, an OGPU agent known as 'Captain Korotnev' insinuated his way into the *Days* office on rue de Vineuse with the intention of assassinating him. Kerensky, however, confronted him and, according to one source, 'talked him out of shooting him'. Korotnev lost his nerve, stole a stash of documents and fled back to Moscow. The Communists published the documents as a pamphlet that blamed Kerensky for the Kronstadt Revolt.[13]

David Soskice and Jacob Gavronsky, who had met Flora through the Russian colony in London, welcomed her as a valued recruit in their mission to free Russia from Communist servitude. Flora, however, judged it a lost cause. 'I suppose revolutions have been created from less,' she said, 'but this hardly struck me as the spearhead of a movement directed to the heart of the Soviet populations. More, it seemed the shadow of the tail of a long-extinct comet.'

Over dinner at Chez Maurice she tried to open Kerensky's eyes to his impossible position, 'reasoning that whatever the crimes of Stalinism, the Soviet masses had at least made a beginning towards cultural and economic progress'. Such an argument was anathema to him. 'It infuriated him,' she said. 'Soviet democracy was a cruel sham, returning Russia to a constitutional ice age.'[14]

Kerensky's beliefs were vindicated when Stalin relaunched the Revolution with the forcible collectivisation of the farms. 'Stalin's present methods will bring on another terrible famine,' Kerensky warned. 'The Soviet is terrorising the peasants, seizing their wheat and paying only one-tenth of the market value. They are also indulging in religious terrorism, shooting many priests on the grounds that they are indulging in anti-Bolshevik propaganda.'

Trotsky, one of the chief persecutors, found himself on the receiving end of Stalin's malice in late 1927 when he was expelled from his Kremlin residence and, on the tenth anniversary of the Revolution, exiled to Alma-Ata in Kazakhstan. His followers – the first Trotskyists - were hunted down and killed. To save his life, Trotsky boarded a ship in Odessa and went into exile in Istanbul with his family. H. G. Wells, John Maynard Keynes, Harold Laski and Beatrice Webb pleaded with the government for him to be given asylum in Britain. Trotsky must have found that amusing - he despised leftwing intellectuals and had they been in Russia he would probably have shot them. Anyway, Stanley Baldwin was too canny to listen to the pleadings of fellow travellers.[15]

When Nell's parents, Frederick and Eliza Tritton, and her youngest brother, Cyril, arrived from Australia on a European tour, she took the train to meet them in Rome. Writing to cousin Gladys Edds in Brisbane from the Grand Hotel Miramare, Geneva, on 21 June 1928, she described a wonderful trip through Italy and added that in a few days they would be leaving for Genoa and Monte Carlo.

Nicholas Nadejine, who had been drinking heavily, had remained in Paris. On Nell's return home they were overjoyed to discover that she was pregnant. During her time in London she had invested in a house in West Hampstead and the couple moved there so that their baby would be born a British citizen. Nell prayed that fatherhood might curtail Nicholas's drinking but she miscarried the baby and became so seriously ill that she lost her sight. Her parents and brother dashed to London and spent many anxious hours at her bedside. It was feared that the blindness resulted from the lead poisoning in childhood but, given rest and good medical treatment, she recovered her sight.[16]

Kerensky made many visits to London, where he attended dinner parties at Flora Solomon's house in Horton Street, Kensington, and saw his sons and grandson, Oleg Jr, born to Oleg and Nathalie on 9 January 1930. Flora's husband Harold had died in July that year and she relied on Kerensky for emotional support. They shared a boating-and-fishing holiday at Annecy during which, she says, he proposed to her but she turned him down because of what she called 'the tedium of the politician passé'.[17]

Passé or not, he still excited the enmity of Reds and Whites alike. When he lectured at Oxford, it was the Communists who protested to the Foreign Office. The next time he applied to enter Britain he was refused a visa unless he gave an undertaking not to talk about Russia. The Labour Government realised this was an unacceptable ban on free speech and withdrew it. Meanwhile, White exiles lost no opportunity to humiliate him. It might be nothing worse than a snub – such as the Tsar's former Gentleman of the Bedchamber, who, on being introduced to him, put his hand behind his back to avoid shaking his hand.

On 17 June 1931 Bruce Lockhart took his friend to lunch at the Carlton Grill to celebrate his fiftieth birthday the previous month. Lockhart was working for the Londoner's Diary gossip column in Lord Beaverbrook's *Evening Standard*. 'The Beaver' was there that day and Lockhart invited him to join them. Beaverbrook asked Kerensky why he hadn't had Trotsky shot in 1917.

Kerensky replied that Trotsky had taken no part in the July rebellion that year and so there were no grounds for executing him. So what, Beaverbrook demanded, was the reason for his collapse? Kerensky replied that the Germans ordered the Bolshevik uprising because their allies Austria, Bulgaria and Turkey were on the brink of making separate peace deals with Russia – indeed, the Austrians had decided to ask for a separate peace less than a fortnight before the October Revolution.

> Beaverbrook: Would you have mastered the Bolsheviks if you had made a separate peace yourselves?
> Kerensky: Of course. We would be in Moscow now.
> Beaverbrook: Why didn't you do it?
> Kerensky: We were too naïve.[18]

Back in Paris Kerensky was reunited with Vladimir Nabokov when the author arrived from Berlin in October to exploit his hard-won fame. He had been publishing his work under the nom de plume V. Sirin, a reference to the mythical creature that possessed the head and chest of a beautiful woman and the body of a bird, the legendary 'firebird' of Russian art. They met at Ilya and Amalia Fondaminsky's home in rue Chernoviz. According to Nabokov, Kerensky looked like 'an old but still hearty actor'.

Pressing a gold lorgnette to his left eye, he congratulated the author on *Kamera Obskura*, a novella about an older man's obsession with a young girl. 'Kerensky,' Nabokov says, 'shook my hand, held the pause, and, in a dramatic whisper: "Amazing!"'[19]

There was no end to the ambition of the émigré publishers. Fondaminsky used family money to launch a Russian quarterly literary review, *Contemporary Annals* (*Sovremennye Zapiski*). According to Nabokov, the former terrorist was 'a saintly and heroic soul, who did more for Russian emigrant literature than any other man'.[20]

Meanwhile, as Kerensky had warned, Stalin had taken 'religious terrorism' to new depths of savagery. In December 1931 the Cathedral of Christ the Saviour in Moscow was dynamited as part of a nationwide purge by the League of Militant Atheists. Protestant churches and seminaries were also closed and their clerics arrested or shot as counter-revolutonaries. Ten thousand mosques were shut down and their imams terrorised as ruthlessly as Christians. In Siberia, shamans were thrown out of planes to see if they could fly.[21]

Stalin turned the cruelty of total state control on ordinary civilians in December 1932 with the introduction of internal passports. These documents decided where they lived, where they worked and whether they had the right to move from one place to another. Peasants were denied passports and were ordered to remain in grain-producing areas. Within three months the OGPU had tracked down 219,500 'illegal' peasants. Most were returned to their villages but thousands were interned in concentration camps.[22]

State control was taken to obscene extremes in the famine that was devastating much of the country. Holodomor ('to kill by starvation'), a man-made famine ordered by Stalin, killed between 3.5 and 4.5 million Ukrainians in 1932 and 1933. Nationwide, government policies led to population losses (including children never born because of the catastrophe) of between 5.5 to seven million, including 1.5 million in Khazakhstan. Officially, there was no famine and to mention it was a serious crime.[23]

The Revolution had moved so far from the joyous ideals of the February Days as to be unrecognisable. In his memoirs Don Gregory wrote, 'Not only does Bolshevism as revealed in practice become a complete perversion of the basic idea of socialism, but, in its virtually mystic garb, it has gone right away beyond collectivism into a sphere totally outside it. It has simply become a jumble of all the oldest religious heresies and the latest material developments of history.'[24]

Days had ceased publication in 1933 and Kerensky was putting down his own experiences of Bolshevik methods in his second book of memoirs, *The Crucifixion of Liberty*. Whenever possible, he returned to London to see his sons and grandson, and on one trip he met Lloyd George for lunch in the Chinese Room of the Metropole Hotel in the Strand. The postwar years had seen a dramatic reversal in his old adversary's reputation. He had been exposed as a philanderer and denounced for selling knighthoods and baronetcies to fund the Liberal Party.[25]

Lloyd George was writing his *War Diaries* and he seized the opportunity to pump Kerensky for information, scribbling notes in a pad as he spoke. He then lived up to his reputation of repaying loyalty with betrayal with this passage:

> Kerensky could never bring himself to take sufficiently rigorous measures against the extreme left, even when they resorted to violent measures to achieve their objects. He was a master of the eloquence that stirs masses, but he trusted too much to his remarkable gifts in that direction, and ignored the fact that there comes a time when words must be translated into action. Able to sway the Duma, the Soviet or the crowd triumphantly with a speech, he relied on his oratorical arts. The man who mattered – Lenin – was not within the sound of his voice, and had he been it would have made no difference to the ruthless fanatic. He despised the Kerensky type.[26]

Kerensky dictated *Crucifixion* in Russian, which Gleb translated into English. The book was published in London and New York in March 1934. In his review in the *New York Times*, Simeon Strunsky wrote:

Kerensky says that the strong appeal which Communism and Fascism make to millions today is less a matter of dogma than of method. It is the crusading spirit in itself that fires the imagination. There is in the world today, he says, a Communist fanaticism and a Fascist fanaticism. Why are there no fanatics of democracy? Why cannot popular government introduce planning into economic life, but planning reconciled with and based upon freedom of the individual and the dignity of the human soul?[27]

Kerensky paid particular attention to 'the annihilation of democracy in Germany', where Nazi paramilitaries had bullied non-Nazi members of the Reichstag into voting for the Enabling Act, which gave Hitler the power to pass whatever laws he wished without consulting parliament. Hitler's chief enabler, President Hindenburg, had signed the Act into law that same day. 'The collapse of the Germany of Weimar into the Hitlerite Third Reich,' Kerensky wrote, 'confronts the whole of European democracy with the fundamental question: must popular government remain, even now, a mere vote-counting machine, or will it be resurrected at long last as a thing of great social and cultural value, the existence of which is unassailable and independent of the ballot-box? The future of the civilised state, the future of civilisation itself depends upon the answer to this question.'[28]

When Hitler reintroduced compulsory military service shortly afterwards, even the French Left, which had stubbornly embraced neo-pacifism and refused to contemplate war with the Nazi regime, was thrown into a state of panic.

Meanwhile, Nell's marriage to Nicholas Nadejine had broken down because of his drinking and infidelity. Nell had had enough of what she called his 'Russian egotism'; she consulted lawyers and started divorce proceedings. In October 1934 she travelled alone in the Italian liner *Romolo* to Sydney. To cover up the failure of her marriage, she told reporters that Nicholas had not been able to accompany her because he was on a concert tour of Scotland. In fact, he was back in the arms of his former lover, Faith Mackenzie. Returning to London in March 1935, Nell sold her house of sad memory in West Hampstead and moved into a flat in bohemian Chelsea. Her divorce decree was granted the following year on the grounds of Nicholas's adultery.

Nell needed to meet new people and to make herself available for new experiences. She accepted an invitation from Flora Solomon to a garden party to raise funds for Alexander Kerensky's latest venture, a newspaper called *New Russia* (*Novaia Rossiia*).[29] Finding 'Madame Nadejine' an attractive addition to his support network, he invited her to have lunch with him on his next visit to London. Nell was not looking for a replacement husband, or even a job, when she turned up at the appointed venue that September. During her marriage she had taken Russian lessons but her Russian was as limited as Kerensky's English, so they conversed in French.

Kerensky was impressed with Nell's intelligence, her command of the French language and the fact that she was a skilful driver. He offered her a job as translator-chauffeur, explaining that money was tight and he could not afford to pay her a proper salary. The thought of returning to Paris appealed to Nell and she moved back to Montparnasse later that month.

On 7 March 1936 German soldiers, with flags flying and drums beating, marched into the Rhineland in breach of the Versailles Treaty and the Locarno pact of 1925. The German force had orders to retreat if challenged but no challenge materialised. Pierre Laval, the pro-Nazi French Prime Minister, did nothing. Stanley Baldwin appealed to the impotent League of Nations. President Franklin D. Roosevelt went fishing. There was no protest from his Secretary of State, Cordell Hull. Hitler was jubilant. At a stroke he had proved that the great democracies were weak and disunited.

After taking tea with Hitler at the Berghof on 4 September 1936, Lloyd George announced that Britain had nothing to worry about. 'German hegemony in Europe, which was the aim and dream of the old pre-war militarism, is not even on the horizon of Nazism,' he said. The Führer was 'the greatest German of the age', 'the George Washington of Germany'.[30]

Nell Tritton worked in the office of *New Russia* in Passy and drove Kerensky to his appointments around the city. He was a difficult taskmaster. He barked orders at his staff, raising his voice and sometimes bursting into song – Verdi's *Aida* was his favourite opera. Some of his editorials were set to verse. For health reasons, he drank no alcohol and, as penance for his failure to save Russia from the Bolsheviks, he denied himself the pleasure of the cinema and the theatre. He more than compensated for those denials with a vigorous appetite for sex and food, particularly sweetmeats.

Through her work at the newspaper, Nell met Nina Berberova and they became friends. Nell told Nina about reading Marya Bashkirtseva's diaries and travelling to Europe in the hope of meeting Russians; how she had fallen in love with Nicholas Nadejine and how he had deceived her 'with some crazy elderly Englishwomen who were rich and idle'.[31]

The friends were united in their condemnation of the Communist regime. Nina's loathing of Stalin was visceral: not a day passed, she said, 'when I did not feel his presence in the world, did not feel hatred, revulsion, degradation, and fear in pronouncing his name'. The thing they could not agree on was Alexander Kerensky. Nina judged him harshly. 'He always appeared to me to be a man of little will power but great intentions, of negligible strength of conviction and mad stubbornness, of great self-assurance and limited intellect,' she wrote in her memoirs. 'I will allow that both the self-assurance and the stubbornness grew in him with the years, that he deliberately cultivated them in defence of himself. A man such as he, who was *killed*, in the full sense of the word, by 1917, had to build his armour to continue to exist: beak, claws, tusks. The most painful punishment for a politician is to be forgotten.' It was precisely these human failings that Nell found attractive. Like her ex-husband, he was fallible but, unlike Nadejine, he denied himself the luxury of self-pity.[32]

The Depression had given the kiss of death to 'Russian Berlin'. Many émigrés could no longer make a living there and so Russian shops and cafés that relied on expatriate trade closed down. *The Rudder*, the paper founded by V. D. Nabokov, vanished from the streets and pro-Hitler Russians took control of the Russian community. Vladimir Nabokov's wife Vera was Jewish and the rise of antisemitism and the appointment of his father's assassin as Hitler's deputy director of Russian émigré affairs made the German capital a dangerous place. When he visited Paris in January 1937 to give further readings of his work, he was intent on making enough money to move Vera and their four-year-old son Dmitri there.

One night Kerensky invited Nell for a meal at the Café des Tourelles. He enjoyed the food there but, more to the point, the waiters addressed him as 'Monsieur Le President'. Nell found herself drawn to this strange individual. He was undeniably a man of great, if uncertain, talent. Part of Kerensky's appeal to the opposite sex was that he had grown more handsome with age. He reminded Flora Solomon of a Shakespearean actor 'whose features have been chiselled from generations close to the climatic extremes of Russia's heartland'.

When Nell learned that he had had a diseased kidney removed and had suffered ever since from a kidney complaint, she switched all of the affection she had felt for Nicholas Nadejine to him. Within a couple of months, she had fallen in love with her 'beloved unicorn', as she called him, a reference to his masculinity, his uniqueness and the threat of extinction that hung over his head.

Kerensky seems to have been slow to react to Nell's advances, probably because of amorous commitments elsewhere. His hyperactive libido eventually took over, however, and they became lovers. He called her 'Thérèse', the name she had used on Capri ten years earlier when she had met Nicholas Nadejine. Kerensky was fifty-five; Nell thirty-seven. The age gap wasn't a concern but whereas Nell was free to remarry, Kerensky was involved in a protracted legal wrangle with Olga over the terms of their divorce.

Nicholas Nadejine did not give up easily. He inveigled his way into the *New Russia* office on the pretext of asking Nell to sign some documents and then made a scene. Kerensky had him thrown out. Nicholas moved in with Faith Mackenzie, of whom Compton Mackenzie's biographer, Andro Linklater, later wrote: 'Her old friend Nadegin (sic) had returned to keep her company after his wife had run off with Kerensky, the last prime minister of pre-Bolshevik Russia, and his presence gave a security she otherwise lacked.' Faith and Nicholas spent the rest of their lives together.[33]

29
The Fury of Comrade Stalin

In his massive work on the Revolution Nikolai Sukhanov wrote that during the October coup d'état 'Stalin gave me the impression...of a grey blur which flickered obscurely and left no trace. There is really nothing more to be said about him.' Leon Trotsky dismissed him as the 'outstanding mediocrity of our party'. Lev Kamenev considered him 'a small-town politician'. But there was nothing mediocre or insignificant about his strategy for destroying his enemies. His attitude was summed up in four words: 'No man, no problem.'

No one was spared, not even Kamenev or Grigory Zinoviev, original members of the Politburo who had formed the Communist Party's ruling troika with him in the 1920s. Back in 1912, Stalin had written to Kamenev, 'I kiss you on the nose, Eskimo-fashion. Dammit! I miss you something awful. I miss you like hell, I swear. I have no one, not a soul to have a proper talk with, damn you.' Now he was just another name on the death list.

The signal for the downfall of the Old Bolsheviks was the assassination of Sergie Kirov, the opera-loving head of the Communist Party in Leningrad. Kirov was shot by Leonid Nikolaev, a mentally disturbed Communist, in the Smolny Institute on 1 December 1934. Stalin was distraught. Following the 1932 suicide of his wife, Nadya, the Soviet leader turned to Kirov who had cared for him like a child.[i] Stalin called him 'my Kirich.'[1]

Taking the night train from Moscow to Leningrad, Stalin supervised the murder investigation himself. Nikolayev had been arrested at the scene of the crime and had confessed. His motive was personal, not political - Kirov had been flirting with his wife – and he had acted

---

[i] Stalin blamed Nadya's suicide on *The Green Hat*, Michael Arlen's 1924 novel about a young woman who kills herself as the only way out of her problems. Nadya was reading the bestseller before she died. Stalin called it a 'vile book'.

alone. At the Leader's urging, the NKVD chief Genrikh Yagoda ignored this statement and linked the killer to Zinoviev and Kamenev. As Trotsky's brother-in-law, the latter bore an added burden of guilt.[2]

After eighteen months of careful rehearsals in their prison cells, Zinoviev, Kamenev and fourteen others, mostly Old Bolsheviks, appeared in court charged with forming a terrorist organisation which had assassinated Kirov and which had also tried to kill Stalin and other luminaries of the Soviet Government. This 'Trial of the Sixteen' was the first of the notorious Moscow show trials of the 1930s. It set the template for subsequent hearings in which the accused confessed to increasingly bizarre crimes of espionage, poisoning and sabotage. Zinoviev and his co-defendants pleaded guilty on 24 August 1936 after Stalin agreed to clemency if they admitted the false charges against them but then, once their confessions were a matter of public record, he ordered their executions.

In an effort to ingratiate himself with Stalin, Vladimir Antonov-Ovsienko, the cavalier conqueror of the Winter Palace, had condemned Kamenev and Zinoviev as 'fascist saboteurs' and said they should be shot. Stalin, however, did not trust him; he was one of the original Trotskyists. He was arrested and shot without trial. 'He said goodbye to us all,' one of his cellmates said, 'took off his jacket and shoes, gave them to us, and went out to be shot half-undressed.'[3]

From his Norwegian refuge, Trotsky declared that Stalin was not only a mediocrity but 'a brutal and ignorant mediocrity'. People who knew him speculated that Nadya's death had triggered an outburst of vengeful rage that 'made the terror inevitable'. Trotsky labelled him an inveterate sadist. 'The best thing in life,' Stalin had told him one night, 'is to choose the right victim, to prepare everything well, to release one's rage ruthlessly, and then go to bed.'[4]

By the mid-1930s the Terror had eliminated most of the Old Bolsheviks, banished all opposition and placed Stalin in an unchallenged position at the pinnacle of Soviet society. The Cult of Stalin had superseded the Cult of Lenin. *Pravda* captured the adulation of Stalin in a speech made by an author named Avdienko at the Seventh Congress of the Soviets of the USSR. 'I write books, I am an author I dream of creating a lasting work. I love a girl in a new way,' he said. 'All this is thanks to thee, O great leader Stalin. Our love, our devotion, our strength, our hearts, our heroism, our life – all are thine. Take them, great Stalin, O leader of this great country.' The speech, *Pravda* noted, was wildly applauded.[5]

Despite such abject sycophancy, Stalin saw conspiracies everywhere. In 1935, 1229 Soviet citizens were sentenced to be shot. After an interlude between February 1935 and August 1936, the total jumped to 353,074 in two years. After that, it accelerated even faster. It was rumoured that Stalin was so paranoid he even killed his pet parrot when it started to mimic him. Even those closest to the dictator were not immune. Members of the Communist Party and the bureaucratic elite – the *nomenklatura* - lived in a state of perpetual dread, waiting for the creak of heavy boots in the hallway and the midnight knock on the door. Before the curtain fell on this grand-guignol of torture and murder, tens of millions of people had been killed, the vast majority almost certainly innocent of the crimes with which they were charged.[6]

The victims include two of Alexander Kerensky's family. His brother-in-law, General Vladimir Baranovsky, was executed without trial on 9 November 1931. If his position as Kerensky's chef-de-cabinet wasn't enough to damn him then his links to Trotsky in his Red Army days ensured his fate. Kerensky's eldest sister, Dr Elena Kerenskaya, the selfless Lyolya who had worked tirelessly for many years as a physician at Obukhov Hospital in Leningrad, disappeared. 'She died of overwork, cold and starvation in the Gulag in 1937 or 1938,' says Stephen Kerensky.[7]

Nikolai Sukhanov lived to regret his 'grey blur' insult about Stalin, which had been published in 1922. He was exiled to Tobolsk at the 1931 Menshevik trial and now, in 1937, he was accused of being a German spy on the grounds that his real name was Nikolai Himmer and he was of German descent. He was sentenced to death and, on Stalin's orders, executed on 29 June 1940. Stalin's paranoid hunt for traitors wreaked havoc in the top echelons of the Red Army that summer when leading generals and their staffs were shot. The dead included three out of five marshals of the Soviet Union, three out of five army commanders, first class, all ten second class, fifty out of fifty-seven corps commanders, 154 out of 196 divisional commanders and 401 out of 436 colonels.

Nor had Stalin forgotten his enemies abroad. Kerensky's circle was rocked by the abduction in Paris of the White Russian leader General Yevgeny Miller. On 22 September 1937 Nikolai Skoblin, an NKVD informer, led Miller to a safe house ostensibly to meet two German agents who were intent on aiding his anti-Bolshevik campaign. The agents were Soviet officers who drugged Miller, locked him in a steamer trunk and smuggled him aboard a Russia-bound ship at Le Havre.

The wily General, however, had left behind a note in which he detailed his suspicions about Skoblin. When he failed to return home from the meeting, his family handed the note to French police who launched a national manhunt to find the missing man and ordered the arrest of Skoblin and his wife, Nadezhda Plevitskaya. Nadezhda was arrested and sent for trial in a French court but Skoblin fled to the Soviet Embassy in Paris and was eventually smuggled out of the country to republican Barcelona.

Back in Moscow, General Miller was tortured to extract information and then shot without trial. According to General Pavel Sudoplatov of the NKVD, 'His kidnapping was a cause célèbre. Eliminating him disrupted his organisation of Tsarist officers and effectively prevented them from collaborating with the Germans against us.'[ii]

On 5 July 1938, while the Miller case was very much on people's minds, Alexander Kerensky addressed a meeting of the Women's Guild of Empire in London. Asked how he had remained free while the Russian secret police were able to seize people all over the world, he replied that Stalin's agents had set several traps for him – one in Paris the previous year - but all their plans had failed. Nell later confirmed that such an attempt had been made:

> My husband was always available to anyone who wished to see him. He could refuse no one. One caller begged for an interview but insisted it must not be at his flat or in a café. He suggested a car. When I heard this I insisted that it should be my car and that I should be the driver. The caller would not consent to this. One week later General Miller, leader of the White Russian Army, disappeared, never to be seen again. I felt it might have been my husband.
>
> Then there was the time in Paris when the telephone suddenly went

---

ii For having his cover blown and thus embarrassing his Moscow handlers, Skoblin was shot as soon as he returned to Soviet Russia. His wife was sentenced to twenty years in a French prison.

out of order. A man arrived at our apartment. He wore the official cap of an officer of the Telephone Department. From that time, the telephone was of little use. At last, we complained to the department, only to receive the reply that none of their mechanics had been to service our instrument. Investigation showed that our line had been tapped.[8]

Proposing a toast on the twentieth anniversary of the Bolshevik seizure of power, Stalin declared, 'We will destroy each and every enemy, even if he was an old Bolshevik; we will destroy all his kin, his family. We will mercilessly destroy anyone who, by his deeds or his thoughts - yes, his thoughts! - threatens the unity of the socialist state.'[9]

From 1934 to 1938 Stalin shot a million of his Communist elite, ultimately killing perhaps twenty million people, with eighteen million incarcerated in slave labour camps. 'Russia has always been a curiously unpleasant country despite her great literature,' Vladimir Nabokov sighed. 'Unfortunately Russians today have completely lost their ability to kill tyrants.'[10]

At the height of the Terror Kerensky's friend Isaak Babel, one of Russia's most popular authors, told a friend, 'Today, a man only talks freely with his wife - at night, with the blankets pulled over his head.' On the night of his arrest at his dacha in the writers' colony of Peredelkino he and his wife, Antonina Pirozhkova, sat calmly holding hands while the NKVD searched through his papers. It was the last time she saw him.[iii][11]

Alexander Solzhenitsyn, who would spend eight years in forced-labour camps for making derogatory remarks about Stalin in a letter to a friend, captured the same terror-induced mentality in a short story: 'Zotov never spoke his thoughts aloud – to do so would be dangerous – but he was afraid even to say them to himself.'[12]

Alexander Kerensky was still a big personality in the United States. The *New York Times* published his speeches and, much to the annoyance of American Communists, routinely described him as 'the leader of the revolution that brought the downfall of the Tsarist regime'. One of the *Times* reporters captured him at his most charismatic after

---

[iii] It was only during 'the Thaw' following Stalin's death in 1953 that the Soviet authorities confirmed that Babel had been shot in 1940 or 1941 after being found guilty at a secret trial of being a member of a Trotskyite organisation and spying for the French and Austrian governments.

a transatlantic trip to New York: 'Seated in the drawing room of the *Berengaria*, the 56-year-old Russian, wearing a neat dark, single-breasted suit, displaying his characteristic crew haircut, and with a gold-rimmed monocle in his left eye, posed for photographers and answered a barrage of questions.'[13]

It was 2 March 1938 and the news from Moscow had brought a swarm of reporters to his ship. The biggest and most important of Stalin's show trials, the public evisceration of the so-called 'Twenty-one', had begun that morning and editors wanted to hear his views. Some of the defendants, such as Nikolai Bukharin, 'one of the most valuable and outstanding theoreticians of the party', and Bukharin's close friend Alexei Rykov, a former Premier of the USSR, were among Stalin's oldest comrades-in-arms.[14]

The trial was taking place in the dome-ceilinged Hall of Columns in the old Nobles' Club, scene of Lenin's hallowed lying-in-state in 1924. The public seats – cushioned wooden benches – were packed with the proletarian elite. Trusted members of the Communist Party laughed and waved to their friends as though at the Bolshoi, all of them keenly aware that they might be next for the Lubianka. The only foreigners permitted to attend the hearings were a few reporters and one diplomat from each embassy.

The British representative was Fitzroy Maclean, a Cairo-born Scot who was known at the Foreign Office as 'Fitzwhiskers' to distinguish him from his contemporary, the Russian spy Donald 'Fancy Pants' Maclean. 'Suddenly, a hush fell over the crowded room,' wrote Fitzroy Maclean.

> Scores of inquisitive, greedy eyes turned in the direction of a little door in the corner at the far end. Through it filed the accused, twenty-one men, paler and smaller, somehow, than ordinary human beings. With them, herding them along, came a dozen giants in the uniform of the special NKVD Security Troops, bearing themselves like guardsmen in their well-fitting tunics and scarlet and blue peaked caps, their fixed bayonets gleaming, their sunburnt faces expressionless.[15]

The President of the Court, Judge V. V. Ulrich, a corpulent, shaven-headed figure with a fat neck and ruddy face, sat behind a table on a dais, with the prisoners corralled in a pen to one side. The Prosecutor-General of the Soviet Union, Andrei Vishinsky, a slight man with thinning reddish hair and a vicious tongue, was a former Menshevik who had once written an article condemning Bolshevik atrocities. It was his fervent hope that his service to Stalin in the show trials would erase that unfortunate misstep.

There were so many charges of high treason, murder, attempted murder, espionage, sabotage and membership of a Trotskyist conspiracy that it took the court secretary an hour and a half to read them out. Under the 'Vishinsky code' practised by Soviet interrogators and prosecutors, the confession of the accused was required as the chief proof of guilt.

One of the accused was Genrikh Yagoda, former boss of the NKVD, who had extracted ludicrous confessions from many defendants in previous show trials. He was, in Kerensky's words, 'a blood-stained executioner hated by the entire country'. One of the charges against Yagoda was that he had murdered his friend and mentor Maxim Gorky with the help of two Kremlin doctors. Fitzroy Maclean wrote:

> For an instant we stared, picking out familiar faces: Bukharin, with his pale complexion and little beard, strangely like Lenin as I had seen him in his glass coffin; Yagoda with his little toothbrush moustache; dark-skinned Faisullah Khojayev [a hero of the Revolution in Central Asia]; Krestinsky, small and nervous-looking.[16]

It was Nikolai Krestinsky who caused a sensation. After his co-defendants had meekly pleaded guilty, the former secretary of the Central Committee who had publicly broken with Trotsky in 1927, piped up in a high-pitched but clearly audible voice: 'Not guilty. I do not admit my guilt. I am not a Trotskyist. I am not a member of the Rightest-Trotskyist Bloc. I did not even know it existed. I am not guilty of any of the crimes with which I am charged.'

This unexpected diversion from the carefully written script left Judge Ulrich momentarily speechless. 'But do you not confirm the admission you made before coming into court?' he spluttered. Krestinsky replied, 'All my previous statements were a deliberate perversion of the truth. I acted thus because I knew that otherwise my words would not reach the ears of the rulers of this country.'[17]

This was unprecedented. The consequences of failing to give Comrade Stalin his pound of flesh carried severe penalties for the transgressor and his family – and possibly more so for the judge, the prosecutor and the NKVD torturers who had been entrusted with delivering a flawless performance. Even when Bukharin and Rykov testified that Krestinsky was still a Trotskyist despite his denials, the little man with steel-rimmed spectacles perched on his beaky nose replied, 'No one is telling the truth except me.'

'When did you begin telling the truth?' sneered the Public Prosecutor.

'Only today.'

Despite two adjournments during which he was exposed to intense pressure to change his plea, Krestinsky, 'looking more than ever like a bedraggled sparrow', maintained his defiance until the court adjourned for the day.

Asked to comment on the trial, Kerensky described the prosecution of the Old Bolsheviks as the death throes of the Soviet regime. Stalin, he said, was so determined to eliminate his former comrades – witnesses to his past crimes - that executions were now running at the rate of twenty or twenty-five a day, while five million people were languishing in prisons and concentration camps. 'The common hatred of Stalin is tremendous,' Kerensky said.

> He brands all opposition as Trotskyist because he knows that the Russian people connect the origin and responsibility for all the horrors they have suffered with Trotsky's name. But his game is contradictory and hopeless. He seeks to divert the wrath of the Russian people from himself by branding all other Bolshevik leaders as traitors.
>
> It should be obvious to even the most ardent apologists that what we are now witnessing is the moral bankruptcy of Bolshevism. Stalin finds himself completely isolated not only in the country but in the governing and administrative apparatus of the dictatorship. He must resort more and more to a rule of fear and terror.[18]

Kerensky was in Manhattan at the start of a lecture tour which would take him across the United States. He was staying with Kenneth Simpson and his wife Helen in their redbrick townhouse at 109 East 91st Street between Park and Lexington Avenues. Simpson had risen to Republican leader of New York County. An early critic of Hitler, he was one of the first politicians to attack American business interests that were sympathetic to the Nazis.

Kerensky's first speech was to the League for Political Education at the Town Hall. Dictatorships that had found their impetus in the Great War were essentially warlike in character and violent in their methods, he said, and if democracies wanted to survive they would have to be dynamic in both policy and action. In a reference to America's isolationism, he added, 'The democrat who does not struggle against all dictatorships actually fights none of them. For he who does not defend freedom everywhere defends it not at all.'[19]

Earlier that day, before Kerensky had got up to speak, little Nikolai Krestinsky in his faraway Moscow courtroom had admitted the error of his ways in daring to challenge the integrity of Stalin's judicial system:

> Yesterday, influenced by a feeling of false shame and by the atmosphere of the court, and by my state of health, I could not bring myself to tell the truth and admit my guilt before the world. Mechanically, I declared myself innocent. I now beg the court to take note of the statement which I now make to the effect that I admit my guilt, completely and unreservedly, under all the charges brought against me, and that I accept full responsibility for my criminal and treacherous behaviour.[20]

'The words were reeled off like a well-learnt lesson,' Fitzroy Maclean noted. 'The night had not been wasted.' Witness after witness supported Prosecutor Vishinsky's horror stories about plots to murder Stalin, poison the new head of the NKVD, dynamite the Kremlin and bring down the beloved Soviet Union. Confirming the method used to murder Gorky, Yagoda admitted that the author, who was ailing from influenza, had been plied with alcohol, exposed to a roaring bonfire and then to a freezing draught to induce pneumonia. He had developed a fever, started spitting blood and died the next day. The partisan crowd lapped up this baloney and drooled for more.[iv][21]

Yagoda obliged. He revealed how he and an accomplice had sprayed poison – 'foreign-made poison', he said, to make it sound more evil - on the walls, curtains and carpets of the office that Nikolai Yezhov would occupy as his replacement as head of the NKVD. Yezhov was nicknamed 'the Poison Dwarf' because of his height – he was barely five-feet tall - and also because of his repellent delight in torturing suspects, including Yagoda, his former mentor.

---

iv Gorky had actually suffered from tuberculosis for many years.

The accused told the court that his motive in attempting to poison Yezhov was to prevent exposure of his own guilty secrets: to wit, that under him the NKVD had become a hive of anti-Soviet activity; that he had killed his former boss, Vyacheslav Menzhinsky, the Old Bolshevik chairman of the OGPU, and that he had then plotted the assassinations of Kirov, Gorky and Gorky's son, Maxim Peshkov (because he was obsessed with Peshkov's wife).

The poison had indeed affected Yezhov – no fewer than six Soviet scientists swore that it was present in his urine and on the office furnishings. 'The Poison Dwarf' had survived, however, and had diligently hunted down these 'enemies of the people'.[22]

Stalin turned up in person to enjoy the entertainment. Fitzroy Maclean spotted him when 'a clumsily directed arc-light dramatically revealed the familiar features and heavy drooping moustache peering from behind the black glass of a small window, high up under the ceiling of the courtroom'.[23]

In summing up the prosecution's case Vishinsky told the court that Comrade Stalin had been correct in stating that the accused, 'whether they called themselves Trotskyists or Bukharinists, had become an unprincipled band of wreckers, spies and assassins, devoid of ideology'. It followed that Bukharin and his fellow accused were not only common criminals but also agents of Britain, Poland, Germany and Japan. And, as Comrade Stalin had rightly ordered, such traitors 'must be mercilessly rooted out.'[24]

The verdicts had been decided in advance of the trial: eighteen of the defendants, including Bukharin, Rykov and Yagoda, were found guilty of all charges and later that night were taken down into the Lubianka cellars and shot. The other three defendants, Christian Rakovski, Bossonov and one of doctors, who had given valuable evidence for the prosecution, received long prison sentences.

Rakovski, former Soviet representative in London, made the startling revelation that Trotsky had been a British agent since 1926, while Bossonov, former counsellor at the Soviet Embassy in Berlin, claimed that he had been the linkman between Trotsky and the wretched Krestinsky.

The American Ambassador, Joseph E. Davies, a corporate lawyer blessed with a Pollyanna attitude towards his Communist hosts, assured President Roosevelt that the evidence had proved conclusively that the eighteen political figures on trial 'had plotted to overthrow the present Soviet government and were therefore guilty of treason under Soviet law'. A. T. Cholerton, the *Daily Telegraph*'s veteran Kremlinologist, however, summed up the trial in one pithy sentence: 'Yes, it was all true – except the facts.'[25]

Alexander Kerensky returned to the trial in the biggest speech of his lecture tour at Carnegie Hall on 9 April when he contrasted Stalin's disastrous economic policy with the ideas of Bukharin and Rykov which might have enabled the Soviet regime to evolve into a peaceful modern state.

> My friends and I place the interests of Russia above all other considerations. Our desire is to see restored the economic welfare of the country, the rebirth if its liberty and the reestablishment of its capacity for defence. It does not matter to us who accomplishes these aims. Any government which will serve the interests of the people and the historic tasks of Russia will have our support, no matter who composes that government or how many crimes they may have committed in the past from the point of view of the interests of the country.

When Kerensky got back to Europe in the *Queen Mary* in May 1938, he had been away from Paris for ten weeks. In that time, Leon Blum's second ministry had come and gone, and Édouard Daladier had been reinstated as Prime Minister. Fearing that Kerensky had been unfaithful during their long separation, Nell had become as jealous and irrational as her mentor, Marie Bashkirtseff, who had written: 'There are no words to express what I feel; but what makes me desperate, what enrages me, what kills me, is jealousy.' When Kerensky accepted another speaking engagement in America, it was agreed that Nell should join him on the trip.

The main objective of Britain's foreign policy under Prime Minister Neville Chamberlain and his Foreign Secretary, Lord Halifax, was to reach a modus vivendi with Hitler. They regarded Russian Communism and National Socialism with equal distaste but chose to appease Hitler rather than Stalin. When Maxim Litvinov suggested a conference of Britain, France, Poland, Romania and Russia in Bucharest, the idea was flatly rejected. Any alliance among those five Powers would amount to the encirclement of Nazi Germany and that would upset the Führer.[26]

Just before Nell and Alexander set sail for New York in the *Normandie*, Chamberlain and Édouard Daladier were complicit in the ultimate act of appeasement: the signing of the Munich Agreement with Hitler and Mussolini to transfer the Czech Sudetenland, which contained three million ethnic Germans, to the Third Reich. In a broadcast to the British people on 28 September Chamberlain spoke about his efforts to obtain a peaceful solution to the Sudeten dispute, which he referred to as a 'quarrel in a faraway country, between people of whom we know nothing'. He conveniently forgot that he had once used the healing waters of the Karlsbad spa in Bohemia to relieve an attack of gout.

Chamberlain's motive in signing the agreement, his supporters later explained, was to win a reprieve that would enable Britain and France to accelerate their rearmament. The truth was quite different. Based on the assessment of Sir Joseph Addison, the British Ambassador in Prague between 1930 and 1936, he believed that the Sudeten Germans had genuine grievances. He also believed he had developed a special relationship with the Führer which would enable him to control his homicidal urges.

His 'peace with honour… peace for our time' assertion outside 10 Downing Street on 30 September was as specious as Daladier's belief that he could count on the British Prime Minister 'in spite of his being a cold and limited man'. The French Premier returned home from Germany uncomfortably conscious of the fact that his betrayal had cost France thirty-five Czech divisions in her defence. 'Imbeciles!' he snorted to an aide, indicating the ecstatic crowds lining the route from the airport. 'If only they knew what they were cheering.'[27]

Relying on Chamberlain and Halifax as his chief sources of information, King George VI supported this blatant betrayal of the Czechs. Urged by Churchill to stand up to Hitler and by Halifax to capitulate, Chamberlain remarked with unintended humour, 'I'm wobbling about all over the place.' His wobbles handed the Nazis the superlative Skoda arms complex, 66 per cent of Czechoslovakia's coal, 70 per cent of her iron and steel, and 70 per cent of her electrical power. The Munich Agreement left the rump Czech state vulnerable to a total German takeover (which Hitler would complete six months later in contravention of his Munich pledges).[28]

Great concern was felt in Moscow about the Nazi's Eastern

encroachment. Stalin decided the agreement was a capitalist conspiracy in which the imperialist nations were ganging up on the Soviet Union. He referred to Britain and France as 'the provocateurs of war who are accustomed to using others as cats'-paws to pull somebody else's chestnuts out of the fire'.[29]

Nell and Alexander arrived in New York on 10 October 1938. Even before Kerensky had stepped ashore, he plunged into the Munich controversy, telling reporters that the pact had prevented a world catastrophe. He challenged the opinion of Americans who believed that it was a 'shameful surrender' to the Nazis. People who held this view were not aware of the 'tremendous difficulties and problems that confronted Mr Chamberlain and M. Daladier', he said. He expressed the opinion that the threat of war had been averted 'for many months' and that the period of respite should be utilised by the free peoples to prepare for future conflict.

> I know that the recent events in Europe produced an unfavourable effect on American public opinion. I have heard people say that the European democracies lost their cause and surrendered to the dictators without a fight. Let me say that such an opinion is entirely erroneous. It is true that the European democracies had to yield on many important points, but as I pointed out on my visit to this country last spring they could not make the stand they would have liked to without the collaboration of the United States and without the support of a strong, free Russia.[30]

Nell and Alexander were in demand socially and met some of the célébrités du jour, including the American actor Frederic March and the French-American soprano Lily Pons, wife of the Saint Petersburg-born conductor Andre Kostelanetz. At a musical evening at the Park Avenue apartment of the opera singer Alma Clayburgh, Nell was reunited with one of her friends from Paris, John Brownlee, the Australian-born baritone who had made a successful début at the Metropolitan Opera as Rigoletto.[31]

Confused about Nell's marital status, Mrs Clayburgh had issued separate invitations to 'Mr Alexander Kerensky' and 'Mrs Thérèse Tritton'. When other hostesses followed her lead, Nell told Alexander that she did not like being treated as his mistress. He was as unbending as ever: his mission was more important than any personal consideration.

By instinct and inclination, the majority of New Yorkers were anti-Nazi without necessarily being pro-British or pro-French and they were appalled about the fate of Czechoslovakia, the most western – and most westernised – of the Slavic nations. Public opinion was also contemptuous of the Allies for their disloyalty towards the popular Czech Prime Minister, Edouard Beneš. Chamberlain's flying visits to Germany convinced them that he must be either pro-Fascist or completely spineless. Dorothy Parker of the *New Yorker* described him in one of her famous epigrams as 'the first Prime Minister to crawl at 250 miles an hour'.

Following a bitter row after yet another social snub, she had packed her bags and flown to Los Angeles en route to Australia. Kerensky wrote frantic letters to her at the West Hollywood home of their friend, Princess Eristoff, begging her to return but Nell's mind was made up. She set sail in the *Monterey*, arriving in Brisbane on 9 March believing that her relationship with Alexander had ended.

Over the next three months Nell lectured to various organisations on international politics and while staying with her parents at 'Elderslie' took Russian lessons with Mikhail Ivanovitch Maximoff, a White Russian refugee who had brought his wife and daughter Nina to Brisbane from Harbin, Manchuria, in 1925.

'There is great heartburn over the Munich pact,' Nell told a reporter from the *Courier-Mail*, 'but surely anything was better than war. The danger has been lessened now that America is more actively cooperating with Britain and France in efforts to make for peace.' Six days later, tearing up the Munich agreement and ignoring the censure of democratic nations, German troops marched into Czechoslovakia to complete the Nazi occupation of that broken little country.[32]

Meanwhile, Nell's abrupt departure had shaken Alexander Kerensky to the core. He found himself facing the prospect of life without her love, her skills and her money. As soon as he could break free from his American commitments, he hurried back to Paris to settle his divorce and was immediately taken ill with a virus which laid him low for several days at his hotel in Avenue du General Mangin, Passy. His illness was considered newsworthy enough to make the columns of *The Times*.[33]

Kerensky visited Vladimir and Véra Nabokov, who were living close to his hotel in a sparsely furnished flat at 59 rue Boileau. From their ragged appearance, it was clear they were struggling to make a living. Vladimir had obtained a carte identité which legalised his presence in France without granting him the right to take a job, so he was still dependent on his writing to provide an income. On 2 May his mother died in Prague but he had no visa to enter Nazi-controlled Czechoslovakia and, anyway, it would have been madness for him to venture there.

Kerensky was appalled at the disunity and rancour among the French cabinet over the key question of national defence. Since 1935 Paul Reynaud, a sixty-two-year-old rightwinger, had played a role similar to Churchill's in warning his countrymen about the growing menace of Nazi militarism. His main opponents were Pierre Laval, the pro-Nazi former Premier, and Georges Bonnet, one of the most snivelling French appeasers ('Let us not be heroic. We're not up to it').

France's security depended on the Maginot Line, the hideously expensive fortifications named after its designer, the Minister of War, André Maginot, to keep the German Army at bay. This elaborate network of dragon-toothed iron tank-traps embedded in concrete, armoured-domed fortresses, machinegun nests, bombproof bunkers and subterranean barracks stretched 140 kilometres from Switzerland to the Belgian border and covered France's entire frontier with her old enemy. It was deemed impenetrable.

Reynaud and his military ally General Maxime Weygand, Foch's great collaborator in World War I, realised the importance of armoured divisions and anticipated the use that the Germans would make of them in the coming conflict. He quoted Colonel Charles de Gaulle's controversial 1934 book, *Vers l'Armée de Métier*, which challenged the omnipotence of the Maginot Line and emphasised the importance of deploying strong armoured and mechanised units to deal with an enemy breakthrough.

But General Maurice Gamelin, the short, prissy Commander-in-Chief, considered de Gaulle a dangerous heretic to the army's military orthodoxy. After the devastation of French towns and villages in World War I, he believed implicitly in the doctrine of forward defence – of fighting the enemy in someone else's country, in this case Holland and Belgium, and thus saving *la Patrie* from the kind of serious damage that might lead to revolution, as witnessed in Russia in 1917 and Germany in 1918.

Nevertheless, it was largely thanks to Gamelin's opposition that France declined to stop Hitler when he marched into the demilitarised Rhineland in 1936 in clear breach of the 1919 Versailles Treaty and the 1925 Treaty of Locarno. Had France acted then, Hitler would have been stopped in his tracks. Instead, Nazism spread to the four corners of the globe.[34]

Travelling around Australia, Nell was astonished to discover that the Nazi Party had opened branches in most capital cities to spread the creed of National Socialism among expatriate German communities through organisations such as the German Labour Front, the Hitler Youth and the League of German Girls. Her family was not immune to the antisemitic poison dripping from these groups. When her twenty-eight-year-old cousin Corbett Tritton was appointed private secretary to the Prime Minister, Robert Menzies, on 2 May 1939, Brisbane Nazis claimed the Tritton family was Jewish and, on account of Nelle's marriage to Nicholas Nadejine, that it hailed from Russia – a clumsy attempt to link the Tritton family to the fictitious Soviet-Jewish conspiracy.[35]

By early June Alexander Kerensky had recovered his health and had persuaded Olga to agree terms for a divorce. Jubilantly, he cabled Nell in Brisbane that he had obtained a decree nisi and pleaded with her to return to New York to marry him. After a farewell party on 17 June, Nell sailed from Sydney to Los Angeles in the *Monterey* and then flew to New York for an emotional reunion with her lover at 109 East 91st Street.

There was then an agonising delay: Alexander's decree had not yet been made absolute, so he was still legally barred from remarrying. Believing she had been misled, Nell moved out of the Simpsons' house into a hotel. 'I am deeply wounded that you made me leave my country without reason,' she wrote to Alexander. 'I am not returning to live a *comedie de la fiancée*.'

Just in time, the decree absolute arrived in the post and Alexander made hurried arrangements for their nuptials with the help of a New York businessman, Victor Soskice (David Soskice's son with his first wife, Anna Sophia Johansen). On 20 August 1939 Nell and Alexander were married by Harry A. Stein, a justice of the peace, in a civil ceremony in the living room of his house at Martins Creek, Pennsylvania.[36]

Nell took her vows under her maiden name, Lydia Ellen Tritton. According to Harry Stein, the groom, replete with monocle and cane, arrived with his bride, 'a light blonde and very pretty, nice-sized'. 'I was thunderstruck when I found out who he was,' Stein said. 'I didn't believe it until I saw his passport and his divorce papers.'

Kerensky had chosen this backwater to avoid publicity but Harry Stein leaked the story to the American news agencies. *Truth* headlined its report 'Brisbane woman's romance: Wed to ex-dictator. Nell Tritton marries M. Kerensky'. Flora Solomon wrote in her memoirs, 'I cannot pretend their marriage didn't sadden me.' The newlyweds were enjoying a motoring honeymoon in Upper New York State on 23 August when Germany signed a non-aggression pact with Soviet Russia. Kerensky cut short his honeymoon and dashed back to New York. Once again events had overtaken him but he was quickly on the attack.

One of his arguments with Flora had been that she regarded Stalin as the Jews best chance of getting rid of Hitler, while Kerensky saw Nazism as the mirror image of Stalinism; both were one-party states based on terror in which people committed acts of evil related to race or class. The Munich Agreement, he said, had denied Hitler the chance of unleashing his forces against Czechoslovakia. However, the German leader was determined to win a violent military victory over neighbouring Poland. The Nazi-Soviet Pact had removed the threat of Russian intervention while he struck that mortal blow. After the Poles had been crushed in their western provinces, he forecast – correctly - that the Red Army would occupy eastern Poland.[v]

Stalin's fellow travellers in the West pointed out that, unlike Chamberlain and Daladier, he had never shaken hands with Hitler. He had been present, however, when the two foreign ministers, Vyacheslav Mikhailovich Molotov and Joachim von Ribbentrop, signed the Russo-German alliance in the Kremlin. Champagne and vodka flowed until dawn. Gloating like a proud father, Stalin proposed a toast to Hitler. 'The Soviet Union is very serious about the new pact,' he told Ribbentrop. 'I give you my word of honour that the Soviet Union will not cheat on its partner.'[37]

---

v It was later revealed that the non-aggression treaty contained secret clauses under which Hitler and Stalin would divide Poland and the Baltic States (Latvia, Lithuania and Estonia) and Finland into German and Soviet spheres of influence.

The only slightly sour note, he added, was the anti-Comintern agreement between Germany, Italy and Japan. How could Ribbentrop explain that? Never lost for words, the former salesman claimed that this pact was actually aimed at disrupting the democracies. Stalin nodded wisely and pretended to accept this explanation.[38]

The apparent rapport between two ideologies shouldn't have surprised Britain and France. Maxim Litvinov, who was Jewish, had been deposed as Commissar for Foreign Affairs by Molotov to smooth the path to a deal with Hitler. He had warned the Allies often enough that it would happen - indeed, an Anglo-French delegation was in Moscow at that very moment attempting to reach a military accord with the Kremlin. Having taken a leisurely fifteen days to reach Moscow, the delegation informed the People's Commissar for Defence, Marshal Kliment Voroshilov, that they lacked the authority to conclude a deal.

When he asked specific questions, such as whether Soviet forces would be permitted to pass through Poland in the event of war with Germany, he was informed that the delegation had no idea whether the Poles would agree to such a thing. After weeks of this sort of fence-sitting, Voroshilov told Stalin that further negotiations were pointless. When news of the non-aggression pact was released, the Anglo-French delegation headed for home complaining bitterly about Soviet treachery.[39]

Stalin's reasons for agreeing to the pact were partly practical, partly intuitive. After the betrayal of Czechoslovakia, he seriously doubted that Britain and France would ever take action to prevent a German attack on the Soviet Union. At the same time he admired Hitler's ruthless, cold-blooded ambition (which was based on his own ruthless, cold-blooded elimination of his enemies). He sensed that in the Führer he had found a kindred spirit and, incredibly, someone he could trust. Indeed, they were both homicidal paranoiacs who were in the process of deporting, enslaving and exterminating entire categories of human beings in pursuit of a perverted totalitarian ideal.[40]

Meanwhile, Hitler had persuaded himself that Communism had ceased to exist in Russia; that the Comintern was no longer a threat to Nazi Germany; and that no real ideological barrier existed between the two countries. That, at least, is what he said. Secretly, he planned to wipe Communism off the face of the earth.[41]

The Kremlin ordered Communist Parties around the globe to cease anti-Nazi propaganda. Cartoonists who routinely portrayed Trotsky in the Soviet press as a pig branded with a swastika dropped the swastika in deference to their new ally (but kept the pig). The Soviet leader's political enemies were also distraught. According to a French police report, White Russian émigrés were the only group of aliens in France who harboured pro-Nazi sympathies because they saw Hitler as their saviour from Communism. Those hopes had now been dashed.[42]

In retaliation for the Nazi-Soviet pact, Daladier outlawed the French Communist Party and the police began rounding up known Communists. By the last week of August, the mobilisation of the French Army was in full swing and trainloads of reservists aged between eighteen and thirty-five took up their posts along the Maginot Line. To the troops manning it, this phenomenally expensive fortification was known dismissively as *'le trou'* (the hole).

Regarded as infallible, the great rampart actually stopped at Montmédy in Northern France and an extension offering weaker protection had been built along the Meuse through Sedan and other towns facing the supposedly impassable Ardennes Forest. This sector was the Third Republic's Achilles' heel.

The West did not have to wait long for the Polish crisis to reach flashpoint. On 28 August Clare Hollingworth, a Leicester-born trainee reporter on the London *Daily Telegraph* who had been helping refugees in Warsaw obtain British visas, paid a visit to the Polish-German border. When a strong wind lifted some canvas camouflage screens, she found herself looking at rows of German tanks and armoured cars. The following day her front-page story in the *Telegraph* was headlined '1000 tanks massed on Polish border. Ten divisions reported ready for swift stroke'.

A *Telegraph* colleague later teased her that there were, in fact, only nine divisions, though he admitted that predicting the outbreak of World War II was 'not bad' for a cub reporter with only three days' experience in the job.[43]

At 8 p.m. on 1 September Major Alfred Naujocks of the SS staged an 'incident' at Gleiwitz near the Polish border.[vi] On the orders of his chief, Reinhard Heydrich, he brought out twelve prisoners from Dachau concentration camp dressed in Polish uniforms. All twelve,

---

vi The SS was the Schutzstaffel, or Hitler's 'Protection Squadron'.

who had been sentenced to death, were killed by lethal injection. Bullets were then fired into their bodies. The story released to the world was that 'Polish soldiers' had crossed the border into Germany and seized the Gleiwitz radio station. After broadcasting an anti-German message in Polish, they had been killed in a firefight with German defenders.[44]

Around 3 a.m. that night, President Roosevelt received an urgent phone call at the White House from his friend William 'Billy' Bullitt, the American Ambassador to France. 'Mr President,' Bullitt said, 'the German army has crossed the border of Poland.' Two days later Hitler's armour rolled into Warsaw, allowing Heydrich to boast, 'I started World War II.'

Neville Chamberlain could no longer evade the issue. At 11.15 a.m. on Sunday 3 September he informed the nation in a broadcast from 10 Downing Street that a state of war existed between Britain and Germany. Chamberlain then went to the House of Commons, where Ivan Maisky, the Soviet Ambassador, leered from the Ambassadors' Gallery. He recorded Chamberlain's demeanour: 'A darkened, emaciated face. A tearful, broken voice. Bitter, despairing gestures. A shattered, washed-up man.'[45]

As the world digested the news, it was raining heavily in Paris. On the Avenue de l'Opéra people queued for gasmasks in little snuff-coloured satchels. The headlights of many vehicles had already been painted blue and the staff of the Dôme were fitting thick blue curtains to its windows. France had sent her own ultimatum to Berlin but war had been expected for so long that it was something of an anti-climax when, at 5 o'clock that evening, Daladier announced that France was also at war with Germany.

Speaking to the Overseas Press Club in New York, Alexander Kerensky urged the Allies to fight 'not only for the victory of democracy over totalitarianism, the overthrow of the Hitler regime and the restoration of Poland and Czechoslovakia, but also for the liberation of the Russian people from Bolshevism'.

> The Russian people hate the Bolshevik dictatorship, as evidenced by the unceasing struggle against it at the cost of millions of lives. Europe can never be reorganised on new foundations of freedom and order without the restoration of liberty in Russia. Stalin duped the Western

democracies with his Popular Front and collective security propaganda, just as Lenin duped the Russian people in 1917. The Russian people hate the Bolshevik dictatorship.[46]

By the end of September, Daladier's anti-Soviet crackdown had prevented thirty-five Communist deputies from taking their seats in the Chamber. Many dangerous Comintern activists who had been instructed to sabotage the French war effort had been being arrested, though the haul also included life-long Socialists who had no truck with Communism. Daladier, however, had done nothing to restrain the advocates of the subversive radical right. When Hitler offered France and Britain a peace proposal on 6 October, several members of the French Government were prepared to take it.[47]

After justifying his campaigns in Austria, Czechoslovakia and Poland, Hitler told the Reichstag that there was no longer any reason for war because his demands had been satisfied. He proposed a summit meeting of the leading European powers to consider 'arms reduction, the return of Germany's colonies and the solution of the Jewish problem'. But the Fuhrer had broken so many promises that not even Chamberlain believed he wanted peace.

Conscription, national service and the grand tradition of the citizen-in-arms had produced a partially trained French Army of three million men whose strength depended almost entirely on defence. It was just as well that hostilities between the warring nations lapsed into a 'Phoney War'. The French called the seven-month respite la drôle de guerre, or, alternatively, la guerre des nerfs – the war of nerves.[vii]

In Colonel de Gaulle's opinion, this hiatus gave France the chance to take positive measures. 'There is nothing more urgent nor more necessary than galvanising the French people, instead of cradling them with absurd illusions of defensive security,' he wrote to Paul Reynaud on 22 October. 'We must, just as soon as possible, be ready to make an active war by getting ourselves all the necessary equipment: planes, ultra-powerful tanks organised in huge armoured divisions.' The Government, however, continued to pour money and manpower into the Maginot fortifications.[48]

---

vii The 'phoney war' tag is attributable to Walter Kerr, who wrote in the *New York Herald Tribune* after failing to find any sign of combat on the front at Metz that this looked like being 'a pretty phoney type of war'.

It was at this inauspicious point that Alexander Kerensky decided to return to Paris. As a Freemason and an outspoken critic of Nazism, he was bound to be on Hitler's death list but he ignored the risk. He saw himself as 'an old soldier of the Revolution' and, he told his American hosts, it was his duty to exploit Anglo-French loathing of the Stalinist regime.

On 2 March 1940 he and Nell set off for Lisbon in the Pan-Am flying boat *Yankee Clipper* on their way to Paris. Kerensky's sudden appearance in wartime France once again demonstrated his flair for being in the wrong place at the wrong time.[49]

30

The Flight from Paris

Paris in March 1940 was a militarised city with an 11 p.m. curfew. After the coldest January in living memory, ice floated in the Seine and there was a dismal wintery air about the City of Light. There were many reminders for Alexander Kerensky of his first visit to Paris in July 1918. Once again sandbags were stacked in bulky khaki heaps to protect Carpeaux's dancers on the Opera House façade and surrounded the base of Napoleon's Column in Place Vendôme.

The windows of public buildings were pasted with brown paper strips to ward against bomb blast, while blackout shutters masked the lights of La Rotonde, La Coupole, Maxim's and Fouquet's. The Flore, the Deux Magots and the Dôme were open for business but sugar rationing had put pâtisseries out of business three days a week. Rina Ketty's haunting ballad *'J'Attendrai'* ('I Will Wait') was the popular song of the period. Parisians, however, had not lost their sense of humour. In the window of Lancel's leather goods emporium two ceramic Aberdeen terriers raised their hind legs over a copy of *Mein Kamph*.[1]

Nell and Alexander moved a short distance from their previous abode in Villa de la Réunion to a bigger flat at 59 rue Nicolo and picked up the threads of their old life. Nobody knew what was going to happen and the atmosphere was tense. French and Russian friends alike bombarded them with questions: would President Roosevelt support France militarily? What was the best way to get an American visa? And, given the comfort and security of New York, why had they come back?

It was a good question. Kerensky, however, revelled in the chance to take the fight to Stalin. In the columns of *New Russia* he attacked the Nazi-Soviet Pact, reporting in one issue that under a new Iran-Soviet trade agreement Moscow had granted Tehran the right to transport raw materials to Germany through the USSR, thus avoiding the Allied blockade. Such a concession, Kerensky noted, had never been granted to a foreign power, even under the Tsar. At a press conference in early April he launched an uncompromising attack which was reported throughout the Western world:

> Hitler has boasted that his agreement with Stalin keeps Germany's back door open against the Allies' blockade. He is right. To close Germany's back door we must move against Russia – that is, Stalin's Russia. Russia is the key to Germany. If you can solve the problem of Russia, you also solve the problem of Germany. If you can free Russia from the grip of Stalin, Ribbentrop's triumph of August 1939 falls to pieces. With Russia working against her, not for her, Nazi Germany is doomed.

One of Kerensky's most persistent inquisitors about life in America was Vladimir Nabokov, who was planning to move there with Vera and their son Dimitri. To qualify for an American entry visa, Vladimir accepted an invitation to teach a summer course on Russian literature at Stanford University. Mark Aldanov had been offered the assignment but his English wasn't up to it. He decided to remain in France for the time being and had recommended Vladimir in his place. The invitation was the first step in a complicated process for entering the United States. Vladimir's green Nansen passport had expired and he still needed American visas, French exit permits and passages on a US-bound ship.

The American visas required supporting affidavits from notable Russians living in the United States. Tolstoy's daughter, Alexandra Tolstoy, organised a glowing testimonial for Vladimir from Serge Koussevitzky, the Russian-born conductor of the Boston Symphony Orchestra, who had performed private concerts at the Nabokov house in pre-revolutionary Saint Petersburg.

The Kerenskys and the Nabokovs spent weekends with Nina Berberova in a converted farmhouse at Longchêne, a hamlet forty kilometres southwest of Paris on the road to Chartres. Since 1933, she had been married to Nikolai Makeyev, a Russian journalist who had been the youngest member of the short-lived Constituent Assembly.[2] The hamlet had no church, school or post office. It consisted of four farms and ten houses built on slightly elevated ground and separated from one another by fields of pasture and rows of poplars Nell took to the country life. She and Nina planted fruit trees, set up beehives and dug a vegetable patch. As they worked, Nell told a Confucian story about how life began on a Chinese farm with the planting of a single peach stone.[3]

Nina's literary career was thriving. As well as poems, short stories, novels and the 1934 novella *The Accompanist* (later filmed), she had written the first full-length biography of Tchaikovsky. Appearing in 1937, the book created a sensation because it dealt openly with the composer's homosexuality. Sexually, Nina identified herself as belonging to 'the people of two-sexes'. She liked to dress up in Nicholai's trousers, jacket and shoes. Hiding her hair under his hat, she would pick up his cane and walk around the country lanes. The thrill was to be mistaken for a man.[4]

The sight of Nell sitting under an almond tree on the terrace between the two wings of the house, 'shelling peas with her pretty fingers with their long and sharp nails', inspired a powerful yearning. 'She was beautiful, calm, intelligent,' Nina recalls, 'and was always recounting something: about Australia where she was born and brought up… Her shoulders and bosom were like Anna Karenina's, her eyes were always lively and some disobedient locks curled around her ears.'[5]

The two women were photographed lying in the tall grass smiling at one another. Katherine Lyall-Watson, a Brisbane playwright, deduced from their correspondence that they had indeed become lovers. Nina's growing dislike of Kerensky could well have been linked to his chauvinist treatment of 'Thérèse', which swung from deep affection to dictatorial abruptness. While her replies were always loving, she expressed anxiety about these outbursts. She made Nina promise that she would come to live 'under my wing', as she put it, once their troubles were over. 'Nell loved our evenings,' Nina says,

> the silent starlit nights always on that terrace, among roses, under the almond tree, the quiet conversation, far-off nocturnal country sounds, the infrequent quick flight of a bat over our heads. She loved to go picking mushrooms and sit for hours under the nut tree on the little bench, looking at the woods…

Paris expected the worst. The Mona Lisa and the Venus de Milo had been evacuated from the Louvre. When air-raid sirens signalled imminent attacks, guests at the Ritz were provided with silken Hermès sleeping-bags and ushered into the cellar. Everyone was on edge waiting for the bombs to fall and yet for days the only warlike things over Paris were ugly grey sausage-shaped barrage balloons.

On 2 May, Parisian society threw its last great party – a charity gala at the Marigny Theatre in the Jardins des Champs Élysées. Among the guests were the Duke and Duchess of Windsor - the former Edward VIII and his American consort, the former Mrs Wallis Simpson - and ex-King Zog, Albania's first (and last) monarch. These two regnal figures summed up the sagging European *zeitgeist*: one a failure, the other a fugitive. The former Ahmet Muhtar Zogolli had crowned himself King of Albania after leading a coup d'état against the government. The Italians had 'bombed' Tirana with confetti to celebrate his coronation but had then deposed him when Mussolini decided to invade his country on the way to attacking Greece. Pausing only to load Albania's gold reserves and the crown jewels into a fleet of large American limousines, King Zog fled to France with his wife, Queen Geraldine, baby son, Prince Leka, six sisters, three nephews, two nieces and twenty-one advisers, courtiers and bodyguards.

The French Government was seriously dysfunctional. Alexander Kerensky was appalled to discover that far from uniting the country, the drôle de guerre had driven people further apart. Having replaced Édouard Daladier as Prime Minister on 21 March 1940, Paul Reynaud was forced to retain him in his cabinet in the vital role of Minister of Defence. Daladier's antipathy then prevented him from carrying out another much-needed change: the dismissal of General Gamelin as Commander in Chief. He did, however, manage to sign a joint declaration with Britain that neither country would make a separate peace with Germany.[6]

Short and dapper, with dyed black eyebrows arched over deep-set Oriental eyes, Reynaud was a lawyer-politician, a fighting cock who enjoyed goading his opponents. He had left his loyal wife Jeanne for a dubious mistress, Countess Hélène de Portes, a shrill Fascist sympathiser whose face was said to bear the traces of an eventful life. Madame de Portes (her Italian title did not apply in the egalitarian Third Republic) lived with the Premier in his cramped apartment overlooking the Place du Palais Bourbon behind the National Assembly.[7]

Like the Empress Alexandra in World War I, her constant interference in matters of state would affect Reynaud's judgment and ultimately destroy him. And yet, like Nicholas II with Alexandra, he was incapable of functioning without her. Pierre Lazareff, the editor of *Paris-Soir*, recalls arriving at the Prime Minister's office expecting to interview him but instead finding Hélène de Portes sitting behind his desk. 'She was presiding over an assorted gathering of generals, high officers, Members of Parliament and officials,' he said. 'She was talking in a peremptory tone of voice, giving advice and orders right and left. Every once in a while she would open the door and step into the next room. One could hear her say, "How are you, Paul? Now just relax and take it easy. Don't worry about a thing. We're working".'[8]

The Jewish editor waged a spirited campaign against Nazism, much to the annoyance of Hélène de Portes and her pro-German clique. His Russian-born Jewish wife, Hélène Gordon-Lazareff, who also worked at the paper, had fled Russia during the Bolshevik coup d'état and was well disposed towards Kerensky. Since the deaths of his friends Albert Thomas (in 1932) and Paul Painlevé (in 1933), he had had little contact with French politicians. When Pierre Lazareff invited him to publish his thoughts on the war in *Paris-Soir*, he jumped at the chance.

The editorial assistant who laid out his articles was the budding Algerian-born author Albert Camus.[i] Having lived through one cataclysmic upheaval, Kerensky feared that the infighting among France's political leaders and the malaise sweeping through her armed forces would lead to another. Just as the Revolution had destabilised the Russian Army, there were signs that French troops had become demoralised over low pay, bureaucratic ineptitude and grinding inactivity.

Money was running short and they decided to move to London, where Nell could access her funds more easily and find work in Fleet Street. There were also family matters to consider. Shortly after the outbreak of war Olga Kerenskaya had lost her typist's job and was reduced to taking lodgers into her house in North London. Both Oleg and Gleb were working in other parts of the country and her ten-

---

i Albert Camus was finishing his first novel, *L'Étranger*, the classic story of Meursault, a French Algerian who, after attending his mother's funeral, kills an Arab man in an apparently motiveless murder.

year-old grandson, Oleg Jr, was boarding at Westminster School. 'When the Blitz began, the lodgers dispersed and she was left alone in an empty flat at the top of an almost empty house,' Gleb Kerensky says. 'She did not go to the air-raid shelters and appeared to be quite philosophical about it but the bombs and the blackout added to her feelings of isolation.'[9]

When Kerensky applied to the British Embassy in Paris for an entry visa, however, he was turned down. At Nell's insistence, he wrote to Bruce Lockhart on 7 May 1940:

> My Dear Friend,
> I would like very much to see you and talk with you about many things but I am in a rather odd position. As is my custom, I wanted to go to London, with my wife, to see my sons and friends but the passport office here refused to even send my application to London if I have only private reasons for visiting England. In order to obtain a visa for England it must be for political or business reasons and I must present documents or letters from someone in London to the Passport Control here.
>   I think you understand that this is an inconvenient and difficult position for me and I can't invent artificial reasons for my visit to London. I hope that you can make the necessary intervention and insist that provision for the visa will be sent to me. Let me hear from you as soon as possible and please make a note of my address and telephone in case you come to Paris before I go to London. I want very much to talk to you.
> Yours very sincerely,
> A. Kerensky.

Time, however, had run out. In the early hours of Friday 10 May the war of nerves ended abruptly when German troops invaded Holland, Belgium and Luxembourg, all neutral countries, and the Luftwaffe bombed targets in Northern France. Within a matter of days, sacred placenames inscribed on the World War I memorials in every French town – the Meuse, the Somme, the Marne, Ypres, Verdun – evoked new terrors in their citizens.

General Gamelin, despite the opposition of some of his own generals, immediately sent three French armies, with the British Expeditionary Force at their centre, streaming into Belgium to block the German advance. The plan was for Allied forces to form a defensive shield stretching from Antwerp in Holland, right across Belgium east of Brussels to link up with the northern extension of the Maginot Line. He then made the disastrous mistake of dispatching his best reserve troops, the Seventh Army under General Giraud, into Belgium to link up with Dutch forces deep in Holland.[10]

'Everybody seems to be very proud of the speed at which our troops were moved at night, and according to a previously elaborated plan, to bring help to our hard-pressed neighbour,' Pierre Lazareff wrote in his memoirs. 'Unfortunately, however, the "previously elaborated plan" was in no way secret as far as the Germans were concerned. We had done them the favour of giving a little dress-rehearsal last January.'[11]

The Wehrmacht's main attack, however, was aimed at the middle of the Allied defensive line. Defying French strategists who believed the rough, heavily timbered terrain of the Ardennes region of southern Belgium to be virtually impassable to tanks, General Gerd von Rundstedt's Army Group A, including seven panzer divisions, swept through the forest into France to attack the lightly manned defences on the Meuse, covering the seventy miles from the German border in just fifty-seven hours. This strategic master-stroke was the brainchild of General Erich von Manstein but Hitler was quick to claim the credit for himself.

In an increasingly tense London the Labour leader Clement Atlee and his MPs refused to join a coalition government under Chamberlain's leadership. Sick in body, mind and spirit, the Prime Minister resigned and the mantle passed to Winston Churchill, who assured Lord Beaverbrook, 'We will come through in triumph but we may lose our tail feathers.' The Gallipoli disaster had taught him that to succeed in military operations he must have total control. Indeed, he spelled this out in his first speech to the House of Commons: 'I have nothing to offer but blood, toil, tears and sweat. You ask, "What is our aim?" I can answer that in one word: Victory – victory at all costs, victory in spite of all the terror; victory, however long and hard the road may be.'[12]

On 12 May Bruce Lockhart contacted the Home Office about Kerensky's visa problem. Acknowledged as one of Stalin's most outspoken enemies, it should have followed that he would be welcome in Britain but Whitehall did not see it that way. To minimise the amount of effort required to keep track of inconvenient Russians living in

Britain, it was easier to ban them all, regardless of their political credentials.

At dawn on 13 May the first of the seven panzer divisions commanded by General Heinz Guderian suddenly and unexpectedly emerged in the meadows on the eastern bank of the Meuse. With Giraud's Seventh Army in the north, Gamelin had no reinforcements to stop them. Two days later, supported by Stuka dive-bombers and mechanised infantry, they crossed the river at Sedan. At 7 a.m. on the fifteenth Churchill was awoken by an urgent call from Paris. Speaking in English, a panic-stricken Paul Reynaud, told him, 'We have been defeated. We are beaten… we have lost the battle… the front is broken at Sedan.'

Churchill thought his French counterpart must be exaggerating and promised to visit him the next day when the picture was clearer but he soon discovered that his panic was justified. Indeed, all eight French divisions defending the Meuse were in full retreat and the road to Paris was open. The much-vaunted French defence system had utterly failed. Poor communications and obsolete tactics had committed tanks and artillery to a static line of defence. The advancing panzers dashed past French troops and literally left them standing.[13]

On the day following Reynaud's panic call Churchill flew to Paris and met the Prime Minister at the Ministry of Foreign Affairs in the Quai d'Orsay. He was appalled at the chaotic state of the French Government and the defeatist mood of the city. Taxis were being used to rush reinforcements to the front and civil servants could be seen burning archives in the grounds of their ministries. Churchill concluded from the evidence of his eyes that Reynaud was preparing to abandon the capital. In response to a plea for greater military aid, Churchill reluctantly agreed to commit an additional ten fighter squadrons which Britain could ill afford to the Battle of France.[14]

Nine days after the invasion had begun and with the Army's morale at rock bottom, Reynaud replaced Gamelin with General Weygand. The new Commander in Chief was seventy-three and had actually retired from the Army in 1935 but had been recalled to become commander of French Forces in the Middle East. He flew in from Beirut to take over his new command. Weygand had two preoccupations: a haunting fear of revolution and an incurable dislike of Reynaud, the man who had appointed him. Unbeknown to Churchill, he was also an Anglophobe who would blame the British for all his military setbacks.[15]

Reynaud's next move would seal France's fate. He invited Marshal Pétain, a bosom friend of General Franco and an outspoken defeatist, to join his government as minister without portfolio. Now eighty-four, Pétain was serving as French Ambassador to Madrid and his appointment puzzled British diplomats. How could he serve Reynaud or the nation when he loathed the Premier's 'immoral' lifestyle and seemed to think that the Battle of France was already lost?

The German advance posed serious problems for Alexander Kerensky and his Russian friends. Ilya Fondaminsky, whose wife Amalia had died in 1935, was determined to stay in Paris but Vladimir and Véra Nabokov were more desperate than ever to escape. After weeks of delay, they had finally obtained passports and American visas. Véra then greased an official palm with a 200-franc bribe to secure French exit visas. Considering that three lives depended on it, the bribe was a paltry sum but it stretched the Nabokovs' finances to the limit. To find the $560 required for half-price fares to the United States, Vladimir held a reading in Paris and tapped friends and supporters in France and America for cash gifts. Rachmaninov, who had fled Russia in 1918 and was living in New York, was one of the contributors.

On 15 May the Nabokovs were packed and ready to leave Paris when rumours swept through the city that a German parachutist had landed in the Place de la Madeleine. Fear gripped the bars and cafés; perhaps this was the start of an airborne invasion similar to the one that had paralysed Belgium. It was several hours before the invader was identified as a deflated barrage balloon. Vladimir called on Nell and Alexander in rue Nicolo to say goodbye and found the Nobel Prize-winning author Ivan Bunin, Zinaida Hippius and Dmitri Merezhkovsky there. Zinaida demanded to know why he was leaving Paris and then insisting that the Nabokovs travel by bus to Calais because, she claimed, the French Army had commandeered all the trains.

Nabokov made his excuses and fled. He stored his collection of South European butterflies and a wickerwork trunk containing his books and papers in Ilya Fondaminsky's basement at 130 avenue de Versailles. Three days later, the family caught a train – not to Calais, which was under fire, but to Saint Nazaire - to board the SS *Champlain*, the most luxurious cabin-class liner afloat. On 19 May she set sail for New York with the Nabokovs among her 1053 passengers. 'My bleakest recollections are associated with Paris,' Vladimir wrote in his memoirs, 'and the relief of leaving it was overwhelming.'

Churchill was in Paris on 22 May to hear Weygand unveil the 'Weygand Plan' for a counterattack in which the French First Army and the British Expeditionary Force on the Channel coast would strike south while a new army group consisting of troops from the Maginot Line, French North Africa and other sources would head north from the Somme to cut off the German force at Saint Quentin. It never happened. The British fought an indecisive battle at Arras but the French units proved as ineffective under Weygand as they had under Gamelin. There was no strike towards Saint Quentin. Civilians driving south reported columns of motorised French troops heading in the same direction.[16]

Churchill placed the blame for this 'colossal military disaster' firmly on the French High Command under Gamelin for failing to withdraw the Northern Armies from Belgium the moment he knew that the French front was decisively broken at Sedan. 'This delay entailed the loss of fifteen or sixteen French divisions and threw out of action for the critical period the whole of the British Expeditionary Force,' he told the Commons.

Bruce Lockhart realised that Alexander Kerensky would almost certainly die in Nazi hands unless something was done to rescue him. On 24 May he wrote to his friend, Fitzroy Maclean, now resident in the FO's Northern Department, urging him to intervene on Kerensky's behalf. Maclean informed Captain Maurice Jeffes, head of the Passport Control Department, that the FO had no objection to Kerensky coming to Britain. Jeffes, however, made it clear that MI5 would do everything in its power 'to prevent doubtful aliens from coming to this country'. Kerensky fitted that description and, again, no visa was forthcoming.

Paris received its first air raid at lunchtime on 3 June when German pilots followed the Seine along the Quai de Javel (now the Quai André-Citroën) from the northeast to the southwest. In rue Nicolo, Nell and Alexander heard the menacing drone of engines overhead and then explosion followed explosion as the planes unloaded their bombs on mainly civilian targets. The bombs blew several apartment houses in Passy and Auteuil to pieces and the west wing of the Citroën car plant at the Pont Mirabeau was set ablaze.

White Russians among Kerensky's neighbours were devastated over the Germans' perfidy. Having lived in hope that Hitler would restore 'Holy Russia' to them, they would never be able to return home now. For Kerensky, the bombing represented a serious downturn in events. A few days earlier he had been warned that fifth columnists were stalking him with the intention of handing him over to the Nazis. The air raid confirmed his fears that the enemy was drawing uncomfortably close and he was still without any means of escape.

Despite the menace of aerial attack tanned young Parisians still swam at the Racing Club pool in the Bois de Boulogne or bought drinks from the open-air bar and sunbathed on the grass. Those members of café society who hadn't been called up for military service carried on as normal at Le Dôme and La Coupole. One thing was missing: crossword puzzles, normally as essential to existence as Gauloises and café crème, had been banned in the press in case they were used to pass subversive messages to fifth columnists.

On 5 June the blitzkrieg outflanked the Maginot Line and French resistance disintegrated. Paul Reynaud, who had moved Daladier to the Foreign Ministry in May and taken over the War portfolio himself, sacked his rival from the government altogether. At Madame de Portes' insistence he appointed one of her favourites, Paul Baudouin, an acolyte of the defeatist Georges Bonnet, in his place.

As the German armour advanced on the capital in a pincer movement from east and west, Russian émigrés huddled together in the Dominique bar in Montparnasse or at the Chez Yar restaurant near the Champs Elysees. Unable to get a British visa for himself, Alexander Kerensky did his best to ensure the safety of his friends and staff. His Passy flat became a nerve centre for worried Russians to swap stories about their encounters with French officialdom and seek assistance.

Then, on Saturday 8 June, an ominous new sound reached Kerensky's ears from the northern battlefield: the *ker-ump* of French cannon firing salvo after salvo at the enemy's forward units. One column of panzers was said to have crossed the Seine at Rouen to the northwest of the capital and others were sighted due north in the forest of Chantilly. All this was gossip – the heavily censored Paris newspapers gave no hint of the impending hammer blow.

Nell and Alexander were due to spend the weekend with Nina Berberova and Nikolai Makeyev at Longchêne. They packed a small suitcase with a few things and set off in their car. Nothing had prepared them for the sight that greeted them at Saint Cloud. All roads leading south were jammed with traffic but it was a traffic jam unlike any they had ever seen before. The German invasion had turned six to eight million people in Holland, Belgium and Northern France into nomads. Antoine de Saint-Exupéry, author of *The Little Prince*, reported that on reconnaissance missions for the French Air Force it seemed a boot had kicked over a giant anthill and the ants were on the march.[17]

The Kerenskys joined uniformed chauffeurs driving the latest limousines as though heading for a day at Longchamps, while farmers manoeuvred huge tractors attached to farm wagons containing entire families and menageries of dogs, cats and canaries. Some cars had mattresses strapped to the roof as flimsy protection against air attack; other people pedalled bicycles or dragged carts laden with boxes and furniture; some walked over broken glass; all sought to dodge the bomb craters pitting the tarmac. Radiators and tempers boiled over; engines seized up.

Past Versailles, the traffic slowed to a crawl. Whenever there was a stoppage, drivers switched off their engines to conserve petrol. Many of the older vehicles had no self-starters and had to be cranked. And all the while thousands of pedestrians - footsloggers whose cars had broken down or who had had no car in the first place – passed the stalled motorists. It was with great relief that Nell turned off the road near Rambouillet and headed for Nina's farmhouse.

Nina and Nikolai had no idea from radio reports – their only source of news - about the tragedy unfolding a few kilometres from their front gate. For weeks, the media had been presenting a totally false, optimistic view of the war and now that the truth could no longer be supressed there was widespread panic. People advised one another to stock up on tinned food and, with a touch of gallows humour, to hoard lots of chewing gum – 'to plug the bullet holes in your petrol tank and to stop your teeth chattering'.

By Sunday morning, the Germans were advancing on a front that stretched across the entire width of France. East of Paris, the same frenzied scenes intensified after two o'clock that afternoon when word spread among the refugees that bridges over the Marne were about to be blown up. As far as General Weygand was concerned, 'if the Germans cross the Seine and the Marne, it is the end'.[18]

Parisians were disgusted to discover that they were being abandoned to the enemy. 'The Government is compelled to leave the capital for imperative military reasons,' French Radio announced. 'The Prime Minister is on his way to the armies.' One after another foreign envoys arrived at the new American Embassy at the corner of Avenue Gabriel and the Place de la Concorde to hand over the keys of their embassies for safekeeping before following Reynaud on his southern odyssey to the new seat of government at Tours, 150 miles away in the Loire Valley.

Following Charles de Gaulle's courageous but unsuccessful attempt to halt the blitzkrieg east of Saint Quentin with the Fourth Armoured Division, Reynaud had promoted him to brigadier-general and given him a seat in the cabinet as Under-Secretary of State for National Defence to counter mounting defeatism among his colleagues. De Gaulle says, 'Suddenly a convoy of luxurious, white-tyred American cars came sweeping along the road, with militiamen on the running-boards and motor-cyclists surrounding the procession; it was the Corps Diplomatique on its way to the châteaux of Touraine.'[19]

Down south on the Cap d'Antibes peninsula, the Duke of Windsor was entertaining Maurice Chevalier to lunch at the Château de la Croë near the Italian border on Monday 10 June when Mussolini announced in Rome that Italy had declared war on Britain and France 'to break the chains which are strangling us in the Mediterranean'. As thirty-two Italian divisions stormed into France, panic gripped the poorly defended Cote d'Azur.[ii]

Thousands of terrified foreigners besieged the British Consulate to plead for visas. Half the population of Monaco disappeared within a matter of hours. Evading Nazi kidnappers, British diplomats and a

---

ii When the Italian Foreign Minister, Il Duce's son-in-law Count Ciano, informed the British Ambassador, Sir Percy Loraine, of Italy's decision, the diplomat remarked mildly, 'I have to remind Your Excellency that England is not in the habit of losing her wars.'

Scotland Yard detective escorted the Duke and Duchess of Windsor to safety through Spain and Portugal.

At dawn on Tuesday 11 June Paul Reynaud reached Orléans. He arranged to meet Churchill at Weygand's new headquarters, the Château du Muguet at Briare, a town on the Loire halfway between Orléans and Tours. Churchill's favourite aircraft was a twin-engine de Havilland Flamingo in which passengers sat in comfortable armchairs. He flew in with a twelve-Spitfire escort that afternoon with his new Secretary of War, Anthony Eden, his new Chief of the General Staff, Sir John Dill, and his trusty cabinet secretary, General Hastings Ismay.

The Château du Muguet was, in General Spears' epicurean phrase, 'a monstrosity of red lobster-coloured brick, and stone the hue of unripe Camembert'. Spears was appalled at the appearance of Reynaud, Weygand and Pétain, who 'sat with white faces, their eyes on the table. They looked for all the world like prisoners hauled up from some dark dungeon'. The exception was Charles de Gaulle, who radiated a haughty self-confidence.

Churchill beamed encouragingly around the room. Drawing on his fast-diminishing reserves of bravado, he urged France's military and political leaders to defend Paris street by street, house by house to hold up the German advance. Weygand, who had travelled to Briare in a luxurious Pullman carriage, replied matter-of-factly. The enemy were too strong for that sort of resistance, he said, and Pétain chimed in that destroying the capital would not alter the outcome of the battle.

At 10 o'clock Churchill was served dinner - 'an omelette or something' - and was disturbed to hear from Reynaud that Pétain believed it would be necessary for France to seek an armistice.[20]

'Think back!' Churchill urged the old man. 'We went through difficult times in 1918 but we got over them. We shall get over these in the same way.'

Pétain was unmoved. Age might have clouded his blue eyes but in a rare moment of clarity he replied in his old caustic manner, 'In 1918, I gave you forty divisions to save the British Army. Where are the forty divisions that we need to save ourselves today?'[21]

Churchill had no answer to that. At the same time in Île-de-France, 200 kilometres closer to the German panzers, the occupants of the Longchêne farmhouse learned from the radio that General Pierre Héring, who had been appointed Military Governor of Paris, had declared Paris an open city. This meant that the capital would be surrendered to the enemy without a shot being fired. Weygand had actually made this decision two days earlier but had neglected to inform Héring's headquarters in Les Invalides. In those forty-eight hours, he had been busily exhorting Parisians to bear arms to fight 'before Paris, in Paris and behind Paris', just as Churchill had hoped.[22]

The news terrified Nell. Since falling in love with Kerensky, she had always known that this day might come. 'The Germans will put Alexander in jail like Schuschnigg,' she told Nina, referring to the brutality meted out to the Austrian Chancellor Kurt von Schuschnigg, whose courageous battle to protect his country's independence had ended in torture and solitary confinement. 'Like Schuschnigg', she repeated and, at the very thought of it, burst into tears.

Her only concern was to save Alexander life. They must flee the country. But how? Australians travelled on British passports and were therefore among the few foreign nationals who could travel in France without a *laissez-passer*. Not so Kerensky; he had only his Nansen refugee passport and had been refused a visa to enter Britain. He knew the Nazis would either shoot him or hand him over to Stalin. Unable to leave France legally, he had no intention of staying put and being arrested.

After dinner that night he told Nell that they must leave Longchêne in the morning and head southwest to the Biscay coast in the hope of getting a boat to England. They would have to pick up a British visa at one of the consulates on the way. 'We had only small suitcases containing a few clothes and jewels which we had made the habit of taking whenever we left Paris to visit friends,' Nell says. 'It was fortunate we did so because we had no time to return home when we learned of the German advance.'[23]

Unable to sleep, Nell and Nina clung to one another on the little bench under the almond tree. Nina vowed never to sit there again until they were reunited. Early on the twelfth, Alexander packed their car with food, water and a few litres of petrol and, with Nell at the wheel, they set off down the country lane to join the route nationale to Chartres, fifty kilometres away. There had been a heavy dew overnight and the dog roses drooped in the hedgerows.

Living through 'l'exode', as the French called this mass evacuation, was to experience the total disintegration of social structures. Localities that should have been able to offer refuge were deserted, some so quickly that half-eaten meals remained on dining-room tables. Even on the Beauce Plain, the agricultural area stretching from the Seine to the Loire, food and fresh water were hard to find. At every village, people queued outside the boulangerie in the hope of buying fresh bread. The shelves of most grocers, butchers and greengrocers had been stripped bare and the bakers – the ones who hadn't fled themselves - were unable to supply the demand.

That day the French Government reached La Touraine, the garden of France. Ministers were billeted at châteaux and villas in the surrounding area. Many of these properties were quite ancient and possessed nothing as new-fangled as an electric telephone, so communication between the various arms of government completely broke down. The retreat had degenerated into a mad scramble in which refugees, reporters and civil servants fought, begged and bribed the local citizenry for a bed, a bath, a meal.

Paul Reynaud pleaded with Churchill to make another trip to France to stiffen the backbone of his cabinet. Boarding the Flamingo the next day, Churchill asked his police bodyguard, Walter 'Tommy' Thompson, if he could borrow his revolver. 'One never knows,' he said sternly. 'I do not intend to be taken alive.'[24]

German Radio was referring to Tours as 'the provisional, the *very* provisional, capital of France'. It had been heavily bombed and the craters on the runway at the airport had only just been filled in when Churchill's aircraft came in to land just after 1 o'clock that afternoon. Two hours later the Supreme War Council met in the ivy-clad Préfecture of Police.[25]

Having abandoned the plan for a Brittany redoubt, Reynaud talked boldly to the visitors about taking his government to French North Africa and continuing the fight from there. He then asked Churchill to release France from her obligation not to negotiate a separate armistice. Churchill refused to allow such a move and instead outlined plans for a rearguard action while the French army withdrew to North Africa. The mood was so grim that Churchill left the meeting around 5 o'clock with tears streaming down his cheeks.

In the courtyard, Hélène de Portes, furious that he stood between France and peace with Germany, physically attacked him in what

Tommy Thompson described as 'a fury of hatred. She came forward with a determination to do him some harm. She had no gun, though we found a knife on her person'. Thompson wrestled the screaming woman to the ground 'and silenced her hysterics'.[26]

Summer in the countryside had been early, hot and dry. Choking dust blew in the air, the heat was suffocating and the smell of petrol fumes overpowering. Nell's face was smeared with grime, her hair streaked red from the dust. She pulled the car over to the side of the road and stopped. Beside her in the passenger seat, Alexander grimaced with pain and pleaded for water.

Nell stepped out of the car into an oil painting from Hell. The roadside was strewn with dead horses, abandoned vehicles and, in some places, hastily buried bodies. Nell's senses reeled from the incessant honking of car horns, the revving of engines, the desperate shouting of adults, the screaming of terrified children. Irene Némirovsky described the scene in *Suite Francaise*, 'Whenever they sank to the ground, they said they would never get up again, they would die right there, that if they had to die it was better to die in peace. But they were the first to stand up when a plane flew near.'[27]

Nell unfolded a map and tried to read it. Suddenly, the piercing wail of 'Jericho trumpets' rent the air. Anxious eyes looked skywards. Swooping down like angry raptors, German Stukas machine-gunned the helpless column, their sirens drowning out the screams of the panic-stricken refugees. 'We were bombed in Paris and on the road to Chartres,' Nell says. 'We saw dreadful things on the way. Each night was an anguish, each day an agony. We saw a child machine-gunned in its mother's arms and the mother refuse to allow people to take the child's body away. She went on clutching it.'

Typhoid fever was endemic in this area of rural France and much of the drinking water was contaminated; notices in public places warned of the danger. Jumping back into the car, Nell turned down a country lane; it would to safer off the beaten track and there would be more chance of finding petrol and drinkable water. They were lucky: in an abandoned farmhouse they found two bottles of mineral water and greedily drank them. At night, they slept under the stars. She recalls, 'One day we lived on a single cup of chocolate; on another day it was a stale loaf of bread salvaged from a deserted village; on a third day it was a tin of herring.'

With so many men under arms, it was a woman's duty to get their families to safety and many of the drivers in these tragic convoys were females. Nell and Alexander arrived in Chartres to find that the population of this proud cathedral town had dropped from 23,000 to just 800. The Hôtel Grand Monarque on the Place des Épars had run out of food and most of the shops were boarded up. Everybody they met seemed jumpy, nervous, irritable.

The same description applied to Kerensky, who found yet again that fate had stacked the odds against him. He had witnessed dire scenes of public disorder and national collapse before in the dreadful summer of 1918 and the panic of their flight from Longchêne brought back unhappy memories of his escape from Moscow. History was repeating itself but with one important difference. Then, he had been the illegally deposed head of the Russian state; now, he was a stateless refugee and as such had no status at all. He was also twenty-two years older. All the props had been kicked away and his life depended on the Australian woman at his side.

At 5.30 that morning - Friday 14 June 1940 – black clouds of burning oil from the storage tanks at the Basse Seine darkened the sky as 'the Teuton onrush', as *The Times* described it, swept into Paris and the swastika flapped over the Eiffel Tower. It seemed Saint Geneviève had abandoned the city to its fate. Premier Reynaud summoned his ministers to a cabinet meeting in Bordeaux, the Government's next port-of-call on its flight southward. 'We know that nothing can do any good,' Saint-Exupéry complained, 'yet we blow up bridges nevertheless, in order to play the game. We burn down real villages, in order to play the game. It is in order to play the game that our men die.'[28]

Between 26 May and 4 June Britain had retrieved 320,000 men – two-thirds British and one-third French – from the forlorn, wind-swept beaches of Dunkirk in an armada of little ships. The survivors owed a great debt to the valiant French rearguard of 25,000 men who kept the Germans at bay during the evacuation. The Royal Navy ensured that many of these brave soldiers escaped on the final night.

Without waiting to hear the result of the French cabinet meeting, the British High Command ordered the start of Operation Ariel, the withdrawal of British troops, diplomats and citizens from other

French ports. Nell and Alexander had no way of knowing that large numbers of ships would shortly be plying across the Channel again but they knew that Alexander would not be admitted to England unless he could procure a British visa. They set off for Bordeaux in the hope that the British Consulate there would provide him with one.

Their most immediate problem was finding fresh water. That afternoon they were so thirsty that they were reduced to drinking rainwater from ditches. 'Driving to Bordeaux,' Nell says, 'we saw two girls take their father, who had died of exhaustion, and bury him in a ditch, scraping the earth over his body with their hands.' Half-starved and desperate, they took refuge in a deserted barn to snatch a few hours' reprieve from the nightmare.

31

The Last Ship Out

Since the start of the German invasion, the population of Bordeaux had doubled to 600,000. Every street and square of the busy inland port were packed with parked cars, half of which contained sleeping refugees and their earthly possessions. The Kerenskys drove slowly along the riverfront looking for food and water, and seeking directions to the British Consulate. Ever since May, it had been too dangerous for transatlantic liners to use Le Havre and Cherbourg, so Bordeaux had become a magnet for foreign travellers. Rich Americans, Argentinians and Brazilians packed the café terraces on both sides of the Hôtel Splendide in the Place des Quinconces, a huge open square with a panoramic view of the Garonne.

From mid-June they were joined for drinks under the hotel's striped umbrellas by French officers, Belgian civilians, British diplomats and the special correspondents of newspapers of many nations, most of whom were as starved of news about the German advance as the general public. Space was at such a premium at the Splendide that people were sleeping in the bathrooms. Hélène de Portes, however, was ushered into an elegant double room, while the former Queen of Portugal was unceremoniously bundled out of the royal suite to make way for Pierre Laval.

Premier Reynaud had sent desperate appeals to President Roosevelt to declare the United States a non-belligerent ally of France in the hope of receiving American arms and planes. Roosevelt, however, was facing re-election in November and all he could offer were stirring words. General Spears was with Reynaud when he received Roosevelt's answer to his final plea. 'As he read it, he grew still paler, his face contracted,' Spears wrote. '"Our appeal has failed," he said in a small toneless voice. "The Americans will not declare war."' Those words effectively signalled the end of Reynaud's resistance.

On the morning of Saturday 15 June military outriders escorted a limousine up to the Splendide's entrance and a short, slim figure with a cavalryman's bandy-legged gait walked smartly up the steps to applause and shouts of 'Weygand! Weygand!' The populace saluted him as the valiant Commander in Chief who would save them from 'les Boches'. As he disappeared into the shadows of the dimly-lit front hall, they had no idea that he had arrived from Tours that day to read the last rites to the Battle of France.

As ministers assembled in the Préfecture for their cabinet meeting that afternoon, thunder echoed around the city like a drumroll of doom. French rightwingers who regarded the Third Republic as corrupt and decadent welcomed its imminent demise. Pierre Laval, usually so sly about showing his hand, openly supported a German victory 'because otherwise Bolshevism would install itself everywhere'. He made no secret of his belief that the 'Anglo-Saxons' would be unable to continue the war against Germany on their own.[1]

With the approval of the Mayor of Bordeaux, Adrien Marquet, Laval set up a pro-German base in the Hotel de Ville, where sycophantic senators and deputies argued that France should not only make peace with Germany but join Hitler in the fight against Britain. 'Peace' demonstrations were organised in the streets and politicians who argued that France should fight on were denounced. The patriotic Léon Blum was called 'a Jewish warmonger' and thrown out of his third-class hotel.[2]

The British Ambassador, Sir Ronald Campbell, signalled the Foreign Office with a French request to ask the United States to act as an intermediary in establishing Germany's terms for an armistice. Churchill rejected the suggestion out of hand, telling the War Cabinet, 'We are fighting for our lives and it is vital that we should allow no chink to appear in our armour.' Once again Reynaud requested the British Government to release France from her obligations under the Anglo-French Agreement and allow the Cabinet to negotiate a separate peace with the Germans. Churchill had no choice but to agree. The French plan was for the President of the Republic, Albert Lebrun, Paul Reynaud and his ministers to make their way to Perpignan near the Spanish border on the east coast and then be ferried across the Mediterranean to Algeria at the last possible moment.

At 10 o'clock that night Reynaud, a nervous tic pulsing in his ashen face, resigned as Premier and at midnight it was announced that President Lebrun had asked Marshal Pétain to form a government. One of his first appointments was to make General Weygand Minister of War, a post that would very shortly cease to have any meaning. Instead of joining the ministerial group heading for North Africa, Reynaud would now become French Ambassador to the United States.

Geneviève Tabouis, foreign editor and columnist of *L'Oeuvre* newspaper, was inside the Préfecture. From a contact in the executive suite, she discovered that Reynaud and Pétain, in collaboration with the High Command, had agreed to order the French forces to surrender within a matter of hours. As she hurried to her hotel to file the story, she passed a crowd of revellers enjoying themselves at a funfair. 'I seethed with rage when I observed a group of people selecting picture-postcards on which the smiling faces of Reynaud and the Marshal emerged from the folds of the tricolour flag,' she wrote in her memoirs. 'But how could the Bordelais even begin to suspect the manoeuvres of these two? How could they know that these two men had just delivered them body and soul to the Nazis?'[3]

That day the British cruiser HMS *Arethusa* arrived from Gibraltar to protect shipping at Le Verdon at the tip of the vast Gironde estuary. Upriver, the destroyer HMS *Berkeley* moored at the quay in central Bordeaux. She would act as a wireless link with the Admiralty and provide a shuttle service taking refugees down to the bigger ships. As they parked their car in the Place des Quinconces and walked along the riverfront towards the British Consulate, the Kerenskys could see the *Berkeley* standing tall among the cranes and gantries. Her grey masts offered hope that help was finally at hand.

The British Consulate was on the first floor of a building across the square from the Hôtel Splendide. Nell and Alexander joined the queue on the wide staircase leading to the consul's office. Such was the demand for British visas that dozens of people of many nationalities were prepared for a long wait. General Spears fought his way through the pandemonium. 'It was an appalling sight,' he said. 'The anxiety of people desperately anxious to get away was very comprehensible.'

Nell and Alexander gave up the unequal struggle and went in search of a place to stay. They were dirty, dispirited and very tired but every hotel room had been taken and they had no luck in finding shelter. It was just as well - had they checked into even the meanest *pension*, the French registration system would have revealed Alexander's presence to the authorities. With the forces of Fascism taking control of Bordeaux, he would have found himself in a cell beneath the very Préfecture in which the cabinet had held its final meeting.

Le Chapon Fin, Bordeaux's finest restaurant, was located in the hotel of the same name a few blocks behind the Splendide in rue Montesquieu. The diners among its grotto-like alcoves that night included Sir Ronald Campbell, General Spears and members of the French and British diplomatic staffs. As the temporary home of the British Embassy, Campbell had taken over the Hotel Montré next to the restaurant. The Ambassador noted with distaste that Pierre Laval was dining at another table with some of his pro-Nazi acolytes. Spears told him that Reynaud and Georges Mandel, the strongest and most-outspoken resister in cabinet, agreed that Laval should be arrested to curtail his treacherous activities but neither was prepared to issue the order.[4]

Had Alexander Kerensky shown his face in the Chapon Fin that night, Laval would have had him arrested and his life would have been forfeit. And yet there were many people in Bordeaux who would have been prepared to help him, including his friend Jean Hugo, a reservist who had retreated there with the French Army; Geneviève Tabouis, who had met him at Aline Ménard-Dorian's salon; Georges Mandel, who had met him in Paris as early as 1918; as well as a dozen assorted British and American correspondents who were familiar with his stand against Hitler and Stalin.

Jean Hugo had spent hours looking for accommodation with the assistance of the local police. 'At three o'clock in the morning, having found nowhere to stay, I lay down in the car in front of the gendarmerie,' he says. 'When a policeman's wife knocked on the window, it was ten o'clock in the morning. I found a room in Le Bouscat on the ground floor overlooking a small suburban garden. You could hardly move in there because the bed was surrounded by ice-chests.'[i][5]

---

[i] Jean Hugo made his way to the family home, 'Mas de Fourques', at Lunel in what would be the Free Zone. In his memoirs he refers to helping two young men to escape across the border into Spain. The Hugo house was an important meeting place for *les Résistants* in the South of France.

The Kerenskys had no way of knowing that these potential saviours were close at hand. Never so alone or more exposed, they were reconciled to the prospect of sleeping in their car when they had a rare stroke of luck. Recognising Alexander from his photograph, a patriotic Frenchman let the fugitives move into his cellar.[6] Early the following day they found a cable office from which Alexander sent a frantic plea to Bruce Lockhart to intercede on his behalf. 'Again I went to the Foreign Office and to the Admiralty,' Lockhart says.

> I met with little sympathy in either department. In 1917, when we were afraid that Russia would make a separate peace, British and French ministers had courted Kerensky as rich and aged plutocrats pay court to a ballerina. To his own detriment, for peace was the winning card of the Bolsheviks, Kerensky carried on the war for nine months until the October Revolution. Now he was forgotten, and a new generation did not even know his name. I pleaded for a transit visa pointing out that Kerensky had friends in the United States. In the end a telegram was sent to Bordeaux but I had little hope that it would produce any result.[7]

Late that morning General de Gaulle drove to Bordeaux airport to see off his friend General Spears on a flight to London. The two men shook hands and appeared to say goodbye to one another in what turned out to be a carefully planned charade. The plane's door was still ajar and as the pilot began to taxi slowly down the airstrip de Gaulle suddenly stepped on board and slammed the door shut. The French police, de Gaulle's staff and airport officials watched dumbfounded as the General soared into the wide blue yonder. The plane landed at Heston, West London, in time for Spears to take de Gaulle to lunch at the Royal Automobile Club in Pall Mall, providing its members with a glimpse of a rare moment in history.

While waiting for a reply to his cable, Nell and Alexander returned to their cellar. It was better to stay out of sight and the obliging Frenchman kept them informed of developments as best he could. On his radio at 12.30 that afternoon they heard Pétain admit in his first broadcast to the nation that France had surrendered. 'It is with heavy heart that I tell you today that we must cease hostilities,' he said. He blamed the French defeat on 'too few allies, too few weapons and too few babies' – in other words, too few replacements for the

Frenchmen slaughtered in the First World War. As a sign of his new political eminence, he signed off this momentous address in the royal plural: *'Nous, Philippe Pétain, Chef de l'État* (Head of State).'

According to Jean Hugo, Pétain's surrender could not prevent Bordeaux from being bombed. 'I slept through the siren and had to be woken up,' he says. 'Rumours were spread that the Germans were close and it caused a panic.'[8] The Gironde teemed with tens of thousands of refugees and retreating Allied troops. There were too many people; too few boats. Among the richer refugees was King Zog, who was desperate to find sanctuary from his Axis enemies. One of his aides asked the British Consul whether His Majesty would be allowed to enter Britain with his family, provided he brought his country's gold reserves and the crown jewels with him. Permission arrived from London within hours.

Zog was advised to go south to Bayonne where four liners – the Polish vessels *Batory* and *Sobieski* plus the British troopships *Ettrick* and *Arandora Star* - had been sent to evacuate refugees and Polish soldiers. Over the next two days some 9000 Poles were embarked in the two Polish transports but it was then decided to shift the operation to better port facilities at Saint Jean de Luz, a fashionable port south of Bayonne in the Basque Country.[9]

Nell and Alexander remained in their French patron's cellar until they were able to return to the consulate to see whether the cable to Bruce Lockhart had met with success. They were overjoyed to discover that the consul had received a telegram from the Foreign Office granting Alexander a transit visa which would enable him to enter a British port on his way to the United States. It had arrived just in time. The legation and consular staff shut up shop that night and went down-river in the *Berkeley* to Le Verdon. On Wednesday 19 June they embarked in the *Arethusa* which sailed for Plymouth the next day with 221 passengers, including the President of Poland and his diplomatic staff.

Even as Pétain's negotiators set out from Bordeaux to make contact with the Nazis, removalists were stacking official boxes, bags and filing cabinets into the backs of lorries. As the hours slipped away, it became evident that no orders have been given to move French warships to British harbours. Word also leaked out that most of the ministers would not be joining the African safari. The *New York Times* lamented, 'For France herself a terrible ordeal now begins.... the most civilised people in the world, deprived of resistance, now stand at the mercy of a barbarian.'[10]

Meanwhile, the barbarians were busy moving the 'Compiègne Wagon-Lit', the old railway dining car in which the 1918 Armistice had been signed, from its museum to the very spot of Germany's humiliation at the hands of Marshal Ferdinand Foch in the Compiègne Forest. On 21 June Hitler was filmed arriving at the site. First, he glared at the imperious, life-sized statue of Foch outside the carriage and then looked even more angrily at a stone plaque on which was inscribed in French: *'Here on 11 November 1918 succumbed the criminal pride of the German Empire, vanquished by the free peoples that it sought to enslave.'* Entering the carriage, Hitler sat in Foch's old chair to receive the French emissaries led by General Charles Huntziger, who had commanded the Second Army in the Battle of Sedan.

Failing to get a ship from Bordeaux or Le Verdon, Nell and Alexander drove down to Saint Jean de Luz only to discover that bad weather had shut down the port. On the gloomy rain-swept docks they learned that the Germans had dropped mines in the Bay of Biscay and it was too risky for local fishermen to venture out to sea. Nevertheless, Nell approached the owner of a Portuguese sailing boat. 'I have refused two fortunes today already,' he told her brusquely and refused to discuss the matter further.

The skipper of a French sardine boat also turned them down. Many other desperate people were trying the same thing: Rolls-Royces and Bentleys lay abandoned at the quayside but no amount of money could buy a boat to take their owners to freedom. It was now a race against time before the Nazis took control of the country. Nell and Alexander decided to try their luck in Spain. Ten days after setting off from Paris, they arrived at Hendaye, the last town on the French side of the border. The frontier post at Irun lay across the bridge over the Bidassoa River. All around, the snow-capped Pyrenees reared up like an impassable barricade.

With just one final hurdle to cross, their luck ran out. At passport control a guardia civil recognised Alexander from press photographs. A Spanish officer told Nell that while she was welcome in Spain, her husband was persona non grata. Nell pleaded with them that

Alexander was travelling through Spain to Portugal and had a visa to enter Britain but Russian revolutionaries were unwelcome in Franco's single-party dictatorship.

Nell refused to give up. Driving to the back of the queue, she scanned the occupants of the waiting cars for a sympathetic face, someone she felt she could trust. Her eyes lighted on a tall, thin, middle-aged man with a toothbrush moustache. He was sitting next to a younger woman and she judged from their appearance that they could only be English. Indeed they were – although she didn't know it the, and would never know it - they were Captain Cecil William Mercer and his wife Elizabeth.

Mercer was an English author who wrote rollicking adventure stories under the penname 'Dornford Yates'. His books were part of the 'Clubland Heroes' collection, which included the works of John Buchan (*The Thirty-Nine Steps*, *Greenmantle*) and Sapper (*Bull-Dog Drummond*, *The Female of the Species*). Dornford Yates's thrillers followed the adventures of the dashing Richard Chandos in tackling criminals, protecting the innocent and romancing beautiful women.[11]

No doubt there were many brave and compassionate British people among the refugees at Irun that day but Mercer/Yates wasn't one of them. He was a strange man. Having driven his first wife into the arms of a lover, he had horsewhipped the man and then divorced her. At Pau in the western Pyrenees he built a house with ninety-three steps despite the fact that his second wife, Elizabeth, had been crippled by polio and walked with a limp. Pau had a prosperous English colony and yet he made no friends and learned no French. He was regarded among expatriates as a crashing bore.[12]

As Nell approached his car, Mercer sat impassively in the passenger seat with an automatic pistol on his knee in case of trouble. Elizabeth was behind the wheel and their wire-haired terrier, Tumble, was on the back seat. Mercer's biographer writes, 'During the wait a redheaded Englishwoman, in great distress, formed up to ask help in getting her husband across the bridge. She could go by herself, she explained, but for him there was flat refusal. It turned out that he was Alexander Kerensky, and the first revolutionary Prime Minister of Russia was unwelcome in Fascist Spain. There was nothing that the Mercers could do for her.'[13]

This was hardly surprising. According to the author George

MacDonald Fraser, Yates was 'quite some distance to the right of Bismarck; if you think Buchan, Sapper and P. C. Wren are the ultimate reactionaries, you haven't met our Dornford'. Among his prejudices were Jews, suffragettes, fellow travellers, Socialists, Lloyd George and George Bernard Shaw. A Socialist Revolutionary like Alexander Kerensky would have been close to the top of his blacklist.[14]

No one knows how many people Nell approached that day before wearily climbing back into her car. Her heart was pounding from the strain of these traumatic weeks and her kidneys ached from the poison in her system. Close to collapse, she faced a stark choice: abandon Alexander, enter Spain on her own and find medical help, or stay with him to the bitter end, even though it meant sacrificing herself. After her experience with Mercer/Yates, it would have been natural if she had felt absolutely crushed but she did not hesitate. Without a second thought, she headed north down the serpentine road leading back to Saint Jean de Luz. She had performed minor miracles to get them this far and she wasn't going to quit now.

The Armistice was signed at 6.50 on the evening of 22 June after the French were warned that if they delayed any longer Germany would occupy the entire country. The treaty decreed that France would be divided into an Occupied Zone and a Free Zone south of the Loire to the Mediterranean (known as Vichy France after its wartime capital, the central spa town of Vichy). The French Army and the French Fleet were to be demobilised and disarmed. French naval commanders would be ordered to sail their ships to specified ports under German or Italian control. The entire French coastline from Belgium to the Spanish frontier would pass into enemy hands at 1.35 a.m. on 25 June.

The French defeat was blamed on many causes ranging from a corrupt press to Léon Blum's forty-hour week, from the 'Munichmen' Édouard Daladier and Georges Bonnet to the fact that the Maginot Line had not been completed to the sea. Saint-Exupéry saw it more simplistically. The French, he explained, were a nation of forty million farmers who stood no chance against a nation of eighty million metal-workers, punch-press operators, blueprint readers, time-study men and belt-line organisers.[15]

France had also concluded a separate peace with the Italians (giving rise to the bon mot 'Veni, vidi, Vichy') and the Côte d'Azur was swarming with Italian soldiers.[16] Somerset Maugham, the author/spy, packed a supply of tea, sugar, macaroni, marmalade and bread, plus a change of clothes, three books, a pillow and blanket, and abandoned his villa, 'La Mauresque' on Cap Ferrat. In Cannes he boarded a small collier and twenty days later arrived in Liverpool haggard, dirty and exhausted after a nightmarish trip.[ii] [17]

On 24 June the weather on the west coast cleared and embarkation began at Saint Jean de Luz. The MV *Ettrick*, a fine-looking 11,200-ton P&O liner newly converted into a troopship, was anchored in the Bay of Biscay protected from the open sea by one of the incurving headlands. The port was located at the mouth of the River Nivelle and its fleet of little sardine boats was being used to ferry passengers out to the ship. Nell joined the queue of cars driving at a crawl past the tall seventeenth and eighteenth century houses lining the narrow streets towards the seafront. Parking the car, the first thing they saw was a squad of French soldiers and sailors holding back hundreds of people who were trying to storm the quayside.

The acting British military attaché, having called for silence, shouted that no one could go on board with hand luggage because there was a big swell and they would need both hands to get up the swaying gangway. The attaché gave instructions that all baggage should be left in a designated spot on the quayside. It would be brought aboard during the night. King Zog and his family, who were queuing up like everybody else, deposited one hundred pieces of luggage, including Albania's gold reserves.

Nell managed to squeeze through the crowd and find the *Ettrick*'s skipper, Captain John Legg, who was standing on the quay. Her dust-streaked hair and grimy clothes were in stark contrast to the smartly dressed women competing for his attention but she collared him for long enough to describe Alexander's predicament and to convince him that the British Government was anxious to speak to him about Russia. Whether it was this argument or her anguish, or perhaps both, Legg agreed to take them on board. As they climbed into one of the sardine boats bound for the *Ettrick*, Nell threw her car keys to a Frenchman who was watching the departures from the quayside.

The troopship had room for just 600 passengers and every cabin was already occupied. Alice Keppel, the last mistress of Edward

---

ii One of Maugham's fellow passengers on the collier was Hedley Hope-Nicholson, whose daughter Loretta married Jean Hugo in 1949.

VII, occupied one room with her husband George and their daughter Violet. George's nerves were in such a bad state that he had broken out in a nasty rash and Violet, who had been driving an ambulance in Paris, complained that rattling over the cobblestones had loosened her teeth. Nell and Alexander settled down on the deck with their meagre possessions. Not for the first time, he had lost all his books, as well as his private papers, while Nelle had forfeited her letters, her poetry and essays, and her designer clothes.[18]

At 10.45 a.m. that day the senior naval officer at Saint Jean de Luz reported to the headquarters of Operation Ariel at Plymouth that 1000 refugees had been loaded into the *Ettrick* but many more were milling around the port. At midday he added, 'Am now filling *Ettrick* to capacity by embarking 300 Polish soldiers. When can we expect another ship?' But there were no other ships and night had already fallen. Because of the risk of mines, the *Ettrick* would not be able to sail until daybreak. Fortunately for King Zog, his chauffeur had time to hire a speedboat and reunite him with his gold bullion.

The Armistice had been in effect for six hours on the twenty-fifth when the *Ettrick* weighed anchor and set sail. She was the last British ship to leave France. It would be four years before the Nazis were removed from French soil and the country could start to rebuild its amour propre.

Once word passed around the liner that Alexander Kerensky was on board, other passengers sought him out. One man who had escaped from Paris two days after the German occupation told him that one of the Nazis' first acts had been to release Communists from prison as a goodwill gesture to Stalin. These men were parading through the streets singing 'The Internationale' and hunting down anti-Communist Russians.

The *Ettrick* refugees were a motley lot. In the packed saloon, Parisiennes in furs, silk stockings, high-heeled shoes, some dripping with jewellery, held themselves aloof from peasant women in old coats and felt slippers. An exiled king and a deposed Russian head of state found themselves in the company of a former royal mistress and three women in the khaki uniforms and blue epaulets of the British Mechanised Transport Corps.

Penelope Otto, Marjorie Juta and Ursula Lloyd-Bennet were members of the Château de Blois Ambulance Corps, whose doctors and nurses had treated the French wounded immediately behind the battlefront. Having seen more action than most soldiers, these courageous young women had been offloaded from another ship to make room for Sir Ronald Campbell and British Embassy staff.[19] Penelope Otto, a twenty-five-year-old Scot, described her fellow passengers on the *Ettrick* as 'one seething mass of questioning, smelly, discontented humanity'.

> Why do I feel such an innate dislike for all these people? Once I was sorry for all refugees but now sympathy is killed by their lack of manners, whining discontent and, worst of all, abuse of the people who are giving them refuge. Was dressing when some Poles came bursting in. These so-and-sos think they own the ship. Having snaffled every first class and other available cabin they have to be unpleasant and grasping for everything else. May I be forgiven for all my uncharitable thoughts.'[20]

Marjorie Juta begged for help from the young third officer. Could he find them somewhere to sleep? He led the ambulance-women up a ladder to the boat deck, where he opened the door to a bright and cheerful children's playroom. The women placed their bedrolls on the floor among the toys and gratefully went to sleep.[21]

Throughout the voyage, Goanese stewards in smart white mess jackets served drinks and meals to all on board and were tipped with huge quantities of francs which everyone assumed would be worthless following the capitulation. It was an anxious journey – they were attacked from the air but Captain Legg's seamanship and the protective guns of a couple of destroyers saw them through.

At 5.15 on the evening of 26 June the *Ettrick* berthed at Plymouth Harbour. 'King Zog and retinue go ashore,' Penelope Otto wrote in her diary. 'We, of course, have to wait till the morning for the immigration officers while a brigand gets away with it.'[22] Alexander Kerensky was forbidden to leave the ship. To prevent him slipping ashore, he and Nell were confined to one of the vacated cabins until the authorities decided what to do with them.

Among the happiest people on board were the Goanese stewards who were informed that the franc had been granted a twenty-four-hour reprieve and that their vast booty of paper money could be cashed at face value for sterling in local banks.

The following day an immigration officer informed Nell and Alexander that they could land on condition that they left for the United States as soon as they could book passage.[23] Wearily, they caught the train to London. Knowing her family in Queensland would be desperately concerned about her, Nell cabled them: 'Have passed through the valley of the shadow of death.'

While the Kerenskys checked into the Cumberland Hotel at Marble Arch, Mrs Keppel and King Zog went to the Ritz. The ex-monarch installed his large entourage on the third floor and paid his bill in gold. Mrs Keppel held court in the Edwardian lounge and was judged to be 'far more regal than the poor Queen of Albania'. Her great enemy, Mrs Ronnie Greville, sighed, 'To hear Alice talk about her escape from France, one would think she had swum the Channel with her maid between her teeth.'[24]

In his biography, Richard Abraham maintained that Kerensky 'unjustly preserved a hostile detachment toward Nell, resenting his second escape from martyrdom. His injustice compounded a trauma in her which never quite healed'. While it was true that the exertions of their escape had permanently damaged Nell's health, her husband's attitude towards her emanated from his short temper, his frustration about his uncertain financial position and his total inability to influence events. Had he desired martyrdom, he would have handed himself over to the French police.[25]

In a valiant attempt to continue the fight against Germany Édouard Daladier and Georges Mandel were among twenty-seven deputies and a solitary senator who had left Bordeaux in the auxiliary cruiser *Massilia* bound for Casablanca in French Morocco. The group reached Casablanca harbour without incident but that was as far as they got. Following the dissolution of the Third Republic, the *Massilia* was ordered to bring them back to Vichy France, where they were imprisoned.

Paul Reynaud and Hélène de Portes drove southeast from Bordeaux intending to stop at Reynaud's holiday home on the Riviera prior to leaving for his ambassadorial appointment in the United States. Anticipating invitations to the White House and a round of cocktail parties on Dupont Circle, de Portes had packed the car with trunkloads of clothing. On the highway near Sète a hatbox tumbled forward and blocked Reynaud's view. The car veered off the road and crashed into a tree. Reynaud was admitted to hospital with minor injuries – the hatbox probably saved his life - but his mistress was all but decapitated.

On 3 July the tragic sequel to the capitulation of France was played out at Oran and Mers-el-Kebir in North Africa. When the main French fleet refused to surrender, Churchill ordered the Royal Navy to sink it. The bombardment killed 1297 French servicemen, sank a battleship and damaged five other vessels. Churchill told Parliament, 'I leave the judgment of our action, with confidence, to Parliament. I leave it to the nation, and I leave it to the United States. I leave it to the world and to history.' France has never forgotten it.

32

The Death of Nell Tritton

The Special Branch logged Kerensky's movements in London and the GPO made a list of every telephone number he dialled from his room at the Cumberland Hotel. There is no record that he met Olga and her telephone number does not appear on that list. 'In private life, grandfather was difficult, sometimes impossible,' says Oleg Kerensky Jr. 'Grandmother could never really forgive him. For many years of exile she refused to see him at all but despite her resentment about their personal relationship, she retained a strong admiration for him as a statesman and was ever-ready to defend him politically.'

Transatlantic travel for civilians was in such demand that Kerensky had difficulty finding passage for Nell and himself to the United States. Cunard had a ship sailing for North America in the middle of July 1940 but he had no hope of making a booking without the assurance of the Foreign Office that they would be granted exit permits. Having battled to get into Britain, he was now fighting to get out.

'I am loath to add to your burdens,' Bruce Lockhart wrote to Fitzroy Maclean on 6 July 1940, 'but I fear we shall have K. on our hands indefinitely unless something can be done. In any event I should like to have him out of the country soon. Otherwise I shall have to apply for a special entertainment allowance and two extra telephones!'[1]

Fitzroy Maclean sent Nell and Alexander's passports to Passport Control with a letter explaining that the couple 'are anxious to leave for the United States towards the middle of the month when they understand from the Cunard Line that a boat will be sailing. They already have American visas, and I should be most grateful if you could arrange for the issue to them of the necessary exit permits, and also do what you can to help them to get passages to the United States. As I told you, MI5 would prefer that they did not remain in this country longer than is necessary'.

British exit permits were forthcoming and Kerensky made bookings in the Cunard liner *Scythia*. Bruce Lockhart visited him at his hotel to say goodbye. 'He is convinced that I had saved him again, and his gratitude was embarrassing,' he says. 'When we said goodbye, he came out with me to the door of the lift and, shaking me violently by the hand, said in a voice trembling with emotion, "You are a real friend, and I have very few friends nowadays. It is in adversity that you know who your real friends are".'[2]

Kerensky's welcome to New York on 12 August was in marked contrast to the niggardly reception he had received in Britain. He had been away from America for 166 days and in that time the map of Europe had been redrawn. Reporters and photographers crammed into his cabin. Next day, in the *New York Times*, Kerensky urged all remaining democracies to assist Britain in her war against Germany. Describing her as 'the last hope of Europe', he enthused,

> I cannot accept any idea but that of an English victory. England has strong will. Not only are the leaders determined to win but the humblest worker. It was not the same in France. France was fatigued; there was psychological collapse. I was astonished to see that in France all political factions continued their fights. It is not the same in England, where there is unity throughout the entire country.[3]

From his MI5 office at 2 Fitzmaurice Place, Mayfair, Bruce Lockhart sent a cutting of the *New York Times* article to Fitzroy Maclean on 21 September 1940 with the comment, 'You will see that (i) the New York paper is giving [Kerensky] a much bigger show than we did, and (ii) that he himself has done us quite proud'.

Nine days after their arrival the Kerenskys were reminded of the unforgiving nature of Stalin's vengeance when Leon Trotsky, an ailing sixty-year-old insomniac, was assassinated in his Mexican stronghold. Ramón Mercader, a Barcelona-born NKVD agent posing as a Canadian travelling salesman, gained access to the fortress by seducing Sylvia Ageloff, an American Trotskyist who was working there.

Trotsky had a weakness for a sweet made of frozen cactus-pulp covered with milk chocolate and sprinkled with bitter cocoa powder and ground almonds. Mercader delivered boxes of the sweet to the house and thus became a familiar figure to Trotsky's guards. One evening he tricked his way into Trotsky's study to discuss a political article he had written and attacked him with a mountaineer's ice-pick concealed in his overcoat.[4]

Kerensky shed no tears for his old enemy. 'Trotsky was the most merciless of all Bolshevist terrorists and died by the same means he brought into being,' he said. 'He was the victim of the system of secret police instituted by him and Lenin against all opponents. His political influence was too weak at this time to have made his death necessary, so his assassination may have been an act of revenge.' He quoted three similar cases in which Stalin's enemies had died at the hands of Soviet secret police: 'a man of great influence in Switzerland in 1937' [a Soviet defector named Ignace Poretsky, a.k.a. Ignace Reiss] and two White Russian generals in Paris [Yevgeny Miller and Alexander Kutepov. The latter was grabbed off the street in January 1930 and never seen again].[5]

Even as he lay dying, Trotsky thought only of world revolution. One of his aides attested that his last words were, 'Please say to our friends that I am sure of the victory of the Fourth International. Go forward!'[6] The *Daily Worker* absolved Stalin of any blame for the murder:

> Leon Trotsky died at the hands of one of that small gang of dubious social elements and provocateurs who alone remained for him to lead after he had long been exposed as an enemy of the working class. Trotsky's activities attracted this kind of irresponsible, criminal element.
>
> The tiny circle of adherents lived in an atmosphere of mutual hatred, suspicion and violence, utterly without principle. It appears now that one of his own followers, one of the members of his degenerate circle, which Trotsky had created for his own designs, struck him down.

Nell feared that Stalin would send his killers after her husband but it did not stop her talking to reporters about the war. 'Stalin is still playing cagey and does not intend to take an active part in the conflict,' she said, 'but he will continue to aid the Axis. In fact, the union between Russia and Germany is so clear that Stalin is likely to fall if Hitler is defeated. But the start of the Allied offensive against the Axis depends largely on American aid to England.'[7]

In the autumn of 1940, Kerensky looked ahead and foresaw with considerable clarity a wider world conflagration in which Hitler, Mussolini and Stalin, together with Japan, would divide the Asian, African and Oceanic possessions of the so-called 'pluto-democracies' among themselves. 'With fire and sword the bearers of the new totalitarian ideology are seeking to establish a "new world order",' he wrote. 'How do they propose to do that? The leaders of the Berlin-Rome-Tokyo military alliance have given us an answer: The British Empire must be destroyed as the basis of the "pluto-democratic" order. For this it is necessary to isolate the British Empire as such from the rest of the world, as a corollary to the isolation of England in Europe; to stop all American aid to Britain; prevent any and all cooperation between the United States and Britain in the Pacific, and in the event of Washington's refusal to obey, to embroil America in the Far East before she is prepared.'[8]

The Kerenskys moved in with Ken and Helen Simpson and in October accompanied them to a buffet supper at the home of Carleton H. Palmer, a pharmaceutical tycoon who, like Simpson, had served as a gunner in France during World War I. Simpson was standing for Congress in the November elections that would return Roosevelt to the White House for an unprecedented third term. The talk was all about Simpson's chances of winning the 'silk stocking district', the diverse and heavily populated Upper East Side of Manhattan.

The excitement reached fever pitch on election night when the results came in and Ken Simpson was duly elected as a Republican Congressman. He took his seat in the House of Representatives in early January 1941. Twenty days later he returned to New York from Washington to spend the weekend with his family and their house guests. He was in his study after dinner when he suffered a heart attack. Helen heard a cry for help and summoned his doctor, who administered stimulants to the stricken man but he died late that night. He was only forty-five. Kenneth Simpson, a true friend to Kerensky, was buried in the family plot in Hudson City Cemetery.

Nell and Alexander moved into their own apartment at 1060 Park Avenue. Nelle's wrote to Nathalie Kerensky from there on 17 February 1941:

My Dear Nathalie,
AF looks forward to letters from you and Oleg and Gleb with about

the same anticipation and anxiety that you must await news of little Oleg. Please send us the address of the school where little Oleg is – AF would like to write to him.

No doubt you know that Krivitsky, that Bolshevik head of the spy system in Western Europe, has died here in Washington by 'suicide'. He wrote *In Stalin's Secret Service* last year and has been tracked ever since. If it was suicide it was forced by the threat to kidnap his 7-year-old son. I expect Jan Valtin, who wrote this dreadful book *Out of the Night*, is the next.[i]

The strength of the fifth columns and Nazi-Communist agents here has been evident by the tone of some of the papers, particularly a paper called *P.M.*; some of the articles in it were about the most offensive and repugnant I have every read anywhere.

The situation in the Far East is increasingly serious and of course it affects me profoundly in <u>all</u> ways. Norman T [cousin Norman Tritton] is in the Air Force but where I do not know. He is a pilot. Cyril T. [cousin Cyril Tritton] is in the Army but still at home. Corbett T. [cousin Corbett Tritton), who is the Prime Minister's private secretary, must be in England now. If Oleg will write to him and see him he will bring a message to AF He is about 30, clever and ambitious and a great admirer of AF. Do not delay. They will come home this way fairly soon. I want you to meet. I am sure you will like him, Oleg.

AF is fit and well but the lack of funds with which to do any active work depresses and irritates him. The sympathy is very strong for England but the isolationists are also very strong and backed by subversive elements. I wish Mr Churchill in his splendid speech had thanked not only the President but the People of the U.S. for we have the spectacle of a President in a crisis losing the support of these people. Many Republicans bitterly attack Wilkie because he supports Roosevelt's foreign policy.

With all wishes and prayers for your safety and health,
Yours very sincerely,
Thérèse.

The complexion of the war – indeed, its outcome - altered completely when Hitler, throwing sanity to the wind, attacked his Russian ally on 22 June 1941 and, following Japan's devastating air raid on Pearl Harbor six months later, declared war on the United States. These two decisions mobilised the ultimately unbeatable forces of America and the Soviet Union on the side of Britain and her Commonwealth allies.

---

i Jan Valtin was the alias of Richard Julius Hermann Krebs, a German writer whose book supposedly described his life as a Soviet secret agent.

Had Hitler concentrated on driving the British out of the Mediterranean, it is difficult to see how he could have lost the war. Instead, on 8 December 1941 – the day after Pearl Harbor – the Red Army halted the Nazi advance a few miles outside Moscow and the pendulum of war started to swing against the Führer.

The breakdown in Soviet–German relations had reached crisis point in November 1940 after Stalin sent Molotov to Berlin to negotiate a new Nazi-Soviet pact. Stalin was concerned about the presence of German troops in Finland and Romania, while Hitler was alarmed at Soviet encroachment in the Balkans. He offered the Soviet Union a junior partnership in the German-Italian-Japanese Axis, which Stalin rejected. There were no further negotiations. On 18 December Hitler issued his directive for 'Operation Barbarossa', the invasion of Russia.[9]

Stalin refused to believe intelligence reports from his spies Anthony Blunt in London and Richard Sorge in Tokyo, as well as official warnings from Churchill and Roosevelt, that the Nazis were planning to attack him. The Soviet leader started drinking heavily and spent more time isolated in his dacha at Kuntsevo. Refusing a plea from General Georgi Zhukov, the new Chief of the General Staff, and Marshal Semyem Timoshenko, the Commissar for Defence, to put the army on alert, Stalin told them, 'You must understand that Germany will never attack Russia - Hitler knows that the Soviet Union isn't Poland or France.' The warnings, he added, were part of a dastardly Western plot to destabilise his relationship with Hitler.[10]

Six days before the Luftwaffe's first bombs fell on the great naval base of Sevastopol, Stalin wrote to Merkulov, head of the NKGB, the new foreign intelligence commissariat, 'You can tell your "source" from the German Air Headquarters that he can go and fuck his mother. This is not a "source", but a disinformant (sic).'[11]

Hitler impressed on his generals that in attacking the Soviet Union they were not fighting a war of attrition against a respected enemy but a war of extermination against a subhuman people. It was Nazi policy to reduce the size of the USSR's urban population in order to generate an agricultural surplus to feed Germany and to create *Lebensraum* (living space) for German émigrés. Not only were Russian prisoners of war to be starved to death in their thousands but civilians, especially Jews, were to be annihilated.[12]

The Germans attacked across a front stretching 1800 miles from the Baltic to the Black Sea with 148 divisions containing 3.8 million men, 4300 tanks, 4389 aircraft, 7200 artillery pieces, 600,000 motor vehicles and 750,000 horses.[13] As the panzers rolled eastward, Russian resistance collapsed and Stalin was devastated. 'Lenin left us a great inheritance and we fucked it up,' he moaned. Unable to face the looming disaster, he retired to his dacha after ordering the chain-smoking Molotov to make the first broadcast to the Russian people about the German attack: 'Citizens and Citizenesses of the Soviet Union! Today, at four o'clock in the morning, without addressing any grievances to the Soviet Union, without declaration of war, German forces fell on our country, attacked our frontiers in many places and bombed our cities... The Red Army and the whole nation will wage a victorious Patriotic War for our beloved country, for honour, for liberty... Our cause is just. The enemy will be beaten. Victory will be ours.'[14]

On the day of the invasion Alexander Kerensky appealed for the United States and Britain to offer military and financial assistance to Russia. A victory for the democracies, he predicted, would end in the collapse of the Nazi and Soviet regimes and lead to a free international order. The situation, he said, was similar to World War I, which had led to the fall of the Tsarist regime. 'The Russian people want to save their country from the German invader, but it is essential they are made to feel that they are fighting not only for the defence of their national frontiers but for a new, free life.[15]

Stalin had no intention of allowing any such thing. Dressed in military tunic and peaked cap, his trousers tucked into soft-leather Caucasian boots, he ordered twenty million people to be evacuated from the frontline areas and relaunched the Stavka, with Timoshenko as its nominal head. The Politburo took to wearing military tunics or soldier's shirts. On 29 June Stalin flew into a rage on hearing about the loss to Belarus following the encirclement of Minsk, the provincial capital, a loss that opened a direct route to Moscow. He retreated to his other dacha in the forest of Poklonnaia Gora and stayed there incommunicado until a deputation including Mikoyan, Molotov and Beria arrived at his front door and begged him to return to the Kremlin. Having feared that his comrades were planning a coup to topple him, Stalin was now in total control of the USSR.[16]

He wrote to Churchill: 'Let me express my gratitude for the two personal messages you have addressed to me. Your messages were the starting point of developments which subsequently resulted in agreement between our two Governments. Now, as you said with full justification, the Soviet Union and Great Britain have become fighting allies in the struggle against Hitlerite Germany. I have no doubt that, in spite of all the difficulties, our two States will be strong enough to crush our common enemy.'[17]

The sudden switch in loyalties created considerable disquiet among members of the Communist Parties of Britain and Australia, which had hitherto opposed the war and actively sabotaged the Western war effort. Churchill detested having to deal with the mass murderer on a personal level. He complained to George VI's private secretary, 'If my shirt were taken off now, it would be seen that my belly is sore from crawling to that man. I do it for the good of the country, and for no other reason.'[ii]

Stalin's son Vasily served as a pilot in the Russian Army. 'Vasily was a good sportsman, superb horseman and brave soldier,' says Artyom Sergeyev, who had lived with Stalin's family until the late 1920s when he rejoined his mother. 'When his half-brother Yakov was captured by the enemy, the military command restricted his flights for fear that Stalin would lose his second son. Vasily wanted to fight, he was brave and not prepared for this "privilege".'[18]

Over the next four years Artyom Sergeyev led a partisan group that fought behind German lines, escaped capture twice and was bayoneted in the liver. A dum-dum bullet all but severed his right hand, which he carried back from the front in a bucket of snow. The leading Soviet surgeon sewed it back on without anaesthetic.

While refusing to leave Moscow himself, Stalin evacuated two million of its citizens eastwards and sent entire factories, including the plant manufacturing the superb T-34 tank, as far as the Urals. Despite a shortage of rolling stock, the Bolshoi Theatre was relocated lock, stock and ballet to Kuibyshev, formerly Samara, 500 miles east

---

ii The pro-Soviet policy intruded into the cloistered world of publishing. Four publishers, including T. S. Eliot at Faber & Faber, rejected George Orwell's classic 1944 novel *Animal Farm*, which the author described as 'a satirical tale against Stalin'. Eliot told Orwell, 'We have no conviction that this is the right point of view from which to criticise the political situation at the present time.'

of Moscow. One train with a refrigeration unit and shock absorbers carried Lenin's mummified remains from its mausoleum in Red Square to a place of safety.[19]

Over the winter months the Battle of Moscow developed into the greatest conflict of World War II in terms of numbers. More than seven million officers and men from both sides took part in an Olympian struggle that saw the huge German war machine bogged down in the quagmires of the autumn *rasputitsa* mud and then frozen solid in temperatures as low as -50 Centigrade. Moscow was the Wehrmacht's first significant defeat of the war but victory was won at the cost of the lives of 926,000 Soviet soldiers.[20]

'Uncle Joe' was lauded in the Western press as an indomitable warrior who was vital to the success of the anti-Hitler alliance. Little personal details were leaked to the press, such as his love of Hollywood movies, especially Frank Capra's *It Happened One Night*, John Ford's *Stagecoach* and Charlie Chaplin's *The Great Dictator*. Roosevelt thought he had Stalin's measure. 'Stalin hates the guts of all your top people,' he wrote to Churchill in March 1942. 'He thinks he likes me better, and I hope he will continue to do so.'

Horror piled upon horror. 'After the Moscow battle of September 1941 to January 1942, I thought the worst was over,' says Artyom Sergeyev, who was a lieutenant colonel in the Russian Army by the age of twenty-three. 'But it was worse at Stalingrad and we lost most of our comrades.' The greatest symbol of Russian defiance was the performance of the Seventh Symphony of Oleg Kerensky's schoolmate Dmitri Shostakovich in Leningrad on 9 August 1942. The concert was broadcast over loudspeakers and reached the German lines. Hitler had designated that day for a lavish banquet at the Hotel Astoria to celebrate the fall of the city. Instead, the half-starved musicians of the Leningrad Radio Orchestra celebrated their city's superhuman feat of endurance.[iii]

Stalingrad was the turning point of the war. Hitler's armies were also starving and few of their soldiers had winter clothes; some had gone into battle wearing patent leather shoes. Field Marshal Friedrich von Paulus, unshaven, pale and sick, surrendered inside the skeleton of the city's Univermag department store. A million Axis troops were

---

iii The Battle of Stalingrad ended on 2 February 1943. The Siege of Leningrad was not lifted until 27 January 1944 after 872 days.

dead and many of the 250,000 who went into captivity were never seen again.[21]

Wartime currency restrictions made it impossible for Nell to access her funds in Australia, so they depended on Alexander's earnings as a guest lecturer to pay the bills. For a time they lived in Vista, a small town in Westchester County, New York, and then moved into a farmhouse at New Canaan in Fairfield County, Connecticut, forty-eight miles northeast of New York. Apart from Alexander's absences on the college lecture circuit, their summers together were idyllic. Nell drove them around in a Ford Deluxe sedan and the farmhouse had plenty of room for house guests. 'My husband adores croquet,' Nell said in an interview. 'And if you think croquet is a gentle, quiet little game then you have never seen Russians play it. You have no idea how dramatic it can be.'[22]

Winters, however, were a nightmare. Nell hated the cold, 'sitting alone thinking of the sorrows of the world & the coming catastrophe'. She yearned for the sunny Queensland skies and the warmth of its sandy beaches. When she complained, Alexander thought she was impugning his manhood; he became angry and shouted at her. She gently rebuked him: 'When you don't want me anymore, my Ala, I fear I won't be desirable any longer.'

Nell applied to the Australian Legation in Washington for permission to travel home with her husband but was turned down. Stalin's celebrity status had reached grotesque proportions in every part of the British Empire. On 21 April 1942 Colonel Longfield Lloyd, director of the Commonwealth Security Service, raised the issue with one of his Canberra colleagues. They agreed that Kerensky's presence in Australia 'might cause difficulties with the Soviet authorities'.

Stalin, the blood-soaked monster, now took precedence over humanitarian considerations and Kerensky was persona non grata in his wife's homeland. The irony was heart-breaking. In the spring of 1943 he read a short poem that Vladimir Nabokov had submitted to a pro-Soviet journal in protest against the glorification of Stalin in the American media:

> *No matter how the Soviet tinsel glitters*
> *upon the canvas of a battle piece;*
> *no matter how the soul dissolves in pity,*

*I will not bend, I will not cease
loathing the filth, brutality, and boredom
of silent servitude. No, no, I shout,
my spirit is still quick, still exile-hungry,
I'm still a poet, count me out!*

The poem's indefatigable spirit touched a chord inside Kerensky and he burst into tears.[23] Nell's health continued to deteriorate. Her kidneys ached and she had palpitations of the heart. Even another personal plea to the head of the Australian legation in May 1944 - 'I am ill. I must avoid the next winter here' – failed to illicit the necessary visa. Back in Brisbane Frederick Tritton knew his daughter would never abandon her husband. He approached Dr Bert Evatt, the Minister for External Affairs, and Senator Joseph Collings, the Minister for the Interior, but his pleas also fell on deaf ears.

Meanwhile, Gleb Kerensky had encountered a case of 'pro-Soviet mania' of his own after arriving in France following the Normandy landings. 'I was an officer in the British Army and very keen on it, even though my near-pacifist parents had forbidden me to play with swords and toy soldiers,' he says. As a captain and then a major in the REME Corps, his job was to inspect Royal Artillery guns to ensure they were in good working order.[24]

Crossing the Rhine, he found the roads clogged with thousands of refugees: displaced persons (DPs) of every nationality heading east and west, many of them ethnic Russians, Belarusians or Ukrainians. In the weeks that followed, he spoke to hundreds of people whose views ranged from 'the Soviet Government is bad and tyrannical' to 'Russia would be a wonderful land without the Communists'. 'A particular source of bitterness against Stalin,' he says, 'was the fact that he had not signed the Geneva Convention, so that Russian prisoners in German hands were treated worse than any others. The reason was clearly and correctly understood: "Stalin does not care a fig how the people suffer but wants his adversaries to ill-treat their prisoners so that those who have surrendered should learn a lesson and those who think of surrendering should think twice."'[25]

Hearing that Major Kerensky spoke Russian, a pro-Soviet British colonel asked him in the officers' mess about his contacts with Russian DPs. Gleb replied truthfully that they were half-expecting to be shot or packed off to concentration camps. 'That's what Stalin has threatened and that's what German propaganda says will happen,' he said. 'It's also what their own knowledge of Soviet life has led them to expect.'[26]

The colonel's face turned purple with rage at such disloyalty towards Comrade Stalin and he stormed out of the mess. The next day Gleb was summoned to a meeting at which the colonel threatened to have him arrested and his views reported to the War Office. 'I replied that I had made the same statement in a memorandum to my Corps HQ, so it was nothing that I might wish to hide from the War Office.'[27]

Gleb heard nothing further about the matter but the world soon learned about the deal that Stalin had cut with Roosevelt and Churchill at the Yalta Conference in February 1945. Under the terms of that agreement people who were Soviet citizens before the Nazi-Soviet pact of August 1939, irrespective of their circumstances during the war, were to be repatriated to the USSR. Britain sent back two and a quarter million soldiers and civilians and the Americans about two million. Stalin regarded people who had lived outside the USSR as a potential threat, so most of the officers were shot and other ranks ended up in the Gulag along with surviving civilians.[iv][28]

In the winter of 1944-45 Nell was so sick that she was admitted to Saint Luke's Hospital in New York to be treated for heart trouble. On her release she and Alexander moved back into the Simpsons' house at 109 East 91st Street. Again, Frederick Tritton appealed to the Government. He wrote that he was seventy-nine and was most eager to see his daughter before he died. 'The United States authorities have not been embarrassed in their relations with the Soviet Union with the fact that Mr Kerensky was admitted as a permanent resident in the United States,' he wrote. 'He would come to Australia purely in a private capacity.'

At this point Nell's cousin Corbett Tritton, Robert Menzies' former

---

[iv] Estonia, Latvia and Lithuania had been part of the USSR since 1940 and Yalta added Albania, Bulgaria, Czechoslovakia, the Germany Democratic Republic (East Germany), Hungary, Poland and Romania to the Soviet bloc. In Churchill's words, 'from Stettin in the Baltic to Trieste in the Adriatic, an iron curtain has descended across the Continent'. His remarks heralded the start of the Cold War. Stalin carried on the persecution of Jews where Hitler had left off with the launch of a massive antisemitic campaign in 1948.

private secretary, intervened and on 13 March 1945 Senator Collings relented. The Department of External Affairs cabled Washington: Permission granted count (sic) Alexander Kerensky accompany his Australian born wife on six months visit to Australia. Even so, Nell was now too ill to travel. Shortly after the War in Europe ended, she wrote to Nina Berberova on 25 June 1945:

> Ma Chere Nina,
> I think of you but it's difficult for me to write. I am ill mentally and spiritually. I live in a nightmare in which I am a victim and pray for some kind of armistice. I'd like to see you and talk again and explain all. Write me, please. I will be better but now I am too tired to continue.
> Je vous embrasse,
> Thérèse

The war against Japan continued until August 1945 when atom bombs reduced Hiroshima and Nagasaki to rubble and killed thousands of Japanese civilians. The Japanese military hierarchy accepted the Allied terms for an unconditional surrender. Echoing the words of his grandfather, Emperor Hirohito told his people, 'The unendurable must be endured.' The senior chemist on the Manhattan Project that produced the bombs was Eugene Rabinowitch, a friend of Kerensky's from the Berlin Poets' Circle which had provided verse for his newspaper.[v]

Nell and Alexander finally left the United States in the *City of Durham* in October, arriving in Melbourne on 8 November. A reporter from *The Argus* asked Kerensky whether he had any regrets.

> Well, he replied, someone had once said that he should have done away with his enemies while he ruled Russia. But that was not his way. He believed that a great pity and kindness was what bound humanity together and how, believing this, could he approve bloodshed and the ruthless liquidation of his enemies?

'The verdict of his enemies that he was weak when he should have been ruthless might be right,' the reporter concluded, 'but he is a

---

[v] After studying chemistry at the University of Berlin under Albert Einstein and Otto Hahn, Eugene Rabinowitch worked in Göttingen with James Franck, the German physicist and Nobel laureate, but lost his post after the Nazis seized power. He moved to Boston with his family in 1938.

serene man with a fine view of the value of human endeavour.' The *Argus* reporter discovered that Kerensky's wife, no longer known as 'the journalist Nell Tritton' but as Thérèse Kerensky, had not lost her fighting spirit, 'She is still a beautiful woman and has a great enthusiasm for her husband's views and his cause. To her, he is a man martyred in the cause of liberty. He had chosen a hard way of life when he could have chosen ease and moneymaking and cultured leisure.'[29]

Five days later the Kerenskys flew into Brisbane and moved into 'Elderslie', the Tritton family home in Adelaide Street, Clayfield. Australians had followed their adventures in the press and their arrival caused quite a stir in the neighbourhood. 'Mr and Mrs Tritton held a ball to welcome them home and my parents were invited,' says Elizabeth-Anne Peters, née Tomlinson. '"Elderslie" was a very stylish house set in a big block of land and that night it blazed with light and music. Everybody loved Nell and we were very sad to hear that she was ill.'[30]

Nell told an interviewer from the *Australian Women's Weekly*, 'My husband has never become reconciled to being an exile. He is always homesick.' Nevertheless, Kerensky tried to make a new life in Australia. He was philosophical when Vladimir Zenzinov told him in a letter that General Denikin was describing him as 'a traitor and a provocateur'. 'One must go his own way until the very end and not demand any understanding from other people,' he said. 'They betray you without even realising it.' He applied for the post of head of the Department of Russian Language and Literature which was being set up at the University of Melbourne. He was eminently qualified for the position but the university authorities considered him a controversial figure and the appointment went to Nina Christesen, daughter of Nell's former Russian teacher M. I. Maximoff.[31]

'I had great admiration for Mr Kerensky,' says Corbett Tritton. 'He was very lonely in Brisbane, although he did give a lecture to the Wider Education Society at Queensland University.' Kerensky told the students, 'The October Revolution was carried out with considerable bloodshed and introduced a regime which was not a true expression of the wishes of the whole of the Russian people. Lenin's justification for accepting German assistance was that he hoped to enlist the aid of the German proletariat in overthrowing the German capitalist regime as well. As well as Karl Marx, his political textbooks included Machiavelli.'

On 11 January 1946 he wrote to Nina Berberova about Nell's illness:

> I'm writing to you, my dear Nina Nikolaevna, on behalf of Thérèse because she isn't able to write herself. The doctors hoped that being under the sun with her parents in a comfortable environment could stop the deterioration and possibly help her recuperate but none of those things has happened. Since Christmas she hasn't been out in the garden and for the last few days she has been lying in bed with a swollen liver and excoriating pains.
>
> The doctors think - and I'm hoping - that this crisis will pass, like it has passed twice before but after each crisis Thérèse doesn't regain her strength. This is the horror of it all and the stalemate. You know, my friend, that I'm not a rational being and I believe in what doctors might think absurd and that is the revival of the Heart because it is the core of oneself.
>
> Write to her, Nina Nikolaevna, as quickly as possible; she loves you very much and she is worried about you not being in touch, but write cheerfully, as if you don't know what I have written to you. She wants you to send a list of things you need and I'll be happy to do all the shopping with one of her cousins. I don't have to tell you that we have been living here in complete privacy and an inner loneliness, especially myself, because I haven't had a chance to be part of their special family relationship.
>
> Teresa's parents think the world of her. Only now I realise why she 'escaped to Europe'; she was never a part of this family (she was a duckling in a family of chickens). Only now I fully understand her life and her personality and this understanding is bitter.

Three weeks later Nell suffered a stroke. Her speech was badly impaired and she became confused. The end was near. Alexander slept on the veranda next to her bedroom to be as close as possible. Nell's nephew Norman Tritton, a pilot in the Royal Australian Air Force, met Kerensky several times at the house. 'Kerensky was a quiet fellow – never said much. He used to walk the garden endlessly, with his hands behind his back, from the front garden, under the house through to the back garden, over and over again. Grandmother said he was meditating.'

Oscillating between hope and despair, Kerensky spent much of his time in his 'hideaway corner' on the veranda writing letters to his family and friends. 'We are living on the outskirts of Brisbane in a Victorian-style house which belongs to Thérèse's parents,' he wrote in one letter.

> In the front, there is a meadow with exotic flowers and trees, and Thérèse planted some sweetcorn and fennel. At the back of the house there are outbuildings, an allotment and a tennis court surrounded by latticework. I walk miles around it like a caged animal. From the veranda there is an amazing view of Moreton Bay and, at night, I can see a magnificent moon. Sometimes there are tropical storms with strong winds and sometimes there is an agonising sultry stillness but more often I can feel a light breeze of sweet, transparent air and hear choirs of mysterious (to me) birds, apart from the Egyptian pigeon. The whole mood of Nature in these parts takes me back to my childhood in Tashkent. So that is the frame our life has been put in and it doesn't fit the framework.

Nell was suffering from chronic nephritis, which occurs when the kidneys suddenly become inflamed and cause high blood pressure and kidney dysfunction. She was constantly feverish and suffered hallucinations. On 10 April she died, aged just forty-six. As her body was placed in a coffin, Kerensky thought she smiled at him. He took this as 'a sign from beyond' and felt unworthy of it. Nell was cremated with Anglican rites and her ashes were buried next to her siblings Lilian and Charles at South Brisbane Cemetery.

Having sacrificed her health for Alexander, her final act of devotion was to name him as the main beneficiary of her estate valued at £11,000 ($800,000 today). In 1917, just as she was beginning her journey as a vibrant young woman in the shadow of illness, Nell ended one of her poems with this thought: *'I wonder does all beauty fade and die?'* Even in her last days, she remained a beautiful woman.

After five hideous years of war, hundreds of thousands of displaced troops were heading for home across the Pacific. Kerensky was unable to make a booking on any ship bound for the United States and was obliged to spend many months in Brisbane with his Australian relatives. Nell's death had shattered his peace of mind. One of her cousins invited him to the family holiday home at Surfers Paradise on the Pacific coast. At a party in his honour he startled his hosts by telling them that one of Stalin's assassins was stalking him and he expected to share Trotsky's fate. He had no doubt about that. When a stranger disturbed him one night, he became so convinced that his life was being threatened that he fled back to 'Elderslie'.

Kerensky returned to America a grieving, unhappy, inconsolable man. The past weighed heavily on him. Flora Solomon's sister, Countess Fira Ilinska, who worked as a fashion consultant with Bonwit Teller, remained close to him. She and her husband, Count Janusz Ilinska, the chairman of the Carlyle Hotel, always welcomed him to their home at 2 Sutton Place. He also became close to Vladimir Nabokov, who worked as a lecturer while developing his literary career. His younger brother Sergei had died in a German concentration camp after denouncing the Nazi regime. Their friend Ilya Fondaminsky fared no better. The Nazis invaded his home, destroyed Nabokov's butterfly collection, scattered his papers in the street and arrested him for being Jewish, even though he was a member of the Russian Orthodox Church. Ilya Fondaminsky died at Auschwitz in 1942.[vi]

Every Sunday Kerensky and Nabokov sat around Eugene Rabinowitch's dinner table at West Brattleboro, Vermont, to engage in debates with other Russian émigrés about their homeland. 'Daily life, their careers, their families - everything had been turned upside down by the October Revolution for these prominent people,' says Eugene's son, the historian Professor Alexander Rabinowitch.

> So it was no wonder that I constantly heard from this circle only the worst things about that great event in world history. They were all agreed that the October Revolution had been a cold-blooded coup on the part of a handful of Lenin's ruthless fanatics - a coup which had absolutely no support from among the people and therefore they had to resort to terror in order to establish its rule. Despite their endless stormy disputes, this was the unifying bond of common belief among the Russian émigrés.[32]

---

vi According to theologian Georgi Fedotov, 'In his last days he wished to live with the Christians and die with the Jews.' In 2003 he was canonised as Saint Ilya Fondaminsky, a Russian Orthodox martyr (an honour he shared with Saint Nicholas II).

Kerensky was instrumental in the first attempt in the United States to unite all anti-Communist Russian émigrés in one organisation. A mass meeting in Manhattan on 13 March 1949 established the Union for the Liberation of the Peoples of Russia, with the aim of overthrowing the Soviet regime. It was an unfortunate name. Ukrainians, Cossacks, Georgians, Crimeans and other national groups objected that 'the Peoples of Russia' inferred that even after liberation from the Third Reich their countries would remain under Russian rule. The old quarrels remained unresolved. Nevertheless, Kerensky told the meeting, 'The Russian people cannot live in slavery any longer. There is a star now in the East that is rising and that star is the desire of the Russians to become a free people.'[33]

Epilogue

The Tiger of History

No country suffered more than Russia in the Twentieth Century. Over a period of forty years from 1905 to1945 the Russians of Alexander Kerensky's generation endured two world wars, three revolutions and a civil war in which a total of perhaps sixty million people died. Millions more died of starvation in the famines of the 1920s and 1930s and in the Stalinist purges of the armed forces, the Communist Party and the *kulaks*.

Lonely and paranoid, Stalin was in his seventy-fifth year when he was felled by a stroke in his dacha around 4 a.m. on Sunday 1 March 1953. He died a slow, agonising death. His successor, Nikita Khrushchev, denounced the Stalinist Terror at a secret session of the Twentieth Congress of the Communist Party of the Soviet Union on 25 February 1956. This was the start of a period of de-Stalinisation known after Ilya Ehrenburg's 1954 novel as 'The Thaw'. But post-Stalinist Russia still had a long way to go before the Communists would loosen the gags on political and religious freedom.

In the summer of 1955 Alexander Kerensky made a two-week trip to Stanford University to sift through the collection of Russian documents at the Hoover Institution of War, Revolution and Peace. He was elated to find an entire archive of relevant material and he spent the next two months reading through it. This sojourn started an eleven-year association with Stanford and with the American historian Robert P. Browder, who was a visiting assistant professor there. Together, they compiled, translated, annotated and published thousands of documents in three volumes entitled *The Russian Provisional Government 1917*.

According to Bernard Butcher, a Stanford *alumnus*, Kerensky became a fixture on campus, giving guest lectures in Russian studies, joining panel discussions and teaching seminars. He remained unfailingly courteous, rising to greet visitors, introducing himself simply as 'Kerensky', giving a little bow and kissing women's hands.

His visits to Britain still made news: 'Alexander Kerensky is in Britain for two months,' *The Observer*'s diarist noted in June 1963. 'Still incredibly active at 82 - he walks two hours every day, talking as he goes – Kerensky has come here to try to finish a book in the vacation quiet of Saint Anthony's College, Oxford. But first a few days in London and Liverpool to see his family, to dine with old friends Manya Harari and Max Hayward, the translators of *Dr Zhivago*, and to stay with Sir Frank and Lady Soskice.'[i][1]

Two years later he heard from a friend that 'Lilya', now known as Hélène Birukoff, had died in Paris, aged seventy-five. Today, she rests in the same grave as her mother Lydia and her sisters Olga and Vera at the New Cemetery at Billancourt.

Since 1954 Olga Kerenskaya had been living with Gleb, his wife Mary, née Hudson, and their three children, Katherine, Stephen and Elizabeth. 'Grandma suffered from PTSD and she took her anguish out on her sons,' says Stephen Kerensky. 'She slept with a photograph of her mother under her pillow and with the bedroom door open and a landing light on. During holidays from boarding school I would spend hours with her while she told me stories about her past life. I became very fond of her and understood her a little better.' One of her proudest moments was a trip to Buckingham Palace to see her elder son, Dr Oleg Kerensky, invested with the CBE for his work in bridge-building.

Oleg Kerensky Jr, who had joined the BBC after leaving Westminster,[ii] drew close to his grandfather during those postwar visits to London and, later, his own visits to New York:

> I came to know the strength of his personality and the devotion (and irritation) this could arouse. I was inclined to find his grand manner

---

i Frank Soskice served as Solicitor-General in Atlee's postwar administration and as Home Secretary in Harold Wilson's 1964 government. Two years later he was elevated to the peerage as Baron Stow Hill of Newport, his Welsh electorate.

ii Oleg Kerensky Jr resigned as deputy editor of The Listener in 1967. He moved to New York, where he worked as a freelance journalist specialising in the arts, particularly ballet. Warren Beatty hired him to play Kerensky in Reds, his 1981 biopic of John Reed, but most of his performance ended up on the cutting room floor.

faintly ridiculous. True, he had been a crucial and memorable figure in Russian history but was it not absurd for him to spend the rest of his life trading on that? Later, I realised it was his burning faith in the Russian people and in himself as their spokesman that kept him going. There was nobody else with the name and the skill to do what he did. His grand manner was to ensure he was taken seriously. We came to understand one another.[2]

Alexander Kerensky spent his last years living alone on the top floor of Mrs Simpson's town house on East 91st Street. From time to time he would recall 'the beauty of the Volga, the chimes of the evening bells, the bishop sitting solemnly in a carriage drawn by four horses, the convicts with heavy chains, the pretty little girls with whom I went to dancing lessons, the ragged, barefoot village boys with whom I played in the summer…'[3]

He had long since become accustomed to the barbed comments of other émigrés. One of Nabokov's friends was Dmitri Vladimirovich Lekhovich, who had fought with Wrangel's army in the Crimea. He had arrived in New York in 1925 and two years later he had been in the Century Theatre when Kerensky was assaulted. Now a successful banker, Lekhovich recalled meeting Kerensky at a party in the Nabokovs' New York apartment:

> We were sitting around – it was quite late; I arrived only after most of the other guests had already left – when suddenly the doorbell rang. Heavy footsteps on the stairs. Nabokov said, 'That must be Alexander Fyodorovich.' The door opened and Kerensky said, as he looked around the room, 'Ah, I see whenever I arrive somewhere all decent people leave!' It was said in such an amusing, self-deprecating way that I decided to stay and see what Kerensky was like at close quarters. Nabokov wanted to draw me into the conversation, and mentioned to Kerensky that I had been to the Lycée [of Tsarskoe Selo, an upper-class college].
>
> 'Ah,' said Kerensky, 'did you leave Russia right after the February Revolution?' (I suppose he thought I was a confirmed monarchist). I replied, 'No, I stayed until 1920 and lived through the mess you created!' I immediately felt very ashamed of myself for this remark; he was, after all, a man considerably older than me, and I was a guest in someone else's house.
>
> When we were leaving, Kerensky offered me a lift home – at that

time he was living in the house of a very rich American woman [and he] very kindly took me home in the chauffeur-driven car that his hostess had put at his disposal.[4]

On 24 April 1970, according to Fira Ilinska, Kerensky entered hospital in New York to recover from a broken elbow and pelvis sustained in a fall. He died of heart disease there on 11 June aged eighty-nine. To the very end, he refused to renounce his Russian citizenship and clung to his tattered little Nansen passport.

Three days later 350 people attended his funeral service at Frank E. Campbell's Funeral Parlour in Madison Avenue. 'The strong features of the former Premier, stony in death, could be seen in the half-opened coffin,' the *New York Times* reporter wrote. 'A white-haired woman in a red raincoat went to the coffin alone before the service and gazed on it for a long moment and, afterwards, several mourners bent low over it as if to bestow a final kiss.'

The *New York Times* editorialised that the tragedy of Alexander Kerensky was that of 'a decent and democratic leader – a man with scruples – called upon to ride the tiger of history in a time of his nation's deepest torment'.

> In the tempestuous autumn of 1917 he could have deprived Lenin of his devastatingly successful peace slogan by surrendering to Germany as the Bolsheviks did a few months later. He could have won the support of the peasant majority by allowing the illegal seizure of the farmlands. With the backing of the troops and the peasants he would have been virtually unassailable. Instead, he attempted to set up a constitutional democracy based on the rule of law. That he failed – and that his failure proved irreversible - is the tragedy of Russia even today.
>
> But in the brief period that he and the Provisional Government ruled Russia, there was a glimpse of forces at work seeking to turn the vast land into a democracy, and to create a new society whose citizens would enjoy both freedom and prosperity. The effort failed and Kerensky is now dead. But the impulses he represented continue to exist. They will not forever be denied by those who even today still walk in Lenin's footsteps.[5]

The priest of the Russian Orthodox Church in New York refused to bury Kerensky's body in the Russian cemetery for fear that outraged monarchists would desecrate his grave. Oleg felt that if his father could not be buried among fellow Russians he should not be buried in New York at all. Consequently, the body was flown to London and on 17 June he was buried by Olga, Oleg and Gleb at Putney Vale Cemetery on Wimbledon Common. During the burial service Olga wept disconsolately. She was unstinting in her praise of the man who had caused her so much pain:

> There was never anything tawdry or Bonapartist about him. From the first to the last he was a political defender, saved hundreds of lives and we barely existed because more often than not he did it gratis. His second dedication was fighting for freedom for Russia, for which he himself became politically persecuted.
>
> There were no Bonapartist expectations of glory for his work. It was self-sacrifice and danger. His every step was watched, our only servant was a spy. The Empress demanded, 'Hang Kerensky'. He knew all that, and a few months before the Revolution he told me that he might be exiled or executed.
>
> Nevertheless, he never stopped his activities; his speeches in the Duma were always a great event and certainly not cheap oratory. They were passionate and sincere and there was never a thought for his personal danger.[6]

Alexander Kerensky never surrendered to what Solzhenitsyn called the 'Soviet Dragon', nor did he ever lose his desire to see the Russian people slay it. 'I may not live to see Russia realise her destiny as a free, humane country with its people dedicated to the betterment of mankind,' he wrote to his sons in his last months. 'But you may see it, and certainly your children will. Russia can never be destroyed – from within or without – and all those who attempt to do so will be doomed to failure. It is with this faith in the Russia that I know and love that I am able to depart in peace.'[7]

Olga Kerenskaya died in her sleep in 1975 and was buried beside her ex-husband. Neither of their sons lived to see the dissolution of the Soviet Union on 31 December 1991: Oleg died in 1984 and Gleb in 1990.[iii] 'My father never spoke about the Revolution, not even to my mother,' says Stephen Kerensky. 'He did not want to burden us with the horror and what he found to be the impossible task of overturning

---

iii The ten Communist regimes in Eastern Europe and Mongolia collapsed between 1989 and 1991. Those in China, Vietnam, Laos, North Korea and Cuba survived.

the ingrained prejudice of British politicians, historians and the media against the views of revolutionary but non-Bolshevik Russians.'[8]

Gleb Kerensky did, however, put his experiences down in *Only One Freedom*, which he finished in 1950 and which remains unpublished. The book begins, 'I have very good and painful reasons for knowing by heart every pro-Communist aberration, illusion and argument that has been current in Britain during the last thirty years. For about fifteen years, from 1930 to 1945, it was next to impossible for any knowledgeable anti-Communist even to state his case.'[9]

Kerensky's daughter Irina lived to see it all. Twice married, she died in France on 8 March 2015 at the age of ninety-seven. Having refused to recognise her father during his lifetime, she later became reconciled to the facts surrounding her birth and accepted that she was his daughter.

Today, fifty years after the death of Alexander Kerensky, his enemies Lenin, Trotsky and Stalin are huge historical celebrities while he is all but forgotten. In *The Crucifixion of Liberty*, he declared, 'Let no one say that Lenin is an expression of some kind of Asiatic elemental Russian force. I was born under the same sky, I breathed the same air, I heard the same peasant songs and played in the same college playground. I saw the same limitless horizons from the same high bank of the Volga, and I know, in my blood and my bones, that it is only by losing all touch with our native land, only by stamping out all native feeling for it, only so could one do what Lenin did in deliberately and cruelly mutilating Russia.'

The Soviet Dragon has indeed been slain but, even in this post-Communist age, Russia's quest for freedom is far from over.

Bibliography

Abraham, Richard, Alexander Kerensky: The First Love of the Revolution, Sidgwick and Jackson, London, 1987

Acton, Edward, Vladimir Iu. Cherniaev and William G. Rosenberg (editors), Critical Companion to the Russian Revolution 1914-1921, Arnold, London, 1997

Adamthwaite, Anthony P., The Making of the Second World War, Routledge, London, 1992

Alanbrooke, Field Marshal Viscount, War Diaries 1939–1945, Alex Danchev and Daniel Todman (editors), Weidenfeld and Nicolson, London, 2001

Allfrey, Anthony, Edward VII and his Jewish Court, Weidenfeld and Nicolson, London, 1991

Andrew, Christopher, Her Majesty's Secret Service, Viking, New York, 1986

— The Defence of the Realm: The Authorised History of MI5, Penguin Books, London, 2009

— The Secret World: A History of Intelligence, Allen Lane, London 2018

Applebaum, Anne, Red Famine: Stalin's War on Ukraine, Penguin, London, 2018

— Gulag: A History of the Soviet Camps, Allen Lane, London, 2003

Asprey, Robert B., The German High Command at War, William Morrow, New York, 1991

Asquith, Margot, An Autobiography, Vol. IV, George H. Doran, New York, 1922

Bailey, Lieutenant-Colonel F. N., Mission to Tashkent, Folio Society, London, 1999

Barber, Noel, The Week France Fell, Stein and Day, New York, 1976

Bashkirtseff, Marie, The Journal of Marie Bashkirtseff, Virago, London, 1985

Baxter, John, Paris at the End of the World: The City of Light during the Great War, Harper Perennial, London, 2014

Beasley, W. G., The Rise of Modern Japan, Weidenfeld and Nicolson, London, 1990

Beckendorff, Count Paul, The Last Days at Tsarskoe Selo, www.alexanderpalace.org

Beer, Daniel, The House of the Dead: Siberian Exile under the Tsars, Penguin, London, 2017

Bennett, Gill, The Zinoviev Letter: The Conspiracy that never dies, Oxford University Press, 2018

Berberova, Nina, The Italics are Mine, Vintage, London, 1993

Bix, Herbert P., Hirohito and the Making of Modern Japan, HarperCollins, New York, 2000

Blake, Robert and William Roger Louis (editors), Churchill, Oxford University Press, 1993

Blatt, Joel (editor), The French Defeat of 1940: Reassessments, Berghahn Books, New York, 1998

Bohlen, Charles E., Witness to History 1929-1969, Weidenfeld and Nicolson, London, 1973

Bond, Brian and Taylor, Michael (editors), The Battle for France and Flanders: Sixty Years On, Leo Cooper, London, 2001

Boterbloem, Kees, A History of Russia and its Empire: From Mikhail Romanov to Vladimir Putin, Rowman and Littlefield, Lanham, Maryland, 1918

Bouverie, Tim, Appeasing Hitler: Chamberlain, Churchill and the Road to War, The Bodley Head, London, 2019

Bowker, Gordon, George Orwell, Little, Brown, London, 2003

Boyd, Brian, Nabokov: The Russian Years, Princeton University Press, 1990

— Nabokov: The American Years, Princeton University Press, 1991

Bradford, Sarah, George VI, Fontana, London, 1991

Brendon, Piers, The Dark Valley: A Panorama of the 1930s, Pimlico, London, 2001

Brenton, Tony (editor), Historically Inevitable? Turning Points of the Russian Revolution, Profile, London, 2016

Brovkin, Vladimir N., The Bolsheviks in Russian Society: The Revolution and the Civil Wars, Yale University Press, New Haven, 1997

Brown, Roland Elliott, Godless Utopia: Soviet Anti-religious Propaganda, Fuel, London, 2019

Browder, Robert Paul, and Alexander F. Kerensky, The Russian Provisional Government 1917, three volumes, Stanford University Press, Stanford, 1961

Bryant, Louise, My Six Months in Russia, George H. Doran, New York, 1918

Buchanan, Sir George, My Mission to Russia, two volumes, Cassell, London, 1923

Buckler, Julie A., Mapping Saint Petersburg, Princeton University Press, 2007

Bullock, Alan, Hitler and Stalin: Parallel Lives, B. C. A., London, 1992

Burleigh, Michael, Moral Combat: A History of World War II, Harper Press, London, 2010

Buruma, Ian, Inventing Japan: From Empire to Economic Miracle, Weidenfeld and Nicolson, London, 2003

— The Wages of Guilt: Memories of War in Germany and Japan, Meridian, London, 1994

Cabanes, Bruno, August 1914: France, the Great War and a month that changed the world forever, Yale University Press, 2016

Calvocoressi, Peter, Guy Wint and John Pritchard, Total War: The Causes and Courses of the Second World War, Penguin, London, 1972

Carey, Joyce, Memoirs of the Bobotes, Michael Joseph, London, 1965

Carlton, David, Churchill and the Soviet Union, Manchester University Press, Manchester, 2000

Carr, E. H., The Russian Revolution from Lenin to Stalin 1917-1929, Macmillan, London, 1980

Carter, Miranda, George, Nicholas and Wilhelm: Three Royal Cousins and the Road to World War I, Knopf, New York, 2010

Caute, David, The Fellow-Travellers, Weidenfeld and Nicolson, London, 1973

Challinger, Michael, Angels in Arkhangel: The Untold Story of Australia and the Invasion of Russia 1918-1919, Hardie Grant Books, Melbourne, 2010

Chamberlain, Lesley, Lenin's Private War: The Voyage of the Philosophy Steamer and the Exile of the Intelligentsia, St Martin's Press, New York, 2006

Chamberlin, William Henry, The Russian Revolution: 1917-1918, two volumes, Universal Library, New York, 1965

Chambers, Roland, The Last Englishman: The Double Life of Arthur Ransome, David R. Godine, Jaffrey, New Hampshire, 2009

Charques, Richard, The Twilight of Imperial Russia, Oxford University Press, 1980

Churchill, Winston S., The World Crisis 1911-1918, three volumes, Odhams Press, London

— The Second World, Penguin, London, 1990

— Their Finest Hour: The Second World War, Vol. II, Penguin, London, 2005

— Great Contemporaries, 1937, Rosetta Books. Kindle Edition

— Secret Session Speeches, Simon and Schuster, New York, 1946

Clark, Christopher, The Sleepwalkers: How Europe Went to War in 1914, Penguin Books, London, 2012

— Kaiser Wilhelm II: A Life of Power, Penguin, London, 2009

— Iron Kingdom: The Rise and Downfall of Prussia 1600-1947, Penguin, London, 2007

Clarkson, Jesse D., A History of Russia, Longmans, London, 1962

Communist International, Second Congress minutes, Vol. I., New Park, London, 1977

Costello, John, Ten Days that Saved the West, Transworld, London, 1991

Corrigan, Gordon, Mud, Blood and Poppycock, Castle, London, 2003

Cox, Geoffrey, Countdown to War: A personal memoir of Europe 1938-1940, William Kimber, London, 1988

Crampton, R. J., Eastern Europe in the Twentieth Century and After, Routledge, London, 2004

Crankshaw, Edward, The Fall of the House of Habsburg, Longmans, Green, London, 1963

— The Shadow of the Winter Palace: The Drift to Revolution 1825-1817, Purnell, Abingdon, 1976

Crim, Brian E., Antisemitism in the German Military Community and the Jewish Response 1914-1938, Lexington Books, Plymouth, 2014

Cronin, Vincent, Paris: City of Light 1919-1939, HarperCollins, London, 1994

Curzon, George, Russia in Central Asia and the Anglo-Russian Question, Longmans, London, 1889

Dallas, Gregor, 1918 War and Peace, John Murray, London, 2000

— Poisoned Peace: 1945: The war that never ended, John Murray, 2005

Davies, Norman, Vanished Kingdoms: The History of Half-Forgotten Europe, Penguin, 2012

Davis, Kenneth, FDR: Into the Storm, Random House, New York, 1993

Davison, Peter (editor), The Complete Works of George Orwell, Secker and Warburg, London, 1998

Dear, I. C. B, and Foot, M. R. D. (editors), Oxford Companion to World War II, Oxford University Press, 2005

de Courcy, Anne, Margot at War: Love and Betrayal in Downing Street 1912-1916, Weidenfeld and Nicolson, London, 2014

de Vries, Suzanna, Trailblazers: Caroline Chisholm to Quentin Bryce, Pirgos Press, Brisbane, 2015

de Jonge, Alex, Stalin and the Shaping of the Soviet Union, Fontana, London, 1987

Deutscher, I, The Prophet Armed: Trotsky 1879-1921, Oxford University Press, 1954

Dickson, Lovat, H. G. Wells: His Turbulent Life and Times, Macmillan, London 1971

Donaldson, Frances, Edward VIII, Book Club, London, 1974

Dorril, Stephen, MI6: Inside the Covert World, The Free Press, New York, 2000

Dowling, Timothy, The Brusilov Offensive, Indiana University Press, 2008

Dull, Paul S., A Battle History of the Imperial Japanese Navy (1941–1945), Naval Institute Press, Annapolis, Maryland, 1989

Durland, Kellogg, The Red Reign in Russia, The Century Company, New York, 1907

Eastman, Max, Reflections on the Failure of Socialism, Devin-Adair, New York, 1955

Egremont, Max, Balfour: A Life of Arthur James Balfour, Phoenix Giant, London, 1998

Emmons, Terence, and Bertrand M. Patenaude (editors), War, Revolution and Peace in Russia: The Passages of Frank Golder 1914-1927, Hoover Institution Press, Stanford, 1998

Engelstein, Laura, Russia in Flames: War, Revolution, Civil War 1914-1921, Oxford University Press, 2018

Ensor, R. C. K., England 1870-1914, Clarendon Press, London, 1952

Evans, Richard J., The Coming of the Third Reich, Penguin, London, 2003

Fairbank, John King, The Great Chinese Revolution 1800-1985, Harper and Row, New York, 1986

Farmborough, Florence, Nurse at the Russian Front: A Diary 1914-1918, Constable, London, 1974

Feiling, Keith, A History of England, Macmillan, London, 1950

Fenby, Jonathan, The Penguin History of Modern China, Penguin, London, 2009

Ferguson, Niall, The Pity of War: Explaining World War I, Basic Books, 1999

Fernandez-Armesto, Felippo, The Times Guide to the People's of Europe, Times Books, London, 1994

Field, Andrew, VN: The Life and Art of Vladimir Nabokov, Futura, London, 1988

Figes, Orlando, A People's Tragedy: The Russian Revolution 1891-1924, Jonathan Cape, London, 1996

— Revolutionary Russia 1891-1991, Pelican, London, 2017

Fitzpatrick, Sheila, On Stalin's Team: The Years of Living Dangerously in Soviet Politics, Princeton University Press, 2015

Flanner, Janet, Janet Flanner's World, Secker and Warburg, London, 1980

Frame, Tom, Pacific Partners: A History of Australian–American Naval Relations, Hodder and Stoughton, Sydney, 1992

Frankel, Jonathan (editor), Vladimir Akimov on the Dilemmas of Russian Marxism 1895-1903, Cambridge University Press, 1969

Frankopan, Peter, The Silk Roads: A New History of the World, Bloomsbury, London, 2015

— The New Silk Roads: The Present and Future of the World, Bloomsbury, London, 2018

Fraser, Rebecca, A People's History of Britain, Chatto and Windus, London, 2003

Freeze, Gregory L., Russia: A History, Oxford University Press, 2009

Gapon, Georgi, The Story of My Life, E. P. Dutton, New York, 1906

Garnett, David, The Golden Echo, Chatto and Windus, London, 1953

Garnett, Olive, Petersburg Tales, Houghton Mifflin, New York, 1900

Garnett, Richard, Constance Garnett: A Heroic Life, Sinclair-Stevenson, London, 1991

Gerhardie, William, God's Fifth Column: Biography of the Age 1890-1940, Hogarth Press, London, 1981

Giffard, Sydney, Japan Among the Powers 1890–1990, Yale University Press, New Haven, 1994

Gilbert, Martin, Second World War, Phoenix, London, 1995

Gilliard, Pierre, Thirteen Years at the Russian Court, www.alexanderpalace.org

Glass, Charles, Americans in Paris: Life and Death under Nazi Occupation 1940-1944, Harper, 2009

Glenny, Michael, and Stone, Norman, The Other Russia: The Experience of Exile, Faber and Faber, London, 1990

Golder, Frank, Documents of Russian History 1914-1917, Andesite Press, New York, 2015

Gorodetsky, Gabriel, The Maisky Diaries: Red Ambassador to the Court of St James's 1932-1943, Yale University Press, New Haven, 2015

Gregory, J. D. On the Edge of Diplomacy: Rambles and Reflections 1902-1928, Hutchinson, London

Gregory, James S., Land of the Soviets, Pelican, London, 1946

Grossman, Vasily, Stalingrad: A Novel (translated by Robert and Elizabeth Chandler; edited by Robert Chandler and Yury Bit-Yunan), Vintage, London, 2019

Hackett, R. F., Yamagata Aritomo in the Rise of Modern Japan 1838-1922, Harvard University Press, Cambridge, Massachusetts, 1971

Hammond, J. L., C. P. Scott of the Manchester Guardian, G. Bell, London, 1934

Hart-Davis, Hugh Walpole: A Portrait of a Man, an Epoch and a Society, Rupert Hart-David, London, 1952

Harvey, Robert, Comrades: The Rise and Fall of World Communism, John Murray, London, 2003

Hawes, James, The Shortest History of Germany, Old Street Publishing, Devon, 2018

Hasegawa, Tsuyoshi, The February Revolution, Petrograd 1917, Brill, New York, 2017

Hankey, Maurice, Politics, Trials and Errors, Pen-in-Hand Publishing, Oxford, 1950

Harding, Neil, Lenin's Political Thought: Theory and Practice in the Democratic and Socialist Revolutions, two volumes, Macmillan, London, 1986

Hastings, Selina, The Secret Lives of Somerset Maugham, John Murray, London, 2009

Hayward, Max, Writers in Russia 1917-1978, Harvill Press, London, 1983

Heffer, Simon, Staring at God: Britain in the Great War, Penguin, London, 2019

Hehn, Paul N., A Low Dishonest Decade 1930-1941, Continuum, New York, 2005

Herwig, Holger H., The First World War: Germany and Austro-Hungary 1914-1914, Bloomsbury Academic, London, 2009

Hickman, Tom, Churchill's Bodyguard: The authorised biography of Walter H. Thompson, Headline, London, 2005

Hoffmann, Major General Max, War Diaries and Other Papers, two volumes, translated by Eric Sutton, Lucknow Books

Hogg, Ivan V., The Guns of World War II, Macdonald and Jane, London

Hogsbawn, Eric, The Age of Empire 1875-1914, Phoenix, London, 1987

Holland, Tom, Dominion: The Making of the Western Mind, Little, Brown, London, 2019

Holmes, Richard (editor), The Oxford Companion to Military History, Oxford University Press, 2001

Hopkirk, Kathleen, Central Asia through Writers' Eyes, Eland, London, 2013

Hopkirk, Peter, The Great Game: On Secret Service in High Asia, John Murray, London, 2006

— Setting the East Ablaze, John Murray, London, 1984

Horne, Alistair, The Price of Glory: Verdun 1916, Penguin, London, 1991

— The Tragedy of War in the Twentieth Century, Weidenfeld and Nicolson, London 2015

— To Lose a Battle: France 1940, Macmillan, London, 2012

Horsbrugh-Porter, Anna (editor), Memories of Revolution: Russian Women Remember, Routledge, London 1993

Hull, Cordell and Andrew Henry Thomas Berding, The Memoirs of Cordell Hull, Vol. I, Macmillan, New York, 1948; Vol. II, Hodder and Stoughton, London, 1948

Ignatieff, Michael, The Russian Album: A Family Sage of Civil War, Revolution and Exile, Penguin, London 1988

Jenkins, Simon, A Short History of Europe, Penguin, London, 2018

Jensen, Marc, A Show Trial Under Lenin: The Trial of the Socialist Revolutionaries, Moscow 1922, Martinus Nijhoff, The Hague, 1982

Judd, Alan, The Kaiser's Last Kiss, HarperCollins, London, 2003

Kagan, Frederick W. and Robin Higham (editors), The Military History of Tsarist Russia, Palgrave Macmillan, Basingstoke, 2002

Kaminski, Valery V. and Valentin A. Veremenko, The Noble Family Baranovsky at the Turn of the Epoch, Central and Eastern European Online Library

Karlinsky, Simon, Marina Tsvetaeva: The Woman, Her World and Her Poetry, Cambridge University Press, 1987

Katkov, George, The Kornilov Affair: Kerensky and the Break-up of the Russian Army, Longman, London, 1980

Keneally, Thomas, The People's Train, Hodder and Stoughton, London, 2010

Kennedy, K. H., Mining Tsar: The Life and Times of Leslie Urquhart, Allen and Unwin, Sydney, 1986

Kennedy, Paul, The Rise and Fall of the Great Powers, Random House, New York, 1987

Kerensky, Alexander, The Prelude to Bolshevism: The Kornilov Rebellion, T. Fisher Unwin, London, 1919

— The Catastrophe, Kerensky's Own Story of the Russian Revolution, D. Appleton, New York, 1927

— The Crucifixion of Liberty, (translated by Gleb Kerensky), Arthur Barker, London, 1934

— The Kerensky Memoirs: Russia and History's Turning Point, Cassell, London, 1966

Kershaw, Ian, To Hell and Back: Europe 1914-1949, Penguin Books, 2016

— Roller-Coaster: Europe 1950-2017, Allen Lane, London, 2019

Knox, Major-General Sir Alfred, With the Russian Army 1914-1917, two volumes, Hutchinson, London, 1921

Kotkin, Stephen, Stalin: Paradoxes of Power 1878-1928, Penguin, London, 2015

— Stalin: Waiting for Hitler 1928-1941, Allen Lane, London, 2017

Kropotkin, Peter, Memoirs of a Revolutionist, Houghton Mifflin, Boston and New York, 1899

— In Russian and French Prisons, Ward and Downey, London, 1887

Lazareff, Pierre, Deadline: The behind-the-scenes story of the last decade in France, Random House, New York, 1942

Lee, Bradford A., Britain and the Sino-Japanese 1937-1939, Stanford University Press, 1973

Le Gates, Marlene, In their Time: A History of Feminism in Western Society, Routledge, London, 2001

Lenin, V. I., On the Foreign Policy of the Soviet State, Progress Publishers, Moscow, 1964

— Collected Works, 4th English Edition, Progress Publishers, Moscow, 1965, Vol. 31

Leonhard, Jorn, Pandora's Box: A History of the First World War, The Belknap Press, Cambridge, Massachusetts, 2018

Linklater, Andro, Compton Mackenzie: A Life, Chatto and Windus, London, 1987

Lieven, Dominic, Towards the Flame: Empire, War and the End of Tsarist Russia, Penguin, 2015

Lloyd George, David, War Memoirs, six volumes, Ivor, Nicholson and Watson, London, 1933

Lockhart, R. H. Bruce, Memoirs of a British Agent, Putnam, London, 1932

— Retreat from Glory, Putnam, London, 1934

— Comes the Reckoning, Putnam, London, 1947

— The Diaries of Bruce Lockhart Vol. I Macmillan, London, 1973

— Giants Cast Long Shadows, Putnam, London, 1960

— The Two Revolutions: An Eyewitness Account of Russia 1917, Dufour Editions, USA, 1967

Lockhart, Robin Bruce, Reilly: Ace of Spies, Futura, London, 1983

Longford, Elizabeth, A Pilgrimage of Passion: The Life of Wilfrid Scawen Blunt, Panther, London, 1979

Lukacs, John, Five Days in London: May 1940, The University Press, New Haven, 2001

Lyandres, Semion, The Fall of Tsarism: Untold Stories of the February 1917 Revolution, Oxford University Press, 2013

Mackenzie, Faith Compton, More than I Should, Collins, London, 1940

Maclean, Fitzroy, Eastern Approaches, Reprint Society, London, 1951

MacClain, James L., Japan: A Modern History, W. W. Norton, New York, 2002

Mackinnon, Stephen R. and Oris Friesen, China Reporting: An Oral History of American Journalism in the 1930s and 1940s, University of California Press, Berkeley, 1987

MacMillan, Margaret, Paris 1919: Six Months that Changed the World, Random House, New York, 2003

— The War That Ended Peace: The Road to 1914, Random House, London, 2013

McCarthy, Dudley, Gallipoli to the Somme, Leo Cooper, London, 1983

McCarthy, James, The Diplomat of Kashgar: A Very Special Agent, Proverse, Hong Kong, 2017

McLellan, David, (editor), Karl Marx: Selected Writings, Oxford University Press, Oxford, 1977

McMeekin, Sean, The Russian Revolution: A New History, Profile Books, London, 2017

Manning, Paul, Hirohito: The War Years, Dodd, Mead, New York, 1986

Marder, Arthur J., Old Friends, New Enemies: The Royal Navy and the Imperial Japanese Navy, Oxford University Press, 1981

Mallinson, Allan, 1914: Fight the Good Fight, Bantam Books, London, 2014

— Fight to the Finish: The First World War Month by Month, Bantam Press, London, 2018

Mansel, Philip, Constantinople: City of the World's Desire 1453 – 1924, Penguin, London, 1995

Marx, Karl and Frederick Engels, The Communist Manifesto, Penguin, London, 2015

Massie, Robert K., Nicholas and Alexandra: The Tragic, Compelling Story of the last Tsar and his Family, Indigo, London, 1996

Maurice, J. F., Hostilities without Declaration of War, HM Stationery Office, London, 1883

Mazour, Anatole G., Russia: Tsarist and Communist, D. Van Nostrand, Princeton, 1962

Mawdsley, Evan, The Russian Civil War, Birlinn, Edinburgh, 2017

Mazower, Mark, What You Did Not Tell: A Russian Past and the Journey Home, Allen Lane, London, 2017.

Meacham, Jon, Franklin and Winston: An Intimate Portrait of an Epic Friendship, Random House, New York, 2003

Melancon, Michael, The Lena Goldfields Massacre, Texas A & M, University Press, 2006

Meriwether, Lee, The War Diary of a Diplomat, Dodd, Mead, New York, 1919

Miéville, China, October: The Story of the Russian Revolution, Verso Books, Brooklyn, 2018

Miles, Jonathan, Saint Petersburg: Three Centuries of Murderous Desire, Windmill Books, London 2018

Miliukov, Paul, Bolshevism, an International Danger, Charles Scribner, New York, 1920

Mitchell, Mairin, The Maritime History of Russia, Sidgwick and Jackson, London, 1949

Merridale, Catherine, Lenin on the Train, Penguin, London, 2016

Medlin, Virgil D. and Steven L. Parsons (editors), V. D. Nabokov and the Russian Provisional Government 1917, Yale University Press, New Haven, 1976

Milton, Giles, Russian Roulette, Bloomsbury Press, London, 2013

Money, James, Capri: Island of Pleasure, Faber and Faber, London, 2012

Montefiore, Hugh Sebag, Somme: Into the Breach, Random House, London, 2016

Montefiore, Simon Sebag, Stalin: The Court of the Red Tsar, Penguin, London, 2017

— The Romanovs 1613-1918, Weidenfeld and Nicolson, London, 2016

Moorehead, Alan, The Russian Revolution, Amberley, Stroud, 2017

Morrison, Simon, Bolshoi Confidential: Secrets of the Russian Ballet, Fourth Estate, London, 2016

Moynaham, Brian, Comrades: 1917 Russia in Revolution, Hutchinson, London, 1992

Muggeridge, Malcolm, The Thirties 1930-1940 in Great Britain, Hamish Hamilton, London, 1940

Nabokov, Konstantin, Ordeal of a Diplomat, Duckworth, London, 1921

Nabokov, Vladimir, Letters to Véra, Random House, London, 2014

— Speak, Memory: An Autobiography Revisited, Penguin, London, 2012

— Think, Write, Speak (Brian Boyd and Anastasia Tolstoy editors), Penguin, London, 2019

Nagorski, Andrew, The Greatest Battle: The Fight for Moscow 1941-1942, Aurum Press, 2007

Neary, Ian, The State and Politics in Japan, Polity Press, Oxford, 2002

Neville, Peter, Russia: The USSR, CIS and the Independent States, Phoenix, London, 2003

Northedge, F. S., and Wells, Audrey, Britain and Soviet Communism: The Impact of a Revolution, Macmillan, London, 1982

Noonan, N. C., Encyclopaedia of Russian Women's Movements, Greenwood Press, Westport, Connecticut, 2001

Norwich, John Julius, Byzantium: The Early Centuries, Penguin, London, 1990

Ohler, Norman, Blitzed: Drugs in Nazi Germany, Allen Lane, London, 2015

Otte, T. G., July Crisis: The World's Descent into War. Cambridge University Press, 2015

Overy, Richard with Andrew Wheatcroft, The Road to War, Penguin, London, 1999

— Russia's War, Penguin, 1997

Owen, Frank, Tempestuous Journey: Lloyd George's Life and Times, Hutchinson, London, 1954

Packard, Jerrold M., Victoria's Daughters, Sutton Publishing, Stroud, 1998

Pares, Bernard, A History of Russia, Jonathan Cape, London, 1947

— Russia, Penguin, London, 1941

Patenaude, Bertrand M., Stalin's Nemesis: The Exile and Murder of Leon Trotsky, Faber and Faber, London, 2009

Perris, G. H., Russia in Revolution, Chapman and Hall, London, 1905

Pipes, Richard, Russia under the Old Regime, Weidenfeld and Nicolson, London 1974

Pitcher, Harvey, Witnesses of the Russian Revolution, Pimlico, London, 2001

Pitzer, Andrea, The Secret History of Vladimir Nabokov, Pegasus Books, New York, 2014

Plowright, John, The Causes, Course and Outcomes of World War Two, Palgrave Macmillan, New York, 2007

Pope-Hennessy, James, The Quest for Queen Mary (Hugo Vickers, editor), Hodder and Stoughton, London, and Zulieka, 2018

Popoff, Alexandra, Vasily Grossman and the Soviet Century, Yale University Press, New Haven 2019

Porter, Cathy, Alexandra Kollontai, Virago, London, 1980

Plowright, John, The Causes, Course and Outcomes of World War Two, Palgrave Macmillan, Hampshire, 2007

Price, Morgan Philips, My Reminiscences of the Russian Revolution, Hyperion, Westport, Connecticutt, 1921

Pritchett, V. S., Midnight Oil, Penguin Books, London, 1974

Pruszynski, Xavier, Russian Year: The Notebook of an Amateur Diplomat, Roy Publishers, New York, 1944

Rabinowitch, Alexander, The Bolsheviks Come to Power: The Revolution of 1917 in Petrograd, Pluto Press, London, 2017

Raleigh, Donald J. (editor), A Russian Civil War Diary: Alexis Babine in Saratov 1917-1921, Duke University Press, Durham and London 1988.

Ramm, Agatha, Europe in the Twentieth Century 1905-1970, Longman, Harlow, 1986

Ransome, Arthur, Russia in 1919, B. W. Huebsch, New York, 1919

Radzinsky, Edvard, The Last Tsar: The Life and Death of Nicholas II, Anchor Books, London, 1993

— Alexander II: The Last Great Tsar, New York, The Free Press, 2005

Rappaport, Helen, Conspirator: Lenin in Exile, Windmill Books, London, 2010

— Caught in the Revolution: Petrograd 1917, Hutchinson, London, 2016

— The Race to Save the Romanovs, Hutchinson, London 2018

Read, Anthony, and Fisher, David, Berlin: The Biography of a City, Pimlico, London, 1994

Reed, John, Ten Days That Shook the World, Penguin Classics, London, 1977

Reynolds, David, and Vladimir Pechatnov, The Kremlin Letters: Stalin's Wartime Correspondence with Churchill and Roosevelt, Yale University Press, New Haven, 2018

Riddell, Lord Riddell's War Diary, Nicholson and Watson, London, 1933

Ridley, Jane, Bertie: A Life of Edward VII, Chatto and Windus, London, 2012

Roberts, Andrew, Salisbury: Victorian Titan, Weidenfeld and Nicolson, London, 1999

Roberts, Geoffrey, Stalin's War: From World War to Cold War 1939–1953, Yale University Press, New Haven, 2006

— Stalin's General: The Life of Georgy Zhukov, Icon Books, London, 2012

Roberts, J. M., Europe 1880-1945, Longman, London, 1992

Roskill, Captain S. W., The War at Sea, Vol. I, HMSO, London, 1954

Ruthchild, Rochelle Goldberg, Equality and Revolution, University of Pittsburg Press, 2010

Rutherford, Ward, The Tsar's War 1914-1918, Ian Faulkner, Cambridge, 1992

Saint-Exupéry, Antoine de, Airman's Odyssey, Harcourt Brace, Orlando, Florida, 1984

Sablinsky, Walter, The Road to Bloody Sunday, Princeton University Press, Princeton, New Jersey, 1976

Salway, Lance, Queen Victoria's Grandchildren, Collins and Brown, London, 1991

Schabas, William A., The Trial of the Kaiser, Oxford University Press, 2018

Sebestyen, Victor, Lenin the Dictator: An Intimate Portrait, Weidenfeld and Nicolson, London, 2017

Second Congress of the Communist International, Vol. I, New Park Publications, New York, 1977

Sheffield, Gary, and John Bourne (editors), Douglas Haig: War Diaries and Letters 1914-1918, Weidenfeld and Nicolson, London, 2005

Service, Robert, Lenin: A Biography, Macmillan, London, 2000

— Trotsky: A Biography, Pan Books, London, 2009

— Spies and Commissars: Bolshevik Russia and the West, Macmillan, London, 2011

— The Last of the Tsars: Nicholas II and the Russian Revolution, Pan Books, London, 2018

— A History of Modern Russia: From Nicholas II to Putin, Penguin, London, 2003

Shepherd, Ben H., Hitler's Soldiers: The German Army in the Third Reich, Yale University Press, New Haven, 2016

Shannon, Richard, The Crisis of Imperialism 1865-1915, Granada, London, 1974

Shipler, David K., Russia: Broken Idols, Solemn Dreams, Time Books, New York, 1985

Shulgin, V. V., Days of the Russian Revolution, Academic International Press, 1990

Sixsmith, Martin, Russia: A 1,000-year Chronicle of the Wild East, BBC Books, London, 2012

Skousen, W. Cleon, The Naked Communist, Ensign, Salt Lake City, 1958

Smith, S. A., Russia in Revolution: An Empire in Crisis 1890-1926, Oxford University Press, 2017

Smithers, A. J., Dornford Yates: A biography, Hodder and Stoughton, London, 1982

Solomon, Flora and Barnett Litvinoff, Baku to Baker Street: Memoirs of Flora Solomon, William Collins, London, 1984

Solzhenitsyn, Alexander, August 1914, The Red Wheel, Node I, Books 1-2, Vintage Books, London, 2014

— November 1916, The Red Wheel, Node II, Books 1-2, Farrar, Straus and Giroux, New York, 1999

— March 1917, The Red Wheel/Node III, Book I, University of Notre Dame Press, Notre Dame, Indiana, 2008

— March 1917, The Red Wheel/Node III, Book II, University of Notre Dame Press, Notre Dame, Indiana, 2019

— Between Two Millstones, Book I, Sketches of Exile 1974-1978, University of Notre Dame Press, Notre Dame, Indiana, 2018

— The Gulag Archipelago, Vintage Books, 2018

— Stories and Prose Poems, Penguin, London, 1974

Sorokin, Professor Pitirim, Leaves from a Russian Diary, the Beacon Press, Boston, 1950

— A Long Journey, Yale University Press, 1963

Smith, Douglas, Rasputin, Macmillan, London, 2016

— Former People: The Last Days of the Russian Aristocracy, Pan Books, 2013

Souter, Gavin, Lion and Kangaroo, William Collins, Sydney, 1976

Spears, Sir Edward, Assignment to Catastrophe: The Fall of France, Vol. II, Windmill Press, Kingswood, Surrey, 1954

— 'Prelude to Victory' in The Penguin Book of War: Great Military Writings, John Keegan (editor), Penguin, London, 2000

Souhami, Diana, Mrs Keppel and Her Daughter, Quercus Editions, London, 2013

Spence, Richard M., Boris Savinkov, Renegade on the Left, East European Monographs, Boulder, Columbia University Press, New York, 1991

Steffens, Lincoln, The Autobiography of Lincoln Steffens, Harcourt, New York, 1931

Steegmuller, Francis, Cocteau: A Biography, Atlantic Monthly Press, Boston, 1969

Stevenson, David, 1917: War, Peace and Revolution, Oxford University Press, 2017

— 1917-1918: A History of the First World War, Penguin, London, 2012

— With Our Backs to the Wall: Defeat and Victory in 1918, The Belknap Press, Cambridge, Massachusetts, 2011

Stoler, Mark A., Allies in War: Britain and America against the Axis Powers 1940–1945, Hodder Arnold, London, 2005

Stone, David R., The Russian Army in the Great War: The Eastern Front 1914-19-17, University Press of Kansas, 2015

Stone, Norman, The Eastern Front 1914-1917, Hodder and Stoughton, London, 1975

Strohn, Matthais, 1918: Winning the War, Losing the War, Osprey, London, 2018

Sukhanov, N. N., The Russian Revolution 1917: A Personal Record, Oxford University Press, 1955

Tabouis, Geneviève, They called me Cassandra, Da Capo Press, New York, 1973

Tansill, Charles Callan, Back Door to War: The Roosevelt Foreign Policy 1933–1941, Henry Regnery, Chicago, 1952

Taylor, A. J. P., English History 1914-1945, Book Club, 1977

— The Struggle for Mastery in Europe 1848-1918, Clarendon Press, Oxford, 2013

Temperley, Harold, and Lillian Penson (editors), Foundations of British Foreign Policy from Pitt 1792 to Salisbury 1902, Cambridge University Press, 1938

Thompson, Peter, The Battle for Singapore, Portrait, London, 2005

— Pacific Fury: How Australia and her Allies defeated the Japanese, Random House Australia, Sydney, 2010

Thompson, Peter and Robert Macklin, The Battle of Brisbane, ABC Books, Sydney, 2001

— Kill the Tiger, Hodder, Sydney, 2002

— Morrison of China, Allen and Unwin, Sydney, 2004

Tompkins, Rosemary Colborn, Alexander Kerensky and the Kornilov Affair, thesis, August 1965, University of North Texas Libraries, Denton, Texas

Trotsky, Leon, The Third International after Lenin, Plough Press, London, 1974

— History of the Russian Revolution, Haymarket Books, Chicago, 2008

— The Young Lenin (translated by Max Eastman), David and Charles, Newton Abbot, 1977

Tuchman, Barbara, The Guns of August, Macmillan, New York, 1962

Turner, John, Lloyd George's Secretariat, Cambridge University Press, 2009

Ullman, Richard H., Intervention and the War: Anglo-Soviet Relations 1917-1921, Oxford University Press, 1951

Volkogonov, Dmitri, Lenin: Life and Legacy, Harper Collins, London, 1994

Waite, Robert G. L., Kaiser and Führer: A Comparative Study of Personality and Politics, University of Toronto Press, Toronto, 2001

Walker, Jonathan, Operation Unthinkable: The Third World War – British Plans to Attack the Soviet Empire, The History Press, 2013

Walton, Calder, Empire of Secrets: British Intelligence, the Cold War and the Twilight of Empire, Harper Press, London, 2013

Waterfield, Gordon, What Happened to France, London, 1940

Watson, Alexander, Ring of Steel: Germany and Austria-Hungary at War 1914-1918, Penguin, London, 2015

— The Fortress: The Great Siege of Przemysl, Penguin, London, 2019

Wawro, Geoffrey, A Mad Catastrophe, Basic Books, New York, 2019

Weintraub, Stanley, Long Day's Journey into War, Truman Talley Books, New York, 1991

Welch, France, The Imperial Tea Party, Short Books, London 2018

Wells, H. G., The Outline of History: The Whole Story of Man, Vol. II, Doubleday, New York, 1971

— Russia in the Shadows, Hodder and Stoughton, London, 1914

Werth, Alexander, The Last Days of Paris, Hamish Hamilton, London, 1942

Westwood, J. N., Endurance and Endeavour: Russian History 1812-2001, Oxford University Press, 2002

Weygand, General Maxime, Memoirs, Vol. III, Flammarion, Paris, 1950

Wheeler, Sara, Mud and Stars; Travels in Russia, Jonathan Cape, London, 2019

Wildman, Allan, K., The Making of a Workers' Revolution: Russian Social Democracy 1891-1903, University of Chicago Press, Chicago, 1967

— The end of the Russian Imperial Army, two volumes, Princeton, 2020

Witte, Count Sergei, Memoirs of Count Witte, (translated and edited by Abraham Yarmolinsky), Doubleday, Page, New York, 1921

Wilson, A. N., Victoria: A Life, Atlantic Books, London, 2014

Wilson, Edmund, To the Finland Station, Fontana Collins, 1970

Wilton, Robert, Russia's Agony, E. P. Dutton, New York, 1919

Winter, Denis, Haig's Command: A Reassessment, Penguin, London, 2001

Winter, Ella, And Not to Yield, Harcourt, Brace and World Inc., New York, 1963

Williams, Charles, Max Beaverbrook: Not Quite a Gentleman, Biteback Publishing, London, 2019

Woodham-Smith, Cecil, The Reason Why, Atheneum, New York, 1982

Wren, Melvin C., The Course of Russian History, Macmillan, New York, 1958

Wright, Damien, Churchill's Secret War with Lenin, Helion, Solihull, 2017

Wright, Mary Clabaugh (editor), China in Revolution: The First Phase 1900-1913, Yale University Press, New Haven, 1968

Young, Kenneth (editor), The Diaries of Sir Robert Bruce Lockhart 1915-1938, Macmillan, London, 1973

Young, Pam, Proud to be a Rebel, Queensland University Press, Brisbane, 1991

Ziegler, Charles E. The History of Russia, Greenwood Press, Westport, Connecticut, 2000

Zupperstein, Steven, Pogrom: Kishinev and the tilt of history, Liveright Publishing, New York, 2019

Zygar, Mikhail, The Empire Must Die: Russia's Revolutionary Collapse 1900-1917, Hachette, New York, 2017

Endnotes

Author's Note

1 A collaborative literary effort by Robert Bruce Lockhart and Alexander Kerensky never got past the synopsis stage. Lockhart's suggested title was *Ordeal by Oratory*.

Prologue: The Russian Unicorn

1 The author in conversation with Anthony Delano, April 2016

2 Muggeridge, Malcolm, 'Russia's last democrat', The Observer, 29 May 1966

3 'Kerensky', New York Times, 12 June 1970

4 Ibid

5 Trotsky, Revolution, p. 133; Abraham, p. 168

6 Edward Acton, 'The Revolution and its Historians', in Acton, Cherniaev, Rosenberg (editors), Critical Companion, p. 7

7 Bernard Butcher, A Doomed Democracy, Stanford Magazine, January-February 2001

8 Ian D. Thatcher, 'Memoirs of the Russian Provisional Government 1917', Revolutionary Russia, Routledge, 2014

9 Louise Bryant, p. 115

10 Christian Neef and Matthias Schepp, 'Interview with Alexander Solzhenitsyn', Spiegel, 23 July 2007

11 Nabokov, Think, Write, Speak, p. 298

12 Sara Wheeler, Mud and Stars, p. 254, p. 5. These are the slogans of the English Socialist Party (INGSOC) in 1984.

13 Michael Hughes, 'The Legacy of Alexander Kerensky', The Independent, 6 November 2017

14 Kerensky, Crucifixion, p. 19

15 Jonathan D. Smele, 'Mania Grandiosa' and the Turning Point in World History: Kerensky in London in 1918', Revolutionary Russia, Vol. 20, 2007, Issue 1

16 Lockhart, Two Revolutions, p. 88; Lockhart, Comes the Reckoning, p. 94

17 'Alexander Kerensky', The Times, 17 June 1970

18 Bernard Butcher, 'A Doomed Democracy', Stanford Magazine, January-February 2001

19 'Alexander Kerensky looks back', The Argus, 10 November 1945

1. The Doomed Dynasty

1 Kerensky, Crucifixion, p. 23

2 Quoted in Constantine de Grunwald, Tsar Nichols I, translated by Brigit Patmore, London, 1954, p. 74

3 Dostoevsky, Notes from the House of the Dead, the first prison-camp novel.

4 Crankshaw, Shadow, p. 41

5 Ibid, pp. 41-2

6 Roberts, Salisbury, p. 29

7 Rebecca Fraser, pp. 557-558; Pares, p. 388; Crankshaw, Shadow, p. 132

8 Victoria's father, the Duke of Kent, was the son of George III and her mother was Princess Victoria of Saxe-Coburg-Saalfeld. Victoria encouraged her children to think of themselves as Germans. They all spoke English with pronounced German accents

9 Neville, p. 126; Crankshaw, Shadow, p. 141

10 Neville, p. 128

11 Tolstoy, Sevastopol in December 1854, p. 18

12 Pares, History of Russia, p. 390

13 Clarkson, Russia, p. 53; Neville, p. 133; Abraham, pp. 3, 6; Michael Lynch, 'The Emancipation of the Serfs 1861, History Review, Issue 47, December 2003

14 Mazour, Russia, p. 259

15 Neville, p. 134; Service, Modern Russia, p. 6

16 Kerensky, Crucifixion, p. 45

17 Service, Modern Russia, pp. 4-6; Stephen Tonge, 'Russia 1870-1917', www.historyhome.co.uk

18 Ziegler, Russia, p. 63; Clarkson, Russia, p. 367

19 Julie A. Buckler, Petersburg, p. 220

20 Crankshaw, Shadow, p. 193

21 Perres, p. 81; Peter Kropotkin, Memoirs of a Revolutionist, pp. 322, 329

22 Pobedonostsev, Reflections of a Russian Statesman, p. 251

23 Robert F. Byrnes, 'Konstantin Petrovich Pobedonostsev', www.britannica.com

24 Radzinsky, Alexander II, p. 415

25 Pares, p. 440; Freeze, pp. 230-231

2. The Sons of Simbirsk

1 Kerensky, Turning Point, p. 18

2 Kerensky, Catastrophe, p. 79. His father's titles were Director of the Simbirsk Classical Gymnasium for Boys and Director of the Simbirsk Marinskaya Gymnasium for Girls.

3 Dearborn Independent, 25 September 1920

4 Kerensky, Crucifixion, p. 57

5 Pipes, Old Regime, p. 311

6 Pares, p. 465; Kerensky, Crucifixion, p. 70

7 Pares, p. 448

8 Kerensky, Crucifixion, p. 70

9 Westwood, p. 125

10 Ibid, p. 126

11 Simon Sebag-Montefiore, Romanovs, Kindle Edition

12 Kerensky, Crucifixion, p. 57

13 Kerensky, Turning Point, p. 11

14 Kerensky, Crucifixion, p. 8

15 Abraham, pp. 6-7

16 Edmund Wilson, p. 360; Abraham p. 7

17 Kerensky, Crucifixion, p. 48. Lenin was eleven years older than Kerensky, so this information must have been second-hand. Service, Lenin, p. 32. Service quotes Lenin's siblings as his source.

18 Service, Lenin, p. 60

19 Kerensky, Crucifixion, p. 13

20 Ibid, p. 12

21 Kerensky, Turning Point, p. 4

22 Ibid, pp. 6-7

23 Sebestyen, p. 60

24 Ibid, p. 61

25 Edmund Wilson, p. 367

26 Harvey, Comrades, p. 24

27 Rappaport, Conspirator, p. xxvi

28 Figes, Tragedy, p. 146

29 Charques, Twilight, p. 77-78

30 Service, Lenin, p. 118

31 Kerensky, Turning Point, pp. 10-11

32 Bailey, Tashkent, p. 17

33 Hopkirk, Great Game, p. 2; Curzon, Russia in Central Asia, p. 241

34 Hopkirk, Great Game, pp. 443-444; Kerensky, Crucifixion, p. 64

35 Kerensky, Turning Point, p. 13

3. The Distorting Mirror

1 Massie, p. 230

2 Kerensky, Crucifixion, p. 147; Flora Solomon has a different version of this incident on p. 138 of her memoirs.

3 Ibid; Jonathan Miles, p. 300

4 Imogen Foulkes, 'Rare window into life of tsarist Russia', BBC News, Geneva, 6 March 2012

5 Simon Sebag Montefiore, Romanovs, Kindle Edition.

6 Quoted in Massie, p. 24 and differently in Figes, p. 17

7 Wren, p. 462

8 Dominic Lieven in Acton, Cherniaev, Rosenberg (editors), Critical Companion, p. 177

9 Simon Sebag Montefiore, Romanovs, Kindle Edition.

10 Morrison, p. 184; Miliukov, Bolshevism, p. 79

11 Thompson, Battle for Singapore, pp. 50-52

12 Simon Sebag Montefiore, Romanovs, Kindle Edition.

13 Morrison, p. 187

14 Witte, p. 86

15 Witte, p. 376

16 Kerensky, Crucifixion, pp. 81, 18

17 Stephen Tonge, 'Russia 1870-1917', www.historyhome.co.uk; Crankshaw, Shadow, p. 288
18 Kerensky, Crucifixion, p. 60
19 Solzhenitsyn, August 1914, p. 650
20 Packard, p. 50
21 Salway, p. 69
22 Simon Sebag Montefiore, Romanovs, Kindle Edition
23 Gareth Russell, 'Could George V have saved the Romanovs?', Daily Telegraph, 16 June 2018
24 Welch, p. 11
25 Kerensky, Crucifixion, p. 61
26 Westwood, p. 88
27 Lieven, p. 75
28 Witte, pp. 179-181
29 Edward Acton, 'The revolution and its historians', in Acton, Cherniaev, Rosenberg (editors), Critical Companion, p. 7
30 Witte, p. 182
31 Mazour, Russia, p. 259; Charques, Twilight, p. 37; Ziegler, Russia, pp. 65-66
32 Kerensky, Crucifixion, p. 50
33 Massie, p. 84; Pares, p. 464
34 World War I Document Archive online
35 Thompson and Macklin, Morrison of China, p. 131
36 Witte, p. 190
37 Witte, p. 186; David Schimmelpenninck van der Oye in Kagan and Higham (editors), p. 185
38 Hackett, Modern Japan. p. 157
39 Thompson, Pacific Fury, p. 17
40 Thompson and Macklin, Morrison of China, p. 179
41 Massie, pp. 54-55; Morrison, p. 192
42 Ziegler, Russia, pp. 65-66
43 Witte, p. 214
44 Alexandra Popoff, p. 12; Mark Mazower, p. 14

45 Shukman, Harold, 1961, 'The Relations between the Jewish Bund and the RSDLP', 1897-1903', (PhD thesis), University of Oxford

46 Frankel (editor), p. 31

47 Kerensky, Turning Point, p. x

48 Pares, p. 473; Witte, pp. 96-97; Keegan, World War I, p. 17

49 Waite, p. 8

50 Ibid. p. 208

51 Kerensky, Turning Point, pp. x-xi

4. The Young Madmen

1 Figes, Tragedy, p. 166

2 Kerensky, Turning Point, p. 20; Kerensky, Crucifixion, p. 77

3 Kerensky, Crucifixion, pp. 78-79

4 Olive Garnett, 'The Case of Vetrova', Petersburg Tales, p. 4

5 Figes, Tragedy, p. 166

6 Kerensky, Crucifixion, p. 101

7 Ibid, p. 102-103

8 Kerensky, Turning Point, pp. 17 and 57

9 Abraham, p. 18; Semion Lyandres, Tsarism, p. 220

10 Kerensky, Turning Point, p. 22

11 Boets and Birukoff, p. 25

12 Valery V. Kaminski and Valentin A. Veremenko, 'The Noble Family Baranovsky at the Turn of the Epoch', Central and Eastern European Online Library

13 Gleb Kerensky, unpublished foreword to his mother's memoirs, Kerensky Family Papers, Cadbury Research Library, University of Birmingham

14 Abraham, p. 16

15 Frankel (editor), Akimov, p. 235

16 Westwood, p. 147

17 Pares, pp. 448-9

18 'The attack on M. Bogolepov', New York Times, 2 March 1901; Solzhenitsyn, November 1916, p. 61

19 Figes, p. 167

20 Kygar, p. 102

21 'Karpovich's secret trial', New York Times, 2 April 1901

22 Charques, Twilight, pp. 179-180

23 Kerensky, Crucifixion, p. 79-80

24 Ibid, p. 102-103

25 Fitzpatrick, Revolution, p. 42

26 Fried, Eric, 'Sergeyev, Fedor Andreyevich (1883-1921)', Australian Dictionary of Biography, Vol. 11, Melbourne University Press, Melbourne, 1988

27 Zupperstein, Kishinev, p. 64

28 Jonathan Miles, p. 310

29 Spence, p. 52

5. The Calamitous Kaiser

1 Victor Hugo letter to Captain Butler, 25 November 1861 ('The Sack of the Summer Palace', UNESCO Courier, November 1985)

2 St Aubyn, Edward VII, pp. 278–279

3 Packard, p. 74

4 Wilson, p. 228

5 Clark, Kaiser Wilhelm II, p. 30; Waite, p. 247 and p. 253

6 Witte, p. 401

7 Clark, Kaiser Wilhelm II, p. 11

8 Waite, p. 8

9 Witte, pp.404-5

10 Feiling, England, p. 1044; Waite, p. 7; Allan Mallinson, 'Deadly arms race that was instigated by the Kaiser', The Times, 7 November 2014

11 Shannon, p. 322

12 Thompson, Shanghai Fury, p. 65

13 Fairbank, p. 137

14 Ibid, p. 5

15 'Before the fighting: an Australian's experience', *Brisbane Courier*, 16 July 1900

16 Thompson and Macklin, Morrison of China, pp. 248-249

17 Witte, p. 127

18 Ibid, p. 127
19 Crossley, Wobbling Pivot, p. 139-140
20 Witte, p. 80
21 Ibid , p. 126
22 Radzinsky, Nicholas II, pp. 68-69
23 'War begun: Russian warships torpedoed', *The Times*, 10 February 1904
24 David Garnett, Golden Echo, p. 75
25 'Count Tolstoy on the War', The Times, 27 June 1904
26 Kerensky, Turning Point, p. 42
27 Abraham, p. 22
28 Kerensky Family Papers, Cadbury Research Library, MS126/1/3/3/2
29 Kerensky Family Papers, Cadbury Research Library, MS126/2/6/3; Nicolai Alexandrovich Vasiliev (29 June 1880 OS – 31 December 1940), was a logician, philosopher, psychologist and poet, was a forerunner of paraconsistent and multi-valued logic.
30 Kerensky, Turning Point, p. 43
31 Massie, p. 105. The previous Tsarevich, Nicholas's younger brother Georgy, died of tuberculosis and his youngest brother, Michael, was never officially named as Tsarevich.
32 David Schimmelpenninck van der Oye in Kagan and Higham (editors), p. 196
33 Kerensky, Turning Point, p. 43
34 Ibid, p. 44
35 Noonan, pp. 49-50
36 Bernard Pares, 'Fedor Rodichev', The Slavonic and East European Review, Vol. 12, No. 34 (July 1933), pp. 199-201
37 Perris, p. 266
38 Robert Gomme, 'Soskice (formerly Soskis), David Vladimirovich (1866–1941)', Oxford Dictionary of National Biography, 23 September 2004
39 David Garnett, Golden Echo, p. 37
40 Robert Gomme, 'Soskice (formerly Soskis), David Vladimirovich (1866–1941)', Oxford Dictionary of National Biography, 23 September 2004
41 Walter Rodney, p. 53
42 Ruthchild, Equality and Revolution, Kindle Edition.
43 Kerensky, Turning Point, p. 45

44 'General Stoessel's last proclamation', *The Times*, 25 January 1905
45 'Port Arthur from Within', *The Times*, 25 January 1905. When General Stoessel arrived back in Saint Petersburg, the Tsar invited him for tea and eagerly listened to his descriptions of his valiant defence of Port Arthur. The truth, however, emerged after the war and he was indicted as a traitor.
46 Massie, p. 96; Abraham, p. 26

6. The Accidental Terrorist

1 'Outbreak in St Petersburg', The Times, 23 January 1905
2 Kerensky, Turning Point, p. 47
3 Sablinksy, Bloody Sunday, p. 15
4 Kerensky, Turning Point, p. 46
5 Figes, p. 174 ; Moorehead, p. 60
6 Pares, p. 463; Kerensky, Turning Point, p. 46
7 Sablinsky, p. 78
8 Gapon, p. 163
9 Sablinsky, p. 34
10 Gapon, p. 170
11 Sablinsky, p. 231
12 Kerensky, Turning Point, p. 48
13 Cathy Porter, Kollontai, p. 92
14 'Outbreak in St Petersburg', The Times, 23 January 1905
15 Quoted in Figes, p. 177
16 Jonathan Miles, p. 315
17 'Outbreak in St Petersburg', The Times, 23 January 1905
18 Gapon, p. 182-183. His recollections were first published in The Strand Magazine, Vol. xxx, numbers 175-179, July-November 1905.
19 Ibid
20 Sablinsky, p. 278
21 Abraham , p. 26; Engelstein, pp. 6-7; S.A. Smith, p. 46; McMeekin, pp. 34-35, Figes, pp. 173-174
22 Kerensky, Crucifixion, p. 95; Kerensky, Turning Point, pp. 49-50
23 Quoted in Simon Sebag-Montefiore, The Romanovs, Orion, Kindle Edition

24 Alexander Pasternak, p. 115
25 Ibid, p. 116
26 Massie, p. 98

7. The Dress Rehearsal

1 Kerensky, Turning Point, p. 330
2 Alexander Pasternak, p. 110
3 Salway, pp. 62-63
4 Jonathan Miles, p. 318
5 'From shoemaker to opera singer', The Times, 30 September 1921
6 Kellogg Durland, p. 285
7 Service, Lenin, p. 173
8 Westwood, p. 151
9 Thompson, Pacific Fury, pp. 19-20
10 Alexander Pasternak, p. 109
11 Marder, p. 5; 'Grave breaches of neutrality', *The Times*, 8 May 1905
12 'The Russian Armada', *Brisbane Courier*, 25 April, 1905
13 Thompson, Shanghai Fury, p. 110
14 Lieven, pp. 85-86
15 Mairin Mitchell, Russia, p. 149-150
16 Lockhart, British Agent, p. 165
17 'The Russian Internal Crisis', The Times, 27 July 1905; 'Funerals of victims held', Los Angeles Herald, 6 November 1905
18 Mazower, p. 43
19 'Trouble throughout Russia', New York Times, 27 June 1905
20 Calvocoressi, Wint and Pritchard, p. 628; Thompson, Pacific Fury, p. 20
21 'Tsushima and its lessons', *Brisbane Courier*, 1 June 1905
22 Jonathan Miles, p. 299
23 Kerensky, Turning Point, p. 53
24 Ibid, p. 54
25 Simon Sebag-Montefiore, Romanovs, Kindle Edition
26 Lockhart, Secret Agent, p. 225
27 Rappaport, Conspirator, p. 122

28 Kerensky, Turning Point, p. 55

29 Ibid, p. 57

30 E. A. Goldenweiser, 'The Russian Duma', Political Science Quarterly, Vol. XXIX, No. 3

31 Witte, p. 190

32 William G. Rosenberg in Acton, Cherniaev, Rosenberg (editors), Critical Companion, p. 256

33 Raymond Pearson p. 169

34 Noonan, p. 79

35 Figes, Tragedy, p. 199

36 Rappaport, Conspirator, p. 130

37 Service, Lenin, p. 177

38 Sebestyen, Lenin, p. 174

39 Witte, p. 189

40 Fried, Eric, 'Sergeyev, Fedor Andreyevich (1883-1921)', Australian Dictionary of Biography, Volume 11, Melbourne University Press, Melbourne, 1988

41 Kerensky, Crucifixion, p. 158; Douglas Smith, p. 65

42 Sablinsky, p. 305. Sergei Zubatov emerged from obscurity to claim that Gapon had accepted a subsidy from him of 100 roubles a month, a claim which created the impression that the priest must have been a paid agent of the Okhrana all along. Many people, including Alexander Pasternak, believed Zubatov's claims, describing Father Gapon in his memoirs as 'the Tsar's secret agent and agent provocateur.' The evidence, however, shows that he received only one payment from Zubatov: a single fee of 100 roubles for a report he had written in the early days of police socialism. Far from concealing his relations with the police, he had kept his assistants informed about his contacts with them and, in his autobiography, he detailed payments made to his cause by agencies and individuals. Professor Walter Sablinsky, a Russian historian who studied Bloody Sunday, concluded that Zubatov's claims should be regarded as 'a vengeful slur'; Georgi Gapon had actually proved to be all too independent of police control for their liking.

43 Peter Rutenberg, 'How Father Gapon was led to his death', New York Times, 7 November 1909

44 Andrew, p. 108; British National Archives, KV 2/659; Solomon, pp. 111-2. Flora Solomon says Rutenberg told her he had shot Gapon in a country shack in Finland but she added that 'he never told the story the same way twice'.

45 Kerensky, Turning Point, pp. 46-47

46 Wren, p. 464

8. The Romantic Assassin

1 Kerensky, Turning Point, p. 62

2 Ibid, p. 65

3 Ibid, p. 67

4 Raymond Pearson, Critical Companion, p. 169

5 Peter Neville, p. 165

6 'Opening of the Duma', The Times, 11 May 1906

7 Kerensky, Turning Point, p. 70

8 Wren, p. 463

9 'Opening of the Duma', The Times, 11 May 1906

10 Ibid

11 E. A. Goldenweiser, 'The Russian Duma', Political Science Quarterly, Vol. XXIX, No. 3

12 V. D. Nabokov, p. 3

13 'Russia Revisited', The Times, 18 October 1906

14 Solzhenitsyn, November 1916, p. 79

15 Kerensky, Turning Point, p. 72

16 Gleb Kerensky, unpublished foreword to his mother's memoirs, Kerensky Family Papers, Cadbury Research Library, University of Birmingham

17 Simon Sebag Montefiore, Romanovs, Kindle Edition

18 Kerensky, Turning Point, p. 77

19 Golder, Passages, p. 6; Kerensky, Turning Point, pp. 74-75

20 Wilcox, Russia's Ruin, p. 190

21 Abraham, p. 48

22 Simon Sebag Montefiore, Romanovs: 1613-1918, Orion. Kindle Edition

23 Figes, p. 34

24 Noonan, p. 75

25 Kevin Windle, 'Brisbane Prison: Artem Sergeev describes Boggo Road', New Zealand Slavonic Journal, Vol. 38, 2004, pp. 159-179

26 Thompson, Shanghai Fury, p. 140

27 Robert A Bickers and Jeffrey N. Wasserstrom, 'Shanghai's "Dogs and Chinese Not Admitted" sign: Legend, history and contemporary symbol', The China Quarterly, No 142, June 1995.' Various signs were displayed at the gardens over the years, the most offensive of which said, '1. No dogs or bicycles are admitted. 5. No Chinese are admitted except servants in attendance upon foreigners.' This was later changed to, '1. The Gardens are reserved for the foreign community. 4. Dogs and bicycles are not admitted.'

28 Thompson and Macklin, Battle of Brisbane, p. 28-29

29 Fried, Eric, 'Sergeyev, Fedor Andreyevich' (1883-1921), Australian Dictionary of Biography, Vol 11, Melbourne University Press, Melbourne, 1988.

30 Kevin Windle, 'Artem Sergeev translator: The image of a Russian revolutionary in Tom Keneally's People's Train', New Zealand Slavonic Journal, Vol. 45 No. 1 (2011)

31 T. Poole and E. Fried, 'Artem: A Bolshevik in Brisbane', *Australian Journal of Politics and History*, Vol 31, No. 2, 1985, pp 243-254

32 Ibid

9. The Kerensky Ascent

1 Kerensky, Turning Point, pp. 80-81

2 Abraham, p. 53

3 Jonathan Daly, p. 58

4 Vladimir Stankevich (Vlados Stanka), 'About A. F. Kerensky' (translated from the Russian daily, *Novoye Russkoe Slovo*), Kerensky Family Papers. Cadbury Research Library, MS126/1/3/3/2

5 'Lena Goldfields', The Times, 9 February 1926; K. H. Kennedy, pp. 217-218

6 Solomon, p. 50

7 Melancon, 48

8 'The Lena Goldfields strike', The Times, 20 March 1912

9 Melancon. P. 92

10 Kerensky, Crucifixion, pp. 123-124

11 'Dreadful massacre in Russia', Bendigo Advertiser, 8 June 1912, reproducing a report from the London correspondent of the 'Daily News' datelined Saint Petersburg, 2 May 1912

12 'The Shooting of the Lena strikers', The Times, 26 April 1912

13 Melancon, p. 7; Abraham, pp. 54-55

14 Solomon, p. 51

15 Kerensky, Crucifixion, p. 124

16 Ibid

17 Kerensky, Turning Point, p. 83

18 Montefiore, Young Stalin, p. 210

19 'The Brisbane Tramways Trouble', The Worker, 27 January 1912

20 Pam Young, Rebel, p. 182. Pam Young writes: 'Not long after the incident it became obvious that the Police Commissioner now walked with a definite limp. It was rumoured to have been caused by Emma's hatpin entering his leg, creating an infection. This was later verified by friends of Cahill.' When Major Cahill died in 1931, the Brisbane Courier commented, 'In the great strike of 1912 Major Cahill handled an ugly position with great tact.'

21 W. Ross Johnston, 'Urquhart, Frederic Charles (1858–1935)', Australian Dictionary of Biography, Vol. 12, MUP, 1990

22 In an article published in Saint Petersburg in 1914, Artem Sergeyev wrote scathingly about his supposed incarceration in Brisbane's Boggo Road Jail for one month during the 'Free Speech Fight' against a regulation that public speakers required a permit from the Police Commissioner. Historians, however, failed to find any reference in Brisbane's police files or court records to Sergeyev's conviction and imprisonment. It seems either Surgeyev (or his publisher) put his name on someone else's experiences of prison life. See Kevin Windle, 'Brisbane Prison: Artem Sergeev describes Boggo Road', New Zealand Slavonic Journal, Vol. 38 (2004).

23 Kerensky, Turning Point, p. 83

24 Zygar, p. 323

25 Abraham, pp. 56-57

26 Ibid, p. 58

27 Quoted in Lipatova, Nadezhda V., "On the Verge of the Collapse of Empire: Images of Alexander Kerensky and Mikhail Gorbachev, Europe-Asia Studies, Volume 65, Number 2, March 2013, pp. 264-289

28 Lockhart, British Agent, p. 50
29 Ibid, p. 18
30 Ibid, p. 60
31 Abraham, p. 66
32 Ibid, pp. 67-8
33 Figes, Tragedy, pp. 242-243
34 Zygar, p 328
35 Abraham, p. 72; Kerensky, Turning Point, p. 85-6
36 Lockhart, British Agent, p. 76
37 Massie, p. 227
38 Douglas Smith, p. 219; Massie, p. 218
39 Rodzianko, p. 45
40 The Biblical seat of judgment.

10. The Damn Fool Thing

1 James Hawes, p. 134
2 Cary, Bobotes, jacket notes
3 Owen, Lloyd George, 1954, pp. 254-256
4 German shipping magnate Albert Ballin to Winston Churchill, summer 1914, Churchill, Crisis, p. 158
5 Kerensky, Crucifixion, p. 172
6 Sebestyen, p. 220
7 Andrew, Secret World, p. 445
8 Edward Crankshaw, Habsburg, p. 342
9 Watson, Ring of Steel, p. 9
10 Christopher Clark, pp. 412-413; A. J. P. Taylor, Mastery, p. 521; Massie, p. 244
11 Stevenson, 1914-1918, p. 8; Otte, p. 83; Ensor, p. 486
12 Szogyenyi to Berchtold, Berlin 6 July 1914, quoted in Christopher Clark, p. 414
13 Stevenon, 1914-1918, p. 14; Rebecca Fraser, p. 650
14 Massie, p. 248
15 Stevenson, 1914-1918, p. 11
16 MacMillan, Peace, p. 569

17 Kerensky, Crucifixion, pp. 173-175

18 Kerensky, Catastrophe, p. 78

19 Kerensky, Alexander, 'Inside the Russian Revolution', New York Times, 8 May 1927; Kerensky, Catastrophe, p. 79

20 Ensor, p. 487; Michael Tillotson, 'The Little Father believed God had chosen him to rule', The Times, 22 February 2014; Massie, p. 249

21 Churchill, Crisis, p. 161

22 Keith Neilson, 'Arthur Nicolson, first Baron Carnock (1849–1928)', Oxford Dictionary of National Biography, 2004; Thomas Laqueur, 'Some Damn Foolish Thing', London Review of Books, 5 December 2013

23 Feiling, England, p. 1055; Michael Tillotson, 'While the British prime minister fell in love, a monster consumed Europe', The Times, 12 July 2014

24 Heffer, Staring at God, p. 26

25 Taylor, Mastery, pp. 511-512

26 Michael Tillotson, 'While the British prime minister fell in love, a monster consumed Europe', The Times, 12 July 2014

27 Crankshaw, Habsburg, p. 286; Otto, p. 357

28 Keith Neilson, 'Arthur Nicolson, first Baron Carnock (1849–1928)', Oxford Dictionary of National Biography, 2004; Grey, Twenty-Five Years, Vol. II, p. 162

29 Ensor, p. 490; Grey, Twenty-Five Years, Vol. II, p. 170; A. J. P. Taylor, Mastery, p. 525

30 Otte, p. 306-307

31 Wawro, p. 171

32 Margot Asquith, Autobiography, Vol. IV, p. 21

33 Massie, p. 257

34 Lieven, p, 337

35 Grey, Twenty-Five Years, Vol. II, p. 227

36 Margot Asquith, Autobiography, Vol. IV, p. 23

37 Massie, p. 263

38 Kerensky, Crucifixion, p. 175

39 Solzhenitsyn, November 1916, pp. 206-207

40 Waite p. 207

41 Plowright, p. 4; Feiling, England, p. 1058

42 Wawro, p. 118

43 Owen, Lloyd George, p. 262

44 Michael Tillotson, 'No one will reproach me again with want of resolution', The Times, 16 May 2014

45 Ibid

46 Waite p. 219

47 Margot Asquith, Autobiography, Vol. IV, p. 26

48 Waite. p. 215

49 Wilfrid Scawen Blunt's 1914 Diary, Fitzwilliam Museum, Cambridge

50 Archibald Hurd, revised by John Van der Kiste Mountbatten, Louis Alexander, first Marquess of Milford Haven (formerly Prince Louis of Battenberg), Oxford Dictionary of National Biography, 2004

51 Grey, Twenty-Five Years, Vol. II, p. 223; Keith Robbins, 'Grey, Edward, Viscount Grey of Fallodon (1862–1933), Oxford Dictionary of National Biography, 2011

52 Margot Asquith, An Autobiography, Vol. IV, p. 70

53 Shannon, p. 460

54 The vast majority of the 12,000 Russian nationals in Australia, however, supported the war effort. Over the next four years one thousand servicemen from the Russian Empire fought in the Australian Imperial Force (AIF) on the battlefields of Turkey, Belgium and France.

11. The Iron Hurricane

1 Waite. p. 23

2 Steegmuller, Cocteau, p. 121

3 Watson, Ring of Steel, p. 246

4 Wawro, p. 121; Watson, Fortress, p. 35

5 Crim, Antisemitism, p. 14

6 Wawro, p. 368

7 Merridale, p. 79; Service, p. 223-224

8 Kerensky, Crucifixion, p. 171; Kygar, p. 335

9 Simon Sebag-Montefiore, Romanovs, Kindle edition; Pierre Gilliard, Thirteen Years at the Russian Court, New York, 1921

10 Wilcox, Russia's Ruin, p. 190

11 Kerensky, Turning Point, p. 131

12 M. N. Pokrovsky (editor), Essays on the History of the October Revolution, Ispart, Moscow, 1927
13 Badayev, The Bolsheviks in the Tsarist Duma, www.marxists.org
14 Lenin, Selected Works, FLPH, Moscow, Vol. I, Part 2, p. 571.
15 Charques, Twilight, p. 37
16 Konstantin Nabokov, p. 99
17 David R. Jones in Kagan and Higham (editors), Tsarist Russia, p. 245; Richard Holmes (editor), Military History, p. 792. The German general was Hugo von Freytag-Loringhoven.
18 Kerensky, Catastrophe, p. 80
19 Buchanan, Vol. I p. 216
20 Lieven, p. 327
21 Watson, Ring of Steel, p. 171
22 Hindenburg, Out of My Life, p. 84
23 Andrew, The Secret World, p. 504
24 Crim, Antisemitism, p. 17; Kerensky, Turning Point, p. 138
25 Christopher Andrew, The Secret History, p. 502
26 Kerensky, Crucifixion.
27 Kerensky, Catastrophe, p. 81
28 Lieven, p.148; Tuchman, p. 62
29 Bruce W. Menning in Kagan and Higham (editors), Tsarist Russia, p. 215
30 Tuchman, p. 61
31 Knox, With the Russian Army, Vol. I, pp. 42, 331
32 Buchanan, Vol. I, pp. 218-220
33 Rutherford, p. 108
34 Lieven, pp. 327-328
35 Lieven, p. 149
36 Keegan, First World War, p. 163; Buchanan, Mission to Russia, Vol. I, pp. 216-217
37 The History of The Times, 1912-1920, 1952, p. 232
38 Feiling, England, p. 1062; Allan Mallinson, 'Churchill struck the decisive blow seven days before the war', The Times, 2 August 2014; Chirol, Fifty Years, p. 885; Bruno Cabanes, p. 19
39 Andrew, Secret World, p. 495; Bruno Cabanes, p. 121

40 Allan Mallinson, 'The tears of a general, then a miracle on the Marne', The Times, 6 September 2014

41 Andrew, Secret World, p. 511

42 Churchill, World Crisis: Eastern Front, p. 84

43 Feiling, England, p. 1063

44 Lockhart, British Agent, p. 98

45 Kerensky, Crucifixion, p. 168

46 Witte, p. viii

47 Buchanan, Vol. I pp 224-225; A. J. P. Taylor, Mastery, pp. 540-541, Feiling, England, p. 1064; Philip Mansel, p. 374

48 David R. Jones in Kagan and Higham (editors), Tsarist Russia, p. 245

49 Ibid, p. 232. Between 1915 and 1918 the Turks massacred ethnic Armenians in the eastern provinces of the Ottoman Empire, while hundreds of thousands were expelled into the Syrian desert. Up to 1.5 million Turkish nationals of Armenian origin perished out of a population of 1.8 million.

50 Abraham, pp. 82-83

51 Ibid

52 Kerensky, Crucifixion, p. 223

53 Kerensky, Turning Point, pp. 134-135

12. The Great Retreat

1 Simion Goldin, 'Anti-Semitism and Pogroms in the Russian Military', 1914-1918 Online

2 Asprey, p. 173

3 Allan Mallinson, 'Welcome to hell — the Gallipoli campaign of 1915', The Times, 10 April 2015

4 Farmborough, p. 49

5 Ibid, p. 56

6 Knox, Vol. I, p. xxiii

7 Heffer, p. 198

8 Feiling, England, p. 1063

9 Lieven, p. 349

10 V. D. Nabokov, p. 108

11 Rutherford, p. 155

12 Clarkson, Russia, p. 507

13 Lieven, p. 348

14 Ibid, pp. 346-347

15 Kerensky, Crucifixion, p. 202

16 Kerensky, Turning Point, pp. 13813-9

17 Lockhart, Diaries, Vol. I, p. 24

18 Buchanan, Vol. II, p. 238

19 Kerensky, Turning Point, p. 160; Kerensky, Crucifixion, p. 153

20 Buchanan, Vol. I, p. 245

21 Solomon, p. 50

22 Witte, p. ix-x

23 Witte, p. 198

24 Buchanan, Volume I, p. x

25 Roger Pethybridge, 'Political Repercussions of the Supply Problem in the Russian Revolution of 1917', The Russian Review, Vol. 29, No. 4, October 1970; Knox, Vol. II, p. 388

26 Knox, Vol. II, pp.334, 388

27 Shulgin, pp. 80-81

28 Pares, p. 523

29 Andrew, Secret World, p. 503

30 Wilcox, Russia's Ruin, p. 191

31 Sukhanov, Revolution, p. 31

32 Wilcox, Russia's Ruin, p. 192

33 Abraham, p. 101

34 Ibid, pp. 105-106

35 'The King on Russian valour', The Times, 10 May 1916

36 'Russian guests in Parliament', The Times, 11 May 1916

37 Konstantin Nabokov, p. 53

38 Simon Sebag Montefiore, Romanovs, Kindle Edition.

39 On 5 June 1916 Lord Kitchener sailed for Russia to discuss coordination between the Western and Eastern Fronts. That evening, in heavy seas off Orkney, his ship, the cruiser HMS Hampshire, struck a German mine and sank with the loss of nearly all aboard, including Kitchener.

40 Paléologue, Memoirs, Vol, III, Ch. II.

41 Oleg Kerensky Jr, unpublished manuscript, Kerensky Family Papers

42 Alexander Watson, Ring of Steel, pp. 293-294

43 Jean Hugo, Le Regard de la Mémoire, pp. 68-69

44 Andrew, Secret History, p. 502; David R. Jones in Kagan and Higham (editors), Tsarist Russia, p. 228; Feiling, England, p. 1067

45 Robin Prior and Trevor Wilson, 'Haig, Douglas, first Earl Haig (1861–1928)', Oxford Dictionary of National Biography, 2011

46 Hindenburg, Out of My Life, p. 273

47 Washburn, Field Notes from the Russian Front, Vol. I, pp. 35-36

48 Cockfield, Jamie H., 'With Snow on their Boots'

49 Timothy Dowling, Brusilov Offensive, p. xv

50 Gert von Hindenburg, Soldier and Statesman, p. 69

51 Ludendorff, pp. 284, 293

52 Hoffmann, Vol. I., Kindle Edition

53 Ibid

13. The Flashes of Lightning

1 Jan Doets and André Birukoff, pp. 62-63

2 Kerensky, Turning Point, p. 148

3 Abraham, p. 108

4 Ibid, p. 107

5 Fitzgerald, Professor Ross, 'Comrade in Arms', Weekend Australian, 15-16 March 2003; Judith Armstrong ('Tritton, Lydia Ellen 'Nellé' 1899–1946)', Australian Dictionary of Biography, 2002

6 Kerensky, Catastrophe, p. 97

7 Kerensky, Turning Point, p. 170

8 The History of The Times, 1912-1920, 1952, p. 243

9 Lockhart, British Agent, p. 160

10 Douglas Smith, p. 565

11 Golder, Documents of Russian History 1914-1917

12 Sorokin, Long Journey, p. 98

13 Merridale, p. 43

14 Documents of Russian History 1914-1917

15 Shulgin, p. 82

16 Watson, Ring of Steel, pp. 451-452

17 Radzinsky, Nicholas II, p. 107

18 Massie, p. 345; Smith, Rasputin, p. 581

19 Clarkson, Russia, p. 367; Fernandez-Armesto (editor), People's of Europe, p. 337

20 Simon Sebag Montefiore, Romanovs, Kindle Edition.

21 Ibid

22 Douglas Smith, pp. 590-592

23 'Death of Rasputin, a sanctimonious adventurer', The Observer, 7 January 1917

24 Radzinsky, Nicholas II, p. 164

25 'The German Propaganda', New York Times, 16 March 1917

26 Figes, Tragedy, p. 289

27 Sorokin, Long Journey, p. 100

28 Babel recalled this incident for Soviet readers in a short story called 'Line and Colour' in which he demonstrated Kerensky's shortsightedness compared with Leon Trotsky's clear vision. Abraham, p. 117

29 Stevenson, Backs to the Wall, p. 19

30 Wilton, Agony, pp. 75, 104. Some historians doubt the existence Protopopov's machineguns. Wilton, however, is sure of his facts.

31 Feldman, Robert S. 'The Russian General Staff and the June 1917 Offensive', Soviet Studies, Vol. 19, No. 4. (1968), pp. 526–543

32 Michael Tillotson, 'The Little Father believed God had chosen him to rule', The Times, 22 February 2014

33 The History of The Times, 1912-1920, 1952, pp. 243-244

34 Lloyd George War Memoirs, Volume III, p. 1564

35 Owen, Lloyd George, p. 375; Keith Jeffery, p. 356

36 Keith Jeffery, 1916, p. 355

37 Wildman, Vol. II, pp. 4, 356

38 Ibid, p. 356

39 Konstantin Nabokov, p. 63

40 Lockhart, British Agent, p. 162; Andrew, HM Secret Service, p. 206

41 Kerensky, Catastrophe, p. 104; Kerensky, Crucifixion, p. 231; Massie, p. 377; Alden Whitman, 'Alexander Kerensky Dies Here at 89', New York Times, 12 June 1970. There are variations of this speech in all of these sources. The version given here draws from all of them.

14. The February Revolution

42 Abraham p. 123; Trotsky, Revolution, p. 59; New York Times, 5 May 1931

43 Simon Sebag Montefiore, Romanovs, Kindle Edition

1 Stevenson, 1917, p. 94; Figes, p. 308

2 Chambers, p. 129

3 Abraham, p. 123

4 Solzhenitsyn, March 1917, I, p. 10; Jonathan Miles, pp. 354-355; Engelstein, p. 105

5 Stevenson, 1917, p. 93; Solzhenitsyn, March 1917, I, p. 132

6 Golder, Passages, p. 34

7 Shulgin, p. 105

8 Buchanan, Mission, Vol. II, pp. 53-54

9 Stevenson, 1917, p. 91

10 Buchanan, Mission, Vol. II, p. 61

11 Buchanan, Mission, Vol. II, p. 58. As Buchanan was on holiday in Finland on 24 February and didn't return to Petrograd until 25 February, he must have been repeating the words of one of his aides.

12 Engelstein, p. 106

13 Ibid, p. 107

14 Sukhanov, p. 16

15 Engelstein, pp. 107-108

16 Semion Lyandres, Tsarism, p 118; Sukhanov, p. 28

17 Robert Wilton, 'The Outbreak of the Revolution', The Times, 21 March, 1917

18 Wilton, Agony, p. 115; Jonathan Miles, pp. 355-356

19 Figes, Tragedy, p. 312

20 Ibid, pp. 313-314

21 Browder and Kerensky, Vol. I, p. 36

22 Hasegawa, February Revolution, p. 271

23 Browder and Kerensky, Vol. I, p. 22

24 Michael's love for a commoner, Natasha Wulfert, the twice-divorced wife of a brother officer, had made him the black sheep of the Imperial Family. Having promised the Tsar that he would keep Natasha as his

mistress, they were married in Vienna and remained abroad in self-imposed exile until the outbreak of war when Nicholas consented to their return. Misha's service with the Savage Division of Caucasian troops redeemed him somewhat in Nicholas's eyes and Natasha, although still persona non grata at court, was now addressed as Countess Brasova.

25 Hasegawa, February Revolution, p. 274
26 Kerensky, Catastrophe, p. 6
27 Ibid, p. 1
28 Shulgin, p. 107
29 Kerensky, Catastrophe, p. 51
30 Sukhanov, p. 21
31 H. G. Wells, Russia in the Shadows, p. 59
32 Hasegawa, February Revolution, p. 280
33 'Revolution in Russia', New York Times, 16 March 1917
34 Sorokin, Long Journey, p. 107
35 Kerensky, Catastrophe, p. 9
36 Sukhanov, p. 35
37 Solzhenitsyn, March 1917, I, p. 334
38 Buchanan, Vol. II, p. 63
39 Ibid, p. 12
40 Hasegawa in Acton and Cherniaev, Critical Companion, p. 55
41 Hsegawa, February Revolution, p. 302
42 Chamberlin, Vol. I, p. 73
43 Semion Lyandres, Tsarism, p. 74. Ensign Medvedev was taken to hospital but his hand had to be amputated. Hasegawa (February Revolution, p. 365) said this incident happened at the gates of the Tauride Palace after one of the Palace guards shot a soldier.
44 Shulgin, p. 118; Hasegawa, February Revolution, p. 366
45 Olga Kerenskaya 1935 memoirs
46 Hasegawa, February Revolution, p. 327
47 Shulgin, pp. 114, 117, 120
48 Ibid, p. 119
49 Hasegawa, February Revolution, p. 368; Semion Lyandres, Tsarism, p. 227

15. The End of Tsarism

1 Solzhenitsyn, March 1917, I, p. 515
2 Hasekawa, February Revolution, p. 301
3 Semion Lyandres, Tsarism, p. 147
4 Semion Lyandres, Tsarism, p. 147, p. 109. According to the Duma Committee's archival record, Savich and Dmitriukov told Michael that 'the course of events' demanded the abdication of Nicholas, with the Grand Duke serving as Regent to the Tsarevich. Such a suggeston would have received the same response: that Michael would have to consult his brother.
5 Browder and Kerensky, p.
6 Chamberlin, Vol. I, p. 81
7 Browder and Kerensky, Vol. I, pp. 87-88
8 Semion Lyandres, Tsarism, p. 148.
9 Simon Sebag Montefiore, Romanovs, Kindle Edition
10 Browder and Kerensky, Vol. I, p. 43
11 Abraham, p. 135; Hasegawa, p. 402
12 Ibid, p. 62
13 Semion Lyandres, Tsarism, p. 267, p.121
14 Semion Lyandres, Tsarism, p. 130
15 Figes, Tragedy, p. 328
16 Solzhenitsyn, March 1917, II, p. 196; Kerensky, Catastrophe, p. 38
17 Morrison, p. 206; Kerensky, Catastrophe, pp. 64-65
18 Figes, Tragedy, pp. 330-331
19 Semion Lyandres, Tsarism, p. 97
20 Sukhanov, p. 117; Figes, Tragedy, p. 334
21 Semion Lyandres, Tsarism p. 231
22 Boris Elkin, The Kerensky Government and its Fate, Slavic Review, Vol. 23, No. 4, December 1964, p. 720
23 Engelstein, p. 129
24 V. D. Nabokov, p. 45
25 Engelstein, p. 128
26 Knox, Vol. II, p. 576
27 Browder and Kerensky, Vol. I, p. 108

28 Kerensky, Catastrophe, p. 66

29 Browder and Kerensky, Vol. I, p. 108

30 Chamberlin, Vol, I, p. 95

31 V. D. Nabokov, p. 50

32 Ibid, p. 18

33 Sorokin, Long Journey, p. 112

34 Browder and Kerensky, Vol. I, p. 196

35 Sorokin, Russian Diary, p. 22

36 V. D. Nabokov, pp. 126-127; Sorokin, Russian Diary, pp. 35-36

37 Sorokin, Russian Diary, p. 35

38 Solzhenitsyn, Millstones, p. 226

39 Browder and Kerensky, Vol. III, p. 1323

40 Harold Williams, Daily Chronicle, 21 March 1917

41 Browder and Kerensky, Vol. I, p. 177

42 Simon Sebag Montefiore, Romanovs, Kindle Edition.

16. The Return of the Exiles

1 Boris I. Kolonitskii, 'Kerensky' in Acton, Cherniaev, Rosenberg (editors), Critical Companion, p. 143

2 Abraham, p. 157

3 Ibid, p. 148

4 Konstantin Nabokov, pp. 102, 107

5 Kerensky, Catastrophe, p. 235; Michael Hughes, 'The Legacy of Alexander Kerensky', The Independent, 6 November 2017

6 Konstantin Nabokov, p. 103

7 'Protest against Russian peace plan', New York Times, 2 December 1917; Abraham, p. 353; Solomon, p. 137

8 Konstantin Nabokov, p. 103

9 Gavronsky in a letter introducing himself to C. W. Bowerman, MP for Deptford and Secretary of the Parliamentary Committee of the Trades Union Congress, 12 January 1918

10 Service, Lenin, p. 256

11 Merridale, p. 62; Andrew, Secret World, p. 544

12 Service, Trotsky, p. 156

13 https://www.marxists.org/archive/lenin/works/1917/lfafar/first.htm
14 Browder and Kerensky, Vol. II, p. 1077-1078
15 Ibid, Vol. II., pp. 1044-1045 (Press interview with Miliukov, Rech' (The Speech), 23 March 1917)
16 V. D. Nobokov, p. 106
17 Browder and Kerensky, Vol. II, pp. 1045-1046
18 Figes, Tragedy, p. 381; Browder and Kerensky, Vol. III, p. 1196
19 Lockhart, Diaries 1915-1938. p. 273
20 Spence, Savinkov, p. 118
21 Paul Benckendorff, Last Days at Tsarskoe Selo, Part II
22 Ibid
23 Kerensky Turning Point, pp. 329-330
24 Radzinsky, Nicholas II, p. 198
25 Sorokin, Long Journey, p. 116
26 Deutscher, p. 247
27 Buchanan, Vol. II, p. 120
28 I. Deutscher, p. 247
29 Kerensky, Turning Point, p. 218
30 Browder and Kerensky, Vol. III, p. 1305
31 V. D. Nabokov, p. 57
32 Ibid, p. 75-76
33 Nabokov, Think, Write, Speak, p. 351
34 Ibid; Field, p. 182
35 Pitcher, Harvey, Witnesses Of The Russian Revolution, Random House, Kindle Edition
36 Buchanan, Vol. II, p. 132
37 Christopher Andrew, Secret World, p. 545
38 Service, Lenin, pp. 31-32; Gina Kolata, Evidence of Dr Harry Vinters, Professor of Neurology and Neuropathology at the University of California in 'Lenin's stroke', New York Times, 7 May 2012
39 Merridale, p. 149
40 Ted Widmer, 'Lenin and the Spark', New Yorker, 20 April 2017

41 Grigory Zinoviev in a speech to the Petrograd Soviet on 6 September 1918, reproduced in a pamphlet, 'Nicholai Lenin: His Life and Work'. Philipp Heinrich Scheidemann (26 July 1865 – 29 November 1939) was a German Social Democrat who, in the midst of the German Revolution of 1918-1919, proclaimed Germany a republic.

42 Stevenson, 1914-1918, p. 350

43 Kerensky, Catastrophe, p. 229; Alden Whitman, 'Kerensky, recalling own role, detects greater freedom', New York Times, 13 March 1967; 'Alexander Kerensky looks back', The Argus, 10 November 1956

44 Kerensky, Catastrophe, p. 229; Chamberlin, Vol. I, p. 117

45 Kotkin, p. 191

46 Trotsky, Revolution, p. 398

47 Golder, Passages, p. 75

48 Dido Davies, p. 60-61

49 'Money from Moscow: A Story of Lenin', The Times, 3 December 1925

50 Richard Garnett, p. 299

51 Konstantin Nabokov, pp. 102, 107

52 Sorokin, Russian Diary, pp. 49-50

53 Ruthchild, Equality and Revolution, Kindle Edition.

54 Ibid

55 Kerensky, Crucifixion, p. 264

56 Stone, Eastern Front, p. 282

57 Lockhart, British Agent, p. 176

58 Lockhart, British Agent, p. 177

59 Philips Price, Reminiscences, p. 21

60 Lockhart, British Agent, p. 184

61 Browder and Kerensky, Vol. II, p. 1098

62 Figes, Tragedy, p. 112; Engelstein, p. 141

63 Lockhart, British Agent, p. 227

64 Trotsky, Revolution, pp. 133-134

65 Service, Trotsky, p. 172

17. The Poison Chalice

1 Browder and Kerensky, Vol. III, pp. 1196-1197

2 Ibid, pp. 1267-1268

3 Figes, Tragedy, p. 383. The other Soviet members were Viktor Chernov (Agriculture), Matvei Skobelev (Labour), Tsereteli (Posts and Telegraphs) and Alexei Peshekhonov (Food).

4 Kerensky, Catastrophe, p. 184

5 Robin Prior and Trevor Wilson, 'Haig, Douglas, first Earl Haig (1861–1928)', Oxford Dictionary of National Biography, 2011

6 Kerensky, Turning Point, p. 254

7 Ibid, p. 255

8 Andrew, The Secret World, p. 550

9 Kerensky, Turning Point, p. 257

10 Knox, Vol. II, p. 617

11 Abraham, p. 196; Browder and Kerensky, Vol. II, p. 880; Allan Wildman in Acton, Cherniaev, Rosenberg (editors), Critical Companion, pp. 73-74

12 Spence, p. 52

13 Browder and Kerensky, Vol. II, p. 933

14 Ibid, p. 932

15 Buchanan, Vol. II, p.112; Stevenson, 1917, p. 162

16 Ibid

17 Kerensky, Turning Point, p. 277; Abraham p. 197

18 Ibid, p. 198

19 Holger H. Herwig, p. 325

20 Knox, Vol. II, p. 628

21 Farmborough, p. 269

22 Ibid, p. 270

23 London *Daily Telegraph*, 25 June 1917

24 Browder and Kerensky, Vol. II, p. 939

25 Figes, Tragedy, pp. 379-380

26 Wrigley, Chris, 'Arthur Henderson (1863-1935)', Oxford Dictionary of National Biography, 23 September 2004

27 Ward Rutherford, pp. 268-269

28 McMeekin, p. 150; Stevenson, 1917, pp, 162-163

29 Farmborough, p. 270

30 Sukhanov, Revolution, p. 380

31 Browder and Kerensky, Vol. III, p. 1305-1306

32 Kerensky Family Papers, Cadbury Research Library, MS126/1/2/6

33 Browder and Kerensky, Vol. III, p. 1305-1306

34 Golder, p. 371

35 Figes, Tragedy, pp. 418-19; Knox, Vol. II, p. 641

36 Kerensky, Catastrophe, p. 221. One of the main factors contributing to the Russian defeat in the June offensive was the poor quality of the guns supplied by the Allies. There was little consolation in Lloyd George's postwar ruminations. 'We could not perceive the approaching catastrophe in Russia and therefore did not take measures to avert it,' he wrote in his memoirs. 'One third of the Somme guns and ammunition transferred in time to the banks of another river, the Dnieper, would have won a great victory for Russia and deferred the Revolution until after the war.' The Dnieper rises near Smolensk and flows through Russia, Belarus and Ukraine to the Black Sea. It was nowhere near the frontline in June/July 1917.

37 Wildman, Vol. II, pp. 89-90; David R. Stone, p. 288; Holger H. Herwig, p. 325

38 Kerensky, Turning Point, p. 284-286; Abraham, p. 217

39 Wildman, Vol. II, p. 91

40 Farmborough, p. 274; Hoffmann, Vol. I, Kindle Edition

41 Wildman, Vol. II, p. 91

42 Stevenson, 1914-1918, p. 325

43 Sorokin, Russian Diary, p. 55; 'Agitators arrested', The Guardian, 4 July 1917

44 Kerensky, Turning Point, p. 285

45 Wildman, Vol. II, pp. 105-106

46 Ibid, p. 106

47 Abraham, p. 217

48 Hoffmann, Vol. I, Kindle Edition; Stevenson, 1917, p. 165

49 Lockhart, British Agent, pp. 177-179

50 Engelstein, p. 153

51 Ibid, p. 422

52 Figes, Tragedy, p. 423

53 Rabinovitch, Bolsheviks, Kindle Edition

54 Service, Lenin, p. 283; Katkov, Kornilov, p. 32

18. The Bolshevik Rising

1 McMeekin, p. 163; Abraham, p. 219
2 Figes, Tragedy, p. 421
3 Stevenson 1917 p. 149
4 Chamberlin, Vol. I, pp. 170-171; Figes, pp. 424-425; Knox, Vol. II, p. 655
5 Browder and Kerensky, Vol. III, p. 1335
6 Rabinowitch, Bolsheviks, Kindle Edition
7 Sorokin, Russian Journal, p. 61; Figes, Tragedy, p. 424
8 Kerensky, Catastrophe, p. 237
9 Figes, Tragedy, p. 425
10 Sorokin, Long Journey, p. 129
11 Golder, Passages, p. 80; Golder, Documents, pp. 445-446; Buchanan, Vol. II, p. 153; Katkov, Kornilov, p. 33
12 Browder and Kerensky, Vol. III, p. 1347
13 Laura Engelstein, p. 155
14 Browder and Kerensky, Vol. III, p. 1378
15 Figes, Tragedy, p. 427; Buchanan, Vol. II, pp. 153-154
16 Rabinowitch, Bolsheviks, Kindle Edition; Figes, Tragedy, p. 428
17 Sorokin, Long Journey, p. 130; Figes, Tragedy, p. 429
18 Rabinowitch, Bolsheviks, Kindle Edition
19 Sorokin, Long Journey, pp. 130-131
20 Rabinowitch, Bolsheviks, Kindle Edition
21 Browder and Kerensky, Vol. III, p. 1365
22 Rabinowitch, Bolsheviks, Kindle Edition
23 Kerensky, Turning Point, pp. 291-293
24 Kerensky, Catastrophe, pp. 241-242
25 Browder and Kerensky, Vol. III, pp. 1388-1389; Abraham, p. 225
26 Spence, Savinkov, pp. 121-122
27 Kerensky, Turning Point, pp. 291-293
28 Wildman, Vol. II, p. 108
29 Ibid
30 Wildman, Vol. II, p. 117; Figes, Tragedy, p. 419; Stevenson, 1917, p. 166; Browder and Kerensky, Vol. III, pp. 1674, 1678

31 Wildman, Allan Wildman in Acton, Cherniaev, Rosenberg (eds), Critical Companion, p. 74; Browder and Kerensky, Vol. II, pp. 967-968

32 Hoffmann, Vol. I, Kindle Edition; Watson, Ring of Steel, pp. 446-447; J. M. Roberts, p. 304

33 'M. Kerensky's heavy task', The Times, 9 August, 2017

34 Abraham, pp. 232-233

35 Spence, Savinkov, p. 127

36 Ibid

37 John Reed, 'Red Russia – Kerensky', *The Liberator,* Vol. 1, No. 2, April, 1918.

38 Author's interview with Stephen Kerensky, 28 December 2019

39 'Kerensky's health causes worry', New York Times, 8 August 1917

40 Kerensky, Catastrophe, pp. 306-307

41 Buchanan, Vol. II, p. 164

42 Bruce Lockhart, British Agent, p. 177

43 Knox, Vol. II, p. 674; Kerensky, Prelude, p. 57

44 Abraham, p. 240; Chamberlin, Revolution, Vol. I, p. 187

45 Rappaport, Romanovs, p. 122

46 Simon Sebag Montefiore, Romanovs, Kindle Edition

47 John Reed, Ten Days, p. 55

48 Trotsky, Revolution, pp. 583-584

49 Sorokin, Russian Diary, p. 76

50 V. D. Nabokov, p. 81

51 'Savinkov, Kerensky and Breshkovskaya, typescript, Soskice Papers, DS/2/1, Box 8, House of Lords Record Office

52 Buchanan, Vol. II, p. 216

53 Abraham, p. 250

54 General Lukomsky's Memoirs of the Russian Revolution quoted in Kerensky, Turning Point, pp. 367-368

55 Ibid, p. 251

56 Spence, Savinkov, p. 128; Abraham, p. 251

57 Figes, Tragedy, p. 446; Abraham, p. 254

58 Moynahan, Comrades, p. 230; Figes, Tragedy, p. 446

59 Figes, Tragedy, p. 445

60 Abraham, p. 255

61 Ibid

62 Sorokin, Russian Diary, pp. 78-79

63 Browder and Kerensky, Vol. II, p. 1456; Sukhanov, p. 494

19. The Kornilov Revolt

1 Philips Price, Reminiscences, p.70

2 Kerensky, Catastrophe, p. 281

3 Philips Price, Reminiscences, p. 71

4 Pitcher, Witnesses, Kindle Edition

5 Katkov, Kornilov, p. 60

6 Kerensky, Catastrophe, p. 315

7 Philips Price, Reminiscences, p. 73

8 Figes, Tragedy, p. 448

9 Buchanan, Vol. II, p. 171

10 Figes, Tragedy, p. 445; McGeekin, Revolution, p. 184

11 Abraham, p. 264

12 Katkov, Kornilov, pp. 61-62; Kerensky, Prelude, p. 13; Abraham, p. 265

13 Abraham, p. 265

14 Rabinowitch, Bolsheviks, Kindle Edition

15 Jorn Leonhard, p. 559; Katkov, Kornilov, p. 32

16 Kerensky, Prelude, p. 180

17 V. D. Nabokov, p. 90

18 Ibid, pp. 91-92; Moynahan, Comrades, p. 234

19 Kerensky, Prelude, pp. 158-159

20 Ibid, p. 159; Kerensky, Turning Point, p. 342-343. It was forty-eight years after the event that Kerensky added this quote to his recollections of the Kornilov Revolt.

21 Kerensky, Prelude, p. 160

22 Abraham, p. 267

23 Buchanan, Vol. II, pp. 175-176

24 Knox, Vol. II., p. 678

25 Figes, Tragedy, p. 449. Quoting General Lukomsky, George Katkov (pp. 79-80) says that Dobrinsky and Aladin accompanied Lvov to Mogilev and were present at some, though not all, of the talks with Kornilov, as were Zavoiko and Filonenko; Michael Tillotson, 'Turning point in revolutionary Russia', The Times, 29 July 2017

26 Kerensky, Turning Point, p. 345

27 Kerensky, Prelude, p. 166

28 Ibid, pp. 166-167

29 Kerensky, Prelude, p. 168; Kerensky, Turning Point, pp. 347-348, Abraham, pp. 272-273. Kerensky says the tape of the Kornilov conversation is preserved in the Archives in Moscow. Transcripts published in The Prelude to Bolshevism, Russia and History's Turning Point, and Richard Abraham's biography all vary to some extent.

30 Spence, p. 141; Browder and Kerensky, Vol. III, pp. 1554-1555

31 Michael Tillotson, 'Turning point in revolutionary Russia', The Times, 29 July 2017

32 Spence, p. 143

33 Allan Wildman in Acton, Cherniaev, Rosenberg (editors), Critical Companion, p. 76; Katkov, p. 78

34 Stevenson, 1914-1918, p. 352; Michael Tillotson, 'Turning point in revolutionary Russia', The Times, 29 July 2017

35 Kerensky, Prelude, p. 131; Alden Whitman, 'Alexander Kerensky Dies Here at 89', New York Times, 12 June 1970; Figes, p. 453

36 Lord Riddell, Lord Riddell's War Diary, London, 1933, entry for 14 September 1917, p. 272

37 Kerensky, Turning Point, p. 23

38 Semion Lyandres, Tsarism, p. 144

39 Browder and Kerensky, Vol. III, pp. 1659-1661

40 Lockhart, British Agent, p. 192

41 Selina Hastings, Maugham, pp. 222-228; Andrew, Secret World, p. 549

42 Ibid

43 Ibid

44 Browder and Kerensky, Vol. III, p. 1729

45 Trotsky, Revolution, p. 577; Sukhanov, Revolution, p. 528

46 Browder and Kerensky, Vol. III., p. 1626

47 Service, Lenin, p. 303; Sukhanov, Revolution, p. 556; Service, Trotsky, p. 183

48 Engelstein, p. 175; Stevenson, 1914-1918; p. 382; McMeekin, p. 203

49 Kerensky, Catastrophe, p. viii

20. The October Coup

1 John Reed, 'Red Russia – Kerensky', The Liberator, Vol. 1, No. 2, April, 1918

2 Ibid

3 Ibid. On page 60 of his book, Ten Days that Shook the World, published in 1919, John Reed tailored this quote to make it appear 'prophetic'. He quotes Kerensky as saying, 'The Russian people are suffering from economic fatigue and from disillusionment with the Allies. The world thinks the Russian Revolution is at an end. Do not be mistaken. The Russian Revolution is just beginning.'

4 Cathy Porter, Kollontai, p. 254

5 V. D. Nabokov, p. 156

6 Kerensky, Prelude, pp. 22-23

7 'Kerensky', Maryborough Chronicle, Maryborough, Queensland, 15 March 1918

8 Alexander Rabinowitch, 'The October Revolution' in Acton, Cherniaev, Rosenberg (editors), Critical Companion, p. 88

9 Boris Elkin, 'The Kerensky Government and its Fate', Slavic Review, Vol. 23, No. 4, December 1964, pp. 717-736

10 Selina Hastings, Maugham, p. 232; Andrew, Secret World, p 552

11 Sukhanov, Revolution, p. 558

12 Rabinowitch, Bolsheviks, Kindle Edition

13 Abraham, p. 314; Chamberlin, Vol. I, p. 308

14 Rabinowitch, Bolsheviks, Kindle Edition

15 David Soskice, 'The Last of the Kerensky Government', The Guardian, 27 December 1917

16 Abraham, p. 315; Engelstein, p. 181

17 Kerensky, Turning Point, p. 435; Abraham, p. 316; Kerensky, Catastrophe', p. 327

18 Figes, p. 483

19 Ibid pp. 483-484; Engelstein, p. 175; Stevenson, 1914-1918, p. 382

20 Figes, Tragedy, p.p. 481-482

21 Kerensky, Catastrophe, p. 331

22 David Soskice, 'The Last of the Kerensky Government', The Guardian, 27 December 1917; Stevenson, 1914-1918, p. 382

23 Jonathan Miles, p. 362; Kerensky, p. 437

24 David Soskice, 'The Last of the Kerensky Government', The Guardian, 27 December 1917

25 Rabinowitch, Bolsheviks, Kindle Edition; Kerensky, Turning Point, p. 438

26 V. D. Nabokov, p. 159

27 Service, p. 311; Engelstein, p. 183

28 David Soskice, 'The Last of the Kerensky Government', The Guardian, 27 December 1917

29 Knox Vol. II, p. 709

30 Reed, Ten Days, pp. 92-93

31 Chamberlin, Vol. I, p. 316

32 Rabinowitch, Kindle Edition

33 McMeekin, p. 208

34 Olga Kerensky's 1935 memoirs

35 Engelstein, p. 185

36 Ibid, pp. 185-186

37 Ibid, pp. 184-185; Alexander Rabinowitch, 'The October Revolution' in Acton, Cherniaev, Rosenberg (editors), Critical Companion, p. 90

38 Kerensky, Catastrophe, pp. 339-340; Abraham, pp. 318-319; McMeekin, p. 205

39 Trotsky, Revolution, pp. 815-816; Engelstein, p. 187; Chamberlin, Vol. I, p. 319

40 Sorokin, Russian Diary, p. 103

41 Engelstein, p. 190

42 Chamberlin, Vol. I, pp. 335-336

43 Engelstein, pp. 190-191

44 Figes, pp. 536-537

45 Chamberlin, Vol. I. p. 327

46 Kerensky, Catastrophe, p. 345

47 Abraham, p. 321

48 Kerensky, Catastrophe, p. 349

49 Spence, p. 164

50 Chamberlin, Vol. I, p. 328

51 Ibid

52 Engelstein, p. 190

53 Chamberlin, Vol. I, p. 331

54 Rabinowitch, Kindle Edition

55 Kerensky, Catastrophe, p. 362

56 Ibid, p. 366

57 Kerensky, Turning Point, p. 448

58 McMeekin, pp. 211, 216

59 'Looks for civil war', New York Times, 22 November 1917

60 Sir George Macartney, 'Bolshevism as I saw it at Tashkent in 1918', Journal of the Central Asian Society, 25 February 2011

61 Engelstein, pp. 195-196

62 Andrew, Secret Service, p. 211, p. 552; Lockhart, Two Revolutions, p. 92

63 Lockhart, British Agent, p. 172

64 Chamberlin, Vol. I, p. 318; Mawdsley, p. 4

21. The Death of Freedom

1 Merridale, p. 88

2 V. D. Nabokov, p. 172

3 Browder and Kerensky, Vol. I, p. 455; Ruthchild, Equality, Kindle Edition; Sorokin, Russian Diary, p. 108

4 Sheila Fitzpatrick, Revolution, pp. 67-68; Sebestyen, Lenin, p. 380

5 V. D. Nabokov, pp. 173-174

6 Figes, p. 508; Sorokin, Russian Diary, p. 109

7 Nikolai N. Smirnov, 'The Constituent Assembly' in Acton, Cherniaev, Rosenberg (editors), Critical Companion, p. pp. 328-329

8 Jonathan Daly, p. 83

9 Watson, Ring of Steel, p. 492; Michael Tillotson, 'Hubris and humiliation at Brest-Litovsk', The Times, 30 December 2017

10 Watson, Ring of Steel, p. 492; Strohn, 1918, p. 164
11 Andrew, Secret Service, p. 212
12 Lockhart, Special Agent, pp. 202-203
13 Ibid
14 Adele Lindenmeyr, 'The First Soviet Political Trial: Countess Sofia Panina before the Petrograd Revolutionary Tribunal', Russian Review, 60: 505–525
15 Jonathan Daly, pp. 83-84
16 Engelstein, p. 204
17 Kerensky, Turning Point, p. 465
18 Abraham, p. 333; Engelstein, p. 208; Service, Lenin, p. 336
19 Kerensky, Turning Point, p. 466
20 Ibid, pp. 466-468
21 Ibid, p. 467
22 'Kerensky', Maryborough Chronicle, Maryborough, Queensland, 15 March 1918
23 Engelstein, p. 208
24 Karl E. Meyer, 'Who killed Russian democracy?', New York Times, 6 July 1989
25 Ruthchild, Equality and Revolution, Kindle Edition
26 'Lenine (sic) dissolves Russian assembly', New York Times, 21 January 1918
27 Chamberlin, Vol. I, p. 369; Engelstein, p. 210; Smirnov, p. 331; Volkogonov, p. 177
28 Ibid
29 Figes, p. 516
30 Smirnov p. 331
31 Volkogonov, p. 177
32 Kerensky, Crucifixion, p. 349
33 Volkogonov, p. 177
34 Kerensky, Turning Point, p. 469
35 Kerensky, Crucifixion, p. 348
36 'Memoirs of Chaliapin', The Times, 11 October 1932
37 Sebestyen, Lenin, p. 384

38 Abraham, p. 442.

39 Kerensky, Turning Point, p. 473

40 Figes, Tragedy, p. 528; Brown, Godless Utopia, pp. 50-51

41 Trotsky, Revolution, p. 898

42 Applebaum, Red Famine, p. 25

43 Hoffmann, Vol. I, Kindle Edition

44 Lockhart, British Agent, pp. 226-227

45 Westwood, pp. 254-254

46 Richard Holmes (editor), Military History, p. 792; Gleb Kerensky, Only One Freedom, unpublished manuscript, p. 121

47 Mawdsley, p. 22

48 Jan Doets and André Birukoff, p, 78

49 J. M. Roberts, p. 308; Asprey, p. 360; Jonathan Daly, p. 85

22. The Lubianka Prisoners

1 Andrew, Secret World, p. 556; Kerensky, Turning Point, p. 474

2 Kerensky, Turning Point, p. 475

3 Sorokin, Long Journey, p. 150; Russian Diary, p. 143

4 Robin Prior and Trevor Wilson, 'Haig, Douglas, first Earl Haig (1861–1928)', Oxford Dictionary of National Biography, 2011; Hindenburg, Out of My Life, p. 336

5 Feiling, England, p. 1071

6 Allan Mallinson, 'First World War: How the 'crisis of the war' put the Allies in sight of victory', The Times 27 April 2018; Strohn, 1918, p. 56

7 Douglas Haig: War Diaries and Letters 1914-1918, Edited by Gary Sheffield and John Bourne, Weidenfeld and Nicolson, London, 2005, p. 499

8 Kerensky, Prelude, p. 23

9 Mawdsley, Civil War, p. 29

10 Abraham, p. 337

11 Kerensky, Turning Point, p. 476

12 Kerensky later explained his mission in these terms: 'I came here to beg the Allies to intervene. I thought they were going to help democratic Russia to continue the common fight against Germany on Russian territory. That was how I formulated the proposal to the British Government and to British public opinion. That is how all democratic and liberal

opinion in Russia, as represented by the Union for the Regeneration of Russia, understood and accepted intervention.' ('The Allies and Russia', Daily News, London, 30 November 1918)

13 Kerensky, Turning Point, p. 480

14 The Secret Intelligence Service had a variety of names in the Twentieth Century including the 'Foreign Intelligence Service', the 'Secret Service', and 'MI1(c)', which was part of the War Office. Around 1920 the Service adopted the title of the Secret Intelligence Service (SIS) and has continued to use it ever since. The 'MI6' abbreviation came in at the start of the Second World War and was used whenever an organisational link needed to be made with MI5 (the Security Service). 'MI6' fell into disuse officially years ago but many writers and journalists continue to use it to describe SIS.

15 British National Archives, KV 2/659

16 Jonathan Daly, p. 85; Challinger, Arkhangel, Kindle Edition

17 Mawdsley, p. 64; Engelstein, p. 395

18 British National Archives, KV 2/658

19 Kerensky, Turning Point, p. 484

20 Sorokin, Russian Diary, p. 144

21 Ibid, p. 233

23. The Entente Outsider

1 Kerensky, Turning Point, p. 485

2 Ibid, p. 489; Baxter, p. 278

3 Konstantin Nabokov, p. 250

4 Turner, p. 55; Sir George Riddell's diary entry for 29 June 1918 quoted in Ullman, p. 209

5 Turner, pp. 76-77

6 Ullman, p. 208; Egremont, p. 301; Abraham, p. 339

7 Lockhart, British Agent, p. 231

8 Kerensky, Turning Point, p. 491

9 Lloyd George, War Memoirs, Vol. VI, p. 3186

10 Ibid

11 Turner, pp. 76-77

12 Lloyd George, War Memoirs, Vol. VI, p. 3186

13 Kerensky, Turning Point, p. 492

14 Author's interview with Stephen Kerensky, 28 December 2019

15 'The Labour Conference', The Times, 27 June 1918

16 Abraham, p. 340

17 'The Fate of Russia', The Times, 28 June 1918

18 Abraham, p. 493-4; Painlevé was referring only to the French section of the Western Front. Field Marshal Sir Douglas Haig lost 275,000 British and Dominion troops in the Third Battle of Ypres – 'Passchendaele' – from 31 July to 6 November 1917.

19 Harold Williams, 'Kerensky, the man who tried to save Russia', the Daily Chronicle, 27 June 1918

20 British National Archives, KV 2/658

21 Quoted in 'Kerensky's Paris visit', Daily Chronicle, 1 July 1918

22 'The safety of Paris', The Times, 20 June 1918

23 Kerensky, Turning Point, p. 499

24 Supreme War Council minutes quoted in Ullman, p. 212

25 Ullman, p. 209; J. H. F. McEwen revised by Ian Nish, 'Lindley, Sir Francis Oswald', Oxford Dictionary of Biography, 2004

26 'Kerensky reveals protest on treaty', New York Times, 6 July 1918

27 Meriwether, p. 294

28 Lee Meriwether's subsequent comments on Kerensky went some way to righting the balance: 'I indulge in these personal remarks because, whatever Kerensky's merits or demerits, whether his downfall resulted from weakness, or from circumstances too overwhelming for even the strongest men to withstand, for a brief period he played a great part in one of the world's greatest upheavals… And so, whatever Fate may do to Kerensky in the future, he will always have a page in the histories of the next thousand years.'

29 Kerensky, Turning Point, p. 496

30 Thompson and Macklin, Morrison of China, p. 205 passim

31 'Le banquet Branting-Kerensky', Le Temps, 11 July 1918

32 Kerensky, Turning Point, p. 497

33 Ibid

34 Louise Bryant, Six Months in Red Russia, p. 113

35 Hammond, p. 76, p. 245

36 Trevor Wilson, 'Scott, Charles Prestwich (1846–1932)', Oxford Dictionary of National Biography, Oxford University Press, 2004; Kerensky, Turning Point, pp. 521-522

37 Kerensky, Turning Point, p. 522

38 Kerensky, Crucifixion, p. 301

24. The Dragon's Teeth

1 Gleb Kerensky, Only One Freedom, unpublished manuscript, p. 119-120

2 Richard B. Spence, 'Sidney George Reilly (1874-1925)', Oxford Dictionary of National Biography, 23 September 2004; Andrew, HM Secret Service, p. 214

3 Lockhart, Robin Bruce, Reilly, pp. 86-87

4 Spence, Savinkov, p. 197

5 Jonathan Daly, p. 87

6 Andrew, Secret World, p. 557

7 Figes, Tragedy, p. 634

8 Ibid

9 Laura Engelstein, p. 268

10 Lockhart, Secret Agent, p. 303; Laura Engelstein, pp. 268-269

11 Challinger, Arkhangel, Kindle Edition; Lockhart, Giants, p. 148

12 McLellan (editor), Karl Marx, p. 272

13 Peter Ryan, Lenin's Terror, p. 2

14 Walter Duranty, 'Soviet's version of Czar's killing', New York Times, 15 July 1923

15 Salway, pp. 62-63

16 Strohn, 1918, p. 30

17 Volkogonov, p. 220; Martin Sixsmith in Historically Inevitable?, pp. 179-184

18 Chamberlin, Vol. II, p. 70

19 Solzhenitsyn, Gulag Archipelago, p. 21

20 Roland Chambers, Ransome, pp. 197-198

21 'In memory of Captain Cromie', The Times, 29 August 1924

22 'The Bolshevist murder', The Times 5 September 1918

23 Chambers, p. 265

24 Abraham, p. 342

25 Mark Honigsbaum, 'A hundred years on, the killer Spanish flu still stalks us', The Observer, 9 September 2018

26 Keegan, First World War, p. 442

27 Read and Fisher, p. 161

28 Christopher Clark, Iron Kingdom, p. 613

29 Schabas, William A., The Trial of the Kaiser, Oxford University Press, Oxford, 2018, p. 24; Waite, p. 223

30 Plowright, p. 6

31 'German soldiers', The Times, 23 November 1918

32 National Archives, KV 2/658

33 Mawdsley, pp. 177-178

34 MacMillan, Paris 1919, p. 71; Ullman, p. 285

35 Egremont, p. 305

36 Peter Hopkirk, Lenin's Dream, Kindle Edition

37 Ibid, Abraham, p. 343. Kerensky never revealed when he learnt of his brother's death and he remained mute about the fate his sisters, Elena (Lyolya), Anna (Nyeta) and Nadezhda (Nadya). Elena died in the Gulag in 1937 or 1938, Nadezhda, an architect, died in Tashkent in 1910, and Anna, a musician who married and divorced a member of the Russian diplomatic service, died in exile in Yugoslavia in 1946.

25. The Suspicious Alien

1 Jan Doets and André Birukoff, p. 106

2 Abraham, pp. 343-4

3 Cronin, Paris, pp. 6-7

4 Williams, Beaverbrook, p. 224

5 MacMillan, Paris, 1919, pp. 63-64

6 Abraham, pp. 343, 345

7 Churchill, Contemporaries, p. 125. In London in December 1922 Savinkov spun Churchill a cock-and-bull story that he had been invited back to Russia to join a new Soviet government. Churchill was so impressed he escorted him to see Lloyd George. Sir Eyre Crowe described Savinkov as 'most unreliable and crooked' but Lloyd George thought him 'a man of action and great determination' and 'the only anti-Bolshevist he

had met who was worth anything'. Churchill later changed his mind and described the terrorist as 'strange and sinister'. (Spence, 324-325)

8 'Clemenceau wounded by anarchist', The Times, 20 February 1919
9 'M. Branting's denunciation of Bolshevism', The Times, 22 April 1919
10 Westwood, pp. 260-261
11 Macmillan, Paris 1919, pp. 81-82; 'To the Editor of The Times', 22 May 1919
12 Abraham, p. 344
13 Macmillan, Paris 1919, p. 82
14 Abraham, p. 345
15 Keith Jeffery, MI6, p. 188
16 British National Archives KV 2/658
17 Cronin, Paris, p. 7
18 The treaty was described as 'savage and vindictive' but its terms had taken into account that, quite apart from the immense loss of life both military and civilian, more than 500,000 French houses and 17,600 French buildings had been partly or completely destroyed; 20,000 French factories and workshops had been damaged or their machinery transported to Germany; 860,400 acres of French farmland had been rendered unproductive and a million head of French cattle had been taken over the border to feed the German people.
19 Ann Douglas, p. 163
20 Clark, Kaiser Wilhelm II, p. 349; Alan Judd, pp. 1-2
21 Taisia Osipova, 'Peasant Rebellions' in Brovkin (editor), pp. 164-165
22 Applebaum, Red Famine, p. 54; Churchill, Contemporaries, p. 133
23 'The Guildhall Banquet', The Times, 10 November 1919
24 'Prime Minister's vagaries', The Times, 14 November 1919. By the time Lloyd George got around to writing the sixth volume of his War Memoirs, the White forces no longer existed. He covered the British abandonment in one sentence, 'When it became clear that their bid for power was doomed to failure, and that the choice of the Russian people was definitely swinging across to support a Bolshevik regime, our withdrawal became inevitable.' (Lloyd George, War Memoirs, Vol. VI, p. 3195). At the time, however, he had misled the House of Commons into believing that Bolshevism was on the wane.
25 'An interview with Kerensky', The Guardian, 30 January 1920

26 British National Archives, KV 2/659

27 'Kerensky spurns peace with Soviet', New York Times, 28 December 1924

28 Laura Spinney, 1 March 2020, Sunday Times

29 The Triad, 10 September 1920

30 'A Critic from "Down Under"', Daily Mail, London, 22 October 1919; The Triad, November 1920; Woods p. 203

26. The Hungry Years

1 Jan Doets and André Birukoff, pp. 114

2 British National Archives, KV 2/659

3 Gregory, p. 148. Under the agreement the Russians pledged to 'refrain from any attempt by military or diplomatic or any other form of action or propaganda to encourage any of the peoples of Asia in any form of hostile action against British interests or the British Empire'. This did not stop Lenin sending Comintern agents to China with orders to fight Chinese feudalism and foreign imperialism.

4 Abraham p. 348; Applebaum, Red Famine, p. 68

5 Boterbloem, Russia, p. 167. The author is Professor of History and Coordinator of Russian, East-European and Eurasian Studies at the University of South Florida

6 Author's interview with Stephen Kerensky, 28 December 2019

7 Gleb Kerensky, Only One Freedom, unpublished manuscript, p. 122

8 Mawdsley, 'The Civil War' in Acton, Cherniaev, Rosenberg (editors), Critical Companion, p. 99

9 Lenin, Collected Works, Vol. 31, pp. 213-263

10 Dr Sokolov later escaped to the United States, where he became a distinguished medical practitioner and scientist, and managing editor of *Growth* magazine. From the time he left Russia, he never ceased to write about the dangers of Communism. 'The only place where there was freedom of speech and thought in Communist Russia,' he said, 'was in prison.' Dr Sokolov died at his home in Lakeland, Florida, on 18 November 1979, five days after his ninetieth birthday.

11 British National Archives, KV 2/659

12 Mawdsley, 'The Civil War' in Acton, Cherniaev, Rosenberg (editors), Critical Companion, pp. 93, 99

13 Engelstein, p. 616; Jonathan Daly, p. 93

14 Read and Fisher, Berlin, p. 171
15 Lockhart, Retreat from Glory, pp. 99-100
16 David Reynolds, 'Did peace come too soon?', New Statesman, 2-8 November 2018
17 Ibid, p. 99
18 Lockhart, Robin Bruce, Ace of Spies, pp. 145-146
19 Spence, p. 309
20 David Hearst, 'Son of leading Bolshevik became Stalin's adopted son', The Guardian, 24 January 2008; T. Poole and E. Fried, 'Artem: A Bolshevik in Brisbane', *Australian Journal of Politics and History*, Vol 31, No 2, 1985, pp 243-254
21 Fyodor Sergeyev's name is commemorated in mines, schools and cities, including Artemovsk, a major industrial centre in the Donets Basin. One of the pallbearers at his funeral was William Earsman, a Scots-born activist who had played a key role in the founding of the Communist Party of Australia.
22 Sorokin, Russian Diary, p, 294
23 Gina Kolata, 'Evidence of Dr Harry Vinters, Professor of Neurology and Neuropathology at the University of California in Lenin's stroke', New York Times, 7 May 2012
24 Ibid, p. 297
25 Jensen, Show Trial, pp. 25-35
26 James Ryan, p. 174
27 Bruce Lockhart, p. 177
28 Vladimir Nabokov, *Think, Write, Speak*, p. 4; Read and Fisher, Berlin, p. 169
29 Boyd, Nabokov: The American Years, p. 190
30 Robert C. Williams, p. 236
31 Kerensky, Turning Point, p. 532
32 Quoted in Plowright, p. 62
33 Kerensky, Turning Point, p. 532, Ben H. Shepherd, p. xix
34 Bellamy, p. 41
35 Karl Schlogel, Professor of East European History, European University, Vladrina Frankfurt, 'Investigating Russian Berlin in Weimar Germany', balticworlds.com, 22 September 2011

36 Abraham, p. 356

37 Jan Doets and André Birukoff, p. 83

27. The French Connection

1 Vasily Grossman, Stalingrad, pp. 513, 517

2 Berberova, pp. 218-223

3 Abraham, p. 358

4 Ibid, p. 354

5 Westwood p. 293

6 'Trotsky attacks Stalin in letter', New York Times, 17 September 1936

7 Kotkin, Vol. II, p. 491

8 Gina Kolata, 'Lenin's stroke', New York Times, 7 May 2012; Alex Dominguez, 'What killed Lenin?', Associated Press, 4 May 2012

9 Ibid

10 Ibid

11 Kerensky Family Papers, Cadbury Research Library, MS126/1/2/6

12 Patenaude, p. 252; Service, Trotsky, pp. 311-2

13 'Bolshevist laments', The Times, 14 January 1924

14 Gregory, p. 148

15 Westwood, p. 294

16 Norman Stone, 'Trotsky on Prinkipo', Cornucopia Magazine, Issue 28

17 Steegmuller, Cocteau, p. 301

18 Author's interview with Jean Baptiste Hugo, 10 December 2019

19 Jean Hugo, Le Regard de la Mémoire, p. 14

20 Tabouis, pp. 74-75

21 Andrew, Secret World, p. 581; Gill Bennett, p. 267-269

22 'Mr MacDonald another Kerensky', The Times, 27 October 1924

23 'The Russian loan', The Times, 16 October 1924

24 Gill Bennett, p. 47

25 It was the beginning of the end of Gregory's career. He was caught up in a financial scandal in 1928 and dismissed from the Diplomatic Service.

26 Hart-Davis, p. 258; Meyers, p. 236

27 'Once an exile', The Argus, 2 April 1930

28 'Czarist dossiers on Reds opened', New York Times, 30 October 1957

29 'Kerensky declares Soviet is doomed', New York Times, 7 February 1926
30 Gregory, p. 145
31 Mackenzie, Faith Compton, Memoir, Vol. I, p. 70; 'Mr H. V. Higgins', The Times, 22 November 1928

28. The Incurable Romantic

1 Abraham, p. 357
2 Built in 1894, Northampton College was actually in Clerkenwell, London, on land presented by the Marquess of Northampton. The college became The City University in 1967.
3 Abraham, p. 359; Simon Karlinsky, Marina Tsvetaeva: The Woman, her World and her Poetry, Cambridge University Press, Cambridge, 1986, p. 159
4 'Alexander Kerensky', New York Times, 4 March 1927
5 Flora Solomon, p. 133
6 Bizarrely, the Soviet Government, having failed to make the Lena Goldfields a going concern, had invited Benenson to return to Russia in 1925 to run the mines on a 50-50 basis. He reorganised and refinanced the operating company and the mine became so successful that the Russians repudiated their agreement with him. Thanks to pressure from the British Foreign Office, he received £3 million in Soviet bonds for his share of the mining company.
7 'Kerensky slapped by woman Tsarist', New York Times, 14 March 1927
8 Flora Solomon, p. 134
9 'Kerensky slapped by woman Tsarist', New York Times, 14 March 1927
10 Flora Solomon, p. 135
11 Kerensky, Catastrophe, p. 42
12 Flora Solomon, pp. 136, 148
13 Stephen Kerensky in conversation with Helen Ivanova, Alexander Kerensky's companion in later life; Abraham, p. 349
14 Flora Solomon, p. 137
15 Service, Trotsky, p. 466
16 The News, Adelaide, 31 January, 1930
17 Flora Solomon, p. 164
18 Lockhart Diaries, 17 June 1931
19 Vladimir Nabokov, Letters to Vera, p. 190

20 Vladimir Nabokov, Speak, Memory, p. 220

21 Tom Holland, Dominion, p. 453

22 Jonathan Daly, p.p. 107-108

23 Ibid, 108

24 Don Gregory, 145-150

25 David Lloyd George, Kenneth O. Morgan, Oxford Dictionary of National Biography, 2004

26 Lloyd George War Memoirs, Vol. IV, pp. 1899-1900

27 Simeon Strunsky, 'A Plea for Democracy', New York Times, 18 March 1934

28 Kerensky, Crucifixion, p. 353

29 'Mme Kerensky tilts at women', The Sun, Sydney, 12 November, 1945; Wilkinson, Betty, 'Never a day without fear', Australian Women's Weekly, 1 December 1945

30 Bouverie, Appeasing Hitler, 2019, pp. 115-16; The Times, 'The Heart of the Peace Problem', 31 Jan 1935

31 Berberova, p. 303

32 Ibid, p. 301

33 Linklater, p. 284

29. The Fury of Comrade Stalin

1 Simon Sebag-Montefiore, Stalin, p. 114

2 Kershaw, To Hell and Back, p. 270. There has been speculation ever since that Stalin ordered Kirov's murder because he resented his popularity. This remains unproven. In honour of his friend, he renamed the then Soviet Ballet, formerly the Imperial Ballet of Saint Petersburg, the Kirov Ballet.

3 Morrison, p. 261

4 Michiko Kakutani, 'His Cure-All Was Murder', New York Times, 16 April 2004; 'Trotsky attacks Stalin in letter', New York Times, 17 September 1936

5 Quoted in Malcolm Muggeridge, The Thirties: 1930-1939, p, 31

6 Kershaw, To Hell and Back, p. 272

7 Abraham, pp. 366-367

8 Betty Wilkinson, 'Never a day without fear', Australian Women's Weekly, 1 December 1945

9 Gary Saul Moron, 'The house is on fire!', The New Criterion, Vol. 35, No. 1, September 2016, quoting Scorched Earth: Stalin's Reign of Terror, by Jörg Baberowski, Yale University Press

10 Boyd, Nabokov: The Russian Years, p. 21

11 'Antonina Pirozhkova', Daily Telegraph, 23 September 2010

12 An Incident at Krechetovka Station, p. 138 in Solzhenitsyn: Stories and Prose Poems

13 'Kerensky asserts Stalin is doomed', New York Times, 3 March 1938

14 Trotsky, The Third International After Lenin, p. 259

15 Maclean, pp. 58-59

16 Ibid, p. 59

17 'Confessions in Moscow', The Times, 3 March 1938

18 'Kerensky asserts Stalin is doomed', New York Times, 3 March 1938

19 'Democratic drive urged by Kerensky', New York Times, 5 March 1938

20 Maclean, pp. 63-64

21 Figes, Tragedy, p. 822

22 Maclean, pp. 80-81

23 Ibid, p. 96

24 Ibid, p. 84

25 Bohlen, p. 52; Malcolm Muggeridge, 'Perceptive correspondent', The Times, 28 March, 1973

26 Northedge and Wells, p. 66

27 Ibid; Hehn, p. 23

28 Bradford, p. 363

29 Bohlen, p. 60

30 'The Munich pact', New York Times, 11 October 1938; Horne, p. 37

31 'Mrs Clayburgh gives dinner and musicale', New York Times, 30 December 1938

32 Courier-Mail, 10 March 1939

33 'Invalids', The Times, 11 May 1939

34 'France under Reynaud and Weygand', The Guardian, 6 June 1940

35 'New secretary for Menzies', The Sun, 3 May 1939

36 During his trip to Australia in September 2007 Vladimir Putin was told that Alexander Kerensky had married an Australian journalist and lived

with her in Brisbane. 'For me it was rather unexpected to know Kerensky visited here,' he said. 'Even more surprised I am that he was married to a representative from the mass media, which is hardly a likely and natural marriage for a former prime minister. I cannot imagine why a prime minister would marry a journalist.'

37 Bellamy, p. 54

38 Ibid

39 Tabouis, p. 410; Bellamy, p. 50

40 Strobe Talbott, New York Times, 18 October 2017

41 Michael Jabara Carley, 'Prelude to Defeat: Franco-Soviet Relations 1918-1939', in The French Defeat of 1940: Reassessments, Joel Blatt (editor), p. 201; Bohlen, p. 84

42 Bohlen, p. 70; Patenaude, pp. 2, 3; Plowright, p.p. 66-67

43 Garrett, Patrick, 'How Clare Hollingworth broke the news of World War II and saved thousands from the Nazis', Daily Telegraph, 12 August 2016

44 Brinkley, David, Washington Goes to War, Andre Deutsch, London, 1989, pp. 24-25

45 Maisky Diaries, p. 223; Chips Channon, p. 215

46 'Pledge to Russians urged by Kerensky', New York Times, 21 September 1939

47 Vicki Caron, 'The Missed Opportunity' in Joel Blatt (editor) The French Defeat of 1940: Reassessments, p. 129

48 De Gaulle, Charles, Lettres, notes et carnets – juin 1919 – juin 1940, Paris, 1980, pp. 485-487

49 Lynne Booker, 'A Fine Balance – Portugal in World War II', Algarve History Association

30. The Flight from Paris

1 Werth, p. 15

2 Nabokov, Letters to Vera, p. 249

3 Berberova, pp. 372-373

4 Collins, Glenn, 'Nina Berberova, 92, poet, novelist and professor', New York Times, 29 September 1993

5 Berberova, p. 303

6 Costello, p. 25

7 Barber, p. 27

8 Lazareff, p. 275

9 Kerensky Family Papers, Cadbury Research Library, MS126/2/2/2/2

10 Cox, p. 163; Julian Jackson, p. 103

11 Lazareff, p. 284

12 John Lukacs, Five Days in London: May 1940, The University Press, New Haven, 2001, p. 210

13 Paxton, p. 4

14 Churchill, Winston, Their Finest Hour, Penguin Books, 1985, p. 42

15 Spears, Assignment to Catastrophe, p. 74, p. 134

16 Churchill's mishandling of the Abdication crisis ensured he remained out of office since 1936 and was therefore untainted by Chamberlain's appeasement policy.

17 Saint-Exupéry, Odyssey, p. 350

18 Weygand, General Maxime, Mémoirs, Volume III, Flammarion, Paris, 1950, pp. 168–88

19 Barber, p. 53; Waterfield, Gordon, What Happened to France, London 1940

20 Horne, p. 497

21 Ibid, p. 498

22 Barber, p. 33

23 'Privations in France: Kerensky's peril', Sydney Morning Herald, 18 July 1940

24 Hickman, Bodyguard, p. 97

25 Ray Moseley, p. 44

26 Hickman, Bodyguard, p. 98; Sandbrook, Dominic, 'A bulletproof team', Daily Telegraph, 9 May 2008

27 Némirovsky, Suite Francaise, p. 50

28 Saint-Exupéry, Odyssey, p. 339

31. The Last Ship Out

1 Kershaw, pp. 398-399

2 Lévy, p. 155; Barber, p. 194

3 Tabouis, p. 3

4 Spears, Assignment to Catastrophe, p. 42

5 Jean Hugo, Le Regard de la Mémoire, pp. 479-480
6 Even at the end of the war, Nell refused to release this man's name to the press on the grounds that disclosure might still be dangerous for him.
7 Lockhart, Reckoning, p. 93
8 Jean Hugo, Le Regard de la Mémoire, p. 481
9 Roskill, War at Sea, p. 238
10 'Tragedy in France', New York Times, 18 June 1940
11 'Dornford' and 'Yates' were the maiden names of Mercer's grandmothers
12 Wordsworth, Christopher, 'Delusions of Grandeur', The Observer, 28 February 1982
13 Smithers, p. 184
14 George MacDonald Fraser, p. 282
15 On Hitler's orders the Armistice site in the forest was demolished and the 'Compiègne Wagon-Lit' was taken to Berlin as a war trophy, along with the shattered pieces of the large stone tablet which had borne the offending inscription. The German Armed Forces had suffered losses of 27,000 dead, 111,000 wounded and 18,000 missing. France had lost 92,000 dead, more than 200,000 wounded and a further two million Frenchmen were in prisoner-of-war camps. Britain's losses were modest in comparison: 10,000 men killed and wounded.
16 Janet Flanner, pp. 61-63
17 Hastings, pp. 446-448
18 Diana Souhami, pp. 366-368
19 'The Zogs and Kerensky in last ship', Daily Mail, 28 June 1940
20 Diary of Penelope Otto, France 4-26 June 1940, entry for 23-24 June, typescript
21 Juta, p. 132
22 Diary of Penelope Otto, 26 June 1940
23 'Kerensky must leave England', New York Times, 29 June 1940
24 Diana Souhami, p. 371
25 Abraham, p. 370

32. The Death of Nell Tritton

1 British National Archives, KV 2/659
2 Lockhart, Reckoning, p. 93

3 'Kerensky arrives in liner Scythia', New York Times, 13 August 1940
4 Norman Stone, 'Trotsky on Prinkipo', Cornucopia magazine, Issue 28, 2003
5 'Woman who introduced killer to Trotsky', New York Times, 23 August 1940.
6 Patenaude, p. 384
7 Belief in Russia 'wishful thinking', Courier-Mail, 10 December 1940
8 'Letters to the Editor', New York Times, 20 October 1940
9 Roberts, p. 89
10 Horne, Hubris, p. 163
11 Bellamy, p. 147
12 Horne, Hubris, p. 168
13 Ibid, p. 165
14 Fitzpatrick, Stalin's Team, pp. 152-153; Horne, Hubris, p. 166
15 'Kerensky in appeal for help for Russia', New York Times, 23 June 1941
16 Bellamy, p. 214
17 Reynolds and Pechatnov, editors, The Kremlin Letters, p. 26
18 David Hearst, 'Son of leading Bolshevik became Stalin's adopted son', The Guardian, 24 January 2008
19 Horne, Hubris, p. 179
20 Ibid, p. 190
21 Ray Moseley, p. 196
22 Betty Wilkinson, 'Never a day without fear', Australian Women's Weekly, 1 December 1945
23 Brian Boyd, Nabokov: The American Years, p. 61
24 Gleb Kerensky, Only One Freedom, unpublished manuscript, p. 185
25 Ibid, p. 205
26 Ibid, pp. 205-206
27 Ibid, p. 205
28 I. C. B. Dear (editor), World War II, p. 804
29 'Alexander Kerensky looks back', The Argus, 10 November 1945
30 Author's interview with Elizabeth-Anne Peters, 20 December 2019

31 'Soviet chief's local link', Courier-Mail, 13 June 1983; Betty Wilkinson, 'Never a day without fear', Australian Women's Weekly, 1 December 1945
32 'Historian Alexander Rabinowitch speaks in Vienna on the Russian Revolution', wsws.org, 15 June 2011. Alexander Rabinowitch later abandoned this view of the October Revolution in his first book, The Bolsheviks in Power: The First Year of Soviet Rule in Petrograd.
33 'Free Russia' move, New York Times, 14 March 1949

Epilogue: The Tiger of History
1 'Gruff voice from old Russia', The Observer, 30 June 1963
2 Oleg Kerensky Jr, 'Grandfather' chapter from his unpublished memoirs
3 Leon Trotsky, The Young Lenin, p. 1; Kerensky, Turning Point, p. 9
4 Glenny and Stone, pp. 287-288
5 'Kerensky', New York Times, 12 June 1970
6 'Alexander Kerensky, The Times, 17 June 1970
7 Brian Boyd, Nabokov: The Russian Years, p. 21; Kerensky Family Papers, Cadbury Research Library, MS126/1/2/6
8 Author's interview with Stephen Kerensky, 28 December 2019
9 Gleb Kerensky, Only One Freedom, unpublished manuscript, Foreword.

Index

Aerowagon, The, 529
Aladin, Alexis F., 384, 387, 388
Albert, Prince of Saxe-Coburg and Gotha (Prince Consort to Queen Victoria), 19, 24, 51, 82
Aldanov, Mark, 539, 593
Alexei Alexandrovich Romanov, Grand Duke, 87
Alexei Nikolaevich, Tsarevich, son of Nicholas II, 45n, 93, 129, 130, 167, 249, 252, 266, 293, 366, 486
Alekseyev, Admiral Evgeni Ivanovich, 87, 88–90, 94, 115
Alekseyev, General Mikhail Vasilievich, 208, 222, 223, 234, 266, 273, 284, 285, 290, 293, 297, 329, 332, 335, 362, 394, 433
Alexander I, Emperor of Russia, 16
Alexander II, 'The Liberator', Emperor of Russia, 20–25, 28, 34, 62, 63, 67, 71
Alexander III, Emperor of Russia, 27, 30–34, 44–54, 84
Alexandra Fyodorovna, Empress of Russia (formerly Princess Alix of Hesse-Darmstadt), 51–60, 93, 94, 109, 127–130, 136, 143, 167, 189, 201, 207, 222–224, 242, 246–254, 257, 258, 260, 267, 284, 289–293, 311–313, 366, 367, 486–487
Alexander Mikhailovich, Grand Duke, 'Sandro' 116, 117

Allied Powers and intervention in Russia, 19, 256, 302, 331, 399, 439, 453, 456, 467, 471, 472, 479, 480, 486, 494, 497, 501, 505, 511
All-Russian Central Executive Committee (VTsIK, Excom), 340, 349, 356, 438
All-Russian Conference of Soviets, 316
All-Russian Congress of Soviets' and Workers' Deputies, 331, 398, 423, 481, 490
All-Russian Communist Party - see Bolshevik Party
All-Russian Constituent Assembly - see Constituent Assembly
All-Russian Democratic Conference and Preparliament, 397, 408, 412
All-Russian Electoral Commission, 428–430
All-Russian Railway Union (Vikzhel), 287, 393, 419, 422
American Relief Administration (ARA), 526, 530
Antisemitism and pogroms, 29, 32, 78, 79, 97, 117, 123, 159, 223, 345, 346, 359, 503, 507, 512, 568, 585, 636n
Antonov, Alexander, 516
Antonov-Ovsienko, Vladimir, 367, 394, 402, 405, 409, 418, 422, 443, 446, 571

ANZAC (Australian and New Zealand Army Corps), the Anzacs, 217, 218, 242
Archangel, 453–455, 472, 480, 483, 484, 497, 510
Armand, Inessa, 317
Armenia, 114, 150, 215, 687
Asquith, Herbert, Prime Minister of Great Britain, 187, 190, 193–197, 211, 212, 215, 220, 256
Assembly of Russian Factory and Mill Workers, 100, 101, 109, 128
Astrakhan, 29, 39, 40
Aurora, Baltic Fleet cruiser, 410, 414, 437
Austria/Austro-Hungarian Empire, 50, 55, 63, 81n, 178–192, 196, 199–209, 234, 237, 254, 318, 336, 341, 344, 430, 444, 446
Autocracy, Romanov, 1, 6, 7, 9, 10, 11, 16, 20, 27, 30, 32, 44, 50, 54, 61, 66, 68, 76, 90, 92, 95, 96, 130, 131, 135, 136, 146, 158, 160, 185, 203, 207, 243, 250, 253, 264, 275, 293, 301, 309, 431
Avinov, N. N., 428, 429
Avksentiev, Nikolai, 121, 306, 307, 365, 369, 398, 408, 438, 451, 495, 498
Axelrod, Paul, 73, 77, 121
Azerbaijan, 114
Azev, Yevno, 79, 114, 129, 132, 146

Babel, Isaak, 253, 574, 574n
Baden, Prince Max von, 495, 496
Baku, 145, 152, 215
Balfour, Arthur (Earl of Balfour), 7, 220, 445, 454, 463–466, 472, 475

Balkans, Balkan Wars, 57, 82, 168, 178–186, 192, 505, 630
Baltic Fleet, 95, 116, 117, 323, 347, 429, 441
Baranovskaya, Elena Lvovna (later Tarchova), younger sister of Olga Kerenskaya, 71, 72, 521, 522
Baranovskaya, Elena Vsevolodovna 'Lilya' - see Birukova, E. V.
Baranovskaya (née Vasilieva), Lydia V., mother of Vera, Elena (Lilya), Olga and Vladimir, 43, 420, 445, 446, 536, 644
Baranovskaya (née Vasilieva), Maria V., mother of Olga Kerenskaya, Elena Tarchova and General Vladimir Baranovsky, 70, 71, 435, 455, 457, 458, 466, 523
Baranovskaya (née Sila-Nowicki), Maria 'Moussia', wife of Vladimir Vsevolodovich Baranovsky, 403, 420, 436
Baranovskaya, Olga Vsevolodovna (later Soumarokova), sister of Vera, Elena (Lilya) and Vladimir, 43, 483
Baranovskaya, Olga Lvovna - see Kerenskaya, Olga Lvovna
Baranovskaya, Vera Vsevolodovna, eldest sister of Elena (Lilya), Olga and Vladimir, 43, 420, 459, 489, 494, 524, 644
Baranovsky, Lieutenant-General Lev Stepanovich, father of Olga Kerenskaya, Elena Tarchova and General Vladimir Baranovsky, 70, 71
Baranovsky, General Vladimir Lvovich, brother of Olga Kerenskaya and Elena Tarchova -

Kerensky's brother-in-law, 109, 329, 389, 390, 417, 445, 457, 485, 521, 572

Baranovsky, Vladimir Vsevolodovich, brother of Vera, Elena (Lilya) and Olga, 403, 420, 436

Baranovsky, Senator Lieutenant-General Vsevolod Stepanovich, father of Vera, Elena (Lilya), Olga and Vladimir, 70, 420, 445, 524

Baratynskaya, Dr Elena, 461, 535

Barclay, Colville, 498

Bashkirtseff, Maria, 240, 241, 241n, 512, 549, 552, 580

Battenberg, Prince Louis of, 110, 196, 196n

Battle of the Marne, Second Battle of the Marne, 211, 476, 488, 494

Battle of Tannenberg, 205, 211

Battle of the Somme, 235, 348, 488, 489

Battle of Tsushima, 116

Battle of Verdun, 233, 233n, 235–237

Battle of Ypres, First, 212

Battle of Ypres, Third ('Passchendaele'), 709n

Beaverbrook, Lord (Max Aitken), 501, 563, 598

Beilis, Mendel, 165, 166, 279

Beliaev, General Mikhail, 273, 274, 283, 284

Belarus, 4, 55n, 62, 205n, 225, 234, 358, 536, 631, 635, 698n

Benckendorff, Count Alexander, 188, 193, 214, 231, 306

Benckendorff, Countess Maria 'Moura' (later Baroness Budberg), 493, 493n, 494

Benckendorff, Count Paul, 311, 312, 312n

Benenson, Fira (later Countess Ilinska), 154, 641, 646

Benenson, Flora - see Solomon, Flora

Benenson, Grigory, 152, 155, 164, 223, 557, 558, 717n

Benenson, Peter (Flora Solomon's son, founder of Amnesty International), 559n

Beneš, Edouard, 501, 525, 545, 583

Benjamin, Metropolitan, 530, 531

Berberova, Nina, 533, 539, 568, 593, 603, 637, 639

Berchtold, Count Leopold, 182–185

Berdyaev, Nikolai, 534

Bernstein, Eduard, 73n

Bessarabia, 79, 502

Bethmann Hollweg, Theobald von, 182, 183, 189, 194, 195, 360

Bezobrazov, General Alexander, 88

Birukova (née Baranovskaya), Dr Elena 'Lilya' Vsevolodovna, lover of Kerensky and mother of his daughter Irina, 13, 43, 228, 240, 252, 253, 293, 301, 323, 329, 361, 364, 403, 420, 435, 436, 450, 483, 484, 489, 495, 500, 513–515, 524, 535, 536, 539, 540, 543, 644

Birukova, Irina, 'Irinouchka', Kerensky's daughter, 435, 483, 484, 500, 515, 524, 536, 539, 648

Birukov, General Nikolai Pavlovich, 229, 361, 514, 539

Birukov, Vsevolod Nikolaevich 'Olik', 229, 420, 445, 446, 514, 515

Bismarck, Prince Otto E. L. von, 50, 51, 57, 101, 180, 383

Black Hundred, 117, 123, 160
Black Sea Fleet, 18, 20, 55, 429
Bliss, General Tasker H., 449
Bloody Sunday, 100, 109, 110, 112, 113, 115, 118, 120, 121, 122, 128, 153, 264
Blum, Leon, 580, 612, 619
Bochkareva, Maria L., 358
Bogolepov, Nikolai, 74, 75
Bogrov, Dimitri, 147
Bolshevik Party, Bolsheviks, Bolshevism (Communist Party, Communists, Communism), 1–13, 23, 38, 72, 77, 78, 103, 124–127, 134, 145, 146, 149, 164, 165, 181, 202, 213, 216, 227, 243, 269, 326, 328–347, 349–372, 389, 394–467, 471–473, 477, 479–493, 497, 499–512, 515–517, 526, 530–535, 542, 547, 551, 515–517, 526, 530–535, 542, 547, 551, 553, 557, 562–590, 621, 629, 632, 635, 642, 643, 643n, 648
Bolshevik Central Committee, 164, 200, 216, 232, 267, 304–305, 325n, 346, 349–351, 367, 367n, 399, 409, 443, 529, 530, 543
Bolshevik Military Committee, 436, 437
Bolshoi Theatre, 344, 372, 382, 384, 481, 482, 632
Bonch-Bruevich, Vladimir, 347, 437, 480
Botkin, Dr Eugene, 167, 366, 486, 487
Botkin, Dr Sergei, 26
Boxers, the (Society of Righteous and Harmonious Fists), 86, 87
Branting, Hjalmar, Prime Minister of Sweden, 467, 502, 545

Breshko-Breshkovskaya, Catherine 'Babushka', 75, 155, 300, 316, 323, 363, 437, 451, 536
Brest-Litovsk, 205n, 219, 235, 238, 430, 433, 434, 448, 468
Brest-Litovsk, Peace of, 446, 453, 476, 481, 501, 534, 542
British Expeditionary Force, (BEF), 'the Old Contemptibles', 199, 210–213, 235
British Foreign Office, 116, 187, 188, 365, 371, 385, 396, 431, 452–454, 462, 463, 471–480, 486, 489, 497, 504, 542, 548, 549, 552, 563, 575, 612, 615, 616, 625
British Labour Party, 220, 335, 467, 471, 485, 542, 545, 546, 549, 598
Browder, Professor Robert P., 1, 643
Brownlee, John, 552, 553n, 582
Brusilov, General Alexei, 234, 234n, 235, 237, 266, 293, 311, 333, 334, 335, 340, 342, 344, 357, 359, 361, 362, 425
Bryant, Louise, 8, 400, 477
Bublikov, Alexander, 287, 290
Buchanan, Sir George, 29n, 127n, 189, 219, 222–225, 262, 271, 282, 314, 331, 332, 352, 365, 369, 371, 385, 390, 396, 398, 404
Bukharin, Nikolai, 367n. 439, 440, 520, 543, 575, 576, 577, 579, 580
Bullitt, William C., 589
Bund, (General Jewish Labour Bund), 61, 118, 148, 317
Bunin, Ivan, 600

Campbell, Sir Ronald, 612, 614, 622
Cary, Joyce, 178, 179, 179n

Catherine the Great, 31, 137, 244, 250
Caucasus, 20, 31, 36, 55, 114, 118, 145, 214, 215, 222, 323, 400, 498, 501
Central Powers, 192, 201, 208, 214, 215, 234, 237, 328, 387, 398, 430, 431, 446, 453, 466, 478
Chaliapin, Fyodor, 113, 344, 441
Chamberlin, William Henry, 273, 298, 422
Cheka, OGPU, 118, 434, 456–459, 480, 482, 484, 489, 490–493, 514, 535, 541, 553n
Cheremisov, General Vladimir, 344, 417
Chernov, Viktor M., 75, 115, 124, 269, 305, 306, 346, 351, 353, 356, 368, 370, 393, 395, 434, 436, 437–440, 442, 527
Chernyshevsky, Nikolai, 22, 23, 38, 76
Chicherin, Georgi, 306, 307, 44, 446
Chinese Eastern Railway, 86, 87
Cheidze, Nikolai, 165, 201, 272, 275, 286, 287, 292, 294–296, 300n, 318, 337, 350, 354, 397, 398
Churchill, Sir Winston S., 7, 180, 186, 196, 197, 212, 213, 215, 218n, 220, 466, 492, 499, 502, 543, 547, 581, 598, 599, 600, 601, 604–624
Cixi, Dowager Empress of China, 86
Clémenceau, Georges, Prime Minister of France, 7, 11, 115, 450, 470, 474–478, 494, 500–506

Comintern (Communist International), 520, 532, 543, 546–548, 550n, 587, 590
Conrad von Hötzendorf, Field Marshal Franz, 199, 200, 209
Constantinople, 18, 214, 215, 217, 247, 256, 309, 310, 511, 512, 524, 525, 536, 539
Constituent Assembly, 75, 98, 102, 127, 227, 294, 299, 322, 348, 356, 388, 397, 406, 409, 412, 428, 429, 30, 433, 434, 436–440, 442, 465, 472, 473, 489, 490, 497, 504, 593
Constitutional Democratic Party - see Kadets
Cossacks, 42, 67, 74, 103, 105, 106, 107, 260, 262, 264, 267, 311, 352, 361, 368, 383, 384, 410, 413, 420–424, 427, 433, 445, 446, 503, 507, 519
Council of Elders, 267, 272, 276, 279, 286
Council of Ministers, 102, 181, 245, 255, 262, 276, 283–286
Council of People's Commissars (Sovnarkom), 420, 429–434, 438, 440, 443, 448
Crimea, Crimean War, 16, 19, 20, 51, 52, 61, 215, 250, 284, 332, 366, 498, 525, 645
Cromie, Captain Francis, 492, 493
Crowe, Sir Eyre, 187, 712n
Curzon, George Nathaniel, (1st Marquess Curzon of Kedleston), 41, 42, 220, 256, 463, 504
Czechoslovakia, 33, 182n, 505, 506, 525, 527, 545, 556, 581, 583, 584, 586, 587, 589, 590, 636n

Czechoslovak Legion, Czechoslovak Rifle Brigade, 340, 341, 343, 453, 465, 467, 486, 487, 489

Daladier, Édouard, Prime Minister of France, 580, 581, 586, 588, 589, 590, 595, 602, 619, 623
Dan, Fyodor, 77, 269, 397, 408, 416
Decembrists, 17, 17n, 73
Declaration of Soldiers' Rights, 330
Declaration of the Rights of the Working and Exploited People, 438, 442
Decree on Land (1918), 440, 442
Decree on Peace (1917), 419
Decree on the Separation of Church and State (1918), 442
de Custine, Marquis, 17, 22
de Gaulle, General Charles, 584, 590, 604, 605, 615
de Lazovert, Colonel Stanislaus, 248
Denikin, General Anton, 234n, 343, 351, 358, 362, 391, 394, 433, 446, 450, 494, 503, 507, 509, 510, 525, 638
Denham, Digby, Premier of Queensland, 157
Derby, Lord, (Edward George Villiers Stanley), 504
Dmitri Pavlovich Romanov, Grand Duke, 248, 251
Dogger Bank Incident, 95, 95n
Donald, William Henry, 117
Donets Basin (Donbas), 443, 446, 447, 520n, 714n
Don Region, 433, 446, 507
Dostoevsky, Fyodor, 17, 90, 98
Dreyfus Affair, 98, 474n, 545n

Dukhonin, General Nikolai, 426
Duma - see State Duma
Durnovo, Peter, 121, 124, 180, 187, 214, 255
Dybenko, Paul, 367, 394, 402, 417, 424, 426, 439
Dzerzhinsky, Felix, 77, 118, 367n, 399, 434, 482, 486, 489, 494, 535

Eastern Front, 204, 205, 209, 211, 212, 213, 217, 220, 233, 234, 235, 237, 239, 329, 360, 400, 430, 431, 445, 451, 471, 473
Ebert, Friedrich, 496
Economism, 73, 73n
Edward VII, (Prince of Wales, 'Bertie'), King of the United Kingdom of Great Britain and Ireland and Emperor of India, 44, 83, 178, 188, 195, 620–621
Edward, VIII, (Prince of Wales and later Duke of Windsor, 'David'), King of the United Kingdom of Great Britain and Ireland and Emperor of India, 512, 595, 604
Efremov, Ivan, 268
Ehrenburg, Ilya, 307, 370, 527, 623
Eisenstein, Sergei, 427
Ekaterinburg, 185, 486, 487
Elizabeth, Princess of Denmark, ('Ella', sister of Tsarina Alexandra), 51, 113, 488
Engelhardt, Colonel Boris, 286, 330
Engels, Friedrich, 38, 62, 277, 505
Enver Pasha, 214, 215
Estonia, 114, 126, 431, 505, 586, 636n

Fabrikant, Vladimir O., 442, 451, 452–454, 462, 470, 474

Falkenhayn, General Erich von, 183, 211, 237
Famine of 1891, Famine of 1921, Famine of 1932, 56, 57, 348, 503, 516, 519, 525, 526, 530, 562, 564, 565
Farmborough, Sister Florence, 219, 333, 336, 341
February Revolution (1917), 1, 3, 5, 7, 259, 281n, 300n, 305n, 319, 329n, 557, 565, 645
Farina, Rafael, 504–510, 515, 523, 524, 548
Figner, Vera, 437
Filonenko, Captain Maximilian, 489, 492
Finland, 11, 31, 55, 111, 124, 126, 139, 203, 318, 322, 387, 394, 442, 501, 503, 505, 586n, 630
First All-Russian Congress of Soviets, 331, 336, 340, 346
First Machine Gun Regiment, 319, 346, 347
First World War - see World War I
Flaxerman, Galina, 399
Fofanova, Margarita, 399, 408
Fondaminsky, Ilya, 141, 307, 501, 564, 600, 641, 641n
Ford Madox Ford, 115n
Ford, Henry, 29n, 538
Fourteen Points, 498
Francis, David R., US Ambassador to Russia, 389
Franz Ferdinand, Archduke of Austria, 181–190, 199, 248n, 505
Franz Josef, Emperor of Austria, King of Hungary, 181–187, 199, 248
French, Field Marshal Sir John, 210, 235

Freemasonry, 161, 165, 330, 362, 395, 398, 528, 591
French Revolution, 241, 326, 338, 339, 401, 473
Friedrich III, 'Fritz', Emperor of Germany, 82

Galicia, 200, 209, 217–219, 333, 342, 359
Gallipoli Campaign 1915, 215–219, 242, 598
Gamelin, General Maurice, 584, 595, 597, 599, 601
Gapon, Father Georgi, 100–111, 114, 115, 128, 129, 413, 487, 512
Gatchina, Great Palace of, 45, 50, 116, 265, 406, 420, 421–425, 434, 502
Gavronskaya, Maria 'Mary', 462, 555
Gavronsky, Dr Jacob Osipovich, 306, 307 462, 464, 466, 467, 470, 473, 474, 508, 511, 534, 555, 561
George V, 'Georgie', King of the United Kingdom of Great Britain and Ireland and Emperor of India, 53, 197n, 230, 486
Georgia, 112, 114, 125, 510, 542
Gerhardie, William, 320
German High Command, 210, 253, 308, 355, 387
German Social Democrats, 202, 203
Gilliard, Pierre, 93, 144, 201, 366
Golder, Frank, 319
Goldman, Emma, 308
Golitsyn, Prince Grigory, 150
Golitsyn, Prince Nikolai, 152, 252, 258, 267, 283, 286

Goremykin, Ivan, 139, 203, 204, 221, 226, 289, 301
Gorky, Maxim (Alexei Peshkov), 72n, 74, 106, 126, 127, 308n, 440, 441, 493n, 526, 529, 576, 578, 579
Gotz, Avram, 269, 307, 408, 531
Gotz, Mikhail, 75
Grant Duff, Sir Mountstuart Elphinstone, 24, 63
Great Russian Retreat, 212, 221
Gregory, J. D. 'Don', 163, 453, 542, 549, 552, 565
Grey, Sir Edward, 186–192, 197, 198, 198n, 214, 215, 310
Guchkov, Alexander, 208, 220, 221, 269, 293, 295–299, 304, 306, 310, 327, 328, 330, 370, 382
Guedalla, Herbert, 152
Gulag, 10, 525, 572, 636
Gutor, Lieutenant-General Alexander, 330, 340, 357

Haldane, Lord, (Richard Burdon Haldane), 196, 220
Hague Conventions, 493
Haig, Field Marshal Sir Douglas, 235, 238, 360, 450, 488
Halifax, Lord, (Edward Frederick Lindley Wood), 580, 581
Hankey, Lieutenant Colonel Maurice, 215
Hapsburg, 81, 181, 185, 206, 234, 343, 505
Hart, Sir Robert, 86
Helphand-Parvus, Alexander, 308
Henderson, Arthur, 220, 256, 335, 467, 468
Helsinki (Helsingfors), 228, 229, 398, 441, 442

Hindenburg, General Field Marshal Paul von, 205, 211, 234, 235, 237, 308, 328, 387, 446, 489, 495, 566
Hippius, Zinaida, 13, 60, 301, 307, 368, 371, 385, 410, 556, 600
Hitler, Adolf, 2, 29n, 538, 566–568, 577, 580, 581, 585–590, 593, 598, 602, 612, 614, 617, 627–630, 633, 636
Hoare, Sir Samuel, 247, 257
Hoffmann, General Maximilian von, 205, 217, 234, 237, 342, 344, 357, 359, 360, 444, 446
Hollingworth, Clare, 588
Holy Synod, 34, 221, 295, 365, 388
Hoover, Herbert, head of ARA (later President of the United States), 506, 526
Hoover Institution of War, Revolution and Peace, 300n, 643
House, 'Colonel' Edward M., 503
Hugo, Jean, 1, 2, 234, 544, 545n, 614, 614n, 616, 620n
Hugo, Jean Baptiste, 1, 544
Hugo, Victor, 81, 234, 544

Ignatiev, Count Nikolai, 32, 221
Intelligentsia, 57, 76, 79, 98, 99, 101, 150
International Court at The Hague, 63, 64, 95n, 186, 191, 192
International League for Human Rights, 545, 545n
International Peace Conference, 63
International Women's Day, 258
Irina Alexandrovna, Grand Duchess, 248, 251, 25
Iskra (Spark), 73, 73n
Ito Hirobumi, Marquis, 88

Ivanova, Helen, 717n
Ivanov, General Nikolai, 208, 209, 282, 288, 290
Ivan the Terrible, 40, 249
Izvestia, 121, 278, 286, 291, 382, 383, 420, 490, 542, 548, 550n

Jaurès, Jean, 114, 164
Jews and Jewish communities, 9, 29, 31, 32, 49, 61, 62, 79, 97, 117, 118, 200, 206, 217, 218, 218n, 346, 499, 568, 590
Joffé, Adolph, 431
Joffre, General Joseph 'Papa', 209, 210n, 220, 328
July Days, 397, 407

Kadets (Constitutional Democratic Party, Party of the People's Freedom), 123, 134, 139, 144, 160, 161, 193, 309, 331, 346, 348, 364, 365, 368, 397, 410, 412, 429, 451, 532
Kaledin, General Alexie, 234n, 433, 445, 446
Kamenev, Lev, 7, 77, 216, 300, 309, 337, 349, 367, 367n, 394, 399, 405, 409, 484, 530, 540, 543, 570, 571
Kannegiser, Leonid, 489
Kaplan, Fania 'Dora', 490
Karakhan, Lev, 520
Karl I, Emperor of Austria, King of Hungary, 248, 248n
Karpovich, Peter, 74
Kazan, 28, 29, 35, 37, 38, 40, 67, 70, 72, 74, 91, 97, 105, 152, 251, 489, 494, 530
Kerenskaya, Anna Fyodorovna 'Nyeta' (later Olferieva), Kerensky's sister, 28, 66, 91, 712n

Kerenskaya, Dr Elena Fyodorovna 'Lyolya', Kerensky's sister, 28, 66, 91, 228, 240, 521, 522, 572, 712n
Kerenskaya, Nadezhda Fyodorovna 'Nadya', (later Svarichevskaya), Kerensky's sister, 29, 40, 712n
Kerenskaya (née Adler), Nadezhda Alexandrovna, Kerensky's mother, 10, 29, 116
Kerenskaya (née Baranovskaya; in exile Kerensky), Olga 'Olya' Lvovna, 1, 2, 13, 69, 72, 75, 91, 92, 95, 131, 133, 140, 143, 165, 229, 230, 232, 233, 239, 240, 253, 268, 276, 277, 293, 295, 301, 361, 415, 415, 416, 420, 425, 451, 454, 455–461, 484, 485, 517–524, 535, 536, 555, 569, 625, 644, 647
Kerensky, Alexander Fyodorovich 'Sasha', 1–14, 16, 21, 45, 49, 50, 54, 57, 64, 98, 119, 122, 130, 131–140, 206–208, 213, 222, 223, 227, 239, 242, 243, 254, 362, 363, 366, 395–599
  background, 28, 29, 29n
  Simbirsk, 30, 33, 34, 36
  Tashkent, 40–43
  university, 65–76
  marriage to Olga Baranovskaya, 91, 92, 95, 116, 143
  legal career, 96, 97, 141, 142, 150, 165, 166
  Bloody Sunday, 100, 101, 105, 106, 109, 112, 129
  Lena Goldfields, 151–156
  Fourth Duma, 158–165, 180, 181, 185, 186, 193, 201, 202, 203, 216, 257
  affair with Elena 'Lilya' Baranovskaya, 228–237, 240, 244–247, 252, 253, 361–363

February Revolution, 259–280, 284–302, 304, 305
Minister of Justice, 306, 311–316, 318, 321, 323, 324, 326
Kerensky Offensive, 328–346, 348, 350, 353
and Lenin, 6, 7, 11, 28, 65, 69, 216, 304, 305, 308, 332, 336–340, 371, 395, 421, 466, 541, 542, 648
Bolshevik Rising, 355–360
Kornilov, 364, 365, 370, 371, 372, 386, 394, 426
Moscow Conference, 368, 369, 382–385
October Revolution, 400–420, 427
at Gatchina, 420–426
and Lloyd George, 394, 396, 404, 426, 463–467
and Clémenceau, 7, 11, 470, 474–478, 494, 500, 504
and Kenneth Simpson, 6, 556, 557, 585, 628, 636, 645
and Flora Solomon, 558, 559, 560, 561, 563, 567, 569, 586
and Nell Tritton, 2, 3, 13, 560, 582, 586, 637–639
last days, 643–648
Kerensky, Elizabeth (Libby Hudson), Gleb and Mary's daughter and Kerensky's granddaughter, 1, 644
Kerensky, Fyodor Fyodorovich 'Fedya', Kerensky's brother, 28, 36, 140, 239, 426, 499
Kerensky, Gleb Alexandrovich, Kerensky's younger son, 1, 2, 13, 70, 71, 133, 143, 158, 159, 165, 232, 240, 277, 301, 315, 425, 444, 450, 454, 458, 460, 479, 485, 519, 521, 522, 523, 532, 535, 555, 556, 565, 596, 597, 628, 635, 636, 644, 647, 648
Kerensky, Katherine (Kate Walker), Gleb and Mary's daughter and Kerensky's granddaughter, 644
Kerensky, Thérèse (née Tritton; formerly Thérèse Nadejine), Lydia Ellen 'Nellé', 2, 3, 13, 198, 240, 241, 512, 513, 549, 550, 560, 561, 562, 567, 582, 585, 586, 591, 592, 594, 596, 597, 600, 601, 603, 606, 608, 609, 610, 611, 613, 615, 623, 629, 637–639
Kerensky, Mary, (née Hudson), Gleb's wife and Kerensky's daughter-in-law, 644
Kerensky, Nathalie, (née Bely), Oleg's wife and Kerensky's daughter-in-law, 555, 563, 628
Kerensky, Dr Oleg Alexandrovich, Kerensky's elder son, 1, 2, 13, 70, 71, 116, 133, 143, 158, 159, 165, 232, 240, 277, 301, 315, 425, 444, 450, 451, 454, 458, 460, 479, 485, 519, 521, 522, 523, 532, 535, 555, 556, 565, 596, 597, 628, 635, 636, 644, 647
Kerensky, Oleg Jr, Oleg's son and Kerensky's grandson, 233, 563, 597, 644n
Kerensky, Stephen, Gleb and Mary's son and Kerensky's grandson, 1, 3, 8, 12, 29, 151, 232, 233, 306, 314, 363, 383, 403, 445, 466, 519, 523, 535, 572, 644, 648
Kerr, Philip (later Lord Lothian), 463, 466, 494, 502
Khabalov, Major General Sergei, 263, 273, 273n, 274, 278, 282, 285, 288

Kharkov (Kharkiv), 79, 112, 126, 443, 446, 447, 495, 495n, 507, 520, 524
Khodasevich, Vladislav, 533, 539, 556
Khodynka Field, 88, 482
Khrushchev, Nikita, 643
Kiev, 32, 74, 97, 97n, 112, 123, 147, 166, 213, 248, 348, 348n, 443, 446, 499, 509, 527
Kingdom of Poland, 118
Kirov, Sergei, 570, 571, 579, 718n
Kishkin, Nikolai, 398, 409, 412
Knox, Major General Sir Alfred, 208, 225, 271, 296, 320, 333, 340, 349, 366, 390, 413
Kokoshkin, Professor Fyodor, 365, 372, 430, 441
Kolchak, Admiral Alexander, 494, 495, 500, 502, 503, 504, 509
Kollontai, Alexandra, 106, 202, 203, 267, 304, 308, 309, 322, 367, 367n, 394, 399, 402, 404, 419, 437, 439, 485
Komuch, (Committee for the Reconvocation of the Assembly), 451, 487, 489
Komuch People's Army, 489
Konovalov, Alexander, 161, 221, 286, 295, 398, 402, 409, 411–414
Kornilov, General Lavr Georgievich, 1, 8, 42, 234n, 310, 311, 324, 325, 330, 336, 343, 357–359, 362, 364, 366–372, 383–395, 426, 427, 433, 446, 448, 450
Krasin, Leonid, 145, 515, 551, 552
Krasnov, General Peter, 417, 418, 420, 423
Kremer, Arkadi, 63

Krestinsky, Nikolai, 367, 576, 579
Kresty Prison (Vyborg One-Night Prison; The Cross), 102, 126, 132, 135, 253, 271, 367, 397
Kronstadt Naval Base, 119, 290, 351
Kronstadt sailors, 326, 347, 352, 367, 410, 414, 420, 422, 424, 437, 439, 525, 526, 541, 561
Kropotkin, Alexandra 'Sasha', 396
Kropotkin, Peter, 23, 23n, 396
Krupskaya, Nadezhda Konstantinovna, 10, 40, 114, 263, 317, 337, 338, 340, 543
Krylenko, Nikolai, 367, 405, 417, 426
Krymov, Lieutenant General Alexander, 384, 390, 391, 393, 394
Kshesinskaya, Matilda, 47, 48, 49, 60, 319, 319n, 320, 321, 326
Kuban region, 420, 446, 450, 507
kulaks, 103, 146, 643
Kuropatkin, General A. N., 58, 63, 115
Kuzmin, Colonel A. I., 355, 411, 423

Lamsdorff, Count Vladimir, 89
Lansing, Robert, 398n, 475
Latsis, Martin, 482, 491
Latvian Riflemen (Latvian Rifle Brigade), 430, 437, 479, 482
Laval, Pierre, 567, 611, 612, 614
League for Women's Equal Rights, 146, 321
Lebedev, V. I., 365, 371
Left SRs, 401, 419, 437, 438, 439, 442, 481, 482, 495, 532
Lemberg (Lvov), 219, 336

Lena Goldfields Massacre, 12, 151–156, 163, 164, 165n, 557, 560
Lenin, Vladimir Ilyich (born Vladimir Ilyich Ulyanov), 2, 5–12, 64, 69, 72, 73, 126, 148, 149, 164, 181, 186, 200, 202, 209, 222, 227, 263, 322, 323–434, 442, 449, 482, 486, 489, 509, 515, 516, 520, 525, 535, 551
  background, 28–30
  brother's execution, 34–36
  education and exile, 35, 37, 39
  marriage, 40
  names Bolsheviks, 76, 77
  1905 Revolution, 112–114, 121, 124, 125, 263, 269, 304, 304n, 307, 308, 317, 326
  and Kerensky, 304, 336, 337, 466, 532, 541, 542, 560, 565, 590, 646, 648
  Bolshevik Rising, 346, 347, 350, 351, 355, 367, 369
  October Revolution, 398, 399, 405, 408–427
  Constituent Assembly, 437–441
  Brest-Litovsk, 433, 445
  Civil War, 428, 429, 443, 499
  War Communism, 481
  shot by Fania Kaplan, 490, 491, 493, 530
  Red Terror, 458, 483, 485, 486, 490, 491
  relationship with Stalin, 125, 309, 540, 541, 542
  death, 541, 542
  Testament, 540, 543
Li Hongzhang, 85–87
Liman von Sanders, Otto, 215
Litvinov, Maxim, 77, 306, 307, 432, 467, 494, 548, 580, 587

Lloyd George, David 'Tom Cat', 7, 11, 179, 215, 220, 256, 257, 323, 335, 360, 384n, 394, 396, 404, 426, 445, 449, 463, 464, 464n, 465, 466, 468, 471, 477, 480, 494, 495n, 496, 499, 502, 504, 506, 509, 515, 534, 547, 565, 567, 619
Lloyd, Colonel Longfield, 634
Locker-Lampson, Commander Oliver, 320, 333
Lockhart, Sir Robert H. Bruce, 3, 12, 162, 163, 166, 167, 222, 244, 257, 302, 308n, 323, 325, 344, 365, 395, 396, 426, 431, 432, 444, 445, 452, 452n, 464, 479, 480, 483, 493, 494, 527, 428, 532, 553, 563, 597, 598, 601, 615, 616, 625, 626
Lopatin, Herman, 277, 277n
Ludendorff, General Erich, 205, 234, 235, 237, 308, 318, 340, 360, 431, 446, 449, 449n, 450, 476, 489, 495, 497, 538
Lukomsky, General Alexander, 370, 388, 392, 394, 433, 511, 702n
Lunacharsky, A. V., 77, 337, 367
Lutherans, 29, 30, 52
Lvov, Prince Georgi, 221, 285, 295, 300, 306, 310, 322, 325, 327, 341, 346, 348, 351, 356, 357, 387, 502
Lvov, Vladimir, 286, 295, 365, 366, 387, 393

MacDonald, Ramsay, 520, 542, 547, 548
Maclean, Donald, 'Fancy Pants', 575
Maclean, Fitzroy 'Fitzwhiskers', 575, 576, 578, 579, 601, 625, 626
Mackensen, Field Marshal August von, 217–219

Maisky, Ivan, 365, 589
Makarov, Alexander, 154, 164, 165n
Maklakov, Nikolai, 166, 203, 220, 221, 301, 470, 471
Maklakov, Vasily, 123, 384, 471n, 502, 504, 551
Makeyev, Nikolai, 593, 603
Malinovsky, Roman, 164, 165, 181, 227, 338n
Manchuria, 47, 49, 58, 59, 85–87, 89, 104, 118, 147, 503
Mandel, Georges, 450, 474, 614, 623
Mannerheim, Marshal of Finland Carl, 442
Manukhin, Senator S. S., 154, 155, 163
Marat, Jean Paul, 25, 38, 305, 326
Maginot Line, 584, 588, 590, 598, 601, 602, 619
Margulies, M. S., 500, 512
Maria Fyodorovna, Empress (formerly Princess Dagmar of Denmark; later Dowager Empress), 27, 30n, 44, 45, 51, 66, 67, 70, 71, 74, 93, 94, 137, 164, 222
Marinsky Palace, 78, 262, 276, 281, 282, 284–286, 301, 301, 315, 322, 325, 348, 397, 407, 412, 428
Martov, Julius (Yuly Tsederbaum), 39, 40, 73, 73n, 77, 124, 127, 269, 416
Marx, Karl, 5, 24, 38, 39, 63, 69, 82, 277, 339, 428, 485, 530, 639
Marxism/Marxists, 6, 7, 23, 25, 39, 40, 40n, 68, 72, 73, 73n, 77, 96, 106, 121,. 144. 149. 201. 216. 308. 318. 339. 400. 428. 577. 535

Masaryk, Tomáš, President of Czechoslovakia, 505, 545
Maugham, (William) Somerset, 396, 397, 403, 404, 426, 619, 620n
May Day celebrations, 324
Mazower, Mark, 61
Meiji, (the Great), Emperor of Japan (Emperor Mutsuhito), 47, 48, 58, 59, 119
Ménard-Dorian, Aline, 2, 544, 545, 545n, 614
Mensheviks, 10, 77, 78, 103, 125–127, 134, 144, 165, 202, 216, 227, 253, 269, 274, 295, 300, 309, 313, 314, 317, 327, 336n, 337, 349, 365, 382, 405, 407, 409, 416, 419, 435, 437, 483, 521, 572, 576
Meriwether, Lee, 473, 474
Military Revolutionary Committee, 399, 401–407, 409, 412, 414, 419, 422
Miliukov, Paul, 96, 98, 123, 124, 134, 139, 144, 146, 181, 221, 230, 231, 244–246, 253, 269, 271, 272, 286, 292, 294, 295, 297–299, 304, 306, 309, 310, 314, 315, 321, 324, 325, 327, 331, 382, 384, 388, 412, 532, 533, 536
Miliukova, Anna, 123, 322n
Miller, Emma, 157
Miller, General Yevgeny, 573, 627
Milner, Lord, (Alfred Milner), 256, 257, 384, 453, 463
Mirbach, Count Wilhelm von, 480, 482, 493
Moiseenko, Boris, 131, 132, 306
Molotov, Vyacheslav Mikhailovich, 308, 309, 551, 586, 587, 630, 631

Moltke, General Helmuth von, 'the Younger', 62, 194, 195, 205, 211
Montagu, Edwin, 220, 220n, 501
Morrison, George Ernest, 99, 475
Moscow, 3, 9, 32, 60, 113, 124, 163, 165, 167, 206, 263, 305, 344, 345, 371, 372, 382, 384, 385, 387, 391, 396, 397, 399, 410, 419, 420, 424, 427, 443, 445, 448, 451, 452, 458, 467, 479–483, 489, 493, 494, 507, 509, 517, 520, 521, 529, 531, 543, 546, 547, 554, 571, 575, 587, 632, 633
Muranov, Matvei, 164, 216, 300, 367n
Murmansk, 256, 336, 452–454, 467
Muromtsev, Professor Sergey, 138, 139, 142
Muslims, 41, 138, 179, 214, 215, 238, 240, 370

Nabokov, Konstantin D., 231, 305, 306, 321, 463, 471, 498
Nabokov, Vladimir D., 98, 123, 139, 220, 231, 244, 293, 299, 309, 315, 316, 368, 388, 390, 395n, 397, 400, 402, 412, 428, 429, 532, 533
Nabokov, Véra, 568, 583, 593, 600
Nabokov, Vladimir V., 9, 98, 315n, 564, 568, 574, 600, 601, 634, 641, 645
Nadejine, Nicholas Alexandrovich, 2, 550–553, 561, 562, 566, 568, 569, 585
Napoleon Bonaparte, Emperor of France, Bonapartism, 12, 13, 104, 234, 237, 311, 314, 315, 323, 331, 384, 647

Nekrasov, Professor Nikolai, 123, 161, 267, 268, 272, 281, 283, 284, 286, 295, 297, 351, 353, 357, 364, 365, 395, 398
New Economic Policy (NEP), 526
New York Times, 6, 90, 115, 118, 129, 270, 363, 438, 533, 556–558, 565, 574, 616, 626, 646
Nicholas I, 'The Flogger', Emperor of Russia, 16, 17, 17n, 18, 19, 26, 29, 30n, 66
Nicholas II, 'Nicky', Emperor of Russia, 1, 4, 8, 12, 54, 56, 58, 61, 63, 119, 122, 140, 147, 164, 179, 182, 224–226, 243, 246, 596, 641n
background, 44, 46
marriage to Princess Alix, 51–53
coronation, 60, 61
antisemitism, 31, 78, 79n, 123, 166, 94, 99
Japan, 47, 48, 82, 87–90, 94, 99, 116, 117
birth of Tsarevich Alexie, 93
Bloody Sunday, 100, 103, 108, 111
and Rasputin, 128, 129, 143, 144, 168, 201, 252
1905 Revolution, 113, 119–122, 124, 126
First Duma, 134–139, 145
World War I, 187, 189, 192, 193, 203, 204, 214, 215, 217, 220, 222, 242, 249, 250, 254, 256
February Revolution, 265–267, 284–286, 289–297, 302, 303
and Kerensky, 258, 305, 312, 313, 366
execution, 486, 487

Nicholas Nikolaevich, 'Nikolasha the Terrible', Grand Duke, 127, 206, 221, 291

Nicolson, Sir Arthur, 179, 188

Nosar (Khrustalev-Nosar) G. S., 121

Noulens, Joseph, 480

October Manifesto, 122, 123, 133, 134, 146, 159

October Revolution, 2, 3, 7, 9, 105n, 305, 367, 398–427, 438, 483

Odessa, 48, 49, 97, 110, 117, 121, 498, 514, 515, 524, 539, 562

O'Grady, Sir James, 316

Okhrana (Department for the Maintenance of Public Safety and Order), 35, 62, 78, 79, 97, 107, 128, 129, 145n, 146, 147, 165, 181, 216, 226–228, 243, 254, 263, 265, 270, 278, 281, 301, 338, 508, 535, 551, 679n

Olga, Tatiana, Maria and Anastasia Romanova, (OTMA), daughters of Nicholas II, 60, 93, 94, 143, 147, 207, 251, 252, 266

Opium Wars, 81

Order Number 1, 11n, 290, 291, 293, 330, 332, 343

Ottoman Empire, 18, 179, 214, 230, 239, 430

Painlevé, Paul, 468, 469, 544, 551, 596

Pale, the (Pale of Permanent Jewish Settlement), 9, 31, 32, 97, 117, 200

Paléologue, Maurice, 44, 168, 232, 251, 271

Panina, Countess Sofia, 96, 146, 262, 322, 322n, 430, 433

Pares, Sir Bernard, 265

Paris Peace Conference, 500, 501, 502, 505

Pasic, Nicholas, Prime Minister of Serbia, 183, 186

Pasternak, Alexander, 110, 113, 115, 679n

Pavlovsky Regiment, 262, 264, 265, 277, 282, 325, 416

Perris, George, 98, 115

Pershing, General John J. 'Black Jack', 449

Peter and Paul Fortress, 17n, 22, 66, 67, 74, 99, 106, 134, 226, 271, 288, 301, 302, 313, 351, 355, 405, 414, 418, 435, 438, 441, 493

Peter the Great, 16, 16n

Peters, Elizabeth-Anne, 3, 638

Peters, Jacob, 494

Petipa, Marius, 48

Petrograd Soviet of Workers' and Soldiers' Deputies, 124, 273, 387, 291, 309, 310, 313, 316, 318, 319, 325, 331, 335, 340, 342, 346, 349, 367, 397, 398, 401, 406, 412, 414, 432

Petrunkevich, Ivan, 54, 98, 138

Pichon, Stephen, 475, 476

Piłsudski, General Józef, President of Poland, 505, 527

Plekhanov, Georgi, 25, 38, 39, 73, 73n, 77, 114, 121, 337, 355

Pleve, Viacheslav, 32, 78, 79, 80, 89, 92, 101

Pobedonostsev, Konstantin Petrovich, 23, 30, 30n, 34, 46, 54, 127, 221

Podvoisky, Nikolai, 402, 409, 414
Poincairé, Raymond, President of France, 184, 193, 476
Pokrovsky, Nikolai, 271, 283, 286
Poland, 31, 55, 114, 118, 124, 182n, 190, 200, 203, 208, 213, 253, 322, 431, 446, 480, 505, 506, 527, 579, 580, 586, 586n, 587, 589, 590, 616, 630, 636n
Poole, Major-General Frederick, 435, 483
Pourtalès, Friedrich, 191, 192
Pravda (Truth), 308, 308n, 319, 355, 367, 399n, 440, 441, 493, 548, 571, 572
Preobrazhensky Regiment, 46, 52, 60, 95, 105, 135, 137, 248, 265, 269, 273, 278, 282, 349
Price, Morgan Phillips, 324, 382, 385
Princip, Gavrilo, 181, 184
Prittwitz, General Maximilian von, 205
Progressive Bloc, 221, 243, 245, 268, 271, 294
prohibition of alcohol, 201, 261
proletariat, 10, 62, 109, 120, 125, 292, 302, 318, 320, 322, 361, 369, 372, 404, 412, 428, 429, 439, 503, 516, 639
Protocols of the Elders of Zion, The, 78, 79, 79n, 492
Protopopov, Alexander, 230, 232, 242, 243, 245–247, 250, 254, 264, 271, 274, 283, 286, 289, 301, 490
Provisional Government, 1, 3, 6–8, 11, 13, 292, 294, 296–303, 306, 308–310, 314, 316, 319, 321, 323, 325, 333–335n, 338, 349, 356, 359, 362, 364, 365, 369, 371, 382, 391, 394–417, 423, 427, 434, 441, 465, 466, 475, 486, 501, 643, 646
Provisional All-Russian Government (the Directory), 489, 495
Przemyśl, Siege of, 209, 217, 219, 234, 310
Pskov, 290, 293, 297, 298, 411, 417
Purishkevich, Vladimir, 247, 248, 251
Pushkin, Alexander, 1, 69, 98, 164, 561
Putilov Iron Works, 102, 102n, 104, 259, 260, 236, 311, 311n, 349, 351, 354, 390

Rabinowitch, Professor Alexander, 641
Rabinowitch, Dr Eugene, 637, 637n, 641
Radek, Karl, 434, 520
Rasputin, Grigory 'Grishka', 127, 127n, 128, 130, 143, 144, 165, 168, 200, 201, 205, 207, 221–223, 226, 231, 232, 242, 245–252, 256, 366
Red Army, 443, 446, 467, 481, 483, 494, 495, 498, 499, 504, 507, 514, 516, 520, 526, 527, 528, 572, 586, 630, 631
Red Guards, 8, 347, 356, 367, 394, 409, 411, 412, 414, 418, 419, 422, 426, 437, 439, 440, 443, 466, 479, 482, 492, 499
Red Terror, 458, 483, 485, 486, 490, 491, 541, 571, 574, 643
Reed, John, 400, 401, 413, 419, 644n, 703n
Reilly, Sidney (Sigmund Rosenblum), 478, 480, 494, 528, 553, 554

Rennenkampf, General Paul von, 205, 206
Repin, Ilya, 137, 160, 301, 316, 400
Reynaud, Paul, Prime Minister of France, 584, 590, 595, 596, 599, 600, 602, 604, 605, 607, 609, 610, 612, 613, 614, 623, 624
Riga, 112, 212, 360, 387, 548
Rimsky-Korsakov, Nikolai, 113, 147, 477
Robbins, Raymond, 121
Rodichev, Fyodor, 54, 96, 123, 141, 141n, 158, 384
Rodzianko, Mikhail, President of the Duma, 160, 168, 181, 221, 225, 244, 246, 258, 265, 266, 267, 269, 271, 272, 276, 278, 279, 280, 281, 284, 289–301, 310, 371, 382
Romania, 117, 179n, 182n, 184, 212, 225, 237, 237n, 333n, 336, 370, 442, 524, 580, 630, 636n
Romanov Dynasty, 16, 48, 112, 128, 200, 227, 259, 269, 271
Russian Democratic Federative Republic, 439
Russian Foreign Ministry, 204, 271, 298, 306, 307, 324, 326, 328, 444, 445, 587
Russian High Command (the Stavka), 205, 205n, 206, 220, 226, 242, 258, 273, 274, 282, 284, 288, 297, 332, 340, 361, 388, 389, 393, 394, 426, 631
Russian Orthodox Church, 12, 16, 18, 28, 30, 31, 34, 49, 52, 53, 70, 101, 158, 322, 366, 442, 530, 641, 641n, 646
Russian Revolution of 1905, 3, 7, 12, 21, 145, 154, 263, 264, 306, 338, 544

Russian Social Democratic Labour Party (RSDLP), 62, 62n, 72, 77, 78, 118, 126, 127, 216, 292, 306
Russo-Japanese War 1904-1905, 82, 90, 118, 179, 189, 236
Russo-Turkish War 1877-1878, 207, 214, 229, 310
Rutenberg, Peter, 104, 108, 128, 129, 413, 511, 512, 68n
Ruzsky, General Nikolai, 266, 250, 362
Rybakov, Nikolai, 25, 27
Rykov, Alexei, 77, 367n, 575, 577, 579, 580

Saint Petersburg/ Petrograd, 8 9, 11, 16n, 17, 18, 20, 22, 25, 29, 29n, 34, 39, 41, 44, 45, 48, 49, 51, 59, 65–69, 73, 78, 79, 88, 90, 91–103, 105, 105n, 108, 110, 111, 112, 113–116, 119–121, 123, 124, 127, 128, 129, 131, 133, 140, 142, 150, 152, 154, 156, 157, 166, 179, 184, 185, 188, 189, 190, 193, 201, 204, 205, 207, 213, 216, 222, 223, 226, 227, 228, 232, 240, 243, 244, 246, 253, 255, 256, 259, 260–263, 266, 268, 269, 273, 273n, 276, 278, 282, 284, 285, 290, 315n
Samara, 39, 40, 56, 185, 451, 453, 465, 489, 534, 633
Samarkand, 41, 42, 239
Samsonov, General Alexander, 205, 206
Saint-Exupéry, Antoine de, 603, 609, 619
Savage Division (of Caucasian troops), 310, 371, 390, 391
Savinkov, Boris, 79, 80, 113, 129, 131, 306, 307, 330, 331, 357,

361–366, 370, 371, 372, 384, 386, 389–395, 421, 423, 479, 480, 482, 483, 492, 502, 504, 527, 528, 553
Sazonov, Serge, 188, 191, 192, 208, 220, 502
Schlieffen Plan, 193–195, 205, 211
Schuschnigg, Kurt von, Austrian Chancellor, 606
Second All-Russian Congress of Soviets, 398, 399, 405, 406, 409, 416, 417, 420, 423
Second World War - see World War II
Serbia, 179, 179n, 182–191, 199, 200, 209
Sergeyev, Fyodor Andreyevich, 'Artem', 3, 77, 78, 126, 127, 147–149, 156–158, 198, 367, 367n, 398, 443, 446, 520, 520n, 528, 682n, 714n
Sergeyev, Tomik Fyodorovich 'Artyom', 529, 632, 633
Serfs, serfdom, 19–21, 29, 30, 30n, 34, 42, 91, 291
Sergei Alexandrovich, Grand Duke, 32, 101, 113, 307, 365, 488
Sevastopol, 16, 19, 20, 155, 156, 630
Shabelsky-Bork, Peter, 533
Sharp, William Graves, 473
Shaw, George Bernard, 432, 466, 459, 550n, 619
Shcheglovitov, Ivan, President of the State Council, 165, 220, 221, 266, 279, 280, 283, 289
Shingarev, Dr Andrei, 123, 230, 231, 254, 268, 295, 297, 304, 430, 441
Shishkina-Iavein, Poliksena, 146, 322

Shliapnikov, Alexander, 266, 267
Shostakovich, Dmitry D., 441, 633
Shulgin, Vasily, 221, 226, 246, 248, 268, 271, 276, 279, 280, 286, 293, 297, 298
Siberia, 12, 16, 17, 17n, 20, 22, 30, 36, 38, 40, 48, 55, 75, 114, 120, 121, 126, 127, 137, 144, 145, 147, 151, 154, 155, 204, 215, 217, 246, 249, 269, 307, 311, 315, 366, 400, 465, 484, 490, 498, 503, 504, 509, 510, 516, 550, 564
Simbirsk/Ulyanovsk, 28–30, 33–36, 39, 68, 158, 159, 243, 542
Simpson, Helen, 6, 577, 628
Simpson, Kenneth F., 6, 556, 557, 577, 628
Simpson, Wallis (later Duchess of Windsor), 595
Skobelev, Matvei, 287, 300, 337
Skobelev, General Mikhail, 310, 310n
Skoblin, Nikolai, 573, 573n
Smolny Institute for Daughters of the Nobility, 70, 72, 367–369, 394, 398, 399, 405, 406–409, 414, 422, 429, 430, 439, 470
Socialist Revolutionaries (SRs), 75, 78, 103, 104, 114, 121, 123, 131, 134, 140, 141, 144, 155, 246, 252, 266, 268, 277, 285, 295, 306, 307, 336n, 349, 382, 401, 405, 409, 416, 417, 421, 422, 428, 429, 435, 437, 438, 439, 451, 454, 458, 465, 483, 490, 491n, 485, 512, 516, 521, 528, 530, 531, 553, 558, 619
Sokolov, Boris Theodore, 2, 521, 522, 715n
Sokolov, Nikolai, 141, 166, 266, 290, 292, 332, 343

Solzhenitsyn, Alexander, 4, 9, 212, 267n, 300, 300n, 515, 574, 657
Solomon (née Benenson), Flora, 129, 152, 305n, 557, 558, 561, 563, 567, 569, 586, 641, 680n
Sorokin, Professor Pitirim, 246, 252, 270, 299, 300, 313, 320, 321, 342, 349n, 350, 354, 368, 372, 418, 429, 430, 435, 438, 448, 461, 530, 535
Soskice, Dr David, 97, 98, 115, 115n, 321, 368, 396, 407, 410, 413, 425, 463, 477, 539, 561
Soskice, Sir Frank (Baron Stow Hill), 644, 644n
Soskice (née Hueffer), Juliet, 97n, 115, 115n, 463, 477
Soskice, Victor, 585
South-Western Front, 204, 234, 235, 330, 336, 340, 356, 357, 521
South Russia, 421, 443, 445, 513, 514, 519
Soviet of Peasant Deputies, 442
Spears, Lieutenant Edward, 210, 329, 605, 611, 613–615
Spiridonova, Maria, 417, 417n, 437, 481, 482, 482n
Stalin, Josef (Josif Vissarionovich Dzhugashvili), 5, 6, 7, 11, 77, 126, 145, 165, 300, 308, 309, 367n, 399, 520, 530, 551, 570, 570n, 571, 582, 593, 606, 628, 658, 718n
  background, 125
  Lena Goldfields Massacre, 156
  relationship with Lenin, 125, 309, 540
  Lenin's death, 541–543, 560, 564
  Artem Sergeyev, 520
  adopts Artem's son, 3, 529
  and Kerensky, 5, 11, 560, 562, 577, 589, 592, 593
  feud with Trotsky, 126, 420, 627
  Holodomor, 564
  show trials, 570, 572, 573, 574, 576–580
  Nazi pact, 2, 586, 586n, 587, 621
  World War II, 630, 631–636, 636n
  death, 643
Stamfordham, Lord, (Lieutenant-Colonel Arthur Bigge), 293
Stankevich, Colonel Vladimir, (also Stanka, Vlados), 151, 161, 332, 422, 423
Stanley, Venetia, (later Venetia Montagu), 187, 211, 212, 220, 220n, 501
Stasova, Elena, 146
State Dumas, First, Second, Third, Fourth - see Duma
Stein, Harry A., 585, 586
Steklov-Nakhamkes, Yuri, 292, 296, 300, 300n
Stevenson, Frances 'Pussy', 464, 464n, 502
Stoessel, Baron Anatoli Mikhailovich, 94, 99, 677n
Stolypin, Peter, 139, 140, 141, 141n, 144–147, 159, 160
Strunsky, Simeon, 556, 565
Struve, Peter, 62, 74, 80, 96, 124, 144
Stürmer, Boris, 226, 232, 239, 240, 244, 245, 246
Sukhanov, Nikolai (Nikolai Nikolaievich Himmer), 227, 263, 269, 290, 292, 300n, 305, 337, 354, 383, 399, 404, 405, 417, 570, 572

Sukhomlinov, Catherine, 207, 242
Sukhomlinov, General Vladimir, 181, 191, 203, 206–208, 214, 219, 220, 221, 226, 291, 292, 301
Sukhotin, Lieutenant Sergei Mikhailovich, 248, 251
Sverdlov, Yakov, 77, 367n, 399n, 438
Svyatopolk-Mirsky, Prince Pyotr Dmitrievich 'Pepka', 95, 98, 103, 110

Taboritsky, Sergei, 533
Tabouis, Geneviève, 545, 613, 614
Tallinn (Reval), 88, 523, 525
Tambov, Tambov Rebellion, 516, 534, 417n
Tashkent, 41–43, 54, 64, 66, 76, 91, 112, 116, 140, 228, 229, 239, 413, 425, 426, 499, 640, 712
Tauride Palace, 7, 134, 135, 137, 139, 260, 267–269, 274–278, 281, 284, 285, 287, 288, 291, 298, 299, 301, 310, 316, 325, 349–352, 356, 366, 409, 429, 430, 434, 436–438, 440–442, 469, 520
Catherine Hall, 137, 159, 201, 248, 268, 274, 278, 288, 290, 291, 292, 295
White Hall, 159, 244, 257, 272, 276, 278, 280, 288, 292, 301, 316, 348, 349n, 350, 354, 430, 437
Tchaikovsky, Peter Ilyich, 594
Tchaikovsky, Nikolai, 483, 502, 504
Tereschenko, Mikhail, 328, 353, 357, 364–366, 368, 375, 398n, 403
The Times of London, 81, 90, 99, 100, 106, 136–139, 236, 243, 264, 361, 467, 468, 470, 475, 493, 497, 503, 506, 510, 563, 609
Third All-Russian Congress of Soviets, 442
Third Cavalry Corps, 370, 384, 389, 391, 393, 417
Third Communist International (the Comintern), 520, 529, 543, 546–548, 550n, 586, 590, 713n
Third Cyclist Battalion, 354, 410
Thomas, Albert, 324, 325, 332, 467, 475, 500, 544, 551, 596
Thorne, Will, 316
Tiflis (Tbilisi), 112, 125, 145, 252
Timashev, S. I., 154, 163
Tisza, István, Prime Minister of Hungary, 183, 184
Tolstoy, Count Leo, 10, 19, 20, 36, 50, 57, 90, 98, 146
Trans-Siberian Railway, 47, 49, 58, 85, 86, 89, 99, 367, 396, 453, 527
Treaty of Portsmouth, 118
Trepov, Alexander, Prime Minister of Russia, 246, 247, 249, 250, 252
Treschenkov, Captain N. V., 153, 156
Tritton, Charles, brother of Nell Tritton, 512, 640
Tritton, Corbett, cousin of Nell Tritton, 585, 629, 637, 638
Tritton, Cyril, brother of Nell Tritton, 562, 629
Tritton, Eliza Ellen (née Worrall), mother of Nell Tritton, 240, 562
Tritton, Frederick William, father of Nell Tritton, 240, 562, 635, 636
Tritton, Ivy, sister of Nell Tritton, 561
Tritton, Lieutenant Joseph, cousin of Nell Tritton, 241, 242

Tritton, Lilian, sister of Nell Tritton, 512, 640
Tritton, Lydia Ellen 'Nell' (Nellé Tritton, later Mrs Thérèse Nadejine and Mrs Thérèse Kerensky) - see Kerensky, Thérèse
Tritton, Norman, cousin of Nell Tritton, 629, 639
Tritton, Roy, brother of Nell Tritton, 550
Trotsky, Leon (Lev Davidovich Bronstein), 2, 5, 6, 7, 33, 62n, 77, 156, 202, 216, 308n, 432, 433, 434, 436, 440, 443, 444, 448, 471, 486, 489, 525, 526, 535, 548
  background, 121
  and Kerensky, 11, 227, 326, 427, 484, 503, 627, 641, 648
  meets Lenin and Stalin, 126
  1905 Revolution, 120, 121
  New York, 269, 308, 313
  Canada, 313, 314, 321
  return to Petrograd, 325, 326
  Bolshevik Rising, 349, 353–355
  October Revolution, 9, 367, 367n, 394, 397, 402, 404–406, 408, 409, 416, 421, 426, 427
  Civil War, 445, 446, 453, 464, 520
  and Stalin, 540, 542, 543, 562, 563, 570, 571, 572, 576, 577, 579
  assassination, 626, 627
Tsaritsyn (Stalingrad, later Volgograd), 520, 447
Tsarskoe Selo, 44, 93, 99, 103, 143, 207, 222, 223, 251, 252, 256, 258, 260, 266, 284, 285, 288, 289, 290, 291, 303, 355, 364, 366, 406, 420, 421, 423

Tsereteli, Irakli, 77, 144, 145, 227, 269, 300, 316, 327, 337, 348, 351, 365, 403, 438, 439
Tsvetaeva, Marina, 556, 556n
Turkestan, 40, 42, 239, 323
Turkey, 202, 214, 498, 524, 525, 527, 563
Turkish Straits, 18, 215
Turner, Anne, 162
Turner, Jean Haslewood, 3, 161, 166, 167, 242, 395, 396
Turner, Major Leonard, 162
Turner, T. Sargent, 162
Tyrkova-Williams, Ariadna, 40, 74, 98, 124n, 146, 322n

Ukraine, 31, 32, 55, 67, 78, 79, 103, 121, 123, 126, 137, 165, 182n, 200, 209, 234, 323, 333, 358, 387, 443, 445, 446, 493n, 503, 516, 520, 520n, 534, 536, 541
Ulyanova, Anna Ilyinichna, elder sister of Lenin, 37, 38
Ulyanova, Maria Alexandrovna (née Blank), mother of Lenin, 29, 30, 37, 39
Ulyanova, Maria Ilyinichna, younger sister of Lenin, 30, 541
Ulyanov, Alexander Ilyich, 34–37
Ulyanov, Ilya Nikolaevich, 28–30, 34
Ulyanov, Vladimir Ilyich - see Lenin, V. I.
Union of Liberation, 96, 98, 535
Union of Struggle for the Liberation of the Working Class, 39
Union for the Defence of the Fatherland and Freedom, 480
Union of Zemstvos, 221, 284

Uritsky, Moisei, 77, 367, 399, 430, 489, 491, 493
Urquhart, Chief Inspector Charles, 157

Vandervelde, Émile, 467, 501, 531, 545, 567
Vasiliev, Sergei, 69, 75, 92, 131–133, 140
Vasiliev, Professor Vasily Pavlovich, 70–72, 91
Versailles Treaty - see also Paris Peace Conference, 534, 567, 585
Vetrova, Maria, 6, 67, 74
Victoria, Queen of the United Kingdom of Great Britain and Ireland and Empress of India, 18, 24, 51, 52, 53n, 82, 85, 109, 178
Victoria, 'Vicky', Empress of Germany, 82–84
Viviani, René, Prime Minister of France, 184, 196
Volunteer Army, 433, 446, 494, 507, 510, 519, 520
Voroshilov, Marshal Kliment, 587
Vyrubova, Anna, 223, 250–252, 254, 311, 312, 366

War Communism, 516, 525, 526, 541
Warsaw, 80, 112, 190, 219, 527, 528, 588, 589
Wells, H. G., 269, 432, 493n, 515, 516, 562
Western Front, 8, 203, 204, 211–213, 218, 218n, 233, 236, 237, 239, 285, 330, 331, 333, 340, 342, 343, 356, 429, 449, 450, 478, 501
Weygand, Maxime, 584, 599, 601, 604–606, 612, 613

What Is To Be Done?, 22, 76
White Russians, White armies, White movement, 4, 12, 31, 55n, 234, 428, 444, 447, 463, 464, 467, 469, 471, 479, 494, 495, 498, 499, 503, 507, 509, 511, 520, 524, 525, 527, 532, 539, 550, 558, 563, 573, 583
Wilcox, E. H., 277
Wilhelm II, 'Willy', Emperor of Germany, 4, 54, 57, 63, 82–85, 88, 179, 182, 184, 184n, 187, 189, 190–192, 194, 195, 199, 211, 214, 334, 397, 498, 506
Williams, Harold, 112, 302, 315, 322n, 383, 469, 491
Wilson, Woodrow, President of the USA, 7, 253, 309, 323, 324, 469, 471, 472, 475, 489, 502n–504, 506
Wilton, Robert, 100, 106, 108, 136, 138, 243, 255, 264, 690n
Winter Palace, 8, 20, 25–27, 44, 45, 53, 54, 61, 89, 93, 99, 102, 108, 135, 138, 140, 193, 271, 277, 278, 299, 363, 364, 368, 370, 371, 389, 391, 392, 394, 396, 398, 400, 405, 407–411, 413, 414, 416, 427, 489, 571
Wiseman, Sir William, 396
Witte, Countess Matilda, 49, 213, 224
Witte, Count Sergei, 48–50, 53, 55, 56, 58, 59, 61, 63, 79, 85–89, 91, 117–121, 123, 124, 126, 136, 213, 214, 224, 224n, 250
World War I, 3, 6, 105, 181, 212, 302, 504, 516, 545, 596, 597, 616, 628, 631
World War II, 2, 506, 545n, 588, 589, 633

Wrangel, General Peter, 520, 525, 645

Yagoda, Genrikh, 571, 576, 578, 579
Yanushkevich, General Nikolai, 188, 208, 209, 219, 222
Yaroslavl, 480, 482–484
Yates, Dornford (Captain Cecil William Mercer), 618, 619
Yeats, William Butler, 402
Yezhov, Nikolai, 578, 579
Yusupov, Prince Felix, 248–252

Zasulich, Vera, 73, 77

Zavoiko, Vasily, 311, 358, 364, 371, 387–389, 471, 478
zemstvos, 21, 54, 208, 221, 284, 382
Zenzinov, Vladimir, 266, 436, 527, 528, 539, 635
Zimmerwald, 302, 302n, 325, 403
Zinoviev, Grigory, 7, 77, 200, 318, 321, 337, 349, 354, 355, 367n, 399, 409, 491, 520, 526, 540, 543, 550n, 570, 571
Zinoviev Letter, 546–549
Zog, King of Albania, (formerly Ahmet Muhtar Zogolli), 595, 616, 620, 621–623